LITERACY SKILLS FOR THE WORLD OF TOMORROW – FURTHER RESULTS FROM PISA 2000

ORGANISATION FOR ECONOMIC CO-OPERATION AND DEVELOPMENT

UNESCO INSTITUTE FOR STATISTICS

Organisation for Economic Co-operation and Development

Pursuant to Article 1 of the Convention signed in Paris on December 14, 1960, and which came into force on September 30, 1961, the Organisation for Economic Co-operation and Development (OECD) shall promote policies designed to:

- achieve the highest sustainable economic growth and employment and a rising standard of living in Member countries, while maintaining financial stability, and thus to contribute to the development of the world economy;

- contribute to sound economic expansion in Member as well as non-member countries in the process of economic development; and

- contribute to the expansion of world trade on a multilateral, non-discriminatory basis in accordance with international obligations.

The original Member countries of the OECD are Austria, Belgium, Canada, Denmark, France, Germany, Greece, Iceland, Ireland, Italy, Luxembourg, the Netherlands, Norway, Portugal, Spain, Sweden, Switzerland, Turkey, the United Kingdom and the United States. The following countries became Members subsequently through accession at the dates indicated hereafter: Japan (April 28, 1964), Finland (January 28, 1969), Australia (June 7, 1971), New Zealand (May 29, 1973), Mexico (May 18, 1994), the Czech Republic (December 21, 1995), Hungary (May 7, 1996), Poland (November 22, 1996), Korea (December 12, 1996) and the Slovak Republic (December 14, 2000). The Commission of the European Communities takes part in the work of the OECD (Article 13 of the OECD Convention).

UNESCO

The constitution of the United Nations Educational, Scientific and Cultural Organization (UNESCO) was adopted by 20 countries at the London Conference in November 1945 and entered into effect on November 4, 1946. The Organization currently has 188 Member States.

The main objective of UNESCO is to contribute to peace and security in the world by promoting collaboration among nations through education, science, culture and communication in order to foster universal respect for justice, the rule of law, and the human rights and fundamental freedoms that are affirmed for the peoples of the world, without distinction of race, sex, language or religion, by the Charter of the United Nations.

To fulfill its mandate, UNESCO performs five principal functions: 1) prospective studies on education, science, culture and communication for tomorrow's world; 2) the advancement, transfer and sharing of knowledge through research, training and teaching activities; 3) standard-setting actions for the preparation and adoption of internal instruments and statutory recommendations; 4) expertise through technical co-operation to Member States for their development policies and projects; and 5) the exchange of specialized information.

UNESCO is headquartered in Paris, France.

The UNESCO Institute for Statistics

The UNESCO Institute for Statistics (UIS) is the statistical office of UNESCO and is the UN depository for global statistics in the fields of education, science and technology, culture and communication.

UIS was established in 1999. It was created to improve UNESCO's statistical programme and to develop and deliver the timely, accurate and policy-relevant statistics needed in today's increasingly complex and rapidly changing social, political and economic environments.

UIS is based in Montréal, Canada.

Photo credit: PhotoDisc.

FOREWORD

Compelling incentives for individuals, economies and societies to raise levels of education have been the driving force for governments to improve the quality of educational services. The prosperity of countries now derives to a large extent from their human capital and the opportunities available for their citizens to acquire knowledge and skills that will enable them to continue learning throughout their lives.

All stakeholders - parents, students, those who teach and run education systems as well as the general public - need to be informed on how well their education systems prepare students to meet the challenges of the future. Many countries monitor student learning in order to provide answers to this question. Coupled with appropriate incentives, assessment and evaluation can motivate students to learn better, teachers to teach more effectively and schools to be more supportive and productive environments. Comparative international analyses can extend and enrich the national picture by providing a larger context within which to interpret national results. They can provide countries with information to judge their areas of relative strength and weakness and to monitor progress. They can stimulate countries to raise aspirations. They can also provide evidence to direct national policy, for schools' curriculum and instructional efforts and for students' learning.

In response to the need for cross-nationally comparable evidence on student performance, the OECD has launched the Programme for International Student Assessment (PISA). PISA represents a new commitment by governments to monitor the outcomes of education systems in terms of student achievement on a regular basis and within an internationally accepted common framework. PISA aims to provide a new basis for policy dialogue and for collaboration in defining and operationalising educational goals – in innovative ways that reflect judgements about the skills that are relevant to adult life.

The first PISA assessment was conducted in 2000 and will now be followed-up with similar assessments every three years. A first report, *Knowledge and Skills for Life*, was published in 2001 and provided evidence on the performance in reading, mathematical and scientific literacy of students, schools and countries, as well as insights into the factors that influence the development of these skills at home and at school, and how these factors interact.

The wide interest generated by PISA beyond the OECD membership has encouraged many non-OECD countries to join the effort. Brazil, Latvia, Liechtenstein and the Russian Federation implemented the first PISA assessment together with 28 OECD countries in 2000. Albania, Argentina, Bulgaria, Chile, Hong Kong-China, Indonesia, Israel, FYR Macedonia, Peru, Romania and Thailand followed in 2002 and further countries have signed up for future rounds.

To respond to this increasing interest in PISA and international assessments more generally, OECD and UNESCO have joined forces with the aims to facilitate the participation of non-OECD countries in PISA and to analyse the resultant data. More broadly, the two organisations are collaborating, in supporting a shift in policy focus from educational inputs to learning outcomes, to assist countries in seeking to bring about improvements in schooling and better preparation for young people as they enter an adult life of rapid change and deepening global interdependence.

This report, *Literacy Skills for the World of Tomorrow - Further results from PISA 2000*, which is the first result of this collaboration, presents the results in PISA for the eleven systems that tested in 2002. The report reveals considerable variation in levels of performance between students, schools and countries. It shows that the socio-economic backgrounds of students and schools exert an important influence on student performance, although this is much less marked in some countries than in others. More importantly, those countries – among them both OECD and non-OECD countries – which have been most successful in mitigating the effect of social disadvantage are among those with the highest levels of overall student performance. These countries demonstrate that it is possible to achieve high quality while reducing inequality. They define an important challenge for other countries by showing what it is possible to achieve. The report also suggests that schools can make an important difference although it will require further analysis to identify precisely how school resources, policies and practices interact with home background to influence student performance.

A series of more detailed thematic reports will be published in 2003 and 2004, including both OECD and non-OECD countries, in pursuit of a deeper understanding of how countries and schools can respond. In the meantime, the mere fact that high-quality learning outcomes are already a reality for the majority of students in some countries is, in itself, an encouraging result that suggests that the challenges ahead can be tackled successfully.

PISA is a collaborative effort, bringing together scientific expertise from the participating countries, steered co-operatively by their governments on the basis of shared, policy-driven interests. A Board of Participating Countries took responsibility for the project at the policy level. Experts from these countries serve on working groups that are charged with linking the PISA policy objectives to the best available substantive and technical expertise in the field of international comparative assessment of educational outcomes. These expert groups ensure that the PISA assessment instruments are internationally valid, that they take into account the cultural and curricular contexts of participating countries, provide a realistic basis for measurement, and emphasise authenticity and educational validity. The frameworks and assessment instruments for PISA 2000 in themselves are the product of a multi-year development process.

This report is the product of close co-operation between the countries participating in PISA, the experts and institutions working within the framework of the PISA Consortium, and the OECD and UNESCO. The report was prepared by the OECD Directorate for Education, the UNESCO Institute for Statistics and the programme on Trade and Development of the Hamburg Institute of International Economics (HWWA), under the direction of Andreas Schleicher (*OECD*) and Albert Motivans (*UNESCO*). Contributing authors are Hannah Cocks (*OECD*), Jeffery Hutcheson (*Vanderbilt University*), Katharina Michaelowa (*HWWA*), Kooghyang Ro (*OECD*), Thomas M. Smith (*Vanderbilt University*), Claudia Tamassia (*OECD*), Sophie Vayssettes (*OECD*) and Yanhong Zhang (*UNESCO*) with production assistance from Cassandra Davis (*OECD*) and Marie-Hélène Lussier (*UNESCO*). The data underlying the report were prepared by the PISA Consortium, under the direction of Raymond Adams and Christian Monseur at the Australian Council for Educational Research.

The development of the report was steered by delegates from the participating non-OECD countries, including Nikoleta Mika and Perparim Shera (*Albania*); Lilia Toranzos (*Argentina*); Alexander Petkov

Lakiurski (*Bulgaria*); Leonor Cariola (*Chile*); Esther Sui Chu Ho (*Hong Kong-China*); Ramon Mohandas and Bahrul Hayat (*Indonesia*); Bracha Kramarski and Zemira Mevarech (*Israel*); Vladimir Mostrov (*FYR Macedonia*); José Rodríguez and Giuliana Espinosa (*Peru*); Adrian Stoica and Roxana Mihail (*Romania*); and, Sunee Klainin (*Thailand*).

The report is published under the joint responsibility of the Secretary-General of the OECD and the Director-General of UNESCO.

Barry McGaw
Director for Education
OECD

Denise Lievesley
Director
UNESCO Institute for Statistics

TABLE OF CONTENTS

Foreword 3

Chapter 1: Programme for International Student Assessment and non-OECD countries ... 11
An overview of PISA 12
Organisation of this report 15
What PISA measures 17
  Reading literacy in PISA 19
  Mathematical literacy in PISA 20
  Scientific literacy in PISA 21
How PISA assesses students and collects information 21
How PISA can inform policy... 24
Social, economic and education contexts of the 14 non-OECD countries........... 24
  Characteristics of youth population... 25
  Educational participation and its returns 26
  Capacities and efforts to invest in education 28
  Summary 30

Readers' guide 32

Chapter 2:The reading performance of 15-year-olds 35
Introduction 36
How reading literacy is assessed in PISA 37
PISA proficiency level 41
Samples of the reading tasks used in PISA 43
Reading literacy profile of 15-year-olds.. 69
Percentage of students proficient at each level of reading literacy................ 69
  The mean performances of countries 74
  The distribution of reading literacy within countries................................ 79
Performance on the subscales of reading literacy..................................... 84
Conclusions 87

Chapter 3: A profile of studentperformance inmathematical and scientific literacy 91
Introduction 92
Student performance in mathematical literacy.. 92
  How mathematical literacy is measured in PISA 92
  The mean performances of countries in mathematical literacy 95
  The distribution of mathematical literacy within countries 101
  Reading and mathematical literacy performance..................................... 103
Student performance in scientific literacy 104
  How scientific literacy is measured in PISA 104
  The mean performances of countries in scientific literacy.......................... 108
  The distribution of scientific literacy within countries 108
  Reading and scientific literacy performance 110
  Reading, mathematical and scientific literacy performance 111
Investment in education and student performance..................................... 111
The income distribution and performance 114
Conclusions 116

Chapter 4: General outcomes of learning 119
  Introduction 120
  Student engagement in schooling and learning 121
    Student engagement with school.. 122
    Students' effort and persistence to learn and instrumental motivation.............. 124
    Student engagement in reading... 127
    Student interest and self-concept in reading and mathematics 129
    Diversity and content of reading - Reader profiles.. 131
  Student learning strategies and preferences 133
    Controlling the learning process 133
    Student use of elaboration and memorisation strategies 135
    Co-operative and competitive learning 137
  Conclusions 138

Chapter 5: Gender differences and similarities in achievement 141
  Introduction 142
  The future labour force 143
  Gender differences in reading, mathematical and scientific literacy...................... 146
  Gender differences in subject interest 150
  Gender differences in engagement in reading... 152
  Gender differences in learning strategies and self-concept 157
  Gender differences in approaches for learning - competitive versus co-operative learning 160
  Conclusions 161

Chapter 6: Family background and literacy performance 163
  Introduction 164
  Social, economic and cultural factors that influence schooling.............................. 164
    Parental occupational status... 165
    Family wealth 167
    Possessions related to "classical" culture 167
    Parental education 167
  Communication with parents on social issues and aspects of culture 169
  Family structure.. 172
  Place of birth and home language 173
  Summarising the relationship between family economic, social and cultural status
  and literacy performance 173
  Is there a trade-off between quality and equity? 178
  Importance of engagement in reading in improving literacy performance........... 180
  Conclusions 184

Chapter 7: School characteristics and student performance.............................. 187
  Introduction 188
  Variation of scores and differences between schools 188
  Physical and human resources at school... 191
    Schools' infrastructure and equipment 192
    Schools' human resources 195
  School organisation and management 201
  School climate 205
  Schools' socio-economic intake 212
    Socio-economic and academic selection 212
    Factors of social selection for different schools... 220
  Conclusions 222

References 227

Annex A 231
    Annex A1: Construction of indices and other derived measures from the student
    and school context questionnaires 232
        Student characteristics and family background 233
        Learning strategies and attitudes 237
        School policies and practices 239
        Classroom practices 241
        School resources and type of school 242
    Annex A2: Explained variation in student performance 244
    Annex A3: The PISA target population and the PISA samples 249
        The PISA concept of "yield" and the definition of the PISA target population 249
        Population coverage 252
        Sampling procedures and response rates 255
    Annex A4: Standard errors, significance tests and multiple comparisons 259
    Annex A5: Quality assurance 260
    Annex A6: Development of the PISA assessment instruments 262
    Annex A7: Reliability of the marking of open-ended items 268

Annex B 269
    Annex B1: Data tables 270

Annex C 385
    Annex C1: The development and implementation of PISA – A collaborative effort 386
        Introduction 386
        Members of the PISA Board of Participating Countries (PISA 2000 and PISA Plus) 387
        PISA National Project Managers (PISA 2000 and PISA Plus) 387
        OECD Secretariat 388
        UNESCO Institute for Statistics 388
        PISA Expert Groups 388
        PISA Technical Advisory Group (PISA) 388
        PISA Consortium (PISA 2000 and PISA Plus) 389

Chapter

PROGRAMME FOR INTERNATIONAL STUDENT ASSESSMENT AND NON-OECD COUNTRIES

An overview of PISA

The Programme for International Student Assessment (PISA) is a collaborative effort among the OECD member countries to measure how well young adults at age 15, and therefore approaching the end of compulsory schooling, are prepared to meet the challenges of today's knowledge societies[1]. The first PISA assessment was conducted in 2000 with an emphasis on the domain of reading. It will be repeated every three years, with the primary focus shifting to mathematics in 2003, science in 2006 and back to reading in 2009. Tests were typically administered to between 4 500 and 10 000 students in each country.

Initial participants in PISA consisted of the 28 OECD countries and four non-OECD countries listed in Figure 1.1. In 2001, in response to interest beyond the OECD, eleven additional non-OECD countries[2] participated in a second administration of the assessment. These are Albania, Argentina, Bulgaria, Chile, Hong Kong-China[3], Indonesia, Israel, FYR Macedonia, Peru, Romania[4] and Thailand. These eleven countries brought the total of non-OECD participants to 15[5].

The results of the first administration of PISA were reported in *Knowledge and Skills for Life* (OECD, 2001*b*). It documented the performance of students, schools and countries in reading, mathematical and scientific literacy and offered insights into the factors that influence the development of these skills at home and at school and how these factors interact. This new report extends the analyses reported in *Knowledge and Skills for Life* to the 14 non-OECD countries listed above. Where applicable, the term "PISA" in the current document refers to the 43 countries that used the same instrument to collect data in either of the two administrations. The focus of this report, however, will be on the 14 non-OECD countries, four from the first administration and ten from the second administration.

PISA is the most comprehensive and rigorous international effort to date that seeks both to assess student performance and to collect data on the student, family and institutional factors that can help to explain differences in performance. Decisions about the scope and nature of the assessments and the background information to be collected were made by leading experts in participating countries and steered jointly by their governments on the basis of common policy interests. Substantial efforts and resources were devoted to achieving cultural and linguistic breadth in the assessment materials. Stringent quality assurance mechanisms were applied in translation, sampling and data collection. As a consequence, the results of PISA have a high degree of validity and reliability, and they can significantly improve our understanding of the outcomes of education.

PISA is based on a dynamic and forward-looking model of lifelong learning in which new knowledge and skills necessary for successful adaptation to a changing world are continuously acquired throughout life. PISA focuses on things that 15-year-olds will need in their future lives and seeks to assess what they can do with what they have learned. The assessment is informed – but not constrained – by the common denominator of national curricula. PISA does assess students' knowledge, but it also examines their ability to reflect on the knowledge and experience and to apply that knowledge and experience to real world issues. For example, in order to understand and evaluate scientific advice on nutrition, an adult would not only need to know some basic facts about the composition of nutrients but also to be able to apply that information. This orientation reflects changes in the goals and objectives of curricula in participating countries, which are increasingly concerned with what students can do with what they learn at school. The term "literacy" is used to encapsulate this broader conception of knowledge and skills.

Figure 1.1
Countries participating in PISA

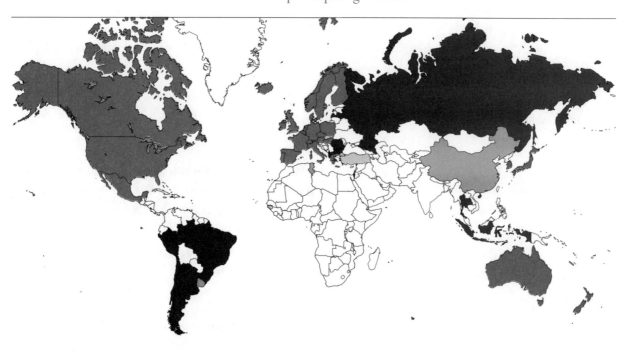

■ **OECD countries participating in PISA 2000**

Australia
Austria
Belgium
Canada
Czech Republic
Denmark
Finland
France
Germany
Greece
Hungary
Iceland
Ireland
Italy
Japan
Korea
Luxembourg
Mexico
Netherlands
New Zealand
Norway
Poland
Portugal
Spain
Sweden
Switzerland
United Kingdom
United States

■ **Additional OECD countries participating in PISA from 2003 onwards**

Slovak Republic
Turkey

■ **Non-OECD countries participating in PISA 2000**

Albania
Argentina
Brazil
Bulgaria
Chile
Hong Kong-China
Indonesia
Israel
FYR Macedonia
Latvia
Liechtenstein
Peru
Romania
Russian Federation
Thailand

■ **Additional non-OECD countries participating in PISA from 2003 onwards**

China
Tunisia
Uruguay

Box 1.1. What is PISA? A summary of key features

Basics

- An internationally standardised assessment that was jointly developed by participating countries and administered to 15-year-olds in schools.

- A survey implemented in 43 countries in the first assessment in 2000.

- Tests typically administered to between 4 500 and 10 000 students in each country.

Content

- PISA 2000 covers the domains of reading, mathematical and scientific literacy not merely in terms of mastery of the school curriculum, but in terms of important knowledge and skills needed in adult life. In 2003, the examination of cross-curriculum competencies will continue to be a part of PISA through the assessment of a new domain of problem solving.

- Emphasis is on the mastery of processes, the understanding of concepts and the ability to function in various situations within each domain.

Methods

- Pencil and paper tests are used, with assessments lasting a total of two hours for each student.

- Test items are a mixture of multiple-choice items and questions requiring students to construct their own responses. The items are organised in groups based on a passage setting out a real-life situation.

- A total of about seven hours of test items is covered, with different students taking different combinations of test items.

- Students answer a background questionnaire, which takes 20-30 minutes to complete, providing information about themselves and their homes. School principals are given a 20-minute questionnaire about their schools.

Assessment cycle

- The assessment takes place every three years, with the first assessment completed in 2000, assessments for 2003 and 2006 are at an advanced planning stage and further assessments beyond the currently being explored.

- Each of these cycles looks in depth at a "major" domain, to which two-thirds of testing time is devoted; the other domains provide a summary profile of skills. Major domains are reading literacy in 2000, mathematical literacy in 2003 and scientific literacy in 2006.

Outcomes

- A basic profile of knowledge and skills among 15-year-old students.

- Contextual indicators relating results to student and school characteristics.

- Trend indicators showing how results change over time.

- A valuable knowledge base for policy analysis and research.

Organisation of this report

As already noted, this new report builds on the analyses reported in *Knowledge and Skills for Life* by examining results from all of the 43 countries that participated in PISA 2000. The current report presents the distributions of performance in each country, not only average scores. In addition, it uses background information on students, their schools and their education systems to examine a range of factors associated with levels of performance. By showing patterns of student proficiency in different countries alongside information about the characteristics and experiences of students, PISA provides a powerful tool to improve understanding of what promotes success in education.

The remainder of *Chapter 1* looks at the PISA approach. It describes what the assessment measures, both overall and within each literacy domain, as well as the methods that were employed. It describes how PISA was developed and discusses potential implications for policy. The 14 non-OECD countries with available data on which this report focuses vary considerably by region, size, per capita wealth, labour market conditions and language, as well as by political and cultural history. It is important to take variations in the contexts within which schools find themselves in these countries into account when interpreting the results from PISA. To address this, the last part of this chapter looks at the broader context that shapes the educational policies. These include youth characteristics, educational paths and the capacity and efforts to finance education.

Chapters 2 and 3 then describe student performance in the three PISA literacy domains, and *Chapter 4* extends this with a profile of students at age 15 with reference to their motivation, engagement, learning strategies and beliefs in their own capacities. *Chapter 5* examines gender differences in student performance in the three literacy domains, both for all students and for specific sub-groups of students.

Chapter 6 situates student performance in the context of students' backgrounds and the broader learning environment. It focuses on a description of the family settings of students, including aspects of their economic, cultural and social backgrounds. This analysis is followed by a discussion of the relationship between school performance and social background through the use of the so-called "social gradients," which allow for the separate estimation of different factors.

Finally, *Chapter 7* examines the conditions of learning environments, including the organisation of schools and how these structures vary across countries. It also looks at the human resources that countries invest in education, selected characteristics of national education systems, and how they are related to learning outcomes.

Box 1.2. The PISA approach

PISA assesses the levels of a wide range of knowledge and skills attained by 15-year-olds. The main features driving the development of PISA have been its:

- policy orientation, with design and reporting methods determined by the need of governments to draw policy lessons;

- innovative approach to literacy, not only in reading but also in science and mathematics;

- focus on the demonstration of knowledge and skills in a form that is relevant to everyday life;

- breadth of geographical coverage, with 43 participating countries that represent one-third of the world population;

- regularity, with a commitment to repeat the survey every three years;

- collaborative nature, with governments from the participating countries jointly steering the project and a consortium of the world's leading institutions in the field of assessment applying cutting-edge scientific know-how.

Through PISA, countries are collaborating to develop comparative indicators on the performance of education systems. This work builds on long-standing work in related areas. For more than a decade, the OECD has been publishing a range of indicators on education systems in its annual publication *Education at a Glance* and it collaborates with the UNESCO Institute for Statistics to extend this work to other countries via the joint World Education Indicators programme. These indicators provide information on the human and financial resources invested in education, on how education and learning systems operate and evolve, and on the individual, social and economic returns from educational investment.

In order to ensure the comparability of the results, PISA needs to assess comparable target populations. Differences between countries in the nature and extent of pre-primary education and care, in the age of entry to formal schooling, and in the structure of the education system, do not allow school grades to be defined so that they are internationally comparable. Valid international comparisons of educational performance must, therefore, define their populations with reference to a target age. PISA covers students who are aged between 15 years and 3 months and 16 years and 2 months at the time of the assessment, regardless of the grade or type of institution in which they are enrolled and of whether they are in full-time or part-time education. PISA excludes 15-year-olds not enrolled in educational institutions. In the remainder of this report "15-year-olds" is used as a shorthand to denote this population. With the exception of Brazil, Luxembourg and Poland, at least 95 per cent of this target population was covered in PISA 2000 by the actual samples, and more than 97 per cent in the majority of countries (for further information on the definition of the PISA population and the coverage of samples see Annex A3). This high level of coverage contributes to the comparability of the assessment results.

As a result, this report is able to make statements about the knowledge and skills of individuals born in the same year and still at school at 15 years of age, but having differing educational experiences, both within and outside school. The number of school grades in which these students are to be found depends on a country's policies on school entry and promotion. Furthermore, in some countries students in the PISA target population represent different education systems, tracks or streams.

What PISA measures

International experts from participating OECD countries defined each of the three literacy domains examined in PISA 2000 – reading, science and mathematics – and drew up a framework for assessing them (OECD, 1999*a*). The concept of literacy used in PISA is broader than the traditional notion of the ability to read and write. Literacy is measured on a continuum, not as something that an individual either does or does not have, even though it may be necessary or desirable for some purposes to define a point on a literacy continuum below which levels of competence are considered inadequate. There is no precise dividing line between a person who is fully literate and one who is not.

The acquisition of literacy is a lifelong process – taking place not just at school or through formal learning but also through interactions with peers, colleagues and wider communities. Fifteen-year-olds cannot be expected to have learned everything they will need to know as adults, but they must have a solid foundation of knowledge in areas such as reading, mathematics and science. In order to continue learning in these domains and to apply their learning to the real world they also need to understand elementary processes and principles and to use these flexibly in different situations. It is for this reason that PISA assesses the ability to complete tasks relating to real life - depending on a broad understanding of key concepts rather than assessing possession of specific knowledge.

In addition to assessing competencies in the three core domains, PISA aims progressively to examine competencies across disciplinary boundaries. PISA 2000 assessed student motivation, other aspects of students' attitudes towards learning, familiarity with computers and, under the heading "self-regulated learning," aspects of students' strategies for managing and monitoring their own learning. In subsequent PISA surveys, further "cross-curricular competencies," such as problem-solving and skills in information technologies, will play a growing role.

To what extent does PISA succeed in measuring "skills for life"? The answer will be based not only on sub-jective judgements about what is important in life, but also on evidence of whether people with the high levels of skills of the type which PISA measures are actually likely to succeed in life. Although the future outcomes for the students participating in PISA cannot yet be known, the International Adult Literacy Survey (IALS) shows that adults' reading literacy skills are closely related to their labour-market success and earnings and have an effect that is independent of their educational attainment (see Box 1.3).

Box 1.3. Does higher reading literacy improve the prospects for employment?

The International Adult Literacy Survey (IALS) found that people with higher levels of reading literacy are more likely to be employed and to have higher average salaries than those with lower levels (OECD and Statistics Canada, 2000). Is this simply because they have better educational qualifications? If it is, then IALS (and PISA) would, at best, be measuring competencies that help people to gain a better education and, through it, better jobs. In IALS, adults who had completed some form of tertiary education scored, on average, between one and two reading literacy levels higher than those who did not complete secondary education. There were, however, significant numbers of adults in the 21 participating countries with a high level of reading literacy and a low level of education, or vice versa. Most importantly, reading literacy levels can help to predict how

---

well people will do in the labour market *over and above* what can be predicted from their educational qualifications alone.

Figure 1.2 illustrates this by showing the likelihood of young people with different combinations of reading literacy and education having a white-collar, highly skilled job. The gaps between the lines show the effects of increasing levels of education; the slopes of the lines show the effect of higher reading literacy at a given level of education. For a person who is between 26 and 35 years of age and working in the business sector, the probability of working in a white-collar, highly skilled job rises rapidly with an increase in reading literacy skills. The independent effect of reading literacy on labour-market outcomes is comparable to the independent effect of educational qualifications. Someone with medium qualifications (upper secondary only) has a two-in-five chance of being in a high-level job if their reading literacy level is 200 (at the low end of the scale) and a four-in-five chance if it is 400 (a high score). Conversely someone with a medium level of reading literacy (a score of 300) has a two-in-five chance of getting such as job with a low level of education (lower secondary education only) and more than a four-in-five chance with a high level of education (a tertiary qualification).

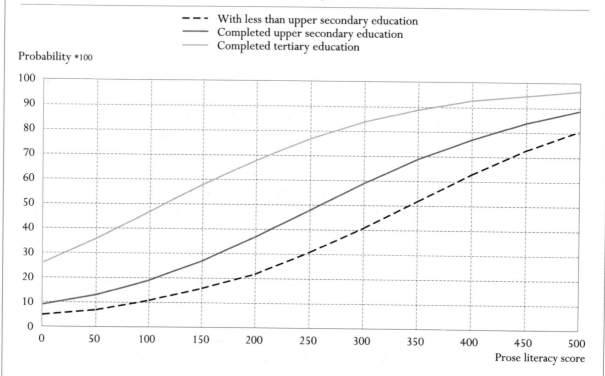

Figure 1.2

Education, literacy and the probability of having a white-collar highly-skilled job
Probability of employment in the white-collar highly-skilled business sector, by level of education and increasing literacy score, all countries combined, IALS prose scale, population aged 26-35, 1994-1998

- - - With less than upper secondary education
—— Completed upper secondary education
········ Completed tertiary education

Probability *100

Source: OECD and Statistics Canada (2000).

The domains covered by PISA are defined in terms of:

- the content or structure of knowledge that students need to acquire in each domain (*e.g.*, familiarity with scientific concepts or various text types);

- the processes that need to be performed (*e.g.*, retrieving written information from a text); and

- the contexts in which knowledge and skills are applied (*e.g.*, making decisions in relation to one's personal life, or understanding world affairs).

Materials in PISA are designed to assess students in each of the three domains. In order to obtain a deeper understanding of each domain over time, however, each cycle of PISA emphasises one domain. PISA 2000 concentrated on reading literacy, to which two-thirds of assessment time was devoted. Consequently, most of this report discusses the results of PISA 2000 in the field of reading literacy.

Reading literacy in PISA

Reading literacy is defined in PISA as the ability to understand, use and reflect on written texts in order to achieve one's goals, to develop one's knowledge and potential, and to participate effectively in society. This definition goes beyond the notion of reading literacy as decoding written material and literal comprehension. Reading incorporates understanding and reflecting on texts. Literacy involves the ability of individuals to use written information to fulfil their goals, and the consequent ability to use written information to function effectively in complex modern societies. PISA 2000 employed about 140 items representing the kinds of reading literacy that 15-year-olds would require in the future. Examples of the assessment items used in PISA to assess reading literacy can be found in Chapter 2 and at the PISA Web site: *www.pisa.oecd.org*.

Readers respond to a given text in a variety of ways as they seek to use and understand what they are reading. This dynamic process has many dimensions, three of which were used to construct the PISA assessments:

- *The form of reading material, or text.* Many past assessments of reading literacy have focused on prose organised in sentences and paragraphs, or "continuous texts". PISA includes continuous prose passages and distinguishes between different types of prose, such as narration, exposition and argumentation. In addition, PISA includes "non-continuous texts," which present information in other ways, including lists, forms, graphs and diagrams. This variety is based on the principle that individuals encounter a range of written texts at school and in adult life that require different information-processing techniques. Flexibility, or the skill to match the type of text to the techniques that are appropriate for locating relevant information in the text, characterises efficient reading.

- *The type of reading task.* This is determined, at one level, by the cognitive skills that are needed to be an effective reader and, at another, by the characteristics of the questions in PISA. The focus of PISA is on "reading to learn", rather than "learning to read". Students are not assessed on the most basic reading skills as most 15-year-olds are assumed to have already acquired these. Rather, they are expected to demonstrate their proficiency in retrieving information, understanding texts at a general level, interpreting them, reflecting on the content and form of texts in relation to their own knowledge of the world, and evaluating and arguing their own point of view.

- **The use for which the text was constructed.** This dimension involves context or situation. For example, a novel, personal letter or biography is written for people's "private" use. Official documents or announcements are for "public" use. A manual or report may be for "occupational" use and a textbook or worksheet for "educational" use.

Mathematical literacy in PISA

Mathematical literacy is defined in PISA as the capacity to identify, understand and engage in mathematics as well as to make well-founded judgements about the role that mathematics plays in an individual's current and future life as a constructive, concerned and reflective citizen. As with reading, the definition revolves around the wider uses of mathematics in people's lives and is not limited to mechanical operations. "Mathematical literacy" is used here to indicate the ability to put mathematical knowledge and skills to use rather than just mastering them within a school curriculum. To "engage in" mathematics covers not just simple calculation (such as deciding how much change to give someone in a shop) but also wider uses, including taking a point of view and appreciating things expressed numerically (such as having an opinion about a government's spending plans). Mathematical literacy also implies not only the ability to pose and solve mathematical problems in a variety of situations but the inclination to do so, a quality that often relies on personal traits such as self-confidence and curiosity.

In order to transform this definition into an assessment of mathematical literacy, three broad dimensions were identified for use in PISA 2000:

- **The content of mathematics.** Content is defined primarily in terms of clusters of relevant, connected mathematical concepts that appear in real situations and contexts. These include quantity, space and shape, change and relationships, and uncertainty. The choice of these topics does not mean that more specific strands of the school curriculum, such as numbers, algebra and geometry, have been ignored. PISA 2000 established tasks that required students to have mastered a balanced mathematical curriculum. However, due to the fact that mathematics was only a minor domain in PISA 2000, the scope of the assessment in this area was more limited, with an emphasis on change and relationships and space and shape. These concepts were selected to allow a wide range of curriculum strands to be represented, without giving undue weight to number skills.

- **The process of mathematics.** Questions in PISA are structured around different types of skills needed for mathematics. Such skills are organised into three "competency clusters". The first cluster – reproduction – consists of simple computations or definitions of the type most familiar in conventional assessments of mathematics. The second – connections – requires the bringing together of mathematical ideas and procedures to solve straightforward and somewhat familiar problems. The third cluster – reflection – consists of mathematical thinking, generalisation and insight and requires students to engage in analysis, to identify the mathematical elements in a situation, to formulate questions and to search for solutions.

- **The situations in which mathematics is used.** Mathematical literacy is assessed by giving students tasks based on situations which, while sometimes fictional, represent the kinds of problem encountered in real life. The situations vary in terms of "distance" from individuals – from those affecting people directly (*e.g.*, deciding whether a purchase offers value for money) to scientific problems of more general interest. In order of closeness to the student, the situations are classified as private life/personal, school life, work and sports, local community and society, and scientific.

Scientific literacy in PISA

PISA defines scientific literacy as the capacity to use scientific knowledge, to identify questions and to draw evidence-based conclusions in order to understand and help make decisions about the natural world and human interactions with it. Scientific literacy is considered a key outcome of education by age 15 for all students, whether or not they continue to study science thereafter. Scientific thinking is demanded of citizens, not just scientists. The inclusion of scientific literacy as a general competency for life reflects the growing centrality of scientific and technological questions. The definition used in PISA does not imply that tomorrow's adults will need large reserves of scientific knowledge. The key is to be able to think scientifically about the evidence that they will encounter. PISA 2000 was developed around three dimensions of scientific literacy:

- *Scientific concepts.* Students need to grasp a number of key concepts in order to understand certain phenomena of the natural world and the changes made to it through human activity. These are the broad integrating ideas that help to explain aspects of the physical environment. PISA asks questions that bring together concepts drawn from physics, chemistry, the biological sciences, and earth and space sciences. More specifically, concepts are drawn from a number of themes, including biodiversity, forces and movement and physiological change.

- *Scientific processes.* PISA assesses the ability to use scientific knowledge and understanding, namely students' ability to acquire, interpret and act on evidence. PISA examines five such processes: the recognition of scientific questions, the identification of evidence, the drawing of conclusions, the communication of these conclusions, and the demonstration of understanding of scientific concepts.

- *Scientific situations and areas of application.* The context of scientific literacy in PISA is primarily everyday life rather than the classroom or laboratory. As with the other forms of literacy, the context thus includes issues that have a bearing on life in general as well as matters of direct personal concern. Questions in PISA 2000 were grouped in three areas in which science is applied: life and health, earth and the environment, and technology.

How PISA assesses students and collects information

PISA 2000 was carefully designed by an international network of leading institutions and experts to serve its purposes. Working in his/her own school, each student participated in a written assessment session of two hours and spent about half an hour responding to a questionnaire about himself or herself. School principals were asked to give further information on school characteristics.

The student assessments followed the same principles in each of the three domains and will do so from one survey to the next, although the amount of assessment material in each domain will differ in each three-year cycle. In PISA 2000, where the main focus was reading literacy, PISA was implemented in the following ways (for details, see the *PISA 2000 Technical Report, OECD, 2002*):

- *A wide range of assessment items.* PISA 2000 assessments were in printed form, with questions taking a range of formats. Students were required to consider written passages and diagrams and to answer a series of questions on each. Much of the material was designed to determine whether students could reflect and think actively about the domain. Examples of items are given in Chapters 2 and 3.

- *Broad coverage of the domain.* Each student was assessed for two hours, although all students were not given the same assessment items. A range of items, equivalent to seven hours of assessment time, was drawn up in order to cover all the areas. Different combinations of items were grouped in nine different assessment booklets. Each item appeared in several booklets, which ensured that each was answered by a representative sample of students. Each student received one booklet.

- *Co-operation between all participating countries in the development of internationally valid assessments.* Using the internationally agreed assessment frameworks and test specifications, countries developed assessment items that were reviewed by subject-matter specialists and assessment experts. Additional items were developed to ensure that all areas of the frameworks were covered adequately. Items were pilot tested, the results were reviewed, and the revised set of items was then validated in a field trial. Finally, in order to ensure that the items were valid across countries, languages and cultures, items were rated by participating countries for cultural appropriateness, curricular and non-curricular relevance, and appropriate level of difficulty.

- *Standardised procedures for the preparation and implementation of the assessment.* PISA represents an effort to achieve comparability of results across countries, cultures and languages. In addition to a comprehensive coverage of 15-year-old students in each country, these efforts have included co-operation with a wide range of experts in all participating countries, the development of standardised procedures for the preparation and implementation of the assessment, and rigorous attention to quality control throughout. The assessment instruments were prepared in both English and French and then translated into the languages of participating countries using procedures that ensured the linguistic integrity and equivalence of the instruments. For non-English and non-French speaking countries, two independent translations of the assessment instruments were prepared and then consolidated, drawing in most cases on both source versions.

Reading literacy was assessed using a series of texts, with a number of tasks on each text. Forty-five per cent of the tasks required students to construct their own responses, either by providing a brief answer from a wide range of possible answers or by constructing a longer response that allowed for the possibility of divergent, individual responses and opposing viewpoints. The latter items usually asked students to relate information or ideas in the stimulus text to their own experience or opinions, and the acceptability of their answer depended less on the position taken by the student than on the ability to use what they had read when justifying or explaining that position. Partial credit was provided for partially correct or less sophisticated answers, and all of these items were marked by hand. A further 45 per cent of the items were asked in multiple-choice format, in which students either made one choice from among four or five given alternatives or a series of choices by circling a word or short phrase (for example "yes" or "no") for each point. The remaining 10 per cent of the items required students to construct their response from a limited range of acceptable answers.

Mathematical literacy was assessed through a combination of question types. As with reading literacy, there were a number of units, each presenting a situation or problem on which students were set several questions or tasks. Different combinations of diagrams and written information introduced each unit. About two-thirds of the items were in a form that could be marked unambiguously as correct or incorrect. Students demonstrated their proficiency by answering problems correctly and showing whether they understood the underlying mathematical principles involved in the task. For more complex items, students could gain full or partial credit.

Scientific literacy was assessed in a manner similar to that of mathematical literacy that employed a series of units, each of which presented a real scientific situation, followed by questions about it. Some two-thirds of the items were in a form that could be marked unambiguously as correct or incorrect. For more complex items, students could gain full or partial credit.

The PISA context questionnaires collected information that was important for the interpretation and analysis of the results. The questionnaires asked about students' characteristics, such as gender, economic and social background, and activities at home and school. As part of an international option, many students also reported on their attitudes towards learning, familiarity with computers and, under the heading "self-regulated learning". strategies for managing and monitoring their own learning. Principals of schools in which students were assessed were asked about the characteristics of their school (such as size and resources) and how learning was organised.

Box 1.4. Developing PISA – a collaborative effort

PISA is a substantial, collaborative effort by participating countries to provide a new kind of assessment of student performance on a recurring basis. The assessments were developed co-operatively, agreed to by participating countries and implemented by national organisations. The constructive co-operation by teachers and principals in participating schools has been a crucial factor contributing to the success of PISA during all stages of the development and implementation.

A Board of Participating Countries, representing participating countries at senior policy levels, laid down policy priorities and standards for the development of indicators, the establishment of the assessment instruments, and the reporting of results. Experts from all participating countries served on working groups linking the programme's policy objectives with the best internationally available technical expertise in the three assessment domains. By participating in these expert groups, countries ensured that the instruments were internationally valid and took into account the cultural and educational contexts of participating countries, that the assessment materials had strong measurement potential and that the instruments emphasised authenticity and educational validity.

Participating countries implemented PISA at the national level through National Project Managers who were subject to technical and administrative procedures common to all participating countries. These managers played a vital role in the development and validation of the international assessment instruments and ensured that the implementation of PISA was of high quality. They also contributed to the verification and evaluation of the survey results, analyses and reports.

The design and implementation of PISA 2000, within the framework established by the Board of Participating Countries, was the responsibility of an international consortium led by the Australian Council for Educational Research (ACER). The other partners in this consortium were the National Institute for Educational Measurement (CITO) in the Netherlands, Westat and the Education Testing Service (ETS) in the United States, and the National Institute for Educational Policy Research (NIER) in Japan.

The OECD Secretariat had overall managerial responsibility for the programme, monitored its implementation on a day-to-day basis, served as the secretariat for the Board of Participating Countries, fostered the building of a consensus between the countries involved and served as the interlocutor between the Board of Participating Countries and the international consortium.

PISA is jointly financed by all participating countries.

How PISA can inform policy

PISA provides a broad assessment of comparative learning outcomes towards the end of compulsory schooling. This assessment can both guide policy decisions and resource allocation and provide insights into the factors that contribute to the development of knowledge and skills and the extent to which these factors are common to different countries. PISA provides international comparisons of the performance of education systems, with cross-culturally valid measures of competencies that are relevant to everyday adult life. Assessments that test only mastery of the school curriculum can offer a measure of the internal efficiency of school systems. They do not reveal how effectively schools prepare students for life after they have completed their formal education.

The information yielded by PISA allows national policy-makers to look closely at the factors associated with educational success, not simply make comparisons between results in isolation. PISA can show, for example, how wide the performance gap is between students from richer and poorer homes in their own country and how this gap compares with those in other countries. PISA also offers insights into the characteristics of schools, such as the way in which learning is organised, and how these characteristics are associated with levels of student performance. Data from PISA can be used to look at which aspects of student attitudes seem to make the greatest contribution to learning. In these and many other ways, PISA offers a new approach to considering school outcomes. It uses as its evidence base the experiences of students across the world rather than in the specific cultural context of a single country.

The international perspective of PISA offers policy-makers a lens through which to recognise the strengths and weaknesses of their own systems. The fact that some countries can achieve a high average level of student performance with only a modest gap between the highest and lowest level of student performance, as shown in Chapters 2 and 3, suggests that large disparities in outcomes do not have to be the price for high average performance. Similarly, the fact that the strength of the relationship between social background and learning outcomes varies widely between countries, as shown in Chapter 6, demonstrates that schools and education systems can succeed in moderating this relationship. Low levels of performance by students from lower social backgrounds are not inevitable. There are things that schools – and policy-makers – can do about poor performance.

Finally, by reporting on student competencies regularly, PISA will enable governments to monitor the progress of their education systems in terms of student outcomes and to evaluate national policies in the light of other countries' performances. The results of PISA 2000 provide a baseline, and every three years countries will be able to see what progress they have made.

In addition to this international report, most participating countries have or are publishing national reports that examine the findings from PISA and consider their policy implications in the national economic, social and educational context. At the international level more detailed thematic reports are being prepared using the outcomes from PISA 2000 to explore specific issues and their implications for policy.

Social, economic and education contexts of the 14 non-OECD countries

Education systems in different countries function within the larger social and economic contexts, which may constitute either advantages or challenges for improving learning outcomes. Given its importance in shaping education systems, understanding the context can provide insights to the challenges that policy-makers face in achieving quality and equity of education for all students. In order to place the PISA findings in a broader context, the remainder of this chapter highlights some key features of the youth population, the educational participation rates and the financial capacities that are regarded as influencing the literacy performance in the participating non-OECD countries.

Characteristics of youth population

Population growth is an important component of the demand for educational services. When the school-age population is becoming large in relation to the size of the working age population, countries must take on extra financial burdens to fund educational services. When youth share of population is declining, governments may be in a position to expand access or shift resources to improve quality.

Between 1990 and 2000 the relative share of the school-age population (5-19 years of age) compared to the total population declined in almost all the 13 non-OECD countries for which data are available, and these proportions are projected to decline further by 2010 (Figure 1.3). The greatest declines in the share of school-age population have been in Thailand, Brazil, Hong Kong-China, Indonesia and Thailand. Nevertheless, the share of school-age population in the non-OECD countries will remain significantly higher than in most OECD countries, with nine out of the 13 countries having a youth share of 20 per cent or higher, compared to an OECD average of 18 per cent.

In countries where populations are largely concentrated in rural areas there are additional challenges providing educational resources. Organizing transportation, communicating between schools and governing organizations, and wiring schools to the Internet tend to be easier in countries with greater population density and a larger proportion of the population living in urban areas. In 2000, while less than 20 per cent of the population of Argentina, Brazil, Chile, Hong Kong-China and Israel live in rural areas, more than 60 per cent of the population in Albania, Indonesia and Thailand do so.

Figure 1.3
Youth aged 5-19 as a percentage of the population, 1990-2010

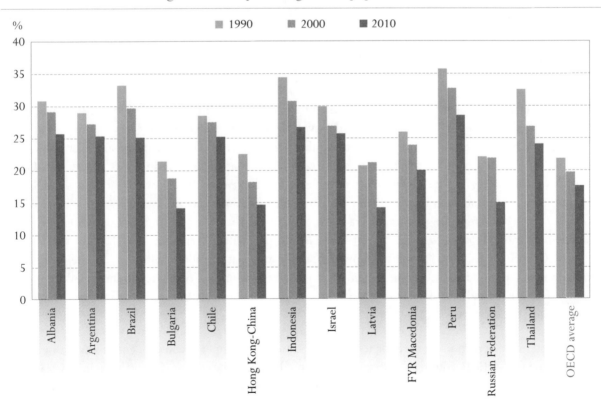

Source: World Population Prospects: The 2000 Revision, United Nations Population Division.

Educational participation and its returns

The literacy skills of 15-year-old students that PISA measures are influenced, among many factors, by the amount of formal schooling – and exposure that students have to different curricula prior to the PISA assessment. In the non-OECD countries, the typical starting age for primary education is age six, although children do not begin primary education until age seven in Brazil, Bulgaria, Indonesia, Latvia and FYR Macedonia. The transition to lower secondary occurs between the ages of ten (Albania and the Russian Federation) and 13 (Indonesia). The transition from lower secondary to upper secondary typically occurs between the ages of 14 (as in Albania and Chile) and 16 (as in Indonesia and Latvia) (see Table 1.1, Annex B1). As a benchmark the average entrance age across OECD countries is six for primary, 12 for lower secondary, and 15 for upper secondary.

Children will reach the end of secondary school by age 15 if they start school at age six or seven and progress on time. A sizeable proportion of children do not make it to secondary education in some of the non-OECD countries. Over 90 per cent of primary students make the transition to secondary education in Albania, Argentina, Bulgaria, Chile, Hong Kong-China Latvia and Peru; about 85 per cent in do so in Thailand; and about 80 per cent make the transition in Indonesia (see Table 1.2, Annex B1). High secondary transition rates indicate that the educational system adequately competes with the youth labour market for students. High enrolment rates in secondary education are an indication that the PISA assessment results reflect the skill levels of most young people in a country, not just a select few who persist to upper secondary schooling. In the non-OECD countries for which data are available, net enrolment rates at the secondary level were below the OECD average of 89 per cent. While they were relatively high in Israel (88 per cent) and Bulgaria (86 per cent), they were considerably lower in Indonesia (48 per cent), Thailand (55 per cent) and Peru (61 per cent). Enrolment rates tend to be similar or favour females in most of the non-OECD countries. Slightly higher proportions of males of secondary education age, however, were attending schools at this level in Bulgaria, Indonesia, FYR Macedonia and Peru (see Table 1.3, Annex B1). To the extent that enrolment rates are an indication of the selectivity of a school system, lower secondary enrolment rates suggest that the PISA results would reflect the literacy performance of the academically successful students in these countries.

Students who start and progress through school on time will reach Grades 9 and 10 by the time when they are 15 years of age. They will be at lower grade levels if they start school late or repeat grades. Thus high rates of grade repetition in a country would mean that many 15-year-old students are at lower grade levels and thus are exposed to less learning than their counterparts at higher grade levels. Some non-OECD countries participating in PISA 2000, especially those in Latin America, experience relatively high rates of repetition. For instance, as many as 9.8 per cent primary school students in Peru and 25.1 per cent in Brazil reported to be repeating a current grade in 1999. At the secondary level, the proportion of students currently repeating a grade was 7 per cent in Peru, 7.6 per cent in Argentina and 15 per cent in Brazil (UNESCO-UIS/OECD, 2001). Some countries practice automatic grade promotion, and hence have few students repeating grades. But to the extent that grade repetition is a result of students' failure to meet locally or nationally defined standards of learning, relatively high repetition rates also suggest that educational quality is a concern.

The programme orientation (general or technical/vocational) of upper secondary enrolments is only available for nine non-OECD countries: Albania, Argentina, Brazil, Chile, Hong Kong-China, Indonesia, Israel, Peru and Thailand (see Table 1.3, Annex B1). Technical/vocational enrolments in upper secondary in these countries run from a low of 5 and 14 per cent in Albania and Hong Kong-China to 58 per cent in Argentina.

Figure 1.4

Earnings differentials by level of educational attainment, population aged 25-64, 1999

■ No schooling   ■ Completed lower secondary (ISCED 2)
■ Completed primary (ISCED 1)   ■ Completed tertiary (ISCED 5A/6)

Males

Multiplier effect relative to upper secondary earnings (log scale)

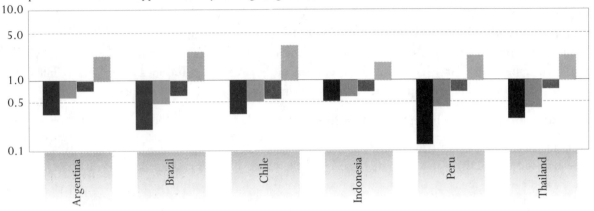

Females

Multiplier effect relative to upper secondary earnings (log scale)

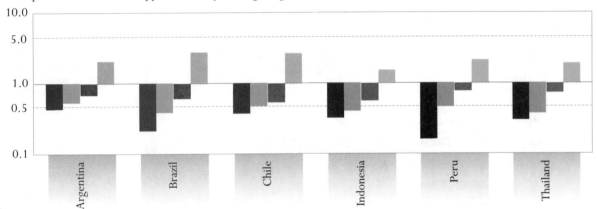

Source: OECD-UNESCO (2003).

The non-OECD countries tend to have a greater percentage of upper secondary students enrolled in general programs than OECD countries. While men are more likely than women to enrol in technical/ vocational programmes as opposed to general programmes in Albania, Chile, Indonesia, Israel, and Thailand, women are more likely than men to enrol in technical/vocational programmes in Argentina.

In most of the developed economies of the OECD, tertiary education has expanded to offer both advanced academic and vocational opportunities to large proportions of young people. The level of access to tertiary education programs varies widely across the non-OECD countries. Gross enrolment ratios in tertiary education range from 15 per cent in Albania and Brazil to between 40 and 50 per cent in Argentina and

Bulgaria, 50 per cent in Israel and Latvia (about the OECD average), to a high of 65 per cent in the Russian Federation. Female enrolment rates tend to be above or similar to male enrolment rates in tertiary education, with the notable exception of Peru (see Table 1.3, Annex B1).

Higher levels of earnings of individuals with more education provide an incentive for people to stay in school. Figure 1.4 shows the ratio of earnings of individuals with different levels of educational attainment relative to those who have completed upper secondary education. For both men and women, those with higher levels of educational attainment had higher earnings. For example, across the 6 non-OECD countries for which earnings data were available by level of educational attainment, men whose highest level of education was primary tended to earn between 40 and 60 per cent less than their counterparts who had completed upper secondary. Tertiary completers earned between 1.8 (Indonesia) and 3.2 (Chile) times more than upper secondary completers. Patterns for employed women were similar.

Capacities and efforts to invest in education

The ability of countries to provide public services, including education, is dependent on their wealth. Gross domestic product (GDP) is an aggregate measure of the value of goods and services that are produced in a country and is thus a measure of a country's productive capacity or wealth. As countries with equal GDPs can have very different numbers of inhabitants, GDP per capita provides a measure of the resources available to a country relative to the size of its population. As Figure 1.5 shows, except Hong Kong-China and Israel, the per capita gross domestic product in all of the non-OECD countries was between 13 per cent and 52 per cent of the OECD average of $24 358, ranging from just over $3 000 in Indonesia to $12 377 in Argentina. This suggests that most of the non-OECD countries need to confront the challenge of financing quality education with fewer resources.

Figure 1.5

GDP per capita (in equivalent US dollars converted using PPPs), 2000

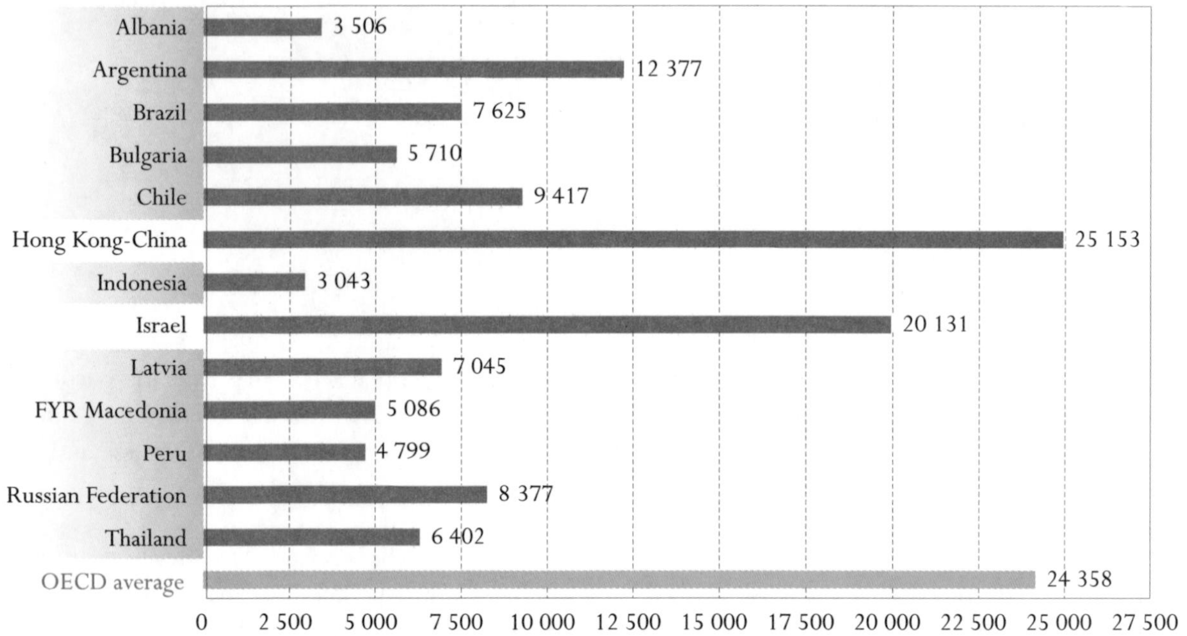

Country	GDP per capita
Albania	3 506
Argentina	12 377
Brazil	7 625
Bulgaria	5 710
Chile	9 417
Hong Kong-China	25 153
Indonesia	3 043
Israel	20 131
Latvia	7 045
FYR Macedonia	5 086
Peru	4 799
Russian Federation	8 377
Thailand	6 402
OECD average	24 358

Source: World Development Indicators 2002, World Bank.
Note: The OECD average is from OECD 2003.

Although it is difficult to assess what level of investment in education best serves the development needs of a country, it is possible to compare the level of "effort" made by the non-OECD countries to invest in their educational systems. One way to benchmark such effort is to compare expenditure on educational institutions as a proportion of GDP. As Figure 1.6 shows, among the non-OECD countries for which public educational expenditure data are available Brazil, Israel, Latvia and Thailand spend 5 per cent or more of their GDP on education, which is the level of spending in all OECD countries on average. By contrast, Indonesia only spends 1.3 per cent of its GDP on education, and the other non-OECD countries spend between 3.4 and 4.9 per cent.

Large disparities in the distribution of wealth within countries can, at least in part, be both a cause and effect of unequal access to educational opportunities. While income disparities exist in all countries, they are more pronounced in some than others. Table 1.4 presents Gini indices of income inequality for the PISA countries with available data, as well as for the average of 28 OECD countries. The indices provide an indication of the disparities in income within countries by measuring the extent to which the distribution of income deviates from a perfectly equal distribution (*i.e.*, where each person has the same income). Theoretical values range from zero (equal distribution of income) to 100, where all income would be concentrated in one unit. In practice, values tend to range from around 20 to 60. Among the non-OECD countries for which data are available, seven – Brazil, Chile, Hong Kong-China, Israel, Peru, the Russian Federation and Thailand – have greater income inequality than the OECD average of 33.2. In each of these

Figure 1.6

Public expenditure on education as percentage of GDP, 1999-2000

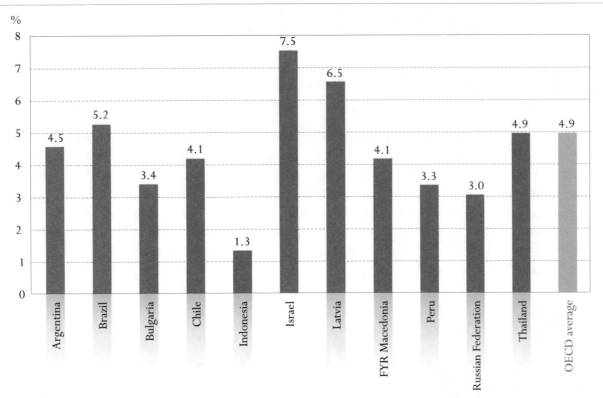

Source: UNESCO Institute for Statistics. Data on Latvia come from European Commission (2002).
Note: Data for Bulgaria and Indonesia refer to 1998/1999. The OECD average is from OECD 2002*e*.

countries, 20 per cent of the population consumes nearly half or more of the country's income. By contrast, Macedonia has the lowest levels of income inequality of the non-OECD countries. Income disparity in Bulgaria, Indonesia and Latvia are closer to the OECD average.

Summary

While the non-OECD countries participating in PISA share some common demographic, educational and economic trends, they differ on others. Even where countries share commonalities, they may face very different challenges in providing quality learning opportunities for all students. In each of the countries, the share of the school-age population in the overall population has been declining and is projected to decline even further over the next two decades. If these countries can maintain the level of per capita resources currently being spent on educational institutions, declines in the student-age population should allow governments to increase access and/or the level of per student resources dedicated to instruction. Projections of increasing retirements over the same period, however, may increase pressures on governments to shift scarce public resource away from education.

Several factors influence the proportion of young people eligible to participate in the PISA assessment in some non-OECD countries. The first is the age at which children start school. While the typical starting age for formal education is similar across the non-OECD countries, the typical ages for the transition from primary to lower secondary and lower secondary to upper secondary vary. The second factor is the proportion of students enrolled in secondary schools. Enrolment rates in many non-OECD countries are lower among students of secondary school age than those in OECD countries. Greater selectivity means that those students targeted by the PISA sample are more likely to be among the academically successful youth cohort. Finally, relatively high rates of grade repetition indicate that a disproportionate number of 15-year-old students attend lower grades than in countries where repetition rates are low. Programmatic options in upper secondary (*e.g.* general vs. vocational) as well as the degree of access to tertiary education could also impact on the incentives for students to stay, and work hard, in school. While mass higher education appears to be a reality in Argentina, Bulgaria, Israel and Latvia, the ability to attend tertiary education is attenuated in other countries, particularly Albania. Countries with above average returns to upper secondary or tertiary completion may provide stronger incentives for young people to stay in school.

The non-OECD countries thus vary widely in their ability to provide quality education services to their population. Cross-country variation in per capita wealth, as well as the internal distribution of that wealth, can affect both the level and distribution of resources for schooling. The wealthiest non-OECD countries participating in PISA have per capita incomes more than four times greater than the poorest countries. Differences in the share of national wealth spent on education also varies considerably across these countries, although the wealthier countries do not necessarily spend a larger share of their wealth on education. The degree to which schools provide equal educational opportunities (a topic addressed in Chapter 7), may be related to variations in income dispersion.

Notes

1. In most OECD countries, the age at which compulsory schooling ends is 15 or 16 years, but in the United States it is 17 years and in Belgium, Germany and the Netherlands it is 18 years (OECD, 2001).

2. For simplicity of expression, the term "country" is used in this report to refer to either a sovereign state or a territory.

3. For China, PISA was conducted only in the Hong Kong Special Administration Region.

4. The data results for Romania are not included in this report due to delayed submission of data.

5. As the Romanian results are not included in this report, the number of non-OECD countries in this report will be referred to as 14 from this point on.

READERS' GUIDE

Data underlying the figures

The data referred to in Chapters 2 to 8 of this report are presented in Annex B1 and, with additional detail, on the web site *www.pisa.oecd.org*. Four symbols are used to denote missing data:

a The category does not apply in the country concerned. Data are therefore missing.

c There are too few observations to provide reliable estimates (*i.e.,* there are fewer than five schools or fewer than 30 students with valid data for this cell).

m Data are not available. Unless otherwise noted, these data were collected but subsequently removed from the publication for technical or other reasons at the request of the country concerned.

x Data are included in another category or column of the table.

Calculation of international averages

An OECD average was calculated for most indicators presented in this report. In the case of some indicators, a total representing the OECD area as a whole was also calculated:

• The **OECD average**, sometimes also referred to as the **country average**, is the mean of the data values for all OECD countries for which data are available or can be estimated. The OECD average can be used to see how a country compares on a given indicator with a typical OECD country. The OECD average does not take into account the absolute size of the student population in each country, *i.e.,* each country contributes equally to the average.

• The **OECD total** takes the OECD countries as a single entity, to which each country contributes in proportion to the number of 15-year-olds enrolled in its schools (see Annex A3 for data). It illustrates how a country compares with the OECD area as a whole.

Three OECD countries are excluded from the calculation of averages or other aggregate estimates: the Netherlands, the Slovak Republic (which became a Member of the OECD in 2000) and Turkey. The Netherlands are excluded because low response rates preclude reliable estimates of mean scores (see Annex A3). The Slovak Republic and Turkey will join PISA from the 2003 survey cycle onwards.

In the case of other countries, data may not be available for specific indicators, or specific categories may not apply. Readers should, therefore, keep in mind that the terms *OECD average* and *OECD total* refer to the OECD countries included in the respective comparisons.

Reporting of student data

The report usually uses "15-year-olds" as shorthand for the PISA target population. In practice, this refers to students who were aged between 15 years and 3 (complete) months and 16 years and 2 (complete) months at the beginning of the assessment period and who were enrolled in an educational institution, regardless of the grade level or type of institution, and of whether they were attending full-time or part-time (for details see Annex A3).

Reporting of school data

The principals of the schools in which students were assessed provided information on their school's characteristics by completing a school questionnaire. Where responses from school principals are presented in this publication, they are weighted so that they are proportionate to the number of 15-year-olds enrolled in the school.

Rounding of figures

Because of rounding, some figures in tables may not exactly add up to the totals. Totals, differences and averages are always calculated on the basis of exact numbers and are rounded only after calculation.

Abbreviations used in this report

The following abbreviations are used in this report:

GDP   Gross Domestic Product

ISCED   International Standard Classification of Education

PPP   Purchasing Power Parity

SD   Standard deviation

SE   Standard error

Country names have been abbreviated in some figures using the International Standards Organisation (ISO) three-digit alphanumeric does as following:

OECD Member countries

Australia	AUS	Korea	KOR
Austria	AUT	Luxembourg	LUX
Belgium	BEL	Mexico	MEX
Canada	CAN	Netherlands	NLD
Czech Republic	CZE	New Zealand	NZL
Denmark	DNK	Norway	NOR
Finland	FIN	Poland	POL
France	FRA	Portugal	PRT
Germany	DEU	Slovak Republic	SVK
Greece	GRC	Spain	ESP
Hungary	HUN	Sweden	SWE
Iceland	ISL	Switzerland	CHE
Ireland	IRL	Turkey	TUR
Italy	ITA	United Kingdom	GBR
Japan	JPN	United States	USA

Non-OECD countries[1]

Albania	ALB	FYR Macedonia	MKD
Argentina	ARG	Latvia	LVA
Brazil	BRA	Liechtenstein	LIE
Bulgaria	BGR	Peru	PER
Chile	CHL	Romania	ROM
Hong Kong-China	HKG	Russian Federation	RUS
Israel	ISR	Thailand	THA
Indonesia	IDN		

Codification used in tables and figures

OECD countries are identified by red text while non-OECD countries are in black. Additionally, countries are classified according to their national income level: low- or middle-income countries are identified by a shaded background. The following have been classified low- and middle-income countries *i*) OECD countries: the Czech Republic, Hungary, Mexico and Poland, and *ii*) Non-OECD countries: Albania, Argentina, Brazil, Bulgaria, Chile, Indonesia, Latvia, FYR Macedonia, Peru, the Russian Federation and Thailand.

◇ OECD countries with high income

◇ OECD countries with low and middle income

◇ Non-OECD countries with high income

◇ Non-OECD countries with low and middle income

In some scatter plot charts, gender was added as differentiation criteria through the following symbols (*e.g.*, Figure 5.5a):

◇ Males, OECD countries (country name in black)

◇ Males, non-OECD countries (country name in black)

☐ Females, OECD countries (country name in red)

☐ Females, non-OECD countries (country name in red)

Further documentation

For further information on the PISA assessment instruments and the methods used in PISA, see the *PISA 2000 Technical Report* (OECD, 2002b) and the PISA Web site (*www.pisa.oecd.org*).

Notes

1. For simplicity of expression, the term "country" is used in this report to refer to either a sovereign state or a territory.

Chapter

2

THE READING PERFORMANCE OF 15-YEAR-OLDS

Introduction

Among the increasing demands placed on the educational development of citizens, reading literacy is fundamental. The emergence of the telephone and television gave rise to the belief that oral and visual modes of communication would soon replace the printed word. Contrary to these expectations, however, the written word has gained in importance as a means of communication.

In our present-day societies literacy bestows advantages on those who have coping skills at the required level. Literacy provides access to literate institutions and resources, and it has an impact on cognition because it shapes the way in which we think. Literacy is also fundamental in dealing with the institutions of a modern bureaucratic society. Law, commerce and science use written documents and written procedures such as legislation, contracts and publications that practitioners must understand in order to function in these domains.

The interest, attitudes and capacity of individuals to access, manage, integrate, evaluate and reflect on written information are all central to the full participation of individuals in modern life. Reading experience adds to our own experience and thus advances and enhances the process of learning to live in our society.

Literacy skills have a significant impact on economic success. The International Adult Literacy Survey (IALS: OECD and Statistics Canada, 1997) shows that, after controlling for educational qualifications, the level of literacy has a strong net direct effect on pre-tax income, on employment, on health and on participation in continued education. This study also shows that people with lower levels of literacy are more likely to depend on public assistance and welfare and to be involved in crime. In addition to the consequences for individuals, such as the lower likelihood of being employed full-time and the greater likelihood of living in poverty, limited overall literacy skills reduce a country's resources and make it less able to meet its goals and objectives, whether they are social, political, civic, or economic.

Reading is also a prerequisite for successful performance in other school subjects. By incorporating the three literacy domains of mathematics, reading and science, PISA 2000 provides information on the relationships between the domains. The correlation between the reading and mathematics scores in PISA for OECD countries is 0.81, and the correlation between reading and science scores is 0.86. Both these correlations are slightly higher if they are computed for girls and boys separately. Reading therefore is not merely a goal; it is also an important tool in education and individual development, both within school and in later life.

Revealing how literacy skills are distributed among young adults and discovering how these skills relate to student background variables are necessary first steps towards remedying lack of sufficient skills by the time young adults leave compulsory education. To address these questions, this chapter reviews the results of PISA in reading literacy by presenting a profile of student performance. The chapter:

- describes the criteria for rating performance in reading literacy and gives examples of easier, medium and harder tasks used in PISA 2000;

- summarises performance in each country by showing the mean scores achieved by students and the distribution of scores across student populations;

- examines how reading performance varies between countries in the combined reading literacy scale as well as in the three reading subscales.

Chapter 3 provides a complementary analysis of student performance in mathematical and scientific literacy and examines how performance in these domains differs from performance in reading literacy. Chapter 4 broadens the profile of PISA findings further by analysing students' reports on their familiarity with computers, their learning strategies, and non-cognitive outcomes of schooling that are important for lifelong learning: motivation, engagement and students' beliefs in their own capacities.

How reading literacy is assessed in PISA

Reading literacy is defined in PISA as the ability to understand, use and reflect on written texts in order to achieve one's goals, to develop one's knowledge and potential, and to participate effectively in society. This definition goes beyond the notion of reading literacy as decoding written material or as literal comprehension. Reading incorporates understanding and reflecting on texts. Literacy equips individuals to use written information to fulfil their goals, and it empowers complex modern societies to use written information to function effectively. PISA 2000 employed tasks reflecting the kinds of reading literacy that 15-year-olds would require in the future.

Readers respond to a given text in a variety of ways as they seek to use and understand what they are reading. This dynamic process has many dimensions, three of which were used to construct the PISA assessments:

- The ***form of reading material***, or text. Many past assessments of reading literacy have focused on prose organised in sentences and paragraphs, or "continuous texts". PISA includes continuous *prose* passages and distinguishes between different types of prose, such as *narration*, *exposition* and *argumentation*. In addition, PISA includes "non-continuous texts," which present information in other ways, including *lists, forms, graphs* and *diagrams*. This variety is based on the principle that individuals encounter a range of written texts at school and in adult life that require different information-processing techniques. Flexibility, or the skill to match the type of text to the techniques that are appropriate for locating relevant information in the text, characterises efficient reading.

- The ***type of reading task***. This is determined, at one level, by the cognitive skills that are needed to be an effective reader and, at another, by the characteristics of the questions in PISA. The focus of PISA is on "reading to learn" rather than "learning to read". Students are thus not assessed on the most basic reading skills because it is assumed that most 15-year-olds have already acquired them. Rather, they are expected to demonstrate their proficiency in *retrieving* information, *understanding* texts at a general level, *interpreting* them, *reflecting* on the content and form of texts in relation to their own knowledge of the world, and *evaluating* and *arguing* their own point of view.

- The ***use for which the text was constructed***. Literacy operates in specific contexts or situations. For example, while a novel, personal letter or biography is written for people's *private* use, official documents or announcements are for *public* use. A manual or report may be for *occupational* use and a textbook or worksheet for *educational* use.

A detailed description of the conceptual framework underlying the PISA assessment of reading literacy is provided in *Measuring Student Knowledge and Skills — A New Framework for Assessment* (OECD, 1999*a*). This concept of reading literacy in PISA has guided the development of the assessment for the PISA survey.

To ensure that the assessment provided the broadest possible coverage of reading literacy as defined here, some 141 reading literacy tasks were constructed and administered to nationally representative samples of

15-year-olds in participating countries. No individual student, however, could be expected to respond to the entire set of tasks. Accordingly, the survey was designed to give each participating student a subset of the total pool of tasks, while at the same time ensuring that each of the tasks was administered to nationally representative samples of students.

One may imagine these 141 reading literacy tasks arranged along a continuum showing the difficulty for students and the level of skills required to answer each task correctly. The procedure used in PISA to capture this continuum of task difficulty and student ability is referred to as Item Response Theory (IRT). IRT is a mathematical model used for estimating the probability that a particular person will respond correctly to a given task from a specified pool of tasks. This probability is modelled along a single continuum which summarises both the proficiency of a person in terms of their ability and the complexity of a task in terms of its difficulty. This continuum of difficulty and proficiency is referred to as a "scale."

A "retrieving information" scale reports on students' ability to locate information in a text. An "interpreting texts" scale reports on the ability to construct meaning and draw inferences from written information. A "reflection and evaluation" scale reports on students' ability to relate text to their knowledge, ideas and experiences. In addition, a combined reading literacy scale summarises the results from the three reading literacy scales.

To facilitate the interpretation of the scores assigned to students, the combined reading literacy scale was designed to have an average score of 500 points for OECD countries, with about two-thirds of students across OECD countries scoring between 400 and 600 points[1]. These reference points provide an "anchor" for the measurement of student performance. The mean scores for the three scales that contribute to the combined reading scale differ slightly from 500.

The scores on the reading literacy scale represent varying degrees of proficiency. A low score indicates that a student has very limited knowledge and skills, while a high score indicates that a student has quite advanced knowledge and skills. Use of IRT makes it possible not only to summarise results for various subpopulations of students, but also to determine the relative difficulty of the reading literacy tasks included in the survey. In other words, just as individuals receive a specific value on a scale according to their performance in the assessment tasks, so each task receives a specific value on a scale according to its difficulty, as determined by the performance of students across the various countries that participated in the assessment.

The complete set of reading literacy tasks used in PISA varies widely in text type, situation and task requirements – and also in difficulty. This range is illustrated in a task map (Figure 2.1). This task map provides a visual representation of the reading literacy skills demonstrated by students along the combined reading literacy scale and the three subscales. The map contains a brief description of a selected number of assessment tasks along with their scale values. These descriptions take into consideration the specific skills the task is designed to assess and, in the case of open-ended tasks, the criteria used for judging the task correct. An examination of the descriptions provides some insight into the range of processes required of students and the proficiencies they need to demonstrate at various points along the reading literacy scales.

Figure 2.1

PISA reading task maps

Task difficulty on PISA scale	Nature of Tasks	Retrieving information	Interpreting texts	Reflection and evaluation
822	**HYPOTHESISE** about an unexpected phenomenon by taking account of outside knowledge along with all relevant information in a **COMPLEX TABLE** on a relatively unfamiliar topic. (score 2)			○
727	**ANALYSE** several described cases and **MATCH** to categories given in a **TREE DIAGRAM**, where some of the relevant information is in footnotes. (score 2)		○	
705	**HYPOTHESISE** about an unexpected phenomenon by taking account of outside knowledge along with some relevant information in a **COMPLEX TABLE** on a relatively unfamiliar topic. (score 1)			○
652	**EVALUATE** the ending of a **LONG NARRATIVE** in relation to its implicit theme or mood. (score 2)			○
645	**RELATE NUANCES OF LANGUAGE** in a **LONG NARRATIVE** to the main theme, in the presence of conflicting ideas. (score 2)		○	
631	**LOCATE** information in a **TREE DIAGRAM** using information in a footnote. (score 2)	○		
603	**CONSTRUE** the meaning of a sentence by relating it to broad context in a **LONG NARRATIVE**.		○	
600	**HYPOTHESISE** about an authorial decision by relating evidence in a graph to the inferred main theme of **MULTIPLE GRAPHIC DISPLAYS**.			○
581	**COMPARE AND EVALUATE** the style of two open **LETTERS**.			○
567	**EVALUATE** the ending of a **LONG NARRATIVE** in relation to the plot.			○
542	**INFER AN ANALOGICAL RELATIONSHIP** between two phenomena discussed in an open **LETTER**.		○	
540	**IDENTIFY** the implied starting date of a **GRAPH**.	○		
539	**CONSTRUE THE MEANING** of short quotations from a **LONG NARRATIVE** in relation to atmosphere or immediate situation. (score 1)		○	
537	**CONNECT** evidence from **LONG NARRATIVE** to personal concepts in order to justify opposing points of view. (score 2)			○
529	**EXPLAIN** a character's motivation by linking events in a **LONG NARRATIVE**.		○	
508	**INFER THE RELATIONSHIP** between **TWO GRAPHIC DISPLAYS** with different conventions.		○	
486	**EVALUATE** the suitability of a **TREE DIAGRAM** for particular purposes.			○
485	**LOCATE** numerical information in a **TREE DIAGRAM**.	○		
480	**CONNECT** evidence from **LONG NARRATIVE** to personal concepts in order to justify a single point of view. (score 1)			○
478	**LOCATE AND COMBINE** information in a **LINE GRAPH** and its introduction to infer a missing value.	○		
477	**UNDERSTAND** the structure of a **TREE DIAGRAM**.		○	
473	**MATCH** to categories given in a **TREE DIAGRAM** to described cases, when some of the relevant information is in footnotes.		○	
447	**INTERPRET** information in a single paragraph to understand the setting of a **NARRATIVE**.		○	
445	Distinguish between variables and **STRUCTURAL FEATURES** of a **TREE DIAGRAM**.			○
421	**IDENTIFY** the common **PURPOSE** of **TWO SHORT TEXTS**.		○	
405	**LOCATE** pieces of explicit information in a **TEXT** containing strong organizers.	○		
397	Infer the **MAIN IDEA** of a simple **BAR GRAPH** from its title.		○	
392	**LOCATE** a literal piece of information in a **TEXT** with clear text structure.	○		
367	**LOCATE** explicit information in a short, specified section of a **NARRATIVE**.	○		
363	**LOCATE** an explicitly stated piece of information in a **TEXT** with headings.	○		
356	**RECOGNISE THEME** of an article having a clear subheading and considerable redundancy.		○	

Source: *Reading for Change: Performance and Engagement across Countries* (OECD, 2002*b*)

An example of how to interpret the task map may be useful. In Figure 2.1, a task at 421 on the combined reading literacy scale requires students to identify the purpose that two short texts have in common by comparing the main ideas in each of them. The score assigned to each task is based on the theory that someone at a given point on the scale is equally proficient in all tasks at that point on the scale. It was decided that, for the purposes of PISA, "proficiency" should mean that students at a particular point on the reading literacy scale would have a 62 per cent chance of responding correctly to tasks at that point. This means that students scoring 421 on the composite reading literacy scale will have a 62 per cent chance of correctly answering tasks graded 421 on the scale. This does not mean that students receiving scores below 421 will always answer incorrectly. Rather, students will have a higher or lower probability of responding correctly in line with their estimated score on the reading literacy scale. Students having scores above 421 will have a greater than 62 per cent chance of responding correctly while those scoring below 421 will be expected to answer a task of that level of difficulty correctly less than 62 per cent of the time. It should be noted that the task will also appear on an aspect subscale as well as on the combined reading literacy scale.

Just as students within each country are sampled from the population of 15-year-old students within the country, each reading literacy task is selected from a class of tasks within the reading literacy domain. Hence, it is indicative of a type of text and of a type of processing that 15-year-old students should have acquired.

Even a cursory glance at Figure 2.1 will reveal that, as might be expected, tasks at the lower end of each scale require very different skills from those at the higher end. A more careful analysis of the range of tasks along each reading literacy scale provides some indication of an ordered set of knowledge-construction skills and strategies. For example, all tasks on the retrieving information scale require students to locate information in prose texts or other forms of writing. The easiest tasks on this scale require students to locate explicitly stated information according to a single criterion where there is little, if any, competing information in the text.

By contrast, tasks at the high end of this scale require students to locate and sequence multiple pieces of deeply embedded information, sometimes in accordance with multiple criteria. Often there is competing information in the text that shares some features with the information required for the answer. Similarly, on the interpreting scale and the reflection and evaluation scale, tasks at the lower end differ from those at the higher end in terms of the process needed to answer them correctly, the degree to which the reading strategies required for a correct answer are signalled in the question or the instructions, the level of complexity and familiarity of the text, and the quantity of competing or distracting information present in the text.

Members of the reading expert group examined each task to identify a set of variables that seemed to influence its difficulty. They found that difficulty is in part determined by the length, structure and complexity of the text itself. They also noted, however, that in most reading units (a unit being a text and a set of questions or directives) the questions or directives range across the reading literacy scale. This means that while the structure of a text contributes to the difficulty of a task, what the reader is asked to do with that text interacts with the text and thus affects overall difficulty.

A number of variables were identified that can influence the difficulty of any reading literacy task. The type of process involved in retrieving information, developing an interpretation or reflecting on what has been read is one salient factor. Processes range in complexity and sophistication from making simple connections between pieces of information to categorising ideas according to given criteria or critically evaluating and hypothesising about a section of text. In addition to the type of process called for, the difficulty of retrieving information tasks is associated with the number of pieces of information to be included in the response, the number of criteria which the information found must satisfy, and whether what is retrieved needs to be sequenced in a particular way. In the case of interpretative and reflective tasks, the amount of a text that needs to be assimilated is an important factor affecting difficulty. In tasks that require reflection on the reader's part, difficulty is also conditioned by the familiarity or specificity of the knowledge that must be drawn on from outside the text. In all aspects of reading, the difficulty of the task depends on how prominent the required information is, how much competing information is present, and whether or not it is explicitly stated which ideas or information are required to complete the task.

PISA proficiency level

In an attempt to capture this progression of complexity and difficulty, the composite reading literacy scale and each of the subscales were divided into five levels:

Level	Score points on the PISA scale
1	335 to 407
2	408 to 480
3	481 to 552
4	553 to 625
5	more than 625

Tasks within each level of reading literacy were judged by expert panels to share specific features and requirements and to differ in systematic ways from tasks at either higher or lower levels. The assumed difficulty of tasks was then validated empirically on the basis of student performance in participating countries. As a result, these levels appear to be a useful way to explore the progression of reading literacy demands within each scale. This progression is summarised in Figure 2.2. As shown, each successive reading level is associated with tasks of ascending difficulty

Students at a particular level not only demonstrate the knowledge and skills associated with that level but also possess the proficiencies required at lower levels. Thus all students proficient at Level 3 are also proficient at Levels 1 and 2. All students at a given level are expected to answer at least half of the tasks at that level correctly.

Students scoring below 335 points, *i.e.,* who do not reach Level 1, are not able routinely to show the most basic skills that PISA seeks to measure. While such performance should not be interpreted to mean that those students have no literacy skills at all[2], performance below Level 1 does signal serious deficiencies in students' ability to use reading literacy as a tool for the acquisition of knowledge and skills in other areas.

The division of the scales into levels of difficulty and of performance makes it possible not only to rank students' performance but also to describe what they can do. This description can be best understood through examination of the tasks.

The discussion of tasks that represent various proficiency levels will provide some insight into the range of processes required of students and the proficiencies that they need to demonstrate at various points along the reading literacy scales.

Figure 2.2

Reading literacy levels map

	Retrieving information	Interpreting texts	Reflection and evaluation
5	Locate and possibly sequence or combine multiple pieces of deeply embedded information, some of which may be outside the main body of the text. Infer which information in the text is relevant to the task. Deal with highly plausible and/or extensive competing information.	Either construe the meaning of nuanced language or demonstrate a full and detailed understanding of a text.	Critically evaluate or hypothesise, drawing on specialised knowledge. Deal with concepts that are contrary to expectations and draw on a deep understanding of long or complex texts.

Continuous texts: Negotiate texts whose discourse structure is not obvious or clearly marked, in order to discern the relationship of specific parts of the text to its implicit theme or intention.
Non-continuous texts: Identify patterns among many pieces of information presented in a display which may be long and detailed, sometimes by referring to information external to the display. The reader may need to realise independently that a full understanding of the section of text requires reference to a separate part of the same document, such as a footnote.

4	Locate and possibly sequence or combine multiple pieces of embedded information, each of which may need to meet multiple criteria, in a text with unfamiliar context or form. Infer which information in the text is relevant to the task.	Use a high level of text-based inference to understand and apply categories in an unfamiliar context, and to construe the meaning of a section of text by taking into account the text as a whole. Deal with ambiguities, ideas that are contrary to expectation and ideas that are negatively worded.	Use formal or public knowledge to hypothesise about or critically evaluate a text. Show accurate understanding of long or complex texts.

Continuous texts: Follow linguistic or thematic links over several paragraphs, often in the absence of clear discourse markers, in order to locate, interpret or evaluate embedded information or to infer psychological or metaphysical meaning.
Non-continuous texts: Scan a long, detailed text in order to find relevant information, often with little or no assistance from organisers such as labels or special formatting, to locate several pieces of information to be compared or combined.

3	Locate, and in some cases recognise the relationship between pieces of information, each of which may need to meet multiple criteria. Deal with prominent competing information.	Integrate several parts of a text in order to identify a main idea, understand a relationship or construe the meaning of a word or phrase. Compare, contrast or categorise taking many criteria into account. Deal with competing information.	Make connections or comparisons, give explanations, or evaluate a feature of text. Demonstrate a detailed understanding of the text in relation to familiar, everyday knowledge, or draw on less common knowledge.

Continuous texts: Use conventions of text organisation, where present, and follow implicit or explicit logical links such as cause and effect relationships across sentences or paragraphs in order to locate, interpret or evaluate information.
Non-continuous texts: Consider one display in the light of a second, separate document or display, possibly in a different format, or combine several pieces of spatial, verbal and numeric information in a graph or map to draw conclusions about the information represented.

2	Locate one or more pieces of information, each of which may be required to meet multiple criteria. Deal with competing information.	Identify the main idea in a text, understand relationships, form or apply simple categories, or construe meaning within a limited part of the text when the information is not prominent and low-level inferences are required.	Make a comparison or connections between the text and outside knowledge, or explain a feature of the text by drawing on personal experience and attitudes.

Continuous texts: Follow logical and linguistic connections within a paragraph in order to locate or interpret information; or synthesise information across texts or parts of a text in order to infer the author's purpose.
Non-continuous texts: Demonstrate a grasp of the underlying structure of a visual display such as a simple tree diagram or table, or combine two pieces of information from a graph or table.

1	Locate one or more independent pieces of explicitly stated information, typically meeting a single criterion, with little or no competing information in the text.	Recognise the main theme or author's purpose in a text about a familiar topic, when the required information in the text is prominent.	Make a simple connection between information in the text and common, everyday knowledge.

Continuous texts: Use redundancy, paragraph headings or common print conventions to form an impression of the main idea of the text, or to locate information stated explicitly within a short section of text.
Non-continuous texts: Focus on discrete pieces of information, usually within a single display such as a simple map, a line graph or a bar graph that presents only a small amount of information in a straightforward way, and in which most of the verbal text is limited to a small number of words or phrases.

Samples of the reading tasks used in PISA

Runners

The first text is a piece of expository prose from a French-Belgian magazine produced for adolescent students. It is classed as belonging to the educational situation. One of the reasons for its selection as part of the PISA 2000 reading instrument is its subject, which was considered of great interest for the PISA population of 15-year-olds. The article includes an attractive cartoon-like illustration and is broken up by catchy sub-headings. Within the continuous text format category, it is an example of expository writing in that it provides an outline of a mental construct, laying out a set of criteria for judging the quality of running shoes in terms of their fitness for young athletes.

The tasks within this unit cover all three aspects – retrieving information, interpreting texts and reflection and evaluation – but all are relatively easy, falling within Level 1.

Two of the four *Runners* tasks are reproduced below.

Feel good in your runners

For 14 years the Sports Medicine Centre of Lyon (France) has been studying the injuries of young sports players and sports professionals. The study has established that the best course is prevention ... and good shoes.

Knocks, falls, wear and tear...

Eighteen per cent of sports players aged 8 to 12 already have heel injuries. The cartilage of a footballer's ankle does not respond well to shocks, and 25% of professionals have discovered for themselves that it is an especially weak point. The cartilage of the delicate knee joint can also be irreparably damaged and if care is not taken right from childhood (10–12 years of age), this can cause premature osteoarthritis. The hip does not escape damage either and, particularly when tired, players run the risk of fractures as a result of falls or collisions.

According to the study, footballers who have been playing for more than ten years have bony outgrowths either on the tibia or on the heel. This is what is known as "footballer's foot", a deformity caused by shoes with soles and ankle parts that are too flexible.

Protect, support, stabilise, absorb

If a shoe is too rigid, it restricts movement. If it is too flexible, it increases the risk of injuries and sprains. A good sports shoe should meet four criteria:

Firstly, it must *provide exterior protection*: resisting knocks from the ball or another player, coping with unevenness in the ground, and keeping the foot warm and dry even when it is freezing cold and raining.

It must *support the foot*, and in particular the ankle joint, to avoid sprains, swelling and other problems, which may even affect the knee.

It must also provide players with good *stability* so that they do not slip on a wet ground or skid on a surface that is too dry.

Finally, it must *absorb shocks*, especially those suffered by volleyball and basketball players who are constantly jumping.

Dry feet

To avoid minor but painful conditions such as blisters or even splits or athlete's foot (fungal infections), the shoe must allow evaporation of perspiration and must prevent outside dampness from getting in. The ideal material for this is leather, which can be water-proofed to prevent the shoe from getting soaked the first time it rains.

Source: Revue ID (16) 1-15 June 1997.

Question 1: RUNNERS

What does the author intend to show in this text?

A   That the quality of many sports shoes has greatly improved.

B   That it is best not to play football if you are under 12 years of age.

C   That young people are suffering more and more injuries due to their poor physical condition.

D   That it is very important for young sports players to wear good sports shoes.

Situation: Educational
Text format: Continuous
Aspect: Interpreting texts
Level: 1
PISA scale score: 356

The easiest task in the unit is an interpreting task [R110Q01][3] falling within Level 1 with a PISA scale score of 356. It requires the reader to recognise the article's main idea in a text about a familiar topic.

The author's main message is not stated directly, or synonymously, so the task is classified as interpreting texts rather than retrieving information. There are at least two features that make this task easy. First, the required information is located in the introduction, which is a short section of text. Secondly, there is a good deal of redundancy, the main idea in the introduction being repeated several times throughout the text. Reading tasks tend to be relatively easy when the information they require the reader to use is either near the beginning of the text or repeated. This task meets both of these criteria.

The question is intended to discover whether students can form a broad understanding. Only small percentages of students did not select the correct answer, and they were spread over the three distractors A, B and C. The smallest percentage and least able selected alternative B, "That it is best not to play football if you are under 12 years of age." These students may have been trying to match words from the question with the text, and linked "12" in distractor B with two references to 12-year-olds near the beginning of the article.

Question 2: RUNNERS

According to the article, why should sports shoes not be too rigid?

Situation: Educational
Text format: Continuous
Aspect: Retrieving information
Level: 1
PISA scale score: 392

A second task [R110Q04] also falls within Level 1 with a PISA scale score of 392 and is classified as retrieving information in terms of aspect. It requires readers to locate a piece of explicitly stated information that satisfies one single criterion.

The reader can directly match the word "rigid" in the question with the relevant part of the text, making the information easy to find. Although the required information is midway through the text, rather than near the beginning as in the previous task, it is quite prominent because it is near the beginning of one of the three sections marked by sub-headings.

In order to receive full credit, students need to refer to *restriction of movement*. However, this is a relatively easy task as full credit can be gained by quoting directly from the text: "It restricts movement". Many students nonetheless used their own words such as:

"They prevent you from running easily."

or

"So you can move around."

No credit is given if students show *inaccurate comprehension* of the material or gave *implausible or irrelevant* answers. A common error was to give an answer such as:

"Because you need support for your foot."

This is the opposite of the answer required, though it is also an idea located in the text. Students who gave this kind of answer may have overlooked the negative in the question ("… not be too rigid"), or made their own association between the ideas of "rigidity" and "support", leading them to a section of the text that was not relevant to this task. Other than this, there is little competing information to distract the reader.

Graffiti

The stimulus for this unit consists of two letters posted on the Internet, originally from Finland. The tasks simulate typical literacy activities, since as readers we often synthesise, and compare and contrast ideas from two or more different sources.

Because they are published on the Internet, the *Graffiti* letters are classified as public in terms of situation. They are classified as argumentation within the broader classification of continuous texts, as they set forth propositions and attempt to persuade the reader to a point of view.

As with *Runners*, the subject matter of *Graffiti* was expected to be interesting for 15-year-olds: the implied debate between the writers as to whether graffiti makers are artists or vandals would represent a real issue in the minds of the test-takers.

The four tasks from the *Graffiti* unit used to measure reading proficiency in PISA 2000 range in difficulty from Level 2 to Level 4 and address the aspects of interpreting texts and reflection and evaluation.

Three of these tasks are presented here.

I'm simmering with anger as the school wall is cleaned and repainted for the fourth time to get rid of graffiti. Creativity is admirable but people should find ways to express themselves that do not inflict extra costs upon society.

Why do you spoil the reputation of young people by painting graffiti where it's forbidden? Professional artists do not hang their paintings in the streets, do they? Instead they seek funding and gain fame through legal exhibitions.

In my opinion buildings, fences and park benches are works of art in themselves. It's really pathetic to spoil this architecture with graffiti and what's more, the method destroys the ozone layer. Really, I can't understand why these criminal artists bother as their "artistic works" are just removed from sight over and over again.

Helga

There is no accounting for taste. Society is full of communication and advertising. Company logos, shop names. Large intrusive posters on the streets. Are they acceptable? Yes, mostly. Is graffiti acceptable? Some people say yes, some no.

Who pays the price for graffiti? Who is ultimately paying the price for advertisements? Correct. The consumer.

Have the people who put up billboards asked your permission? No. Should graffiti painters do so then? Isn't it all just a question of communication — your own name, the names of gangs and large works of art in the street?

Think about the striped and chequered clothes that appeared in the stores a few years ago. And ski wear. The patterns and colours were stolen directly from the flowery concrete walls. It's quite amusing that these patterns and colours are accepted and admired but that graffiti in the same style is considered dreadful.

Times are hard for art.

Sophia

Source: Mari Hamkala.

Question 3: GRAFFITI

The purpose of each of these letters is to

A   explain what graffiti is.

(B) present an opinion about graffiti.

C   demonstrate the popularity of graffiti.

D   tell people how much is spent removing graffiti.

Situation: Public
Text format: Continuous
Aspect: Interpreting texts
Level: 2
PISA scale score: 421

This Level 2 interpreting task [R081Q01] with a PISA score of 421 requires students to identify the purpose that two short texts have in common by comparing the main ideas in each of them. The information is not prominent, and low-level inference is required. The intention of the question is to establish whether the student can form a broad understanding and recognise the purpose of the text. The reader needs to follow logical connections, synthesising information from both texts in order to infer the authors' purposes. The need to compare and contrast the two letters makes this task more difficult than, for instance, a task which asks the purpose of a single letter only.

Of those who did not select the correct alternative, B, the largest proportion selected D, "Tell people how much is spent removing graffiti". Although this is not the main idea of even one of the letters, it does relate strongly to the first few lines of the first letter, and thus its choice may reflect the characteristic difficulty of less proficient readers in getting beyond the first part of a text.

Question 4: GRAFFITI

Why does Sophia refer to advertising?

Situation: *Public*
Text format: *Continuous*
Aspect: *Interpreting texts*
Level: *3*
PISA scale score: *542*

This more difficult Interpreting task based on the *Graffiti* texts [R081Q05] falls within Level 3 with a PISA score of 542. The task requires students to follow an implicit logical link between sentences, in this case a comparison between advertising and graffiti. The relative difficulty of the task can be attributed to the fact that the comparison must be construed from a series of questions and challenges. In order to answer the question correctly, the student must recognise that a *comparison* is being drawn between graffiti and advertising. The answer must be consistent with the idea that advertising is a legal form of graffiti. Or the student must recognise that referring to advertising is a *strategy to defend graffiti*. Typical full-credit answers ranged from those that gave a relatively detailed and specific explanation such as:

   "Because there are many billboards and posters that are an eyesore but these are legal."

to those that merely recognised the writer's comparison between graffiti and advertising such as:

   "She says advertising is like graffiti."

No credit is given for *insufficient or vague* answers, or if the student shows *inaccurate comprehension* of the material or gave an *implausible or irrelevant answer*.

Question 5: GRAFFITI

We can talk about **what** a letter says (its content).

We can talk about **the way** a letter is written (its style).

Regardless of which letter you agree with, in your opinion, which do you think is the better letter? Explain your answer by referring to **the way** one or both letters are written.

Situation: *Public*

Text format: *Continuous*

Aspect: *Reflection and evaluation*

Level: *4*

PISA scale score: *581*

The most difficult task associated with the *Graffiti* texts [R081Q06B] falls within Level 4 with a PISA score of 581. It requires students to use formal knowledge to evaluate the writer's craft by comparing the two letters. In the five-aspect categorisation, this task is classified as reflection on and evaluation of the form of a text, since to answer it, readers need to draw on their own understanding of what constitutes good writing.

Full credit may be given for many types of answers, including those dealing with one or both writers' tone or argumentative strategies, or with the structure of the piece. Students are expected to explain opinion with *reference to the style or form* of one or both letters. Reference to criteria such as style of writing, structure of argument, cogency of argument, tone, register used and strategies for persuading the reader are given full credit, but terms such as "better arguments" need to be substantiated.

Some typical answers that earned full credit were:

"Helga's letter was effective because of the way she addressed the graffiti artists directly."

"In my opinion, the second letter is better because it has questions that involve you making you feel that you are having a discussion rather than a lecture."

Answers that were not given credit were often vague or could apply equally to either letter, such as:

"Helga's was better because it was more trustworthy."

"Sophia's was written better."

or they related to content rather than style, such as:

"Helga's. I agree with what she said."

"Sophia, because graffiti is a form of art."

or they clearly misunderstood the rhetorical tone of the letters, especially the second:

"Helga's was better, because Sophia didn't show her opinion, she just asked questions."

The relative difficulty of the task, and of other similar tasks in the PISA reading assessment, suggests that many 15-year-olds are not practised in drawing on formal knowledge about structure and style to make critical evaluations of texts.

The gift

The tasks in this unit are classified as personal in the situation dimension, and as continuous in the text format category. The text type is narrative.

This short story from the United States represents the humane, affective and aesthetic qualities of literature that make reading this kind of text an important part of many people's personal lives. A significant reason for its inclusion in the PISA assessment was the literary quality of the piece: its spare, precise use of language and its strong yet subtle rendering of the woman's state of mind and evolving response to the panther.

Another reason for including *The gift* in the PISA assessment was its length. It is a relatively *short* story in comparison with many others that have been published, but it is a long piece compared with the material generally presented to students in assessments of this kind. The international reading expert panel that developed the reading framework and oversaw the test development considered that perseverance in reading longer texts was an important facet in reading proficiency that ought to be addressed in the PISA assessment.

In PISA, the number of tasks attached to each text is roughly proportionate to the amount of reading required. As the longest text, *The gift* supported the greatest number of tasks. Five of the seven tasks are presented here with commentary. The full set of *The gift* tasks covers all three aspects and all five levels of difficulty.

How many days, she wondered, had she sat like this, watching the cold brown water inch up the dissolving bluff. She could just faintly remember the beginning of the rain, driving in across the swamp from the south and beating against the shell of her house. Then the river itself started rising, slowly at first until at last it paused to turn back. From hour to hour it slithered up creeks

5   and ditches and poured over low places. In the night, while she slept, it claimed the road and surrounded her so that she sat alone, her boat gone, the house like a piece of drift lodged on its bluff. Now even against the tarred planks of the supports the waters touched. And still they rose.

As far as she could see, to the treetops where the opposite banks had been, the swamp was an

10   empty sea, awash with sheets of rain, the river lost somewhere in its vastness. Her house with its boat bottom had been built to ride just such a flood, if one ever came, but now it was old. Maybe the boards underneath were partly rotted away. Maybe the cable mooring the house to the great live oak would snap loose and let her go turning downstream, the way her boat had gone.

No one could come now. She could cry out but it would be no use, no one would hear. Down

15   the length and breadth of the swamp others were fighting to save what little they could, maybe even their lives. She had seen a whole house go floating by, so quiet she was reminded of sitting at a funeral. She thought when she saw it she knew whose house it was. It had been bad seeing it drift by, but the owners must have escaped to higher ground. Later, with the rain and darkness pressing in, she had heard a panther scream upriver.

20   Now the house seemed to shudder around her like something alive. She reached out to catch a lamp as it tilted off the table by her bed and put it between her feet to hold it steady. Then creaking and groaning with effort the house struggled up from the clay, floated free, bobbing like a cork and swung out slowly with the pull of the river. She gripped the edge of the bed. Swaying from side to side, the house moved to the length of its mooring. There was a jolt and

25   a complaining of old timbers and then a pause. Slowly the current released it and let it swing back, rasping across its resting place. She caught her breath and sat for a long time feeling the

---

slow pendulous sweeps. The dark sifted down through the incessant rain, and, head on arm, she slept holding on to the bed.

Sometime in the night the cry awoke her, a sound so anguished she was on her feet before she
30 was awake. In the dark she stumbled against the bed. It came from out there, from the river. She could hear something moving, something large that made a dredging, sweeping sound. It could be another house. Then it hit, not head on but glancing and sliding down the length of her house. It was a tree. She listened as the branches and leaves cleared themselves and went on down-stream, leaving only the rain and the lappings of the flood, sounds so constant now that they
35 seemed a part of the silence. Huddled on the bed, she was almost asleep again when another cry sounded, this time so close it could have been in the room. Staring into the dark, she eased back on the bed until her hand caught the cold shape of the rifle. Then crouched on the pillow, she cradled the gun across her knees. "Who's there?" she called.

The answer was a repeated cry, but less shrill, tired sounding, then the empty silence closing
40 in. She drew back against the bed. Whatever was there she could hear it moving about on the porch. Planks creaked and she could distinguish the sounds of objects being knocked over. There was a scratching on the wall as if it would tear its way in. She knew now what it was, a big cat, deposited by the uprooted tree that had passed her. It had come with the flood, a gift.

Unconsciously she pressed her hand against her face and along her tightened throat. The rifle
45 rocked across her knees. She had never seen a panther in her life. She had heard about them from others and heard their cries, like suffering, in the distance. The cat was scratching on the wall again, rattling the window by the door. As long as she guarded the window and kept the cat hemmed in by the wall and water, caged, she would be all right. Outside, the animal paused to rake his claws across the rusted outer screen. Now and then, it whined and growled.

50 When the light filtered down through the rain at last, coming like another kind of dark, she was still sitting on the bed, stiff and cold. Her arms, used to rowing on the river, ached from the stillness of holding the rifle. She had hardly allowed herself to move for fear any sound might give strength to the cat. Rigid, she swayed with the movement of the house. The rain still fell as if it would never stop. Through the grey light, finally, she could see the rain-pitted flood and far
55 away the cloudy shape of drowned treetops. The cat was not moving now. Maybe he had gone away. Laying the gun aside she slipped off the bed and moved without a sound to the window. It was still there, crouched at the edge of the porch, staring up at the live oak, the mooring of her house, as if gauging its chances of leaping to an overhanging branch. It did not seem so frightening now that she could see it, its coarse fur napped into twigs, its sides pinched and ribs
60 showing. It would be easy to shoot it where it sat, its long tail whipping back and forth. She was moving back to get the gun when it turned around. With no warning, no crouch or tensing of muscles, it sprang at the window, shattering a pane of glass. She fell back, stifling a scream, and taking up the rifle, she fired through the window. She could not see the panther now, but she had missed. It began to pace again. She could glimpse its head and the arch of its back as it passed
65 the window.

Shivering, she pulled back on the bed and lay down. The lulling constant sound of the river and the rain, the penetrating chill, drained away her purpose. She watched the window and kept the gun ready. After waiting a long while she moved again to look. The panther had fallen asleep, its head on its paws, like a housecat. For the first time since the rains began she wanted to cry, for

70   herself, for all the people, for everything in the flood. Sliding down on the bed, she pulled the quilt around her shoulders. She should have got out when she could, while the roads were still open or before her boat was washed away. As she rocked back and forth with the sway of the house a deep ache in her stomach reminded her she hadn't eaten. She couldn't remember for how long. Like the cat, she was starving. Easing into the kitchen, she made a fire with the few

75   remaining sticks of wood. If the flood lasted she would have to burn the chair, maybe even the table itself. Taking down the remains of a smoked ham from the ceiling, she cut thick slices of the brownish red meat and placed them in a skillet. The smell of the frying meat made her dizzy. There were stale biscuits from the last time she had cooked and she could make some coffee. There was plenty of water.

80   While she was cooking her food, she almost forgot about the cat until it whined. It was hungry too. "Let me eat," she called to it, "and then I'll see to *you*." And she laughed under her breath. As she hung the rest of the ham back on its nail the cat growled a deep throaty rumble that made her hand shake.

After she had eaten, she went to the bed again and took up the rifle. The house had risen so

85   high now it no longer scraped across the bluff when it swung back from the river. The food had warmed her. She could get rid of the cat while light still hung in the rain. She crept slowly to the window. It was still there, mewling, beginning to move about the porch. She stared at it a long time, unafraid. Then without thinking what she was doing, she laid the gun aside and started around the edge of the bed to the kitchen. Behind her the cat was moving, fretting. She

90   took down what was left of the ham and making her way back across the swaying floor to the window she shoved it through the broken pane. On the other side there was a hungry snarl and something like a shock passed from the animal to her. Stunned by what she had done, she drew back to the bed. She could hear the sounds of the panther tearing at the meat. The house rocked around her.

95   The next time she awoke she knew at once that everything had changed. The rain had stopped. She felt for the movement of the house but it no longer swayed on the flood. Drawing her door open, she saw through the torn screen a different world. The house was resting on the bluff where it always had. A few feet down, the river still raced on in a torrent, but it no longer covered the few feet between the house and the live oak. And the cat was gone. Leading from

100   the porch to the live oak and doubtless on into the swamp were tracks, indistinct and already disappearing into the soft mud. And there on the porch, gnawed to whiteness, was what was left of the ham.

Source: Louis Dollarhide, "The Gift" in *Mississippi Writers: Reflections of Childhood and Youth*, Volume 1, edited by Dorothy Abbott, University Press of Mississippi, 1985.

Question 6: GIFT

Here is part of a conversation between two people who read "The gift":

Give evidence from the story to show how each of these speakers could justify their point of view.

Speaker 1 ....

Speaker 2 ....

Situation: *Personal*
Text format: *Continuous*
Aspect: *Reflection and evaluation*
Levels: *Level 2 and Level 3*
PISA scale scores: *480 and 537*

As the easiest among the reflection and evaluation tasks associated with *The gift*, this task [R119Q09] requires students to make comparisons and connections between the text and outside knowledge, drawing on their personal experience and attitudes. In order to gain credit for this task, a connection has to be made between the behaviour of a character in the story and personal values, by drawing on ideas about compassion and cruelty and using evidence from the text.

This task is marked using the full-credit/partial-credit rule, and therefore yields two levels of difficulty. To receive partial credit (Level 2, PISA score of 480), the student needs to find evidence of *either* compassion *or* cruelty in the story. For full credit (Level 3, PISA score of 537), the student needs to find evidence of *both* compassion *and* cruelty. The full-credit score reflects the ability to deal with contrary concepts or ambiguities, a capacity associated with proficiency higher than that typically found at Level 2. No credit is given for insufficient answers or for showing inaccurate comprehension of the material.

The content of the answer does not need to be very elaborate to gain credit. A full-credit answer is typically, for Part A, "Because she was going to shoot the panther" and, for Part B, "Because she fed the panther in the end".

Other tasks, such as the following two, give more credit for more sophisticated readings.

Question 7: GIFT

Do you think that the last sentence of "The gift" is an appropriate ending?

Explain your answer, demonstrating your understanding of how the last sentence relates to the story's meaning.

Situation: *Personal*
Text format: *Continuous*
Aspect: *Reflection and evaluation*
Level: *Level 4 and Level 5*
PISA scale scores: *567 and 652*

This second reflection and evaluation task [R119Q05], like the first discussed here, is marked using the full-credit/partial-credit rule, with the partial-credit score falling within Level 4 with a PISA score of 567 and the full-credit score falling within Level 5 with a PISA score of 652.

For full credit, the reader has to *go beyond a literal interpretation* and is required to evaluate the text critically, drawing on specialised knowledge and a deep understanding of a long and complex text. The reader needs to *comment critically on the appropriateness of the ending* of the narrative by reflecting on how it connects with the general theme or mood of the text. Readers need to draw inferences, making use of ideas activated during reading but not explicitly stated. The reader must implicitly base the response on an internalised sense of what makes an ending "appropriate", and the standards referred to for this level of response are deep or abstract rather than superficial and literal. For example, the full-credit response might comment on the metaphorical significance of the bone, or on the thematic completeness of the ending. These concepts, drawing on formal literary ideas, can be regarded as specialised knowledge for 15-year-olds. The range of interpretations of the story is suggested by the following examples of full-credit answers.

"Yes. I suppose that what was left of the ham by the panther was also a gift, the message being 'live and let live'."

"I think the ending is appropriate because I believe the panther was the gift to stop the flood. Because she fed it instead of shooting it the flood stopped, and almost like a mystery, on the porch lay the remains of the meat almost like a thank you."

"The flood was over and all that was left was the damages and basically that's what the last line says, that the whiteness of the bone was all that was left of the ham."

For partial credit, the task requires students to evaluate the appropriateness of the ending *at a more literal level* by commenting on its consistency with the narrative. Like the full-credit response category, the partial-credit category also requires an evaluation (either positive or negative) based on an idea about what constitutes appropriateness in an ending; but the partial-credit response refers to the *superficial features* of the story, such as consistency of plot. The relative difficulty of this score category (Level 4) reflects the fact that the answer must refer in some way to formal standards of appropriateness and, perhaps more importantly, that it must indicate accurate understanding of a long and complex text. Some examples of partial-credit answers were:

"I think it is a pretty good ending. When she gave it food all was well. The animal left her alone and all had changed."

"Yes, it is finished because the meat is finished and so is the story."

"I think it was a stupid ending, which is perfect to finish off a stupid story! Of course the ham is going to be eaten,

I knew that but I never thought the author — would be ignorant enough to bother mentioning it."

As can be seen from these examples, and as is the case in similar tasks, credit is available for both positive and negative evaluations. The adequacy of the answer is judged according to the quality of insight into the text and the sophistication of critical tools, rather than any idea of a "right" or "wrong" point of view on the reader's part.

Some answers to this task were not given any credit; these included implausible or downright inaccurate readings such as:

"I think it is an appropriate ending. It shows that maybe there never was a panther, and the ham that she threw out of the window is still there to prove this point."

and responses that were considered too vague:

"Yes it is because it tells you what happened in the end."

Like the first two reflection and evaluation tasks, the following interpreting task is marked using the full-credit/ partial-credit scoring rule, with the full-credit score falling within Level 5 with a PISA score of 645 and the partial-credit score within Level 3 with a PISA score of 539. The levels of difficulty of these two categories of response are thus more than 100 points apart — over one standard deviation — on the reading literacy scale.

Question 8: GIFT

Here are some of the early references to the panther in the story.

"the cry awoke her, a sound so anguished…" (line 29)

"The answer was a repeated cry, but less shrill, tired sounding…" (line 39)

"She had…heard their cries, like suffering, in the distance." (lines 45-46)

Considering what happens in the rest of the story, why do you think the writer chooses to introduce the panther with these descriptions?

Situation: *Personal*
Text format: *Continuous*
Aspect: *Interpreting texts*
Level: *Level 3 and Level 5*
PISA scale scores: *539 and 645*

For full credit, the task [R119Q07] requires the reader to construe the meaning of language containing nuances while dealing with ideas that are contrary to expectation. The reader needs to negotiate a text whose discourse structure is not clearly marked, in order to discern the relationship of specific parts of the text (indicated in the question) to its implicit theme.

The text deliberately creates ambiguity through ideas that are contrary to expectation. Although the main response of the woman when she realises there is a panther nearby is fear, the carefully chosen descriptions of the panther's cries — "anguished", "tired-sounding" and "suffering" — suggest pathos rather than threat. This hint, near the beginning of the story, is important for a full understanding of the woman's "unexpected" behaviour at the end, and hence to an understanding of the story's implicit theme. Thus, to receive full credit, students must recognise that the *descriptions are intended to evoke pity.*

Partial credit is given for answers that treat the text at a more straightforward level, linking the phrases highlighted in the question with the plot. Students may refer to possible *intentions (or effects) of the quoted descriptions, other than that of evoking pity*. At this level the task is to follow implicit logical links between sentences by inferring that the panther is crying because it is hungry. A second kind of response receiving partial credit brings together different parts of the text so as to identify a main idea. This kind of response identifies the atmosphere of the story at this point. Students may refer to the *literal information given in the quoted descriptions*.

Question 9: GIFT

When the woman says, "and then I'll see to **you**" (line 81) she means that she is

A   sure that the cat won't hurt her.

B   trying to frighten the cat.

C   intending to shoot the cat.

D   planning to feed the cat.

Situation: *Personal*
Text format: *Continuous*
Aspect: *Interpreting texts*
Level: *Level 4*
PISA scale score: *603*

This task [R119Q04] requires a high level of text-based inference in order to construe the meaning of a section of text in context, dealing with ambiguities and ideas that may be contrary to expectation. The reader needs to infer psychological meaning, following thematic links over several paragraphs, in deciding which of the four alternatives is the best answer.

Taken out of context, the sentence that the task focuses on is ambiguous and even in context there are apparently plausible alternative readings. The task is designed specifically to assess proficiency in dealing with this kind of ambiguity. One of the translation notes that was sent to national teams along with the test material (in the source languages of French and English) says of this passage, "'Please ensure that the phrase, "and then I'll see to *you*" allows both of the following interpretations: "and then I'll feed you" and "and then I'll shoot you."' Nevertheless, only one reading is consistent with the psychological sequence of the story: the woman must be intending to shoot the panther, since just after this moment she takes up the rifle and thinks that "she could get rid of the cat while light still hung in the rain." The woman's eventual compassion towards the panther is powerful distracting information, contrary to the expectations set up elsewhere in the story. The multiple-choice alternative that reflects this reading – "planning to feed the panther" – attracted almost half of the students. These readers were clearly following the storyline at one level, recognising a main theme and construing meaning within a limited part of the text (skills identified with Levels 1 and 2 tasks) but they were not dealing with ambiguities and ideas that were contrary to expectations to the degree demanded by a Level 4 interpreting task.

While the tasks based on this long and relatively subtle text are generally difficult, the unit also contains one Level 1 task:

Question 10: GIFT

"Then creaking and groaning with effort the house struggled up …" (lines 21-22)

What happened to the house in this part of the story?

A It fell apart.

(B) It began to float.

C It crashed into the oak tree.

D It sank to the bottom of the river.

Situation: *Personal*
Text format: *Continuous*
Aspect: *Retrieving information*
Level: *Level 1*
PISA scale score: *367*

For this task [R119Q06], the reader needs to locate a piece of explicitly stated information in a short section of text and match it to one of four alternatives stated in the question.

Although the whole text is long, for this task the section of text that the reader needs to refer to is short and is very clearly marked in the question, both by being quoted directly and by reference to line numbers. The correct answer, "It began to float", uses a word directly matching a word closely following the quoted section: "Then creaking and groaning with effort the house struggled up from the clay, floated free … "

Lake Chad

The tasks related to this stimulus are classified as non-continuous on the text format dimension. The *Lake Chad* unit presents two graphs from an archaeological atlas. Figure A in *Lake Chad* is a line graph, and Figure B is a horizontal histogram. A third non-continuous text type is represented in this unit, by a small map of the lake embedded in Figure A. Two very short passages of prose are also part of the stimulus.

By juxtaposing these pieces of information the author invites the reader to infer a connection between the changing water levels of *Lake Chad* over time, and the periods in which certain species of wildlife inhabited its surroundings.

This is a type of text that might typically be encountered by students in an educational setting. Nevertheless, because the atlas is published for the general reader the text is classified as public in the situation dimension. The full set of five tasks covers all three aspects. The tasks range in difficulty from Level 1 to Level 4.

Four of the tasks from *Lake Chad* are reproduced here.

Figure A shows changing levels of Lake Chad, in Saharan North Africa. Lake Chad disappeared completely in about 20 000 BC, during the last Ice Age. In about 11 000 BC it reappeared. Today, its level is about the same as it was in AD 1000.

Figure A
Lake Chad: changing levels

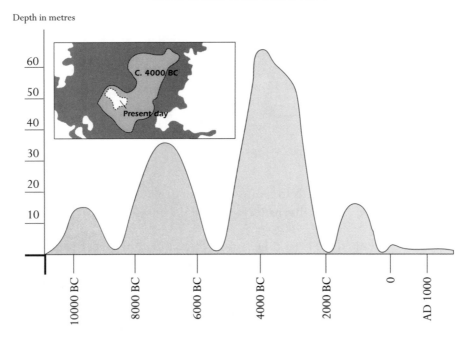

Figure B shows Saharan rock art (ancient drawings or paintings found on the walls of caves) and changing patterns of wildlife.

Figure B
Saharan rock art and changing patterns of wildlife

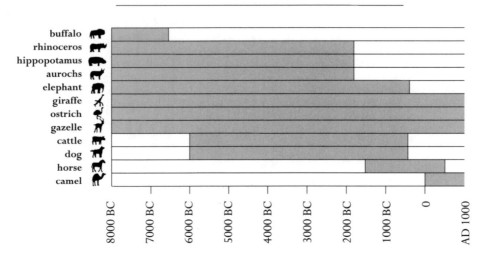

Source: Copyright Bartholomew Ltd. 1988. Extracted from *The Times Atlas of Archaeology* and reproduced by permission of Harper Collins Publishers.

Question 11: LAKE CHAD

What is the depth of Lake Chad today?

A About two metres.

B About fifteen metres.

C About fifty metres.

D It has disappeared completely.

E The information is not provided.

Situation: *Public*
Text format: *Non-continuous*
Aspect: *Retrieving information*
Level: *Level 2*
PISA scale score: *478*

This first task [R040Q02] is a Level 2 retrieving information task with a PISA score of 478 that requires students to locate and combine pieces of information from a line graph and the introduction.

The word "today" in the question can be directly matched in the relevant sentence of the introduction, which refers to the depth of the lake "today" being the same as it was in AD 1000. The reader needs to combine this information with information from Figure A by locating AD 1000 on the graph and then by reading off the depth of the lake at this date. Competing information is present in the form of multiple dates in Figure A, and the repetition of "AD 1000" in Figure B. Nevertheless, the task is relatively easy because key information is supplied explicitly in the prose introduction. Most students who did not select the correct alternative A, "About two metres", selected E, "The information is not provided." This is probably because they looked only at Figure A, rather than combining the relevant part of Figure A with information from the introduction. Level 2 tasks based on non-continuous texts – like this one – may require combining information from different displays, whereas Level 1 non-continuous tasks typically focus on discrete pieces of information, usually within a single display.

Question 12: LAKE CHAD

In about which year does the graph in Figure A start?

Situation: *Public*
Text format: *Non-continuous*
Aspect: *Retrieving information*
Level: *Level 3*
PISA scale score: *540*

This second, more difficult retrieving information task [R040Q03A] is at Level 3 with a PISA score of 540.

For this task students need to locate and recognise the relationship between pieces of information in the line graph and the introduction, and to deal with prominent competing information.

As in the previous task, the reader has to locate relevant information in the introduction ("In about 11000 BC it reappeared") and relate it to the identified part of the graph (the origin). This task might appear to be easier than the previous one, in that students are explicitly directed to look at Figure A. However, the competing information in this task is stronger. The lure of competing information is demonstrated in a common error made in this task, which was to mistake the first date marked on the horizontal axis of Figure A (10000 BC) for the beginning of the line graph representing the depth of Lake Chad, at about 11000 BC.

Although this is classified as a retrieving information task since it primarily requires the locating of information in a text, interpretative strategies must also be drawn upon to infer the correct information from the graph. In addition, readers need to reflect on what they know about dating conventions, drawing on the contextual knowledge that BC dates go "backwards". This suggests that there is considerable overlap between the three aspects of retrieving information, interpreting texts and reflection and evaluation: most tasks make a number of different demands upon readers, and individual readers may approach a task in different ways. As noted in the reading literacy framework (OECD, 1999*a*), the assignment of a task to one of the aspect scales often involves making judgements about what the most salient features of the task are and about the approach that readers are most likely to take when responding to it.

Question 13: LAKE CHAD

Figure B is based on the assumption that

A the animals in the rock art were present in the area at the time they were drawn.

B the artists who drew the animals were highly skilled.

C the artists who drew the animals were able to travel widely.

D there was no attempt to domesticate the animals which were depicted in the rock art.

Situation: *Public*
Text format: *Non-continuous*
Aspect: *Interpreting texts*
Level: *Level 1*
PISA scale score: *397*

The easiest task associated with *Lake Chad* [R040Q04], with a PISA scale score of 397, is classified as interpreting texts. This Level 1 task requires students to recognise the main idea of a chart, where the information is not prominent and the focus is on a single display with little explanatory text.

The *Lake Chad* stimulus comprises two figures, but the reader is directed in the question to look at only one of them, Figure B. This figure has few labels (the dates and names of animals) and the symbols are representative rather than abstract; in other words, only fairly low-level processing is needed to interpret the figure. On the other hand the required information in the text is not prominent, since there is no explicit statement that artists painted what they saw – indeed, there is no direct reference to the artists at all. Clearly, however, students did not find it difficult to make this inference.

Question 14: LAKE CHAD

For this question you need to draw together information from Figure A and Figure B.

The disappearance of the rhinoceros, hippopotamus and aurochs from Saharan rock art happened

A   at the beginning of the most recent Ice Age.

B   in the middle of the period when Lake Chad was at its highest level.

C   after the level of Lake Chad had been falling for over a thousand years.

D   at the beginning of an uninterrupted dry period.

Situation: *Public*
Text format: *Non-continuous*
Aspect: *Interpreting texts*
Level: *Level 3*
PISA scale score: *508*

This more difficult interpreting task [R040Q06] (Level 3, PISA score of 508) in the *Lake Chad* unit requires students to draw together several parts of the non-continuous texts in order to understand a relationship. They need to compare information given in two graphs.

The requirement to combine information from two sources contributes to the task's moderate level of difficulty (Level 3). An added feature is that two different types of graph are used (a line graph and a histogram), and the reader needs to have interpreted the structure of both in order to translate the relevant information from one form to the other.

Of those students who did not select the correct answer, the largest proportion chose distractor D, "at the beginning of an uninterrupted dry period." If one disregards the texts, this seems the most plausible of the wrong answers, and its popularity indicates that these students might have been treating the task as if it were a Level 2 reflection and evaluation task, where it would be appropriate to hypothesise about the explanation for a feature of the text, drawing on familiar outside knowledge.

Labour

Tasks in the *Labour* unit are classified as non-continuous in terms of text format. The unit is based on a tree diagram showing the structure and distribution of a national labour force in 1995. The diagram is published in an economics textbook for upper secondary school students, so that the text is classified as educational in terms of situation. The specific information contained in the diagram relates to New Zealand, but the terms and definitions used are those established by the OECD and the stimulus can therefore be regarded as, essentially, international.

This unit does not have the immediate appeal of some of the material presented earlier in this selection. The content is unlikely to excite lively interest among 15-year-olds, and the form of presentation is uncompromisingly academic. Compare, for example, the text of the last unit presented in this selection, which includes some small illustrations to give a more friendly touch to the tabular and numerical information. Nonetheless, the *Labour* unit represents a kind of reading text that adults are likely to encounter and need to be able to interpret in order to participate fully in the economic and political life of a modern society.

The full *Labour* unit comprises five tasks representing all three aspects and spanning Levels 2 to 5. Four of the tasks are reproduced here.

The tree diagram below shows the structure of a country's labour force or "working-age population". The total population of the country in 1995 was about 3.4 million.

The labour force structure, year ended 31 March 1995 (000s)[1]

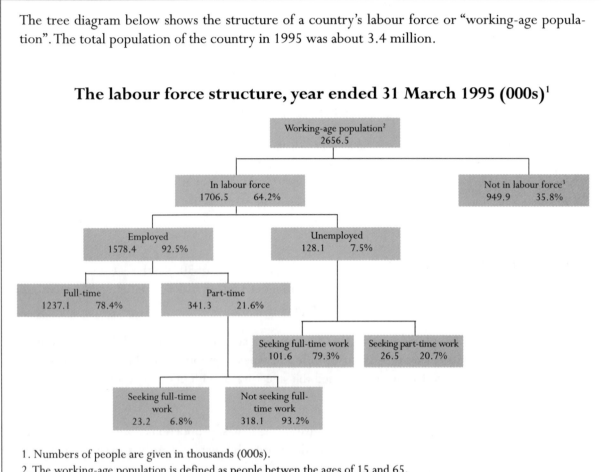

1. Numbers of people are given in thousands (000s).
2. The working-age population is defined as people betwen the ages of 15 and 65.
3. People "Not in the labour force" are those not actively seeking work and/or not available for work.
Source: D. Miller, *Form 6 Economics*, ESA Publications, Box 9453, Newmarker, Auckland, NZ, p. 64.

Question 15: LABOUR

How many people of working age were not in the labour force? (Write the **number** of people, not the percentage.)

Situation: *Educational*
Text format: *Non-continuous*
Aspect: *Retrieving information*
Levels: *Level 3 and Level 5*
PISA scale scores: *485 and 631*

The first task presented here [R088Q03] yields two levels of difficulty, with the partial-credit response category falling within Level 3 with a PISA scale score of 485 and the full-credit category within Level 5 with a PISA scale score of 631. The latter is one of the most difficult retrieving information tasks in the PISA reading assessment.

For full credit (Level 5) students are required to locate and combine a piece of numerical information in the main body of the text (the tree diagram) *with information in a footnote* – that is, outside the main body of the text. In addition, students have to apply this footnoted information in determining the correct number of people fitting into this category. Both of these features contribute to the difficulty of this task.

For partial credit (Level 3) this task merely requires students to locate the number given in the appropriate category of the tree diagram. *They are not required to use the conditional information provided in the footnote to* receive partial credit. Even without this important information the task is still moderately difficult.

Typically, the requirement to use conditional information – that is, information found outside the main body of a text – significantly increases the difficulty of a task. This is clearly demonstrated by the two categories of this task, since the difference between full-credit and partial-credit answers is, substantively, the application or non-application of conditional information to correctly identified numerical information in the body of the text. The difference in difficulty of these two categories of response is more than two proficiency levels.

Question 16: LABOUR

In which part of the tree diagram, if any, would each of the people listed in the table below be included?

Show your answer by placing a cross in the correct box in the table.

The first one has been done for you.

	"In labour force: employed"	"In labour force: unemployed"	"Not in labour force"	Not included in any category
A part-time waiter, aged 35	☒	☐	☐	☐
A business woman, aged 43, who works a sixty-hour week	☒	☐	☐	☐
A full-time student, aged 21	☐	☐	☒	☐
A man, aged 28, who recently sold his shop and is looking for work	☐	☒	☐	☐
A woman, aged 55, who has never worked or wanted to work outside the home	☐	☐	☒	☐
A grandmother, aged 80, who still works a few hours a day at the family's market stall	☐	☐	☐	☒

Situation: Educational
Text format: Non-continuous
Aspect: Interpreting texts
Levels: Level 2 and Level 5
PISA scale scores: 473 and 727

A second task based on the tree diagram [R088Q04] is classified as interpreting texts. It too yields two levels of difficulty, with the partial-credit response category falling within Level 2 with a PISA score of 473 and the full-credit category within Level 5 with a PISA score of 727.

The task requires students to analyse several described cases and to match each case to a category given in the tree diagram. The described cases are designed to determine whether the reader has understood, fully and in detail, the distinctions and definitions provided by the diagram. Again, some of the relevant information is in footnotes that are external to the main display.

For the Level 5 category of response, students need to demonstrate a full and detailed understanding of the text, sometimes referring to information external to the main display. To receive full credit, students need to answer all five parts correctly.

For the Level 2 with a PISA score of 473 or partial-credit category of response, students need to demonstrate some understanding of the text by correctly matching three or four of the five described cases with the appropriate labour force category. In PISA 2000, students most often chose the correct category of the labour force for the second and fourth cases listed, those for which it is not necessary to deal with the information in footnotes 2 and 3 (definitions of "working-age population" and "not in labour force"). The cases that are most difficult to categorise correctly are the third, fifth and sixth – those that require assimilation of footnoted information. As in the previous task, conditional information increases the overall difficulty. Another feature contributing to the difficulty of this task is the fact that it requires students to provide several independent answers.

Question 17: LABOUR

Suppose that information about the labour force was presented in a tree diagram like this every year.

Listed below are four features of the tree diagram. Show whether or not you would expect these features to change from year to year, by circling either "Change" or "No change". The first one has been done for you.

Features of Tree Diagram	Answer
The labels in each box (*e.g.* "In labour force")	Change / ⟨No change⟩
The percentages (*e.g.* "64.2%")	⟨Change⟩ / No change
The numbers (*e.g.* "2656.5")	⟨Change⟩ / No change
The footnotes under the tree diagram	Change / ⟨No change⟩

Situation: *Educational*
Text format: *Non-continuous*
Aspect: *Reflection and evaluation*
Levels: *Level 2*
PISA scale score: *445*

This third task based on Labour is a relatively easy reflection and evaluation task [R088Q05], falling within Level 2 with a PISA score of 445.

This task requires students to recognise features of the text, demonstrating a grasp of the underlying structure of a tree diagram by distinguishing between variables and invariables. Although it is not necessary to know the technical terms "variable" and "invariable", successful completion of this task requires a grasp of the underlying structure of the text. This task is classified as reflection and evaluation, not because it is critically evaluative or because it asks for a personal answer, but because it asks the reader to consider the text as an artefact, in terms of its form and structure. To obtain full credit, students need to answer all three parts correctly. Students with two or fewer parts correct are given no credit.

Question 18: LABOUR

The information about the labour force structure is presented as a tree diagram, but it could have been presented in a number of other ways, such as a written description, a pie chart, a graph or a table.

The tree diagram was probably chosen because it is especially useful for showing

A   changes over time.

B   the size of the country's total population.

C   categories within each group.

D   the size of each group.

Situation: *Educational*
Text format: *Non-continuous*
Aspect: *Reflection and evaluation*
Level: *Level 3*
PISA scale score: *486*

This last task [R088Q07] based on the *Labour* diagram requires an evaluation of a feature of the text. The task is to consider the suitability of the tree diagram for particular purposes in comparison with the suitability of other forms of presentation. Formal knowledge of text structures and their advantages and disadvantages is a relatively unfamiliar area of knowledge for 15-year-olds, contributing to the medium level of difficulty (Level 3). Whereas the previous *Labour* question only implicitly requires the reader to demonstrate understanding of the text's structure, this question makes the requirement explicit. To gain credit for this task the student has to recognise the appropriateness of a tree diagram for showing categories within groups. The more explicitly abstract approach of the question may contribute to the comparative difficulty of this task. The second and fourth distractors, which drew significant numbers of students, focus on information that is presented in the diagram, but the structure of the diagram does not particularly emphasise those features. Students who selected these distractors seemed to be treating the question as if it involved retrieving information ("Which of these kinds of information is shown in the diagram?"), rather than evaluating the structure of the presentation.

PLAN International

The third and last non-continuous text presented here is a table containing information about the types of programmes offered by an international aid agency, PLAN International. It is taken from a public report distributed by the agency, and is therefore classified as public in terms of situation.

The table shows the countries in one region of PLAN International's operation, the type of aid programmes it offers (27 categories of aid programme grouped under three main headings) and the amount of work accomplished in each country within each category of aid. There is a great deal of information presented in a rather dense fashion in the table, which might overwhelm the less proficient reader. Confident readers would be most likely to scan the text to gain a broad impression of its structure and content, rather than slavishly read every detail of the table indiscriminately.

Only one task associated with the *PLAN International* text was used in constructing the PISA scale of reading literacy.

PLAN International Program Results Financial Year 1996

REGION OF EASTERN AND SOUTHERN AFRICA — RESA

Growing up Healthy

	Egypt	Ethiopia	Kenya	Malawi	Sudan	Tanzania	Uganda	Zambia	Zimbabwe	Totals
Health posts built with 4 rooms or less	1	0	6	0	7	1	2	0	9	26
Health workers trained for 1 day	1 053	0	719	0	425	1 003	20	80	1 085	4 385
Children given nutrition supplements > 1 week	10 195	0	2 240	2 400	0	0	0	0	251 402	266 237
Children given financial help with health/dental treatment	984	0	396	0	305	0	581	0	17	2 283

Learning

	Egypt	Ethiopia	Kenya	Malawi	Sudan	Tanzania	Uganda	Zambia	Zimbabwe	Totals
Teachers trained for 1 week	0	0	367	0	970	115	565	0	303	2 320
School exercise books bought/donated	667	0	0	41 200	0	69 106	0	150	0	111 123
School textbooks bought/donated	0	0	45 650	9 600	1 182	8 769	7 285	150	58 387	131 023
Uniforms bought/made/donated	8 897	0	5 761	0	2 000	6 040	0	0	434	23 132
Children helped with school fees/a scholarship	12 321	0	1 598	0	154	0	0	0	2 014	16 087
School desks built/bought/donated	3 200	0	3 689	250	1 564	1 725	1 794	0	4 109	16 331
Permanent classrooms built	44	0	50	8	93	31	45	0	82	353
Classrooms repaired	0	0	34	0	0	14	0	0	33	81
Adults receiving training in literacy this financial year	1 160	0	3 000	568	3 617	0	0	0	350	8 695

Habitat

	Egypt	Ethiopia	Kenya	Malawi	Sudan	Tanzania	Uganda	Zambia	Zimbabwe	Totals
Latrines or toilets dug/built	50	0	2 403	0	57	162	23	96	4 311	7 102
Houses connected to a new sewage system	143	0	0	0	0	0	0	0	0	143
Wells dug/improved (or springs capped)	0	0	15	0	7	13	0	0	159	194
New positive boreholes drilled	0	0	8	93	14	0	27	0	220	362
Gravity feed drinking water systems built	0	0	28	0	1	0	0	0	0	29
Drinking water systems repaired/improved	0	0	392	0	2	0	0	0	31	425
Houses improved with PLAN project	265	0	520	0	0	0	1	0	2	788
New houses built for beneficiaries	225	0	596	0	0	2	6	0	313	1 142
Community halls built or improved	2	0	2	0	3	0	3	0	2	12
Community leaders trained for 1 day or more	2 214	95	3 522	232	200	3 575	814	20	2 693	13 365
Kilometres of roadway improved	1.2	0	26	0	0	0	0	0	5.34	80.6
Bridges built	0	0	4	2	11	0	0	0	1	18
Families benefited directly from erosion control	0	0	1 092	0	1 500	0	0	0	18 405	20 997
Houses newly served by electrification project	448	0	2	0	0	0	0	0	44	494

Source: Adapted from PLAN International Program Output Chart financial year 1996, appendix to Quarterly Report to the International Board first quarter 1997.

Question 19A: PLAN INTERNATIONAL

What does the table indicate about the level of PLAN International's activity in Ethiopia in 1996, compared with other countries in the region?

A   The level of activity was comparatively high in Ethiopia.

B   The level of activity was comparatively low in Ethiopia.

C   It was about the same as in other countries in the region.

D   It was comparatively high in the Habitat category, and low in the other categories.

Question 19B: PLAN INTERNATIONAL

In 1996 Ethiopia was one of the poorest countries in the world.

Taking this fact and the information in the table into account, what do you think might explain the level of PLAN International's activities in Ethiopia compared with its activities in other countries?

Situation: Public
Text format: Non-continuous
Aspect: Reflection and evaluation
Levels: Level 5
PISA scale scores: 705 and 822

The marking rules for this task [R099Q04B] are somewhat complicated. Although students are asked two questions within this task – one multiple-choice and one constructed-response – only the second of these is counted for scoring purposes. As this task contributes to the reflection and evaluation scale, the multiple-choice component of the task, which predominantly requires retrieval of information, does not earn any credit on its own. However, the multiple-choice question is taken into account in that a correct answer to this question is a necessary condition for earning credit on the second, constructed-response question.

The second question is given either full credit or partial credit, both score categories falling within Level 5 with PISA scale scores of 705 and 822). For this task students must hypothesise about the content of the text, drawing on specialised knowledge, and must deal with a concept contrary to expectations. They also need to identify patterns among the many pieces of information presented in this complex and detailed display.

Specifically, students need to reflect on the amount of aid given to Ethiopia by PLAN International, in comparison with the amount given to other countries in the region. This requires them to form a hypothesis, rather than simply to explain something, given that very few 15-year-olds are likely to know as a matter of fact what might have prompted the aid agency to give the amount of aid it did to Ethiopia. It is specialised knowledge to the extent that thinking about the work of international aid agencies is not familiar territory for most adolescents, although it is a reasonable expectation that 15-year-olds will have some basic knowledge about what aid agencies do. On the other hand, it is not reasonable to assume that students will have specific knowledge about the economic status of a particular country, and for that reason, the information about Ethiopia's poverty is supplied. The task includes reference to a phenomenon that is contrary to expectation: that an aid agency gives a relatively small amount of aid to a very poor country.

In order to gain full credit for this task, students *must have answered 19A correctly* and *then draw on all the information supplied*. They are required to form a hypothesis about why PLAN International gave relatively little aid to Ethiopia, taking into account all the relevant information in the table – both the amount and the type of aid – as well as the information supplied in the question. A number of different hypotheses were offered by students, drawing on all the information given in the table. Among the responses that received full credit were:

> "PLAN helped community leaders to try to get them to be self-sufficient. As they are an aid organisation this may seem the best idea."

> "The only help to Ethiopia has been with training of community leaders. Ethiopia may not let PLAN International be involved in other aspects of the country."

For partial credit, students also need to have *answered 19A correctly* and must then take into account *some, but not all*, of the relevant information in the table: the amount, but not the type of aid given. In addition, the hypothesis needs to be consistent with broad background knowledge about the work of aid agencies. Some of the more common hypotheses offered, and awarded partial credit, were:

> "There may have been floods or something happened in the country to stop them helping."

> "PLAN International may have just been introduced to that community and therefore they were low on activities."

> "Maybe other aid organisations are already helping in Ethiopia, so they don't need as much from PLAN."

> "It's just too hard to help there."

This task is particularly difficult for a number of reasons in addition to those discussed above. First, it requires many pieces of information – both internal and external to the text – to be synthesised. Second, there is minimal direction as to which part of the text needs to be consulted for full credit: specifically, there is no indication that the *type* of aid given in Ethiopia needs to be referred to for the full credit score. This means that the information required is not given any prominence, either in the question or by a marker in the text itself. For a combination of all of these reasons this is probably one of the most difficult tasks in the PISA reading assessment.

Reading literacy profile of 15-year-olds

Percentage of students proficient at each level of reading literacy

If students' proficiency is described in terms of five levels of reading literacy, it is possible either to indicate what proportion of them are proficient *at* a particular level or to identify the percentage that are proficient *at most* at that level (as presented in Tables 2.1a-d, Annex B1) – meaning that it is their highest level of proficiency. However, knowing that 10 per cent of students in one country and 20 per cent in another are exactly at, say, Level 3 is not especially meaningful without also knowing the percentages at the other levels. It is therefore generally more useful to know the percentage who are *at most* proficient at a given level, since this information indicates what proportion of students are able to cope with certain demands of everyday life and work. For the purposes of analysis, later in this report and elsewhere, the attributes of groups of students who perform at a certain level may nevertheless be useful, in order to explore the limits of their proficiency.

Figure 2.3 presents an overall profile of proficiency on the combined reading literacy scale (see also Table 2.1a, Annex B1), the length of the segments showing the percentage of students proficient at each level. Countries are listed according to the proportion of students who reached at least Level 3.

Figure 2.3

Percentage of students performing at each of the proficiency levels on the combined reading literacy scale

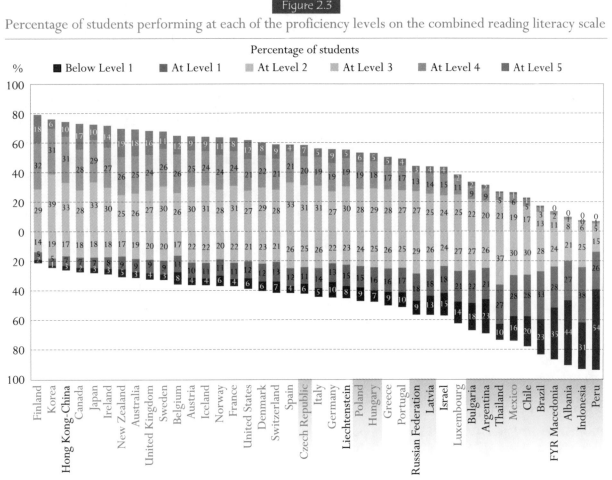

Source: OECD PISA database, 2003. Table 2.1a.

Proficiency at Level 5 (above 625 points)

Students proficient at Level 5 on the combined reading literacy scale are capable of completing sophisticated reading tasks, such as managing information that is difficult to find in unfamiliar texts; showing detailed understanding of such texts and inferring which information in the text is relevant to the task; and being able to evaluate critically and build hypotheses, draw on specialised knowledge, and accommodate concepts that may be contrary to expectations. See Figure 2.2 for a more detailed description.

Students performing at the highest PISA proficiency levels are likely to enhance their country's pool of talent. Today's proportion of students performing at these levels may also influence the contribution which that country will make to the pool of tomorrow's world-class knowledge workers in the global economy. Comparing the proportions of students reaching the highest level of reading proficiency is, therefore, of relevance in itself.

Among the non-OECD countries, the proportion of students who reached Level 5 shows substantial variation, from 10 per cent in Hong Kong-China to 0.1 per cent or less in Albania, Indonesia, FYR Macedonia and Peru. By contrast, in the combined OECD area, 10 per cent of the students reach Level 5, and more than 15 per cent of students in Australia, Canada, Finland, New Zealand and the United Kingdom reach this level (see Table 2.1a, Annex B1).

It is important to keep in mind that the proportion of students performing at Level 5 is influenced not only by the overall performance of countries in reading literacy but also by the variation that exists within countries between the students with the highest and the lowest levels of performance. While there is a general tendency for countries with a higher proportion of students scoring at Level 5 to have fewer students at Level 1 and below, this is not always the case. In Finland, for example, 19 per cent of students reach Level 5 while only 2 percent are below Level 1. By contrast, Belgium and the United States, which also have high percentages reaching Level 5, have relatively high proportions of students scoring below Level 1 as well (8 and 6 per cent, respectively). In Korea, one of the countries that performs at a very high level in all three domains in PISA, less than 6 per cent of students reach Level 5 and less than 1 per cent score below Level 1.

Examining the three components of the combined reading literacy scale shows even more variation, particularly in those countries with an above-average percentage of students performing at Level 5 on the combined reading literacy scale. In Hong Kong-China, for example, 16 per cent of students reach Level 5 on the reflection and evaluation scale (see Table 2.1d, Annex B1). This is the sixth highest proportion of students at Level 5 followed by Ireland and Finland. But Hong Kong-China has only 8 per cent of students at Level 5 on the interpreting texts scale (OECD average 10 per cent) (see Table 2.1c, Annex B1). A similar picture, though less pronounced, can be observed in Argentina, Bulgaria, Canada, Israel and United Kingdom. In the case of Canada, Hong Kong-China, and the United Kingdom, the high overall performance on the combined reading literacy scale is achieved by strong performance in tasks that require students to engage in critical evaluation, to use hypotheses and to relate texts to their own experience, knowledge and ideas (see Tables 2.1b, c and d, Annex B1)[4].

Proficiency at Level 4 (from 553 to 625 points)

Students proficient at Level 4 on the combined reading literacy scale are capable of difficult reading tasks, such as locating embedded information, construing meaning from nuances of language and critically evaluating a text (see Figure 2.2 for a detailed description). In the combined OECD area, 32 per cent of students are proficient at Level 4 and beyond (that is, at Levels 4 and 5) (see Table 2.1a, Annex B1). Among the non-OECD countries, Hong Kong-China (41 per cent) has higher percentages of students than the OECD average. Liechtenstein has 25 per cent of students at Level 4 and beyond, followed by Israel (19 per cent), Latvia (18 per cent), the Russian Federation (16 per cent), Bulgaria (11 per cent) and Argentina (10 per cent). Among OECD countries, half of the students in Finland and 40 per cent or more of those in Australia, Canada, Ireland, New Zealand and the United Kingdom attain at least Level 4. With the exception of the seven countries mentioned above, less than one in twenty students in seven remaining non-OECD countries reaches Level 4 and beyond.

Proficiency at Level 3 (from 481 to 552 points)

Students proficient at Level 3 on the combined reading literacy scale are capable of reading tasks of moderate complexity, such as locating multiple pieces of information, making links between different parts of a text and relating it to familiar everyday knowledge (see Figure 2.2 for a detailed description). In the combined OECD area, 60 per cent of students are proficient at least at Level 3 (that is, at Levels 3, 4 or 5) on the combined reading literacy scale (see Table 2.1a, Annex B1). In Hong Kong-China, three out of four students have reached at least Level 3, whereas in Indonesia and Peru less than one out of twelve students perform at or beyond Level 3.

Proficiency at Level 2 (from 408 to 480 points)

Students proficient at Level 2 are capable of basic reading tasks, such as locating straightforward information, making low-level inferences of various types, working out what a well-defined part of a text means, and using some outside knowledge to understand it (see Figure 2.2 for a detailed description). In the combined OECD area, 82 per cent of students are proficient at Level 2 or above on the combined reading literacy scale.

In every OECD country at least half of all students are at Level 2 or above, whereas the percentage among the non-OECD countries varies from 21 per cent in Peru to 91 per cent in Hong Kong-China (see Table 2.1a, Annex B1). In Hong Kong-China, more than nine in ten students reached Level 2 and beyond. In Albania, Brazil, Indonesia, FYR Macedonia and Peru, more than half of the students have not reached Level 2. Almost half of the non-OECD countries, including Argentina, Bulgaria, Chile, Israel, Latvia, the Russian Federation and Thailand, have the largest proportion of students at Level 2.

It is interesting to contrast Thailand's performance with Israel's: similar proportions of students are at least at Level 2 (63 and 67 per cent, respectively) but the proportion in Israel at Level 4 is almost three times higher than that in Thailand. It is the large proportion (37 per cent) of students at Level 2 that moves overall performance up in Thailand, whereas in Israel it is a small percentage of students performing very well (see Table 2.1a, Annex B1).

Proficiency at Level 1 (from 335 to 407 points) or below (less than 335 points)

Reading literacy, as defined in PISA, focuses on the knowledge and skills required to apply "reading for learning" rather than on the technical skills acquired in "learning to read". Since comparatively few young adults in participating countries have not acquired technical reading skills, PISA does not therefore seek to measure such things as the extent to which 15-year-old students are fluent readers or how well they spell or recognise words. In line with most contemporary views about reading literacy, PISA focuses on measuring the extent to which individuals are able to construct, expand and reflect on the meaning of what they have read in a wide range of texts common both within and beyond school. The simplest reading tasks that can still be associated with this notion of reading literacy are those at Level 1. Students proficient at this level are capable of completing only the least complex reading tasks developed for PISA, such as locating a single piece of information, identifying the main theme of a text or making a simple connection with everyday knowledge (see Figure 2.2 for a detailed description).

Students performing below 335 points, *i.e.* below Level 1, are not capable of the most basic type of reading that PISA seeks to measure. This does not mean that they have no literacy skills. In fact, at least among OECD countries, most of these students can probably read in a technical sense, and the majority of them (54 per cent on average across OECD countries[5]) are able to solve successfully at least 10 per cent of the non-multiple choice[6] reading tasks in PISA (and 6 per cent a quarter of them). Nonetheless, their pattern of answers in the assessment is such that they would be expected to solve fewer than half of the tasks in a test made up of items drawn solely from Level 1, and therefore perform below Level 1. Such students have serious difficulties in using reading literacy as an effective tool to advance and extend their knowledge and skills in other areas. Students with literacy skills below Level 1 may, therefore, be at risk not only of difficulties in their initial transition from education to work but also of failure to benefit from further education and learning opportunities throughout life.

Education systems with large proportions of students performing below, or even at, Level 1 should be concerned that significant numbers of their students may not be acquiring the necessary literacy knowledge and skills to benefit sufficiently from their educational opportunities. This situation is even more troublesome in light of the extensive evidence suggesting that it is difficult in later life to compensate for learning gaps in initial education. OECD data suggest, indeed, that job-related continuing education and training often reinforce the skill differences with which individuals leave initial education (OECD, 2001*a*). Adult literacy skills and participation in continuing education and training are strongly related, even after controlling for other characteristics affecting participation in training. Literacy skills and continuing education and training appear to be mutually reinforcing, with the result that training is least commonly pursued by those adults who need it most.

In the combined OECD area, 12 per cent of students perform at Level 1, and 6 per cent below Level 1, but there are wide differences between countries. In Finland and Korea only around 5 per cent of students perform at Level 1, and less than 2 per cent below it, but these countries are exceptions. In all other OECD countries, between 10 and 44 per cent of students perform at or below Level 1 (see Table 2.1a, Annex B1). Over 2 per cent and, in half of the OECD countries over 5 per cent, perform below Level 1.

Among the non-OECD countries, Hong Kong-China has 9 per cent of students at or below Level 1. The large proportion of students at Level 3 and Level 4 (33 and 31 per cent respectively) and the small percentage of students at the lower end of proficiency level means that Hong Kong-China ranks with the top performing OECD countries in reading literacy.

All other non-OECD countries have much larger proportion of students at Level 1 or below (Figure 2.4). Peru has the highest proportion of students at Level 1 or below (80 per cent). Albania, Indonesia and FYR Macedonia also have more than 60 per cent of students at Level 1 or below (70, 69 and 63 per cent, respectively).

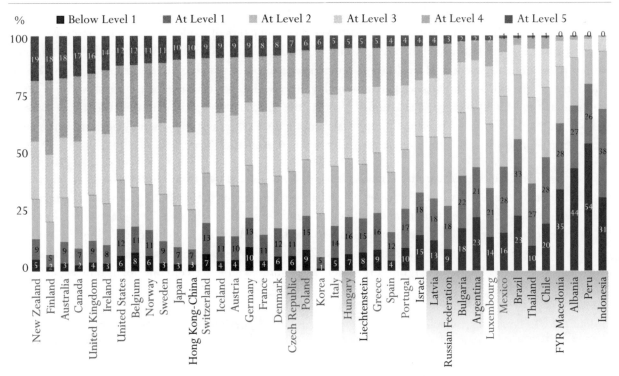

Figure 2.4

Percentages of students at Level 5 and below Level 2 on the combined reading literacy scale

Source: OECD PISA database, 2003. Table 2.1a.

Students at Level 1 and below are not a random group. Although the specific characteristics of these students can best be examined in the national context, some commonalities are apparent. In virtually all countries, for example, the majority of these students are male (see Chapter 5), and many of them come from disadvantaged backgrounds. Moreover, in many countries a comparatively high proportion of students at Level 1 or below are foreign-born or have foreign-born parents. In Germany and Luxembourg, two of the four OECD countries with the highest proportion of students performing at or below Level 1, more than 26 and 34 per cent of these students, respectively, are foreign-born, whereas among the students performing above Level 1, the corresponding figures are only 8 and 11 per cent respectively[7]. A more systematic analysis of gender differences among the students with the lowest level of performance follows in Chapter 5, and background characteristics of students with particularly low or high levels of performance are analysed in Chapters 6 and 7.

Among the non-OECD countries student performance at or below Level 1 does not show substantial differences between the three reading literacy scales. This suggests that students whose literacy skill is weak in one aspect may show weak performance in the other aspects. This pattern contrasts with the situation in some OECD countries. In Greece, Mexico, Portugal and Spain, the weaknesses in student performance are greatest on the retrieving information scale, the proportion of students at or below Level 1 being between 5 and 15 percentage points higher than on the reflection and evaluation scale. Conversely, in France, Germany and Switzerland, the proportion of students at or below Level 1 is at least 2 percentage points lower on the retrieving information scale than on the reflection and evaluation scale. In Brazil more than half of the students do not reach beyond Level 1 on the combined reading literacy scale. On the retrieving information scale, more than two-thirds of students in Brazil fail to go beyond Level 1, but only 46 per cent on the reflection and evaluation scale (see Tables 2.1b-d, Annex B1).

To what extent is the pattern of proficiency similar across countries? To examine this, consider the ten countries that have between two-thirds and just over three-quarters of students at Level 3 or above. These are, in order, Finland, Korea, Hong Kong-China, Canada, Japan, Ireland, New Zealand, Australia, the United Kingdom and Sweden. How do these countries do in other respects? In one country, Hong Kong-China, the proportion of students who are also highly literate (9.5 per cent performing at Level 5) is about the same as the OECD average. The country also has the third highest proportion of students at Level 3 and beyond on the combined reading literacy scale among the PISA countries – mainly because of the large proportion of highly literate students on the reflection and evaluation scale.

In a further five countries, Australia, Canada, Ireland, New Zealand and the United Kingdom, there are large numbers at the highest level (between 14 and 19 per cent), but the percentage with performance at or below Level 1 is higher than in Finland, between 10 and 14 per cent (the OECD average is 18 per cent). These countries perform well in getting students to the highest level of proficiency but they do less well in reducing the proportion with low skills. In New Zealand, more students than in any other country are proficient at Level 5 (19 per cent), but a relatively high number (14 per cent) perform only at or below Level 1.

Unlike OECD countries, which have varying patterns of proportion of students at various proficiency levels in relation to the overall performance, the non-OECD countries are rather consistent in terms of proficiency distribution. That is, a country whose overall performance is low tends to have a larger proportion of students at the lower levels.

The results for Hong Kong-China and Korea show that low disparities in literacy skills at a relatively high level is an attainable goal: approximately three-quarters of their students are proficient at least at Level 3 and only 9 and 6 per cent respectively are at or below Level 1.

The mean performances of countries

The discussion above has focused on comparisons of the distribution of student performance between countries. Another way to summarise student performance and to compare the relative standing of countries in reading literacy is to examine their mean scores. To the extent that high average performance at age 15 is predictive of a highly skilled future workforce, countries with high average performance will have a considerable economic and social advantage.

It should be appreciated, however, that average performance figures mask significant variation in performance within countries, reflecting different levels of performance among many different student groups. As in previous international studies of student performance, such as the IEA Third International Mathematics and Science Study (TIMSS), only around one tenth of the total variation in student performance in PISA lies between countries and can, therefore, be captured through a comparison of country averages. The remaining variation in student performance occurs within countries – either between education systems and programmes, between schools, or between students within schools.

Box 2.1. Interpreting sample statistics

Standard errors and confidence intervals. The statistics in this report represent estimates of national performance based on samples of students rather than on the values that could be calculated if every student in every country had answered every question. Consequently, it is important to know the degree of uncertainty inherent in the estimates. In PISA, each estimate has an associated degree of uncertainty, which is expressed through a standard error. The use of confidence intervals provides a means of making inferences about the population means and proportions in a manner that reflects the uncertainty associated with sample estimates. It can be inferred that the observed statistical result for a given population would lie within the confidence interval in 95 out of 100 replications of the measurement, using different samples drawn from the same population.

Judging whether populations differ. This report tests the statistical significance of differences between the national samples in percentages and in average performance scores in order to judge whether there are differences between the populations whom the samples represent. Each separate test follows the convention that, if in fact there is no real difference between two populations, there is no more than a 5 per cent probability that an observed difference between the two samples will erroneously suggest that the populations are different as the result of sampling and measurement error. In the figures and tables showing multiple comparisons of countries' mean scores, the significance tests are based on a procedure for multiple comparisons that limits to 5 per cent the probability that the mean of a given country will erroneously be declared to be different from that of any other country, in cases where there is in fact no difference (for details see Annex A4).

Figure 2.5 summarises the performance of participating countries on the combined reading literacy scale, and Tables 2.2a, b and c show the corresponding information for the three component scales. Figure 2.5 also shows which countries perform above, below, or at the OECD average.

Finland's performance on the combined reading literacy scale is higher than that of any other OECD country (Figure 2.5). Its country mean, 546 points, is almost two-thirds of a proficiency level above the OECD average of 500 (or in statistical terms almost half the international standard deviation above the mean). Countries with mean performances significantly above the OECD average include Australia, Austria, Belgium, Canada, Finland, Hong Kong-China, Iceland, Ireland, Japan, Korea, New Zealand, Sweden and the United Kingdom. Five countries perform around the OECD average (Denmark, France, Norway, Switzerland and the United States). Except for Hong Kong-China, all non-OECD countries have performance that is significantly below the OECD average.

As discussed in Box 2.1, when interpreting mean performance, only those differences between countries that are statistically significant should be taken into account. Accordingly, a country's ranking in Figure 2.5 should be read in the light of whether countries ranked close to it are significantly different from it. Figure 2.5 shows those pairs of countries where the difference in their mean scores is sufficient to say with confidence that the higher performance by sampled students in one country holds for the entire population of enrolled 15 year-olds. Read across the row for a country to compare its performance with the countries listed along the top of the figure. The symbols indicate whether the average performance of the country in the row is significantly lower than that of the comparison country, not statistically different, or significantly higher. For example, Bulgaria is shown in Figure 2.5 to be significantly lower than most of the OECD countries except for Luxembourg and Mexico, and significantly higher than Chile, Brazil, FYR Macedonia, Indonesia, Albania and Peru.

Figure 2.5

Multiple comparisons of mean performance on the combined reading literacy scale

Combined reading literacy scale	Mean	S.E.
Finland	546	(2.6)
Canada	534	(1.6)
New Zealand	529	(2.8)
Australia	528	(3.5)
Ireland	527	(3.2)
Hong Kong-China	525	(2.9)
Korea	525	(2.4)
United Kingdom	523	(2.6)
Japan	522	(5.2)
Sweden	516	(2.2)
Austria	507	(2.4)
Belgium	507	(3.6)
Iceland	507	(1.5)
Norway	505	(2.8)
France	505	(2.7)
United States	504	(7.1)
Denmark	497	(2.4)
Switzerland	494	(4.3)
Spain	493	(2.7)
Czech Republic	492	(2.4)
Italy	487	(2.9)
Germany	484	(2.5)
Liechtenstein	483	(4.1)
Hungary	480	(4.0)
Poland	479	(4.5)
Greece	474	(5.0)
Portugal	470	(4.5)
Russian Federation	462	(4.2)
Latvia	458	(5.3)
Israel	452	(8.5)
Luxembourg	441	(1.6)
Thailand	431	(3.2)
Bulgaria	430	(4.9)
Mexico	422	(3.3)
Argentina	418	(9.9)
Chile	410	(3.6)
Brazil	396	(3.1)
FYR Macedonia	373	(1.9)
Indonesia	371	(4.0)
Albania	349	(3.3)
Peru	327	(4.4)

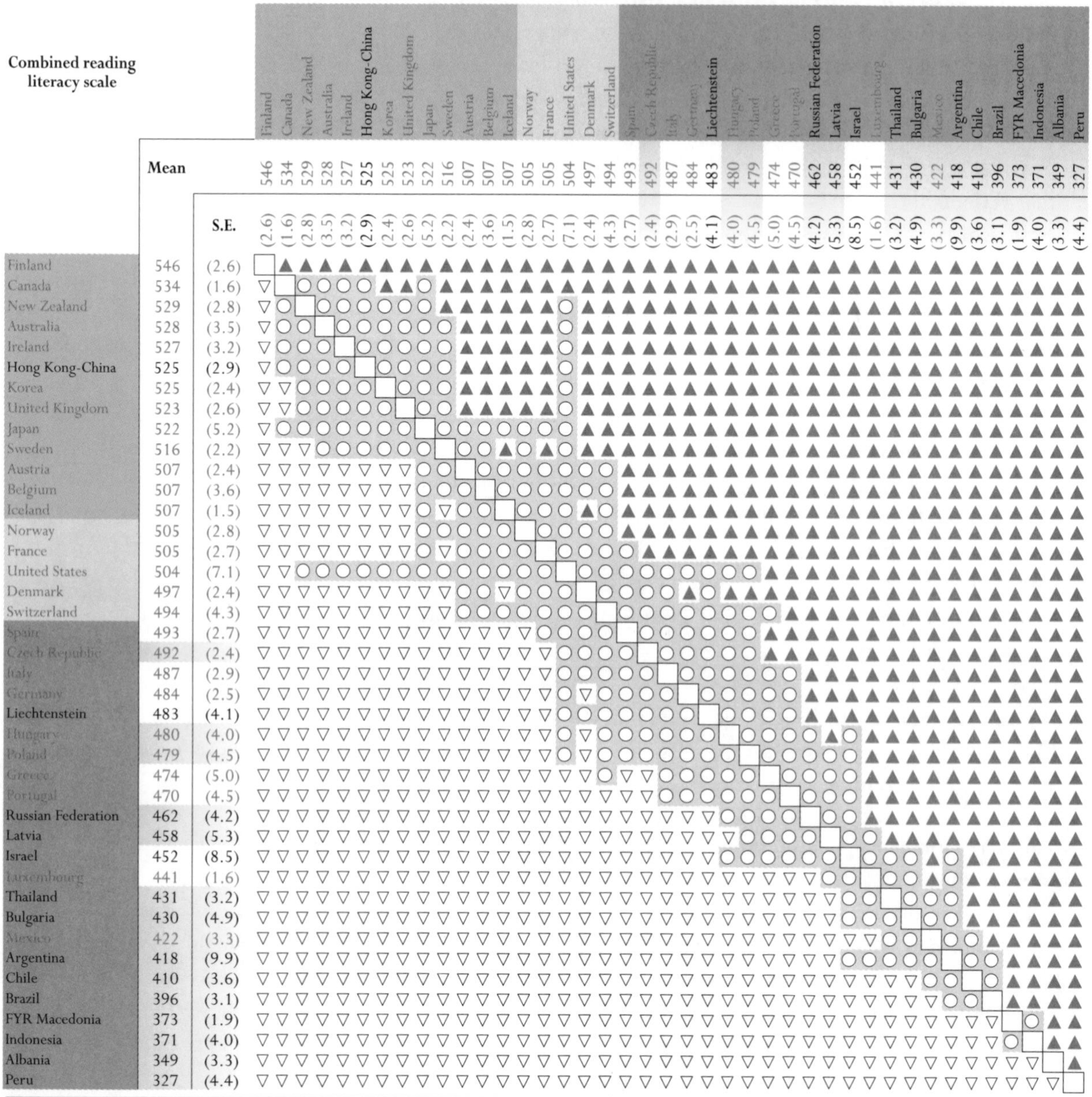

Instructions: Read across the row for a country to compare performance with the countries listed along the top of the chart. The symbols indicate whether the average performance of the country in the row is significantly lower than that of the comparison

▲ Mean performance statistically significantly higher than in comparison country.

○ No statistically significant difference from comparison country.

▽ Mean performance statistically significantly lower than in comparison country.

OECD countries

Non-OECD countries

Statistically significantly above the OECD average

Not statistically significantly different from the OECD average

Statistically significantly below the OECD average

Low- and middle-income countries

Source: OECD PISA database, 2003.

Peru's performance is lower than those of all other countries and more than two full proficiency levels below the OECD average. In fact, the difference in the country mean score between Finland, the top performing country, and Peru is equivalent to three proficiency levels. Thus the average Finnish student performs at the upper end of Level 3, while the average Peruvian student performs below Level 1.

Brazil and Mexico also have performances that are significantly lower than those of most of the OECD countries. When their mean scores are interpreted, however, it needs to be borne in mind that 15-year-old students in both countries are spread across a wide range of grade levels. Fifteen-year-olds in these countries who are enrolled in grade 10 (the modal grade of 15-year-olds in OECD countries) score on average 463 and 467 points respectively, *i.e.*, between the average scores of the Russian Federation and Portugal (for data see *www.pisa.oecd.org*). Similar results can be found for the other Latin American countries.

For another picture of the general level of achievement in each country it is useful to observe where the largest proportion of each population is situated. In the case of 24 countries, this is at Level 3, as Figure 2.6 shows. In Belgium, Finland and New Zealand, the most common level is Level 4. The most common level for students in Argentina, Bulgaria, Chile, Israel, Latvia, Luxembourg, Mexico, the Russian Federation and Thailand is Level 2, and for Brazil and Indonesia, it is Level 1. The three nations of Albania, FYR Macedonia and Peru have the largest proportion of students below the basic reading literacy level.

Figure 2.6

Proficiency level accounting for the highest proportion of students in each country
on the combined reading literacy scale

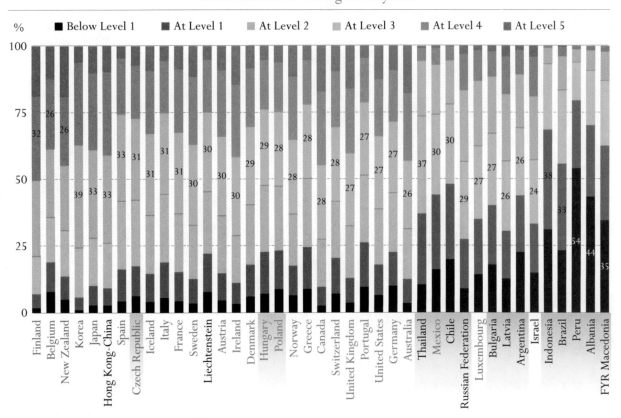

Source: OECD PISA database, 2003. Table 2.1a.

Box 2.2. Mean scores and performance distributions

Mean scores provide a general indication of the overall performance of each country, but they provide no information about the range and distribution of performances within countries. It is possible for countries to achieve similar means yet to have quite different score patterns. Consider the graph of three hypothetical countries' performance on the combined reading literacy scale, as shown in Figure 2.7.

Country A has a mean score well above the OECD average and a narrow distribution of results on the combined reading literacy scale. Country B has a mean below that of Country A, but still above the mean for the OECD average, and a narrow distribution of results. The mean for Country C is identical to that of Country B, but its scores are more widely distributed than those in Country C. This means that there are more high achievers at the extreme top end of the range and more low achievers at the extreme bottom end.

There would be little argument that, of these three countries, Country A has the most desirable set of results. The students in Country A perform relatively well on average, with the best students achieving excellent results and even the least able students achieving close to the international mean. One could infer either that the population is homogeneous to begin with or that the education system is succeeding in minimising any inequalities. Whatever the explanation, the high general level of achievement combined with a compact spread of scores indicates that most students have the necessary literacy skills to benefit from and contribute to modern society and to develop their potential as individuals.

Now consider Countries B and C. Which of these countries offers the more desirable distribution of results? In Country B with even the lowest performing students achieving reasonable levels of proficiency, almost everyone is able to deal with the normal literacy demands occurring in the daily

Figure 2.7

Performance of three hypothetical countries

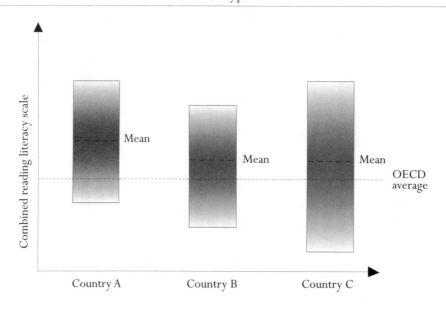

Source: OECD PISA database, 2003.

life of an adult. For example, they will be able to follow current events in a newspaper, to apply for a job, to make sense of the policy statements of a local government candidate or to read a novel for pleasure. On the other hand, the most proficient readers in this population are not on a par with the best readers worldwide. The country may lack a critical mass of people who are able to compete with the best and brightest internationally, and this situation may put the country as a whole at a disadvantage. It is also possible that the potential of the most able students is not being fulfilled, although comparatively large resources are being devoted to the least able.

In Country C the highest performing students are at least as proficient as the best in either of the other countries, and they are potentially in a position to lead their country in global contexts. Conversely, it is unlikely that the least proficient students in Country C can meet many of the literacy demands of adult life. This may not matter in a narrow economic sense (even today there are occupations requiring little or no reading), and, indeed, some would argue that providing high levels of education for everyone leads to shortages of workers for unskilled positions. But individuals are not merely economic units: they have families, live in communities and vote for their representatives in government. It is not desirable to have a large proportion of the adult population unable to function in family, cultural and political contexts. In a modern democracy it is desirable for everyone to be able to fulfil the literacy demands imposed by family life (*e.g.,* reading an article about baby care), by community life (*e.g.,* reading a notice of a public information evening about a shopping centre development) and by political life.

Clearly, similar mean performances in two different countries may mask very different distributions of ability. But whatever a country's decision about how best to organise its education system and its resources, it is surely a matter of social justice that education systems should aim to equip all students to fulfil their potential.

The distribution of reading literacy within countries

Mean performance scores are typically used to assess the quality of schools and education systems. However, the preceding analysis has shown that mean performance does not provide a full picture of student performance and can mask significant variation within an individual class, school or education system. Moreover, countries aim not only to encourage high performance but also to minimise internal disparities in performance. Both parents and the public at large are aware of the gravity of low performance and the fact that school-leavers who lack fundamental skills face poor prospects of employment. A high proportion of students at the lower end of the reading literacy scale may give rise to concern that a large proportion of tomorrow's workforce and voters will lack the skills required for the informed judgements that they must make.

The analysis in this section needs to be distinguished from the examination of the distribution of student performance across the PISA proficiency levels discussed above. Whereas the distribution of students across proficiency levels indicates the proportion of students in each country that can demonstrate a specified level of knowledge and skills, and thus compares countries on the basis of *absolute* benchmarks of student performance, the analysis below focuses on the *relative* distribution of scores, *i.e.,* the *gap* that exists between students with the highest and the lowest levels of performance *within* each country. This is an important indicator of the equality of educational outcomes in the domain of reading literacy (see Box 2.3).

Figure 2.8

Distribution of student performance on the combined reading literacy scale

■ Gradation bars extend from the 5th to the 95th percentiles   ■ Mean score of females
— Mean score on the combined reading literacy scale   ▫ Mean score of males
■ 95% confidence interval around the mean score   ······ OECD average

Performance on the combined reading literacy scale

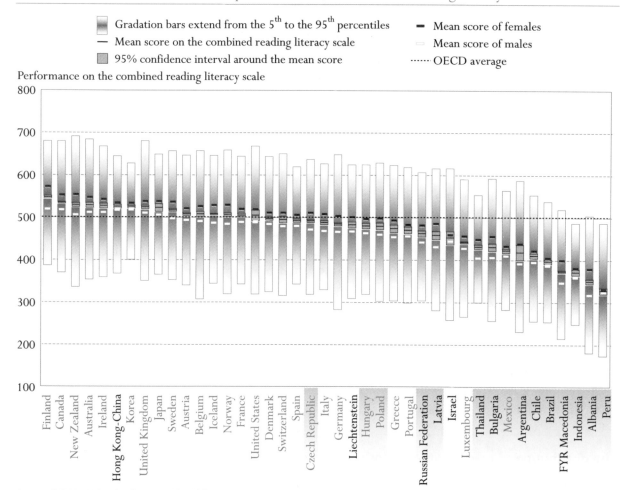

Source: OECD PISA database, 2003. Table 2.3a.

Figure 2.8 shows the distribution of performance scores on the combined reading literacy scale (see Table 2.3a, Annex B1). Since the results are relatively similar for each of the three component scales, these scales are not examined separately in this section. The data for the distribution of performance scores on the component scales can be found in Tables 2.3b, c and d.

The gradation bars in Figure 2.8 show the range of performance in each country between the 5th percentile (the point below which the lowest-performing 5 per cent of the students in a country score) and the 95th percentile (the point below which 95 per cent of students perform or, alternatively, above which the 5 per cent highest-performing students in a country score). The density of the bar represents the proportion of students performing at the corresponding scale points. The horizontal black line near the middle shows the mean score for each country (*i.e.,* the subject of the discussion in the preceding section) and is located inside a shaded box that shows its confidence interval.

Figure 2.8 shows that there is wide variation in student performance on the combined reading literacy scale within countries. The middle 90 per cent of the population shown by the length of the bars exceeds by far the range between the mean scores of the highest and lowest performing countries. In almost all

OECD countries, this group includes some students proficient at Level 5 and others not proficient above Level 1. However, in five countries, namely Albania, Brazil, Indonesia, FYR Macedonia and Peru, the top performing students do not reach Level 4 (*i.e.*, below 553 points) and the lowest performing students are well below the basic literacy level. In all countries, the range of performance in the middle half of the students exceeds the magnitude of one proficiency level, and in Argentina, Australia, Belgium, Germany, Israel and New Zealand it exceeds twice this difference (OECD average 1.8).

Figure 2.9 shows that in some countries with high average performance, such as Australia, New Zealand and the United Kingdom, the 25th percentile on the combined reading literacy scale lies well within proficiency Level 2 (around 458 points), indicating that students at the 25th percentile are doing reasonably well in absolute terms. Nevertheless, the large difference between student performance at the 25th and 75th percentiles of the national performance distribution in these countries could indicate that the students at the 25th percentile are substantially below what is expected of them within their national education system.

Figure 2.9

Differences in scores at 25th and 75th percentiles on the combined reading literacy scale

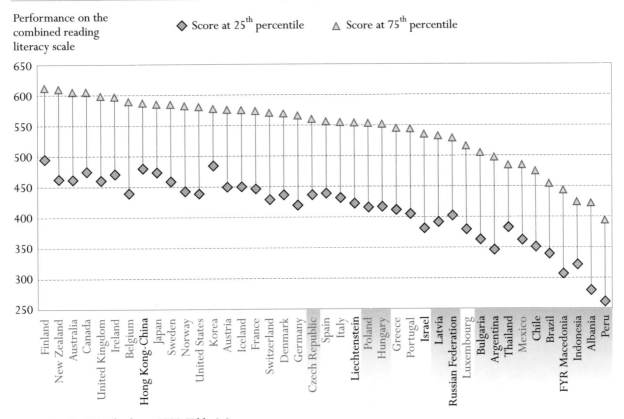

Source: OECD PISA database, 2003. Table 2.3a.

Box 2.3. Interpreting differences in PISA scores: How large a gap?

What is meant by a difference of, say, 50 points between the scores of two different groups of students? A difference of 73 points on the PISA scale represents one proficiency level in reading literacy. A difference of one proficiency level can be considered a comparatively large difference in student performance in substantive terms. For example, on the interpreting scale, Level 3 describes students who can typically integrate several parts of a text, can understand a relationship or construe the meaning of a word or phrase and can compare, contrast and categorise competing information according to a range of criteria. Such students differ from those at Level 2, who can be expected only to identify the main idea in a text, to understand relationships, to make and apply simple categories, and to construe meaning within a limited part of a text where information is not prominent and only low-level inferences are required (see also Figure 2.1).

Another benchmark is that the difference in performance on the combined reading literacy scale between the OECD countries with the third highest and the third lowest mean performance is 59 points; and the difference between the fifth highest and the fifth lowest OECD countries is 48 points.

Differences in scores can also be viewed in terms of the differences in student performance demonstrated by different groups of students on the combined reading literacy scale:

- The difference in performance between the highest national quarters of students on the PISA international socio-economic index of occupational status and the bottom quarters equals, on average across OECD countries, 81 points (Table 6.1a, OECD 2001*b*). That is, on average across OECD countries, 81 points separate students who report that their parents are, for example, secondary school teachers or managers of a small business enterprise from those whose parents are bricklayers, carpenters or painters.

- The difference in student performance between students whose mothers have completed tertiary education and those who have not completed upper secondary education equals, on average across OECD countries, 67 points (Table 6.7, OECD, 2001*b*).

- The difference in student performance between students who speak the language of the assessment most of the time and those who do not equals, on average across OECD countries, 68 points (Table 6.11, OECD 2001*b*).

To what extent are differences in student performance a reflection of the natural distribution of ability and, therefore, difficult to influence through changes in public policy? It is not easy to answer such a question with data from PISA alone, not least because differences between countries are influenced by the social and economic context in which education and learning take place. Nonetheless, several findings suggest that public policy can play a role:

- First, the within-country variation in performance in reading literacy varies widely between countries, the difference between the 75th and 25th percentiles ranging from less than 101 points in Indonesia, Korea and Thailand to more than 150 points in Argentina and Israel. The within-country difference in these two countries is even larger than that of Belgium, which registers the largest difference among the OECD countries (see Table 2.3a, Annex B1). The five Asian countries showed the five smallest differences.

- Second, countries with similar levels of average performance show a considerable variation in disparity of student performance. For example, Indonesia and FYR Macedonia have similar mean performance on the combined reading literacy (371 and 373 respectively). The difference between the 75th and 25th percentiles in Indonesia is 101 points, significantly below the OECD average, but in FYR Macedonia it is 135 points, which is the average difference for the OECD countries. The same can be observed in the OECD countries scoring below the average. Germany and Italy, two countries that perform at around 486 points, significantly below the OECD average, vary in their internal differences. The difference between the 75th and 25th percentiles is 124 points in Italy, but it is 146 points in Germany. Bringing the bottom quarter of students closer to their current mean would be one way for countries with wide internal disparities to raise the country's overall performance.

- Third, it is evident from a comparison between the range of performance within a country and its average performance that wide disparities in performance are not a necessary condition for a country to attain a high level of overall performance. As an illustration, the four of the seven countries with the smallest differences between the 75th and 25th percentiles, Finland, Hong Kong-China, Japan and Korea are also among the best-performing countries in reading literacy. Conversely, two countries are among these with the highest performance differences, Argentina and Israel, score significantly below the OECD average. In most of the non-OECD countries, the large within-country difference is due to the large proportion of students at the extreme lower end of the scale. Therefore, most of these countries are faced with a double challenge to enhance the performance of all students and to narrow the gap between the top and low performers.

Examining the range from the 25th to the 5th percentiles provides an indication of performance by the least successful students relative to the overall performance of the respective country. Does the range of performance become wider at the bottom end of the distribution? Generally, countries with a narrow range between the 75th and 25th percentiles, such as Finland, Japan, Korea and Spain, also show a narrow range of distribution at the bottom end, between the 25th and 5th percentiles.

In some countries with below-average performance, the students who perform best nevertheless do extremely well. For example, 5 per cent of students in Germany score above 650 points, while the top 5 per cent of students in Korea only score above 629 points – even though the mean score of Germany is significantly below, and that of Korea significantly above, the OECD average. Conversely, the least proficient students can do poorly in countries with good average performance. In one of the countries with the highest average reading performance, New Zealand, 5 per cent of the population are below the comparatively low score of 337 - a higher proportion of low scores than in several countries with only moderate average performance.

Where does performance variation originate from? Fifteen-year-olds in OECD countries attend schools in a variety of educational and institutional settings. In certain countries, some students enrol in vocationally oriented schools while others attend schools designed to prepare students for entry into university-level education. Similarly, in countries where the transition from lower to upper secondary education occurs at around the age of 15, some students surveyed by PISA may still be attending school at the lower secondary level, while others may have already progressed to the upper secondary level. Furthermore, while the majority of students in all but two OECD countries attend public schools, a significant minority of students in several OECD countries attend schools that are privately managed and, in some cases, privately financed.

The analysis in this chapter has shown that, in most countries, there are considerable differences in performance within each education system. This variation may result from the socio-economic backgrounds of students and schools, from the human and financial resources available to schools, from curricular differences, from selection policies and practices and from the way in which teaching is organised and delivered (see also Chapters 6 and 7). Some countries have non-selective school systems that seek to provide all students with the same opportunities for learning and that allow each school to cater for the full range of student performance. Other countries respond to diversity explicitly by forming groups of students of similar performance levels through selection either within or between schools, with the aim of serving students according to their specific needs. And in yet other countries, combinations of the two approaches occur. Even in comprehensive school systems, there may be significant variation between schools due to the socio-economic and cultural characteristics of the communities that the schools serve or to geographical differences, such as differences between regions, provinces or states in federal systems, or differences between rural and urban areas. Finally, there may be significant variation between individual schools that cannot be easily quantified or otherwise described, part of which could result from differences in the quality or effectiveness of the teaching that those schools provide.

How do the policies and historical patterns that shape each country's school system affect and relate to the overall variation in student performance? Do countries with explicit tracking and streaming policies show a higher degree of overall disparity in student performance than countries that have non-selective education systems? These questions are further examined in Chapter 7 of this report.

Performance on the subscales of reading literacy

Table 2.2a compares the performances of countries in the retrieving information aspect of reading literacy, and indicates whether the performance of any one country is significantly higher than, lower than, or not different from, the performance of every other participating country. The OECD average score for retrieving information is 498. The mean scores for 13 countries are significantly above the OECD average, 22 are significantly below it, and 6 countries have scores not significantly different from the OECD average (see Table 2.2a, Annex B1). Countries' mean scores range from 556 (Finland) to 289 (Peru). This range of mean performance scores (267 score points), the equivalent of almost three and half proficiency levels, is the widest among the three aspects of reading literacy.

Table 2.2b compares the performances of countries in the interpreting texts aspect, and indicates whether the performance of any one country is significantly higher than, lower than, or no different from, the performance of every other participating country. On this subscale, country mean scores range from 555 in Finland to 342 in Peru (see Table 2.2b, Annex B1). The range of mean scores (213) is equivalent to almost three proficiency levels.

Table 2.2c compares the performances of countries in the reflection and evaluation aspect and shows whether the performance of any one country is significantly higher than, lower than, or no different from, the performance of every other participating country. In the case of reflection and evaluation, the highest mean score is 542 in Canada, and the lowest is 323 in Peru (see Table 2.2d, Annex B1). The range of country means (219 score points) is equivalent to three proficiency levels, which is less than for the retrieving information but almost the same as for the interpreting texts subscale.

While the OECD averages on the three aspect subscales are almost identical (498, 501 and 502 score points in retrieving information, interpreting texts and reflection and evaluation respectively), each of the aspects appears to have been easier for some countries, and more difficult for others. (Figure 2.10a).

Figure 2.10a
Difference in performance between the retrieving information and the reflection and evaluation subscales

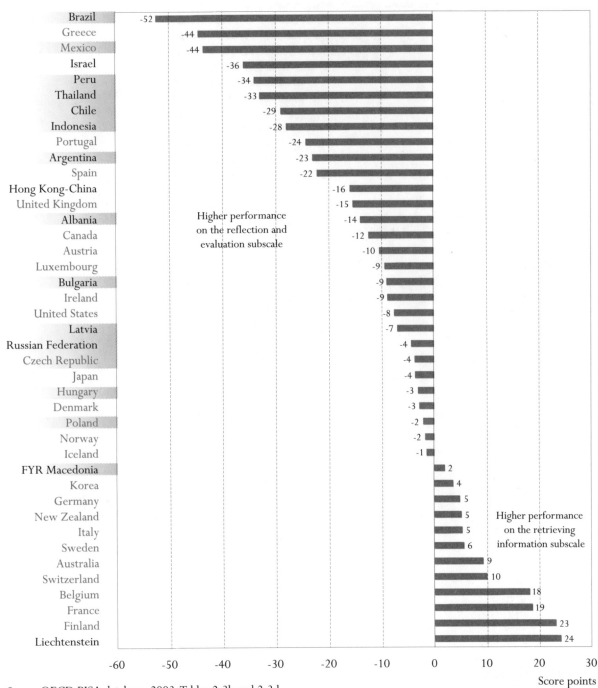

Source: OECD PISA database, 2003. Tables 2.3b and 2.3d.

Figure 2.10b

Difference in performance between the retrieving information and the interpreting subscales

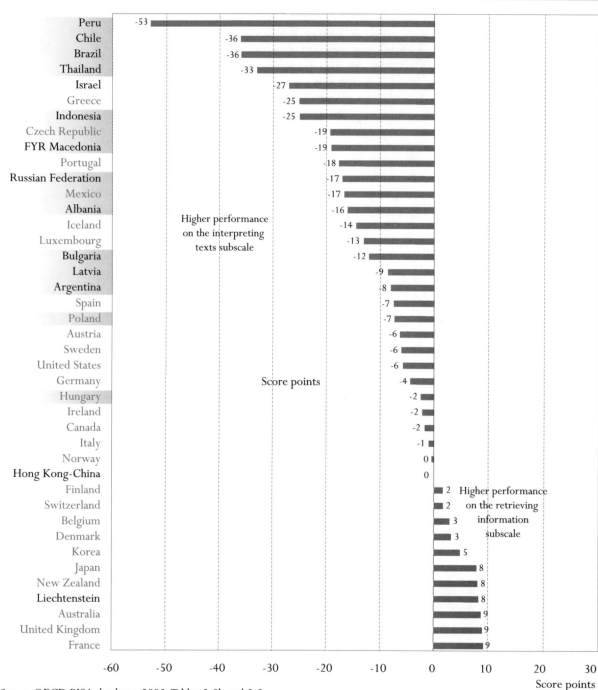

Source: OECD PISA database, 2003. Tables 2.3b and 2.3c.

In addition to this proportion of students not reaching Level 1, there are those who perform only at Level 1, which means that they are capable only of completing the most basic reading tasks, such as locating a simple piece of information, identifying the main theme of a text or making a simple connection with everyday knowledge. Adding these two categories together brings the proportion of low performers to an average of 18 per cent across OECD countries and to well over 50 per cent in many of the non-OECD

> ## Box 2.4. Evaluating within-country differences in performance on subscales
>
> Results for retrieving information, interpreting texts and reflection and evaluation are not independent measures, since the levels of difficulty of all the tasks were estimated in the same analysis. The same holds true for the continuous texts and non-continuous texts subscales. Standard tests of significance are therefore not appropriate. The discussion of within-country profiles of performance on the three aspect subscales, and on the two text format subscales, is based on the observation of patterns in the data, rather than on statistical tests of significance.

The mean score on the reflection and evaluation scale is more than 20 points higher than that on the retrieving information subscales in Argentina, Brazil, Chile, Greece, Hong Kong-China, Indonesia, Israel, Mexico, Peru, Portugal, Spain and Thailand. Three countries – Finland, France and Liechtenstein – show the opposite pattern of relatively stronger performance in retrieving information, with a difference of approximately 20 points between mean proficiency in reflection and evaluation and in retrieving information in favour of the latter (see Figure 2.10a).

Chile, Peru and the Russian Federation perform best, relative to other subscales, on the interpreting texts subscale. Seven countries including Brazil, Chile, Indonesia, Israel, Greece, Peru and Thailand have score differences of more than 20 points between the mean score in interpreting texts and the mean score in retrieving information. The higher score being attained for interpreting texts (see Figure 2.10b).

Conclusions

The results of PISA show wide differences between countries in the knowledge and skills of 15-year-olds in reading literacy. Two-hundred and nineteen score points, which is three proficiency levels, separate the highest and lowest average performances by participating countries on the combined reading literacy scale. Differences *between* countries represent, however, only a fraction of overall variation in student performance, for differences in performance within countries are on average about ten times as great as the variation between country means. Catering for such a diverse client base and narrowing the gaps in student performance represent formidable challenges for all countries.

In every country, some proportion of 15-year-olds reach the highest proficiency level in PISA, demonstrating the ability to complete sophisticated reading tasks, to show detailed understanding of texts and the relevance of their components, and to evaluate information critically and to build hypotheses drawing on specialised knowledge. At the other end of the scale, 6 per cent of students among OECD countries and well over one-third of the student population in some of the non-OECD countries do not reach proficiency Level 1. They fail to demonstrate routinely the most basic knowledge and skills that PISA seeks to measure. These students may still be able to read in a technical sense, but they show serious difficulties in applying reading literacy as a tool to advance and extend their knowledge and skills in other areas. Even in countries which do well overall, the existence of a small but significant minority of students who, near the end of compulsory schooling, lack the foundation of literacy skills needed for further learning, must be of concern to policy makers seeking to make lifelong learning a reality for all. This is particularly significant given mounting evidence that continuing education and training beyond school tend to reinforce rather than mitigate skill differences resulting from unequal success in initial education.

countries. Parents, educators, and policy-makers in systems with large proportions of students performing at or below Level 1 need to recognise that significant numbers of students are not benefiting sufficiently from available educational opportunities and are not acquiring the necessary knowledge and skills to do so effectively in their further school careers and beyond. In countries such as Brazil and Mexico, which have comparatively low levels of national income and where spending on educational institutions per student up to age 15 is only around one fourth of the OECD average (see Chapter 3), fostering the education of those most in need represents a considerable challenge, and specific policies to that end have often only been recently introduced.

Wide variation in student performance does not, however, always mean that a large part of the student population will have a low level of reading literacy. In fact, in some countries with high average performance, such as Australia, New Zealand and the United Kingdom, the 25th percentile on the combined reading literacy scale lies well within proficiency Level 2 (around 458 points), indicating that students at the 25th percentile are doing reasonably well by international comparative standards. Nevertheless, the variation in the distribution of student performance in these countries suggests that the students at the 25th percentile may be performing substantially below expected benchmarks of good performance in the countries in question.

To what extent is the observed variation in student performance on the PISA assessments a reflection of the innate distribution of students' abilities and thus a challenge for education systems that cannot be influenced directly by education policy? This chapter shows not only that the magnitude of within-country disparities in reading literacy varies widely between countries but also that wide disparities in performance are not a necessary condition for a country to attain a high level of overall performance. Although more general contextual factors need to be considered when such disparities are compared between countries, public policy may therefore have the potential to make an important contribution to providing equal opportunities and equitable learning outcomes for all students. Showing that countries differ not just in their mean performance but also in the extent to which they are able to close the gap between the students with the lowest and the highest levels of performance and to reduce some of the barriers to equitable distribution of learning outcomes is an important finding which has direct relevance to policy making.

Many factors contribute to variation in student performance. Disparities can result from the socio-economic backgrounds of students and schools, from the human and financial resources available to schools, from curricular differences, and from the way in which teaching is organised and delivered. As the causes of variation in student performance differ, so too do the approaches chosen by different countries to address the challenge. Some countries have non-selective school systems that seek to provide all students with the same opportunities for learning and require each school to cater for the full range of student performance. Other countries respond to diversity by forming groups of students of similar levels of performance through selection either within or between schools, with the aim of serving students according to their specific needs. Chapter 7 takes this analysis further and seeks to address the question of the extent to which such policies and practices affect actual student performance.

Notes

1. Technically, the mean score for student performance across OECD countries was set at 500 points and the standard deviation at 100 points, with the data weighted so that each OECD country contributed equally.

2. The concept of literacy used in PISA is much broader than the historical notion of the ability to read and write. In particular, the PISA definition goes beyond the notion that reading literacy means decoding written material and literal comprehension, so that the PISA tests did not seek to measure that kind of technical literacy. Those who fail to reach Level 1 may well be literate in the technical sense.

3. In PISA each item has a unique code. The item code is presented in brackets *e.g.,* [R110Q01] in this chapter. This identification code helps users who wish to retrieve student responses to the item from the online database for PISA 2000 (*http://www.pisa.oecd.org/pisa/outcome.htm*).

4. In order to confirm that these differences are statistically significant, the relative probability of each country assuming each rank-order position on each reading scale was determined from the country's mean scores, their standard errors and the covariance between the performance scales. This reveals whether, with a likelihood of 95 per cent, a country would rank statistically significantly higher, at the same level, or statistically significantly lower in one reading scale than in the other reading scale. For details on the methods employed see the *PISA 2000 Technical Report* (OECD, 2002*a*).

5. For data see the *PISA 2000 Technical Report* (OECD, 2002*a*).

6. Multiple-choice items were excluded from this comparison because students might answer these correctly simply by guessing at random.

7. In Germany, 11.3 per cent of students are foreign-born (standard error 0.59); 5.1 per cent of students are foreign-born students and score at Level 1 or below (standard error 0.51); 88.7 per cent of students were born in Germany (standard error 0.59); 14.4 per cent of students were born in Germany and score at Level 1 or below (standard error 0.82). In Luxembourg, 18.6 per cent of students are foreign-born (standard error 0.64); 11.5 per cent of students are foreign-born and score at Level 1 or below (standard error 0.55); 81.5 per cent of students were born in Luxembourg (standard error 0.64); 22.3 per cent of students were born in Luxembourg and score at Level 1 or below (standard error 0.62).

Chapter

3

A PROFILE OF STUDENT PERFORMANCE IN MATHEMATICAL AND SCIENTIFIC LITERACY

Introduction

For much of the last century, the content of school mathematics and science curricula was dominated by the need to provide the foundations for the professional training of a small number of mathematicians, scientists and engineers. With the growing role of science, mathematics and technology in modern life, however, the objectives of personal fulfilment, employment and full participation in society increasingly require that all adults, not just those aspiring to a scientific career, should be mathematically, scientifically and technologically literate.

Mathematical and scientific literacy are important for understanding environmental, medical, economic and other issues that confront modern societies, which rely heavily on technological and scientific advances. Further, the performance of a country's best students in mathematics and scientific subjects may have implications for the part which that country will play in tomorrow's advanced technology sector and for its general international competitiveness. Conversely, deficiencies in mathematical and scientific literacy can have negative consequences for individuals' labour-market and earnings prospects and for their capacity to participate fully in society.

Consequently, policy-makers and educators alike attach great importance to mathematics and science education. Addressing the increasing demand for mathematical and scientific skills requires excellence throughout education systems, and it is important to monitor how well countries provide young adults with fundamental skills in this area. Mathematical and scientific knowledge and skills, therefore, form an integral part of the PISA literacy concept. The definition of mathematical and scientific literacy used in PISA, which is described in Chapter 1, makes the results more relevant to modern societies than assessments that focus solely on the common denominators to be found in national curricula.

This chapter reviews the results of PISA in mathematical and scientific literacy, and examines the degree to which these coincide with or differ from the results in reading presented in Chapter 2. The chapter:

- describes the criteria for rating performance in mathematical and scientific literacy and gives examples of easier, medium and harder tasks used in PISA 2000;

- summarises performance in each country in terms of the mean scores achieved by students and the distribution of scores across student populations;

- examines how performance varies between reading, mathematical and scientific literacy.

PISA 2000 devoted major attention to reading literacy. For this reason, the assessment of mathematical and scientific literacy was more limited, and the analysis of the results is not as detailed as in the case of reading. This analysis will be deepened in PISA 2003, when primary attention will be given to mathematics, and in PISA 2006, when the most attention will be given to science. Descriptions of the conceptual frameworks underlying the PISA assessments of mathematical and scientific literacy are provided in *Measuring Student Knowledge and Skills – A New Framework for Assessment* (OECD, 1999a).

Student performance in mathematical literacy

How mathematical literacy is measured in PISA

Performance in mathematical literacy is marked on a single scale that, as in the case of reading literacy, was constructed with an average score of 500 points and a standard deviation of 100 points for OECD countries, and with about two-thirds of students across OECD countries scoring between 400 and 600 points[1]. This scale measures the ability of students to recognise and interpret mathematical problems encountered in their world, to translate these problems into a mathematical context, to use mathematical knowledge and procedures to solve the problems within such a context, to interpret the results in terms of the original problem, to reflect upon the methods applied and to formulate and communicate the outcomes.

The criteria that define the level of difficulty of tasks involve:

- *The number and complexity of processing or computational steps involved in the tasks.* Tasks range from single-step problems requiring students to recall and to reproduce basic mathematical facts or to complete simple computations to more complex problems calling for advanced mathematical knowledge and complex decision-making, information processing and problem-solving and modelling skills.

- *The requirement to connect and integrate material.* The simplest tasks typically require students to apply a single representation or technique to a single piece of information. More complicated tasks require students to integrate more than one piece of information using different representations, or different mathematical tools or knowledge in a sequence of steps.

- *The requirement to represent and interpret material and to reflect on situations and methods.* Such tasks range from recognising and using a familiar formula to the formulation, translation or creation of an appropriate model within an unfamiliar context, and the use of insight, reasoning, argumentation and generalisation.

As previously mentioned, PISA 2000 assessed mathematical and scientific literacy as a minor domain. Thus the limited data available for these domains in this cycle does not permit the development of subscales. Moreover, no attempt was made to define levels of proficiency, as was done in reading. It is nonetheless possible to provide a broad description of performance in mathematics and science with reference to the knowledge and skills that students need to demonstrate at various points on the relevant scales.

In the case of the mathematical literacy scale, this description is as follows.

- Towards the top end, around 750 points, students typically take a creative and active role in their approach to mathematical problems. They interpret and formulate problems in mathematical terms, handle more complex information, and negotiate a number of processing steps. Students at this level identify and apply relevant tools and knowledge (frequently in an unfamiliar problem context), use insight to identify a suitable way of finding a solution, and display other higher-order cognitive processes, such as generalisation, reasoning and argumentation to explain and communicate results.

- At around 570 points on the scale, students are typically able to interpret, link and integrate different representations of a problem or different pieces of information; use and manipulate a given model, often involving algebra or other symbolic representations; and verify or check given propositions or models. Students typically work with given strategies, models or propositions (*e.g.*, by recognising and extrapolating from a pattern), and they select and apply relevant mathematical knowledge in order to solve a problem that may involve a small number of processing steps.

- At the lower end of the scale, around 380 points, students are usually able to complete only a single processing step consisting of reproducing basic mathematical facts or processes or of applying simple computational skills. Students typically recognise information from diagrammatic or text material that is familiar and straightforward and in which a mathematical formulation is provided or readily apparent. Any interpretation or reasoning typically involves recognition of a single familiar element of a problem. The solution calls for application of a routine procedure in a single processing step.

To put these scales into context, across OECD countries the best performing 5 per cent of students achieved 655 points. However, the performance of this top 5 per cent of students varied widely across countries: The performance levels of the top 5 per cent of students ranged from over 680 points in Hong Kong-China, Japan, New Zealand and Switzerland to less than 500 points in Brazil and Peru, *i.e.*, the top students in these latter countries only reach the average level of performance across OECD countries. At the lower end of the scale, more than three-quarters of students in OECD countries achieved at least 435 points, more than 90 per cent 367 points, and more than 95 per cent, 326 points (see Table 3.1, Annex B1).

The tasks used for the assessment of mathematical literacy in PISA vary widely in difficulty. Figure 3.1 shows the tasks from two of the 16 units used for the assessment of mathematical literacy along with a description of the criteria used to mark students' answers (a more complete set of sample tasks can be found at *Sample Tasks from the PISA 2000 Assessment – Reading, Mathematical and Scientific Literacy*, OECD, 2002c or *www.pisa.oecd.org*).

Question 3 in the unit *Apples* was the most difficult of the sample questions shown in Figure 3.1. Students were given a hypothetical scenario involving planting apple trees in a square pattern, with a "row" of protective conifer trees around the square. The scenario required students to show insight into mathematical functions by comparing the growth of a linear function with that of a quadratic function. Students were asked to construct a verbal description of a generalised pattern and to develop an argument using algebra. In order to answer correctly, students had to understand both the algebraic expressions used to describe the pattern and the underlying functional relationships in such a way that they could see and explain the generalisation of these relationships in an unfamiliar context. To receive full credit for Question 3, which corresponds to a score of 723 points on the mathematical literacy scale, students had to provide the correct answer as well as a valid explanation. Students with a score of 723 points should theoretically be able to answer questions of this level of difficulty correctly 62 out of 100 times (see also Box 2.1). On average across OECD countries, 8 per cent of students received full credit for this open-ended question. A further 10 per cent received partial credit (see *PISA 2000 Technical Report*, OECD, 2002a).

In Question 2 in the same unit – a slightly less difficult question with a difficulty of 655 points on the PISA mathematical literacy scale – students were given two algebraic expressions describing the growth in the number of trees as the orchard increased in size. Students were asked to find a value for which the two expressions coincide. This question required students to interpret expressions containing words and symbols and to link different representations (pictorial, verbal and algebraic) of two relationships (one quadratic and one linear). Students had to find a strategy for determining when the two functions had the same solution and then communicate the result by explaining the reasoning and calculation steps involved. On average across OECD countries 25 per cent of students received full credit for this open-ended question.

The easiest question in the unit *Apples* asked students to complete a table of values generated by the functions describing the number of trees as the size of the orchard increased. The question required students to interpret a written description of a situation, to link this to a tabular representation of some of the information, to recognise a pattern and then to extend this pattern. Students had to work with given models and then relate two different representations (pictorial and tabular) of two relationships (one quadratic and one linear) in order to extrapolate from the pattern. On average across OECD countries, 50 per cent of students received full credit for this open-ended question, while an additional 13 per cent received partial credit.

The second sample unit shown in Figure 3.1, *Racing Car,* provides questions illustrating the middle and the lower end of the mathematical literacy scale. In Question 5, which is located at 492 points on the mathematical literacy scale, students were given a graph showing the speed of a car as it moves around a racetrack. They were asked to interpret the graph to find a distance that satisfies a given condition. Students needed to interpret the graph by linking a verbal description with two particular features of the graph (one simple and straightforward, one requiring a deeper understanding of several elements of the graph and what it represents), and then to identify and read the required information from the graph, selecting the best option from among a number of given alternatives. On average across OECD countries, 67 per cent of students answered this multiple-choice question correctly (see *PISA 2000 Technical Report*, OECD, 2002*a*). However, this task was shown to be more difficult for non-OECD countries, with an average of 49 per cent of students answering it correctly in these countries, ranging from 28 and 29 per cent in Peru and Indonesia to 68 per cent in the Russian Federation.

At the lower end of the mathematical literacy scale, Question 7 (with a level of difficulty of 413 points) asked students to interpret the speed of the car at a particular point in the graph. The question required students to read information from a graph representing a physical relationship (speed and distance of a car). Students had to identify the place in the graph referred to in a verbal description, to recognise what happens to the speed of a vehicle at that point, and then to select the best option from among a number of given alternatives. On average 83 per cent of students in the OECD countries and 67 per cent in the non-OECD countries answered this multiple-choice question correctly.

The mean performances of countries in mathematical literacy

For policy-makers in the participating countries, international comparisons of student performance have become an essential tool for assessing the outcomes of their countries' education systems. Such comparisons offer an external point of reference for the objective evaluation of the effectiveness of education systems. The first question that is often asked is how nations compare in their mean performance. As with reading, performance in mathematical literacy can be summarised by countries' mean scores.

Figure 3.2 orders countries by the mean performance of their students on the mathematical literacy scale. The figure also shows which countries have a level of performance above, below or about the same as the OECD average.

As in the case of reading literacy, only those differences between countries that are statistically significant should be considered. Figure 3.2 shows the pairs of countries where the difference in their mean scores is large enough to say with confidence that the higher performance by sampled students in one country would hold for the entire student population in both countries. The reader should read across the row for each country to compare its mean performance with those of the countries listed along the top of the figure. The symbols indicate whether the average performance of the country in the row is statistically significantly lower than that of the comparison country, not statistically different from it or significantly higher.[2]

Students in Hong Kong-China, Japan and Korea display the highest mean scores in mathematical literacy. The other countries that also score above the OECD average are Australia, Austria, Belgium, Canada,

Figure 3.1
Samples of the mathematics tasks used in PISA

APPLES

A farmer plants apple trees in a square pattern. In order to protect the trees against the wind he plants conifers all around the orchard.

Here you see a diagram of this situation where you can see the pattern of apple trees and conifers for any number (n) of rows of apple trees:

✖ = conifer

● = apple tree

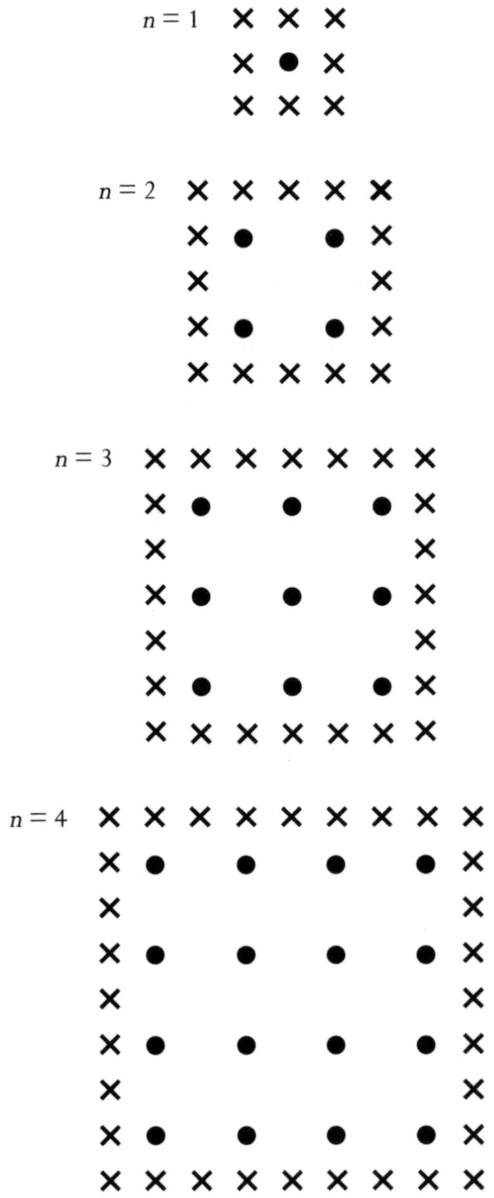

$n = 1$

✖ ✖ ✖
✖ ● ✖
✖ ✖ ✖

$n = 2$

✖ ✖ ✖ ✖ ✖
✖ ●　　● ✖
✖　　　　✖
✖ ●　　● ✖
✖ ✖ ✖ ✖ ✖

$n = 3$

✖ ✖ ✖ ✖ ✖ ✖ ✖
✖ ●　● 　● ✖
✖　　　　　✖
✖ ●　● 　● ✖
✖　　　　　✖
✖ ●　● 　● ✖
✖ ✖ ✖ ✖ ✖ ✖ ✖

$n = 4$

✖ ✖ ✖ ✖ ✖ ✖ ✖ ✖ ✖
✖ ●　● 　● 　● ✖
✖　　　　　　　✖
✖ ●　● 　● 　● ✖
✖　　　　　　　✖
✖ ●　● 　● 　● ✖
✖　　　　　　　✖
✖ ●　● 　● 　● ✖
✖ ✖ ✖ ✖ ✖ ✖ ✖ ✖ ✖

**TASK
DIFFICULTY**

QUESTION 3

APPLES

Suppose the farmer wants to make a much larger orchard with many rows of trees. As the farmer makes the orchard bigger, which will increase more quickly: the number of apple trees or the number of conifers?

Explain how you found your answer.

Score 2 (723)*

— Answers which are correct (apple trees) AND which give some algebraic explanations based on the formulae n^2 and $8n$.

Score 1

— Answers which are correct (apple trees) AND are based on specific examples or on extending the table.

— Answers which are correct (apple trees) and show SOME evidence that the relationship between n^2 and $8n$ is understood, but not so clearly expressed as in Score 2.

highest

750

This task requires students to show insight into mathematical functions by comparing the growth of a linear function with that of a quadratic function. Students are required to construct a verbal description of a generalised pattern, and to create an argument using algebra. Students need to understand both the algebraic expressions used to describe the pattern and the underlying functional relationships, in such a way that they can see and explain the generalisation of these relationships in an unfamiliar context. A chain of reasoning is required, and communication of this in a written explanation.

This task requires students to interpret expressions containing words and symbols, and to link different representations (pictorial, verbal and algebraic) of two relationships (one quadratic and one linear). Students have to find a strategy for determining when the two functions will have the same solution (for example, by trial and error, or by algebraic means), and to communicate the result by explaining the reasoning and calculation steps involved.

middle

QUESTION 2

APPLES

There are two formulae you can use to calculate the number of apple trees and the number of conifers for the pattern described above:

• number of apple trees $= n^2$

• number of conifers $= 8n$

• where n is the number of rows of apple trees.

There is a value of n for which the number of apple trees equals the number of conifers. Find the value of n and show your method of calculating this.

Score 2 (655)*

— Answers which give n=8, with the algebraic method explicitly shown.

— Answers which give n=8, but no clear algebra is presented, or no work shown.

— Answers which give n=8 using other methods, *e.g.*, using pattern expansion or drawing.

570

Students are given a hypothetical scenario involving planting an orchard of apple trees in a square pattern, with a row of protective conifer trees around the square. They are asked to complete a table of values generated by the functions that describe the number of trees as the size of the orchard is increased. This question requires students to interpret a written description of a problem situation, to link this to a tabular representation of some of the information, to recognise a pattern and then to extend this pattern. Students need to work with given models and to relate two different representations (pictorial and tabular) of two relationships (one quadratic and one linear) in order to extend the pattern.

lowest

QUESTION 1

APPLES

Complete the table:

n	Number of apple trees	Number of conifers
1	1	8
2	4	16
3	9	24
4	16	32
5	25	40

Score 2 (548)*

— Answers which show all 7 entries correct.

380

Source: OECD PISA, 2001.

*Thresholds, based on RP $= 0.62$ (see Box 2.1).

Figure 3.1 (continued)

Samples of the mathematics tasks used in PISA

SPEED OF A RACING CAR

This graph shows how the speed of a racing car varies along a flat 3 kilometre track during its second lap.

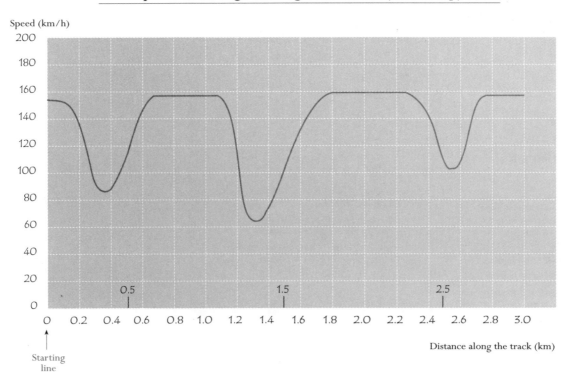

Speed of a racing car along a 3 km track (second lap)

TASK DIFFICULTY

QUESTION 8

SPEED OF A RACING CAR

Here are pictures of five tracks: Along which one of these tracks was the car driven to produce the speed graph shown earlier?

Score 1 (655*)
— Answer B.

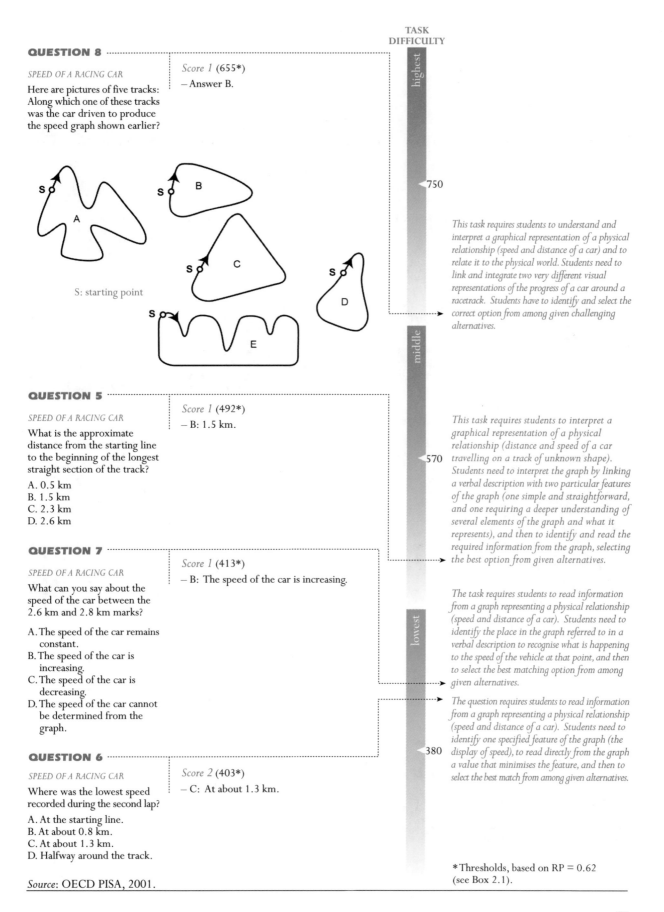

S: starting point

highest

—750

This task requires students to understand and interpret a graphical representation of a physical relationship (speed and distance of a car) and to relate it to the physical world. Students need to link and integrate two very different visual representations of the progress of a car around a racetrack. Students have to identify and select the correct option from among given challenging alternatives.

middle

QUESTION 5

SPEED OF A RACING CAR

What is the approximate distance from the starting line to the beginning of the longest straight section of the track?

A. 0.5 km
B. 1.5 km
C. 2.3 km
D. 2.6 km

Score 1 (492*)
— B: 1.5 km.

—570

This task requires students to interpret a graphical representation of a physical relationship (distance and speed of a car travelling on a track of unknown shape). Students need to interpret the graph by linking a verbal description with two particular features of the graph (one simple and straightforward, and one requiring a deeper understanding of several elements of the graph and what it represents), and then to identify and read the required information from the graph, selecting the best option from given alternatives.

QUESTION 7

SPEED OF A RACING CAR

What can you say about the speed of the car between the 2.6 km and 2.8 km marks?

A. The speed of the car remains constant.
B. The speed of the car is increasing.
C. The speed of the car is decreasing.
D. The speed of the car cannot be determined from the graph.

Score 1 (413*)
— B: The speed of the car is increasing.

lowest

The task requires students to read information from a graph representing a physical relationship (speed and distance of a car). Students need to identify the place in the graph referred to in a verbal description to recognise what is happening to the speed of the vehicle at that point, and then to select the best matching option from among given alternatives.

The question requires students to read information from a graph representing a physical relationship (speed and distance of a car). Students need to identify one specified feature of the graph (the display of speed), to read directly from the graph a value that minimises the feature, and then to select the best match from among given alternatives.

—380

QUESTION 6

SPEED OF A RACING CAR

Where was the lowest speed recorded during the second lap?

A. At the starting line.
B. At about 0.8 km.
C. At about 1.3 km.
D. Halfway around the track.

Score 2 (403*)
— C: At about 1.3 km.

*Thresholds, based on RP = 0.62 (see Box 2.1).

Source: OECD PISA, 2001.

Figure 3.2

Multiple comparisons of mean performance on the mathematical literacy scale

Mathematical literacy scale	Mean	S.E.	Hong Kong-China	Japan	Korea	New Zealand	Finland	Australia	Canada	Switzerland	United Kingdom	Belgium	France	Austria	Denmark	Iceland	Liechtenstein	Sweden	Ireland	Norway	Czech Republic	United States	Germany	Hungary	Russian Federation	Spain	Poland	Latvia	Italy	Portugal	Greece	Luxembourg	Israel	Thailand	Bulgaria	Argentina	Mexico	Chile	Albania	FYR Macedonia	Indonesia	Brazil	Peru
	Mean		560	557	547	537	536	533	533	529	529	520	517	515	514	514	514	510	503	499	498	493	490	488	478	476	470	463	457	454	447	446	433	432	430	388	387	384	381	381	367	334	292
		S.E.	(3.3)	(5.5)	(2.8)	(3.1)	(2.2)	(3.5)	(1.4)	(4.4)	(2.5)	(3.9)	(2.7)	(2.5)	(2.4)	(2.3)	(7.0)	(2.5)	(2.7)	(2.8)	(2.8)	(7.6)	(2.5)	(4.0)	(5.5)	(3.1)	(5.5)	(4.5)	(2.9)	(4.1)	(5.6)	(2.0)	(9.3)	(3.6)	(5.7)	(9.4)	(3.4)	(3.7)	(3.1)	(2.7)	(4.5)	(3.7)	(4.4)
Hong Kong-China	560	(3.3)		○	○	▲	▲	▲	▲	▲	▲	▲	▲	▲	▲	▲	▲	▲	▲	▲	▲	▲	▲	▲	▲	▲	▲	▲	▲	▲	▲	▲	▲	▲	▲	▲	▲	▲	▲	▲	▲	▲	▲
Japan	557	(5.5)	○		○	○	▲	▲	▲	▲	▲	▲	▲	▲	▲	▲	▲	▲	▲	▲	▲	▲	▲	▲	▲	▲	▲	▲	▲	▲	▲	▲	▲	▲	▲	▲	▲	▲	▲	▲	▲	▲	▲
Korea	547	(2.8)	○	○		○	○	○	▲	▲	▲	▲	▲	▲	▲	▲	▲	▲	▲	▲	▲	▲	▲	▲	▲	▲	▲	▲	▲	▲	▲	▲	▲	▲	▲	▲	▲	▲	▲	▲	▲	▲	▲
New Zealand	537	(3.1)	▽	○	○		○	○	○	○	○	▲	▲	▲	▲	▲	○	▲	▲	▲	▲	▲	▲	▲	▲	▲	▲	▲	▲	▲	▲	▲	▲	▲	▲	▲	▲	▲	▲	▲	▲	▲	▲
Finland	536	(2.2)	▽	▽	○	○		○	○	○	○	▲	▲	▲	▲	▲	○	▲	▲	▲	▲	▲	▲	▲	▲	▲	▲	▲	▲	▲	▲	▲	▲	▲	▲	▲	▲	▲	▲	▲	▲	▲	▲
Australia	533	(3.5)	▽	▽	○	○	○		○	○	○	○	▲	▲	▲	▲	○	▲	▲	▲	▲	▲	▲	▲	▲	▲	▲	▲	▲	▲	▲	▲	▲	▲	▲	▲	▲	▲	▲	▲	▲	▲	▲
Canada	533	(1.4)	▽	▽	▽	○	○	○		○	○	▲	▲	▲	▲	▲	○	▲	▲	▲	▲	▲	▲	▲	▲	▲	▲	▲	▲	▲	▲	▲	▲	▲	▲	▲	▲	▲	▲	▲	▲	▲	▲
Switzerland	529	(4.4)	▽	▽	▽	○	○	○	○		○	○	○	○	○	○	○	▲	▲	▲	▲	▲	▲	▲	▲	▲	▲	▲	▲	▲	▲	▲	▲	▲	▲	▲	▲	▲	▲	▲	▲	▲	▲
United Kingdom	529	(2.5)	▽	▽	▽	○	○	○	○	○		○	▲	▲	▲	▲	○	▲	▲	▲	▲	▲	▲	▲	▲	▲	▲	▲	▲	▲	▲	▲	▲	▲	▲	▲	▲	▲	▲	▲	▲	▲	▲
Belgium	520	(3.9)	▽	▽	▽	▽	▽	○	▽	○	○		○	○	○	○	○	○	▲	▲	▲	○	▲	▲	▲	▲	▲	▲	▲	▲	▲	▲	▲	▲	▲	▲	▲	▲	▲	▲	▲	▲	▲
France	517	(2.7)	▽	▽	▽	▽	▽	▽	▽	○	▽	○		○	○	○	○	○	▲	▲	▲	○	▲	▲	▲	▲	▲	▲	▲	▲	▲	▲	▲	▲	▲	▲	▲	▲	▲	▲	▲	▲	▲
Austria	515	(2.5)	▽	▽	▽	▽	▽	▽	▽	○	▽	○	○		○	○	○	○	▲	▲	▲	○	▲	▲	▲	▲	▲	▲	▲	▲	▲	▲	▲	▲	▲	▲	▲	▲	▲	▲	▲	▲	▲
Denmark	514	(2.4)	▽	▽	▽	▽	▽	▽	▽	○	▽	○	○	○		○	○	○	○	▲	▲	○	▲	▲	▲	▲	▲	▲	▲	▲	▲	▲	▲	▲	▲	▲	▲	▲	▲	▲	▲	▲	▲
Iceland	514	(2.3)	▽	▽	▽	▽	▽	▽	▽	○	▽	○	○	○	○		○	○	▲	▲	▲	○	▲	▲	▲	▲	▲	▲	▲	▲	▲	▲	▲	▲	▲	▲	▲	▲	▲	▲	▲	▲	▲
Liechtenstein	514	(7.0)	▽	▽	▽	○	○	○	○	○	○	○	○	○	○	○		○	○	○	○	○	▲	▲	▲	▲	▲	▲	▲	▲	▲	▲	▲	▲	▲	▲	▲	▲	▲	▲	▲	▲	▲
Sweden	510	(2.5)	▽	▽	▽	▽	▽	▽	▽	▽	▽	○	○	○	○	○	○		○	○	▲	○	▲	▲	▲	▲	▲	▲	▲	▲	▲	▲	▲	▲	▲	▲	▲	▲	▲	▲	▲	▲	▲
Ireland	503	(2.7)	▽	▽	▽	▽	▽	▽	▽	▽	▽	▽	▽	▽	○	▽	○	○		○	○	○	▲	○	▲	▲	▲	▲	▲	▲	▲	▲	▲	▲	▲	▲	▲	▲	▲	▲	▲	▲	▲
Norway	499	(2.8)	▽	▽	▽	▽	▽	▽	▽	▽	▽	▽	▽	▽	▽	▽	○	○	○		○	○	○	○	▲	▲	▲	▲	▲	▲	▲	▲	▲	▲	▲	▲	▲	▲	▲	▲	▲	▲	▲
Czech Republic	498	(2.8)	▽	▽	▽	▽	▽	▽	▽	▽	▽	▽	▽	▽	▽	▽	○	▽	○	○		○	○	○	○	▲	▲	▲	▲	▲	▲	▲	▲	▲	▲	▲	▲	▲	▲	▲	▲	▲	▲
United States	493	(7.6)	▽	▽	▽	▽	▽	▽	▽	▽	▽	○	○	○	○	○	○	○	○	○	○		○	○	○	○	○	▲	▲	▲	▲	▲	▲	▲	▲	▲	▲	▲	▲	▲	▲	▲	▲
Germany	490	(2.5)	▽	▽	▽	▽	▽	▽	▽	▽	▽	▽	▽	▽	▽	▽	▽	▽	▽	○	○	○		○	○	▲	▲	▲	▲	▲	▲	▲	▲	▲	▲	▲	▲	▲	▲	▲	▲	▲	▲
Hungary	488	(4.0)	▽	▽	▽	▽	▽	▽	▽	▽	▽	▽	▽	▽	▽	▽	▽	▽	○	○	○	○	○		○	○	○	▲	▲	▲	▲	▲	▲	▲	▲	▲	▲	▲	▲	▲	▲	▲	▲
Russian Federation	478	(5.5)	▽	▽	▽	▽	▽	▽	▽	▽	▽	▽	▽	▽	▽	▽	▽	▽	▽	▽	○	○	○	○		○	○	○	▲	▲	▲	▲	▲	▲	▲	▲	▲	▲	▲	▲	▲	▲	▲
Spain	476	(3.1)	▽	▽	▽	▽	▽	▽	▽	▽	▽	▽	▽	▽	▽	▽	▽	▽	▽	▽	▽	○	▽	○	○		○	○	▲	▲	▲	▲	▲	▲	▲	▲	▲	▲	▲	▲	▲	▲	▲
Poland	470	(5.5)	▽	▽	▽	▽	▽	▽	▽	▽	▽	▽	▽	▽	▽	▽	▽	▽	▽	▽	▽	○	▽	○	○	○		○	○	○	○	▲	▲	▲	▲	▲	▲	▲	▲	▲	▲	▲	▲
Latvia	463	(4.5)	▽	▽	▽	▽	▽	▽	▽	▽	▽	▽	▽	▽	▽	▽	▽	▽	▽	▽	▽	▽	▽	▽	○	○	○		○	○	○	▲	○	▲	▲	▲	▲	▲	▲	▲	▲	▲	▲
Italy	457	(2.9)	▽	▽	▽	▽	▽	▽	▽	▽	▽	▽	▽	▽	▽	▽	▽	▽	▽	▽	▽	▽	▽	▽	▽	▽	○	○		○	○	▲	○	▲	▲	▲	▲	▲	▲	▲	▲	▲	▲
Portugal	454	(4.1)	▽	▽	▽	▽	▽	▽	▽	▽	▽	▽	▽	▽	▽	▽	▽	▽	▽	▽	▽	▽	▽	▽	▽	▽	○	○	○		○	○	○	▲	▲	▲	▲	▲	▲	▲	▲	▲	▲
Greece	447	(5.6)	▽	▽	▽	▽	▽	▽	▽	▽	▽	▽	▽	▽	▽	▽	▽	▽	▽	▽	▽	▽	▽	▽	▽	▽	○	○	○	○		○	○	○	○	▲	▲	▲	▲	▲	▲	▲	▲
Luxembourg	446	(2.0)	▽	▽	▽	▽	▽	▽	▽	▽	▽	▽	▽	▽	▽	▽	▽	▽	▽	▽	▽	▽	▽	▽	▽	▽	▽	▽	▽	○	○		○	▲	○	▲	▲	▲	▲	▲	▲	▲	▲
Israel	433	(9.3)	▽	▽	▽	▽	▽	▽	▽	▽	▽	▽	▽	▽	▽	▽	▽	▽	▽	▽	▽	▽	▽	▽	▽	▽	▽	○	○	○	○	○		○	○	▲	▲	▲	▲	▲	▲	▲	▲
Thailand	432	(3.6)	▽	▽	▽	▽	▽	▽	▽	▽	▽	▽	▽	▽	▽	▽	▽	▽	▽	▽	▽	▽	▽	▽	▽	▽	▽	▽	▽	▽	○	▽	○		○	▲	▲	▲	▲	▲	▲	▲	▲
Bulgaria	430	(5.7)	▽	▽	▽	▽	▽	▽	▽	▽	▽	▽	▽	▽	▽	▽	▽	▽	▽	▽	▽	▽	▽	▽	▽	▽	▽	▽	▽	▽	○	○	○	○		▲	▲	▲	▲	▲	▲	▲	▲
Argentina	388	(9.4)	▽	▽	▽	▽	▽	▽	▽	▽	▽	▽	▽	▽	▽	▽	▽	▽	▽	▽	▽	▽	▽	▽	▽	▽	▽	▽	▽	▽	▽	▽	▽	▽	▽		○	○	○	○	○	▲	▲
Mexico	387	(3.4)	▽	▽	▽	▽	▽	▽	▽	▽	▽	▽	▽	▽	▽	▽	▽	▽	▽	▽	▽	▽	▽	▽	▽	▽	▽	▽	▽	▽	▽	▽	▽	▽	▽	○		○	○	○	▲	▲	▲
Chile	384	(3.7)	▽	▽	▽	▽	▽	▽	▽	▽	▽	▽	▽	▽	▽	▽	▽	▽	▽	▽	▽	▽	▽	▽	▽	▽	▽	▽	▽	▽	▽	▽	▽	▽	▽	○	○		○	○	○	▲	▲
Albania	381	(3.1)	▽	▽	▽	▽	▽	▽	▽	▽	▽	▽	▽	▽	▽	▽	▽	▽	▽	▽	▽	▽	▽	▽	▽	▽	▽	▽	▽	▽	▽	▽	▽	▽	▽	○	○	○		○	○	▲	▲
FYR Macedonia	381	(2.7)	▽	▽	▽	▽	▽	▽	▽	▽	▽	▽	▽	▽	▽	▽	▽	▽	▽	▽	▽	▽	▽	▽	▽	▽	▽	▽	▽	▽	▽	▽	▽	▽	▽	○	○	○	○		○	▲	▲
Indonesia	367	(4.5)	▽	▽	▽	▽	▽	▽	▽	▽	▽	▽	▽	▽	▽	▽	▽	▽	▽	▽	▽	▽	▽	▽	▽	▽	▽	▽	▽	▽	▽	▽	▽	▽	▽	○	▽	○	○	○		▲	▲
Brazil	334	(3.7)	▽	▽	▽	▽	▽	▽	▽	▽	▽	▽	▽	▽	▽	▽	▽	▽	▽	▽	▽	▽	▽	▽	▽	▽	▽	▽	▽	▽	▽	▽	▽	▽	▽	▽	▽	▽	▽	▽	▽		▲
Peru	292	(4.4)	▽	▽	▽	▽	▽	▽	▽	▽	▽	▽	▽	▽	▽	▽	▽	▽	▽	▽	▽	▽	▽	▽	▽	▽	▽	▽	▽	▽	▽	▽	▽	▽	▽	▽	▽	▽	▽	▽	▽	▽	

Instructions: Read across the row for a country to compare performance with the countries listed along the top of the chart. The symbols indicate whether the average performance of the country in the row is significantly lower than that of the comparison country, significantly higher than that of the comparison country, or if there is no statistically significant difference between the average achievement of the two countries.

▲ Mean performance statistically significantly higher than in comparison country.

○ No statistically significant difference from comparison country.

▽ Mean performance statistically significantly lower than in comparison country.

OECD countries

Non-OECD countries

Statistically significantly above the OECD average

Not statistically significantly different from the OECD average

Statistically significantly below the OECD average

Low- and middle-income countries

Source: OECD PISA database, 2003.

Denmark, Finland, France, Iceland, Liechtenstein, the Netherlands[3], New Zealand, Sweden, Switzerland and the United Kingdom.

Although the tasks for the PISA assessment of mathematical literacy were designed so that students not using calculators would not be disadvantaged, students were allowed to use their own calculators or those provided by test administrators. At least for OECD countries, there is no indication that the use of calculators provided an advantage to students in terms of their performance in PISA.[4]

The distribution of mathematical literacy within countries

While there are large differences in mean performance between countries, the variation in performance between students within each country is, as in the case of reading literacy, many times larger. Mean performance does not therefore provide a full picture of student performance, and it can mask significant variation within an individual class, school or education system. One of the major challenges faced by education systems is to encourage high performance while at the same time minimising internal disparities.

Figure 3.3 shows the distribution of performance scores on the mathematical literacy scale. The gradation bars show the range of performance in each country between the 5th and 95th percentiles. The density of the bar represents the proportion of students performing at the corresponding scale points. The middle of each bar shows the mean country score, which was the subject of the discussion in the preceding section, together with its confidence interval. In addition, Table 3.1 shows the 25th and 75th percentiles, *i.e.*, the scale points that mark the bottom and top quarters of performers in each country.

In every country, education systems, educational programmes, schools and teachers are called to meet the needs of students with a wide range of knowledge, skills and interests. In 27 countries, more than 10 per cent of students do not reach the mean score of the OECD country with the lowest level of performance, 387 points. Indeed, the average scores reached by students in Brazil and Peru are lower than those reached by ninety per cent of students in OECD countries (see Table 3.1, Annex B1). Students in such low-performing countries will typically find it difficult to complete simple tasks consisting of reproducing basic mathematical facts or processes, or applying simple computational skills. Furthermore, tasks requiring interpretation or reasoning skills that go beyond recognition of a single familiar element of the problem — as well as solution processes more complex than the application of a routine procedure in a single processing step - will normally be beyond the level of knowledge and skills of these students. In fact, all of the sample questions shown in Figure 3.1 are typically beyond the ability of students performing below the mean performance level of Mexico (387 points).

At the other end of the scale, all OECD countries but one have at least 10 per cent of students performing above the mean of the two highest performing countries, Hong Kong-China (560 points) and Japan (557 points). In six of the non-OECD member countries (of which three are low- and middle-income countries), at least 10 per cent of students reach these scores.

These findings suggest that education systems in many countries are faced with a wide range of student knowledge and skills - from students with greatest difficulties to those who perform exceptionally well.

Differences in mathematical performance within countries are also pronounced, but, as in the case of reading, some countries succeed in reaching high levels of student performance without large disparities. It is striking that five out of the seven countries with the smallest differences between the 75th and 25th percentiles — Canada, Finland, Iceland, Japan and Korea — all perform statistically significantly above the

Figure 3.3

Distribution of student performance on the mathematical literacy scale

Gradation bars extend from the 5ᵗʰ to the 95ᵗʰ percentiles   ▬ Mean score of males
▬ Mean score on the mathematical literacy scale   ▭ Mean score of females
▨ 95% confidence interval around the mean score   ⋯⋯⋯ OECD average

Performance on the mathematical literacy scale

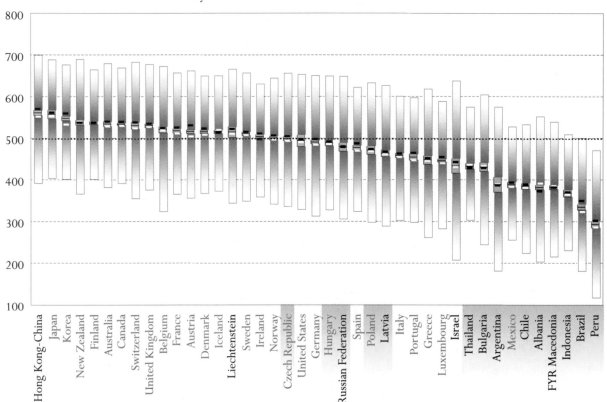

Source: OECD PISA database 2003. Table 3.1.

OECD average (see Table 3.1, Annex B1). Likewise, the five countries with the most unequal distribution of mathematical literacy skills – Albania, Argentina, Bulgaria, Greece and Israel – all perform significantly below the OECD average.

On the other hand, the five OECD countries with the most unequal distribution of mathematical literacy skills as measured by the difference between the 75ᵗʰ and 25ᵗʰ percentiles – Albania, Argentina, Bulgaria, Greece and Israel – perform statistically significantly below the OECD average, Belgium is the exception, having a very unequal distribution of scores but a mean above the OECD average.

In OECD countries, the pattern in the distribution of student performance on the mathematical literacy scale tends to be similar to that in reading literacy. Belgium, Germany, Greece, Hungary, New Zealand, Poland, Switzerland and the United States show a relatively large gap between the 75ᵗʰ and 25ᵗʰ percentiles, between 135 and 149 points on the mathematical literacy scale and between 134 and 150 points on the combined reading literacy scale. On the other hand, Finland, Iceland, Ireland, Japan and Korea show comparatively small disparities, less than 113 points separating their 75ᵗʰ and 25ᵗʰ percentiles on the mathematical literacy scale and less than 125 on the combined reading literacy scale. The pattern is the same for non-OECD countries. Albania, Argentina, Bulgaria, Israel, Latvia, FYR Macedonia and Peru show a wide unequal distribution of mathematical literacy skills as well as reading literacy skills - between 135 and 182 points on the mathematical literacy scale and between 133 and 153 points on the combined reading literacy scale - while Indonesia and Thailand show small differences between the 75th and 25th percentiles –116 and 106 points on the mathematical literacy scale and 101 points on the combined reading literacy scale. Thailand, which is a low- or middle-income country, shows the smallest disparity among all the OECD and non-OECD countries. There are, however, exceptions. Australia shows comparatively large disparities on the combined reading literacy scale (144 points) while its difference between the 75th and 25th percentiles in mathematical literacy, 121 points, is below the OECD average interquartile range. The Russian Federation, with a gap of 145 points on the mathematical literacy scale (above the OECD average interquartile range) shows smaller disparities on the combined reading literacy scale with 126 points (see Tables 3.1 and 2.3a, Annex B1).

Although the interquartile range is very useful for examining the middle part of the distribution, it is also important to examine the fuller extent of the performance distribution. The length of the bars presented in Figure 3.3. shows the range between the 5th and 95th percentiles of national performance distributions. The widest distribution in performance is found in Israel with, where 431 points separate the lowest from the highest 5 percent of performers. While 5 percent of students in Israel do not perform beyond 206 points (compared to the OECD average of 318 points), there are 5 percent of the students who perform at a score of 637 or beyond (compared to the OECD average of 655 points). Out of the ten countries with the widest distribution of performance, namely Albania, Argentina, Belgium, Bulgaria, Greece, Israel, Latvia, Peru, Poland and the Russian Federation, all, with the exception of Belgium, show average level of performance below the OECD average, and six of them are in the low- and middle-income category.

Reading and mathematical literacy performance

It is not appropriate to compare numerical scale scores directly between the reading and mathematical literacy scales (the mean scores for reading and mathematical literacy provided in brackets below are for reference only). Nevertheless, it is possible to determine the relative strengths of countries in the two domains on the basis of their relative rank-order positions on the reading and mathematical literacy scales.[5] Note that this comparison does not compare performance between countries, but rather between the domains within countries.

• On the basis of this comparison, Albania (349, 381), Denmark (497, 514), Hungary (480, 488), Latvia (458, 463), Japan (522, 557), Korea (525, 547), Liechtenstein (483, 514), the Russian Federation (462, 478) and Switzerland (494, 529) show better performance in mathematical literacy than in reading literacy.

• Canada (534, 533), Finland (546, 536), Greece (474, 447), Indonesia (371, 367), Ireland (527, 503), Italy (487, 457), Norway (505, 499), Spain (493, 476), Sweden (516, 510) and the United States (504, 493) perform better in reading.

• The relative strengths of the remaining countries are essentially the same on both scales.

Student performance in scientific literacy

How scientific literacy is measured in PISA

Like performance in mathematical literacy, performance in scientific literacy is marked in PISA on a single scale with an average score of 500 points for OECD countries, a standard deviation of 100 points and with about two-thirds of students across OECD countries scoring between 400 and 600 points. The scale measures students' ability to use scientific knowledge (understanding of scientific concepts), to recognise scientific questions and to identify what is involved in scientific investigations (understanding of the nature of scientific investigation), to relate scientific data to claims and conclusions (use of scientific evidence), and to communicate these aspects of science.

The criteria defining the increasing difficulty of tasks along the scale take account the complexity of the concepts used, the amount of data given, the chain of reasoning required and the precision required in communication. In addition, the level of difficulty is influenced by the context of the information, the format and the presentation of the question. The tasks in PISA require scientific knowledge involving (in ascending order of difficulty): recall of simple scientific knowledge or common scientific knowledge or data; the application of scientific concepts or questions and a basic knowledge of investigation; the use of more highly developed scientific concepts or a chain of reasoning; and knowledge of simple conceptual models or analysis of evidence in order to try out alternative approaches.

- Towards the top end of the scientific literacy scale (around 690 points) students are generally able to create or use conceptual models to make predictions or give explanations; to analyse scientific investigations in order to grasp, for example, the design of an experiment or to identify an idea being tested; to compare data in order to evaluate alternative viewpoints or differing perspectives; and to communicate scientific arguments and/or descriptions in detail and with precision.

- At around 550 points, students are typically able to use scientific concepts to make predictions or provide explanations; to recognise questions that can be answered by scientific investigation and/or identify details of what is involved in a scientific investigation; and to select relevant information from competing data or chains of reasoning in drawing or evaluating conclusions.

- Towards the lower end of the scale (around 400 points), students are able to recall simple factual scientific knowledge (*e.g.*, names, facts, terminology, simple rules) and to use common scientific knowledge in drawing or evaluating conclusions.

A description of the conceptual framework underlying the PISA assessment of scientific literacy is provided in *Measuring Student Knowledge and Skills – A New Framework for Assessment* (OECD, 1999a).

In order to put these scores into context, on average across OECD countries, the best 5 per cent of students achieved 657 points, the top 10 per cent reached 627 points and the best performing quarter of students reached 572 points on average across countries. At the lower end of the scale, more than three-quarters achieved at least 431 points, more than 90 per cent reached 368 points and more than 95 per cent, 332 points. In non-OECD countries, only one country, Hong Kong-China, performed above the OECD averages with scores of 671, 645, 488, 426 and 391 points for the 95th, the 90th, the 25th, the 10th and the 5th percentiles respectively (see Table 3.2, Annex B1).

The tasks used for the assessment of scientific literacy in PISA vary widely. Figure 3.4 shows the tasks from one of the 13 units used along with a description of the criteria used to mark students' answers (a more complete set of sample tasks can be found at *www.pisa.oecd.org* or OECD, 2002*c*). The sample unit refers to Semmelweis' research on the causes of puerperal fever. Semmelweis was puzzled by a remarkably high death rate due to puerperal fever in a maternity ward. The students are presented with this finding by way of graphs and then confronted with the suggestion that puerperal fever may be caused by extraterrestrial influences or natural disasters, not an uncommon thought in Semmelweis' time. The physician tried to convince his colleagues to consider more rational explanations. Students are invited to imagine themselves in Semmelweis' position and to use the data that he collected to defend the idea that earthquakes are an unlikely cause of the disease. The graphs show a similar variation in death rate over time, the first ward consistently having a higher death rate than the second ward. If earthquakes were the cause, the death rates in both wards should be about the same. The graphs suggest that something about the wards explains the difference. Figure 3.4 shows an extract of the criteria used to mark students' answers.

To receive full credit for Question 1 in this sample unit, students needed to refer to the idea that death rates in both wards should have been similar over time if earthquakes were the cause. Full credit for this question corresponds to a score of 666 points on the scientific literacy scale. Students with a score of 666 points should theoretically be able to answer questions of this level of difficulty correctly 62 out of 100 times (see also Box 2.2). On average, 22 per cent of students across OECD countries and 19 per cent across non-OECD countries answered this question correctly (for data see *www.pisa.oecd.org*). Some students provided answers that referred not refer to Semmelweis' findings but to a characteristic of earthquakes that made it unlikely that they were the cause, such as their infrequent occurrence, while the fever was present all the time. Other students provided original and justifiable statements, such as "If it were earthquakes, why do only women get the disease, and not men?" or "If so, women outside the wards would also get that fever." Although it can be argued that these students did not consider the data that Semmelweis collected, as the question asks, they received a partial score because their answers demonstrated an ability to use scientific facts to reach a conclusion. On average, 28 per cent of students across OECD countries and 16 per cent across non-OECD countries received at least partial credit for this question (see *PISA 2000 Technical Report*, OECD, 2002*a*).

Question 2 in the same sample unit asked students to identify Semmelweis' idea that was most relevant to reducing the incidence of puerperal fever. Students needed to put two pieces of relevant information from the text together: the behaviour of a medical student and the death of Semmelweis' friend of puerperal fever after the student had dissected a cadaver. This question exemplifies average performance, at a level of difficulty of 493 points. The question required students to refer to given data or information in order to draw a conclusion and assessed their understanding of the nature of scientific investigation. On average, 64 and 49 per cent of students across OECD and non-OECD countries respectively answered this question correctly, by choosing the response option stating that having students clean themselves after dissection should lead to a decrease in puerperal fever.

Most people are now aware that bacteria cause many diseases and that heat can kill these bacteria. However, many people may not realise that routine procedures in hospitals use this observation to reduce the risks of fevers and other diseases. Question 3 in the sample unit asked students to apply the common scientific knowledge that heat kills bacteria to explain why these procedures are effective. This is another example of a question of low to moderate difficulty, with a value of 467 points on the scientific literacy scale. On

A sample of the science tasks used in PISA

SEMMELWEIS' DIARY – TEXT 1

'July 1846. Next week I will take up a position as "Herr Doktor" at the First Ward of the maternity clinic of the Vienna General Hospital. I was frightened when I heard about the percentage of patients who die in this clinic. This month not less than 36 of the 208 mothers died there, all from puerperal fever. Giving birth to a child is as dangerous as first-degree pneumonia.'

Number of deaths per 100 deliveries from puerperal fever

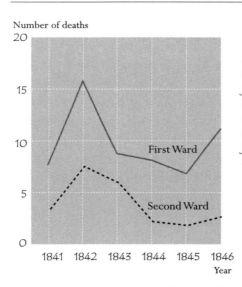

Number of deaths

First Ward

Second Ward

1841 1842 1843 1844 1845 1846
Year

These lines from the diary of Ignaz Semmelweis (1818-1865) illustrate the devastating effects of puerperal fever, a contagious disease that killed many women after childbirth. Semmelweis collected data about the number of deaths from puerperal fever in both the First and the Second Wards (see diagram).

Physicians, among them Semmelweis, were completely in the dark about the cause of puerperal fever. Semmelweis' diary again:

'December 1846. Why do so many women die from this fever after giving birth without any problems? For centuries science has told us that it is an invisible epidemic that kills mothers. Causes may be changes in the air or some extraterrestrial influence or a movement of the earth itself, an earthquake.'

Nowadays not many people would consider extraterrestrial influence or an earthquake as possible causes of fever. We now know it has to do with hygienic conditions. But in the time Semmelweis lived, many people, even scientists, did! However, Semmelweis knew that it was unlikely that fever could be caused by extraterrestrial influence or an earthquake. He pointed at the data he collected (see diagram) and used this to try to persuade his colleagues.

SEMMELWEIS' DIARY – TEXT 2

Part of the research in the hospital was dissection. The body of a deceased person was cut open to find a cause of death. Semmelweis recorded that the students working on the First ward usually took part in dissections on women who died the previous day, before they examined women who had just given birth. They did not pay much attention to cleaning themselves after the dissections. Some were even proud of the fact that you could tell by their smell that they had been working in the mortuary, as this showed how industrious they were!

One of Semmelweis' friends died after having cut himself during such a dissection. Dissection of his body showed he had the same symptoms as mothers who died from puerperal fever. This gave Semmelweis a new idea.

TASK
DIFFICULTY

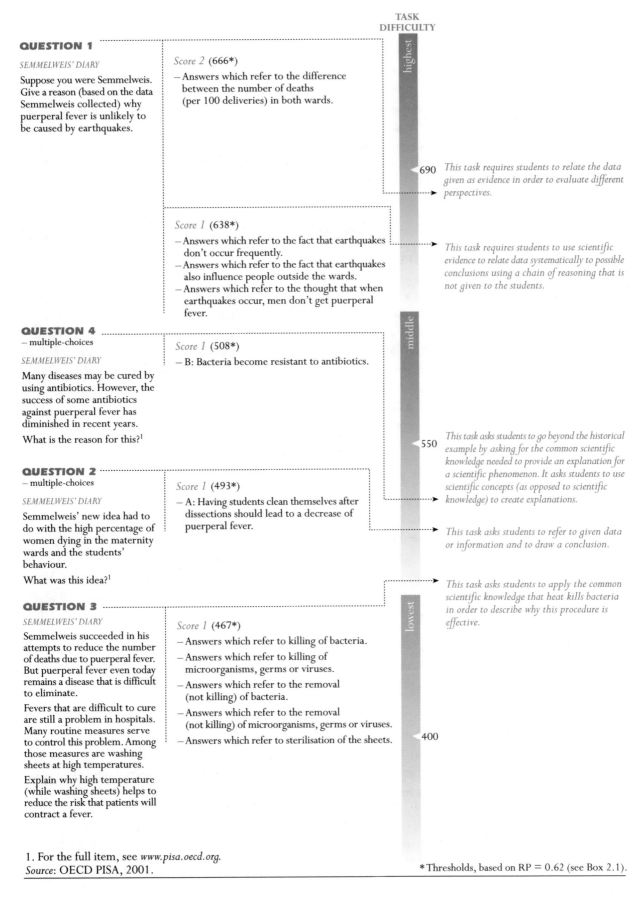

QUESTION 1

SEMMELWEIS' DIARY

Suppose you were Semmelweis. Give a reason (based on the data Semmelweis collected) why puerperal fever is unlikely to be caused by earthquakes.

Score 2 (666*)
— Answers which refer to the difference between the number of deaths (per 100 deliveries) in both wards.

◄ 690   *This task requires students to relate the data given as evidence in order to evaluate different perspectives.*

Score 1 (638*)
— Answers which refer to the fact that earthquakes don't occur frequently.
— Answers which refer to the fact that earthquakes also influence people outside the wards.
— Answers which refer to the thought that when earthquakes occur, men don't get puerperal fever.

► *This task requires students to use scientific evidence to relate data systematically to possible conclusions using a chain of reasoning that is not given to the students.*

QUESTION 4
— multiple-choices

SEMMELWEIS' DIARY

Many diseases may be cured by using antibiotics. However, the success of some antibiotics against puerperal fever has diminished in recent years.

What is the reason for this?[1]

Score 1 (508*)
— B: Bacteria become resistant to antibiotics.

◄ 550   *This task asks students to go beyond the historical example by asking for the common scientific knowledge needed to provide an explanation for a scientific phenomenon. It asks students to use scientific concepts (as opposed to scientific knowledge) to create explanations.*

QUESTION 2
— multiple-choices

SEMMELWEIS' DIARY

Semmelweis' new idea had to do with the high percentage of women dying in the maternity wards and the students' behaviour.

What was this idea?[1]

Score 1 (493*)
— A: Having students clean themselves after dissections should lead to a decrease of puerperal fever.

► *This task asks students to refer to given data or information and to draw a conclusion.*

QUESTION 3

SEMMELWEIS' DIARY

Semmelweis succeeded in his attempts to reduce the number of deaths due to puerperal fever. But puerperal fever even today remains a disease that is difficult to eliminate.

Fevers that are difficult to cure are still a problem in hospitals. Many routine measures serve to control this problem. Among those measures are washing sheets at high temperatures.

Explain why high temperature (while washing sheets) helps to reduce the risk that patients will contract a fever.

► *This task asks students to apply the common scientific knowledge that heat kills bacteria in order to describe why this procedure is effective.*

Score 1 (467*)
— Answers which refer to killing of bacteria.
— Answers which refer to killing of microorganisms, germs or viruses.
— Answers which refer to the removal (not killing) of bacteria.
— Answers which refer to the removal (not killing) of microorganisms, germs or viruses.
— Answers which refer to sterilisation of the sheets.

◄ 400

1. For the full item, see *www.pisa.oecd.org.*
Source: OECD PISA, 2001.

*Thresholds, based on RP = 0.62 (see Box 2.1).

average, 68 and 49 per cent of students across OECD and non-OECD countries respectively received full credit for answering correctly this open-ended question.

Finally, Question 4 went beyond the historical example and asked students to provide an explanation for a scientific phenomenon. Students were required to explain why antibiotics have become less effective over time. In order to answer correctly, they needed to know that the frequent and extended use of antibiotics creates strains of bacteria resistant to the initially lethal effects. This question is located at a moderate level on the scientific literacy scale, 508 points, because it asks students to use scientific concepts (as opposed to common scientific knowledge, which is at a lower level) to find explanations. On average, 60 and 40 per cent of students across OECD and non-OECD countries respectively answered this question correctly, by choosing the multiple-choice option that bacteria become resistant to antibiotics.

The mean performances of countries in scientific literacy

As with mathematical literacy, performance in scientific literacy can be summarised by way of countries' mean scores (see Figure 3.5). Japan, Korea and Hong Kong-China show the highest performance on the scientific literacy scale. Other countries that score statistically significantly above the OECD average are Australia, Austria, Canada, the Czech Republic, Finland, Ireland, New Zealand, Sweden and the United Kingdom. Mean scores in Belgium, France, Hungary, Iceland, Norway, Switzerland and the United States are not significantly different from the OECD average.[6] Except for the Czech Republic and Hungary, all other low- and middle-income countries score below the OECD average of 500 points. The range of average scores between the highest and the lowest performing countries is also very large. Very high performing countries score around one-half standard deviation above the OECD average, while the five lowest performing countries perform on average between one and one and one-half standard deviation below the OECD average of 500.

The distribution of scientific literacy within countries

Figure 3.6 shows the distribution of performance scores on the scientific literacy scale in a format parallel to that of Figure 3.3. The overall pattern of results is similar to the one found for mathematical literacy, which can be in part explained by the high inter-correlation between these two domains – a latent correlation of 0.85 for OECD countries[7]. The top ten per cent of the students in the OECD countries score 627 points. Sixteen participating countries reach that threshold, including one non-OECD country, Hong Kong-China at 645 points. It also includes two countries from the low- and middle-income category, namely the Czech Republic at 632 points and Hungary at 629 points.

On the other end of the distribution, three-quarters of the students in twelve participating countries (10 non-OECD and 10 low- and middle-income) reach the level of performance that is reached by ninety-five percent of students in the three highest performing countries.

The distribution of scores as shown by the interquartile range is again very small for Indonesia and Thailand, which is consistent with the findings for reading and mathematics. Interquartile ranges of 99 and 100 points as shown by Indonesia and Thailand are much smaller than the OECD average of 141 points, and the largest range of 177 points is shown by Israel (standard deviation of 125 points), which once again is consistent with the findings for mathematics.

Consistent with Figure 3.3, the bars presented in Figure 3.6 show a wider perspective of the distribution of scores - between the 5th and 95th percentiles of the national distributions. The widest distribution in per-

Figure 3.5

Multiple comparisons of mean performance on the scientific literacy scale

Scientific literacy scale	Mean	S.E.	Korea 552 (2.7)	Japan 550 (5.5)	Hong Kong-China 541 (3.0)	Finland 538 (2.5)	United Kingdom 532 (2.7)	Canada 529 (1.6)	New Zealand 528 (2.4)	Australia 528 (3.5)	Austria 519 (2.6)	Ireland 513 (3.2)	Sweden 512 (2.5)	Czech Republic 511 (2.4)	France 500 (3.2)	Norway 500 (2.8)	United States 499 (7.3)	Hungary 496 (4.2)	Iceland 496 (2.2)	Belgium 496 (4.3)	Switzerland 496 (4.4)	Spain 491 (3.0)	Germany 487 (2.4)	Poland 483 (5.1)	Denmark 481 (2.8)	Italy 478 (3.1)	Liechtenstein 476 (7.1)	Greece 461 (4.9)	Russian Federation 460 (4.7)	Latvia 460 (5.6)	Portugal 459 (4.0)	Bulgaria 448 (4.6)	Luxembourg 443 (2.3)	Thailand 436 (3.1)	Israel 434 (9.0)	Mexico 422 (3.2)	Chile 415 (3.4)	FYR Macedonia 401 (2.1)	Argentina 396 (8.6)	Indonesia 393 (3.9)	Albania 376 (2.9)	Brazil 375 (3.3)	Peru 333 (4.0)
Korea	552	(2.7)		○	○	▲	▲	▲	▲	▲	▲	▲	▲	▲	▲	▲	▲	▲	▲	▲	▲	▲	▲	▲	▲	▲	▲	▲	▲	▲	▲	▲	▲	▲	▲	▲	▲	▲	▲	▲	▲	▲	▲
Japan	550	(5.5)	○		○	○	○	▲	▲	▲	▲	▲	▲	▲	▲	▲	▲	▲	▲	▲	▲	▲	▲	▲	▲	▲	▲	▲	▲	▲	▲	▲	▲	▲	▲	▲	▲	▲	▲	▲	▲	▲	▲
Hong Kong-China	541	(3.0)	○	○		○	○	▲	▲	○	▲	▲	▲	▲	▲	▲	▲	▲	▲	▲	▲	▲	▲	▲	▲	▲	▲	▲	▲	▲	▲	▲	▲	▲	▲	▲	▲	▲	▲	▲	▲	▲	▲
Finland	538	(2.5)	▽	○	○		○	○	○	○	▲	▲	▲	▲	▲	▲	▲	▲	▲	▲	▲	▲	▲	▲	▲	▲	▲	▲	▲	▲	▲	▲	▲	▲	▲	▲	▲	▲	▲	▲	▲	▲	▲
United Kingdom	532	(2.7)	▽	○	○	○		○	○	○	▲	▲	▲	▲	▲	▲	▲	▲	▲	▲	▲	▲	▲	▲	▲	▲	▲	▲	▲	▲	▲	▲	▲	▲	▲	▲	▲	▲	▲	▲	▲	▲	▲
Canada	529	(1.6)	▽	▽	▽	○	○		○	○	▲	▲	▲	▲	▲	▲	▲	▲	▲	▲	▲	▲	▲	▲	▲	▲	▲	▲	▲	▲	▲	▲	▲	▲	▲	▲	▲	▲	▲	▲	▲	▲	▲
New Zealand	528	(2.4)	▽	▽	▽	○	○	○		○	○	▲	▲	▲	▲	▲	▲	▲	▲	▲	▲	▲	▲	▲	▲	▲	▲	▲	▲	▲	▲	▲	▲	▲	▲	▲	▲	▲	▲	▲	▲	▲	▲
Australia	528	(3.5)	▽	▽	○	○	○	○	○		○	○	▲	▲	▲	▲	▲	▲	▲	▲	▲	▲	▲	▲	▲	▲	▲	▲	▲	▲	▲	▲	▲	▲	▲	▲	▲	▲	▲	▲	▲	▲	▲
Austria	519	(2.6)	▽	▽	▽	▽	▽	▽	○	○		○	○	○	▲	▲	○	▲	▲	▲	▲	▲	▲	▲	▲	▲	▲	▲	▲	▲	▲	▲	▲	▲	▲	▲	▲	▲	▲	▲	▲	▲	▲
Ireland	513	(3.2)	▽	▽	▽	▽	▽	▽	▽	○	○		○	○	○	○	○	▲	▲	▲	▲	▲	▲	▲	▲	▲	▲	▲	▲	▲	▲	▲	▲	▲	▲	▲	▲	▲	▲	▲	▲	▲	▲
Sweden	512	(2.5)	▽	▽	▽	▽	▽	▽	▽	▽	○	○		○	○	○	○	▲	▲	▲	○	▲	▲	▲	▲	▲	▲	▲	▲	▲	▲	▲	▲	▲	▲	▲	▲	▲	▲	▲	▲	▲	▲
Czech Republic	511	(2.4)	▽	▽	▽	▽	▽	▽	▽	▽	○	○	○		○	○	○	○	▲	○	○	▲	▲	▲	▲	▲	▲	▲	▲	▲	▲	▲	▲	▲	▲	▲	▲	▲	▲	▲	▲	▲	▲
France	500	(3.2)	▽	▽	▽	▽	▽	▽	▽	▽	▽	○	○	○		○	○	○	○	○	○	○	▲	○	▲	▲	○	▲	▲	▲	▲	▲	▲	▲	▲	▲	▲	▲	▲	▲	▲	▲	▲
Norway	500	(2.8)	▽	▽	▽	▽	▽	▽	▽	▽	▽	○	○	○	○		○	○	○	○	○	○	▲	○	▲	▲	○	▲	▲	▲	▲	▲	▲	▲	▲	▲	▲	▲	▲	▲	▲	▲	▲
United States	499	(7.3)	▽	▽	▽	▽	▽	▽	▽	▽	○	○	○	○	○	○		○	○	○	○	○	○	○	○	○	○	▲	▲	▲	▲	▲	▲	▲	▲	▲	▲	▲	▲	▲	▲	▲	▲
Hungary	496	(4.2)	▽	▽	▽	▽	▽	▽	▽	▽	▽	▽	▽	○	○	○	○		○	○	○	○	○	○	○	▲	○	▲	▲	▲	▲	▲	▲	▲	▲	▲	▲	▲	▲	▲	▲	▲	▲
Iceland	496	(2.2)	▽	▽	▽	▽	▽	▽	▽	▽	▽	▽	▽	▽	○	○	○	○		○	○	○	○	○	▲	▲	○	▲	▲	▲	▲	▲	▲	▲	▲	▲	▲	▲	▲	▲	▲	▲	▲
Belgium	496	(4.3)	▽	▽	▽	▽	▽	▽	▽	▽	▽	▽	▽	○	○	○	○	○	○		○	○	○	○	○	▲	○	▲	▲	▲	▲	▲	▲	▲	▲	▲	▲	▲	▲	▲	▲	▲	▲
Switzerland	496	(4.4)	▽	▽	▽	▽	▽	▽	▽	▽	▽	▽	○	○	○	○	○	○	○	○		○	○	○	○	▲	○	▲	▲	▲	▲	▲	▲	▲	▲	▲	▲	▲	▲	▲	▲	▲	▲
Spain	491	(3.0)	▽	▽	▽	▽	▽	▽	▽	▽	▽	▽	▽	▽	○	○	○	○	○	○	○		○	○	○	○	○	▲	▲	▲	▲	▲	▲	▲	▲	▲	▲	▲	▲	▲	▲	▲	▲
Germany	487	(2.4)	▽	▽	▽	▽	▽	▽	▽	▽	▽	▽	▽	▽	▽	▽	○	○	○	○	○	○		○	○	○	○	▲	▲	▲	▲	▲	▲	▲	▲	▲	▲	▲	▲	▲	▲	▲	▲
Poland	483	(5.1)	▽	▽	▽	▽	▽	▽	▽	▽	▽	▽	▽	▽	○	○	○	○	○	○	○	○	○		○	○	○	○	▲	○	▲	▲	▲	▲	▲	▲	▲	▲	▲	▲	▲	▲	▲
Denmark	481	(2.8)	▽	▽	▽	▽	▽	▽	▽	▽	▽	▽	▽	▽	▽	▽	○	○	▽	○	○	○	○	○		○	○	▲	▲	▲	▲	▲	▲	▲	▲	▲	▲	▲	▲	▲	▲	▲	▲
Italy	478	(3.1)	▽	▽	▽	▽	▽	▽	▽	▽	▽	▽	▽	▽	▽	▽	○	▽	▽	▽	▽	○	○	○	○		○	○	○	○	▲	▲	▲	▲	▲	▲	▲	▲	▲	▲	▲	▲	▲
Liechtenstein	476	(7.1)	▽	▽	▽	▽	▽	▽	▽	▽	▽	▽	▽	▽	○	○	○	○	○	○	○	○	○	○	○	○		○	○	○	○	▲	▲	▲	▲	▲	▲	▲	▲	▲	▲	▲	▲
Greece	461	(4.9)	▽	▽	▽	▽	▽	▽	▽	▽	▽	▽	▽	▽	▽	▽	▽	▽	▽	▽	▽	▽	▽	○	▽	○	○		○	○	○	○	▲	▲	○	▲	▲	▲	▲	▲	▲	▲	▲
Russian Federation	460	(4.7)	▽	▽	▽	▽	▽	▽	▽	▽	▽	▽	▽	▽	▽	▽	▽	▽	▽	▽	▽	▽	▽	▽	▽	○	○	○		○	○	○	▲	▲	○	▲	▲	▲	▲	▲	▲	▲	▲
Latvia	460	(5.6)	▽	▽	▽	▽	▽	▽	▽	▽	▽	▽	▽	▽	▽	▽	▽	▽	▽	▽	▽	▽	▽	○	▽	○	○	○	○		○	○	○	▲	○	▲	▲	▲	▲	▲	▲	▲	▲
Portugal	459	(4.0)	▽	▽	▽	▽	▽	▽	▽	▽	▽	▽	▽	▽	▽	▽	▽	▽	▽	▽	▽	▽	▽	▽	▽	▽	○	○	○	○		○	▲	▲	○	▲	▲	▲	▲	▲	▲	▲	▲
Bulgaria	448	(4.6)	▽	▽	▽	▽	▽	▽	▽	▽	▽	▽	▽	▽	▽	▽	▽	▽	▽	▽	▽	▽	▽	▽	▽	▽	▽	○	○	○	○		○	○	○	▲	▲	▲	▲	▲	▲	▲	▲
Luxembourg	443	(2.3)	▽	▽	▽	▽	▽	▽	▽	▽	▽	▽	▽	▽	▽	▽	▽	▽	▽	▽	▽	▽	▽	▽	▽	▽	▽	▽	▽	○	▽	○		○	○	▲	▲	▲	▲	▲	▲	▲	▲
Thailand	436	(3.1)	▽	▽	▽	▽	▽	▽	▽	▽	▽	▽	▽	▽	▽	▽	▽	▽	▽	▽	▽	▽	▽	▽	▽	▽	▽	▽	▽	▽	▽	○	○		○	▲	▲	▲	▲	▲	▲	▲	▲
Israel	434	(9.0)	▽	▽	▽	▽	▽	▽	▽	▽	▽	▽	▽	▽	▽	▽	▽	▽	▽	▽	▽	▽	▽	▽	▽	▽	▽	○	○	○	○	○	○	○		○	○	▲	○	▲	▲	▲	▲
Mexico	422	(3.2)	▽	▽	▽	▽	▽	▽	▽	▽	▽	▽	▽	▽	▽	▽	▽	▽	▽	▽	▽	▽	▽	▽	▽	▽	▽	▽	▽	▽	▽	▽	▽	▽	○		○	▲	○	▲	▲	▲	▲
Chile	415	(3.4)	▽	▽	▽	▽	▽	▽	▽	▽	▽	▽	▽	▽	▽	▽	▽	▽	▽	▽	▽	▽	▽	▽	▽	▽	▽	▽	▽	▽	▽	▽	▽	▽	○	○		▲	○	▲	▲	▲	▲
FYR Macedonia	401	(2.1)	▽	▽	▽	▽	▽	▽	▽	▽	▽	▽	▽	▽	▽	▽	▽	▽	▽	▽	▽	▽	▽	▽	▽	▽	▽	▽	▽	▽	▽	▽	▽	▽	▽	▽	▽		○	○	▲	▲	▲
Argentina	396	(8.6)	▽	▽	▽	▽	▽	▽	▽	▽	▽	▽	▽	▽	▽	▽	▽	▽	▽	▽	▽	▽	▽	▽	▽	▽	▽	▽	▽	▽	▽	▽	▽	▽	○	○	○	○		○	○	○	▲
Indonesia	393	(3.9)	▽	▽	▽	▽	▽	▽	▽	▽	▽	▽	▽	▽	▽	▽	▽	▽	▽	▽	▽	▽	▽	▽	▽	▽	▽	▽	▽	▽	▽	▽	▽	▽	▽	▽	▽	○	○		▲	▲	▲
Albania	376	(2.9)	▽	▽	▽	▽	▽	▽	▽	▽	▽	▽	▽	▽	▽	▽	▽	▽	▽	▽	▽	▽	▽	▽	▽	▽	▽	▽	▽	▽	▽	▽	▽	▽	▽	▽	▽	▽	○	▽		○	▲
Brazil	375	(3.3)	▽	▽	▽	▽	▽	▽	▽	▽	▽	▽	▽	▽	▽	▽	▽	▽	▽	▽	▽	▽	▽	▽	▽	▽	▽	▽	▽	▽	▽	▽	▽	▽	▽	▽	▽	▽	○	▽	○		▲
Peru	333	(4.0)	▽	▽	▽	▽	▽	▽	▽	▽	▽	▽	▽	▽	▽	▽	▽	▽	▽	▽	▽	▽	▽	▽	▽	▽	▽	▽	▽	▽	▽	▽	▽	▽	▽	▽	▽	▽	▽	▽	▽	▽	

Instructions: Read across the row for a country to compare performance with the countries listed along the top of the chart. The symbols indicate whether the average performance of the country in the row is significantly lower than that of the comparison country, significantly higher than that of the comparison country, or if there is no statistically significant difference between the average achievement of the two countries.

▲ Mean performance statistically significantly higher than in comparison country.

○ No statistically significant difference from comparison country.

▽ Mean performance statistically significantly lower than in comparison country.

OECD countries

Non-OECD countries

Statistically significantly above the OECD average

Not statistically significantly different from the OECD average

Statistically significantly below the OECD average

Low- and middle-income countries

Source: OECD PISA database, 2003.

Figure 3.6

Distribution of student performance on the scientific literacy scale

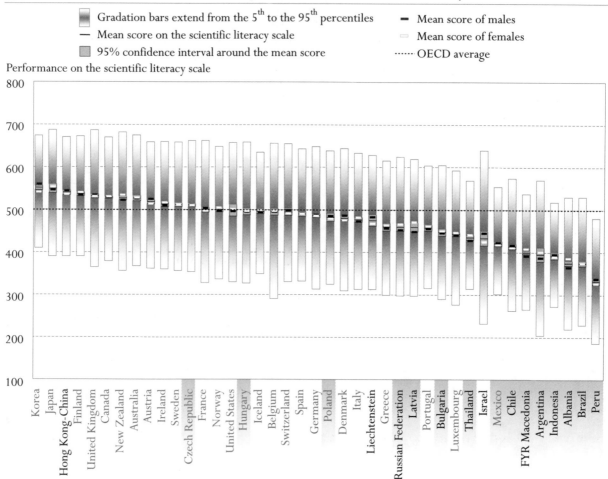

Source: OECD PISA database 2003. Table 3.2.

formance is again found in Israel, where 407 points separate these two extremes. Out of ten countries with the widest distribution of performance, five also showed the widest distributions in mathematical literacy outcomes, namely Argentina, Belgium, Germany, Israel and the Russian Federation.

Reading and scientific literacy performance

Most countries rank about the same in scientific as in reading literacy; but there are exceptions. A comparison of the relative rank order of countries reveals the following concerning the performance of students in reading and scientific literacy. Values in parenthesis indicate mean scores for reading and scientific literacy respectively:

• Countries showing better performance in scientific literacy than in reading literacy are: Austria (507, 519), Bulgaria (430, 448), Chile (410, 415), the Czech Republic (492, 511), Hungary (480, 496), Japan (522, 550), Korea (525, 552), FYR Macedonia (373, 401) and the United Kingdom (523, 532).

- Countries whose students perform better in reading literacy than in scientific literacy are: Argentina (418, 396), Belgium (507, 496), Canada (534, 529), Denmark (497, 481), Finland (546, 538), Iceland (507, 496), Ireland (527, 513), Israel (452, 434) and Italy (487, 478).

- The relative rank order positions of the remaining countries are essentially the same on both scales.

Reading, mathematical and scientific literacy performance

Some countries have mean scores significantly above the OECD average in all three domains: Australia, Austria, Canada, Finland, Japan, Korea, New Zealand, Sweden, the United Kingdom and Hong Kong-China, the only non-OECD country.

The performances of countries differ widely, especially on the mathematical literacy scale, with 173 points (more than one and a half international standard deviations) separating the two OECD countries with the highest and lowest mean scores on the mathematical literacy scale, and with 111 points separating the two OECD countries with the second highest and the second lowest mean scores. If the non-OECD countries are included in this comparison, the performance gap between the highest and lowest performing countries increases by almost another 100 points in mathematical literacy and a little less in the other domains (see Tables 2.1a and 3.2, Annex B1).

While in the OECD countries the variation in mean performance between countries was somewhat smaller in scientific literacy and smallest in reading literacy[8], a different picture appeared with the introduction of the non-OECD countries. Similar gaps between the highest and the lowest performing countries now exist in reading and scientific literacy. Although further studies are necessary, it may be that because learning in mathematics and science is more closely related to schooling than is proficiency in reading. Thus differences between education systems in these domains are more pronounced than in reading.

Investment in education and student performance

In any comparison of the outcomes of education systems it is necessary to take into account countries' economic circumstances and the resources that they can devote to education. The relative prosperity of some countries allows them to spend more on education, while other countries find themselves constrained by a relative lack of national income.

Figure 3.7a displays the relationship between adjusted national income (GDP) per capita and the average performance of students in the PISA assessment in each country. For this comparison, the mean performance of countries has been averaged across the reading, mathematical and scientific literacy domains. The GDP values represent GDP per capita in 2000 at current prices, adjusted for differences in purchasing power between countries (see Table 3.3, Annex B1). The figure also shows a trend line that summarises the relationship between GDP per capita and mean student performance across the three literacy domains. It should be borne in mind, however, that the number of countries involved in this comparison is small and that the trend lines are therefore strongly affected by the countries included in this comparison.

The scatter plot suggests that countries with higher national income tend to perform better on the combined reading, mathematical and scientific literacy scale than countries with lower national income. In fact, the relationship suggests that 43 per cent of the variation between countries' mean scores can be predicted on the basis of their GDP per capita. Moreover, excluding Luxembourg, which is an extreme outlier due to its high per capita income, the overall correlation coefficient across all participating countries increases to 60 per cent.

Figure 3.7a

Student performance and national income

Relationship between average performance across the combined reading, mathematical and scientific literacy scales and GDP per capita, in US$, converted using purchasing power parities (PPPs)

◇ OECD country with high income   ◇ Non-OECD country with high income
◈ OECD country with low and middle income ◈ Non-OECD country with low and middle income

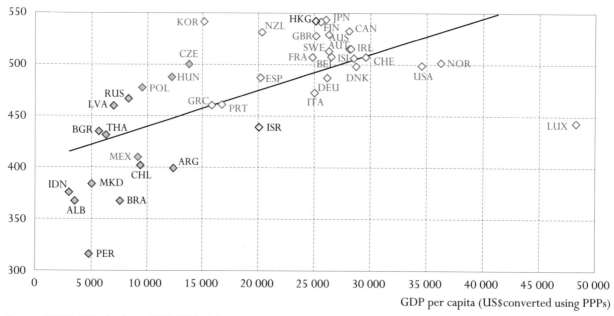

Average performance
(reading, mathematical and scientific literacy)

GDP per capita (US$ converted using PPPs)

Source: OECD PISA database, 2003. Table 3.3.

Countries close to the trend line are where the predictor GDP per capita suggests that they would be; examples include Greece, Iceland, Portugal, Switzerland and Thailand. For example, Iceland outperforms Greece in all three assessment domains to an extent that one would predict from the difference in their GDP per capita, as shown in Figure 3.7a. Countries above the trend line have higher average scores on the PISA assessments than would be predicted on the basis of their GDP per capita (and on the basis of the specific set of countries used for the estimation of the relationship). Among non-OECD countries, Hong Kong-China, Latvia and the Russian Federation perform better than the estimates from their GDP would suggest. Countries below the trend line show lower performance than would be predicted from their GDP per capita, including the following non-OECD countries: the Latin American countries, Albania, Indonesia, Israel and FYR Macedonia.

Obviously, the existence of a correlation does not necessarily mean that there is a causal relationship between the two variables. Indeed, there are likely to be many other factors involved. Figure 3.7a does suggest, however, that countries with higher national income are at a relative advantage. This should be taken into account, in particular, in the interpretation of the performance of countries with comparatively low levels of national income.

GDP per capita provides a measure of a country's ability to pay for education but does not directly measure the financial resources actually invested in education. Figure 3.7b compares the money that countries

Figure 3.7b

Student performance and spending per student

Relationship between average performance across the combined reading, mathematical and scientific literacy scales and cumulative expenditure on educational institutions up to age 15 in US$, converted using purchasing power parities (PPPs)

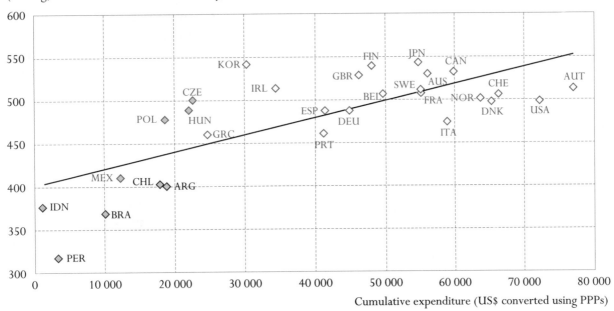

◇ OECD country with high income   ◇ Non-OECD country with high income

◆ OECD country with low and middle income   ◆ Non-OECD country with low and middle income

Average performance
(reading, mathematical and scientific literacy)

Cumulative expenditure (US$ converted using PPPs)

Source: OECD PISA database, 2003. Table 3.3.

spend per student, on average, from the beginning of primary education up to the age of 15, with average student performance across the three assessment domains. Spending per student is approximated by multiplying public and private expenditure on educational institutions per student in 1998 at each level of education by the theoretical duration of education at the respective level, up to the age of 15[9]. The results are expressed in U.S. dollars using purchasing power parities (OECD, 2002e).

Without establishing a causal link, the figure shows a positive relationship between spending per student and mean country performance averaged across the three assessment domains (see Table 3.3, Annex B1). As expenditure per student on educational institutions increases, so also does a country's mean performance, with expenditure per student explaining 54 per cent of the variation between countries in mean performance[10].

Deviations from the trend line, however, suggest that modest spending per student cannot automatically be equated with poor performance by education systems. Italy spends about twice as much per student as Korea but, whereas Korea is among the best performing countries in all literacy areas assessed by PISA, Italy performs significantly below the OECD average. Many similar exceptions to the overall relationship between spending per student and student performance suggest that, as much as spending on educational institutions is a necessary prerequisite for the provision of high-quality education, spending alone is not sufficient to achieve high levels of outcomes. This becomes most clearly visible in the performance of the

Latin American countries and in Indonesia: Although expenditure per student in these countries is comparatively low, the performance of students in these countries lags considerably behind the investments. While PISA does not provide insights into the underlying nature of the relationship, the data suggest that other factors, including the effectiveness with which resources are invested, may play a crucial role.

The income distribution and performance

It is not only average wealth that counts in the financing of education, but inequalities in the distribution of national income can also impose constraints on financing and, by implication, the quality of educational outcomes. One measure for inequalities in the distribution of national wealth is the Gini index of income inequality (see also Chapter 1). It ranges from 0 (perfect equality) to 100 (total inequality). Figure 3.8a shows the relationship between the Gini index of income inequality and the average performance of students in the PISA assessment in each country. Similar to the methodology used in Figure 3.7a, the mean performance of countries has been averaged across the reading, mathematical and scientific literacy domains. Overall, the relationship is negative: higher levels of income inequality are associated with lower levels of average performance. The relationship is fairly consistent, with the Gini index explaining 26 per cent of the variation in performance for these participating countries. Japan, Korea and Hong Kong-China show similar levels of high performance with very different levels on the Gini index of income inequality (24.9, 31.6 and 43.4 respectively). Another picture emerges when the four Latin American countries – Brazil, Chile, Mexico and Peru – are examined. They show relatively low performance with the four highest levels of income inequality among all of the participating countries with an average index of 54 – Brazil shows the most unequal distribution of income inequality among all of the participating countries with a Gini index of 59.1. On the other hand, the Central and Eastern European countries (except the Russian Federation) with an average level of the Gini index of income inequality at around 29.0 show relatively low performance. The Russian Federation with a high level of income inequality (45.6) has a higher average score on the PISA assessments than would be predicted on the basis of the Gini index.

In addition to examining income inequality and performance, the level of income inequality in relation to investments in education is also important. Figure 3.8b shows the relationship between expenditure per student and the Gini index of income inequality. As seen, the relationship is also negative, higher levels of spending are associated with higher levels of income equality with expenditure explaining about 20 per cent of the variation in the Gini index. Additional spending of US$ 10 000 per student are associated with a 2 points decrease in the Gini index of income inequality.

Figure 3.8a

Student performance and the Gini index of income inequality

◇ OECD country with high income   ◇ Non-OECD country with high income
◆ OECD country with low and middle income   ◈ Non-OECD country with low and middle income

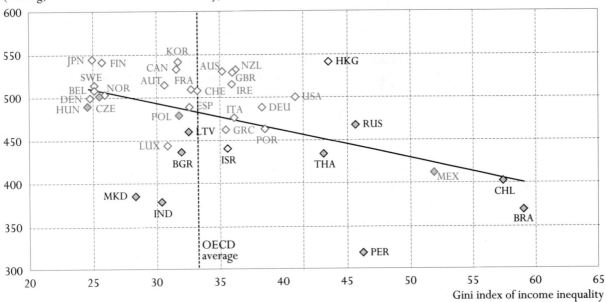

Average performance
(reading, mathematical and scientific literacy)

Source: OECD PISA database, 2003. Tables 1.4 and 3.3.

Figure 3.8b

Spending per student and the Gini index of income inequality

◇ OECD country with high income   ◇ Non-OECD country with high income
◆ OECD country with low and middle income   ◈ Non-OECD country with low and middle income

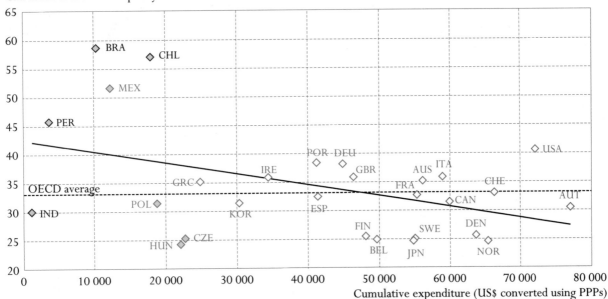

Gini index of income inequality

Source: OECD PISA database, 2003. Tables 1.4 and 3.3.

Conclusions

In an increasingly technological world, all adults, not just those aspiring to a scientific career, need to be mathematically and scientifically literate. The wide disparities in student performance on the mathematical and scientific literacy scales that emerge from the analysis in this chapter suggest, however, that this remains a remote goal and that countries need to serve a wide range of student abilities, including both those who perform exceptionally well and those most in need.

At the same time, the fact that five out of the seven OECD countries with the smallest internal variation on the mathematical literacy scale all perform statistically significantly above the OECD average suggests that wide disparities in performance are not a necessary condition for a country to attain a high level of overall performance.

Although the variation in student performance within countries is many times larger than the variation between countries, significant differences between countries in the average performance of students should not be overlooked. To the extent that these are predictive of student career paths, these differences may, particularly in subject areas such as mathematics and science, raise questions about countries' future competitiveness. In addition, differences in countries' relative performance across the three subject areas may point to significant systemic factors influencing student performance.

The economic situation of countries can be associated with outcomes in reading, mathematical and scientific literacy. As shown in the chapter, countries from low- and middle-income tend to have much lower performance than countries in high-income. Like a comparison between national income and student performance, a comparison between spending per student and mean student performance across countries cannot be interpreted in a causal way. Nevertheless, the data reveal a positive association between the two. At the same time, as much as spending on educational institutions is a necessary prerequisite for the provision of high-quality education, the comparison also suggests that spending alone is not sufficient to achieve high levels of outcomes and that other factors, including the effectiveness with which resources are invested, play a crucial role.

Notes

1. Technically, the mean score for student performance across OECD countries was set at 500 points and the standard deviation at 100 points, with the data weighted so that each OECD country contributed equally.

2. Poland's performance may be overestimated slightly, due to the exclusion of the 6.7 per cent of 15-year-olds enrolled in primary schools. This exclusion is unlikely to affect its rank-order position on the mathematical literacy scale (for details see Annex A3).

3. The performance of students in the Netherlands cannot be estimated accurately because the response rate of its schools was too low. It can, however, be said with confidence that the Netherlands would lie between the 1st and 4th position among OECD countries on the mathematical literacy scale. Therefore, the Netherlands does not appear in Figure 3.2 [for details see Annex A3].

4. In Australia, Austria, Canada, the Czech Republic, Denmark, Finland, Germany, Greece, Iceland, Liechtenstein, Mexico, the Netherlands, New Zealand, Norway, Portugal, Sweden, Switzerland, the United Kingdom and the United States, between one half and three quarters of students used calculators during the PISA assessment. In Belgium, France, Hungary, Italy, Latvia, the Russian Federation and Spain, between one third and one half of students used calculators. Lower rates of calculator use were reported in Poland (31 per cent), Ireland (27 per cent), Luxembourg (7 per cent) and Brazil (6 per cent). Students did not use calculators in Japan. No information was available for Korea. With the exception of Brazil and Greece, scores on the mathematical literacy scale for students who used calculators in the PISA assessment tended to be higher than for students who did not use them. However, the differences between the scores of students on the mathematical literacy scale who used calculators and those who did not are very closely mirrored by the differences in scores on the reading literacy scale between these two groups (which did not involve numerical calculations). There is therefore no indication that the use of calculators provided an advantage to students in terms of their performance in PISA.

5. The relative probability of each country assuming each rank-order position on each scale can be determined from the country's mean scores, their standard errors and the covariance between the performance scales of two domains. This reveals whether, with a likelihood of 95 per cent, a country would rank statistically significantly higher, at the same level, or statistically significantly lower in one domain than in the other domain. For details on the methods employed see *PISA 2000 Technical Report* (OECD, 2002a).

6. Poland's performance may be overestimated slightly, due to the exclusion of the 6.7 per cent of 15-year-olds enrolled in primary schools. As a result of this, Poland's performance on the scientific literacy scale may be overestimated by two rank-order positions. The performance of students in the Netherlands cannot be estimated accurately because the response rate of its schools was too low. It can, however, be said with confidence that the Netherlands would lie between the 3rd and 14th position among OECD countries on the scientific literacy scale. (for details see Annex A3)

7. See *PISA 2000 Technical Report* (OECD, 2002a), Chapter 13.

8. Differences in performance between countries can also be summarised in terms of the overall variation in performance of the combined OECD student population that is accounted for by differences between countries. This amounts to 14 per cent on the mathematical literacy scale, 8 per cent on the combined reading literacy scale and 9 per cent on the scientific literacy scale.

9. Cumulative expenditure for a given country is approximated as follows: let $n(0)$, $n(1)$, $n(2)$ and $n(3)$ be the typical number of years spent by a student from the beginning of pre-primary education up to the age of 15 years in pre-primary, primary, lower secondary and upper secondary education. Let $E(0)$, $E(1)$, $E(2)$ and $E(3)$ be the annual expenditure per student in U.S. dollars converted using purchasing power parities in pre-primary, primary, lower secondary and upper secondary education, respectively. The cumulative expenditure is then calculated by multiplying current annual expenditure E by the typical duration of study n for each level of education i using the following formula:

$$CE = \sum_{i=0}^{3} n(i) * E(i)$$

Estimates for $n(i)$ are based on the International Standard Classification of Education (ISCED) (OECD, 1997).

10. The correlation for the overall relationship is 0.74. Taken separately, the correlation is 0.75 for the combined reading literacy scale, 0.75 for the mathematical literacy scale and 0.69 for the scientific literacy scale.

Chapter

GENERAL OUTCOMES OF LEARNING

Introduction

Most children come to school ready and willing to learn. How can schools foster and strengthen this predisposition and ensure that young adults leave school with the motivation and capacity to continue learning throughout life? Students need effective approaches to learning both to succeed at school and to meet their learning needs later in life. In particular, they need to regulate the learning process, taking responsibility for reaching particular goals. These types of outcomes are not pursued as a specific part of the curriculum, yet they can be strongly influenced by students' experiences at school and play a crucial part in their futures.

This chapter looks at what PISA found out about students approaches to learning. Specifically, it examines the way they handle and address learning tasks in school and the extent to which they are able to identify and pursue their own learning goals by applying strategies and drawing on their motivation.

PISA set out to measure "self-regulated learning" through a questionnaire that asked a wide range of questions about students' learning habits, attitudes and preferences. The questionnaire was given to about half of the students taking part in the survey. PISA looks in particular at three aspects that may influence students' capacity to regulate their learning. The first is the use of effective learning strategies. For example, students who regularly review what they have learned relative to their learning goals are likely to be more effective at reaching these goals. The second is motivation. Students who enjoy reading, for example, tend to make better progress in developing strong reading literacy skills. The third is a positive self-concept since an important ingredient in learning successfully is having confidence in one's own abilities.

All three of these features play a complex part in the learning process and can be a result of students' school achievements (*e.g.,* being good at reading helps one enjoy it) as well as contributing to it. However, research in this area has demonstrated that being able to regulate one's learning is central to success in school and influences the degree to which people engage in further learning. Thus self-regulated learning is desirable both as a factor that can help raise the sort of student performance measured in PISA and as an end in itself.

While effective lifelong learning strategies warrant examination as an important outcome of schooling, questions naturally arise about the extent to which effective learning strategies are also prerequisites for success at school. To address these questions, this chapter not only reviews the nature and distribution of students' attitudes towards learning and their use of particular learning strategies but also tries to establish the relationship between these factors and the results of the PISA assessments.

This approach in turn leads to questions about the direction of such relationships and causality. But, pertinent as these questions are, they remain difficult to answer. It may be, for example, that good performance and attitudes towards learning are mutually reinforcing or that students with higher natural ability both perform well and use particular learning strategies. There may also be third factors, such as home background or differences in the schooling environment to which students are exposed. In what follows, readers are therefore cautioned that the exact nature and strength of cause-and-effect relationships are uncertain and, indeed, beyond the scope of this first report on PISA. Demonstration of the fact that such relationships exist, however, may stimulate policy discourse and future research.

The important issue of how attitudes, motivation and self-concept differ between males and females is discussed in Chapter 5. Other factors relating to student learning outcomes such as student engagement in reading, students' capacity for self-regulated learning and student engagement in school are discussed in three PISA thematic reports entitled *Reading for Change* (OECD, 2002b), *Learners for Life: Approaches to Learning* (OECD, 2003a) and *Student Disaffection with School* (OECD, 2003b).

Box 4.1. Interpreting students' self-reports

Most of the measures presented in this chapter are based on self-reported behaviours and preferences and on students' assessments of their own abilities. These measures rely on reports from the students themselves rather than on external observations, and they may be influenced by cross-cultural differences in response behaviour or the social desirability of certain responses. Comparisons must therefore be undertaken with care, even though the instruments used to assess students' approaches to learning and their beliefs in their own abilities are based on well-established research and were tested extensively before their use in PISA 2000.

Several of the measures are presented as indices that summarise student responses to a series of related questions. The questions were selected from larger constructs on the basis of established theoretical considerations and previous research (see *PISA 2000 Technical Report,* OECD, 2002a). Structural equation modelling was used to confirm the theoretically expected results of the indices and to validate their comparability across countries. For this purpose, a model was estimated separately for each country and, collectively, for all OECD countries.

The indices were constructed in such a way that two-thirds of the OECD student population are between the values of −1 and 1, with an average score of 0 (*i.e.,* the mean for the combined student population from participating OECD countries is set at 0 and the standard deviation is set to 1). It is important to note that negative values on an index do not necessarily imply that students responded negatively to the underlying questions. A negative value merely indicates that a group of students (or all students, collectively, in a single country) responded less positively, than all students did, on average, across OECD countries. For detailed information on the construction of indices, see Annex A1.

Student engagement in schooling and learning

Student motivation and engagement in schooling and learning are important outcomes of education. Students who leave school with the autonomy to set their own learning goals and with a sense that they can reach those goals are potential learners throughout life. Motivation and engagement can also affect students' quality of life during their adolescence and can influence whether they will successfully pursue further educational or labour market opportunities. There are many intrinsic and extrinsic factors – student's level of self-confidence in learning, support and interest of parents, teachers and peer group, school policy and practice, promise of good grades, employment prospects - associated with students' motivation to learn and with their behaviour and attitudes towards school.

While some students display positive attitudes towards schooling and are highly motivated to learn, others may not see the value of education nor feel a strong sense of attachment to their school and may be reluctant to participate in school life. Research suggests that although these relationships are complex, understanding the factors that shape students' motivations and engagement with school can help teachers, parents and policymakers to gain insight into how students have become disengaged with school, thus addressing the important issues of school dropout and truancy. Research also indicates that high levels of student engagement and motivation in school can be associated with higher performance at school, although many students with high achievement are not engaged in schooling and vice-versa.

Student engagement with school

Disruptive behaviour, poor attendance and negative attitudes towards school may often be associated with low academic performance and the decision to withdraw from school. On the other hand, research has shown that if students become involved in their school curricula or extra-curricular activities and develop strong ties with other students and teachers, they are more likely to do well in their studies and to complete secondary school. PISA examined two aspects of student engagement with school: students' sense of belonging and school attendance.

Students' sense of belonging

Most students suffer from disaffection from school at some stage in their schooling careers, often as a result of academic, peer group or family-related pressures. In PISA, 15-year-old students were asked about their attitudes towards school[1]. More than 18 per cent of students in Argentina, Hong Kong-China and Peru agree or strongly agree that school is a place where they feel like an outsider; and a similar percentage of students in Peru and Thailand reported that they feel lonely and awkward and out of place at school. By contrast, around 90 per cent of students in Brazil, Hong Kong-China and Thailand agree or strongly agree that they "make friends easily" at school, and around 85 per cent of students in Brazil, Chile and Israel reported that other students seem to like them.

An index of sense of belonging was constructed to summarise students' attitudes towards school, with the average score across countries set at 0 and two-thirds scoring between 1 and −1. A positive value on the index indicates that students reported a sense of belonging that is higher than the OECD average and a negative value a sense of belonging lower than the OECD average. The index of sense of belonging was derived from students' responses to questions about the extent to which students feel like an outsider (or left out of things), make friends easily, feel like they belong, feel awkward and out of place, think that other students seem to like them and feel lonely (for the definition of the index see Annex A1). The upper part of Figure 4.1 shows the distribution of countries on the index of sense of belonging. While Albania, Hong Kong-China, Japan, Korea, Latvia, Poland and Thailand score at least one third of a standard deviation lower than the OECD average on the index, other countries such as Austria, Brazil, Chile, Israel, Liechtenstein, Sweden and Switzerland report an index value of at least 0.20 index points above the OECD average. The five Asian countries all show below average levels of sense of belonging below the OECD average.

Table 4.1 shows that within countries the difference in performance between the bottom and top quarters of students on the index of belonging is statistically significant in all non-OECD countries, and in Argentina and Peru this difference is greater than one proficiency level on the combined reading literacy scale (about 80 points). The issue of whether students with a strong sense of belonging tend to perform better at school is examined in more detail in a forthcoming PISA thematic report on student disaffection with school (OECD, 2003*b*).

School attendance

Student absenteeism is a common problem in many schools. Students who are frequently absent from school not only miss out on the opportunities for learning and socialisation that schools can provide but may also jeopardise their potential future careers, studies and relationships.

Figure 4.1

Sense of belonging and student performance on the combined reading literacy scale

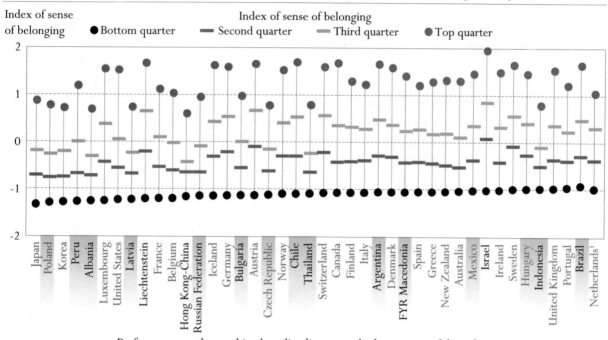

Index of sense of belonging ● Bottom quarter ━ Second quarter ━ Third quarter ● Top quarter

Performance on the combined reading literacy scale, by quarters of the index

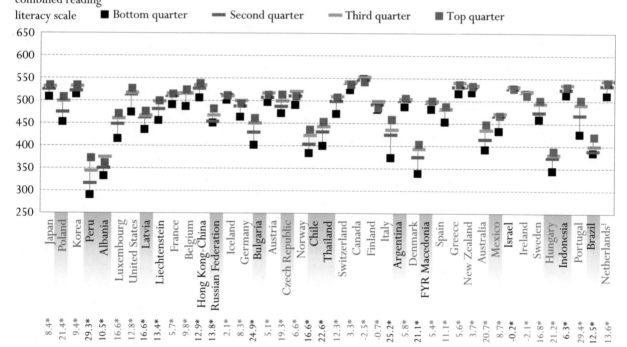

Performance on the combined reading literacy scale ■ Bottom quarter ■ Second quarter ▬ Third quarter ■ Top quarter

*Change in the combined reading literacy score per unit of the index of engagement in reading.
For the definition of the index, see Annex A1.
1. Response rate is too low to ensure comparability (see Annex A3).
Source: OECD PISA database, 2003. Table 4.1.

With the exception of Hong Kong-China, Indonesia and Liechtenstein, students in non-OECD countries reported much lower attendance at school than students in OECD countries. Figure 4.2 shows the percentage of students who reported skipping class in the last two weeks along with their performance on the combined reading literacy scale[2]. Around 10 per cent of students in Argentina, Brazil and Bulgaria reported that they skipped class five or more times during the previous two school weeks, which is more than three times the reported OECD average of 3 per cent (see Table 4.2, Annex B1). The difference in performance between those students who reported not skipping class and those who reported skipping class five or more time is between 75 and 100 score points in eight countries, including Argentina, Chile and Thailand and 100 points or more in Belgium, France and the United States. Similarly, more than 5 per cent of students in Bulgaria, Israel, Spain and the Russian Federation reported arriving late at school five or more times over this same period.

Although there is a large amount of variation between schools and students within countries, some of which may be attributed to gender and the socio-economic background of the school and student, the high proportion of both disaffected and absent students across OECD and non-OECD countries highlights the need for schools and teachers to create a positive, encouraging learning environment that focuses on both the pedagogical and affective needs of students, particularly for those at risk of dropping out of school. More research needs to be undertaken to investigate the causes and relationships between student engagement with school and academic performance.

Students' effort and persistence to learn and instrumental motivation

Improving the level of student motivation has become an important policy focus in recent years, often as a means of combating problems of school dropout, student disaffection with school and low academic achievement (OECD, 2002b). Understanding what actually motivates students to learn is the first step in creating a learning environment that will allow students to "learn how to learn" under self-motivated and self-managed conditions.

Students may be motivated to learn by various factors. Intrinsically-motivated students are motivated by a personal enjoyment and satisfaction derived from learning for its own sake, while instrumentally motivated students are motivated by a reward or punishment that is external to the activity itself, such as the prospect of employment or financial security. PISA asked students in 33 countries, including 11 non-OECD countries, about the extent to which certain external and internal forces motivated them to learn.[3]

Figure 4.3 shows four items relating to students' effort and persistence to learn[4] (intrinsic motivation) and three items relating to students' instrumental[5] motivation. Concerning instrumental motivation, between 40 and 50 per cent of students in 11 countries, including Albania, Brazil, Bulgaria, Chile, FYR Macedonia and the Russian Federation reported that they "almost always" study to get a good job, to increase their job opportunities and to ensure that their future will be financially secure. Similar patterns emerge for students reporting their effort and persistence for learning. In Albania, Bulgaria, Brazil, Chile, FYR Macedonia and Portugal, more than one third of students "almost always" agreed that they work as hard as possible when studying; and over 40 per cent of students in Albania, Chile and FYR Macedonia reported "almost always" putting forth their best effort. Hong Kong-China, Latvia and Thailand are the three countries where students consistently reported levels of intrinsic motivation well below the OECD average, while students in countries such as Albania, Brazil, Chile and FYR Macedonia indicated levels of intrinsic motivation that are more than twice the OECD average (see Table 4.3, Annex B1 and *www.pisa.oecd.org* for data).

Figure 4.2

Student attendance and student performance on the combined reading literacy scale

Percentage of students who reported that in the previous two school weeks they...

- skipped class five or more times
- skipped class three or four times
- skipped class once or twice
- did not skip class

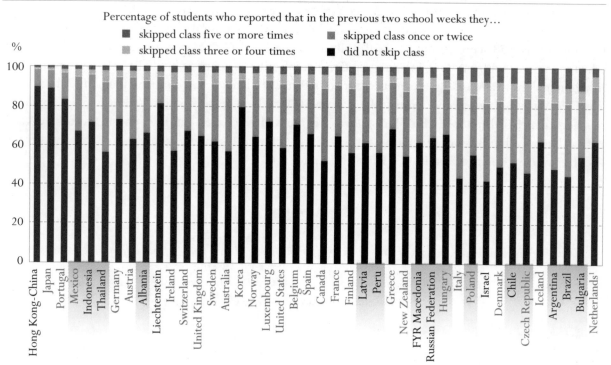

Performance on the combined reading literacy scale of students who reported that in the previous two school weeks they...

Performance on the combined reading literacy scale

- skipped class five or more times
- skipped class three or four times
- skipped class once or twice
- did not skip class

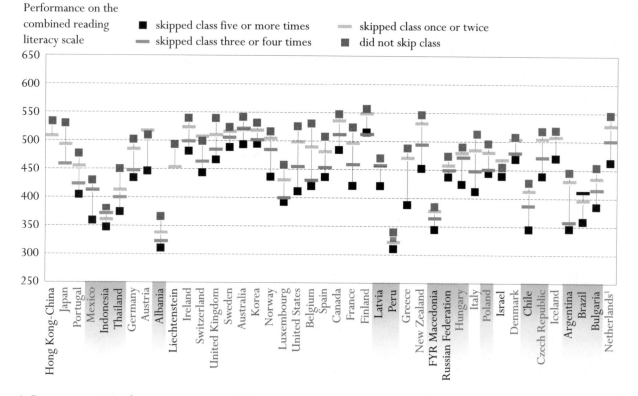

1. Response rate is too low to ensure comparability (see Annex A3).
Source: OECD PISA database, 2003. Table 4.2.

Do high levels of motivation expressed by students translate into better student performance? Interestingly, performance is higher for students who reported high levels of effort and persistence to learn, especially for students in many non-OECD countries. For example, the average difference in performance between students who reported that they "almost never" and "almost always" work as hard as possible is between 61 and 73 score points in Brazil, Bulgaria, Denmark, FYR Macedonia and Hong Kong-China, which compares with the OECD average difference of only 13 score points. The relationship between instrumental motivation and performance is mixed. While students in 13 countries, including Chile, Israel and FYR Macedonia who reported that the statement "I study to get a good job" "almost never" applies to them score higher than those who "almost always" agree with the statement, the opposite occurs in Brazil, Latvia, Norway, the Russian Federation and Thailand (differences ranging from 48 points in the Russian Federation to 81 points in Brazil) (see Table 4.3, Annex B1).

Figure 4.3

Effort, persistence and motivation of students to learn

Distribution of mean percentages of students who often or almost always agree with the following statements

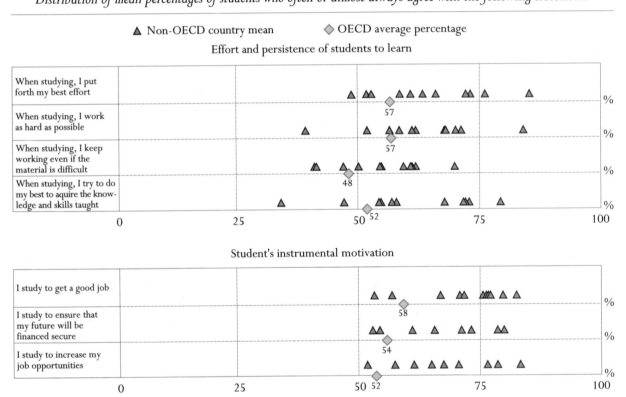

Source: OECD PISA database, 2003. For data see *www.pisa.oecd.org.*

Further analysis is required to understand these patterns of student motivation at the individual, school and country levels and to evaluate the effect on student motivation of contextual factors such as gender, attitudes of parents and teachers, and school and student socio-economic background.

Student engagement in reading

Reading activities and engagement in reading are decisive factors in the maintenance and further development of reading skills. The International Adult Literacy Survey findings that reading skills can deteriorate after the completion of initial education if they are not used (OECD and Statistics Canada, 1995) points to the importance of the maintenance of literacy skills. Positive reading activities and engagement in reading are, therefore, important outcomes of initial education as well as predictors of learning success throughout life. Similarly, students' reports on the frequency with which, for example, they read for pleasure, enjoy talking about books or visit bookstores and libraries, and the general importance they attach to reading, can indicate the degree to which they will read in the future.

Previous research conducted on student engagement in reading in PISA suggests not only that students who express positive attitudes to reading, who read a variety of materials, and who spend time reading are on average much better readers, but that reading engagement can compensate for disadvantage in students' social background (see OECD, 2002*b*).

Students in PISA were not only asked if they enjoyed reading but also how much time they spent reading for enjoyment and the frequency with which they read certain materials. This allowed the construction of reader profiles based on the types of materials that 15-year-olds reported reading as well as a single composite index of reading engagement, which is described below.

Reading engagement is defined here as the time that students report reading for pleasure, the time students spend reading a diversity of material, and students' interest in, and attitudes towards, reading (OECD, 2002*b*). This index is an extension of the index reported in *Knowledge and Skills for Life: First Results from PISA* (OECD, 2001*b*), which mainly focused on students' attitudes about reading. The index of engagement in reading is constructed with the average score across OECD countries set at 0 and two-thirds scoring between 1 and –1. A positive value on the index indicates that students' reported reading engagement is higher than the OECD average, while a negative value is lower than the OECD average (for the definition of the index see Annex A1).

The upper part of Figure 4.4 shows the distribution on the index of engagement in reading. Compared to OECD countries, 10 out of 14 non-OECD countries show higher values on the index. Albania, Finland, Hong Kong-China and FYR Macedonia have index values that are more than one-third of a standard deviation higher than the OECD average on the index of engagement in reading. Within-country differences in student performance on the combined reading literacy scale between those students on the bottom and top quarters of the index are statistically significant in all participating countries. While these differences are not as substantial in non-OECD countries – the OECD average difference is 95 score points – in seven non-OECD countries the difference in student performance between the top and bottom quarters of the index is more than 70 points, which is about the size of a whole proficiency level (see Table 4.4, Annex B1).

An important ingredient in reading engagement is the actual time that students devote to reading for enjoyment on a typical day. For many students this time may be restricted due to the length of the school day, homework requirements or other out-of-school activities such as sporting commitments.

More than 10 per cent of students reported that they read for enjoyment for more than two hours each day in Albania, Brazil, FYR Macedonia, Peru and the Russian Federation, which is more than twice the OECD

Figure 4.4

Engagement in reading and student performance on the combined reading literacy scale

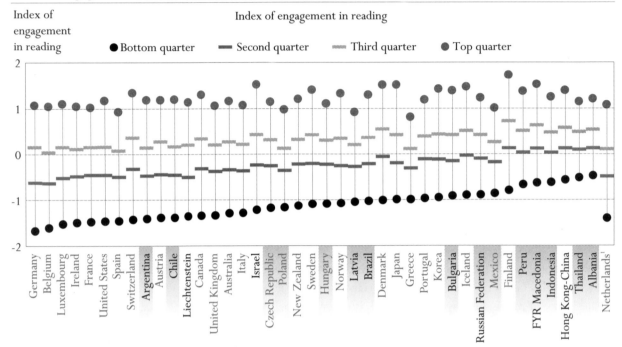

Index of engagement in reading

● Bottom quarter ▬ Second quarter ▬ Third quarter ● Top quarter

Performance on the combined reading literacy scale, by quarters of the index

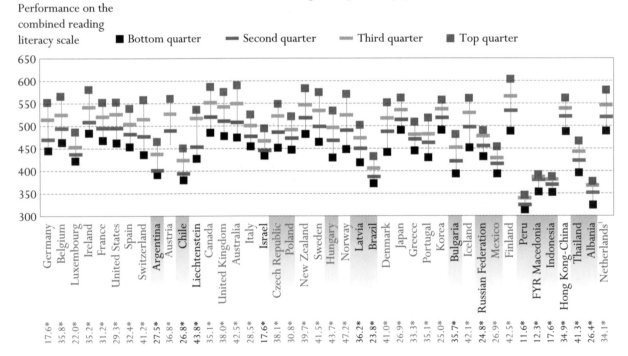

■ Bottom quarter ▬ Second quarter ▬ Third quarter ■ Top quarter

*Change in the combined reading literacy score per unit of the index of engagement in reading.
For the definition of the index, see Annex A1.
1. Response rate is too low to ensure comparability (see Annex A3).
Source: OECD PISA database, 2003. Table 4.4.

average percentage of students who reported reading the same amount of time per day. While more than one-third of student in 13 countries including Israel and Liechtenstein reported that they did not read for enjoyment – which is just above the OECD average for this response category (32 per cent) - less than 10 per cent of students reported this in Albania and Peru (see Table 4.5, Annex B1).

The average difference between the performance of students who reported reading for enjoyment for more than two hours per day and those who reported not reading for enjoyment is between 40 and 60 score points in Chile, Hong Kong-China, Indonesia, Latvia, the Russian Federation and Thailand as well as in 12 OECD countries. This difference is more than 80 points in Finland. This is considerably larger than the OECD average of 33. By contrast, students reporting more time spent reading for pleasure in Albania, FYR Macedonia and Peru performed score points lower than students who reported that they did not.

Student interest and self-concept in reading and mathematics

Interest in particular subjects affects both the degree and continuity of engagement in learning and the depth of understanding reached. This effect is largely independent of students' general motivation to learn. For example, a student who is interested in mathematics and therefore tends to study diligently may or may not show a high level of general learning motivation, and vice versa. Hence, an analysis of the pattern of students' interest in various subjects is of importance. Such an analysis can reveal significant strengths and weaknesses in attempts by education systems to promote motivation to learn in various subjects among differing sub-groups of students.

Figure 4.5 shows the distribution of mean percentages of students in non-OECD countries for six questions relating to students' interest and confidence in reading, relative to the OECD average[6]. An index of interest in reading was constructed using students' reported responses about the extent to which they agree that reading is fun and would not want to give it up, that they read in their spare time, and that they sometimes become totally absorbed in reading. An index of self-concept in reading was also constructed using students' reported responses about the extent to which they agree that they are hopeless, they learn things quickly and get good marks in the <test language> class. The indices have an average score across OECD countries set at 0 and a standard deviation of 1. A positive value on the indices means that students reported interest and confidence in reading are higher than the OECD average, while a negative value indicates that interest and confidence in reading are lower than the OECD average (for the definition of the index see Annex A1).

In most non-OECD countries, students reported consistently higher levels of interest in reading than the OECD average. More than 70 per cent of students in Albania and Thailand reported often or always read in spare time, while more than three-quarters of students in Brazil, Hong Kong-China and Thailand indicated that they become totally absorbed when reading (see Table 4.6, Annex B1).

Students were also asked about their interest in mathematics. An index of interest in mathematics was constructed using students' reported responses about the extent to which they agree that when they do mathematics, they sometimes become completely absorbed, that because mathematics is fun they would not want to give it up, and that mathematics is important to them personally[7]. A positive value on the index indicates that students reported interest in mathematics is higher than the OECD average, while a negative value means that interest in mathematics is lower than the OECD average (for the definition of the index see Annex A1). Compared to OECD countries, students in non-OECD countries reported comparatively high levels of interest in mathematics. The average index value in Albania, Brazil and Hong Kong-China is

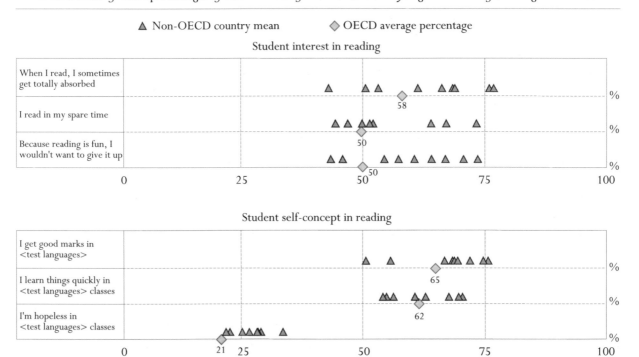

Figure 4.5

Student interest and self-concept in reading

Distribution of mean percentages of students who often or almost always agree with the following statements

Source: OECD PISA database, 2003. For data see *www.pisa.oecd.org.*

more than half a standard deviation higher than the OECD average. Liechtenstein was the only country that reported levels of interest in mathematics that were slightly lower than the OECD average.

Students in non-OECD countries generally also report higher levels of reading confidence on the index of self-concept in reading compared to OECD countries (see Table 5.8a, Annex B1). Between half and three-quarters of students in non-OECD countries reported that they often or always learn things quickly and receive good marks in the <test language> class – from more than 50 per cent of students in Hong Kong-China and Israel, to around 70 per cent of students in Albania, Chile, Latvia and FYR Macedonia.

But do students with high levels of interest and confidence in reading and mathematics perform better than their peers? What the results do show is that, within countries, students with greater interest and self-concept in reading and mathematics tend to perform significantly better than students who report less interest and self-concept in reading and mathematics. On average, the difference in performance on the combined reading literacy scale between students in the top and bottom quarters of the index of interest in reading is between 56 and 83 score points in Bulgaria, Hong Kong-China, Latvia and the Russian Federation. On the mathematical literacy scale the score differences in these same countries in between 43 and 69 score points (see Tables 4.6 and 4.7, Annex B1). Similar patterns can be seen in reading and mathematics on the index of self-concept for non-OECD countries. On the mathematical literacy scale, this difference is about the size of one proficiency level in Latvia, Liechtenstein and the Russian Federation. On the combined reading literacy scale this difference is at least one proficiency level in Albania, Latvia, FYR Macedonia and the Russian Federation (see Table 5.8a and 5.8b, Annex B1).

Diversity and content of reading - Reader profiles

While students who enjoy reading for pleasure and are interested and confident about reading are more likely to perform better in reading-related activities than other students, what students are reading can also influence students' reading practices and their performance in reading.

In PISA, four broad reader profiles, or "clusters," were identified according to the frequency and diversity of the material students read, such as magazines, comic books, newspapers, and fiction and non-fiction books[8]. Each of these clusters is also associated with levels of student performance on the combined reading literacy scale. Mean percentages of students in each of these clusters are shown in Figure 4.6.

Students in Cluster 1 are the least diversified readers. Almost one third of students in ten countries including Albania, Brazil and Chile are in this cluster. These students frequently read magazines, while a small percentage frequently read fiction or comics. In both OECD and non-OECD countries students in this cluster have the lowest average score on the combined reading literacy scale. Students in this Cluster score more than 40 score points lower than the country mean on the combined reading literacy scale in Bulgaria, Hong Kong-China, Japan, Latvia, Liechtenstein, Thailand, as well as in the five Nordic countries (see Table 4.8, Annex B1).

Students in Cluster 2 are classified as moderately diversified readers who frequently read magazines and newspapers, probably for the purpose of obtaining information. More than one-third of students in 11 countries, among them Bulgaria, Israel, Latvia and Liechtenstein are in this cluster. They rarely report reading books or comics. Students in Cluster 3 are similar to those in Cluster 2, but they also read comic books and are moderate readers of fiction. More than one third of students in Hong Kong-China, Indonesia, FYR Macedonia and Thailand plus seven OECD countries are in this cluster. In most countries, students in Cluster 3 perform above students in Cluster 2 and below those in Cluster 4. However, in several Eastern European countries, such as Hungary, Latvia, Poland, FYR Macedonia and the Russian Federation, students in Cluster 2 outperform students involved in more diversified reading (Cluster 3).

Cluster 4 contains students who are classified as diversified readers and the focus here is on more demanding and longer texts. In OECD countries, between 3 (Japan) and 40 per cent (New Zealand) of students are in this cluster; in non-OECD countries, between 17 (Indonesia) and 50 per cent (Russian Federation) of students are in this cluster. In all OECD and most non-OECD countries students in Cluster 4 have a higher average score than students in other clusters. In Argentina, Bulgaria, Latvia, and Liechtenstein students in this Cluster score more than 40 score points above the country mean on the combined reading literacy scale.

With few exceptions, the pattern seen in OECD countries across reading clusters is consistent with patterns observed for non-OECD ones. In most cases, students who are among the least diversified readers have, on average, the lowest mean scores; while students who are the most diversified readers have higher mean scores. In contrast, the pattern amongst Eastern European countries, whereby students in Cluster 2 outperform those in Cluster 3, indicates that students who reported reading a greater diversity of materials, especially comics and to a lesser extent books, perform less well than students who report only reading newspapers and magazines. A similar pattern can also be seen amongst English-speaking countries. Relationships between clusters and gender, and socio-economic background are explored further in Chapters 5 and 6.

Figure 4.6

Percentage of students in each reading profile cluster and student performance on the combined reading literacy scale

■ Cluster 1 - Least diversified readers   ▨ Cluster 2 - Moderately diversified readers
▨ Cluster 3 - Diversified readers in short texts   ▨ Cluster 4 - Diversified readers in long texts

Performance on the combined
reading literacy scale

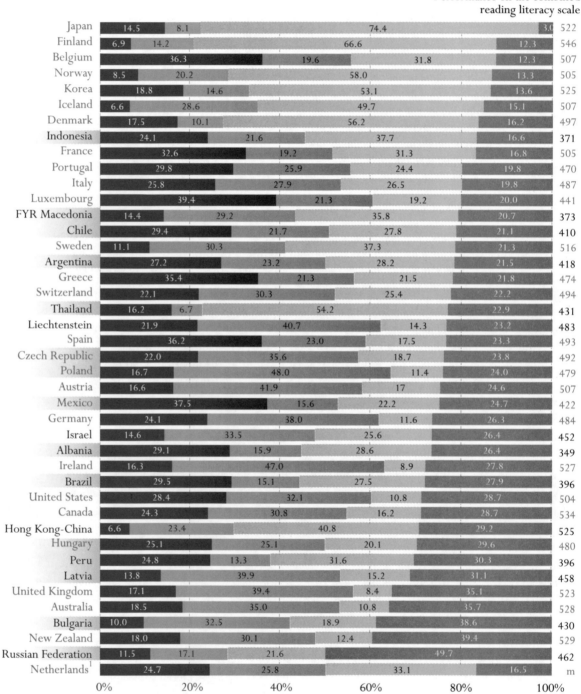

	Performance on the combined reading literacy scale
Japan	522
Finland	546
Belgium	507
Norway	505
Korea	525
Iceland	507
Denmark	497
Indonesia	371
France	505
Portugal	470
Italy	487
Luxembourg	441
FYR Macedonia	373
Chile	410
Sweden	516
Argentina	418
Greece	474
Switzerland	494
Thailand	431
Liechtenstein	483
Spain	493
Czech Republic	492
Poland	479
Austria	507
Mexico	422
Germany	484
Israel	452
Albania	349
Ireland	527
Brazil	396
United States	504
Canada	534
Hong Kong-China	525
Hungary	480
Peru	396
Latvia	458
United Kingdom	523
Australia	528
Bulgaria	430
New Zealand	529
Russian Federation	462
Netherlands[1]	m

1. Response rate is too low to ensure comparability (see Annex A3).

Source: OECD PISA database, 2003. Table 4.8.

Student learning strategies and preferences

In order for students to be able to manage their own learning effectively they must be able to set realistic goals, overcome obstacles and understand how to use appropriate learning strategies to achieve these goals. They must learn how to learn. The ability to regulate one's own learning behaviour can be seen as an important outcome of schooling because it equips students for lifelong learning and adult like. The use of self-regulated learning strategies by students is the subject of the upcoming PISA thematic report entitled *Learners for Life: Approaches to Learning* (OECD, 2003*a*).

Students were asked to report on how they used learning strategies to monitor and control the learning process, to evaluate the relevance of material learned and to memorise information. Students were also asked about their learning preferences, or, more precisely, if they preferred to compete against or work together with their peers. The results are examined in the following.

Controlling the learning process

Students do not passively receive and process information. They are active participants in the learning process, constructing meaning in ways shaped by their own prior knowledge and new experiences. Students with a well-developed ability to manage their own learning are able to choose appropriate learning goals, to use their existing knowledge and skills to direct their learning, and to select learning strategies appropriate to the task in hand. While the development of these skills and attitudes has not always been an explicit focus of teaching in schools, they are increasingly being identified explicitly as major goals of schooling and should, therefore, also be regarded as significant outcomes of the learning process.

An effective learner processes information efficiently. This requires more than the capacity to memorise new information. It calls for the ability to relate new material to existing knowledge and to determine how knowledge can be applied in the real world. A good understanding of learning strategies strengthens students' capacity to organise their own learning. Good learners can apply a variety of learning strategies in a suitably flexible manner. On the other hand, students who have problems learning on their own often have no access to effective strategies to facilitate and monitor their learning, or fail to select a strategy appropriate to the task in hand.

Students who can selectively process, monitor and organise information as they learn will be able to use this learning strategy to support their learning in school and throughout life. An index of control strategies was constructed from students' responses to questions about the frequency with which they figure out exactly what they need to learn, check to see if they have remembered what they have learned, figure out the concepts that they have not really understood, make sure they remember the important things, and look for additional information to clarify areas where they have not understood something. The index was constructed with the average score across OECD countries set at 0 and the standard deviation a 1 (for the definition of the index see Annex A1).

Figure 4.7 compares countries' mean scores on the index of control strategies and their performance on the combined reading literacy scale by quarters of the index of control strategies. Students in all non-OECD countries, with the exception of Hong Kong-China, Latvia and Thailand, reported more frequent use of control strategies than the OECD average with particularly high values found in Albania and Chile, as well as in Austria (see Table 4.9, Annex B1). Additionally, in half of the participating countries females favour the use of these strategies over males.

Figure 4.7

Controlling the learning process and student performance on the combined reading literacy scale

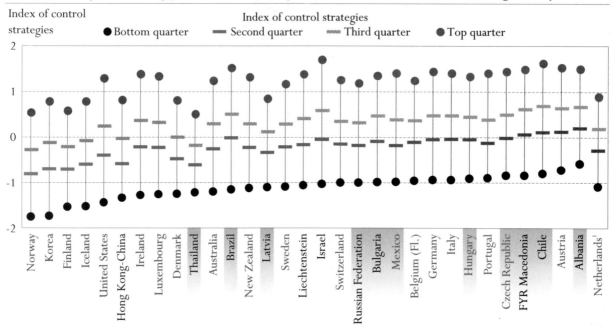

Index of control strategies

Index of control strategies

● Bottom quarter ▬ Second quarter ▭ Third quarter ● Top quarter

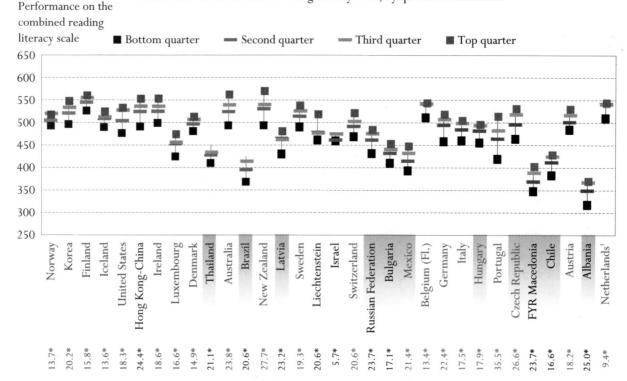

Performance on the combined reading literacy scale, by quarters of the index

Performance on the combined reading literacy scale

■ Bottom quarter ▬ Second quarter ▭ Third quarter ■ Top quarter

Norway	13.7*
Korea	20.2*
Finland	15.8*
Iceland	13.6*
United States	18.3*
Hong Kong-China	24.4*
Ireland	18.6*
Luxembourg	16.6*
Denmark	14.9*
Thailand	21.1*
Australia	23.8*
Brazil	20.6*
New Zealand	27.7*
Latvia	23.2*
Sweden	19.3*
Liechtenstein	20.6*
Israel	5.7*
Switzerland	20.6*
Russian Federation	23.7*
Bulgaria	17.1*
Mexico	21.4*
Belgium (Fl.)	13.4*
Germany	22.4*
Italy	17.5*
Hungary	17.9*
Portugal	35.5*
Czech Republic	26.6*
FYR Macedonia	23.7*
Chile	16.6*
Austria	18.2*
Albania	25.0*
Netherlands[1]	9.4*

*Change in the combined reading literacy score per unit of the index of control strategies.
For the definition of the index, see Annex A1.
1. Response rate is too low to ensure comparability (see Annex A3).
Source: OECD PISA database, 2003. Table 4.9.

The use of control strategies is positively related to performance in all countries, although a causal relationship cannot be established. Within each country, with the exception of Israel, students who use control strategies more frequently tend to perform statistically significantly better on the combined reading literacy scale than those who do not. The difference in student performance on the combined reading literacy scale between the top and bottom quarters of the index is 52 points on average for OECD countries, and range from 11 points in Israel to 64 points in Hong Kong-China reaching 78 points in New Zealand and 96 points in Portugal.

Student use of elaboration and memorisation strategies

Memorisation strategies (*e.g.*, reading material aloud several times and learning key terms) are important in many tasks, but they commonly lead only to verbatim representations of knowledge or new information being stored in the memory with little further processing. Where the learner's goal is to be able to retrieve the information as presented memorisation is an appropriate strategy, but such "learning by rote" rarely leads to deep understanding. In order to achieve understanding, new information must be integrated into a learner's prior knowledge base. Elaboration strategies (*e.g.*, exploring how the material relates to things one has learned in other contexts, or asking how the information might be applied in other contexts) can be used to reach this goal.

In PISA, students were asked about their use of elaboration and memorisation strategies. On the basis of their responses an index was created for each of these learning strategies. The index of memorisation strategies was derived from students' responses to questions about the frequency with which students try to memorise everything that might be covered, memorise as much as possible, memorise all material so that they can recite it, and practice by reciting the material over and over again. The index of elaboration strategies was derived from students' responses to questions about the frequency with which they try to relate new material to things learned in other subjects, discern the information that may be useful in the real world, try to understand new material by relating it to that already known, and figure out how material fits with that which has already been learned. The indices were constructed with the average score across OECD countries set at 0 and the standard deviation a 1 (for the definition of the index see Annex A1).

Figure 4.8 shows the mean scores on the indices of elaboration and memorization strategies for participating countries. Students in non-OECD countries report frequent use of both strategies, although countries tend to favour the use of elaboration strategies. In Albania, Brazil, Bulgaria, Chile and FYR Macedonia, the elaboration strategies index score is around half a standard deviation higher than the OECD average (see Table 4.11, Annex B1). Students in Albania and Hungary reported the greatest use of memorisation strategies at 0.82 and 0.89 index points respectively, while students in other countries reported less frequent use of this learning strategy, particularly in Italy and Norway (see Table 4.10, Annex B1).

There is also a strong positive association between the use of elaboration strategies and academic performance in all countries except Belgium (Fl.), Israel and the United States. Performance differences between the bottom and top quarters of the index of elaboration strategies are statistically significant and vary between 26 and 47 score points in all non-OECD countries except Israel and reaching 60 points in Korea and Portugal. For the index of memorisation strategies, however, students in several countries who reported low use of such strategies actually perform better than those who reported frequent use, particularly in FYR Macedonia where this difference reached 86 points (more than a proficiency level).

Figure 4.8
Learning strategies and preferences

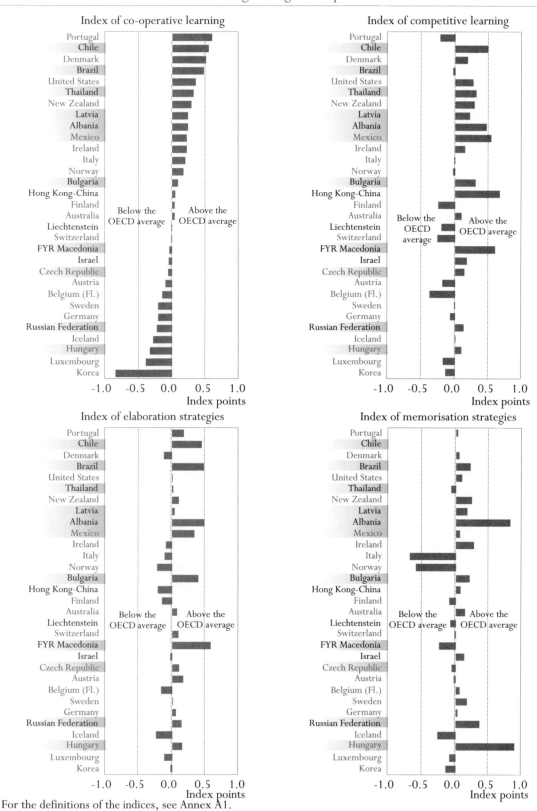

For the definitions of the indices, see Annex A1.
Source: OECD PISA database, 2003. Tables 4.10, 4.11, 4.12 and 4.13.

In both OECD and non-OECD countries, data suggest that elaboration strategies are strongly related to student performance. As with control strategies, schools need to help students to develop the strategies that best enhance their leaning. However, further consideration needs to be given to the cultural and educational context of the country concerned before any firm conclusions can be drawn from these data.

Co-operative and competitive learning

Learning in adult life occurs most frequently in circumstances in which people work together and depend on one another. In formal education, particularly at the secondary and tertiary levels, learning often occurs in isolation and in a context of preparation for competitive assessment. Although co-operative learning and competitive learning can be in conflict, both can lead to high performance. The results of PISA suggest that, if acquired in tandem, both types of learning may add to learning efficiency.

Separate PISA indices for co-operative and competitive learning were created from students' reports. The co-operative learning index is derived from responses to questions about whether students like working with others, like helping others do well in a group, learn most when working with others and perform best when working with others. The competitive learning index is derived from responses to questions about whether students like trying to do better than others, like being the best at something, work well when trying to be better than others and learn faster when trying to be better than others. Note that it was possible for students to provide positive or negative answers independently of either set of questions. The indices are constructed with the average score across OECD countries set at 0 and the standard deviation set at 1 (for the definition of the indices and references to their conceptual underpinning see Annex A1).

Figure 4.8 shows the mean scores on the indices of co-operative and competitive learning for participating countries. In general, students in non-OECD countries reported strong preferences for more competitive learning compared with OECD countries. However, many students – especially those in Latvia and Thailand - reported using both strategies. Students in Brazil and Liechtenstein were the only non-OECD countries that reported no preference for competitive learning styles (see Table 4.13, Annex B1). The preference for co-operative learning was particularly clear in Chile, Denmark and Portugal with average index scores of more than half of one standard deviation higher than the OECD average, while in Korea the opposite occurred. In Albania, Chile, Hong Kong-China, FYR Macedonia and Mexico, the average index score for competitive learning was as high as half a standard deviation higher than the OECD average (see Table 4.13, Annex B1).

Both competitive and co-operative learning tends to be positively related to performance in most countries, although this relationship is stronger in non-OECD countries for co-operative learning and in OECD countries for competitive learning. In non-OECD countries the differences in performance on the combined reading literacy scale between the top and bottom quarters of the index of competitive learning are not statistically significant in 8 countries including Albania, Brazil, Israel, Liechtenstein or FYR Macedonia. However, this difference is between 48 and 66 score points in Hong Kong-China, Latvia and the Russian Federation.

While students who like competitive learning perform better than those who do not - and while those who like co-operative learning perform better than those who do not - many students report using both learning styles. Thus, students as active learners are not limiting themselves to a single learning strategy that may not be the most appropriate in a given situation. Further research is needed to explore these aspects in detail.

Conclusions

Lifelong learning is a well-recognised need for individuals that contemporary education policy increasingly seeks to address. The need raises important questions of opportunities and access beyond formal education as well as important questions about how to develop the capacities of individuals to benefit from those opportunities.

Developing the predisposition of students to engage with learning and the capacity to do so effectively is an important goal of school education, and these objectives are becoming increasingly explicit in national education policies, especially with an eye to fostering lifelong learning. Students who leave school with the autonomy to set their own learning goals and with a sense that they can reach those goals are potential learners for life. Motivation and engagement can also affect students' quality of life during the adolescence, and they can influence whether they will successfully pursue further educational or labour market opportunities.

The results of PISA show that those most likely to memorise information do not always achieve the best results, while those who process or elaborate what they learn generally do well. Finally, PISA does not indicate that co-operative learning is superior to competitive learning, or vice versa. The evidence suggests, rather, that the two strategies can be used in a complementary fashion to promote higher performance. Since the use of co-operative learning in particular is closely dependent on the way in which learning opportunities are organised in schools, this conclusion is relevant for both education policy and educational practice.

Given the substantial investment that all countries make in education, it is unsatisfactory that a significant minority of students in all countries display negative attitudes towards learning and a lack of engagement with school, even if this may to some extent be determined by the age of the population assessed. Not only do negative attitudes seem to be associated with poor student performance, but students who are disaffected with learning at school will also be less likely to engage in learning activities, either inside or outside of school, in later life.

Of course, the links between attitudes, motivation and performance are complex, and the analysis in this chapter does not pretend to have established causal links. Indeed, for performance and attitudes, the relationship may well be reciprocal, students liking what they do well at, and doing well at what they like. Schools and education systems need to aim at both performance and satisfaction, and should not take the risk of addressing one in the belief that the other will follow. If both are achieved, a more secure foundation for productive engagement with lifelong learning will have been established.

Notes

1. The scale had the response categories "strongly disagree", "disagree", "strongly agree" and "agree".

2. The scale had the response categories "none", "1 or 2", "3 or 4" and "5 or more".

3. The scale had the response categories "almost never", "sometimes", "often" and "almost always".

4. The index of effort and perseverance was constructed using the four items shown in Figure 4.3. For more information on the creation of this index and the associated data, see the *PISA 2000 Technical Report* (OECD, 2002*a*) and *www.oecd.pisa.org.*

5. The index of instrumental motivation was constructed using the four items shown in Figure 4.3. For more information on the creation of this index and the associated data, see the *PISA 2000 Technical Report* (OECD, 2002*a*) and *www.oecd.pisa.org.*

6. The scale had the response categories "agree", "agree somewhat", "disagree" and "disagree somewhat".

7. The scale had the response categories "agree", "agree somewhat", "disagree" and "disagree somewhat".

8. See the PISA thematic report *Reading for Change* (OECD, 2002*b*), Chapter 5, for further information on the cluster analysis.

Chapter

GENDER DIFFERENCES AND SIMILARITIES IN ACHIEVEMENT

Introduction

Recognising the impact that education has on participation in labour markets, occupational mobility and the quality of life, all countries emphasise the importance of reducing educational disparities between males and females.

Significant progress has been achieved in reducing the gender gap in educational attainment. Younger women today are far more likely to have completed a tertiary qualification than women 30 years ago. In 13 of the 30 OECD countries with comparable data, more than twice as many women aged 25 to 34 have completed tertiary education as women aged 55 to 64 years. Furthermore, university-level graduation rates for women now equal or exceed those for men in 17 of the 30 OECD countries and in all but one of the non-OECD countries participating in PISA for which comparable data are available (OECD, 2001*a*; OECD, 2002*e*).

Nevertheless, in certain fields of study, gender differences in tertiary qualifications remain persistently high. The proportion of women among university graduates in mathematics and computer science is below 31 per cent, on average, among OECD countries. In Austria, the Czech Republic, Hungary, Iceland, the Netherlands, Norway and Switzerland, the proportion is between 12 and 19 per cent. Though much smaller in scale, a gender gap in university-level graduation rates is also evident in the life sciences and physical sciences (OECD, 2002*e*). In this context, it is noteworthy that past international assessments indicate that relatively small gender differences in favour of males in mathematics and science performance in the early grades become more pronounced and pervasive in many countries at higher grade levels (see Box 5.1).

Box 5.1. Changes in gender differences in mathematics and science performance, as students get older

In 1994/95, the IEA Third International Mathematics and Science Study (TIMSS) revealed statistically significant gender differences in mathematics among 4th-grade students in only three out of the 16 participating OECD countries (Japan, Korea and the Netherlands), in favour of males in all cases. However, the same study showed statistically significant gender differences in mathematics at the 8th-grade level in six of the same 16 OECD countries, all in favour of males. And finally, in the last year of upper secondary schooling, gender differences in mathematics literacy performance in the TIMSS assessment were large and statistically significant in all participating OECD countries except Hungary and the United States (again, all in favour of males). A similar and even more pronounced picture emerged in science (Beaton *et al.*, 1996; Mullis *et al.*, 1998).

Although the groups of students assessed at the two grade levels were not made up of the same individuals, the results suggest that gender differences in mathematics and science become more pronounced and pervasive in many OECD countries at higher grade levels.

Despite this general tendency, TIMSS also showed that some countries were managing to contain the growth in gender disparities at higher grade levels (OECD, 1996; OECD, 1997).

Why are males so much more prevalent in some professions than females? Why do fields of study and work differ substantially between the two genders? And how does all of this relate to student performance in school?

These are questions that have been central to educational research in many countries, and international assessments provide an important means to benchmark progress in countries in closing gender gaps.

In the past, concern about gender differences has almost universally addressed the underachievement of females. However, as females have first closed the gap and then surpassed males in many aspects of education, there are now many instances in which there is concern about the underachievement of males.

A key question is the extent to which these gender differences can be influenced through education systems and public policy more generally. It is difficult to answer this question, but an analysis of how gender differences vary across countries can provide important benchmarks on what can be achieved in terms of minimising gender differences early at school. To address these questions, this chapter concludes the profile of student performance begun in the preceding chapters by examining gender differences in student performance in the three literacy domains. It also describes differences by gender in the interest that students show in various subject areas, in motivation, in "self-concept" and in learning styles.

The future labour force

PISA explored students' expected occupations at the age of 30 in order to understand the future aspirations and expectations for their own future. These expectations are likely to affect their academic performance as well as the courses and educational pathways that they pursue. Students with higher academic aspirations are also more likely to be engaged with school and related activities.

Perhaps not surprisingly, PISA suggests that students' expected occupations are associated with their parents' professions, although the correlations are only weak to moderate. On average across countries the correlation of students' expected occupations with fathers' occupations is 0.19 and that of mothers' occupations is 0.15.

More importantly, the occupations that students expect to have at the age of 30 seem to be predictive for the career choices that they make later on. For example, female students in the participating countries are far more likely than males to report expected occupations related to life sciences and health, including biology, pharmacy, medicine and medical assistance, dentistry, nutrition and nursing, as well as professions related to teaching. Twenty per cent of females expect to be in life sciences or health related professions compared to only 7 per cent of males; 9 per cent of females compared to 3 per cent of males expect to be in occupations associated with teaching. Male students, on the other hand, more often expect careers associated with physics, mathematics or engineering (18 per cent of males versus 5 per cent of females) or occupations related to metal, machinery and related trades (6 per cent of males versus less than 1 per cent of females).

PISA classified students' expected professions at the age of 30 into four socio-economic categories, namely *white-collar high-skilled[1]*, *white-collar low-skilled[2]*, *blue-collar high-skilled[3]* and *blue-collar low-skilled[4]*. This taxonomy shows that in 40 out of the 42 countries females seem to have higher expectation towards their future occupations than males. Figure 5.1 indicates this relationship. Each symbol represents one country, with diamonds representing the percentage of students expecting a *white-collar* occupation at the age of 30 and squares representing the percentage of students expecting to have a blue-collar occupation at the age of 30. In Belgium, Czech Republic, Denmark and the Russian Federation 25 per cent more females than males expect to have a *white-collar* occupation at the age of 30. Argentina, Brazil, FYR Macedonia, Mexico and Korea are countries where large percentages of males and females seem to have high expectations for a *white-collar* occupation (more than 80 per cent), with small differences found in this expectation between males and females (less than 10 per cent). Liechtenstein and Israel, on the other hand, have males and females with similar levels of expectations: approximately 53 and 69 per cent respectively, levels lower than the OECD averages (67 per cent for males and 85 per cent for females) (see Table 5.1, Annex B1).

Figure 5.1

Expectations of 15-year-old students to have a white-collar or blue-collar occupation at the age of 30, by gender

◇ OECD countries, white-collar occupation expected ◼ OECD countries, blue-collar occupation expected
◇ Non-OECD countries, white-collar occupation expected ☐ Non-OECD countries, blue-collar occupation expected

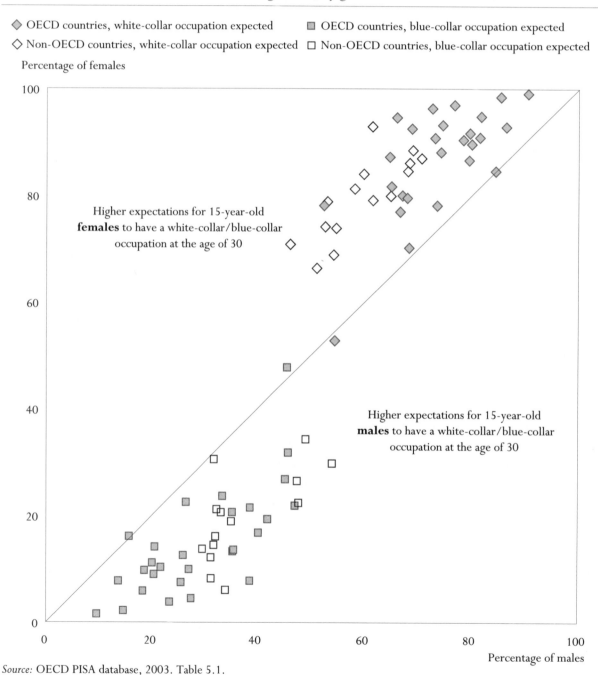

Source: OECD PISA database, 2003. Table 5.1.

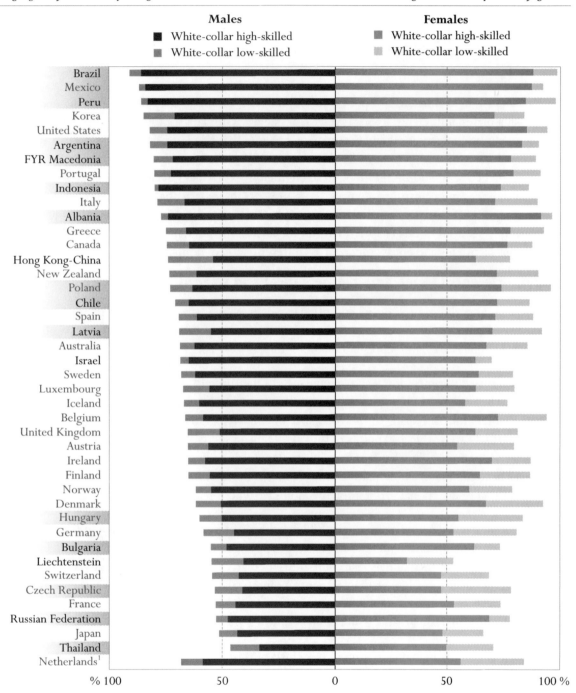

Figure 5.2

15-year-olds' expectations of having a white-collar occupation at age 30

Percentage of 15-year-olds expecting to have a white-collar low-skilled or white-collar high skilled occupation, by gender

1. Response rate is too low to ensure comparability (see Annex A3).
Note: For this classification, see Annex A1.
Source: OECD PISA database, 2003. Table 5.1.

Figure 5.2 provides further detail on this by showing the percentage of male and female students who expect to have a *white-collar* profession, either *high-* or *low-skilled*. The left side of the figure shows the percentage of males and the right side the percentage for females. The percentages of females expecting to hold a *white-collar* position at the age of 30 range from more than 95 per cent in Albania, Brazil, Poland, Peru to 53 per cent in Liechtenstein. Similar patterns are found for males ranging from 85 per cent or more in Brazil, Mexico and Peru to 51 and 46 per cent in Japan and Thailand, respectively (see Table 5.1, Annex B1).

These results are of significance for policy development. Combining the PISA data on the occupations that 15-year-olds males and females expect to have at age 30 with data on today's gender patterns in choices relating to educational pathways and occupations suggests that gender differences in occupational expectations at age 15 are likely to persist and to have a significant influence on the future of students. An important policy objective should therefore be to strengthen the role that education systems play in moderating gender differences in occupational expectations and - to the extent that these are related to gender patterns in student performance and student interest - to reduce performance gaps in different subject areas. The remaining sections of this chapter focus on the latter aspect, examining gender differences in student performance, attitudes and engagement across different subject domains.

Gender differences in reading, mathematical and scientific literacy

Studies on gender differences on in educational performance have historically focused on the underachievement of females. PISA suggests that patterns have changed and that females have often surpassed males and that males are, overrepresented among the poorest performers.

Figure 5.3 shows differences in mean performance in the three PISA assessment domains (see Table 5.2a, Annex B1). The scale used for comparing the performance of males and females is the same as that used in previous chapters for comparing the performance of countries. On that scale, about two-thirds of 15-year-olds in the OECD are within 100 points of the OECD mean score of 500, and one proficiency level is equal to just over 70 points. As in Chapters 2 and 3, it also needs to be taken into account that the mean score differences between males and females in this chapter may mask significant variation in gender differences between different educational programmes, schools or types of students.

In every country females, on average, reach higher levels of performance in reading literacy than males. This difference is significant in all countries except Israel and Peru. The better performance of females in reading is not only universal but also substantial, particularly in Albania, Finland, Latvia and FYR Macedonia, where it is equal to or higher than 50 score points, half of one international standard deviation. On average across all 42 countries, this difference is 32 points, which still represents almost half of one proficiency level, and generally greater than the typical difference in mean scores between countries.

The average gap in mathematics is around one third of this value, 11 points in favour of males. In science gender differences average out across countries. In mathematical literacy there are statistically significant differences in 15 countries where males perform better and one country, Albania, where females perform statistically better than males. In scientific literacy there are fewer differences between males and females, and the pattern of the differences is not consistent. Thirty-three countries show no statistically significant gender differences in science performance. Better performance of males is found in Austria, Denmark and Korea and better science performance for females is found in Albania, Latvia, FYR Macedonia, New Zealand, the Russian Federation and Thailand.

Figure 5.3

Gender differences in student performance
Differences in PISA scale scores

Difference in performance on the combined reading literacy scale

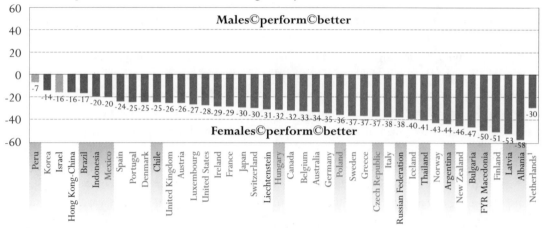

Difference in performance on the mathematical literacy scale

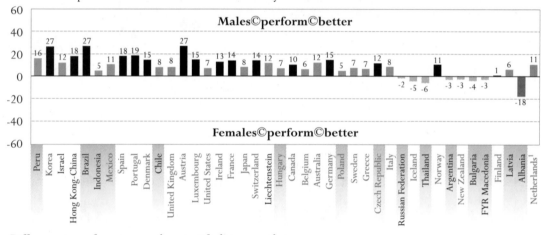

Difference in performance on the scientific literacy scale

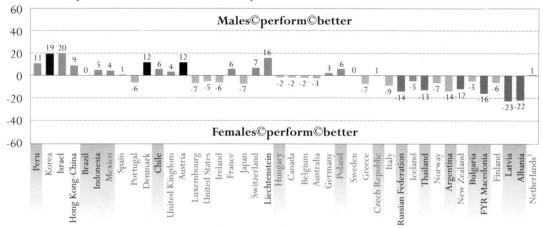

1. Response rate is too low to ensure comparability (see Annex A3).
Statistically significant differences are marked in black and dark red.
Source: OECD PISA database, 2003. Tables 4.10, 4.11, 4.12 and 4.13.

The significant advantage of females in reading literacy in all countries, and the advantage of males in mathematical literacy in many countries, may be the result of the broader societal and cultural context or of educational policies and practices. Whatever the cause, however, the results suggest that countries are having differing success at eliminating gender gaps.

Whatever the variations, the data suggest that the current differences are not the inevitable outcomes of differences between young males and females in learning styles. These gaps can be closed. Some countries do appear to provide a learning environment that benefits both genders equally, either as a direct result of educational efforts or because of a more favourable societal context. In reading literacy, Hong Kong-China, Korea and, to a lesser extent, Ireland, Japan and the United Kingdom, achieve both high mean perform-ance and limited gender differences. In mathematical literacy, Belgium, Finland, Japan, New Zealand and the United Kingdom achieve both high mean performance and small gender differences (see Table 5.2a, Annex B1).

At the same time, some of the countries with the largest gender gaps have high mean performances. In Fin-land, for example, it is not that males do poorly in reading literacy – their scores are well above the average for all students in PISA and there is no other country where males do better – but rather that females score exceptionally well: 18 points ahead of the country with the next highest-scoring females, New Zealand (see Table 5.2a, Annex B1)

With the exception of Bulgaria, differences in reading performance between males and females tend to be larger on the reflection and evaluation scale, that is, on tasks requiring critical evaluation and the relating of text to personal experience, knowledge and ideas. On average, gender differences are 45 points on the reflection and evaluation scale in favour of females, compared with 29 points on the interpretation scale and 26 points on the retrieving information scale (see Table 5.2b, Annex B1). In Finland, the country with one of the greatest gender differences, females have an exceptionally high mean score on the reflection and evaluation scale, 564 points, while males score only at the OECD average, 501 points. Particularly striking are the results for Albania, Latvia and FYR Macedonia, where on the reflection and evaluation scale girls score, on average, more than one proficiency level higher than boys (*i.e.*, more than 71 points). These find-ings may be associated with the types of reading material to which young men and women are exposed or which they tend to favour (see below). Brazil, Korea and Peru are countries with the smallest differences in all three subscales. While Korea has been able to minimise gender differences with very high outcomes for both groups, this is not the case for Brazil and Peru.

Gender differences in mathematical and scientific literacy, in which males have often been more proficient in the past, tend to be much smaller than the difference in favour of females in reading. These results are quite different from those of the IEA Third International Mathematics and Science Study (TIMSS), where gender differences in science performance among 8th-grade students were much larger, almost always favouring males.

The differences in results between PISA and TIMSS may be explained in part by the fact that the PISA assessment of scientific literacy placed greater emphasis than TIMSS on life sciences, an area in which females tended to perform well. By contrast, TIMSS placed greater emphasis than PISA on physics, in which males generally tend to perform well. In addition, PISA placed greater emphasis on scientific proc-esses and the application of knowledge. Finally, the fact that PISA had a higher proportion of open-ended and contextualised items, in which females tend to do better, rather than multiple-choice items, in which males tend to do better, may also have contributed to the higher performance by females.

In all countries, gender patterns tend to be similar in the three content areas of reading, mathematical and scientific literacy. This pattern suggests that there are underlying features of education systems and/ or societies and cultures that affect gender differences in performance throughout school careers. Nonetheless, some important differences do exist between domains. Finland, for example, shows very high gender differences on the combined reading literacy scale (51 points in favour of females), while its gender differences on the mathematical and scientific literacy scales are small. Albania, which reported the highest difference in reading towards females, also shows significant differences favouring females in mathematics and science. Indeed, it reported the only significant difference in mathematics favouring females (18 points). Conversely, Korea shows the lowest gender differences in reading literacy (14 points in favour of females) while gender differences in mathematical literacy (27 points in favour of males) and scientific literacy (19 points in favour of males) are among the largest in the OECD. Such variation across the domains suggests that these differences are the result of students' learning experiences and thus amenable to changes in policy.

The large gender differences among the students with the lowest levels of performance are of concern to policy-makers (see Figure 5.4 and Table 5.3a, Annex B1). In all countries, males are more likely than females to be among the lowest-performing students, *i.e.* to perform at or below Level 1 on the combined reading literacy scale. The ratio of males to females at this level ranges from less than 1.5 in Brazil, Mexico and Luxembourg to 6.8 in Thailand. Particularly striking are the results for Thailand, where only 8 per cent of females perform at or below Level 1 as opposed to 51 per cent of males. In Canada, Finland, Japan and Korea, 6 per cent or less of females perform at Level 1 or below, compared with between 7 and 14 per

Figure 5.4

Percentage of males and females among the lowest performers on the combined reading literacy scale
Percentage of males and females at or below Level 1

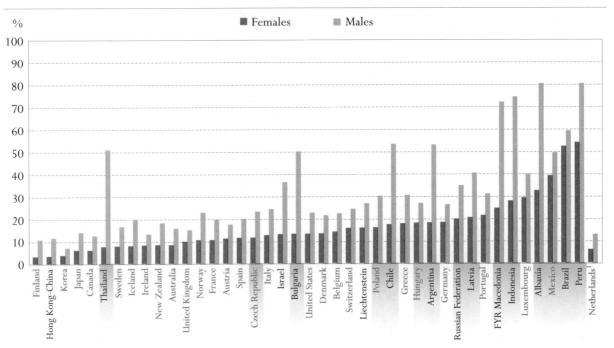

1. Response rate is too low to ensure comparability (see Annex A3).
Source: OECD PISA database, 2003. Table 5.3b.

cent of males. Even in the country with the highest performance, Finland, only 3 per cent of females are at Level 1 or below, compared with 11 per cent of males. Similar results found for Albania, Indonesia, FYR Macedonia and Thailand show 40 per cent or more males than females scoring at or below Level 1.

These findings suggest that the underachievement of young men in reading is a significant challenge for education policy that will need particular attention if the gender gap is to be closed and the proportion of students at the lowest levels of proficiency is to be reduced.

On the mathematical literacy scale males tend to perform better than females overall. However, much of this difference is attributable to larger differences in favour of males among the better students, not to a relative absence of males among the poorer performers. Among students who perform at least 100 points below the international average on the mathematical literacy scale (*i.e.,* those students typically able to complete only a single processing step consisting of reproducing basic mathematical facts or processes or applying simple computational skills), the proportion of females and males is roughly equal, although a higher proportion of females in this category is found in Brazil (9 per cent) and higher proportions of males in Albania (*i.e.,* 7 per cent) (see Table 5.3b, Annex B1). By contrast, in 17 of the participating countries males are more likely to be among the best-performing students – scoring more than one standard deviation above the OECD average – while in no country is the reverse the case.

Gender differences in subject interest

Figure 5.5a compares students' interest in reading (horizontal axis) with performance on the combined reading literacy scale (vertical axis). The index of interest in reading is described in Chapter 4. Each

Figure 5.5a

Relationship between interest in reading and performance on the combined reading literacy scale for males and females

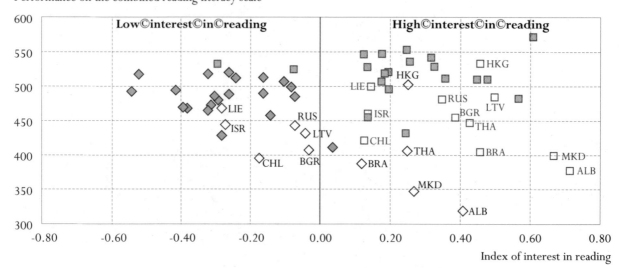

Note: For the definition of the indices, see Annex A1.
Source: OECD PISA database, 2003. Tables 4.6 and 4.7.

country is represented by two symbols in this diagram. The diamonds show the mean index of interest in reading for males and their mean performance on the combined reading literacy scale. The corresponding country positions for females are shown by squares, with open symbols representing non-OECD countries. The top of the vertical axis represents high mean performance in reading literacy. The right-hand end of the horizontal axis indicates that, on average, students frequently report that they often read in their spare time, that reading is important to them personally, that they would not want to give up reading because it is fun, and that they sometimes become totally absorbed in reading (see Table 4.1, Annex B1). Figure 5.5b shows the pattern of interest in mathematics and performance on the mathematical literacy scale (see Table 4.2, Annex B1).

Figures 5.5a and 5.5b show clearly that females tend to express greater interest in reading than males, while the reverse is the case in mathematics. Gender differences in performance in reading and mathematical literacy are thus closely mirrored in student interest in the respective subject areas. Higher interest in reading for females is true in all countries (see Table 4.6, Annex B1), with differences larger than half a standard deviation in 13 countries. The smallest gender differences are found for students in Hong Kong-China, Korea, Mexico and Thailand. Except for Korea, these small differences are generally due to positive views of males towards reading. In mathematics (see Table 4.7, Annex B1), the majority of countries show males to have higher interest for mathematics, with Portugal and FYR Macedonia the only two countries where females report a higher level of interest than males. Liechtenstein, the Netherlands, Norway and Switzerland show the largest differences on interest in mathematics and favour males.

The causal nature of this relationship associating interest with performance cannot be asserted from these data, and causality is no doubt complex in that interest and performance reinforce one another. Nonethe-

Figure 5.5b

Relationship between interest in mathematics and performance on the mathematical literacy scale for males and females

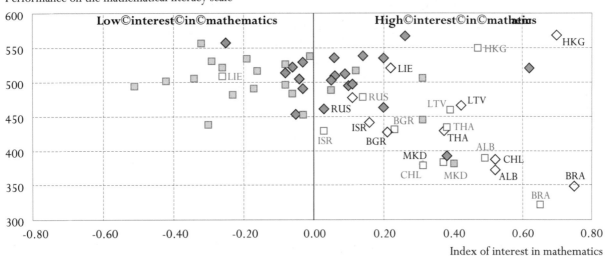

Note: For the definition of the indices, see Annex A1.
Source: OECD PISA database, 2003. Tables 4.6 and 4.7.

less, the fact that subject interest differs consistently between the genders and that it is so closely interrelated with learning outcomes in the respective domains is, in itself, of relevance for policy development. It reveals inequalities between the genders in the way schools and societies promote motivation and interest in the different subject areas.

Gender differences in engagement in reading

Gender differences in favour of females are also reflected in the broader engagement of students in reading activities, which PISA measures through self-reports on the frequency with which students read for pleasure, enjoy talking about books, visit bookstores and libraries, spend time reading for enjoyment, the diversity and content of the materials they read, and their interest and attitudes towards reading.

Figure 5.6 shows the relationship between engagement in reading for males and females. In all participating countries females have higher levels of engagement in reading than males. Only in Korea and Peru the differences are almost non-existent. The largest differences are found in Austria, Brazil, the Czech Republic, Finland, Germany, Norway and Switzerland, where the differences in engagement in reading between females and males are larger than half of one standard deviation. Females in Albania, Denmark, Finland, Hong Kong-China and FYR Macedonia and males in Albania, Hong Kong-China, FYR Macedonia and Peru show the highest levels of engagement in reading. Finland and Hong Kong-China are two countries where

Figure 5.6

Gender differences in engagement in reading

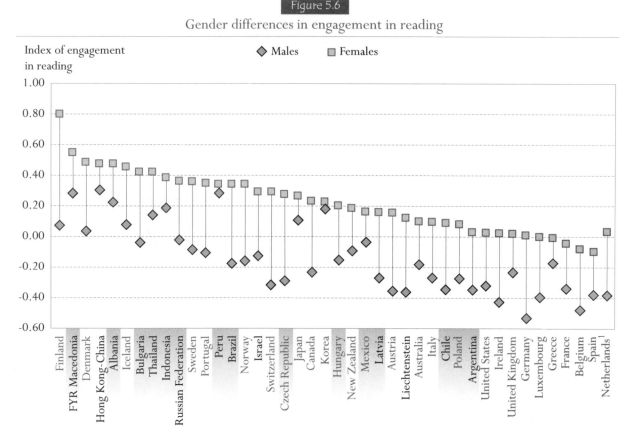

1. Response rate is too low to ensure comparability (see Annex A3).
Note: For the definition of the indices, see Annex A1.
Source: OECD PISA database, 2003. Table 4.4.

high engagement in reading is associated with high performance in reading, but it is important to note that in Finland very large differences in engagement in reading are found, with females showing a level of reading engagement at 0.82 and males 0.08. In Hong Kong-China this difference is much smaller, with males showing levels of engagement at 0.30, below the females' level of 0.49 (see Table 4.4, Annex B1).

The index of engagement in reading examines three important aspects for engagement and the next sections will examine these aspects independently. The first of these aspects is students' general attitude towards reading. Figure 5.7 shows how countries differ with regard to the attitudes of males and females towards several statements about reading. The average percentages for OECD countries, as well as the individual values for each non-OECD member country are included in this graph, with male and female students shown separately. There appears to be only limited engagement in reading among 15-year-old males beyond what is required of them. On average across the OECD countries, 46 per cent of male students agree with the statement that they "read only if they have to," whereas this is true for only 26 per cent of female students. Although this difference is larger than 20 per cent in half of the participating countries, students from the five eastern Asian countries - Hong Kong-China, Indonesia, Japan, Korea and Thailand – show this difference to be less than 10 per cent. However, the percentage of students agreeing with this

Figure 5.7

Gender differences in engagement in reading – attitudes towards reading
Distribution of mean percentages of males and females who agree or strongly agree with the following statements

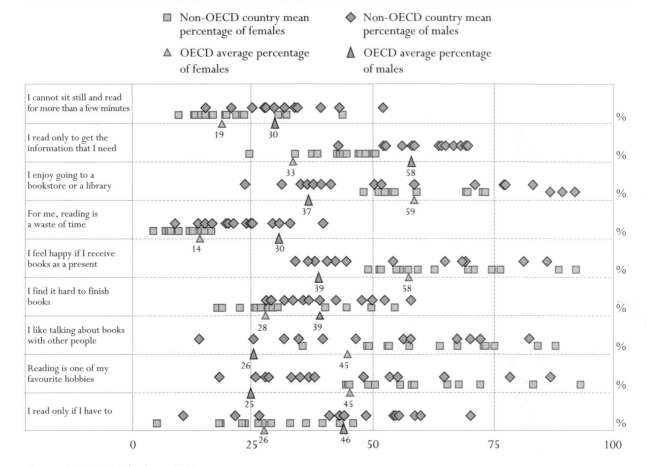

Source: OECD PISA database, 2003.

statement is extremely high in four of these countries. In Thailand, for example, 61 per cent of females and 70 per cent of males read only if they have to. In 17 of the participating countries the percentage of males is higher than 50 per cent. On the other hand, more than 50 per cent of the males in Albania, Indonesia, FYR Macedonia, Mexico and Peru consider "reading as one of their favourite hobbies".

Fifty-eight per cent of males (compared with 33 per cent of females) report that they read only to get the information they need. This figure is particularly high in Argentina, Chile, Latvia and the Russian Federation, where between 68 and 70 per cent of males and less than 50 per cent of females read with this in mind. More alarming is the finding that twice as many males as females see reading as a waste of time. In 25 out of the 42 participating countries between a quarter and half of the male students see reading as a waste of time.

Together, these data suggest that many education systems have not been able to sufficiently engage students – especially males – in reading activities.

Considering the above results, it is perhaps not unexpected that males also tend to spend much less time reading for enjoyment than females. On average across participating countries, 49 per cent of females report that they read for enjoyment for more than 30 minutes each day. The proportion ranges from 27 per cent of females in Japan to more than twice that figure in Albania, Brazil, Bulgaria, Chile, the Czech Republic, Finland, Indonesia, Latvia, Peru, Poland, Portugal and the Russian Federation. The comparable figure for males is 30 per cent, with the proportion ranging from 20 per cent or less in Austria, the Netherlands and Switzerland to over 40 per cent in Greece, Korea and Poland (see Figure 5.8 and Table 5.5, Annex

Figure 5.8

Gender differences in engagement in reading – time spent reading for enjoyment
Percentages of males and females who read for more than 30 minutes per day for enjoyment

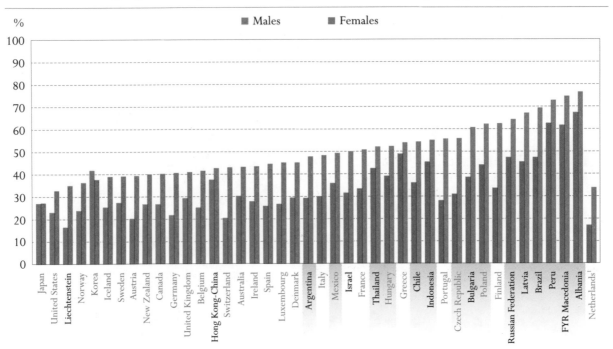

1. Response rate is too low to ensure comparability (see Annex A3).
Source: OECD PISA database, 2003. Table 5.5.

B1). The fact that 21 per cent of females and 36 per cent of males report not reading for enjoyment at all warrants attention. This is particularly striking for Japan, where 55 per cent of females report not reading for enjoyment, and in the Austria, Belgium, Germany, Japan, the Netherlands and the United States, where more than 50 per cent of males do not read for enjoyment.

Although these findings do not permit the establishment of causal links, they suggest that the differing reading habits of females and males may have far-reaching consequences for learning that need to be addressed if gender equality is to be achieved within school systems.

Finally, 15-year-old males and females differ not only with regard to their engagement in reading, but also in the materials that they read voluntarily (Figure 5.9, Table 5.6). On average across OECD countries, females are more likely than males to read fiction books (37 per cent of females read fiction books several times per month or several times per week compared with 19 per cent of males) and magazines. Males are more likely than females to read newspapers (68 per cent of males read newspapers several times per month or per week compared with 60 per cent of females), comic books (35 per cent of males several times per month or per week, compared with 24 per cent of females) and e-mails and Web pages (50 per cent of males several times per month or per week, and 40 per cent of females). Females and males are, on average across countries, equally likely to read non-fiction (19 per cent of both females and males several times per month or per week). Countries do, however, vary widely with regard to the diversity of reading material that males and females report to read.

Figure 5.9

Gender differences in engagement in reading – diversity of reading materials
Distribution of mean percentages of males and females who report reading the following materials several times a month or several times per week

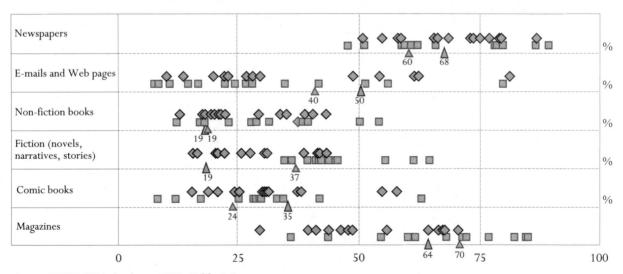

Source: OECD PISA database, 2003. Table 5.6.

Figure 5.10

Percentage of students in each reading profile cluster, by gender

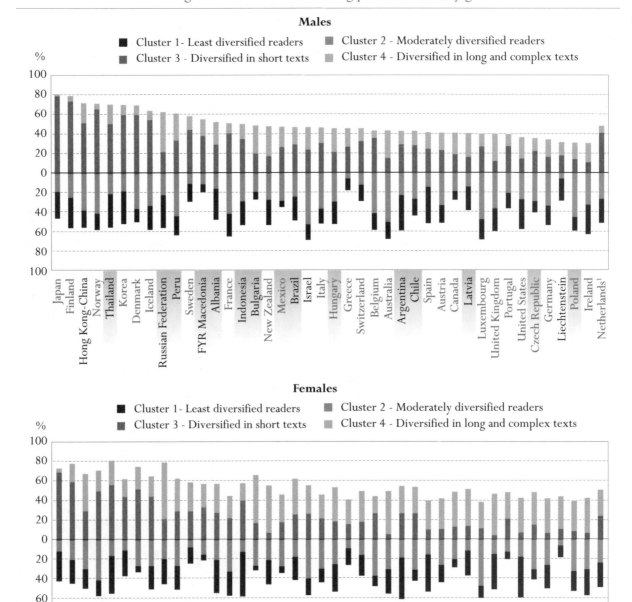

1. Response rate is too low to ensure comparability (see Annex A3).
Source: OECD PISA database, 2003. Table 5.7.

In addition to examining these three aspects of reading separately — frequency, diversity and time spent on reading for enjoyment — students were also grouped into four broad reader profiles, or "clusters," according to the frequency and diversity of the material students read, such as magazines, comic books, newspapers, and fiction and non-fiction books[5]. The mean percentages of students, by gender, in each of these clusters is shown in Figure 5.10 and Table 5.7.

Cluster 1 represents the least diversified readers among the four clusters. Students in this cluster frequently read magazines with a very small percentage reading fiction or comics. At the international level approximately one-fifth of the students are in this cluster, but this distribution varies considerably when examined at the country level (see Chapter 4) and at the gender level. The percentage of males in this cluster ranges from less than 10 per cent in Finland, Hong Kong-China, Iceland and Norway to more than 30 per cent in nine countries including the four Latin American countries — Argentina, Brazil, Chile and Mexico. The situation of females varies substantially. In addition to Finland, Hong Kong-China, Iceland and Norway, also Bulgaria and the Russian Federation show percentages of females below 10 per cent. The largest differences occurred in Greece (20 per cent more females than males) and Thailand (10 per cent more males than females). Nine of the non-member countries showed a higher percentage of males than females in this cluster.

Cluster 2 comprises the moderately diversified readers, who often read magazines and newspapers. Very low percentage of males and females in Japan and Thailand are in this cluster. More than 50 per cent of males are in this cluster in Liechtenstein and Ireland. Among the non-OECD countries, Argentina, Chile, Latvia, Peru and Thailand show very small differences between males and females. From all participating countries, 15 per cent more males than females are classified in this cluster in the Czech Republic, Greece, Liechtenstein and Portugal.

Students classified in Cluster 3 are more diversified in short texts and are moderate readers of fiction. At the OECD level, this cluster holds the largest proportion of males at 34 per cent. More than 50 per cent of males in 8 countries, including the four Asian countries — Hong Kong-China, Japan, Korea and Thailand are in this cluster as opposed to 30 per cent of females in Hong Kong-China (the largest difference between males and females in Cluster 3), 44 per cent in Korea, 57 per cent in Thailand, with the highest percentage found in Japan — 70 per cent.

Cluster 4 represents the most diversified readers, but focusing on longer texts. At the OECD level, 29 per cent of females are in this cluster — the largest among all four clusters.

Except for Israel, in all of the non-OECD countries, the majority of females are in Clusters 3 or 4, more diversified readers. Japan, Finland and Korea show very high percentages of students in Cluster 3 while Hong Kong-China shows high percentages of males only. Chile, Argentina and Brazil show the highest percentages of males in Cluster 1 while the highest percentages of females are in Clusters 3 or 4. The English speaking countries — Australia, Canada, Ireland, New Zealand, United Kingdom and the United States — all show the highest percentage of males in Cluster 2 while females in these countries are mostly classified in Cluster 4 (except for Ireland).

Gender differences in learning strategies and self-concept

Chapter 4 provided an overall profile of student learning strategies that 15-year-old students report to employ. This chapter extends this analysis to an examination of important differences in self-reports about learning strategies among males and females.

In the majority of countries, 15-year-old females report emphasising memorisation strategies more than males, with only three countries showing a statistically significant difference in the other direction (see Table 4.6, Annex B1). Conversely, males report using elaboration strategies more often than females, there being only one country in which a statistically significant proportion of females report more frequent use of elaboration strategies (see Table 4.7, Annex B1).

In almost all countries with statistically significant gender differences, however, females report using control strategies more often than males (see Table 4.9, Annex B1). This suggests that females are more likely to adopt a self-evaluating perspective during the learning process, although, in most countries they could benefit from training in the use of elaboration strategies. Males, on the other hand, could benefit from more general assistance in planning, organising and structuring learning activities.

Finally, there is abundant evidence that individuals' beliefs about themselves are strongly related to successful learning. Successful learners are confident of their abilities and believe that investment in learning can make a difference. Students with high self-concept are likely to approach school-related tasks with confidence, and success on those tasks reinforces this confidence. The opposite pattern is likely to occur for children with low academic self-concepts. Additionally, students who lack confidence in their ability to learn what they judge to be important are exposed to failure, not only at school but also in their adult lives. For this reason, PISA examined students' "self-concept" in reading and mathematics. This is shown in two indices that summarise student responses to a series of related questions on self-concept that, in turn, were selected from constructs used in previous research (see also Annex A1). The scale used in the indices places two-thirds of the OECD student population between the values of -1 and 1, with an average score of zero.

Figure 5.11a shows the relationship between self-concept in reading and performance on the combined reading literacy scale. The symbols represent the average position of males (represented by diamonds) and females (represented by squares) in participating countries. In 20 out of 26 countries, females state more frequently that they receive good marks in language-related subjects and that they learn things quickly. The differences are especially pronounced in Albania, Bulgaria, Finland, Germany, Italy and the United States (see Table 5.8a, Annex B1). In the remaining countries, namely Brazil, Latvia, Liechtenstein, the Netherlands and the Russian Federation males showed higher levels of self-concept in reading than females. Female students in Denmark, Italy, FYR Macedonia and the United States show the highest levels of self-concept in reading.

In all countries (see Figure 5.11b) males tend to express a higher level of self-concept in mathematics than females, particularly in Germany, the Netherlands, Norway and Switzerland (see Table 5.8b, Annex B1). These gender differences have a close relationship with gender differences in student performance in reading and mathematics. PISA suggests that self-concept relates positively to student performance, more so in mathematics than in reading. All this suggests that gender differences in student performance need to be reviewed and analysed in close relationship with the habits, attitudes and self-concepts of young males and females.

Figure 5.11a

Relationship between self-concept in reading and performance on the combined reading literacy scale, by gender

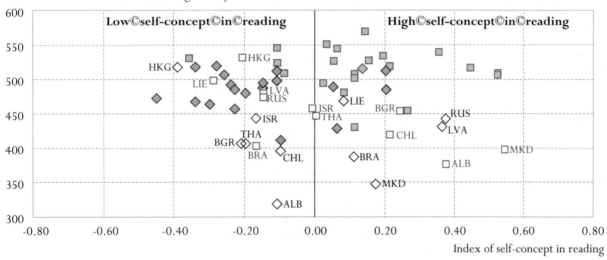

Note: For the definition of the indices, see Annex A1.
Source: OECD PISA database, 2003. Tables 5.8a and 5.8b.

Figure 5.11b

Relationship between self-concept in mathematics and performance on the mathematical literacy scale, by gender

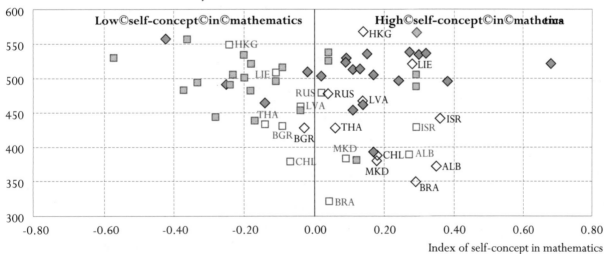

Note: For the definition of the indices, see Annex A1.
Source: OECD PISA database, 2003. Tables 5.8a and 5.8b.

Gender differences in approaches for learning - competitive versus co-operative learning

PISA also examined students' reports on the extent to which they feel comfortable with co-operative and competitive learning styles. In co-operative learning, students work in groups to achieve shared goals. In competitive learning, students usually achieve goals that only few can attain.

Figure 5.12 shows differences between males and females concerning their preference for competitive or co-operative learning styles (see Tables 4.12 and 4.13, Annex B1). With the exception of Korea, in all countries female students show a higher level of comfort with a co-operative learning approach than

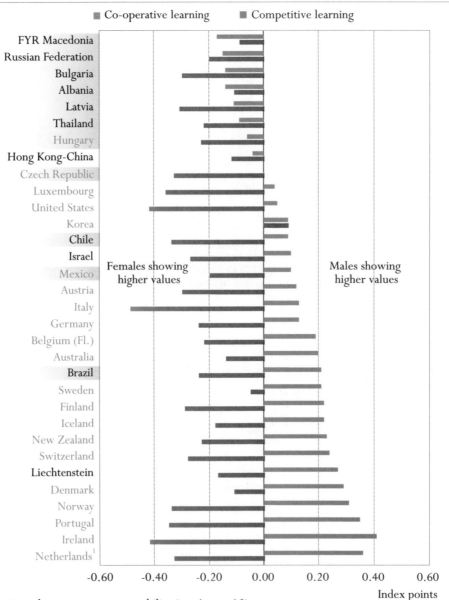

Figure 5.12

Gender differences in learning style preferences

■ Co-operative learning   ■ Competitive learning

1. Response rate is too low to ensure comparability (see Annex A3).
Note: For the definitions of the indexes, see Annex A1.
Source: OECD PISA database, 2003. Tables 4.12 and 4.13.

males. This is particularly true for Italy, United States and Ireland. For co-operative learning, gender patterns are less pronounced and vary across countries.

Conclusions

Policy-makers have given considerable priority to issues of gender equality, with particular attention being paid to the disadvantages faced by females. The results of PISA point to successful efforts in many countries but also to a growing problem for males, particularly in reading literacy and at the lower tail of the performance distribution. In mathematics, females on average remain at a disadvantage in many countries, but in those countries where this persists the advantage of males is mainly due to high levels of performance of a comparatively small number of males.

At the same time, there is significant variation between countries in the size of gender differences. The evidence from those countries where females are no longer at a disadvantage is that effective policies and practices can overcome what were long taken to be the inevitable outcomes of differences between males and females in learning style - and even in underlying capacities. Indeed, the results of PISA make clear that some countries provide a learning environment or broader context that benefits both genders equally. The enduring differences in other countries, as well as the widespread disadvantage now faced by young males in reading literacy, require serious policy attention.

The analysis also reveals inequalities between the genders in the effectiveness with which schools and societies promote motivation and interest in different subject areas. The close interrelationship between subject interest and learning outcomes also suggests that the differing habits and interests of young females and males have far-reaching consequences for learning, and that education policy needs to address these consequences.

Education systems have made significant strides towards closing the gender gap in educational attainment in recent decades (OECD, 2001*a*), but much remains to be done. At age 15, many students are about to face the transition from education to work. Their performance at school along with their motivation and attitudes in different subject areas can have a significant influence on their further educational and occupational pathways. These pathways, in turn, will have an impact not only on individual career and salary prospects, but also on the broader effectiveness with which human capital is developed and utilised in modern economies and societies. Improving the level of engagement of males in reading activities, and stimulating interest and self-concept among females in mathematics, need to be major policy objectives if greater gender equality in educational outcomes is to be achieved.

Notes

1. *White-collar high-skilled*: Legislators, senior officials and managers, and professional, technicians and associate professionals.

2. *White-collar low-skilled*: Service workers and shop and market sales workers and clerks.

3. *Blue-collar high-skilled*: Skilled agricultural and fishery workers and craft and related trades workers.

4. *Blue-collar low-skilled*: Plant and machine operators and assemblers and elementary occupations.

5. See the PISA thematic report *Reading for Change* (OECD, 2002b), Chapter 5, for further information on the cluster analysis.

FAMILY BACKGROUND AND LITERACY PERFORMANCE

Introduction

Students' learning is influenced by an interplay of their individual, family and school characteristics. Families differ widely in how they shape their children's behaviour and attitudes towards schools and in their ability to provide learning opportunities for their children. Such differences influence children's readiness to learn even before they come to school. As children progress through the school system, the early differences in their academic competencies may be either reduced or exacerbated depending upon their schooling experiences.

To ensure that children reach their full potential, it is important for educational systems to provide appropriate and equitable learning opportunities to students from all family backgrounds. If policies are successful, students in an educational system would have high levels of average performance. At the same time, there would be small gaps between females and males, individuals from disadvantaged and well-to-do families, and students in rural and urban areas. How successful are the educational systems in the PISA countries in achieving an equitable distribution of literacy performance among their 15-year-old students? If some countries are able to achieve high levels of learning outcomes for students from different backgrounds, the implication for others is that it is feasible to meet both equity and quality goals.

By identifying the characteristics of students most likely to perform poorly, educators and policy-makers can determine where best to intervene in order to ensure the successful learning of all students. Similarly, in order for policy-makers to promote high levels of performance it is useful to identify the characteristics of students who are successful academically despite adverse family conditions.

This chapter looks at how the literacy performance compares across students from different family backgrounds. Family background in this case is measured by the occupational status and educational attainment of their parents, home possessions, the country of birth and the language spoken at home. The chapter explores whether trade-offs between high levels of performance and inequality in literacy performance are inevitable. It also looks at the potential role of policies that promote reading engagement in compensating for disadvantaged family backgrounds.

Social, economic and cultural factors that influence schooling

Family characteristics are a major source of disparity in students' educational outcomes. More family financial resources, which are associated with parents' occupation and educational attainment, often imply increased learning opportunities both at home and in school. Better-educated parents can contribute to their children's learning through their day-to-day interactions with their children and involving themselves in their children's school work. With their social networks and knowledge of social norms, better-educated parents – who often also have better jobs – also tend to be able to offer more educational and career options for their children, which may have an impact on children's motivation to learn. Parents with higher occupational status and educational attainment may also have higher aspirations and expectations for their children's occupation and education, which in turn can influence their commitment to learning.

PISA captures a number of family economic, social and cultural characteristics as reported by students. The following measures are used in this report:

- *Parental occupational status*, which is measured by the *international socio-economic index of occupational status* and that captures the attributes of occupation that convert a person's education into income

(Ganzelboom *et al.*, 1992). The index is constructed in such a way that greater values represent higher occupational status. The index has a mean of 49 and a standard deviation of 16 for all OECD countries.

- **Home possessions**, which includes an *index of family wealth* and an *index of possessions related to "classical" culture* in the family home. The *index of family wealth* is based on student reports on availability of various items at home. The *index of cultural possessions* is based on students' responses to questions regarding whether they have assess to classic literature, books of poetry and works of art (such as paintings) in their homes. The OECD countries were used as a benchmark to create these summary indices. Thus for the OECD countries as a group the three indices have a mean of zero and standard deviation of one. Greater values represent more possessions and smaller values indicate fewer possessions.

- **Parents' educational attainment,** which is indicated by three highest levels of schooling that the student's mother completed: primary or lower secondary, upper secondary and tertiary. These categories are defined on the basis of the International Standard Classification of Education (ISCED, OECD, 1999*b*) and are therefore internationally comparable.

Parental occupational status

PISA data consistently show a relationship between advantaged family backgrounds and higher levels of literacy performance for students in every country. Figure 6.1 demonstrates the differences in performance in reading literacy that are associated with the international socio-economic index of parents' occupational status within each country. As can be seen, in every country, students in a higher quartile on the socio-economic index perform, on average, better than their counterparts in a lower quartile on the index in all three domains (see Tables 6.1a, 6.1b and 6.1c, Annex B1).

However, while visible in all countries, the effects of parental occupational status on literacy performance are different across the PISA countries. This can be seen in the differences in reading scores between students in the top and bottom national quartiles on the index of parental occupational status. These differences range from 33 points in Korea to 115 points in Switzerland. In half of the non-OECD countries, these differences are either equal to, or larger than, 81 points, which is the average difference for OECD countries as a whole. While such differences in terms of points on the combined literacy scale are 40 in Hong Kong-China, 46 in Thailand and 62 in Indonesia, they are 100 in Peru and 104 in Argentina.

The cross-country variation of the influence of parental occupational status on literacy performance can also be seen in the last two columns of Table 6.1a. The data here suggest that with each standard deviation difference on the index of parental occupational status (16.3 units), the difference in performance on the combined literacy scale ranges from almost 15 points in Korea, 19 points in Iceland, 20 points in Hong Kong-China, 21 points in Finland, Indonesia, Thailand and Latvia to 39 points or more in Bulgaria, Chile, Luxembourg, Hungary, Switzerland, the Czech Republic and Germany. The last column of Table 6.1a also suggests that students in the bottom national quartile of the index of parental occupational status are less likely to be in the bottom quartile of the literacy performance scale in Asian and Scandinavian countries than in several countries in Central and Eastern Europe, as well as in Switzerland, Germany, Luxembourg and Belgium.

Differences in literacy performance associated with parental occupational status are, however, relative across countries. A student in the bottom quartile of the index of parental occupational status in one country may perform at a very different level than a counterpart in the bottom quartile of the index in another country. Figure 6.1 and Table 6.1a show that the average scores of students in the bottom quartile are 508

Figure 6.1

Occupational status of parents and student performance

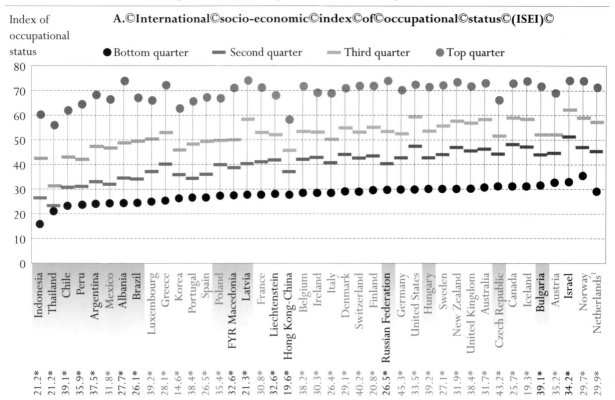

A. International socio-economic index of occupational status (ISEI)

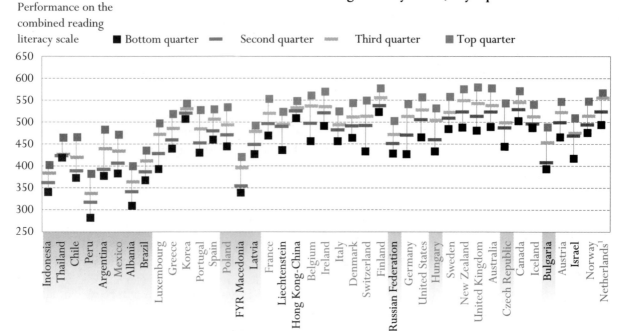

B. Performance on the combined reading literacy scale, by quarter of the index

*Change in the combined reading literacy score per 16.3 units of the international socio-economic index of occupational status
1. Response rate is too low to ensure comparability (see Annex A3).
Note: For the definition of the index see Annex A1.
Source: OECD PISA database, 2003. Table 6.1a.

points in Hong Kong-China, 445 points in the Czech Republic and Poland and 435 in Hungary – all higher than the average scores of students in the top quartile in Peru (383 points), Albania (400 points), Indonesia (403 points) and FYR Macedonia (420 points).

Family wealth

Table 6.2 shows the average scores on the combined reading literacy scale of students by quartiles on the index of family wealth. In every country except Albania and Iceland, students from wealthier families on average tend to have higher reading scores. The difference in performance on the combined reading literacy scale between the top and bottom quartiles of the index of family wealth is 34 points for OECD countries on average. The average difference, however, should not mask wide variation across PISA countries. The gaps in reading scores between the top and bottom quartiles of the index of family wealth range from 16 points or less in Japan, Latvia, FYR Macedonia, Norway and Sweden to 91 points in Argentina. These gaps are particularly large in the United States (85 points), Chile (82 points), Israel (77 points), Portugal (75 points), Mexico (72 points), Peru (70 points) and Brazil (67 points). Table 6.2 also shows that with each unit change on the national index of family wealth, the differences in the performance on the combined literacy scale are as large as 25 points or more in nine countries including Argentina, Brazil, Chile and Peru. Indeed it seems that in Latin American countries, the gaps in reading performance associated with the index of family wealth tend to be larger than most of the other countries.

Possessions related to "classical" culture

Figure 6.2 and Table 6.3 show the proportion of students in each quartile on the index of possessions in the family home related to "classical" culture and the average reading scores for each group. For all the OECD countries, the difference between students from the top and bottom quartiles of the index is 68 points in reading scores. The gaps in literacy performance between students from families with different levels of cultural possessions are larger in some countries than in others. The differences in mean scores on the combined literacy scale between the top and bottom quartiles of the national index of cultural possessions range from 10 points in Indonesia, 12 points in Thailand and 34 points in Peru to 86 points in Albania and 87 in Hungary and the United States to 100 points in Luxembourg. In five of the non-OECD countries, such gaps are larger than the OECD average of 68 points. The last column of Table 6.3 also shows that with each unit difference on the index of cultural possessions, the differences in performance on the combined literacy scale are approximately 4 points in Indonesia and Thailand. In contrast, such differences are almost 43 points in Bulgaria, 40 points in Albania and 34 points in Latvia. The gaps associated with cultural possessions seem smallest in the Asian countries that participated in PISA.

Parental education

Another aspect of family background is the level of educational attainment of parents. Figure 6.3 and Table 6.5 show the relationship between mothers' educational attainment and students' literacy performance. Mothers' educational attainment is chosen here because literature suggests that this is a stronger predictor of children's learning outcomes than fathers' education. In all countries students whose mothers have completed upper secondary education have on average higher levels of performance in the three domains of literacy than students whose mothers have not completed an upper secondary education. In all non-OECD countries but the Asian ones, the gaps in mean reading scores between students whose mothers have completed upper secondary education and those whose mothers have not are 47 points or higher. In comparison, the mean difference for all OECD countries is 44 points. The gaps are particularly large in FYR Macedonia (78 points), Bulgaria (69 points), Argentina (63 points) and Albania (60 points).

Figure 6.2

Cultural possessions and student performance

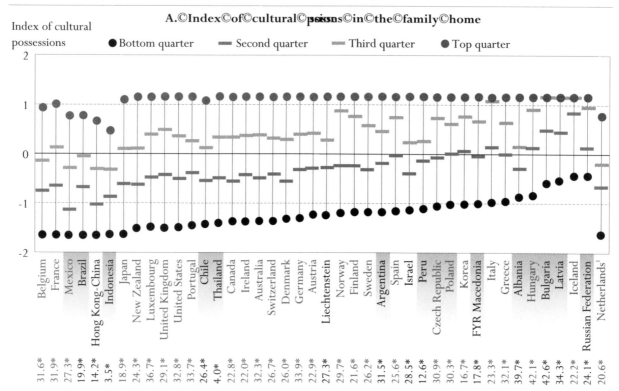

A. Index of cultural possessions in the family home

B. Performance on the combined reading literacy scale, by quarter of the index

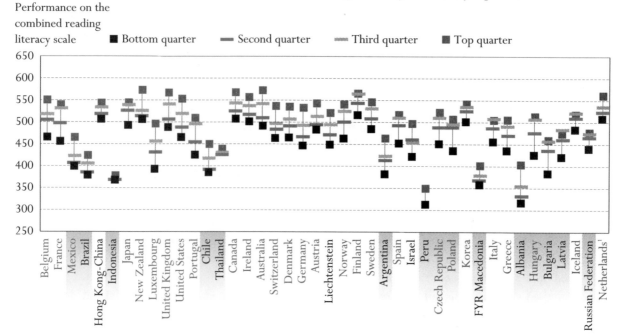

*Change in the combined reading literacy score per unit of the index of cultural possessions
1. Response rate is too low to ensure comparability (see Annex A3).
Note: For the definition of the index see Annex A1.
Source: OECD PISA database, 2003. Table 6.3.

In most countries, students whose mothers have completed tertiary education perform even better than those whose mothers have completed upper secondary education, particularly in Bulgaria (60 points) and Israel (43 points).

The extent of disadvantage associated with those students whose mothers have not completed upper secondary education is evident in the second panel of Figure 6.3. It shows that these students are on average much more likely to be among the bottom quartile of the national distribution in reading performance than the rest of the students .

The "low" levels of literacy performance of students whose mothers have not completed upper secondary education should, however, be put in perspective. In Hong Kong-China, the mean reading score of students with the least educated mothers is 518, higher than the mean scores of students whose mothers have completed upper secondary or even tertiary education in most of the other non-OECD countries. To a lesser extent, students with the least educated mothers in Liechtenstein, the Russian Federation an Thailand achieve 468, 413 and 425 points respectively on the combined reading scale, which are also higher than the mean scores of students whose mothers have completed upper secondary education in several non-OECD countries. Such results suggest that other educational and societal factors can compensate for the deficits in learning that are due to different family backgrounds.

Communication with parents on social issues and aspects of culture

Various family resources – financial, social and cultural – are important for students' educational pursuits in that such resources create conditions for students to succeed. Nevertheless, it is also important for parents to offer encouragement, set expectations, demonstrate interest in their children's academic work and convey their concern for their children's progress both in and out of school. Considerable research has demonstrated that parental involvement plays an important role in fostering their children's academic success.

In PISA, students reported how often they interacted or communicated with their parents in the following six areas: discussing political or social issues; discussing books, films or television programmes; listening to music together; discussing how well the student was doing in school; eating the main meal with the student; and spending time just talking. Responses to the first three questions were combined to create an *index of cultural communication* and responses to the last three questions were combined to create an *index of social communication*. Both indices were standardised to have a mean of zero and a standard deviation of one for OECD countries. Greater values indicate more frequent communication between students and their parents, while smaller values indicate less frequent communication. Note that negative values do not mean an absence of communication. Rather they mean that the communication between students and parents is less frequent than the average of OECD countries.

Students in the Russian Federation, Bulgaria and Chile report that they communicate with their parents frequently on social issues. Parents in half of the non-OECD countries -- namely Albania, Argentina, Brazil, Bulgaria, Chile, Latvia, FYR Macedonia and the Russian Federation -- also seem to communicate with their children on social issues more frequently than parents in OECD countries as a whole (see Tables 6.5 and 6.6, Annex B1 and Figure 6.4). In all non-OECD countries except Liechtenstein and Indonesia, students report that their parents communicate with them on cultural issues more often than students in OECD countries on average.

Figure 6.3
Mothers' education and student performance

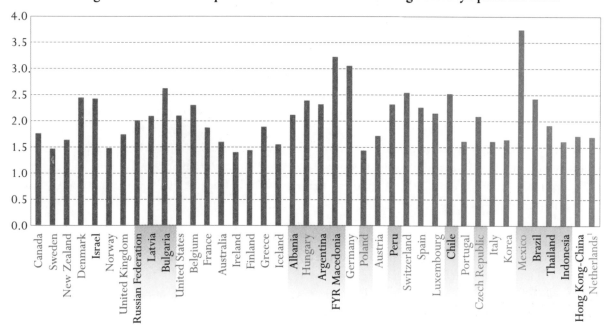

1. Response rate is too low to ensure comparability (see Annex A3).
2. For all countries, the ratio is statistically significantly greater than one.
Source: OECD PISA database, 2003. Table 6.4.

Figure 6.4

Social and cultural communication with parents and student performance
Index of social communication and index of cultural communication

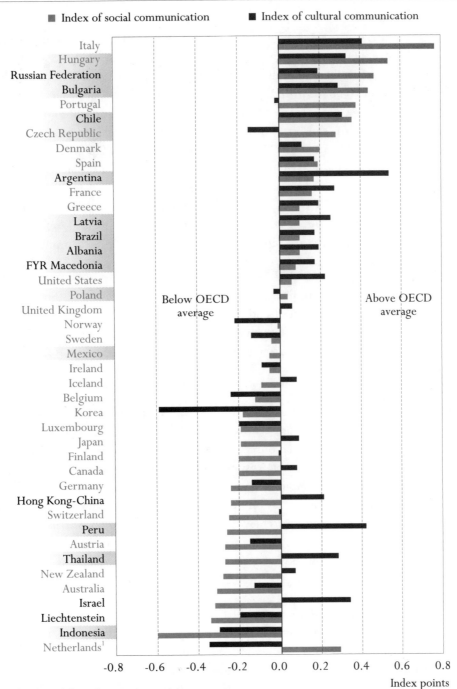

■ Index of social communication   ■ Index of cultural communication

Note: For the definition of the index see Annex A1.
1. Response rate is too low to ensure comparability (see Annex A3).
Source: OECD PISA database, 2003. Tables 6.5 and 6.6.

Students who report more frequent interaction with their parents on both social and cultural issues tend to perform better on the combined reading literacy scale in every country (see Tables 6.5 and 6.6, Annex B1). The average difference in mean reading scores between students in the top and bottom national quartiles of the index of social communication is 30 points across the OECD countries. The difference ranges from 8 points in Israel to 55 points and more in Albania, Argentina, Hong Kong-China and FYR Macedonia. In all but three non-OECD countries, the relationship between students' reading scores and communication on social issues seems to be stronger than for OECD countries on average. The evidence comes from the last column of Table 6.5 which shows that one unit change of the index of social communication is associated with a difference of more than 10 points in all the non-OECD countries except Israel, Latvia and Thailand. Cultural communication is also closely related to reading performance. The difference in mean reading scores between students in the top and bottom national quartiles of the index of social communication ranges from 31 points in Thailand to 72 points in Argentina and more than 80 points in Australia, Denmark and Portugal. The last column of Table 6.6 shows that in only four non-OECD countries is one unit change in the index of cultural communication associated with a difference of more than 20 points in the reading scores, which corresponds to the OECD average. Thus social communication is more closely related to reading scores in most non-OECD countries than cultural communication is. The opposite is true in most OECD countries, where reading scores are more closely related with cultural communication than with social communication.

These findings suggest that communication and interaction between students and their parents may help create the positive synergies between school and home environments that benefit children's academic work. A useful policy tool is to encourage parents to get more involved with their children's learning activities. This may be particularly important for students from families with limited financial resources.

Family structure

Providing a supportive learning environment at home requires parents' time as much as financial resources. Single-parent families have on average lower income than two-parent families and are thus more constrained in ensuring adequate financial resources to meet their children's learning needs. In addition, since single parents must cope with the double responsibility of work and child-rearing, it may be more challenging for them to provide and maintain a supportive learning environment for their children. The PISA questionnaire asked students for information on the family members who live at their home. Based on students' responses, their families comprise several different types. About one in every five students is from single-parent families in Argentina, Brazil, Chile, Peru, Latvia and the Russian Federation (see Table 6.7, Annex B1). By contrast, only about one in every ten or more students is from a single-parent family in Albania, Hong Kong-China, Indonesia, Israel, FYR Macedonia and Thailand.

The relative performance in reading literacy of students from single-parent families is quite mixed for the non-OECD countries. In Israel and Liechtenstein students from single-parent families, on average, perform about 24 and 18 points lower on the combined reading literacy scale than students from other types of families. To a lesser extent, students from single-parent families in Latvia and Hong Kong-China also have lower reading scores than their counterparts from other types of families. However, in other non-OECD countries, students from single-parent families have roughly similar levels of reading literacy than students from other types of families. These results are quite different from OECD countries, where students from single-parent families have reading scores that are on average 12 points lower than students from other types of families. In countries with a higher percentage of students from single-parent families, like the United Kingdom or the United States, the gaps are even larger.

As will be shown later in this chapter, the issue of family structure should be considered in the context of other family and student characteristics. The relevant questions are how to ensure students have adequate resources to meet their learning needs as well as how to facilitate productive home support for children's learning in ways that do not demand more time than single parents are able to provide.

Place of birth and home language

Aside from family structure, another important issue related to student family background is place of birth and language spoken at home. Based on students' responses, the migrant status of students is divided into three categories: "native students" were born in the country of assessment and have parents who themselves were born in the country of assessment; "first-generation students" were born in the country of assessment but their parents were foreign-born; and "non-native students" who were foreign-born and have parents who were also foreign-born. Migration seems less common in non-OECD countries participating in PISA than in OECD members. In most of the non-OECD countries that participated in PISA, the student population from migrant families is quite small (see Table 6.8, Annex B1 and upper panel of Figure 6.5), and only a few of them have sizeable proportions of students who are "non-native students." These are Latvia (20.6 per cent), Hong Kong-China (17.4 per cent), Liechtenstein (10.4 per cent) and Israel (8.9 per cent). In Liechtenstein, the reading performance of these three groups of students resembles that of the three groups in most OECD countries, where there are also a large numbers of "non-native" students. That is, first-generation students have lower levels of literacy performance than native students, and non-native students have the lowest levels of literacy performance. In Hong Kong-China native students and first-generation students have similar levels of literacy performance, although non-native students perform at somewhat lower levels. In Latvia and Israel, there is virtually no difference between the non-native students and the other students.

The influence of migration on students' literacy performance is complex. The differential relationships between migration status and literacy performance may be partly due to migration policies, *i.e.* the extent to which countries filter immigrants by economic or educational background. However, the fact that some countries succeed in bringing children with a migrant background to performance levels comparable to those of native students while others show large gaps could also suggest that public policy could have an impact.

For many non-native and first-generation students, the language of assessment and instruction is different from the language that is spoken at home. For some of these students, this may pose a problem when trying to acquire the necessary knowledge and skills for completing academic tasks. Table 6.9 and the lower panel of Figure 6.5 show the proportion of students for whom the language spoken at home is different from the language of test and instruction together with their average literacy scores. The proportions of students who speak a different language at home are 20.7 per cent in Liechtenstein, 9.8 per cent in Israel, 7.3 per cent in the Russian Federation, 5.3 per cent in Hong Kong-China and 3.8 per cent in Bulgaria. Large and statistically significant differences in reading scores are found only in Bulgaria (121 points), Hong Kong-China (64 points), Liechtenstein (53 points) and the Russian Federation (33 points).

Summarising the relationship between family economic, social and cultural status and literacy performance

So far, the chapter has shown how various family background characteristics are each individually related to students' literacy performance across the PISA countries. How do these these characteristics interact and jointly related to students' reading literacy performance in each country? To answer this question, an index of family economic, social and cultural status has been created. It is based on the index of parents'

Figure 6.5
Place of birth, home language and student performance

Percentage of non-native and first-generation students (left scale) and performance of non-native,
first generation and native students on the combined reading literacy scale (right scale)

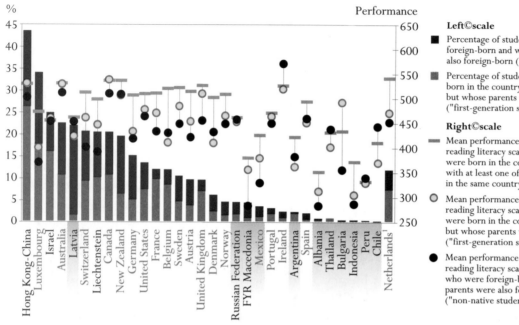

Percentage of students who speak a language at home most of the time that is different from the language of
assessment, from other official languages or from other national dialects (left scale)
and performance of students on the combined literacy scale by language group (right scale)

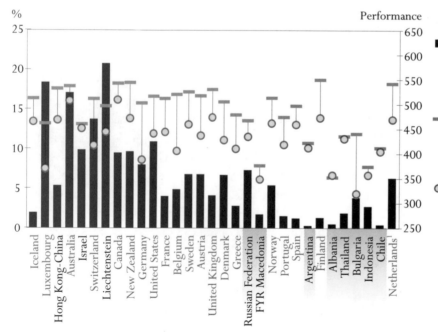

1. Response rate is too low to ensure comparability (see Annex A3).
Source: OECD PISA database, 2003. Tables 6.8 and 6.9.

occupational status and years of schooling that the parents completed as well as the indices of family wealth, home educational resources and possessions related to "classical" culture (see Annex A1 for details). The index is standardised across all the OECD countries to have a mean of zero and a standard deviation of one. Greater values represent more advantaged social backgrounds and smaller values represent less advantaged social backgrounds. A negative value implies that the social economic status is below the OECD mean, and a positive value means that it is above the OECD mean.

Figure 6.6 is a graphic presentation of the relationship between students' economic, social and cultural status and reading scores in each country. The relationship is shown in the form of social economic gradient lines. The top panel highlights high-income countries while the bottom one highlights low- and middle-income countries. Additionally, the impact of socio-economic background on student performance is represented by the type or colour of the line. Further details of the social economic gradients are also given in Table 6.10. The gradients can be understood in terms of their level, slope and length.

The level of the gradient line represents the average reading score adjusted for students' economic, social and cultural status in each country. Put differently, the level of the gradient line is the expected average reading score in a country if the economic, social and cultural background of the student population in that country were identical to the OECD average. The second column of Table 6.10 estimates the level of the gradient line for each country. In more than half of the countries, the adjusted mean reading scores that result when the level of socio-economic is accounted for, are higher than the actual mean scores. The differences are particularly striking in the low- and middle-income countries. Take Peru as example. The average student in Peru scores 327 points on the combined reading literacy scale. However, students in Peru also tend to have relatively low scores on the index of economic, social and cultural status. If students in Peru had a similar economic, social and cultural background as an average student from OECD countries, the average student in Peru would expect to have a score of 383 points on the combined reading scale, 56 points higher than their actual score Similarly, the average reading scores in Argentina, Brazil, Indonesia, Mexico, Thailand and would be raised by 36 points or more if students in these countries had similar socio-economic backgrounds as their counterparts in OECD countries do. The adjusted readings scores in Hong Kong-China – where the actual average reading scores are 525 points, well above the OECD mean – would be even higher.

Two points become evident from the above comparison. First, the average reading scores adjusted for students' socio-economic backgrounds are higher than the actual performance in many countries that perform below the OECD average, especially the poorer countries. This suggests the lower levels of students' performance in reading literacy in these countries are partly attributable to students' overall lower socio-economic status. Second, the average reading scores adjusted for students' socio-economic background in many of these are still below the OECD average of 500 points, indicating that even though the lower social economic background contributes to the lower levels of literacy performance, it is not the only reason. Attention should be paid to factors beyond students' socio-economic background in order to find effective ways to improve student learning.

Column 3 of Table 6.10 presents the slope of the gradient line – the difference in reading scores that is associated with each unit change in the index of the economic, social and cultural status. The slope of the gradient line is an indication of the extent of inequality in reading performance attributable to students' socio-economic background. Steeper gradients indicate a greater impact of family background on reading performance. In contrast, gentler gradients indicate a lower impact of family background. Figure 6.6 is a

Figure 6.6

Relationship between student performance and socio-economic background in high-income and low- and middle-income countries

- - - Below average impact of socio-economic background on student performance
——— Impact of socio-economic background not statistically different from OECD average impact
——— Above average impact of socio-economic background on student performance

A. High income countries

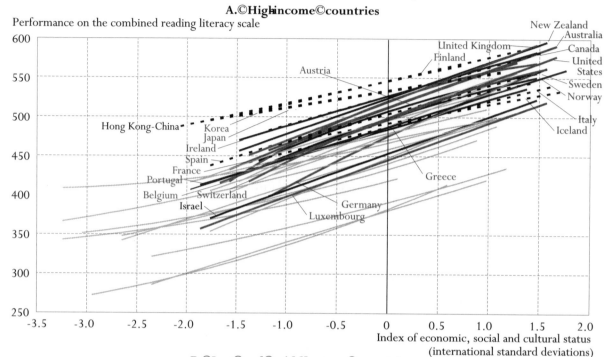

B. Low and middle income countries

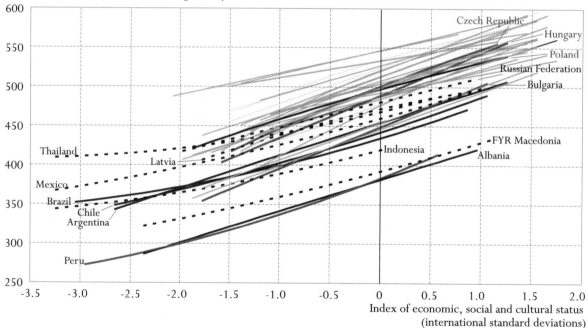

1. Response rate is too low to ensure comparability (see Annex A3).
Source: OECD PISA database, 2003. Table 6.10.

graphic display of the slopes of the gradient lines for high-income countries and low- and middle-income countries. The average slope for OECD countries can be used as a benchmark for comparing the relative levels of equality of educational outcomes between different socio-economic groups. The high-income countries that have relatively high levels of equality include Japan, Korea, Iceland, Kong-China, Sweden and Canada. By contrast, Germany, Switzerland, the United Kingdom and the United States, among others, have relatively low levels of equality. In about one-third of the high-income countries, the socio-economic gradients are not statistically significant from the OECD average

The low- and middle-income countries participating in PISA follow a similar pattern. In about one-third of these countries the performance gaps among different socio-economic groups are smaller than the OECD average. They are Indonesia, Latvia, FYR Macedonia, Mexico the Russian Federation and Thailand, In Albania, Argentina, Brazil Chile and Poland, the level of inequality in reading among various socio-economic groups is about the same as that of OECD average. Relatively large gaps in reading literacy performance are found in Bulgaria, the Czech Republic, Hungary and Peru. In general, the performance gaps associated with students' socio-economic background seem relatively moderate in Asian countries, and are quite pronounced in Germany and several Central and Eastern European countries.

Both Figure 6.6 and Table 6.10 show that the gradient lines are slightly curved in some countries. In Brazil, Chile, Indonesia, Liechtenstein, FYR Macedonia, Mexico, Peru and Thailand, and the gradients are relatively moderate at low levels of the social economic index, but they become steeper at higher levels of the index. This may indicate that differences in social economic status below a minimal level have little impact on the reading performance of students. By contrast, in Latvia, as well as Austria, Belgium and Switzerland the gradients are relatively steeper at lower levels of the socio-economic index and become moderate at higher levels of the index.

In general the curvature of the gradient line is so slight that it is hardly discernible in Figure 6.6, where the gradients look roughly straight, indicating that each increment on the index of economic, social and cultural status is associated with a roughly equal increase in the combined reading literacy score. This result suggests that it is difficult to establish a "threshold point" in terms of the economic, social and cultural status for designing special educational programmes for the most disadvantaged students in order to raise their performance. It may be that the programmes that can improve the performance of these students can equally effectively improve the performance of students from higher socio-economic backgrounds. The difficulty in establishing such a threshold point does not mean that special support for disadvantaged students is not warranted. On the contrary, many educational systems have been successful in reducing the disadvantage in the learning outcomes of female students. Carefully designed programs that meet the learning needs of students from disadvantaged family backgrounds can also be effective at reducing the disparities in learning outcomes.

The last column of Table 6.10 displays the length of the gradient line for each country that measures the range of the index of economic, social and cultural status for the middle 90 per cent of students, those between the 5th and 95th percentiles. The range of the index of economic, social and cultural status varies widely among the PISA countries, with the span noticeably large in the Latin American countries as well as in Indonesia, FYR Macedonia, Portugal and Thailand. Most of the countries with relatively large variability in students' socio-economic status are have lower levels of wealth than the richer OECD countries. They face greater challenges in meeting the learning needs of even more diverse student populations.

Is there a trade-off between quality and equity?

Educational policies in many low- and middle-income countries have long faced the dual challenge of improving overall learning outcomes while reducing disparities in access to learning opportunities. Some believe that, when resources are scarce, an effective way to raise the performance of the population is to focus the resources on a relatively limited proportion of the student population rather than to spread efforts and resources too thinly across a wide population. In other words, it is suggested that there is a trade-off between average level of learning outcomes and their equitable distribution.

PISA data throws this line of argument into serious doubt. The four areas in Figure 6.7 represent different possible scenarios for a country in terms of its overall mean reading performance and distribution of reading scores by socio-economic status. The upper right quadrant represents the most desirable scenario for education policy makers – one where a country has a high mean score and the gap in literacy performance among students from different family backgrounds is relatively small. Among the non-OECD participants of PISA, – only Hong Kong-China falls into this category. Among the OECD member countries, Korea, Japan, the three Scandinavian countries as well as Canada, Iceland and Ireland also fall into this category. The symbols in the upper-left quadrant represent countries where students display high levels of performance in reading literacy and also relatively large gaps in reading performance between students from well-to-do families and their counterparts from disadvantaged backgrounds.

All the low- and middle-income countries, both OECD and non-OECD, fall below OECD mean scores of reading literacy performance. In most of these countries, the gaps in reading scores associated with students' socio-economic backgrounds are smaller than the OECD average. Such countries are located in the lower right quadrant of the figure. Among them, Indonesia, Latvia, the Russian Federation and Thai-

Figure 6.7

Performance in reading and the impact of family background
Relationship between the average performance of countries on the PISA reading literacy scale and the socio-economic distribution of student performance

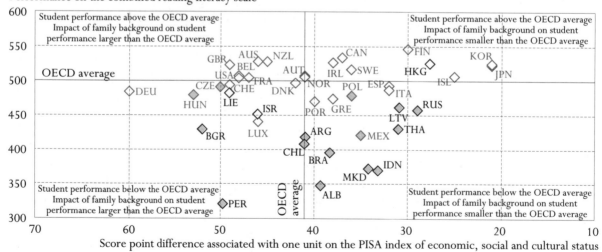

Source: OECD PISA Database, 2003, Tables 2.3a and 6.10.

land have the smallest gaps. The other low- and middle-income countries, by contrast, have relatively low average reading scores and large gaps among students from different socio-economic backgrounds. These include the Czech Republic, Bulgaria, Hungary and Peru.

Chapter 5 showed that female students in every country outperformed male students in reading performance and that the gender differences are larger in some countries than in others. Are the high-performing countries successful in reducing the female-male gaps in reading literacy? Figure 6.8 provides the mean scores and the female-male gaps in combined reading performance of individual countries. Hong Kong-China shows high mean level of performance and relatively smaller gender gap in reading performance. Argentina, Bulgaria, the Czech Republic, Hungary, Israel and Liechtenstein have scores below the OECD mean and relatively large gender gaps. On the other hand, in most of the non-OECD countries, the mean reading scores are lower than the OECD average, and the female-male gaps in reading performance are also smaller.

In summary PISA data do not suggest a direct relationship between average level of performance and the extent of inequality in performance between students from different socio-economic backgrounds and between females and males. There are countries where the performance gaps between different groups of students are small and the average reading scores are high. There are also countries where the inequalities in reading performance among different groups students are relatively pronounced yet the average levels of performance are low. High levels of performance do not necessarily occur at the expense of equity. On the contrary, it is possible for educational systems simultaneously to achieve high average levels of learning outcomes and to reduce disparities among students. In order to achieve this goal, educational policies need to consider the learning needs of different students and to provide the learning experiences that are appropriate to all students.

Figure 6.8

Relationship between gender differences and performance on the combined reading literacy scale

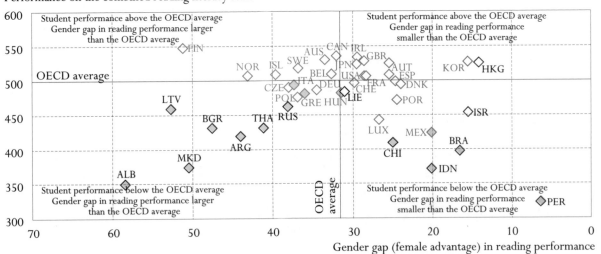

Source: OECD PISA database, 2003. Tables 2.3a and 5.2a

Importance of engagement in reading in improving literacy performance

Even though family background is an important influence on students' learning outcomes, it is important to understand that family background is not the only determinant. Examples abound of students from disadvantaged backgrounds who manage to overcome adverse conditions and to flourish in their academic pursuits. An important characteristic of such students may be how they approach learning. This analysis focuses on how engagement in reading is related to performance on the combined reading literacy scale across all countries. As described in Chapter 4, the concept of engagement in reading in PISA includes the time students report that they spend reading for pleasure, the time they spend reading a diversity of materials, and students' interest in and attitudes towards reading (see Annex A1 for a definition of the construct). The following analysis extends the discussion in Chapter 4 by examining how engagement in reading is related to reading literacy performance after taking into consideration a variety of the students' family and individual characteristics, such as gender, place of birth, family structure, number of siblings and family socio-economic status.

In order to better understand this issue, imagine a group of 1,000 students in each country with the same profile as a group sampled randomly across all the countries that participated in PISA. As the first column of Table 6.11 indicates, this group of 1000 students would, on average, contain:

- 507 females and 493 males

- 952 students born in the country of testing and 48 born outside of the country of testing

- 147 students from single-parent families

- Almost two siblings per student

- An average score of –0.23 on the index of economic, social and cultural status

- 357 students from low- and middle-income countries

- An average score of 0.051 on the index of engagement in reading

The results of the analysis are summarised in Table 6.11. The second column presents the relationship between performance on the combined reading literacy scale and various individual and family characteristics. Across all 42 countries participating in PISA, females on average scored 32 points higher than males did after taking into consideration their immigrant status, family structure, number of siblings, family economic, social and cultural status as well as the level of wealth of the country. Native or first-generation students scored 13 points higher than students born outside of the country of assessment, but the difference is, on average, not statistically significant. Once the other individual and family characteristics are considered, there is no difference in reading scores between students from single-parent families and those from two-parent families. Students with multiple siblings tend to have lower reading scores, while students with one additional sibling on average scored almost 8 points less on the combined reading literacy scale. Students from families of higher social economic status tend to have higher levels of performance on the combined reading literacy scale. A difference of one standard deviation, on the socio-economic index is associated with a difference of 36 points on the combined reading literacy scale. After considering these individual and family characteristics, students from low- and middle-income countries scored on average 53 less than their counterparts from high-income countries.

To what extent are the differences in reading scores between these various groups of students attributable to the way they approach reading? The next column of Table 6.11 provides clues to the importance of reading engagement in predicting a student's performance in reading literacy. The coefficient of the variable representing reading engagement is positive, implying that students who spend more time reading for pleasure, read a greater variety of materials and exhibit a more positive attitude towards reading. They tend to have higher scores on the combined reading literacy scale, even after taking into consideration the impact of gender, immigrant status, single-parent family status, number of siblings, economic, social and cultural status as well as the level of wealth of the country. More importantly, the coefficients on the variable representing female students become 23.6 and that for family socio-economic status 31.8. This suggests that reading engagement accounts for part of the advantage in reading performance that female students and students from more privileged family backgrounds have.

Further analysis reveals that the effects of reading engagement differ according to students' social economic backgrounds and the wealth level of the country (see the last column of Table 6.11, Annex B1). The relationship between performance in reading literacy and reading engagement is illustrated in Figure 6.9 for females and males and in Figure 6.10 for students from different socio-economic backgrounds and countries of various levels of wealth.

Figure 6.9 presents the predicted literacy scores of two pairs of female and male students who have the same family characteristics as described above but differ on the level of reading engagement. One pair – a female and male – report a higher level of reading engagement, while the other pair report a lower level of reading engagement. Hence, the first pair has a score of one standard deviation above the mean of the index of reading engagement, while the latter pair has a score of one standard deviation below the mean of the index. For the pair reporting higher level of reading engagement, the female student is expected to score 22 points more than the male student on the combined literacy scale. For the pair reporting a lower level of reading engagement, the female student also outperforms the male student by 22 points.

Figure 6.9

Expected performance for males and females with different levels of engagement in reading but the same family characteristics

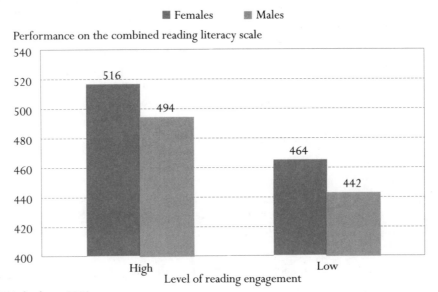

Source: OECD PISA database, 2003.

The importance of reading engagement on reading performance can be understood in the following two comparisons. First, the gap in reading scores attributable to different levels of reading engagement is far greater than differences attributable to gender. The female student with a higher level of reading engagement is predicted to score 516 while the female student with a lower level of reading engagement would score only 464. At the same time, the two male students are expected to score 494 and 442 points respectively. The difference in reading scores between the two pairs of students (52 points) is more than twice as large as between females and males from similar family backgrounds (22 points). Second, despite the persistent gender gap among students reporting similar levels of reading engagement, male students who are more engaged in reading tend to outperform female students who are less engaged in reading. Such results suggest that reading engagement is an important factor that distinguishes between high-performing and low-performing students, regardless of their gender.

Figure 6.10 presents the relationship between reading scores and socio-economic status by level of reading engagement and the country's wealth. The vertical axis represents the performance on the combined reading literacy scale, while the horizontal axis represents the index of economic, social and cultural status in standard deviations. Each point along the horizontal axis for the pair of red lines represent two groups of students from high-income countries that have the same proportion of female students, the same proportion of native or first-generation students, the same proportion of students from single-parent families and who have the same number of siblings. In fact the only difference between the two groups of students is level of reading engagement. One group reports a higher level of reading engagement and is indicated by one standard deviation above the mean on the index, while the other group reports a lower level of engagement and has a value of one standard deviation below the mean on the index. The pair of black lines represent two groups of students from low- and middle-income countries who share the same characteristics as mentioned above except the level of reading engagement.

The two pairs of lines in Figures 6.10 go upward, confirming that, across all the PISA countries, students from more advantaged family backgrounds tend to have higher levels of performance in reading literacy. In addition, at each specific point on the horizontal axis the pair of red lines lies above the pair of black lines. This pattern implies that students from high-income countries, on average, have higher reading scores than their counterparts from middle-income countries, even though they have the same value on the index of family economic, social and cultural status. Schools in richer countries tend to have better trained teachers and more resources, which may explain the better performance of students from high-income countries after considering reading engagement and the other individual and family characteristics.

Figure 6.10 shows that at each specific point of the socio-economic index the red solid line lies above the red dotted line, and the black solid line lies above the black dotted line. This suggests that students who are more engaged in reading tend to have better reading scores regardless of their socio-economic background. The effects of reading engagement seem to differ more in high-income countries than in low- and middle-income countries. Take two students for example, one spends more time reading for pleasure, reading a diversity of materials and possesses more positive attitudes towards reading. Hence the student has a score of one standard deviation above the mean on the index of reading engagement. The other student is less engaged in reading and has a score of one standard deviation below the mean. While the difference in reading scores between such students is expected to be 50 points in high-income countries, it would be 31 points in low- and middle-income countries. In Figure 6.10, the varying size of the difference is represented by the distance between each pair of the lines: the distance between the pair of red lines is larger than between the pair of black lines.

Figure 6.10

Relationship between performance in reading literacy and engagement in reading
and family socio-economic background

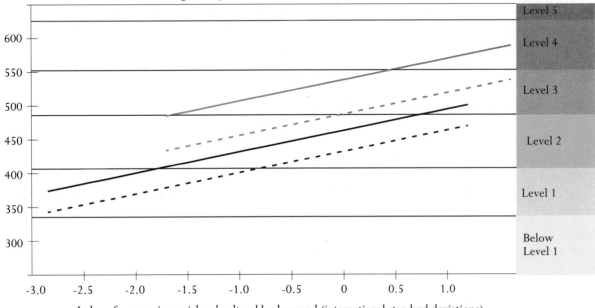

Source: OECD PISA database, 2003.

Engagement in reading appears to be an important factor that distinguishes between different levels of performance in reading literacy. Even though females in general are better readers than males, male students who are more engaged in reading tend to have higher levels of performance in reading literacy than females who are not very engaged in reading. Engagement in reading is also strongly associated with reading performance in richer countries. These results should not be taken as evidence of the causal relationship between reading engagement and reading performance. Readers who perform better may show a stronger interest in reading, spend more time reading or read a greater diversity of materials than less proficient ones. However, it would be difficult to imagine that students can become good readers without spending considerable time learning or practising reading skills. Therefore, reading engagement and reading performance may be mutually reinforcing. In this sense, an important policy tool is to encourage schools and parents to cultivate good reading habits in students.

Figure 6.10 also indicates that a large proportion of students from low- and middle-income countries would perform below the OECD average in reading literacy regardless of their level of reading engagement and socio-economic background. To the extent that a country's wealth reflects its level of spending on education, as Chapter 3 demonstrates, the gap in performance in reading literacy between richer countries and poorer countries suggests that students in poorer countries would benefit substantially from increased inputs and better school quality.

Conclusions

An important goal of educational policy is to provide appropriate and equitable opportunities that meet the learning needs of all individuals, regardless of the differences in their family backgrounds. The PISA data show that family background is a consistent source of disparity in learning outcomes in many countries. However, the fact that some countries are able to attain both a high average level of literacy performance and small disparities between students from various family backgrounds suggests that quality and equity in learning outcomes do not necessarily exist at the expense of each other. On the contrary, some countries show that it is possible to achieve educational quality and equity simultaneously.

In terms of the relationship between family background and literacy performance, this chapter shows specifically that:

• Various aspects of the family economic, social and cultural conditions have a consistent impact on the literacy performance of students in all countries. Students whose parents have better jobs and higher levels of educational attainment and who are exposed to more educational and cultural resources at home tend of have higher levels of literacy performance. Educational systems face the challenging task of compensating students from less advantaged backgrounds, for the deficit in economical, social and cultural capital they experience at home. Expanding students' knowledge of occupational choices and increasing their occupational aspirations may help them to become more motivated learners. Educational benefits can reinforced by making available literature and other cultural possessions accessible to students, especially those from poor families in low- and middle-income countries.

• Students who communicate and interact with their parents frequently on social and cultural issues tend to be better readers. An important issue is how to support parents, particularly those with limited educational attainment, to facilitate their interaction with their children and with their children's schools in ways that enhance their children's learning.

• Some countries are more successful than others in reducing the gaps in literacy performance that are related to students' family background. Significantly, however, there is no relationship between average performance and the gaps in performance related to family background. Quality and equity are not necessarily achieved at the expense of each other.

• An important distinction between students who have higher scores and those who have lower scores on the combined reading literacy scale is how they approach reading. Those who spend more time reading for pleasure, read a great variety of materials and show more positive attitudes towards reading. They tend to be better readers, regardless of their family background and the wealth level in the country that they are from. Particularly interesting is the finding that high levels of engagement in reading may potentially mitigate the adverse effects of poorer school quality in low- and middle-income countries.

These PISA findings have important implications for educational and social policies. Literacy skills are becoming crucial for the economic and social success of individuals in the many low- and middle-income economies where drastic transformation is taking place in the workplace as well as in people's daily lives. Individuals with weak skills are the most vulnerable in that they are least likely to find employment opportunities that offer the promise of economic prosperity. At a societal level, in order for development to continue and be sustained, it is important to provide appropriate learning opportunities for such individuals so that they can break this vicious cycle. This chapter shows that independent of financial, social and cultural resources, there is a role for parents and schools to play in improving the chances of their children's academic success by motivating students and encouraging them to be more engaged in reading.

SCHOOL CHARACTERISTICS AND STUDENT PERFORMANCE

Introduction

The preceding chapters focussed on differences in performance between students with different individual or family characteristics. Building on this, this chapter analyses the students' school environment and relates this to student performance patterns. Since the learning environment at school is most directly linked to educational reform, information on the policy levers that shape this learning environment and an assessment of their effectiveness is of particular relevance for educational policy.

The school environment is characterised by various elements. Some of them, like the school's physical infrastructure or typical class-size, can be easily assessed and measured. Other important factors are more difficult to measure, such as aspects of school organisation and management as well as the attitudes of both teachers and students that relate to the school climate. However, all of these aspects need to be considered to obtain an overall impression of students' learning opportunities at school.

The school environment is also characterised by peer effects among the students in each school. The same student may develop very different performance patterns depending on the motivation, performance and socio-economic background of his or her classmates. Students' individual or family characteristics that were already discussed in previous chapters of this report, must therefore be re-examined from different perspectives: What is the impact of the schools' socio-economic environment on student performance, measured by the average socio-economic background of students within the same school? To what extent do differentiation policies have an impact on this relationship?

Variation of scores and differences between schools

As shown in Chapters 2 and 3 there are considerable differences between the highest and lowest perform-ing students in all countries. This variation in performance within a given education system may result from the socio-economic backgrounds of students and schools, from the human and financial resources available to schools, from curricular differences, from selection policies and practices, and from the way in which teaching is organised and delivered. In preceding chapters, some of these differences in perform-ance were accounted for by students' individual characteristics and their family background. However, this is only part of the explanation, and the explaination needs to be further developed by considering factors which characterise schools.

Some countries have non-selective school systems that seek to provide all students with the same learning opportunities and that allow each school to cater to the full range of student performance. Other coun-tries respond to diversity directly by forming groups of students of similar performance levels through a selection process either within or between schools, with the aim of serving students according to their specific needs. In other countries, combinations of the two approaches are adopted. Even in comprehen-sive school systems, there may be significant variation between schools due to the socio-economic and cultural characteristics of the communities that the schools serve or because of geographical differences (such as differences between regions, provinces or states in federal systems, or differences between rural and urban areas). Finally, there may be significant variation between individual schools that cannot easily be measured or explained, part of which could result from differences in the quality or effectiveness of the teaching that those schools provide.

In many cases, the policies and historical patterns that shape each country's school system also affect and relate to the overall variation in student performance. Do countries with explicit tracking and streaming policies show a higher degree of overall disparity in student performance than countries that have non-selective education systems? Such questions arise especially in countries marked by large variations in overall student performance, such as Argentina, Belgium, Germany, Israel, New Zealand, Norway and the United States.

Figure 7.1 shows total variation of scores on the combined reading literacy scale in each country as a percentage of the OECD average. Total variation is represented by the total length of the bars (adding left and right hand side) and it is surrounded by a black frame wherever it exceeds the OECD average of 100 (see Table 7.1a, Annex B1). Most noticeably, it remains far below the average in all Asian countries in PISA, *i.e.,* in Hong Kong-China, Indonesia, Japan, Korea and Thailand. The situation is similar for mathematical and scientific literacy (see Table 7.1b, Annex B1).

In order to assess the impact of school characteristics on performance patterns, it is useful to consider the extent to which overall variation in student performance within each country can be attributed to performance differences between schools rather than to variation between students within schools. If variation between students within a given school environment accounts for most of the overall variation, then school characteristics do not play a dominant role in explaining student performance. If, however, performance differences between schools account for a significant part of total variation, then school characteristics may have an important impact and therefore would be highly relevant levers for educational policy.

The share of performance differences between schools in total variation is represented by the length of the bar to the left of the vertical line down the centre of Figure 7.1, and variation within schools is represented by the length of the bar to the right of that vertical line. Longer segments to the left of the vertical line indicate greater variation in the mean performance of schools. Longer segments to the right of the vertical line indicate greater variation among students within schools.

As shown in Figure 7.1, in most countries a considerable proportion of the variation in student performance lies between schools. In 25 countries, differences between schools exceed one third of the overall variation in student performance of a typical OECD country. These are the countries depicted in the upper part of Figure 7.1 (above the United Kingdom). Independently of whether overall variation is large or small, between-school variation amounts to more than half of total variation in 13 countries and accounts for about 60 per cent or more in Austria, Belgium, Germany, Hungary and Poland. While non-OECD countries do not belong to the five most extreme cases, with the exception of Latvia and Thailand, they all show larger performance differences between schools than at the OECD average where between-school variance represents 35 per cent of the total variation in student performance. This means that in all of these countries students encounter a quite different learning environment in terms of average academic standards. Furthermore, these differences in academic standards may be closely related to differences in the learning environment offered by the respective schools and their local communities, *i.e.,* their equipment, management, social intake, learning climate etc.

To some extent, the large cross-country differences that can be observed from Iceland at one end of the scale to Belgium at the other end, may be related to countries' deliberate decisions to create homogeneous school environments. If countries choose education policies which favour within-school homogeneity this can easily translate into higher between-school variation. In some countries, it is widely believed that overall performance levels are maximised by stratification policies that track or stream students into homogenous groups. However, as already pointed out in other reports (OECD, 2001*b*, Chapter 2), this belief is not empirically supported by the PISA data. In fact, cross-country comparisons reveal a negative

Figure 7.1

Variation in student performance between schools and within schools
on the combined reading literacy scale

Expressed as a percentage of the average variation in student performance in OECD countries

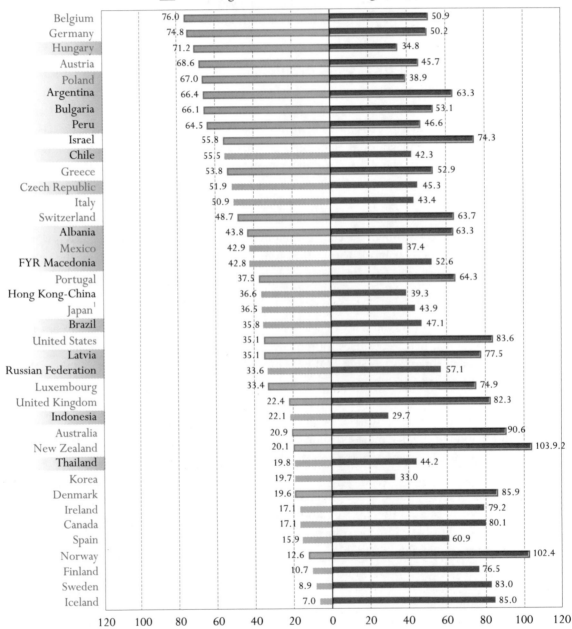

■ Between-school variance
■ Within-school variance
☐ Variance greater than the OECD average (100)

Country	Between-school variance	Within-school variance
Belgium	76.0	50.9
Germany	74.8	50.2
Hungary	71.2	34.8
Austria	68.6	45.7
Poland	67.0	38.9
Argentina	66.4	63.3
Bulgaria	66.1	53.1
Peru	64.5	46.6
Israel	55.8	74.3
Chile	55.5	42.3
Greece	53.8	52.9
Czech Republic	51.9	45.3
Italy	50.9	43.4
Switzerland	48.7	63.7
Albania	43.8	63.3
Mexico	42.9	37.4
FYR Macedonia	42.8	52.6
Portugal	37.5	64.3
Hong Kong-China	36.6	39.3
Japan[1]	36.5	43.9
Brazil	35.8	47.1
United States	35.1	83.6
Latvia	35.1	77.5
Russian Federation	33.6	57.1
Luxembourg	33.4	74.9
United Kingdom	22.4	82.3
Indonesia	22.1	29.7
Australia	20.9	90.6
New Zealand	20.1	103.9.2
Thailand	19.8	44.2
Korea	19.7	33.0
Denmark	19.6	85.9
Ireland	17.1	79.2
Canada	17.1	80.1
Spain	15.9	60.9
Norway	12.6	102.4
Finland	10.7	76.5
Sweden	8.9	83.0
Iceland	7.0	85.0

120   100   80   60   40   20   0   20   40   60   80   100   120

1. Due to the sampling methods, the between-school variance in Japan includes variation between classes
within schools.
Source: OECD PISA database, 2003. Table 7.1a.

Figure 7.2
Performance in reading and intra-school homogeneity in student performance

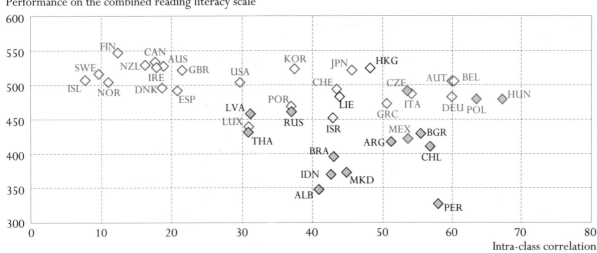

Source: OECD PISA database, 2003. Tables 2.3a and 7.1a.

relationship between the proportion of variation in student performance that is accounted for by differences between schools, on the one hand, and student performance, on the other.

The cross-country correlation coefficient between average performance on the combined reading literacy scale and the intra-class correlation is -0.43. Figure 7.2 summarises the positions of countries both with regard to their overall performance levels and the relative share of variation in student performance that is accounted for by differences between schools. The most noteworthy countries in this analysis are Finland and Sweden. These are countries with strong overall performance and, at the same time, the smallest variation in reading performance among schools, with differences between schools accounting for only between 7 and 11 per cent of the average between-student variation in OECD countries. Moreover, in these countries, performance is largely unrelated to the schools in which students are enrolled. They are thus likely to encounter a similar learning environment in terms of the distribution of students by ability. These countries thus succeed both in minimising differences between schools and in containing the overall variation in student performance in reading literacy, at an overall high level of student performance.

These results suggest that intended or unintended differentiation between schools tends to be negatively associated with overall student performance levels. These findings underline the importance of analysing both the determinants of a school environment that are conducive to successful learning and the factors that account for differences among schools. This analysis follows in the subsequent sections of this chapter.

Physical and human resources at school

A school's available physical and human resources are factors most closely associated with the quality of learning opportunities at school. They will be addressed first while other school characteristics such as school management, school climate and schools' social intake, will be discussed subsequently.

In all schools participating in PISA, principals were asked to give an appraisal of the extent to which the quality of the physical and human resources at their disposal hinders learning. It should be noted that no attempt was made to compare the quality of physical and human resources across countries. Rather, the objective was to assess the views of school principals on the relationship between the quality of the school resources and the quality of learning opportunities. While the following discussion primarily relies on these assessments, additional objective and quantitative indicators are used to complement principals' views in some cases.

Schools' infrastructure and equipment

With respect to physical resources, a distinction can be made between the physical infrastructure (*e.g.*, the condition of buildings, the instructional space, and heating, cooling and lighting systems) and educational resources (*e.g.*, computers, library material, multi-media resources, science laboratory equipment and facilities for the fine arts). Figures 7.3a and 7.3b presents the inter-quartile range of the various indices[1]. With respect to the physical infrastructure, the best-equipped quarter of schools reaches the maximum of the index in a large majority of countries, independently of their national income level. However, some of the lower income countries show considerable differences, with some schools assessed very positively and

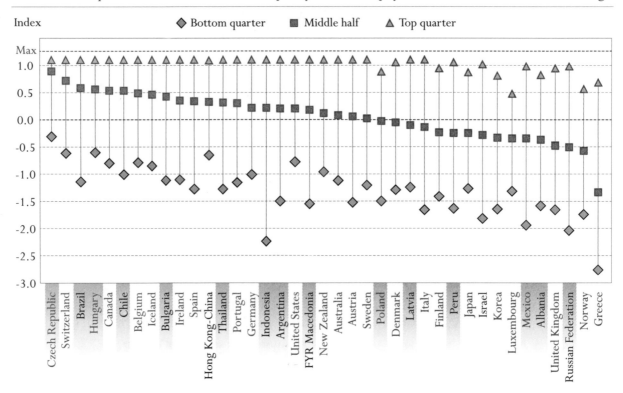

Figure 7.3a

Index on the perceived extent to which the quality of schools' physical infrastructure hinders learning

Source: OECD PISA database, 2003. Table 7.2

Figure 7.3b

Index on the perceived extent to which the quality of schools' educational resources hinders learning

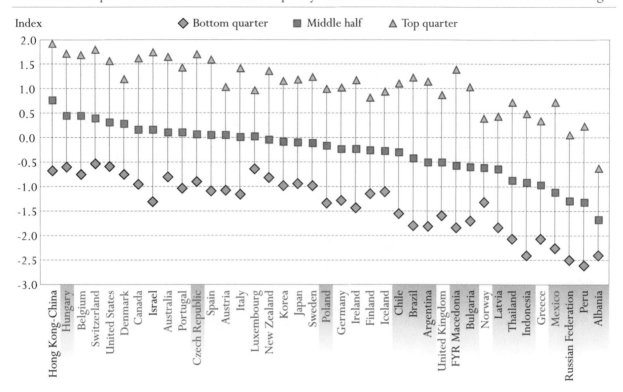

Source: OECD PISA database, 2003. Table 7.3.

others very negatively. In Greece, Indonesia, Mexico and the Russian Federation, principals' perceptions of deficiencies in the physical infrastructure in the bottom quarter of schools are two or more international standard deviations below the OECD country mean (see Table 7.2, Annex B1).

With respect to school principals' perceptions of the adequacy of educational resources, differences within countries appear to be less pronounced. At the same time, variation between countries is much stronger, and principals in low- and middle-income countries generally report the greatest deficiencies.

Figure 7.4 compares the two indices based on national averages. With references to the index of the quality of the schools' physical infrastructure, the figure shows that principals' perceptions do not give any general indication of a greater impact of deficiencies of the physical infrastructure on learning in non-OECD than in OECD countries. Non-OECD countries are quite evenly spread within the range of -0.52 (Russian Federation) and 0.29 (Chile), which also contains the bulk of OECD countries. It is interesting to note that there is hardly any correlation between the mean index of the quality of the schools' physical infrastructure and per capita income. Using GDP per capita for the year 2000 (in current USD, PPP)[2] the correlation coefficient across all countries is 0.07.

Box 7.1. Interpreting the PISA indices

In order to summarise students' or school principals' responses to a series of related questions, various indices were created for PISA 2000. These indices cover various fields of the learning environment, such as resources available in schools, school management, and students' socio-economic background. A detailed description of the underlying questions and the methodology used to compute these indices is provided in Annex A1.

For reasons of comparison, if not otherwise specified, all indices used in this chapter were standardised at OECD level with mean 0 and a standard deviation of 1. Therefore, negative values of the indices do not necessarily correspond to negative responses but rather to values below the OECD mean. Only with respect to variables used in the framework of multivariate regression models was standardisation carried out at the national rather than the international level. This was done in order to facilitate the comparison of different coefficients within each country regression.

Apart from technical considerations, several limitations of the information collected through the questions underlying these indices should be taken into account. In particular, all indices rely on the judgement by school principals rather than on external observations and may therefore be influenced by cross-cultural differences in the perception about standards or by the social desirability of certain responses. Moreover, indices based on responses by principals rely on a comparatively small number of observations (around 150 for most countries).

Wherever information collected from school principals is presented in this report, it has been weighted in order to reflect the number of 15-year-olds enrolled in each school.

With respect to the index of the quality of the schools' educational resources, however, the situation is different. Here the correlation coefficient with GDP per capita is 0.61 indicating a strong relationship between a country's overall financial resources and the availability of instructional material as perceived by principals. Correspondingly, with the exception of Hong Kong-China and Israel, all non-OECD countries for which data are available, show very low values with respect to this index. Among these countries, Chile presents the most positive results with an index of -0.29 (as compared to the OECD mean of 0.0). In only four OECD countries (Greece, Mexico, Norway and the United Kingdom), are the values of the index below the value for Chile (see Table 7.3, Annex B1).

It is interesting to note, in Figure 7.4, that with the exception of Hong Kong-China and Israel, all non-OECD countries appear to the left side of the OECD average. While non-OECD countries are relatively close to and relatively evenly scattered around the OECD country mean of the index of the quality of schools' physical infrastructure, they deviate substantively from the OECD country mean of the index of the quality of schools' educational resources. This indicates that, among non-OECD countries, school principals perceive the quality of educational resources to be a more important barrier to learning than their counterparts in OECD countries whereas the picture is not systematically different from OECD countries with regard to the quality of the physical infrastructure. If principals' perceptions are considered to truly reflect the existing deficiencies, this suggests that education policy in non-OECD countries may have given too much priority to the physical infrastructure of schools while neglecting instructional resources.

Figure 7.4

Countries' priorities: Perceived adequacy of the physical infrastructure
of the school and schools' educational resources

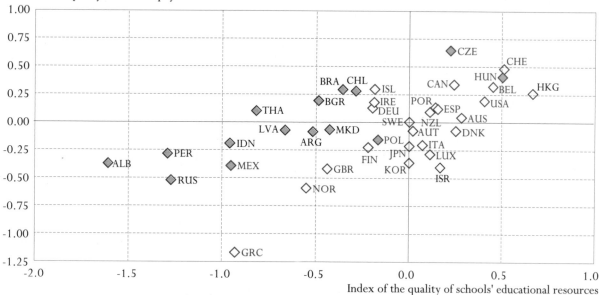

Source: OECD PISA database, 2003. Tables 7.2 and 7.3.

Do these perceptions of school principals matter? The data suggest that school principals' perceptions about the quality of educational resources are consistently related to performance while this is not the case with regard to the quality of the physical infrastructure. In only eleven out of the 41 participating countries is student performance between schools (see Table 7.2, Annex B1) in the top and bottom quarters of schools on the index of the quality of the schools' physical infrastructure significantly different. By contrast, in around half of the participating countries, there is a significant performance difference between schools in the top and bottom quarters of the index of the quality of schools' educational resources (see Table 7.3, Annex B1)[3].

Figure 7.5 illustrates that the marginal effect of an increase in the quality of educational resources tends to be highest in countries where deficiencies reported by principals are particularly pronounced. This negative relationship may suggest diminishing returns to investment in educational resources. However, the value of coefficients varies widely across countries. In Argentina, Mexico and Peru, but also in Germany, a one unit change of the index is associated with difference in scores by 25 points or more, corresponding to an improvement of more than a third of a proficiency level on the combined reading literacy scale.

Schools' human resources

With respect to human resources, principals of schools were asked to report the extent to which learning by 15-year-old students is hindered by the shortage or inadequacy of teachers. A corresponding index of teacher shortage was then constructed. Non-OECD countries figure both at the top and bottom of the index of teacher shortage. In none of the OECD countries, did school principals assess the availability of qualified teachers as positively as in Bulgaria and FYR Macedonia, or as negatively as in Indonesia and Thai-

Figure 7.5

School principals' perception about the extent to which the quality of school educational resources hinders learning and its relationship with student performance

◇ OECD country with high income   ◇ Non-OECD country with high income
◆ OECD country with low and middle income ◆ Non-OECD country with low and middle income

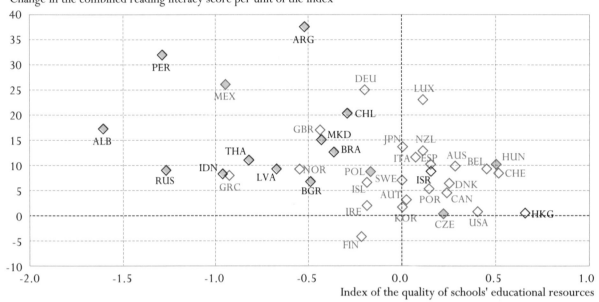

Change in the combined reading literacy score per unit of the index

Index of the quality of schools' educational resources

Source: OECD PISA database, 2003. Table 7.3.

land (see Table 7.4, Annex B1). Principals' perception of teacher shortage appear to be unrelated either to countries' national income level, or to the observed marginal effect on students' performance. Some of the countries already expressing high overall satisfaction with the availability of qualified teachers such as Austria, the Czech Republic and FYR Macedonia show, nevertheless, a close relationship between the index and student performance, suggesting that further improvements in the availability of qualified teachers may make a difference.

It is important to keep in mind that the indicators discussed so far reflect principals' perceptions of obstacles to effective learning and do not allow for cross-country comparisons of the absolute levels of the quality of resources. Indicators that can be directly compared across countries are class size or student-teaching staff ratios. In PISA, student-teacher ratios are computed on the basis of principals' reports for their schools as a whole. In addition, students were asked individually to report the number of students in their class.

Figure 7.6 reports the average sizes of language classes together with information on the proportion of teachers with a university-level degree (ISCED 5A) in the subject taught.

Non-OECD countries, together with Japan, Korea and Mexico, are at a clear disadvantage with respect to class sizes. Among non-OECD countries, only Bulgaria, Latvia, the Russian Federation and Liechtenstein have comparatively low class sizes. Generally, the average class size in participating countries tends to be closely related to GDP per capita - a fact that is not surprising given that teacher salaries account for the majority of current education expenditure and that, in addition, the share of population at school-age in the low- and middle-income countries tends to be the highest. The cross-country correlation coefficient between class size and GDP per capita is -0.50. Between class size and the share of the population below 15 years of age[4], it is 0.51.

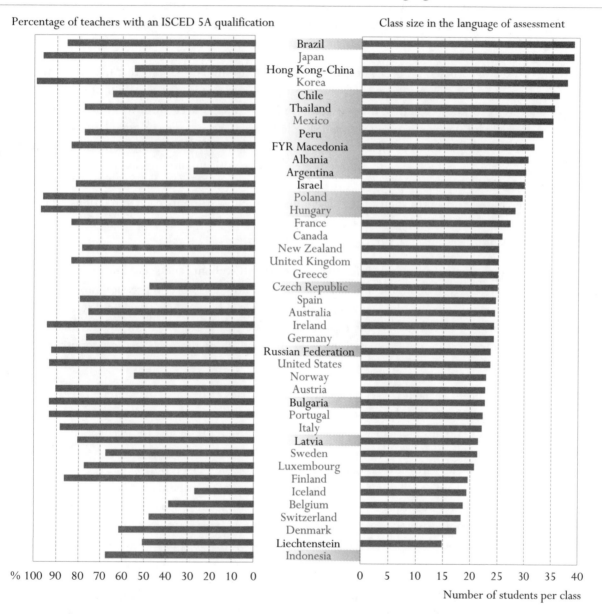

Figure 7.6

Class size and teacher qualification in classes of the language of assessment

Note: For Indonesia, no data on class size are available. Data on language teachers' qualification in the language of assessment are missing for Albania, Canada and Greece.
Source: OECD PISA database, 2003. Tables 7.4 and 7.5.

Box 7.2. Measuring the effect of school inputs on performance

In order to correctly interpret the impact of school inputs on performance, it is necessary to distinguish between the different tools of analysis used. Some of the discussion in this chapter draws on simple bivariate relationships based on correlation coefficients or coefficients of bivariate regression models. In this case, analysis leads to the estimation of an overall relationship between two variables, irrespective of other variables that may have an impact on the relationships. For instance, it may be interesting to consider the gross effect of students' socio-economic background on performance (discussed later in this chapter) irrespective of whether this background is, in turn, related to factors such as immigration which may themselves influence student performance. In this case, a simple bivariate regression model is sufficient to provide the requested estimates. If, however, only socio-economic background net of immigration effects is of interest, immigration needs to be included in the regression model as a control variable. In this case a multivariate regression model is needed.

In some cases, results based on bivariate analyses may lead to interpretations that overlook important third variables. A relevant example is the number of students in a class. While the interest of policy makers is to know whether this variable can be used as a direct tool to influence student performance, the influence measured through simple bivariate regressions or correlations is generally blurred by multiple indirect effects. For instance, students with a favourable socio-economic background might have the means to choose better schools with smaller class sizes. The measured effect of class size may then simply reflect their higher socio-economic background. Similarly, class size may be related to factors such as the disciplinary climate, student-teacher relations, and the grade level. It is therefore important to account for these variables when interpreting the results. To do this, the chapter uses multivariate regression models.

Multivariate regressions that include information from both students and schools also need to take into account the nested structure of the data. For each country, two-level regression models can be estimated, taking into account the fact that students are nested in schools (Bryk and Raudenbush, 1992; Goldstein, 1999). All net effects reported in this chapter are based on the coefficients of a two-level hierarchical model estimated individually for each of the participating countries (see Tables 7.15 and 7.16, Annex B1).

For a further group of variables, variation between countries is of particular interest. This is the case, for instance, for the variables related to school autonomy which generally do not vary much within a given country. These variables do not represent relevant predictors for performance within a two-level regression model and become significant only when the country-level is added to the analysis. A corresponding three-level model was estimated for the PISA report *Knowledge and Skills for Life* (OECD, 2001*b*, Chapter 8, Table 8.5). An alternative way of proceeding is to consider the gross effect at the country level by simply computing bivariate relationships such as cross-country correlations between the country averages of the variables of interest. This simpler approach without control for indirect effects through other variables has been used where appropriate in this Chapter.

On average, lower-income countries also have a smaller share of teachers with a university degree in the relevant subject matter. Nevertheless, in all low- and middle-income countries apart from Argentina and Mexico more than 50 per cent of the language teachers hold ISCED 5A qualifications for the subject taught.

Given that average class size is so much higher in most low- and middle-income countries than in the typical OECD country, it appears relevant to ask to what extent this puts these countries at a disadvantage with respect to student performance. Generally, for OECD countries, the PISA report *Knowledge and Skills for Life* suggests that the related link between student-teaching staff ratios and student performance is rather weak, at least in the relevant range of ratios between 10 and 20 (OECD, 2001*b*, pp. 202f.).

However, the situation is potentially different in countries where average class sizes are considerably higher. In order to detect possible differences between countries, the analysis presented here is based on separate estimations for each country. Computations were based on a multivariate regression model in order to take into account the interactions of class size with other variables (for details, see Table 7.16, Annex B1, and Box 7.2).

The results show that there are considerable similarities for countries within given regions, notably, the East-Asian countries, the Latin-American countries and the Nordic countries. For these groups of countries, the estimated relationship between class size and student performance on the combined reading literacy scale is presented in Figure 7.7.

For the Nordic countries, the results suggest a decline in student performance from around 22 students per class onwards. This is different from the typical OECD country where such a decline is observed only for classes larger than 30 students. Within the OECD, the Nordic countries thus present an untypical picture wherein adding additional students tends to have a negative effect at comparatively low class sizes.

The situation is different for the East-Asian countries that participated in PISA. It might be that this is the result of cultural factors or that these countries might have developed particularly efficient pedagogical strategies to deal with large class sizes. It might also be that these countries tend to place weaker students in smaller classes in order to devote more individual attention to them. On average, in these countries, no negative effect of adding additional students can be discerned at any relevant class size. The estimated coefficients of class size generally remain insignificant.

At a lower level of student performance, the situation is similar in Latin-America. It is less pronounced, however, with an average Latin-American class size of 35 students and an estimated decline in performance from about 38 students onwards.

It is interesting to note that in all country groups, including the Nordic countries, the average class size lies within a range where adding additional students does not lead to discernible negative effects. Irrespective of average class size, in most participating countries, only a relatively small share of classes falls into the range where student numbers appear to adversely affect learning.

It follows that, in most countries, class size alone does not seem to have a significant negative impact on student performance. This is in line with previous research findings for many countries.[5] Nevertheless, it should be kept in mind that even though the estimations are based on multivariate regressions, some relevant factors influencing both student performance and class size might not have been controlled for. First of all, some countries deliberately place disadvantaged or low performing students in smaller classes, in order to provide a more supportive learning environment for them. Further, class sizes in technical or vocational streams may generally be lower than in academic streams due to the laboratory and practical work that characterises the former. At the same time, reading performance can be often expected to be higher in the latter. Similarly, there tends to be a difference in class size between urban and rural schools

Figure 7.7

Regional differences in the relationship between class size and
performance on the combined reading literacy scale

◆ Country mean of class size in the lowest quarter
☐ Overall country mean of class size in the region
△ Country mean of class size in the highest quarter

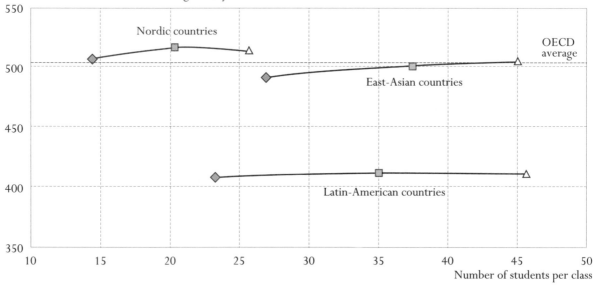

Note: Nordic countries include Denmark, Finland, Norway and Sweden.
East-Asian countries include Hong Kong-China, Japan, Korea and Thailand.
Latin-American countries include Argentina, Brazil, Chile and Mexico.
The y- and x-axis show performance on the combined reading literacy scale and class size respectively. Computations are based on the regional country averages of the coefficient estimates of the two-level regression model presented in Table 7.16, Annex B1. Indonesia and Peru could not be included in the regional averages since not all data required for this computation was available.
Source: OECD PISA Database, 2003. Tables 2.3a and 7.5.

whereby the former might have both higher class sizes and higher student performance. The influence of these variables was not monitored because their inclusion into the model would have implied considerable loss of observation. However, at least for some countries, omitting these variables may have led to an underestimation of the true affect of class size.

Overall, the discussion of schools' available physical and human resources suggests that the most visible resources such as the physical infrastructure and the number of teachers per student are not necessarily ones that relate most closely to student performance. In low- and middle-income countries, the obstacles to learning most deplored by principals do not reflect deficiencies in the physical infrastructure or a shortage of teachers, although the latter, is clearly more prevalent there than in a typical OECD country. What principals in these countries do point out is the shortage of adequate educational resources. Indeed, the corresponding PISA index is associated with student performance in almost all low- and middle-income non-OECD countries. Priority investments in educational resources may therefore help to bridge the performance gap between high- and low-income countries.

As mentioned earlier, other factors such as the management and organisation of schools can also contribute significantly to students' performance. What impact do these factors have? Are there similar differences to be observed between countries of different income groups? In fact, if factors related to school management and organisation have a significant impact on performance, they might be particularly relevant for educational policy since changes in these variables do not necessarily require additional financial resources.

School organisation and management

One aspect of school management concerns the distribution of decision-making responsibilities between the different stakeholders in education systems and, particularly, the roles that schools play in the decision making process. This section focuses on how much freedom education systems give individual schools to determine particular aspects of school organisation and management and on the extent to which teachers take part in these decisions. This section covers various fields of management and organisation and addresses questions related to the courses offered and the pedagogical material used, budgetary issues, teachers' appointments and pay. Figure 7.8 compares OECD and non-OECD countries with respect to the autonomy of schools in each of these areas.

In most countries, decisions involving direct interaction with students are generally taken at school level. On average, in both OECD and non-OECD countries, more than 80 per cent of students are enrolled in schools that carry at least some responsibility for student disciplinary policies, assessment policies and decisions on students' admission. In addition, schools usually have some responsibility for the courses offered, for course content and for the textbooks used. In all these areas, Figure 7.8 shows most countries to the right hand side, between the 75 per cent and the 100 per cent marks. There are only few countries where less than 75 per cent of schools report to have some responsibilities in these areas.

Decisions on budget allocations within the school are also often taken at school level. This responsibility has to be distinguished from decisions about the formulation of school budgets. Schools tend to have more autonomy with respect to budgetary allocation within their institution than with respect to the formulation of their school budgets. However, many schools also have some responsibility for the formulation of their school budget. Despite considerable cross-country variation, about 70 per cent of students on average are enrolled in schools with at least some responsibility in this field. The results also indicate that responsibility for budgetary issues seems to be considerably more frequent in OECD countries than in non-OECD countries. Cross-country averages of the share of students enrolled in schools with some autonomy in this field differ by over 15 percentage points between the two groups.

Among the categories examined, schools appear to have least responsibility for decisions related to the appointment and dismissal of teachers. Nevertheless, across all countries, a majority of students attend schools that retain at least some responsibility regarding the appointment and dismissal of teachers. About a quarter of students are enrolled in schools that even have some responsibility for teachers' remuneration. In all these areas, cross-country variation is very high.

In addition to the autonomy of schools, Figure 7.9 goes one step further to indicate the extent to which teachers have the main decision making responsibility for the issues that have been examined above.

In most countries, the choice of textbooks in particular, seems to be a decision largely taken by teachers themselves. In many schools, teachers also have the main responsibility with respect to student assessment and disciplinary policies as well as with respect to the course programme and content offered. However,

Figure 7.8

Percentage of students enrolled in schools which have at least some responsibility
for the following aspects of school policy and management

*Results based on reports from school principals and reported proportionate to the
number of 15-year-olds enrolled in the school*

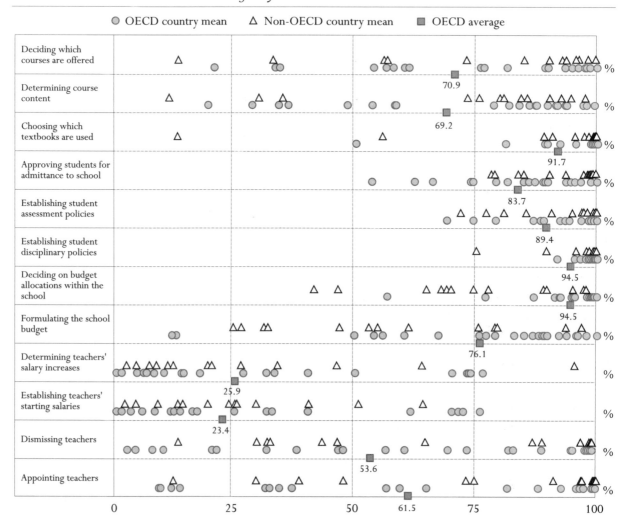

Source: OECD PISA database, 2003. Table 7.6.

the difference between autonomy at school and teacher levels is significant. With reference to decisions about the courses offered, for instance, less than 35 per cent of students, on average, are enrolled in institutions where this is part of teachers' responsibilities. At the same time, more than 70 per cent of students attend institutions where this is part of schools' responsibilities.

Teachers' responsibilities are rare when it comes to budgetary issues as well as to students' admissions. Finally, not surprisingly, teachers have little influence on their appointment and salaries.

It is interesting to note that, although general patterns in the distribution of decision-making are similar for OECD and non-OECD countries, teachers in OECD countries appear to retain considerably more responsibilities than in non-OECD countries.

Figure 7.9

Percentage of students enrolled in schools in which teachers have the main responsibility
for the following aspects of school policy and management
*Results based on reports from school principals and reported proportionate to the
number of 15-year-olds enrolled in the school*

● OECD country mean   △ Non-OECD country mean   ■ OECD average

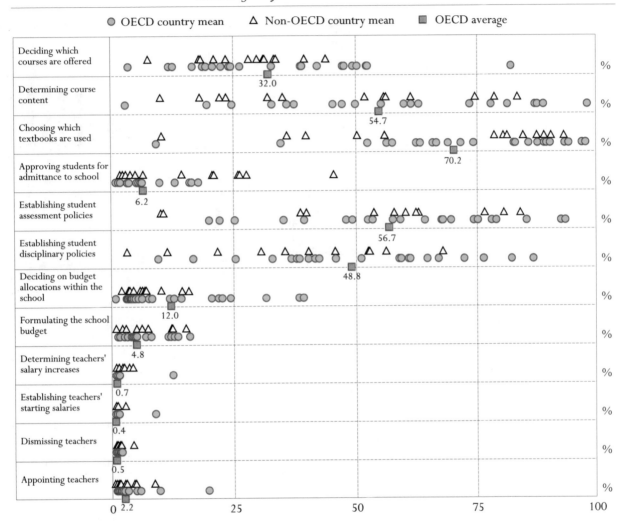

Source: OECD PISA database, 2003. Table 7.7.

Cross-country correlations between the individual categories presented above and student performance provide some indication of the impact of school and teacher autonomy on student performance. Across all countries, sizeable correlations can be observed between performance and schools' responsibilities for budgetary allocations within schools, the choice of textbooks, disciplinary policies and courses offered. Correlation coefficients are all positive, ranging from 0.65 for budgetary allocations to 0.37 for establishing disciplinary policies (Table 7.6, Annex B1).

Figure 7.10 reports the percentage of students enrolled in schools in which teachers have the main responsibility for students' admittance. Six of the non-OECD countries show the highest percentages of teacher responsibility for student admissions, and all Latin-American countries seem to assign teachers a high degree of decision-making responsibility for student admissions.

Figure 7.10

Percentage of students enrolled in schools in which teachers
have the main responsibility for students' admittance

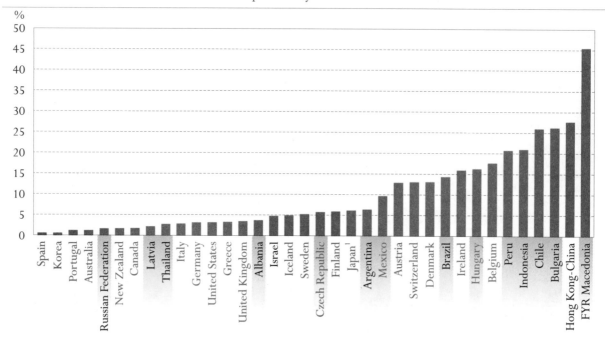

1. Due to the sampling methods used in Japan, the between-school variance in Japan includes variation between classes within schools.
Source: OECD PISA database, 2003. Table 7.7.

Figure 7.11 contrasts schools' and teachers' responsibility with regard to courses on offer. Finland is the country where both schools and teachers enjoy the greatest autonomy with respect to the courses offered by their schools. In all Asian countries, school responsibility in this field is almost at 100 per cent while teachers' responsibility varies between below 20 per cent in Korea and about 40 per cent in Indonesia. In other regions, Chile and Israel fall into the same range. Among all PISA countries, Albania is the country where schools and teachers have the least autonomy.

One hypothesis is that the different indicators of autonomy relate to the prevalence of private schooling. While this is generally true within countries, the relationship at the cross-country level is rather weak. In fact, at the confidence level of 95 per cent, there is no significant positive correlation between any of the categories of schools' and teachers' autonomy and the share of schools that are both publicly managed and financed. Only at a lower confidence level of 90 per cent, can a positively significant correlation be observed with respect to the choice and contents of the course schools make.

Generally, it seems that the structures of education systems vary widely across countries, and that publicly managed and financed schools in some countries enjoy considerably greater autonomy than privately managed and financed schools in others. A good example is Finland where, both schools and teachers enjoy remarkable autonomy whereas privately managed and funded schools are negligible (see Figure 7.11).

While it should be kept in mind that substantial decentralisation generally requires complementary measures (to ensure transparency and accountability for example) and that no causal inferences can be made from the data shown, the analysis has revealed various areas where, on average, higher school autonomy tends to go hand in hand with higher average student performance. With respect to budgetary allocations within schools, the choice of textbooks, disciplinary policies, courses offered, and other related areas, countries currently adopting a more centralised role might consider devolving some responsibilities in these areas to schools.

There are other variables related to the organisation of schools that are less a matter of structures but more a matter of pedagogical approaches, teacher training, personnel management or even individual attitudes, cultural aspects and values. Some of these aspects are considered in the following section.

Figure 7.11

Teachers' versus schools' responsibility for decisions on the courses to be offered[1]

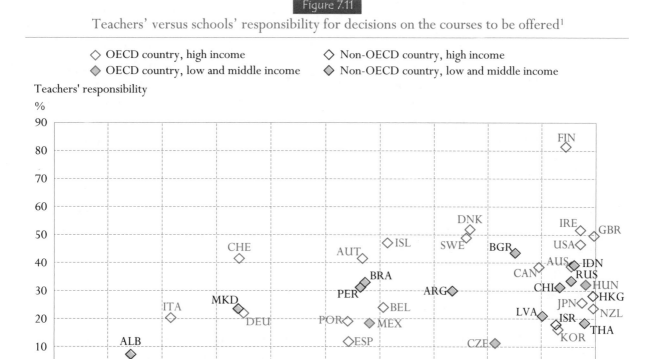

1. As measured by the percentage of students enrolled in schools which have at least some responsibility, or in schools where teachers have the main responsibilty in this field (based on reports from school principals).
Source: OECD PISA database, 2003. Tables 7.6 and 7.7.

School climate

The learning climate of a school encompasses many aspects and cannot be easily quantified. Any indicator of school climate is necessarily based on subjective impressions. Nevertheless, trying to measure differences in school climate may give valuable insights into relevant differences in learning opportunities that might otherwise be overlooked.

In PISA, several indices were constructed to capture relevant aspects of school climate and to contrast the views of students and school principals on this issue. These indices capture elements of both teachers' and students' behaviour and of the working relationships between students and teachers.

Figure 7.12 presents the national mean values for three indices of school climate related to teacher behaviour.

• The first index reflects school principals' perceptions about teachers' morale and commitment. It reports on their morale in general, their enthusiasm for their work, their pride in their school and their evaluation of academic performance.

• The second index focuses on teacher-related factors affecting school climate. It comprises principals' perceptions about: teachers' expectations for students' learning, student-teacher relations, the extent to which teachers meet the needs of students, teacher absenteeism, the attitude of staff towards change, strictness with students and the encouragement of students to achieve their full potential.

• The third index reflects students' opinions about teachers' attitudes towards them, especially on teacher support. The literature on school effectiveness suggests that students (particularly those with a low level of performance) benefit from teaching practices that demonstrate teachers' interest in the progress of their students, giving the clear message that all students are expected to attain reasonable performance standards, and showing willingness to help all students to meet these standards. In order to examine the extent to which such practices are common in different countries, as well as the extent to which they promote higher levels of performance, students were asked to indicate the frequency with which teachers in the language of assessment show an interest in each student's learning, give students an opportunity to express opinions, help students with their work and continue to explain until students understand.

Since the last two indices are both based primarily on the interaction between students and teachers, one might expect to find a high positive correlation between their values. However, as shown in Figure 7.12, the perceptions of principals and students often diverge. Among non-OECD countries, only in Brazil, Bulgaria and FYR Macedonia do students and principals share a positive, *i.e.*, above the OECD average, view about teacher-student interactions. In Indonesia and Thailand, their views also converge, but at a level slightly below the OECD country mean.

It is remarkable that in ten of the fourteen non-OECD countries, notably in Albania, Argentina, Bulgaria, Chile, Israel, FYR Macedonia and Peru, students give a higher evaluation to teacher support than students in the average OECD country. Generally, countries on the American continent show relatively high levels of student satisfaction with teacher support. By contrast, students' reports in Asian countries are rather negative. Hong Kong-China, Indonesia and Thailand as well as the OECD countries Japan and Korea all show indices below the OECD average, with Korea at the bottom of all countries considered here.

With respect to the index reflecting principals' views on the teacher-related factors that affect school climate, only five non-OECD countries reach national mean values above the OECD average. These countries are Bulgaria, Brazil, Hong Kong-China, Latvia and FYR Macedonia. The index of teachers' morale and commitment, also reported by principals is above the OECD average in only two of the non-OECD countries. Again, Bulgaria is one of them, making it the only non-OECD country, and one of only five countries overall, for which all three indices take values above the OECD average. The second country is Indonesia, where the index of teachers' morale and commitment exceeds the values for all other OECD and non-OECD countries for which data are available. This high general evaluation of teachers by principals reflects the overall respect for the profession in this country.

Somewhat surprisingly, as with the index of teacher support and the index of teacher-related factors affecting school climate, there is no apparent cross-country correlation between teacher-related factors affect-

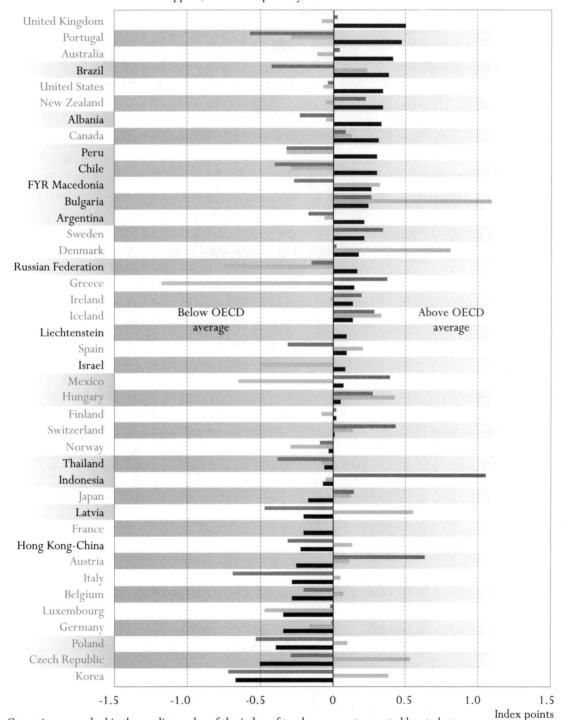

Figure 7.12

Perceptions of school climate related to teachers

- ◼ Index of teachers' morale and commitment, based on reports by school principals
- ◼ Index of teacher-related factors affecting school climate, based on reports by school principals
- ◼ Index of teacher support, based on reports by students

Note: Countries are ranked in descending order of the index of teacher support reported by students.
For France and Liechtenstein no data are available for both indices based on principals' perceptions.
For the definition of the indices see Annex A1.
Source: OECD PISA database, 2003. Tables 7.8, 7.9 and 7.10.

ing school climate and the index of teachers' morale and commitment. It seems that, at least to a certain extent, principals' overall evaluation of teachers is independent of their reports about teachers' attitudes towards students.

As mentioned earlier, students' individual behaviour also contributes considerably to the climate prevailing in their schools. Figure 7.13 presents two different indices reflecting student-related factors. The index of student related factors affecting school climate summarises school principals' reports about: student absenteeism, disruption of classes by students, students skipping classes, students' lack of respect for teachers, the use of alcohol or illegal drugs, and the intimidation or bullying amongst students. Students' own perceptions are captured by the index of disciplinary climate that includes issues such as the time the teacher has to wait until students quieten down and until he or she can effectively start teaching, the prevalence of noise and disorder in class, and whether students listen to what the teacher says.

Within the 14 non-OECD countries, five countries show values above the OECD average, and two countries (Brazil and Israel) show values below this average for both of the indicators. Divergence of views about students' discipline can be found only in the Russian Federation and in the three remaining Latin-American countries. Particularly notable is Argentina, where principals' perception is the most positive of all OECD and non-OECD countries. At the same time, students themselves paint a rather negative picture of their behaviour and place their country just before Greece at the very end of the list.

Generally, students' own perception of their discipline appears to be rather modest in Latin American countries. Argentina, Brazil and Chile are among the five countries with the lowest overall value of the index, and the index remains below the OECD average in Peru as well. Only in Mexico is the index positive. As far as the two North American countries are concerned, the index is clearly negative for Canada but slightly positive for the United States.

By contrast, in none of the Asian countries does the index of disciplinary climate as reported by students fall below the OECD average. The index falls at exactly this average value in Hong Kong-China and above this value in Indonesia and Thailand as well as in the OECD countries Japan and Korea.

It is interesting to note that these regional similarities do not, at the country level, relate to the general standard of living or other indicators of economic development. They might therefore rather reflect cultural patterns prevailing in different world regions.

Comparing students' reports on disciplinary climate to their reports on teacher support provides an additional perspective on the issue. Across all countries, a negative correlation coefficient of -0.26 can be calculated for the national mean values of the two indicators, and such contrasts come out most clearly for Asia and Latin America. If students' perceptions are correct, Asian students are very disciplined, while their teachers are very demanding and do not give much support to students who lag behind. The opposite seems to be the case in Latin-America. There, teachers are perceived by students to care much more about making sure all students understand and helping them if they don't. At the same time, students characterise themselves as being much less disciplined, not always listening to the teacher and sometimes creating noise and disorder. If this is a cultural disposition, and both teachers and students are used to the situation, they might also have developed particular ways to cope with it. In any case, in Latin-America, students' lack of discipline does not seem to be taken as a reflection of disrespect. This may explain why, despite students' negative evaluation of their own behaviour, principals in all Latin-American countries except Brazil convey rather positive impressions about student-related factors affecting school climate.

Figure 7.13
Perceptions of school climate related to students

■ Index of student-related factors affecting school climate, based on reports by school principals
■ Index of disciplinary climate, based on reports by students

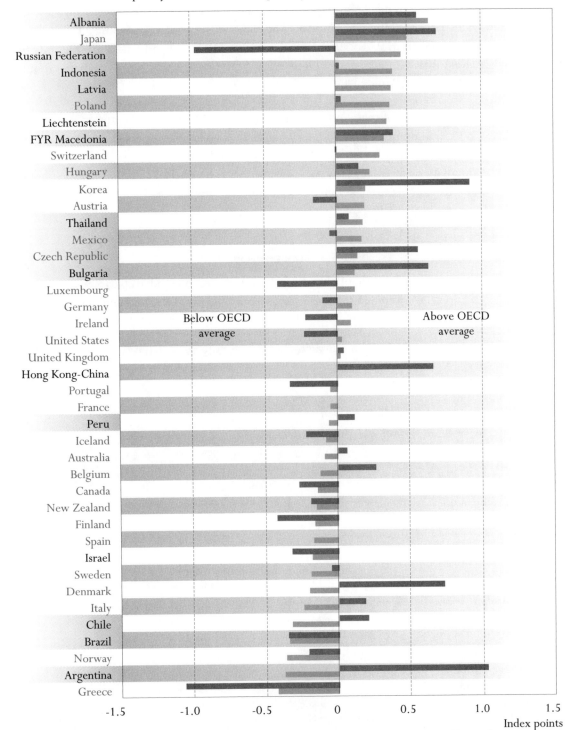

Note: Countries are ranked in descending order of the index of disciplinary climate support reported by students.
For France and Liechtenstein no data are available for the index based on principals' perceptions.
For the definition of the indices see Annex A1.
Source: OECD PISA database, 2003. Tables 7.11 and 7.12.

With regard to the impact of school climate as experienced by principals and students on student performance, students' reports concerning their own behaviour seem to be somewhat less clearly related to outcomes than the reports of principals'. Figure 7.14 shows that in eight out of 13 non-OECD countries for which data are available, a more positive evaluation of students' behaviour by principals is significantly and positively correlated with higher student performance on the combined reading literacy scale. In two of the remaining countries, coefficients could also be classified as positively significant if the accepted confidence level is decreased from 95 to 90 per cent. Albania, Indonesia and Latvia are the only non-OECD countries where no positive influence of student-related factors affecting school climate on outcomes can be discerned (see Table 7.11, Annex B1).

When considering the impact of these indices one should generally keep in mind that the above discussion relates to bivariate relationships. The incidence of disorder, noise, disrespect or even violence in schools may, however, be closely related to other factors, most notably the school's social intake. If these factors are considered simultaneously in a multivariate framework, the coefficients tend to shrink considerably. Table 7.15 (Annex B1) shows the coefficients reflecting the impact of disciplinary climate net of other influences.

Figure 7.14

Indices related to school climate and their impact on student performance
on the combined reading literacy scale, for non-OECD countries

School climate related to teachers			
Indices	**Positive impact**	**Insignificant impact**	**Negative impact**
Index of teachers' morale and commitment, based on reports by principals	Argentina, Bulgaria, Chile, Hong Kong-China, Israel, FYR Macedonia, Peru, Russian Federation, Thailand	Albania, Brazil, Indonesia, Latvia	
Index of teacher-related factors affecting school climate, based on reports by principals	Argentina, Brazil, Chile, Hong Kong-China, FYR Macedonia, Russian Federation	Albania, Bulgaria, Indonesia, Israel, Latvia, Peru, Thailand	
Index of teacher support, based on reports by students	Brazil, Bulgaria, Indonesia, Latvia, Peru, Russian Federation, Thailand	Albania, Argentina, Chile, Hong Kong-China, Israel, FYR Macedonia	Liechtenstein

School climate related to students			
Indices	**Positive impact**	**Insignificant impact**	**Negative impact**
Index of student-related factors affecting school climate, based on reports by principals	Argentina, Brazil, Bulgaria, Chile, Hong Kong-China, FYR Macedonia, Peru, Russian Federation	Albania, Indonesia, Israel, Latvia, Thailand	
Index of disciplinary climate, based on reports by students	Bulgaria, Chile, Hong Kong-China, Latvia, FYR Macedonia, Russian Federation, Thailand	Albania, Indonesia, Liechtenstein, Peru	Argentina, Brazil, Israel

Note: The level of significance is set at $\alpha=0.05$.

For Liechtenstein, no data are available for the indices based on principals' perceptions.

Source: OECD PISA database 2003. Tables 7.8, 7.9, 7.10, 7.11 and 7.12.

Besides teachers' and students' interaction and their general behaviour and commitment, the climate for learning may depend on whether students feel that their school is a place they belong to. In order to test this relationship, students were asked to state their agreement or disagreement with the following statements about their current school: I feel left out of things; I make friends easily; I feel like I belong; I feel awkward and out of place; and other students seem to like me.

Among OECD countries, the observed correlation between students' sense of belonging to their school and performance is weak, especialy after an adjustment for other variables (see Table 7.15, Annex B1) is made. Among non-OECD countries, however, the relationship between students' sense of belonging to their school and performance is clearly positive. Figure 7.15 shows that for this group of countries, coefficients are significantly different from zero in all countries except Brazil, Hong Kong-China, Latvia, Israel and the Russian Federation. Generally, in low- and middle-income countries, the positive association between students' sense of belonging and performance tends to be stronger than in economically more advanced countries. The cross-country correlation between the value of the coefficient and GDP per capita is -0.53. Replacing GDP per capita by the country means of the PISA index of family wealth, it is -0.65.

Figure 7.15

Difference in student performance associated with a change of one national standard deviation on the index of students' sense of belonging

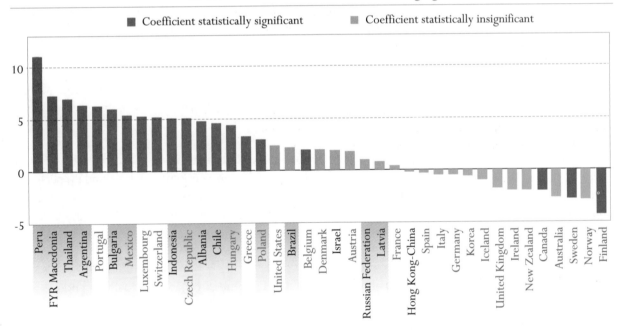

Note: Coefficients are based on a multivariate, multilevel model. For the complete model, see Table 4.15, Annex B1. Countries are ranked in descending order of coefficients.
Source: OECD PISA database, 2003. Table 7.15.

Schools' socio-economic intake

Socio-economic and academic selection

Some of the indicators discussed in the context of school climate shed light on the relevance to consider the performance of individual students in the context of their peers. Such an analysis is carried out below.

Schools often vary quite substantially with respect to their socio-economic composition. As already discussed in Chapter 6, students' socio-economic background is a strong predictor of learning outcomes. Consequently, if a school tends to predominantly enrol students with a favourable family background, results of students from this school are likely to be superior. In addition, due to positive spill-over effects, even a student whose individual socio-economic background is unfavourable may benefit from the positive environment in this school. This effect of the socio-economic background of the peer-group needs to be distinguished from the impact of the socio-economic background of the individual student on his or her performance. While Chapter 6 provided an overview about the individual effects, this section focuses on the peer-group effects and compares the two.[6]

Giving all young people equal access to high quality education and fostering the interaction between students of different backgrounds within the same school can represent a powerful tool to overcome social inequalities. Conversely, social segregation leading to high quality schools for some students and low quality schools for others, may reinforce existing inequalities. Given the inequality in the income distribution in some of the non-OECD countries, the question of whether education enhances or mitigates the existing inequalities appears to be particularly relevant. Generally, Gini-coefficients indicating income and consumption inequalities are particularly high in Latin-America, ranging from 59.1 per cent in Brazil to 46.2 per cent in Peru. With a coefficient of 45.6 per cent, the Russian Federation falls into a similar range (see Table 1.4, Annex B1). In both Hong Kong-China and Thailand income inequalities are less pronounced. Nevertheless, compared to the level of inequality prevailing in these countries, even the United States, with a Gini coefficient of 40.8, presents a comparativly equal income distribution. Among non-OECD countries, only the Eastern European countries as well as Indonesia and Israel show comparatively small inequalities in income distribution.[7]

For the predominately high-income OECD countries, an analysis of distribution effects of the education system can be limited to the evaluation of the impact of students' socio-economic background on performance (OECD, 2001b, Chapter 6 and OECD, 2002b, Chapter 7). Many of the economically less advanced non-OECD countries, however, have only relatively low secondary enrolment rates, so that the first step should be to examine the selection process that takes place before children even reach the age of 15 years which is examined by PISA.

Indeed a closer look at net secondary enrolment rates (Table 1.3, Annex B1) reveals that in all non-OECD countries except Bulgaria, Israel and Latvia for which data are available, less than 80 per cent of the 15-year-olds are enrolled in school. Within the OECD, this is true only for Ireland and Mexico . Net enrolment rates of 15-year-olds below 75 per cent are observed in Albania, Brazil, Chile, Hong Kong-China, Indonesia, Mexico, Peru and Thailand.

It is therefore necessary to examine the extent to which the selection process is driven by socio-economic factors. In order to do so, one can relate one of the indicators of PISA students' family background to another socio-economic variable based on information for the whole population. GDP per capita is a readily available variable to convey information for the population as a whole. Among the indicators available

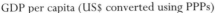

Figure 7.16

Per capita income in the total population and family wealth among 15-year-old students

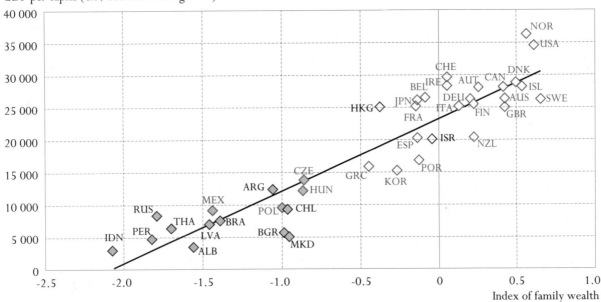

Note: Luxembourg was not represented on this graph. It is an extreme outlier with per capita GDP of $48 239 and a value of the PISA index of family wealth of only 0.32.
Source: OECD PISA database, 2003. Tables 3.3 and 6.2.

within PISA, the PISA index of family wealth appears to be the most appropriate choice. It is constructed in such a way as to capture information related to wealth, and both variables are therefore highly correlated across countries. In fact, excluding Luxembourg which is an extreme case due to its high per capita income, the overall correlation coefficient across all participating countries is 93 per cent.

In Figure 7.16, the average relationship between GDP per capita and the index of family wealth is indicated by the regression line. Countries to the right of this line show a higher family wealth for the student population represented in PISA than would be expected on the basis of their GDP per capita. This should be the case for all countries with strong income based pre-selection for secondary education. Countries on the line show the average level of income based selection. Finally, in countries to the left of the line, there is a less than average dependency on family income for secondary enrolment, so that the index of family wealth observed for PISA students is lower than GDP per capita would suggest.

Surprisingly, none of the six countries with the lowest secondary enrolment rates appear among the countries on the right hand side of the regression line. The countries with the relatively strongest income-based selection seem to be FYR Macedonia and Bulgaria. Among all participating countries, they are the furthest away from the trend line. In most Latin-American countries social intake into secondary education does not appear to be more dependent on family wealth than in the average country in the sample.

Even for those countries where a slight divergence can be observed, it should also be noted that this may be related to measurement differences of the two indicators (GDP per capita and family wealth), rather than to a real selection effect. This is best illustrated by all countries with universal (or close to universal) secondary enrolment, and their variance on both sides of the line. By definition, no real selection effect can take place in these countries.

All in all, it can be concluded that non-OECD countries, despite their generally lower secondary enrolment rates, do not seem to diverge significantly from the typical OECD country with respect to the income based pre-selection of students for secondary education. Moreover, since family wealth is directly related to (and highly correlated with[8]) students' overall socio-economic background, it can be expected that, with respect to socio-economic background in general, the population of 15-year-old students does not differ markedly from the population as a whole - even in non-OECD countries. This implies that looking at the impact of students' socio-economic background on students' performance within the PISA data set is not likely to lead to strongly biased estimates. Consequently, this analysis can be carried out and interpreted in analogy to the analysis carried out for the OECD countries that participated in PISA 2000 (OECD, 2002*b*, Chapter 7). Throughout this chapter, socio-economic background is measured through the PISA international socio-economic index of occupational status (ISEI, see Annex A1 for the exact definition).

Figure 7.17 presents the results differentiating between the overall (gross) effect computed through simple bivariate regression, and the net effect that is obtained by controlling for indirect influences of other variables (such as migration, family structure etc.[9]) using a multivariate regression model. In order to distinguish peer-group effects from the effects of inter-individual differences, the net effect is split into two parts measuring *i*) the impact of differences in socio-economic background for different students within the same school environment (individual effect), and *ii*) the impact of the school average socio-economic background on differences between schools (peer-group effect).

In Figure 7.17, the light red columns to the left depict the gross effect of an individual student's socio-economic background on performance on the combined reading literacy scale. The length of the bars corresponds to the coefficients of Table 6.1a, Annex B1.[10]

In none of the non-OECD countries is the overall effect of students' socio-economic background as strong as in the Czech Republic, Germany and Switzerland. Nevertheless, Argentina, Bulgaria, Chile and Peru also show large coefficients - indicating that an improvement of the index by one national standard deviation would imply an improvement in performance by at least half a proficiency level. By contrast, in Hong Kong-China, Indonesia and Thailand, the effect is much smaller so that, together with Finland, Iceland and Korea, they are the best performing countries on this measure. Albania, Israel and FYR Macedonia fall somewhere in between.

Looking at regional patterns, the East-Asian countries all seem to have educational systems where socio-economic background seems to matter comparatively less. In the Eastern European countries, the opposite seems to be true. Evidence in Latin-America is mixed: While in most countries, socio-economic background appears to be highly predictive for student performance, Brazil and Mexico present noticeable exceptions.

It is interesting to relate these results to the earlier discussion of the distribution of national resources. While the Eastern European countries tend to show a relatively equal distribution of national income in the population, their education systems nevertheless, yield high levels of social disparities in student performance. In some of the Latin-American countries, the already existing strong income inequalities may be

Figure 7.17

Socio-economic background and its relationship to student performance
on the combined reading literacy scale

- ▨ Gross effect of a unit improvement of an individual student's socio-economic background (overall effect)
- ■ Net effect of a unit improvement of an individual student's socio-economic background (individual effect)
- ■ Net effect of a unit improvement of the average socio-economic background of students in the same school (peer-group effect)

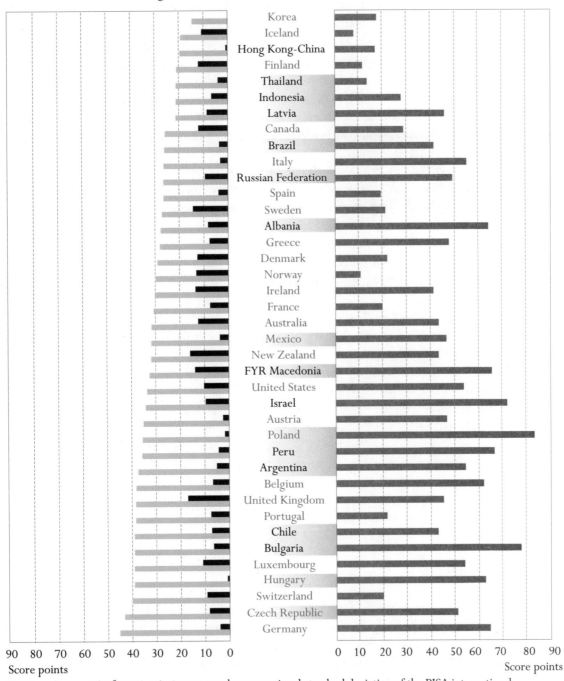

Note: Unit improvement refers to an improvement by one national standard deviation of the PISA international socio-economic index of occupational status (ISEI).
Source: OECD PISA database, 2003. Tables 6.1a and 7.15.

reinforced by an education system offering lower quality education to students from lower socio-economic backgrounds. By contrast, in Hong Kong-China, the impact of social background on student performance is comparatively small, despite large inequalities in the income distribution in the population. Although this may also reflect wider aspects of social policy or culture, it is possible that the education system in Hong Kong-China caters to better integration of students from disadvantaged backgrounds than in most other countries.

The net effect of the socio-economic background, presented by the black bars (individual effect) and red bars (peer-group effect) in Figure 7.17, is the overall effect corrected for simultaneous influences by other variables separately introduced into the regression model. These variables are: students' grade level, migration status, family structure and communication, educational resources at home (including books), school climate, and engagement in homework and reading (see Table 7.15, Annex B1, for the regression results and the definition of variables). It should be noted that both socio-economic background and engagement in reading were introduced at both the individual and school level in order to obtain separate estimates for the impact of differences between individuals within given school environments and between schools.

The black bars indicating the net individual effects of different socio-economic backgrounds are drawn to the left of graph, like the gross effects. When the two coefficients are compared, net individual effects turn out to be substantially smaller than gross effects. This indicates that, once indirect influences and, in particular, the overall socio-economic environment of the school (peer-effect) are corrected for, individual students' socio-economic background appears to be a much less relevant predictor of students' performance. In six countries, the individual students' socio-economic background no longer shows a significant impact once the schools social impact and the other variables are accounted for.

By contrast, differences in the socio-economic background between schools do play an extremely important role (peer-group effect, red bars). The impact of a change in the school's average socio-economic background by one national standard deviation of the PISA international socio-economic index of occupational status is associated with a difference of more than 50 points on the combined reading literacy scale for six of the 13 non-OECD countries. With coefficients at the school level of 63.7 and 82.6 respectively, Germany and Poland showed the strongest impact within OECD countries, but Albania, Bulgaria, Israel, FYR Macedonia and Peru all fall within the same range. In Argentina, the influence of the school's socio-economic background is slightly lower, while in Chile, it comes relatively close to the OECD country mean of 37.8. The only non-OECD countries in which schools' socio-economic background seems to matter less than average are, once again, the Asian countries of Hong Kong-China, Indonesia and Thailand.

Figure 7.18 allows a direct comparison of the impact of the socio-economic background at the individual student's level (within a given school) with the impact of the socio-economic background of the school. Note that the two axes use unequal scales and that even in countries where individual effects can be considered as relatively strong from a cross-country perspective, they generally remain weak when compared to the corresponding peer-group effects.

In countries towards the left, the impact of students' socio-economic background matters relatively little, at either the student or the school level. This is where all Asian countries are located irrespective of their level of economic development and their initial income distribution. They compare well even with the regional cluster of the Nordic countries at the right side of the figure, where socio-economic background plays an equally small role in explaining differences in performance between schools, but a relatively important role in explaining differences in performance for individual students within schools.

Most of the countries in transition are located towards the upper part of the graph, with the non-OECD country Bulgaria topping the list just after Poland. In Israel the situation is similar, with a slightly less pronounced impact of socio-economic background at school level, but a slightly stronger student level effect.

The picture is mixed for the Latin-American countries. While the effect of socio-economic background at the individual student's level does not seem to be particularly pronounced in any of these countries, the impact at school level varies from intermediate (Brazil, Chile, Mexico) to high (Peru).

How should these differences between countries and regions be interpreted? In fact, if school-level socio-economic differences explain a major part of performance differences between schools, this indicates relatively strong socio-economic segregation, *i.e.*, major differences in schools' socio-economic intake. Could the relevance of schools' socio-economic background be a simple reflection of purposeful academic selection into different institutions with the objective of building academically homogeneous clusters of students? The advantage of analysing net effects is that this academic and not directly socially based selection can be corrected for a variable is introduced into the regression model which can be considered as an indicator of prior academic performance. One variable already introduced in the multivariate regression discussed above is students' engagement in reading. Since engagement in reading is highly correlated with reading proficiency, and, at the same time, reading proficiency is highly correlated with proficiency

Figure 7.18

Effects of students' socio-economic background and schools' socio-economic background
on performance on the combined reading literacy scale

◇ OECD country with high income   ◇ Non-OECD country with high income
◆ OECD country with low and middle income   ◆ Non-OECD country with low and middle income

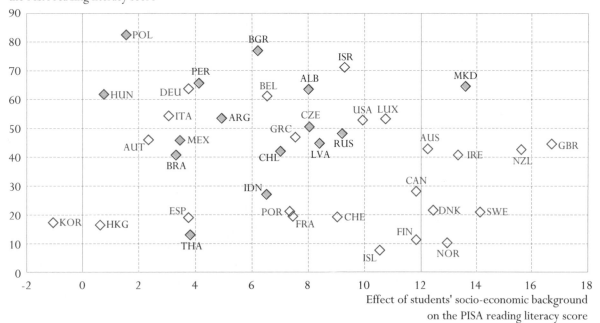

Source: OECD PISA database, 2003. Table 7.15.

in mathematics and science, it does not seem inappropriate to consider the effect of the school mean for engagement in reading as an indicator of academic selection (OECD, 2002*b*, Chapter 7, p. 154). Since this variable was already introduced into the regression model, the net effect of the socio-economic variable considered above does not include the effect of academic selection, at least to the extent that engagement in reading is a valid predictor for academic selection. Similarly, since engagement in reading was introduced as a separate variable at student level, the net effect of each student's socio-economic background within a given school can be considered as corrected for his or her prior academic achievement.

Interpreting the impact of engagement in reading on performance as an indicator of the effect of students' academic ability, it is interesting to compare the relevance of the student and school level effects, *i.e.*, the impact of students' individual skills versus the impact of being surrounded by peers with a certain average academic ability. To allow for this comparison, Figure 7.19 replicates Figure 7.18, but based on reading engagement.

Again, peer-group effects appear, on average, to be much more relevant than individual effects, although the differences are not as striking as with respect to socio-economic background. In four out of the thirteen non-OECD countries, reading engagement seems to have a relatively low influence on the whole, with regard to both individual students and peer-effects. These countries are Albania, Indonesia, FYR Macedonia and Peru. In Argentina, Brazil and Israel, reading engagement does not explain much of the variation between schools either, but it is a more relevant predictor of performance at the individual level. In none of the non-OECD countries, however, does individual engagement in reading play such a strong role as in the Nordic countries and Iceland (at the extreme right of Figure 7.19). In these countries, engagement in reading has a strong impact on student performance, but it does not seem to be very relevant for explaining differences between schools. The opposite is true for most of the Asian countries, notably for Hong Kong-China, and, to a lesser extent, for Korea and Thailand. In Bulgaria, Greece and Poland, the situation is similar. In all these countries, academic skills as indicated by reading engagement appear to be an extremely relevant determinant of performance differences between schools while being of only intermediate importance at the individual student level. Academic selection appears to play a particularly strong role in these countries.

It is worth noting the particular situation of Chile because the country's voucher system was the subject of considerable controversy, precisely because of its potential to accentuate segregation by skills.[11] In this country, the coefficient of average reading engagement at school level indicating academic selection remains close to the country average, although it is higher than in the other Latin-American countries.

Finally, Figure 7.20 compares socio-economic selection with academic selection as indicated by the peer-group effects of the index of students' socio-economic background and students' reading engagement respectively. Drawing a diagonal through the origin helps to examine the relative prevalence of socio-economic segregation (to the right of the line) and academic segregation (to the left of the line). In countries situated close to the origin neither of the two selection mechanisms play a very important role. The Nordic countries and Iceland are among these. Among the thirteen non-OECD countries, ten are located clearly to the right of the line. At their respective level of the effect of schools' engagement in reading, Albania, Bulgaria, Israel, FYR Macedonia and Peru show the highest impact of schools' socio-economic background, *i.e.*, the highest socio-economic segregation of all countries in the PISA sample.

Looking at regional similarities, it can be noted that all Latin-American countries share a low to intermediate relevance of academic selection, though at widely diverging levels of socio-economic selection.

Figure 7.19

Effects of students' reading engagement and schools' average reading engagement
on performance on the combined reading literacy scale

◇ OECD country with high income   ◇ Non-OECD country with high income
◆ OECD country with low and middle income   ◆ Non-OECD country with low and middle income

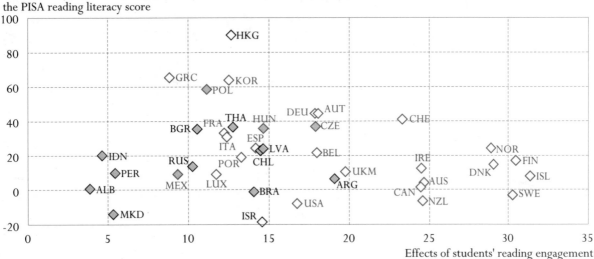

Effects of schools' reading engagement on
the PISA reading literacy score

Effects of students' reading engagement
on the PISA reading literacy score

Source: OECD PISA database, 2003. Table 7.15.

The Eastern European countries Bulgaria, Czech Republic, Hungary and Poland as well as Austria and Germany present a similar diversity with respect to schools' socio-economic selection, albeit at a higher level of academic selection. In these countries, both social and academic selection appear to be highly relevant.

The East-Asian countries including Korea and the non-OECD countries of Hong Kong-China, Indonesia and Thailand, are among the minority of countries where socio-economic segregation does not clearly predominate. While Indonesia remains slightly to the right of the line, all other Asian countries are located clearly to the left. Hong Kong-China is the most extreme case, with selection strongly based on academic criteria. While there is considerable diversity with respect to academic selection among the different Asian countries, they all share relatively low levels of socio-economic selection which makes them comparable to the Nordic countries.

The data show that reduced socio-economic segregation does not necessarily lead to worse results with respect to students' overall performance. Canada, Finland, Hong Kong-China, Korea and Sweden, are among the top ten performers on the combined reading literacy scale. None of the countries with high socio-economic segregation is represented in that group.

Since regression results reveal that, in many countries, the impact of schools' socio-economic background is much stronger than the effect of any other variable (including, school climate, homework, reading engagement etc., see Table 7.15, Annex B1), policy reform in this area appears to be particularly important.

The following section provides an overview of some factors that might account for social segregation. These factors may provide a starting point for further analysis on a country-by-country basis.

Figure 7.20

Effects of schools' socio-economic background versus schools' reading engagement
on performance on the combined reading literacy scale

◇ OECD country with high income   ◇ Non-OECD country with high income
◆ OECD country with low and middle income   ◆ Non-OECD country with low and middle income

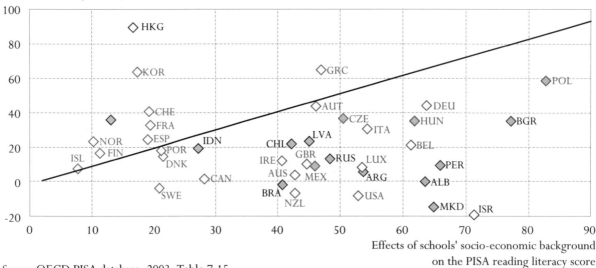

Effects of schools' reading engagement on
the PISA reading literacy score

Effects of schools' socio-economic background
on the PISA reading literacy score

Source: OECD PISA database, 2003. Table 7.15.

Factors of social selection for different schools

In order to go beyond the mere observation of social segregation, it is necessary to analyse the structural features of national education systems. One explanation for social segregation can be differences between public and private schools, especially if enrolment in the latter requires substantial fees. A second explanation may be diversified institutional structures with streaming into general or vocational / technical orientations. While the intention is generally to create academically rather than socially homogeneous groups, selection at early grade levels as well as selection primarily based on parental choice may lead to a predominance of socio-economic criteria. A third explanation may simply be local or regional variations in the socio-economic background of the population.

Figure 7.21 shows all participating countries ranked by the relevance of social selection as indicated by the school level coefficient (peer-group effect, see Table 7.15 Annex B) of students' socio-economic background. The figure also presents some evidence on the relevance of the different structural features of the education system for explaining the extent of socio-economic segregation. Intermediate figures and early ages for streaming are marked in bold grey; very high figures or very early streaming are marked in bold black.

Among the ten countries with the most pronounced socio-economic segregation observed in PISA, all carry out selection procedures that channel students into different streams of secondary education before or at the age of assessment. In Belgium, Germany, Hungary and Israel, students have to choose particularly early, at the ages of 10 to 12, between different orientations. In all four countries, among the structural variables presented here, streaming seems to be the most relevant. Government-independent private schools either do not play an important role within the education system or do not seem to discriminate

Figure 7.21
Structural features of the education system and socio-economic segregation

Country Ranked by order of socio-economic selection effect	Relevance of private schools		Streaming Age of first streaming	Socio-economic advantage of urban schools
	Percentage of students in government-independent private schools	Differences in mean ISEI[1] for public and government-independent private schools		Differences in mean ISEI[1] for schools in cities with less than 15 000 inhabitants, and cities between 100 000 and 1 000 000 inhabitants[2]
Poland	2.9	12.3	15	8.2
Bulgaria	0.6	**18.7**	14	7.3
Israel	4.2	11.7	**12**	1.8
Peru	6.7	14.8	15	a
FYR Macedonia	0.0	13.0	15	5.0
Germany	a	a	**10**	4.4
Albania	3.9	9.7	14	**12.0**
Hungary	0.3	-11.4	**11**	7.5
Belgium	m	m	**12**	3.5
Italy	5.1	6.8	14	7.4
Argentina	6.5	**25.2**	18	9.3
Luxembourg	a	a	**13**	4.4
United States	4.3	3.5	a	5.2
Czech Republic	0.2	c	**11**	3.6
Russian Federation	a	a	15	5.8
Greece	4.1	**20.6**	15	7.8
Austria	5.0	10.1	**10**	4.1
Mexico	**14.9**	**18.5**	**12**	12.8
Latvia	a	a	15	2.5
United Kingdom	9.2	14.7	a	-2.0
Australia	m	m	a	8.0
New Zealand	4.8	12.3	a	**9.8**
Chile	**12.9**	**21.9**	14	7.9
Brazil	10.5	15.4	18	7.5
Ireland	2.9	**18.0**	15	3.1
Canada	2.6	12.1	a	a
Indonesia	**46.6**	-0.6	15	**9.9**
Denmark	a	a	16	5.9
Portugal	1.5	12.3	15	7.6
Sweden	a	a	16	**9.3**
France	m	m	15	**9.2**
Switzerland	4.7	15.1	15	8.1
Spain	9.2	**21.5**	16	7.4
Korea	**33.6**	1.3	14	7.1
Hong Kong-China	0.5	**19.2**	19	5.6
Thailand	**17.5**	4.0	14	**12.9**
Finland	a	a	16	**10.4**
Norway	a	a	16	7.3
Iceland	0.8	c	16	a

1. For the definition of the index see Annex A1.

2. Information for schools in cities with more than 1 000 000 inhabitants is equally available. However, specific features of megacities tend to blur the typical rural-urban divide. This is why the cities in the lower size category were used for the comparison of means.

General note: Relatively high figures / early streaming are marked in bold black, intermediate figures are marked in bold gray and low figures / late or no streaming are marked in normal font.

Sources: Annex B1, Table 4.13 for the relevance of private schools; Annex B1, Table 4.14 for the socio-economic advantage of urban schools; for the age of first streaming: OECD (1999*b*), European Commission (2002, chapter B), Macedonian Ministry of Education and Science (2001), Institute of International Education Hong Kong (2003), Israeli Ministry of Education (2002, p. 12).

against students from lower social backgrounds. At the same time, there is not much evidence for social segregation due to geographical reasons either, though it should be taken into account that, in addition to the urban-rural divide for which the evidence is provided here, there may be other geographical divides, *e.g.*, between certain quarters within a city, or between different regions.

Looking at regional similarities, it can be noted that early streaming before the age of 13 is predominantly observed in German speaking and Eastern European education systems.

A common feature of all East-Asian countries except Hong Kong-China is the high share of students enrolled in private schools.[12] This may be surprising given their position at the very end of the list in Figure 7.21. In fact, in these countries, the institutional choice does not seem to be strongly related to students' socio-economic background. In Indonesia and Korea where enrolment rates in government-independent private schools are far higher than in all participating countries, the difference of the average socio-economic background between the two types of institutions is not significantly different from zero (see Table 7.13, Annex B1).

The opposite is true for all Latin-American countries. While the share of students in government-independent private schools is considerably lower (varying from close to 7 per cent in Argentina and Peru to almost 15 per cent in Mexico), those students who do attend private schools are generally selected from families with a significantly higher socio-economic background.

The socio-economic divide between schools in urban and rural (or smaller urban) areas does not seem to follow any regional patterns. Among non-OECD countries, it is particularly relevant for Albania, Argentina, Indonesia, and Thailand.

Conclusions

Home background influences educational success, and socio-economic status may reinforce its effects. Although PISA shows that poor performance in school is not automatically related to a disadvantaged socio-economic background, it appears to be one of the most powerful factors influencing performance on the PISA reading, mathematical and scientific literacy scales.

This represents a significant challenge for public policy, which strives to provide learning opportunities for all students irrespective of their home backgrounds. National research evidence from various countries has generally been discouraging. Schools have appeared to make little difference. Either because privileged families are better able to reinforce and enhance the effect of schools, or because schools are better able to nurture and develop young people from privileged backgrounds. It has often been apparent that schools reproduce existing patterns of privilege rather than deliver equal opportunities in a way that can distribute outcomes more equitably.

The international evidence of PISA is more encouraging. While all countries show a clear positive relationship between home background and educational outcomes, some countries demonstrate that high average quality and equality of educational outcomes can go together: Canada, Finland, Hong Kong-China, Iceland, Japan, Korea and Sweden all display above-average levels of student performance on the combined reading literacy scale and, at the same time, a below-average impact of economic, social and cultural status on student performance. Conversely, average performance in reading literacy in the Czech Republic, Germany, Hungary and Luxembourg is significantly below the OECD average while, at the same time, there are above-average disparities between students from advantaged and disadvantaged socio-economic backgrounds.

One of the most important findings of PISA is that the student's own home background is only part of the story of socio-economic disparities in education – and in most countries the smaller part. The combined impact of the school's socio-economic intake can have an appreciable effect on the student's performance, and generally has a greater effect on predicted student scores than the student's own family characteristics.

A second key finding from the analysis of PISA results is that beneficial school effects are reinforced by socio-economic background. Schools with more resources and policies and practices associated with better student performance tend, to varying degrees, to have more advantaged students. The net result of this effect is that in countries where there is a high degree of segregation along socio-economic lines, students from disadvantaged socio-economic backgrounds do worse. This, in turn, means that some of the inequality of outcomes observed in the analysis of socio-economic gradients is associated with inequality of opportunity. In such circumstances, talent remains unused and human resources are wasted.

In some countries, students are highly segregated along socio-economic lines, in part because of residential segregation and economic factors, but also because of features of the education system. Education policy in such countries might attempt to moderate the impact of socio-economic background on student performance by reducing the extent of segregation along socio-economic lines, or by allocating resources to schools differentially. In these countries, it may be necessary to examine how the allocation of school resources within a country relates to the socio-economic intake of its schools. In other countries, there is relatively little socio-economic segregation, i.e. schools tend to be similar in their socio-economic intake. Education policy in these countries might aim to moderate the impact of socio-economic background through measures targeted at improving school resources and reducing within-school segregation according to students' economic, social and cultural status. Of course, what matters most in the end is how effectively resources are used. Approaches might include, for example, eliminating classroom streaming or providing more assistance for students with a poor level of performance.

In countries where the impact of socio-economic background on student performance is moderate, not all successes can be credited to the education system and, in countries where gradients are steep, not all of the problems should be attributed to schools either. The analysis has shown that the challenges which education systems face as a result of the differences in the distribution of socio-economic factors in the student population differ widely. Many of the factors of socio-economic disadvantage are also not directly linked to education policy, at least not in the short term. For example, the educational attainment of parents can only gradually improve, and family wealth will depend on long-term national economic development.

But PISA results suggest that school policy and schools themselves can play a crucial role in moderating the impact of social disadvantage on student performance. The results reveal some school resource factors, school policies and classroom practices that appear to make a significant difference to student performance. The extent to which students make use of school resources, and the extent to which specialist teachers are available, can both have an impact on student performance. According to principals' perceptions of teacher-related factors affecting school climate, teacher morale and commitment, and some aspects of school autonomy, also appear to make a difference. Finally, there are aspects of classroom practice that show a positive relationship with student performance, such as teacher-student relations and the disciplinary climate in the classroom.

PISA results suggest that there is no single factor that explains why some schools or some countries have better results than others. Successful performance is attributable to a variety of factors, including school resources, school policy and practice, and classroom practice. It will require much further research and analysis to identify how these factors operate, interact with home background, and influence student performance.

In pursuit of this deeper understanding, a series of thematic PISA reports in 2003 and 2004 will analyse the impact of school and system-level factors on student performance more extensively, and will seek to understand in more detail why some countries achieve better and more equitable learning outcomes than others. In the meantime, the mere fact that high-quality learning outcomes are already a reality for most students in some countries is, in itself, an encouraging result that shows that the challenges ahead can be tackled successfully.

Notes

1. For the exact definition of the indices, see Annex A1.

2. The source of this indicator, here and elsewhere in this chapter, is World Bank (2002).

3. For several developing countries, Pritchett and Filmer (1999) directly compare the efficiency of an improvement in school infrastructure and educational resources on the basis of a one-unit rise in expenditures. They find a much higher impact of change in educational resources and suggest a politico-economic model to explain the frequently observed and inefficient policy emphasis on infrastructure and other even less relevant determinants of student performance.

4. For the data on population, see World Bank (2002).

5. For an overview on the evidence of class size, see Hanushek (1998).

6. Starting with the seminal papers of Summers and Wolfe (1977) and Henderson, Mieszkowski and Sauvageau (1978), a huge scientific literature has developed around the topic of peer-effects within schools. More recent examples are Hoxby (2000), Sacerdote (2001) or McEvan (2003).

7. For the data on Gini-coefficients, see Table 1.4, Annex B1. No data are available for Albania and Argentina.

8. The cross-country correlation of country means is 0.72.

9. See Table 7.15, Annex B1 for the full regression.

10. To be precise, slight differences may exist between the coefficients reported here and the coefficients reported in Table 6.1a, Annex B1. Differences are due to the fact that for the purpose of comparing different coefficients within one country regression, the socio-economic index of occupational status (ISEI) was standardised at the national level here while it was standardised at the international level earlier. Since in general, national standard deviations of ISEI do not diverge much from its international standard deviation, observed differences in coefficients remain very small (changes visible only at the second or third decimal point).

11. See *e.g.,* Hsieh, Chang-Tai and Miguel Urquiola (2002).

12. Including Japan, although this country is not included on Figure 7.21 due to missing data for socio-economic segregation. For the Japanese data on private schools, see Table 7.13, Annex B1.

REFERENCES

Audas, R. and **J.D. Willms** (2000), *Engagement and Dropping out of School: A life-course perspective,* Report prepared for Human Resources Development, Canada.

Baumert, J., S. Gruehn, S. Heyn, O. Köller and **K.U. Schnabel** (1997), *Bildungsverläufe und Psychosoziale Entwicklung im Jugendalter (BIJU): Dokumentation - Band 1,* Max-Planck-Institut für Bildungsforschung, Berlin.

Baumert, J., S. Heyn and **O. Köller** (1994), *Das Kieler Lernstrategien-Inventar (KSI),* Institut für die Pädagogik der Naturwissenschaften an der Universität Kiel, Kiel.

Beaton, A.E., I.V. Mullis, M.O. Martin, E.J. Gonzalez, D.L. Kelly and **T.A. Smith** (1996), *Mathematics Achievement in the Middle School Years,* Center for the Study of Testing, Evaluation and Educational Policy, Boston College.

Brookover, W.B., J.H. Schweitzer, J.M. Schneider, C.H. Beady, P.K. Flood and **J.M. Wisenbaker** (1978), "Elementary school social climate and school achievement", *American Educational Research Journal,* Vol. 15, pp. 301-318.

Bryk, A.S. and **S.W. Raudenbush** (1992), *Hierarchical Linear Models: Application and Data Analysis Models,* Advanced Qualitative Techniques in the Social Sciences No. 1, London (Sage).

Centre for Development of Teaching and Learning (CDTL) (2001), "Facilitating students' learning: Co-operation or competition?", *Ideas on teaching,* Issue 20.

Eignor, D., C. Taylor, I. Kirsch and **J. Jamieson** (1998), *Development of a Scale for Assessing the Level of Computer Familiarity of TOEFL Students,* TOEFL Research Report No. 60, Educational Testing Service, Princeton, NJ.

European Commission (2002), Key Data on Education in Europe. Brussels, Belgium.

Fiszbein, A. (1999), *Institutions, Service Delivery and Social Exclusion: A Case Study of the Education Sector in Buenos Aires,* Human Development Department, LCSHD Paper Series No. 47, World Bank, Latin America and the Caribbean Regional Office, Washington.

Ganzeboom, H.B.G., P. De Graaf and **D.J. Treiman** (with J. De Leeuw) (1992), "A standard international socio-economic index of occupational status", *Social Science Research,* Vol. 21(1), pp. 1-56.

Ganzeboom, H.B.G., D.J. Treiman and **J. Donald** (1996), "Internationally comparable measures of occupational status for the 1988 International Standard Classification of Occupations", *Social Science Research,* Vol. 25, pp. 201-239. Henderson, V., Mieszkowski, P. and Sauvageau, Y. (1978), "Peer group effects and educational production functions", *Journal of Public Economics,* Vol. 10, pp. 97-106.

Goldstein, H. (1999), *Multilevel Statistical Models, Kendal's Library on Statistics,* Internet Edition, *http://www.arnoldpublishers.com/ support/goldstein.htm* (26/02/03).

Hanushek, E.A. (1998), *The Evidence on Class Size,* Occasional Paper No. 98-1, W. Allan Wallis Institute of Political Economy, University of Rochester.

Henderson, V., P. Mieszkowski and Y. Sauvageau (1978), "Peer Group Effects and Educational Production Functions", *Journal of Public Economics,* Vol. 10, No. 1, pp. 97-106.

House, J., R. Kessler, R. Herzog, R.P. Mero, A.M. Kinney and **M.J. Breslow** (1990), "Age, socioeconomic status, and health", *The Millbank Quarterly,* Vol. 68, pp. 383-411.

Hoxby, C. (2000), *Peer Effects in the Classroom: Learning from Gender and Race Variation,* NBER Working Paper No: 7867.

Hsieh, C. and **M. Urquiola** (2002), *When Schools Compete, How Do They Compete? An Assessment of Chile's Nationwide School Voucher Program,* Princeton University and Cornell University mimeo, *http://www.worldbank.org/research/projects/service_delivery/paper_ hsieh.pdf* (26/02/03).

INSEE-DPD (1999), *Etude de la fiabilité des déclarations des élèves de 15 ans dans le cadre de l'opération PISA 2000,* document interne, DPD-INSEE, France.

Institute of International Education Hong Kong - China (2003), *Hong Kong - China: Local and International Education, http://www.iiehongkong.org/hked/hkeducation.htm* (6/2/03).

Israeli Ministry of Education (2002), *Structure of the Education System*, *www.education.gov.il/minhal_calcala/ download/ facts2.pdf* (6/2/03).

Kerckhoff, A.C. (1986), "Effects of ability grouping in British secondary schools", *American Sociological Review*, Vol. 51, pp. 842-858.

Macedonian Ministry of Education and Science (2001), *Structure of Education System in Macedonia*, *http:// www.euroeducation.net/prof/macenco.htm* (6/2/03).

McEvan, P. J. (2003), "Peer Effects on Student Achievement: Evidence from Chile", *Economics of Education Review*, Vol. 22, pp. 131-141.

Marsh, H.W., R.J. Shavelson and **B.M. Byrne** (1992), "A multidimensional, hierarchical self-concept", in R. P. Lipka and T. M. Brinthaupt (Eds.), *Studying the Self: Self-perspectives across the life-span*, State University of New York Press, Albany.

Mirowsky, J. and **P. Hu** (1996), "Physical impairment and the diminishing effects of income", *Social Forces*, Vol. 74(3), pp. 1073-1096.

Mullis, I.V. et al. (2000), *TIMSS 1999 International Mathematics Report*, Boston.

Mullis, I.V., M.O. Martin, A.E. Beaton, E.J. Gonzalez, D.L. Kelly and **T.A. Smith** (1998), *Mathematics and Science Achievement in the Final Year of Secondary School*, Center for the Study of Testing, Evaluation and Educational Policy, Boston College.

OECD (1996), *Education at a Glance - OECD Indicators*, Paris.

OECD (1997), *Education at a Glance - OECD Indicators*, Paris.

OECD (1999*a*), *Measuring Student Knowledge and Skills – A New Framework for Assessment*, Paris.

OECD (1999*b*), *Classifying Educational Programmes. Manual for ISCED-97 Implementation in OECD Countries*, Paris.

OECD (2000*)*, *Motivating Students for Lifelong Learning*, Paris.

OECD (2001*a*), *Education at a Glance - OECD Indicators*, Paris.

OECD (2001*b*), *Knowledge and Skills for Life - First Results from PISA 2000*, Paris.

OECD (2002*a*), *PISA 2000 Technical Report*, Paris.

OECD (2002*b*), *Reading for Change – Performance and Engagement across Countries*, Paris.

OECD (2002*c*), *Sample Tasks from the PISA 2000 Assessment – Reading, Mathematical and Scientific Literacy*, Paris.

OECD (2002*d*), *Thematic Review of National Policies for Education - Albania*, CCNM/DEELSA/ED(2001)2, Paris.

OECD (2002*e*), *Education at a Glance*, Paris.

OECD (2003*a*, in press), *Learners for Life: Approaches to Learning*, Paris.

OECD (2003*b*, in press), *Student Disaffection with School*, Paris.

OECD (2003*c*, in press), *Education at a Glance*, Paris.

OECD and **Statistics Canada** (1995), *Literacy, Economy and Society: Results of the First International Adult Literacy Survey*, Paris and Ottawa.

OECD and **Statistics Canada** (2000), *Literacy in the Information Age*, Paris and Ottawa.

Owens, L. and **J. Barnes** (1992), *Learning Preferences Scales*, ACER, Victoria, Australia.

Pelgrum, W.J. and **R.E. Anderson** (1999), *ICT and the Emerging Paradigm for Lifelong Learning: a worldwide educational assessment of infrastructure, goals, and practices*, International Association for the Evaluation of Educational Achievement (IEA), Amsterdam.

Pintrich, P.R., D.A.F. Smith, T. Garcia and **W.J. McKeachie** (1993), "Reliability and predictive validity of the motivated strategies for learning questionnaire (MLSQ)", *Educational and Psychological Measurement*, Vol. 53, pp. 801-813.

Pritchett, L. and **D. Filmer** (1999), "What Education Production Functions Really Show, A Positive Theory of Education Expenditure", *Economics of Education Review*, Vol. 18, pp. 223-239.

Rumberger, R. and **J.D. Willms** (1992), "The impact of racial and ethnic segregation on the achievement gap in California high schools", *Educational Evaluation and Policy Analysis*, Vol. 14(4), pp. 377-396.

Sacerdote, B. (2001), "Peer Effects with Random Assignment: Results for Dartmouth Roommates", *Quarterly Journal of Economics*, Vol. 116, No. 2, pp. 681-704.

Shavit, Y. and **R.A. Williams** (1985), "Ability grouping and contextual determinants of educational expectations in Israel", *American Sociological Review*, Vol. 50, pp. 62-73.

Summers, A.A. and **B.L. Wolfe** (1977), "Do schools make a difference?", *American Economic Review,* Vol. 67, pp. 639-652.

UIS (2002), Statistical Tables, *http://portal.unesco.org/uis/ev.php?URL_ID=5187&URL_DO=DO_TOPIC&URL_SECTION=201* (20/02/03).

UNESCO-UIS/OECD (2000), *Investing in Education - Analysis of the 1999 World Education Indicators*, Montreal and Paris.

UNESCO-UIS/OECD (2001), *Teachers for Tomorrow's Schools: Analysis of the World Education Indicators*, Paris and Montreal.

UNESCO-UIS/OECD (2003), *Financing Education - Investments and Returns: Analysis of the World Education Indicators*, Montreal and Paris.

Warm, T.A. (1985), "Weighted maximum likelihood estimation of ability in Item Response Theory with tests of finite length", *Technical Report CGI-TR-85-08,* U.S. Coast Guard Institute, Oklahoma City.

Wilder, G.Z. and **K. Powell** (1989), *Sex differences in test performance: A survey of the literature*, College Board Report No.89-3.

Willms, J.D. (1986), "Social class segregation and its relationship to pupils' examination results in Scotland", *American Sociological Review,* Vol. 51, pp. 224-241.

Willms, J.D. and **M. Chen** (1989), "The effects of ability grouping on the ethnic achievement gap in Israeli elementary schools", *American Journal of Education*, Vol. 97(3), pp. 237-257.

Wolfson, M., G. Rowe, J.F. Gentleman and **M. Tomiak** (1993), "Career earnings and death: A longitudinal analysis of older Canadian men", *Journal of Gerontology*, Vol. 48(4), pp. S167-S179.

World Bank (2002), *World Development Indicators*, CD ROM, Washington.

ANNEX A

Annex A1: Construction of indices and other derived measures from the student and school context questionnaires

Several of PISA's measures reflect indices that summarise responses from students or school representatives (typically principals) to a series of related questions. The questions were selected from larger constructs on the basis of theoretical considerations and previous research. Structural equation modelling was used to confirm the theoretically expected behaviour of the indices and to validate their comparability across countries. For this purpose, a model was estimated separately for each country and, collectively, for all OECD countries.

This section explains the indices derived from the student and school context questionnaires that are used in this report. For a detailed description of other PISA indices and details on the methods see the *PISA 2000 Technical Report* (OECD, 2002a).

Unless otherwise indicated, where an index involves multiple questions and student responses, the index was scaled using a weighted maximum likelihood estimate, using a one-parameter item response model (referred to as a WARM estimator; see Warm, 1985) with three stages:

- The question parameters were estimated from equal-sized sub-samples of students from each OECD country.

- The estimates were computed for all students and all schools by anchoring the question parameters obtained in the preceding step.

- The in dices were then standardised so that the mean of the index value for the OECD student population was zero and the standard deviation was one (countries being given equal weight in the standardisation process).

It is important to note that negative values in an index do not necessarily imply that students responded negatively to the underlying questions. A negative value merely indicates that a group of students (or all students, collectively, in a single country) or principals responded less positively than all students or principals did on average across OECD countries. Likewise, a positive value on an index indicates that a group of students or principals responded more favourably, or more positively, than students or principals did, on average, in OECD countries.

Terms enclosed in brackets < > in the following descriptions were replaced in the national versions of the student and school questionnaires by the appropriate national equivalent. For example, the term <qualification at ISCED level 5A> was translated in the United States into "Bachelor's Degree, post-graduate certificate program, Master's degree program or first professional degree program". Similarly the term <classes in the language of assessment> in Luxembourg was translated into "German classes" or "French classes" depending on whether students received the German or French version of the assessment instruments.

For the reliabilities of the indices, see the *PISA 2000 Technical Report (OECD, 2002a)*.

Student characteristics and family background

Family structure

Students were asked to report who usually lived at home with them. The response categories were then grouped into four categories: *i)* **single-parent family** (students who reported living with one of the following: mother, father, female guardian or male guardian); *ii)* **nuclear family** (students who reported living with a mother and a father); *iii)* **mixed family** (students who reported living with a mother and a male guardian, a father and a female guardian, or two guardians); and *iv)* **other response combinations.**

Number of siblings

Students were asked to indicate the number of siblings older than themselves, younger than themselves, or of the same age. For the analyses in Chapter 8, the numbers in each category were added together.

Country of birth

Students were asked if they, their mother and their father were born in the country of assessment or in another country. The response categories were then grouped into three categories: *i)* **"native"** students (those students born in the country of assessment and who had at least one parent born in that country); *ii)* **"first-generation"** students (those born in the country of assessment but whose parents were born in another country); and *iii)* **"non-native"** students (those born outside the country of assessment and whose parents were also born in another country).

Language spoken at home

Students were asked if the **language spoken at home** most of the time is the language of assessment, another official national language, other national dialect or language, or another language. The responses were then grouped into two categories: *i)* the language spoken at home most of the time is different from the language of assessment, from other official national languages, and from other national dialects or languages, and *ii)* the language spoken at home most of the time is the language of assessment, other official national languages, or other national dialects or languages.

Economic, social and cultural status

Students were asked to report their mothers' and fathers' occupations, and to state whether each parent was: in full-time paid work; part-time paid work; not working but looking for a paid job; or "other". The open-ended responses were then coded in accordance with the International Standard Classification of Occupations (ISCO 1988).

The PISA **International Socio-Economic Index of Occupational Status** (ISEI) was derived from students' responses on parental occupation. The index captures the attributes of occupations that convert parents' education into income. The index was derived by the optimal scaling of occupation groups to maximise the indirect effect of education on income through occupation and to minimise the direct effect of education on income, net of occupation (both effects being net of age). For more information on the methodology, see Ganzeboom *et al.* (1992). The PISA International Socio-Economic Index of Occupational Status is based on either the father's or mother's occupations, whichever is the higher.

Values on the index range from 0 to 90; low values represent low socio-economic status and high values represent high socio-economic status.

To capture wider aspects of a student's family and home background in addition to occupational status, the PISA *index of economic, social and cultural status* was created on the basis of the following variables: the International Socio-Economic Index of Occupational Status (ISEI) (see Table 6.1a, Annex B1); the highest level of education of the student's parents, converted into years of schooling (for data on parental levels of education see Table 6.5, for the conversion coefficients see Table A1.1); the PISA index of family wealth (see Table 6.2, Annex B1); the PISA index of home educational resources; and the PISA index of possessions related to "classical" culture in the family home. The ISEI represents the first principle component of the factors described above. The index has been constructed such that its mean is 0 and its standard deviation is 1.

Table A.1.1
Levels of parental education converted into years of schooling

	Did not go to school	Completed <ISCED Level 1 (primary education)>	Completed <ISCED Level 2 (lower secondary education)>	Completed <ISCED Levels 3B or 3C (upper secondary education aimed at direct entry into the labour market)>	Completed <ISCED Level 3A (upper secondary education aimed at entry into tertiary education)>	Completed <ISCED Level 5A, 5B or 6 (tertiary education)
Albania	0.0	4.0	8.0	12.0	12.0	16.0
Argentina	0.0	6.0	9.0	12.0	12.0	16.0
Australia	0.0	7.5	11.0	13.0	13.0	16.5
Austria	0.0	4.0	8.0	11.0	13.0	15.5
Belgium (Fl.)	0.0	6.0	8.0	12.0	12.0	16.5
Belgium (Fr.)	0.0	6.0	8.5	12.0	12.0	16.5
Brazil	0.0	6.0	9.0	12.0	12.0	15.5
Bulgaria	0.0	4.0	8.0	10.0	11.0	14.0
Canada	0.0	6.0	9.0	12.0	12.0	14.5
Chile	0.0	6.0	8.0	12.0	12.0	16.0
Czech Republic	0.0	5.0	9.0	12.0	13.0	16.0
Denmark	0.0	6.0	9.5	12.0	12.0	15.0
Finland	0.0	6.0	9.0	12.0	12.0	15.0
France	0.0	5.0	9.0	12.0	12.0	15.0
Germany	0.0	4.0	9.5	12.5	13.0	18.0
Greece	0.0	6.0	9.0	11.5	12.0	16.0
Hong Kong-China	0.0	6.0	9.0	12.0	13.0	16.5
Hungary	0.0	4.0	9.0	11.5	12.5	15.0
Iceland	0.0	7.0	11.0	13.5	14.0	18.0
Indonesia	0.0	6.0	9.0	12.0	12.0	14.5
Ireland	0.0	8.0	11.0	12.0	13.5	15.5
Israel	0.0	6.0	9.0	12.0	12.0	14.5
Italy	0.0	5.0	8.0	12.0	13.0	16.5
Japan	0.0	6.0	9.0	12.0	12.0	15.5
Korea	0.0	5.0	9.0	12.0	12.0	16.0
Liechtenstein	0.0	5.0	9.0	13.0	13.0	16.0
Luxembourg	0.0	6.0	8.5	13.0	13.0	15.5
FYR Macedonia	0.0	4.0	8.0	12.0	12.0	15.5
Mexico	0.0	6.0	9.5	12.0	12.0	15.0
New Zealand	0.0	6.0	10.0	12.0	13.0	16.0
Norway	0.0	6.0	9.0	12.0	12.0	15.5
Peru	0.0	6.0	9.0	11.0	11.0	14.5
Poland	0.0	8.0	11.0	12.5	16.0	16.0
Portugal	0.0	6.5	9.0	12.0	12.0	16.0
Russian Federation	0.0	4.0	8.0	11.0	11.0	16.0
Spain	0.0	6.0	9.5	11.5	11.5	15.0
Sweden	0.0	9.0	11.0	12.0	12.0	15.5
Switzerland	0.0	6.0	9.5	11.5	12.5	16.0
Thailand	0.0	6.0	9.0	12.0	12.0	15.5
United Kingdom	0.0	6.0	9.0	11.0	12.5	14.5
United States	0.0	6.0	9.0	12.0	12.0	14.5
Netherlands[1]	0.0	6.0	9.5	12.0	12.0	16.5

1. Response rate is too low to ensure comparability (see Annex A3).
Source: UNESCO-UIS/OECD WEI (2003); UNESCO Institute for Statistics (UIS).

Among these components, the data most commonly missing relate to the International Socio-Economic Index of Occupational Status (ISEI), parental education, or both. Separate factor analyses were therefore undertaken for all students with valid data for: *i)* the socio-economic index of occupational status, the index of family wealth, the index of home educational resources and the index of possessions related to "classical" culture in the family home; *ii)* years of parental education, the index of family wealth, the index of home educational resources and the index of possessions related to "classical" culture in the family home; and *iii)* the index of family wealth, the index of home educational resources and the index of possessions related to "classical" culture in the family home. Students were then assigned a factor score based on the amount of data available. For this to be done, students had to have data on at least three variables. In the case of France, questions remain about the reliability of students' responses regarding parental occupation and education (see INSEE-DPD, 1999).

Socio-economic categories

Students were asked to report their mothers' and fathers' occupations, and to state whether each parent was: in full-time paid work; part-time paid work; not working but looking for a paid job; or "other". The open-ended responses were then coded in accordance with the International Standard Classification of Occupations (ISCO 1988). Students were also asked to report on their occupation at age 30. These three variables – mother, father and students – were transformed into four *socio-economic categories*: *i)* white-collar high-skilled: legislators, senior officials and managers, and professional, technicians and associate professionals; *ii)* white-collar low-skilled: service workers and shop and market sales workers and clerk, *iii)* blue-collar high-skilled: skilled agricultural and fishery workers and craft and related trades workers; and *iv)* blue-collar low-skilled: plant and machine operators and assemblers and elementary occupations.

Parental education

Students were asked to classify the highest level of education of their mother and father on the basis of national qualifications, which were then coded in accordance with the International Standard Classification of Education (ISCED 1997) in order to obtain internationally comparable categories of educational attainment. The resulting categories were: did not go to school; completed <ISCED Level 1 (primary education)>; completed <ISCED Level 2 (lower secondary education)>; completed <ISCED Level 3B or 3C (upper secondary education, aimed in most countries at providing direct entry into the labour market)>; completed <ISCED Level 3A (upper secondary education, aimed in most countries at gaining entry into tertiary education)>; and completed <ISCED Level 5A, 5B or 6 (tertiary education)>.

Parental interest

The PISA index of *cultural communication* was derived from students' reports on the frequency with which their parents (or guardians) engaged with them in the following activities: discussing political or social issues; discussing books, films or television programmes; and listening to classical music.

The PISA index of *social communication* was derived from students' reports on the frequency with which their parents (or guardians) engaged with them in the following activities: discussing how well they are doing at school; eating <the main meal> with them around a table; and spending time simply talking with them.

Students responded to each statement on a five-point scale with the response categories: 'never or hardly ever', 'a few times a year', 'about once a month', 'several times a month' and 'several times a week'. Both indices were derived using the WARM estimator described above.

Participation in additional courses

Students were asked if they had sometimes or regularly **attended any special courses** outside school during the previous three years in order to improve results. The response categories were then grouped into two categories: *i)* students who attended additional courses in the <language of assessment>, courses in other subjects or extension or other additional courses outside school; and *ii)* students who attended remedial courses in the <language of assessment>, remedial courses in other subjects outside school or other training to improve study skills or private tutoring.

Cultural activities

The PISA index of **activities related to "classical" culture** was derived from students' reports on how often they had participated in the following activities during the preceding year: visited a museum or art gallery; attended an opera, ballet or classical symphony concert; and watched live theatre. Students responded to each statement on a four-point scale with the following categories: 'never or hardly ever', 'once or twice a year', '3 or 4 times a year', and 'more than 4 times a year'. The index was derived using the WARM estimator described above.

Family possessions

The PISA index of **family wealth** was derived from students' reports on: *i)* the availability, in their home, of a dishwasher, a room of their own, educational software, and a link to the Internet; and *ii)* the number of cellular phones, television sets, computers, motor cars and bathrooms at home.

The PISA index of **home educational resources** was derived from students' reports on the availability and number of the following items in their home: a dictionary, a quiet place to study, a desk for study, textbooks and calculators.

The PISA index of **possessions related to "classical" culture in the family home** was derived from students' reports on the availability of the following items in their home: classical literature (examples were given), books of poetry and works of art (examples were given).

These indices were derived using the WARM estimator (Warm, 1985) described above.

Learning strategies and attitudes

Engagement in reading

The PISA index of **engagement in reading** is derived from three components: *i)* the amount of time students spend on reading in general; *ii)* the diversity of the materials students read (e.g., magazines, comic books, fictions, non-fiction, books, newspapers); and *iii)* students' attitude towards reading by their level of agreement with the following statements: I read only if I have to; reading is one of my favourite hobbies; I like talking about books with other people; I find it hard to finish books; I feel happy if I receive a book as a present; for me reading is a waste of time; I enjoy going to a bookstore or a library; I read only to get information that I need; and, I cannot sit still and read for more than a few minutes; which were all answered in a four-point scale with the response categories 'strongly disagree', 'disagree', 'agree' and 'strongly agree' was used. The indices were derived using the WARM estimator described above. See Annex A2 from *Reading for Change: Performance and Engagement across Countries* (OECD, 2002*b*) for more information on this index.

Student interest in reading

The PISA index of **interest in reading** was derived from students' level of agreement with the following statements: because reading is fun, I wouldn't want to give it up; I read in my spare time; and, when I read, I sometimes get totally absorbed. A four-point scale with the response categories 'disagree', 'disagree somewhat', 'agree somewhat' and 'agree' was used. The indices were derived using the WARM estimator described above. For information on the conceptual underpinning of the index see Baumert *et al.* (1997).

Student interest in mathematics

The PISA index of **interest in mathematics** was derived from students' level of agreement with the following statements: when I do mathematics, I sometimes get totally absorbed; mathematics is important to me personally; and because doing mathematics is fun, I wouldn't want to give it up. A four-point scale with the response categories 'disagree', 'disagree somewhat', 'agree somewhat' and 'agree' was used. The indices were derived using the WARM estimator described above. For information on the conceptual underpinning of the index see Baumert *et al.* (1997).

Control strategies

The PISA index of **control strategies** was derived from the frequency with which students used the following strategies when studying: I start by figuring out what exactly I need to learn; I force myself to check to see if I remember what I have learned; I try to figure out which concepts I still haven't really understood; I make sure that I remember the most important things; and, when I study and I don't understand something, I look for additional information to clarify this. A four-point scale with the response categories 'almost never', 'sometimes', 'never' and 'almost always' was used. The indices were derived using the WARM estimator described above. For information on the conceptual underpinning of the index see Baumert (1994).

Memorising

The PISA index of **memorisation strategies** was derived from the frequency with which students use the following strategies when studying: I try to memorise everything that might be covered; I memorise as much as possible; I memorise all new material so that I can recite it; and I practice by saying the material to myself over and over. A four-point scale with the response categories 'almost never', 'sometimes', 'never' and 'almost always' was used. The indices were derived using the WARM estimator described above. For information on the conceptual underpinning of the index see Baumert *et al.* (1994) and Pintrich *et al* (1993).

Elaboration

The PISA index of **_elaboration strategies_** was derived from the frequency with which students use the following strategies when studying: I try to relate new material to things I have learned in other subjects; I figure out how the information might be useful in the real world; I try to understand the material better by relating it to things I already know; and, I figure out how the material fits in with what I have already learned. A four-point scale with the response categories 'disagree', 'disagree somewhat', 'agree somewhat' and 'agree' was used. The indices were derived using the WARM estimator described above. For information on the conceptual underpinning of the index see Baumert *et al.* (1994).

Co-operative and competitive learning

The PISA index of **_co-operative learning_** was derived from students' level of agreement with the following statements: I like to work with other students; I learn the most when I work with other students; I do my best work when I work with other students; I like to help other people do well in a group; and, it is helpful to put together everyone's ideas when working on a project. A four-point scale with the response categories 'disagree', 'disagree somewhat', 'agree somewhat' and 'agree' was used. The indices were derived using the WARM estimator described above. For information on the conceptual underpinning of the index, see Owens and Barnes (1992).

The PISA index of **_competitive learning_** was derived from the students' level of agreement with the following statements: I like to try to be better than other students; trying to be better than others makes me work well; I would like to be the best at something; and, I learn things faster if I'm trying to do better than the others. A four-point scale with the response categories 'disagree', 'disagree somewhat', 'agree somewhat' and 'agree' was used. The indices were derived using the WARM estimator described above. For information on the conceptual underpinning of the index see Owens and Barnes (1992).

Student self-concept in reading

The PISA index of **_self-concept in reading_** was derived from students' level of agreement with the following statements: I'm hopeless in <classes of the language of assessment>; I learn things quickly in the <classes of the language of assessment>; and, I get good marks in the <language of assessment>. A four-point scale with the response categories 'disagree', 'disagree somewhat', 'agree somewhat' and 'agree' was used. The indices were derived using the WARM estimator described above. For information on the conceptual underpinning of the index see Marsh *et al.* (1992).

Student self-concept in mathematics

The PISA index of **_self-concept in mathematics_** was derived from students' level of agreement with the following statements: I get good marks in mathematics; mathematics is one of my best subjects; and, I have always done well in mathematics. A four-point scale with the response categories 'disagree', 'disagree somewhat', 'agree somewhat' and 'agree' was used. The indices were derived using the WARM estimator described above. For information on the conceptual underpinning of the index see Marsh *et al.* (1992).

Student sense of belonging

The PISA index of **_sense of belonging_** in the school was derived from the students' responses to the following statement concerning their school: I feel like an outsider (or left out of things); I make friends easily; I feel like I belong; I feel awkward and out of place; other students seem to like me; and , I feel lonely. The indices were derived using the WARM estimator described above.

Interest in computers

The PISA index of **_interest in computers_** was derived from the students' responses to the following statements: it is very important to me to work with a computer; to play or work with a computer is really fun; I use a computer because I am very interested in this; and, I forget the time, when I am working with the computer. A two-point scale with the response categories 'yes' and 'no' was used. The indices were derived using the WARM estimator described above. For information on the conceptual underpinning of the index see Eignor *et al.* (1998).

Comfort with and perceived ability to use computers

The PISA index of **_comfort with and perceived ability to use computers_** was derived from students' responses to the following questions: How comfortable are you with using a computer?; How comfortable are you with using a computer to write a paper?; How comfortable are you with taking a test on a computer?; and, If you compare yourself with other 15-year-olds, how would you rate your ability to use a computer? For the first three questions, a four-point scale was used with the response categories 'very comfortable', 'comfortable', 'somewhat comfortable' and 'not at all comfortable'. For the last questions, a four-point scale was used with the response categories 'excellent', 'good', 'fair' and 'poor'. The indices were derived using the WARM estimator described above. For information on the conceptual underpinning of the index see Eignor *et al.* (1998).

Time spent on homework

The PISA index of **_time spent on homework_** was derived from students' reports on the amount of time they devote to homework per week in the <language of assessment>, mathematics and science. Students rated the amount on a four-point scale with response categories 'no time', 'less than 1 hour per week', 'between 1 and 3 hours per week', '3 hours or more per week'. The indices were derived using the WARM estimator described above.

School policies and practices

Use of student assessments

School principals reported on the frequency with which 15-year-olds in their school are assessed using: standardised tests; tests developed by teachers; teachers' judgmental ratings; student <portfolios>; and student assignments/projects/homework. School principals rated each form of assessment on a five-point scale with the response categories: 'never', 'yearly', '2 times a year', '3 times a year', and '4 or more times a year'. School principals also provided information on whether the assessment of 15-year-old students was used to: compare a school's performance with <district or national> performance; monitor the school's progress from year to year; and make judgements about teachers' effectiveness.

The PISA index of the **_use of formal assessments_** was derived from school principals' reports on the frequency with which standardised tests were used, and on their reports on how those assessments were used. The indices were derived using the WARM estimator described above. High values on the index identify schools where standardised assessment played an important role as a monitoring tool.

The PISA index of the **_use of informal assessments_** was derived from principals' reports on the frequency with which tests developed by teachers, teachers' judgmental ratings, student <portfolios> and student assignments/projects/homework were used, and on their reports on the uses made of those assessments.

The indices were derived using the WARM estimator described above. High positive values on the index identify schools where informal assessment plays an important role as a monitoring tool.

School and teacher autonomy

School principals were asked to report whether teachers, department heads, the school principal, an appointed or elected board or an education authorities at a higher level had the main responsibility for: appointing teachers; dismissing teachers; establishing teachers' starting salaries; determining teachers' salary increases; formulating school budgets; allocating budgets within the school; establishing student disciplinary policies; establishing student assessment policies; approving students for admittance to school; choosing which textbooks to use; determining course content; and deciding which courses were offered.

The PISA index of *school autonomy* used in Chapter 8 was derived from the number of categories that principals classified as not being a school responsibility. The scale was then inverted so that high values indicate a high degree of autonomy.

The PISA index of *teacher autonomy* used in Chapter 8 was derived from the number of categories that principals identified as being mainly the responsibility of teachers.

The indices were derived using the WARM estimator described above.

Staff professional development

School principals reported the percentage of teachers involved in *professional development programmes*. Professional development included formal programmes designed to enhance teaching skills or pedagogical practices. Such programmes might or might not lead to a recognised qualification. For the purpose of this question, a programme had to be at least one full day in length and to focus on teaching and education.

School principals' perceptions of teacher-related factors affecting school climate

The PISA index of the *principals' perceptions of teacher-related factors affecting school climate* was derived from principals' reports on the extent to which the learning by 15-year-olds was hindered by: low expectations of teachers; poor student-teacher relations; teachers not meeting individual students' needs; teacher absenteeism; staff resisting change; teachers being too strict with students; and students not being encouraged to achieve their full potential. A four-point scale with the response categories 'not at all', 'very little', 'to some extent' and 'a lot' was used. The indices were derived using the WARM estimator described above. This index was inverted so that lower values indicate a poorer disciplinary climate.

School principals' perception of teachers' morale and commitment

The PISA index of the *principals' perception of teachers' morale and commitment* was derived from the extent to which school principals agreed with the following statements: the morale of the teachers in this school is high; teachers work with enthusiasm; teachers take pride in this school; and teachers value academic achievement. A four-point scale with the response categories 'strongly disagree', 'disagree', 'agree' and 'strongly agree' was used. The indices were derived using the WARM estimator described above.

Shortage of teachers

The PISA index of the *teacher shortage* was derived from the principals' view on how much learning by 15-year-old students was hindered by the shortage or inadequacy of teachers in general, teachers in the

<language of assessment>, mathematics or science. The index was derived using the WARM estimator described above. This index was inverted so that low values indicate problems with teacher shortage.

Classroom practices

Teacher support

The PISA index of **teacher support** was derived from students' reports on the frequency with which: the teacher shows an interest in every student's learning; the teacher gives students an opportunity to express opinions; the teacher helps students with their work; the teacher continues teaching until the students understand; the teacher does a lot to help students; and, the teacher helps students with their learning. A four-point scale with the response categories 'never', 'some lessons', 'most lessons' and 'every lesson' was used. The index was derived using the WARM estimator (Warm, 1985) described above.

Disciplinary climate

The PISA index of **disciplinary climate** summarises students' reports on the frequency with which, in their <class of the language of assessment>: the teacher has to wait a long time for students to <quieten down>; students cannot work well; students don't listen to what the teacher says; students don't start working for a long time after the lesson begins; there is noise and disorder; and, at the start of class, more than five minutes are spent doing nothing. A four-point scale with the response categories 'never', 'some lessons', 'most lessons' and 'every lesson' was used. This index was inverted so that low values indicate a poor disciplinary climate.

The PISA index of the **principals' perceptions of student-related factors affecting school climate** was derived from principals' reports on the extent to which learning by 15-year-olds in their school was hindered by: student absenteeism; disruption of classes by students; students skipping classes; students lacking respect for teachers; the use of alcohol or illegal drugs; and students intimidating or bullying other students. A four-point scale with the response categories 'not at all', 'very little', 'to some extent' and 'a lot' was used. This index was inverted so that low values indicate a poor disciplinary climate. The indices were derived using the WARM estimator described above.

Pressure to achieve

The PISA index of **achievement press** was derived from students' reports on the frequency with which, in their <class of the language of assessment>: the teacher wants students to work hard; the teacher tells students that they can do better; the teacher does not like it when students deliver <careless> work; and, students have to learn a lot. A four-point scale with the response categories 'never', 'some lessons', 'most lessons' and 'every lesson' was used. The indices were derived using the WARM estimator described above with 'never' coded as 1 and all other response categories coded as 0.

Teacher-student relations

The PISA index of **teacher-student relations** was derived from students' reports on their level of agreement with the following statements: students get along well with most teachers; most teachers are interested in students' well-being; most of my teachers really listen to what I have to say; if I need extra help, I will receive it from my teachers; and most of my teachers treat me fairly. A four-point scale with the response categories 'strongly disagree', 'disagree', 'agree' and 'strongly agree' was used. The indices were derived using the WARM estimator described above with 'strongly agree' coded as 1 and all other response categories coded as 0.

School resources and type of school

Quality of the schools' physical infrastructure

The PISA index of the **quality of the schools' physical infrastructure** was derived from principals' reports on the extent to which learning by 15-year-olds in their school was hindered by: poor condition of buildings; poor heating and cooling and/or lighting systems; and lack of instructional space (*e.g.,* in classrooms).

A four-point scale with the response categories 'not at all', 'very little', 'to some extent' and 'a lot' was used. The index was derived using the WARM estimator described above. This index was inverted so that low values indicate a low quality of physical infrastructure.

Quality of the schools' educational resources

The PISA index of the **quality of the schools' educational resources** was derived based on the school principals' reports on the extent to which learning by 15-year-olds was hindered by: not enough computers for instruction; lack of instructional materials in the library; lack of multi-media resources for instruction; inadequate science laboratory equipment; and inadequate facilities for the fine arts.

A four-point scale with the response categories 'not at all', 'very little', 'to some extent' and 'a lot' was used. The index was derived using the WARM estimator described above. This index was inverted so that low values indicate a low quality of educational resources.

Availability of computers

School principals provided information on the total number of computers available in their schools and, more specifically, on the number of computers: available to 15-year-olds; available only to teachers; available only to administrative staff; connected to the Internet; and connected to a local area network. The PISA index of the **availability of computers** was derived by dividing the total number of computers available to 15-year-olds by the total number of computers in the school.

Student-teaching staff ratio and class size

School principals indicated the number of full-time and part-time teachers employed in their schools. Principals also specified: the numbers of teachers that were <language of assessment> teachers, mathematics teachers and science teachers; the number of teachers fully certified as teachers by the <appropriate national authority>; and the numbers of teachers with a qualification at <ISCED level 5A> in <pedagogy>, at <ISCED level 5A> in the <language of assessment>, at <ISCED level 5A> in <mathematics>, and at <ISCED level 5A> in <science>. The proportions of teachers in the respective categories are used in Chapter 8.

The **student-teaching staff ratio** was defined as the number of full-time equivalent teachers divided by the number of students in the school. In order to convert head-counts into full-time equivalents, a full-time teacher, defined as a teacher employed for at least 90 per cent of the statutory time as a classroom teacher, received a weight of 1 and a part-time teacher, defined as a teacher employed for less than 90 per cent of the time as a classroom teacher, received a weight of 0.5.

An estimate of **class size** was obtained from students' reports on the number of students in their respective <language of assessment>, mathematics and science classes.

Use of school resources

The PISA index of the ***use of school resources*** was derived from the frequency with which students reported using the following resources in their school: the school library; calculators; the Internet; and <science> laboratories. Students responded on a five-point scale with the following categories: 'never or hardly ever', 'a few times a year', 'about once a month', 'several times a month' and 'several times a week'. The index was derived using the WARM estimator described above.

Hours of schooling

The PISA index of ***hours of schooling per year*** was derived from the information which principals provided on: the number of weeks in the school year for which the school operates; the number of <class periods> in the school week; and the number of teaching minutes in a single <class period>. The index was derived from the product of these three factors, divided by 60.

School type

A school was classified as either public or private according to whether a public agency or a private entity had the ultimate power to make decisions concerning its affairs. A school was classified as ***public*** if the school principal reported that it was: controlled and managed directly by a public education authority or agency; or controlled and managed either by a government agency directly or by a governing body (council, committee, etc.), most of whose members were either appointed by a public authority or elected by public franchise. A school was classified as ***private*** if the school principal reported that it was controlled and managed by a non-governmental organisation (*e.g.*, a church, a trade union or a business enterprise) or if its governing board consisted mostly of members not selected by a public agency.

A distinction was made between "government-dependent" and "independent" private schools according to the degree of a private school's dependence on funding from government sources. School principals were asked to specify the percentage of the school's total funding received in a typical school year from: government sources; student fees or school charges paid by parents; donations, sponsorships or parental fund-raising; and other sources. Schools were classified as ***government-dependent private*** if they received 50 per cent or more of their core funding from government agencies. Schools were classified as ***government-independent private*** if they received less than 50 per cent of their core funding from government agencies.

Annex A2: Explained variation in student performance

In several tables, the change in student performance associated with one unit change on a given measure has been estimated by means of regression methods. The variation in student performance that is explained by this regression is shown in Table A2.1 and conventionally referred to as R^2. For the definitions of the indices, see Annex A1.

Table A2.1
Explained variation in student performance (R²)
Results are expressed as percentages

	Index of comfort with and perceived ability to use computers	Index of competitive learning	Index of control strategies	Index of co-operative learning	Index of activities related to "classical" culture in the family home	Index of cultural communication	Index of possessions related to "classical" culture in the family home
Albania	a	0.3	4.7	0.2	0.8	2.6	10.2
Argentina	a	a	a	a	2.3	6.6	7.8
Australia	2.9	3.2	5.7	0.2	7.1	9.7	10.3
Austria	a	1.0	3.4	1.5	7.0	6.6	5.7
Belgium	0.6	0.1	1.6	0.1	11.8	1.9	8.8
Brazil	4.5	0.0	7.2	0.6	0.2	6.8	4.8
Bulgaria	0.3	1.8	2.7	2.5	4.4	5.7	12.3
Canada	2.1	a	a	a	7.0	5.0	5.9
Chile	3.8	0.2	3.4	1.1	4.2	8.5	8.0
Czech Republic	2.9	3.2	8.4	1.8	7.3	5.4	9.2
Denmark	1.1	3.1	1.7	0.3	5.5	11.4	6.9
Finland	0.2	3.6	2.4	1.4	2.9	6.1	5.8
France	a	a	a	a	7.2	5.4	12.1
Germany	0.0	2.1	4.8	0.8	9.0	5.1	8.9
Greece	a	a	a	a	0.8	4.0	8.4
Hong Kong-China	a	5.5	7.0	1.3	4.0	4.9	2.6
Hungary	1.3	3.6	3.1	0.0	6.7	2.9	15.3
Iceland	a	5.0	2.0	1.3	5.1	4.5	3.4
Indonesia	a	a	a	a	1.1	2.8	0.2
Ireland	2.0	2.8	4.8	0.0	2.6	3.8	5.6
Israel	0.0	0.1	0.4	0.0	0.5	1.9	5.9
Italy	a	0.3	3.3	0.2	3.8	3.8	5.4
Japan	a	a	a	a	3.9	5.9	5.1
Korea	a	7.1	8.9	1.5	1.1	3.6	4.8
Latvia	0.4	6.2	3.3	3.0	1.7	2.5	7.5
Liechtenstein	0.9	0.0	4.7	0.1	7.1	4.7	7.2
Luxembourg	0.1	0.1	3.8	0.1	5.6	3.0	14.6
FYR Macedonia	a	0.1	6.0	0.8	4.4	2.2	3.1
Mexico	4.8	1.6	5.7	0.8	9.4	6.6	10.1
New Zealand	2.3	3.4	6.9	0.3	2.0	2.4	5.1
Norway	0.0	7.3	1.7	3.6	3.6	8.2	8.6
Peru	a	a	a	a	2.3	2.2	1.4
Poland	a	a	a	a	5.4	2.8	7.6
Portugal	a	0.3	11.7	1.9	5.1	12.4	11.9
Russian Federation	1.5	4.0	5.4	1.7	3.7	2.8	3.9
Spain	a	a	a	a	10.5	11.0	8.5
Sweden	0.2	1.6	3.8	0.0	2.6	6.1	7.7
Switzerland	1.3	0.1	3.6	1.3	5.6	7.1	6.7
Thailand	1.2	2.5	3.7	2.4	0.0	2.2	0.3
United Kingdom	a	a	a	a	8.7	6.6	9.5
United States	4.5	6.5	4.0	2.5	7.1	4.7	10.4
OECD average	1.4	2.3	4.2	0.9	4.5	5.0	7.5
Netherlands[1]	a	0.0	0.8	0.7	10.0	7.5	4.7

1. Response rate is too low to ensure comparability (see Annex A3).

Table A2.1(continued)
Explained variation in student performance (R²)
Results are expressed as percentages

	Index of disciplinary climate	Index of elaboration strategies	Index of engagement in reading	Index of family wealth	Index of home educational resources	Index of interest in computers	Index of interest in mathematics	Index of interest in reading
Albania	0.1	2.4	3.5	0.0	13.3	a	0.1	2.5
Argentina	1.2	a	7.8	11	15.7	a	a	a
Australia	2.3	1.5	17.4	2.0	5.4	0.1	0.1	11.7
Austria	0.4	1.3	16.6	0.8	4.0	a	0.4	10.9
Belgium	0.1	0.0	13.2	0.5	11.2	0.0	0.1	5.3
Brazil	0.3	3.7	6.9	10.0	10.8	1.5	1.0	0.9
Bulgaria	1.2	3.0	11.2	2.3	12.1	0.6	1.1	4.3
Canada	1.7	a	15.8	1.7	3.1	a	a	a
Chile	0.6	2.8	10.0	12.1	9.2	0.4	0.4	3.3
Czech Republic	2.2	4.3	17.4	1.1	9.8	0.0	0.2	12.0
Denmark	0.6	1.7	18.5	0.9	4.8	0.1	2.0	10.6
Finland	1.0	2.5	23.4	1.0	1.8	1.0	3.5	17.9
France	0.0	a	12.0	4.7	7.6	a	a	a
Germany	1.1	4.0	17.0	3.8	7.9	0.1	0.0	10.7
Greece	0.1	a	6.4	1.8	6.8	a	a	a
Hong Kong-China	2.3	2.9	11.2	1.6	7.9	a	3.7	6.7
Hungary	2.9	1.2	17.1	4.4	9.5	0.2	0.6	10.6
Iceland	0.7	2.0	20.4	0.2	1.1	a	4.0	12.9
Indonesia	0.0	a	3.5	5.7	5.2	a	a	a
Ireland	3.5	0.5	15.2	1.2	6.7	0.1	0.2	13.1
Israel	0.6	0.0	3.5	6.5	9.0	0.2	0.4	0.6
Italy	2.3	0.6	9.1	0.7	2.7	a	0.1	6.4
Japan	4.7	a	10.3	0.1	3.8	a	a	a
Korea	1.0	11.6	12.5	2.1	3.2	a	6.9	9.4
Latvia	0.8	0.9	8.3	0.4	3.7	0.7	1.3	8.8
Liechtenstein	0.1	1.7	20.2	1.6	7.5	a	1.3	9.4
Luxembourg	0.1	1.0	6.3	5.2	11.2	0.1	0.6	3.6
FYR Macedonia	0.6	3.7	1.5	0.7	14.5	a	0.7	1.4
Mexico	0.0	1.5	5.8	10.8	13.5	4.3	0.3	0.5
New Zealand	1.2	0.6	12.5	3.3	9.8	0.3	0.0	10.8
Norway	0.4	2.7	20.0	0.1	9.4	a	1.8	13.8
Peru	0.1	a	1.1	9.3	9.1	a	a	a
Poland	5.2	a	7.6	0.8	8.3	a	a	a
Portugal	0.8	5.1	10.2	9.1	8.0	a	0.7	6.9
Russian Federation	1.3	1.3	5.3	1.4	5.9	5.8	1.4	5.3
Spain	2.0	a	14.2	2.9	4.6	a	a	a
Sweden	1.3	1.8	20.4	0.5	2.1	0.2	0.1	13.7
Switzerland	0.9	1.9	20.7	1.3	5.7	0.1	0.3	10.1
Thailand	1.0	2.6	13.0	3.7	9.5	2.1	1.1	2.2
United Kingdom	4.3	a	13.9	1.6	6.5	a	a	a
United States	1.8	0.7	9.3	8.6	11.2	4.1	0.5	6.9
OECD average	*1.2*	*2.4*	*12.4*	*3.1*	*7.2*	*0.4*	*1.3*	*8.2*
Netherlands[1]	0.1	0.0	14.5	0.1	8.4	a	0.3	7.7

1. Response rate is too low to ensure comparability (see Annex A3).

Table A2.1 (continued)
Explained variation in student performance (R^2)
Results are expressed as percentages

	Index of memorisation strategies	Index of the principal's perception of teachers' morale and commitment	Index of school autonomy	Index of self-concept in mathematics	Index of self-concept in reading[1]	Index of social communication	Index of the principals' perceptions of student-related factors affecting school climate	Index of teacher autonomy
Albania	2.8	0.3	0.6	0.0	7.3	6.7	0.1	0.1
Argentina	a	1.9	8.5	a	a	4.0	3.8	0.6
Australia	0.8	2.7	2.5	2.5	7.5	2.9	4.9	0.7
Austria	1.7	0.5	0.2	0.9	7.0	1.3	1.8	3.6
Belgium	0.9	8.0	0.7	0.0	1.8	0.9	18.4	0.0
Brazil	2.2	0.7	10.4	1.0	2.8	2.9	2.9	0.1
Bulgaria	0.2	1.8	0.3	2.3	5.5	5.6	4.1	0.3
Canada	a	0.3	0.2	a	a	2.0	1.1	0.1
Chile	4.1	3.9	7.4	0.3	6.9	3.0	11.2	1.2
Czech Republic	1.6	0.2	0.0	2.3	6.4	1.2	8.5	0.6
Denmark	0.2	0.6	0.0	7.1	13.1	4.0	1.7	0.5
Finland	0.5	0.3	0.0	8.9	12.8	0.4	0.1	0.0
France	a	m	m	a	a	1.6	m	m
Germany	0.0	1.1	0.0	0.6	4.7	0.5	12.3	2.9
Greece	a	0.9	0.1	a	a	0.9	0.0	0.1
Hong Kong-China	4.0	9.6	0.1	0.6	1.9	7.0	9.3	0.1
Hungary	2.1	2.7	0.4	2.7	8.2	1.7	13.5	0.1
Iceland	0.0	0.1	0.0	11.1	10.6	1.5	0.4	0.0
Indonesia	a	0.1	3.2	a	a	5.2	0.3	0.8
Ireland	0.4	0.6	1.9	2.7	1.4	1.1	3.3	0.0
Israel	1.5	5.4	1.0	0.6	3.8	0.1	1.3	0.0
Italy	2.4	0.1	0.1	2.2	6.6	0.5	13.3	0.2
Japan	a	7.5	0.0	a	a	6.3	16.0	1.3
Korea	0.8	2.4	0.0	4.2	7.8	9.0	10.2	0.1
Latvia	0.7	0.3	0.2	0.8	11.2	0.8	0.6	0.1
Liechtenstein	0.1	0.0	1.3	0.1	4.5	1.6	1.9	13.0
Luxembourg	0.1	4.0	a	0.0	9.7	1.3	0.6	a
FYR Macedonia	11.0	1.8	0.3	0.3	11.3	6.4	3.8	0.0
Mexico	0.0	0.5	8.2	0.3	1.7	3.4	0.3	0.1
New Zealand	1.3	1.1	0.3	4.3	5.4	1.7	3.5	0.3
Norway	0.1	0.0	a	9.1	12.1	2.4	0.1	a
Peru	a	1.7	7.4	a	a	4.1	3.1	0.1
Poland	a	6.5	a	a	a	2.4	16.7	a
Portugal	0.0	0.8	1.0	1.7	9.3	4.6	1.3	0.1
Russian Federation	1.6	3.5	1.1	4.8	8.3	1.8	1.1	0.1
Spain	a	2.9	4.1	a	a	1.7	4.8	1.8
Sweden	0.6	0.4	0.0	5.3	11.0	0.3	1.4	0.3
Switzerland	0.0	0.2	0.0	0.0	4.3	1.6	2.4	0.1
Thailand	2.0	0.8	0.2	0.1	4.4	1.5	0.5	0.0
United Kingdom	a	2.8	0.5	a	a	1.9	11.8	0.2
United States	0.0	1.4	0.4	3.6	9.8	1.8	1.3	0.5
Country average	*1.3*	*2.2*	*1.6*	*2.4*		*2.7*	*5.4*	*1.1*
Netherlands[1]	0.3	0.8	0.1	0.2	2.1	7.1	21.3	1.6

1. Response rate is too low to ensure comparability (see Annex A3)

Table A2.1 (continued)
Explained variation in student performance (R²)
Results are expressed as percentages

	Index of teacher shortage	Index of teacher support	Index of the principals' perceptions of teacher-related factors affecting school climate	Index of teacher-student relations	Index of the quality of schools' educational resources	Index of the quality of the schools' physical infrastructure	Index of time spent on homework	International Socio-Economic Index of Occupational Status (HISEI)
Albania	0.8	0.0	0.0	5.2	1.6	0.3	5.7	11.8
Argentina	0.7	0.1	2.9	1.8	17.0	13.7	1.0	15.8
Australia	1.8	0.5	2.1	2.6	0.9	0.0	7.0	10.2
Austria	3.5	0.0	1.5	0.1	0.1	0.1	0.1	11.0
Belgium	3.8	0.2	5.1	0.0	0.7	1.3	8.6	14.0
Brazil	0.5	0.3	0.8	0.1	3.1	1.2	2.6	10.4
Bulgaria	0.1	0.5	0.0	0.0	0.5	1.4	5.3	13.6
Canada	0.1	0.2	0.2	2.1	0.2	0.0	4.5	7.4
Chile	0.8	0.0	2.2	0.0	5.7	2.1	3.8	17.7
Czech Republic	7.2	0.0	0.0	0.3	0.0	0.2	2.0	15.0
Denmark	0.4	1.1	0.3	3.0	0.3	0.1	0.4	9.3
Finland	0.0	0.3	0.1	1.4	0.2	0.1	1.5	5.5
France	m	m	m	0.1	m	m	9.0	12.8
Germany	11.9	1.5	1.2	0.1	4.1	1.2	0.9	15.8
Greece	0.2	0.0	0.1	0.0	0.7	1.2	15.2	10.3
Hong Kong-China	1.2	0.0	4.0	1.3	0.0	1.2	7.3	3.5
Hungary	1.5	0.1	1.3	1.0	1.0	0.9	7.8	16.8
Iceland	0.3	0.8	0.4	3.4	0.3	0.0	0.2	4.7
Indonesia	0.3	1.7	0.6	0.9	1.7	0.2	2.7	11.1
Ireland	0.1	0.0	0.0	1.4	0.0	0.2	2.2	9.9
Israel	0.2	0.5	0.4	0.1	0.9	0.0	0.1	10.6
Italy	0.1	1.2	0.8	0.2	1.6	0.5	7.0	8.1
Japan	2.1	0.6	4.0	3.8	1.9	0.2	6.5	0.7
Korea	0.9	0.5	1.3	0.9	0.0	0.2	6.2	3.5
Latvia	0.3	1.6	0.4	0.6	0.7	0.0	2.4	5.8
Liechtenstein	22.7	1.7	9.6	0.0	0.1	5.3	0.2	11.1
Luxembourg	0.2	0.3	0.5	0.1	2.5	6.3	0.1	16.2
FYR Macedonia	4.7	0.0	0.5	1.4	4.1	3.3	3.0	13.6
Mexico	0.2	0.1	0.0	0.1	13.0	4.9	1.4	14.9
New Zealand	1.3	0.2	1.8	1.5	1.1	0.1	3.3	9.7
Norway	0.2	1.8	0.2	3.1	0.4	0.0	1.9	7.6
Peru	5.6	1.2	1.1	0.1	14.1	11.1	a	14.4
Poland	0.6	0.7	1.3	0.2	0.6	3.0	8.8	12.4
Portugal	0.0	0.0	0.4	0.3	0.3	2.4	1.6	15.4
Russian Federation	0.0	0.4	0.5	0.1	1.0	2.5	9.9	9.2
Spain	0.1	0.1	1.3	0.6	1.6	1.3	8.8	10.2
Sweden	0.7	0.4	0.1	1.7	0.4	0.4	0.0	8.8
Switzerland	2.0	1.6	0.1	0.1	0.5	0.8	0.1	15.9
Thailand	1.9	0.4	0.1	0.2	2.7	0.0	2.9	6.5
United Kingdom	3.8	0.4	4.9	2.9	2.8	0.8	7.9	14.7
United States	1.5	0.5	1.1	3.5	0.0	0.0	7.6	11.3
Country average	*2.4*	*0.5*	*1.5*	*1.1*	*1.8*	*1.5*	*4.1*	*10.8*
Netherlands[2]	2.8	0.3	6.8	0.5	1.8	0.1	1.0	11.6

1. This index (SCVERB) is different from the one published in OECD, 2001*b*.
2. Response rate is too low to ensure comparability (see Annex A3).

Annex A3: The PISA target population and the PISA samples

The PISA concept of "yield" and the definition of the PISA target population

PISA provides an assessment of the cumulative yield of education and learning at a point at which most young adults are still enrolled in initial education.

A major challenge for an international survey is to operationalise such a concept in ways that guarantee the international comparability of national target populations.

Differences between countries in the nature and extent of pre-primary education and care, the age of entry to formal schooling, and the institutional structure of educational systems do not allow the definition of internationally comparable grade levels of schooling. Consequently, international comparisons of educational performance typically define their populations with reference to a target age. Some previous international assessments have defined their target population on the basis of the grade level that provide maximum coverage of a particular age cohort. A disadvantage of this approach is that slight variations in the age distribution of students across grade levels often lead to the selection of different target grades in different countries, or between education systems within countries, raising serious questions about the comparability of results across, and at times within, countries. In addition, because not all students of the desired age are usually represented in grade-based samples, there may be a more serious potential bias in the results if the unrepresented students are typically enrolled in the next higher grade in some countries and the next lower grade in others. This would exclude students with potentially higher levels of performance in the former countries and students with potentially lower levels of performance in the latter.

In order to address this problem, PISA uses an age-based definition for its target population, *i.e.* a definition that is not tied to the institutional structures of national education systems: PISA assessed students who were aged between 15 years and 3 (complete) months and 16 years and 2 (complete) months at the beginning of the assessment period and who were enrolled in an educational institution, regardless of the grade levels or type of institution in which they were enrolled, and regardless of whether they were in full-time or part-time education (15-year-olds enrolled in Grade 6 or lower were excluded from PISA but, among the countries participating in PISA 2000 and PISA Plus, such students only exist in significant numbers in Brazil and to a lesser degree in Peru and Argentina). Educational institutions are generally referred to as *schools* in this publication, although some educational institutions (in particular some types of vocational education establishments) may not be termed schools in certain countries. As expected from this definition, the average age of students across OECD countries was 15 years and 8 months years, a value which varied by less than 0.2 years between participating countries).

As a result of this population definition, PISA 2000 and PISA Plus makes statements about the knowledge and skills of a group of individuals who were born within a comparable reference period, but who may have undergone different educational experiences both within and outside schools. In PISA, these knowledge and skills are referred to as the *yield* of education at an age that is common across countries. Depending on countries' policies on school entry and promotion, these students may be distributed over a narrower or a wider range of grades. Furthermore, in some countries, students in PISA's target population are split between different education systems, tracks or streams.

If a country's scale scores in reading, scientific or mathematical literacy are significantly higher than those in another country, it cannot automatically be inferred that the schools or particular parts of the education system in the first country are more effective than those in the second. However, one can legitimately conclude that the cumulative impact of learning experiences in the first country, starting in early childhood and up to the age of 15 and embracing experiences both in school and at home, have resulted in higher outcomes in the literacy domains that PISA measures.

The PISA target population did not include residents attending schools in a foreign country.

To accommodate countries that desired grade-based results for the purpose of national analyses, PISA 2000 provided an international option to supplement age-based sampling with grade-based sampling.

Population coverage

All countries attempted to maximise the coverage of 15-year-olds enrolled in education in their national samples, including students enrolled in special educational institutions. As a result, PISA 2000 and PISA Plus reached standards of population coverage that are unprecedented in international surveys of this kind.

The sampling standards used in PISA permitted countries to exclude up to a total of 5 per cent of the relevant population either by excluding schools or by excluding students within schools. All but three countries achieved the required coverage of at least 95 per cent of the national desired target population, and half of countries achieved 98 per cent or more. The ceiling for population exclusions of 5 per cent ensures that potential bias resulting from exclusions is likely to remain within one standard error of sampling.

Exclusions within the above limits include:

- *At the school level*: i) schools which were geographically inaccessible or where the administration of the PISA assessment was not considered feasible; and ii) schools that provided teaching only for students in the categories defined under "within-school exclusions", such as schools for the blind. The percentage of 15-year-olds enrolled in such schools had to be less than 2.5 per cent of the nationally desired target population. The magnitude, nature and justification of school-level exclusions is documented in the *PISA 2000 Technical Report (OECD, 2002a)*.

- *At the student level*: i) students who were considered in the professional opinion of the school principal or of other qualified staff members, to be educable mentally retarded or who had been defined as such through psychological tests (including students who were emotionally or mentally unable to follow the general instructions given in PISA); ii) students who were permanently and physically disabled in such a way that they could not perform in the PISA assessment situation (functionally disabled students who could respond were to be included in the assessment); and iii) non-native language speakers with less than one year of instruction in the language of the assessment. Students could not be excluded solely because of normal discipline problems. The percentage of 15-year-olds excluded within schools had to be less than 2.5 per cent of the ***nationally desired target population***.

Table A3.1
PISA target populations and samples

	Population and sample information						
	(1)	(2)	(3)	(4)	(5)	(6)	(7)
	Total population of 15-year-olds	Total enrolled population of 15-year-olds	Total in national desired target population	School-level exclusions	Total in national desired target population after school exclusions and before within-school exclusions	Percentage of school-level exclusions	Number of participating students
	SF 2[a]	SF 2[b]	SF 3[a]	SF 3[b]	SF 3[c]	3[b] / 3[a]	
Albania	58 720	25 080	25 080	94	24 986	0.37	4 980
Argentina	662 014	505 404	505 404	5 736	499 668	1.13	3 983
Australia	266 878	248 908	248 738	2 850	245 888	1.15	5 176
Austria	95 041	90 354	90 354	32	90 322	0.04	4 745
Belgium	121 121	119 055	118 972	1 091	117 881	0.92	6 670
Brazil	3 464 330	1 841 843	765 502	6 633	1 830 603	0.36	4 893
Bulgaria	96 000	92 200	92 200	1 200	91 000	1.30	4 650
Canada	403 803	396 423	391 788	2 035	389 990	0.52	29 687
Chile	263 863	230 538	229 757	3 738	226 019	1.63	4 889
Czech Republic	134 627	132 508	132 508	2 181	130 327	1.65	5 365
Denmark	53 693	52 161	52 161	345	51 816	0.66	4 235
Finland	66 571	66 561	66 319	550	65 769	0.83	4 864
France	788 387	788 387	750 460	17 728	732 732	2.36	4 673
Germany	927 473	924 549	924 549	5 423	919 126	0.59	5 073
Greece	128 175	124 656	124 187	200	123 987	0.16	3 644
Hong Kong-China[1]	80 000	77 567	77 567	1 408	76 159	1.82	4 405
Hungary	120 759	115 325	115 325	0	115 325	0.00	4 887
Iceland	4 062	4 044	4 044	18	4 026	0.45	3 372
Indonesia[2]	4 558 817	3 247 422	3 102 630	7 611	3 095 019	0.25	7 368
Ireland	65 339	64 370	63 572	1 021	62 551	1.61	3 854
Israel[3]	128 913	108 784	108 784	1 441	107 343	1.32	4 498
Italy	584 417	574 864	574 864	775	574 089	0.13	4 984
Japan	1 490 000	1 485 269	1 459 296	34 124	1 425 172	2.34	5 256
Korea	712 812	602 605	602 605	1 820	600 785	0.30	4 982
Latvia	38 000	35 981	35 981	886	35 095	2.46	3 920
Liechtenstein	415	326	326	0	326	0.00	314
Luxembourg	4 556	4 556	4 556	416	4 140	9.13	3 528
FYR Macedonia	33 420	20 312	20 166	218	19 948	1.08	4 511
Mexico	2 127 504	1 098 605	1 073 317	0	1 073 317	0.00	4 600
New Zealand	54 220	51 464	51 464	976	50 488	1.90	3 667
Norway	52 165	51 587	51 474	420	51 054	0.82	4 147
Peru[4]	546 601	358 780	355 422	12 244	343 178	3.44	4 429
Poland	665 500	643 528	643 528	56 524	587 004	8.78	3 654
Portugal	132 325	127 165	127 165	0	127 165	0.00	4 585
Russian Federation	2 268 566	2 259 985	2 259 985	10 867	2 249 118	0.48	6 701
Spain	462 082	451 685	451 685	2 180	449 505	0.48	6 214
Sweden	100 940	100 940	100 940	1 360	99 580	1.35	4 416
Switzerland	81 350	79 232	79 232	954	78 278	1.20	6 100
Thailand[5]	968 760	765 502	765 502	7 655	757 847	1.00	5 340
United Kingdom	731 743	705 875	705 875	17 674	688 201	2.50	9 340
United States	3 876 000	3 836 000	3 836 000	0	3 836 000	0.00	3 846
Netherlands[6]	178 924	178 924	178 924	7 800	171 124	4.36	2 503

1. The reported figure for Hong Kong-China concerning the total population of 15-year-olds was 80 000-90 000, so 80 000 was used above.

2. Indonesia seems to have a high drop out rate among the older half of this age cogort.

3. Israel sent updated numbers for 15-year-olds in 2002 (103 207) which, after applying ratios based on their sampling form information, arrives at a 3[c] value that is much closer to their P+E value.

4. Peru included grades 4 and below in sf2[b] and then took them off in exclusions. This was revised to that above.

5. Thailand did not list all students in some of the largest schools.

6. Response rate is too low to ensure comparability (see Annex A3).

For details see the *PISA 2000 Technical Report (OECD, 2002a)*.

Table A3.1 (continued)
PISA target populations and samples

	Population and sample information					Coverage indices	
	(8)	(9)	(10)	(11)	(12)	(13)	(14)
	Weighted number of participating students	Number of excluded students	Weighted number of excluded students	Within-school exclusion rate (%)	Overall exclusion rate (%)	Coverage Index 1: Coverage of national desired population	Coverage Index 2: Coverage of national enrolled population
	P		E	$E / (P+E)$		$P/(P+E) * (3[c] / 3[a])$	$P/(P+E) * (3[c]/2[b])$
Albania	23 773	1	6	0.02	0.40	1.00	1.00
Argentina	512 687	23	2 424	0.47	1.60	0.98	0.98
Australia	229 152	63	2 688	1.16	2.29	0.98	0.98
Austria	71 547	41	500	0.69	0.73	0.99	0.99
Belgium	110 095	100	1 596	1.43	2.33	0.98	0.98
Brazil	2 402 280	14	7 842	0.33	0.69	0.99	0.99
Bulgaria	87 781	33	394	0.45	1.74	0.98	0.98
Canada	348 481	1 584	16 197	4.44	4.94	0.95	0.94
Chile	216 305	9	616	0.28	1.91	0.98	0.98
Czech Republic	125 639	13	297	0.24	1.88	0.98	0.98
Denmark	47 786	119	1 195	2.44	3.08	0.97	0.97
Finland	62 826	58	673	1.06	1.88	0.98	0.98
France	730 494	59	8 208	1.11	3.45	0.97	0.92
Germany	826 816	60	9 163	1.10	1.68	0.98	0.98
Greece	111 363	21	682	0.61	0.77	0.99	0.99
Hong Kong-China[1]	69 967	0	0	0.00	1.82	0.98	0.98
Hungary	107 460	34	765	0.71	0.71	0.99	0.99
Iceland	3 869	79	79	2.01	2.44	0.98	0.98
Indonesia[2]	1 796 969	0	0	0.00	0.25	1.00	0.95
Ireland	56 209	134	1 734	2.99	4.55	0.95	0.94
Israel[3]	78 507	130	1 623	2.03	3.32	0.97	0.97
Italy	510 792	117	12 247	2.34	2.47	0.98	0.98
Japan	1 446 596	0	0	0.00	2.34	0.98	0.96
Korea	579 109	6	826	0.14	0.44	1.00	1.00
Latvia	30 063	62	402	1.32	3.75	0.96	0.96
Liechtenstein	325	2	2	0.61	0.61	0.99	0.99
Luxembourg	4 138	0	0	0.00	9.13	0.91	0.91
FYR Macedonia	20 001	0	0	0.00	1.08	0.99	0.98
Mexico	960 011	2	564	0.06	0.06	1.00	0.98
New Zealand	46 757	137	1 590	3.29	5.12	0.95	0.95
Norway	49 579	93	944	1.87	2.67	0.97	0.97
Peru[4]	274 185	9	775	0.28	3.72	0.96	0.95
Poland	542 005	53	5 484	1.00	9.70	0.90	0.90
Portugal	99 998	122	2 777	2.70	2.70	0.97	0.97
Russian Federation	1 968 131	22	4 960	0.25	0.73	0.99	0.99
Spain	399 055	153	8 998	2.21	2.68	0.97	0.97
Sweden	94 338	174	3 349	3.43	4.73	0.95	0.95
Switzerland	72 010	62	822	1.13	2.32	0.98	0.98
Thailand[5]	525 912	0	0	0.00	1.00	0.99	0.99
United Kingdom	643 041	219	15 990	2.43	4.87	0.95	0.95
United States	3 121 874	211	132 543	4.07	4.07	0.96	0.96
Netherlands[6]	157 327	1	23	0.01	4.37	0.96	0.96

1. The reported figure for Hong Kong-China concerning the total population of 15-year-olds was 80 000-90 000, so 80 000 was used above.

2. Indonesia seems to have a high drop out rate among the older half of this age cohort.

3. Israel sent updated numbers for 15-year-olds in 2002 (103 207) which, after applying ratios based on their sampling form information, arrives at a 3[c] value that is much closer to their P+E value.

4. Peru included grades 4 and below in sf2[b] and then took them off in exclusions. This was revised to that above.

5. Thailand did not list all students in some of the largest schools.

6. Response rate is too low to ensure comparability (see Annex A3).

For details see the *PISA 2000 Technical Report (OECD, 2002a)*.

Table A3.1 describes the target population of the countries participating in PISA 2000. Further information on the target population and the implementation of PISA sampling standards can be found in the *PISA 2000 Technical Report (OECD, 2002a)*.

- **Column 1** shows the total number of 15-year-olds according to 2000 national population registers.

- **Column 2** shows the number of 15-year-olds enrolled in schools (as defined above), which is referred to as the *eligible population*.

- **Column 3** shows the national desired target population. As part of the school-level exclusions, countries were allowed to exclude up to 0.5 per cent of students *a priori* from the eligible population, essentially for practical reasons. The following a priory exclusions exceed this limit but were agreed with the PISA Consortium: **Canada** excluded 1.17 per cent of the eligible population, of which 0.73 per cent accounted for schools on Federal Indian reservations and 0.43 per cent were in the Yukon, Northwest, and Nunuvuk territories. In the case of France, the eligible population included students in the Territoires d'Outre-Mer, but because countries were not required to assess students in outlying territories not subject to the national education systems, it was permissible to exclude these students. French students in outlying *départements* were, as required, included in PISA 2000. **Ireland** excluded 1.61 per cent of the eligible population. This covered 1.15 per cent of students enrolled in schools not aided by the Department of Education and Science, 0.36 per cent in very small schools, and 0.12 per cent in "designated disadvantaged schools". **Japan** excluded 4.0 per cent of the eligible population, of which 1.7 per cent were students educated by mail and students in "other small streams (Bekka, Koto-senmon-gakko)", and 2.3 per cent were in part-time education ('Teiji-sei"). **Mexico** excluded 2.3 per cent of its eligible population in geographically remote schools. Both Chile and Peru excluded schools with only one or two eligible students in them, accounting for 0.78 per cent of the eligible population for Chile, and 3.44 per cent of the eligible population for Peru. Among the non-OECD countries, **Brazil** excluded 15-year-olds enrolled in grades 1 to 6 which accounted for 16 per cent of 15-year-olds enrolled in Brazil. This exclusion was legitimate because such students are not part of the PISA target population. Additionally, Albania, Argentina, Bulgaria, Chile, and Peru also excluded 15-year-olds in grades below grade 7, but only Peru and Argentina had any significant percentage of these at about 10 per cent and 4 per cent respectively. Subtracting the students excluded *a priori* from the eligible population results in the national desired target population in Column 3.

- **Column 4** shows the number of students enrolled in schools that were excluded from the national desired target population.

- **Column 5** shows the size of the national desired target population after subtracting the students enrolled in excluded schools. This is obtained by subtracting Column 4 from Column 3.

- **Column 6** shows the percentage of students enrolled in excluded schools. This is obtained by dividing Column 4 by Column 3.

- **Column 7** shows the *number of students participating in PISA 2000*. Note that this number does not account for 15-year-olds assessed as part of additional national options. These national options account for an additional 82105 15-year-old students across all countries.

- **Column 8** shows the *weighted number of participating students*, *i.e.*, the number of students in the nationally defined target population that the PISA sample represents.

- Each country attempted to maximise the coverage of PISA's target population within the sampled schools. In the case of each sampled school, all eligible students, namely those 15 years of age, regardless of grade, were first listed. Sampled students who were to be excluded had still to be included in the sampling documentation, and a list drawn up stating the reason for their exclusion. **Column 9** indicates the number of *excluded students, i.e.* students who fell into one of the categories specified above. **Column 10** indicates the *weighted number of excluded students*, *i.e.*, the overall number of students in the nationally defined target population represented by the number of students excluded from the sample.

- **Column 11** shows the *percentage of students excluded within schools.* This is calculated as the weighted number of excluded students (Column 10) divided by the weighted number of excluded and participating students (Column 8 plus Column 10).

- **Column 12** shows the *overall exclusion rate* which represents the weighted percentage of the national desired target population excluded from PISA either through school-level exclusions or through the exclusion of students within schools. It is obtained by multiplying the percentage of school-level exclusions (Column 6) by 100, minus the percentage of students excluded within schools (Column 11) and adding the percentage of students excluded within schools (Column 11) to the result.

- **Column 13** presents an *index of the extent to which the national desired target population is covered by the PISA sample*. The index is expressed in per cent of the national desired target population covered. Luxembourg, Poland and Brazil are the only countries in which less than 95 per cent of the population that PISA seeks to cover is represented by the PISA samples. In the case of **Poland**, the exclusion rate is 10 per cent. This includes the 6.7 per cent of 15-year-olds enrolled in primary schools. The performance of these students in the PISA assessments can be expected to be lower than the performance of 15-year-olds in secondary schools, and this exclusion may imply that the performance of Polish students on the combined reading literacy scale is overestimated by two rank-order positions and on the scientific literacy scale by about three rank-order positions. No rank-order shifts are expected on the mathematical literacy scale. **Luxembourg** has an exclusion rate of 9.1 per cent, due largely to students instructed in languages other than the languages of assessment in Luxembourg. Permissible exclusions included 28 students with special needs; 297 students attending the European School; 32 students attending the American International School; 45 students attending other schools not under the authority of the Ministry of Education; and 14 students attending small schools. It is not expected that the exclusions in Luxembourg overestimate its rank-order position on the PISA scales. Among non-OECD countries, in **Brazil**, the school-level exclusion rate is 18 per cent but much of this is explained by 15-year-olds enrolled in Grade 5 and 6 who do not belong to the PISA target population. No rank order shifts are expected of the exclusions in Brazil. For further information see the *PISA 2000 Technical Report (OECD, 2002a)*.

- **Column 14** presents an *index of the extent to which 15-year-olds enrolled in schools are covered by the PISA sample*. The index measures the overall proportion of the national enrolled population that is covered by the non-excluded portion of the student sample. The index takes into account both school-level and student-level exclusions. Values close to 100 indicate that the PISA sample represents the entire education system as defined for PISA 2000. The index is the weighted number of participating students

(Column 9) divided by the weighted number of participating and excluded students (Columns 9 plus Column 11), times the nationally defined target population (Column 5) divided by the national desired target population (times 100).

Sampling procedures and response rates

The accuracy of any survey results depends on the quality of the information on which national samples are based as well as on the sampling procedures. Quality standards, procedures, instruments and verification mechanisms were developed for PISA that ensured that national samples yielded comparable data and that the results could be compared with confidence.

Most PISA samples were designed as two-stage stratified samples (where countries applied different sampling designs, these are documented in the *PISA 2000 Technical Report, OECD, 2002a*). The first stage consisted of sampling individual schools in which 15-year-old students were enrolled. Schools were sampled systematically with probabilities proportional to size, the measure of size being a function of the estimated number of eligible (15-year-old) students enrolled. A minimum of 150 schools were selected in each country (where this number existed), although the requirements for national analyses often required a somewhat larger sample. As the schools were sampled, replacement schools were simultaneously identified, in case a sampled school chose not to participate in PISA 2000.

In the case of **Iceland**, **Liechtenstein** and **Luxembourg**, all schools and all eligible students within schools were included in the sample. However, since not all students in the PISA samples were assessed in mathematical and scientific literacy, these national samples represent a complete census only in respect of the assessment of reading literacy, and a partial census of the assessment of mathematical and scientific literacy.

Experts from the PISA Consortium monitored the sample selection process in each participating country.

The second stage of the selection process sampled students within sampled schools. Once schools were selected, a list of each sampled school's 15-year-old students was prepared. From this list, 35 students were then selected with equal probability (all 15-year-old students were selected if fewer than 35 were enrolled).

Data quality standards in PISA required minimum participation rates for schools as well as for students. These standards were established to minimise the potential for response biases. In the case of countries meeting these standards, it is likely that any bias resulting from non-response will be negligible, *i.e.*, typically smaller than the sampling error.

A minimum response rate of 85 per cent was required for the schools initially selected. Where the initial response rate of schools was between 65 and 85 per cent, however, an acceptable school response rate could still be achieved through the use of replacement schools. This procedure brought with it a risk of increased response bias. Participating countries were, therefore, encouraged to persuade as many of the schools in the original sample as possible to participate. Schools with a student participation rate between 25 and 50 per cent were not regarded as participating schools, but data from these schools were included in the database and contributed to the various estimations. Data from schools with a student participation rate of less than 25 per cent were excluded from the database.

PISA 2000 also required a minimum participation rate of 80 per cent of students within participating schools (original sample and replacement). This minimum participation rate had to be met at the national level, not necessarily by each participating school. Make-up sessions were required in schools in which too few students had participated in the original assessment sessions. Student participation rates were calculated over all participating schools, whether original sample or replacement schools, and from the participation of students in both the original assessment and any make-up sessions. A student who did not participate in the first assessment session was not regarded as a participant but was included in the international database and contributed to the statistics presented in this publication if he or she participated in the second assessment session and provided at least a description of his or her father's or mother's occupation.

Table A3.2 shows the response rates for students and schools, before and after replacement.

- **Column 1** shows the ***weighted participation rate of schools before replacement.*** This is obtained by dividing Column 2 by Column 3. The Netherlands, the United Kingdom and the United States did not meet PISA's requirements for response rates before replacement. In the **United Kingdom,** the initial response rate fell short of the requirements by 3.7 per cent and in the **United States** by 8.6 per cent. Both countries provided extensive evidence to the PISA Consortium that permitted an assessment of the expected performance of non-participating schools. On the basis of this evidence, PISA's Technical Advisory Group determined that the impact of these deviations on the assessment results was negligible. The results from these countries were included in all analyses. The initial response rate for the **Netherlands** was only 27 per cent. As a result, the PISA Consortium initiated supplementary analyses that confirmed that the data from the Netherlands might be sufficiently reliable and could be used in some relational analyses. Despite this conclusion, the response rate was too low to give confidence that the sample results reflect those for the national population reliably, with the level of accuracy and precision required in PISA 2000. Assuming negligible to moderate levels of bias due to non-response, the rank-order position of the Netherlands may be expected, with 95 per cent confidence, to lie between 2nd and 14th among countries on the combined reading literacy scale, between 1st and 4th on the mathematical literacy scale, and between 3rd and 14th on the scientific literacy scale (for further details see the *PISA 2000 Technical Report, OECD, 2002a*). Mean performance scores for the Netherlands can, therefore, not be compared with those from other countries. In tables where the focus is on the comparison of mean scores, the Netherlands has been excluded. Where the performance of sub-groups is shown, only the relative differences in performance between the relevant sub-groups within the Netherlands should be considered, and the sub-group means should not be compared with those from other countries.

- **Column 2** shows the ***weighted number of responding schools before school replacement*** (weighted by student enrolment)

- **Column 3** shows the ***weighted number of sampled schools before school replacement*** (including both responding and nonresponding schools).

- **Column 4** shows the ***weighted participation rate of schools after replacement.*** This is obtained by dividing Column 5 by Column 6.

- **Column 5** shows the ***weighted number of responding schools after school replacement*** (weighted by student enrolment).

Table A3.2
Response rates

	Initial sample - before school replacement			Final sample - after school replacement			Final sample - students within schools after school replacement				
	(1)	(2)	(3)	(4)	(5)	(6)	(7)	(8)	(9)	(10)	(11)
	Weighted school participation rate before replacement (%)	Number of responding schools (weighted by enrolment)	Number of schools sampled (responding and non-responding) (weighted by enrolment)	Weighted school participation rate after replacement (%)	Number of responding schools (weighted by enrolment)	Number of schools sampled (responding and non-responding) (weighted by enrolment)	Weighted student participation rate after replacement (%)	Number of students assessed (weighted)	Number of students sampled (assessed and absent) (weighted)	Number of students assessed (unweighted)	Number of students sampled (assessed and absent) (unweighted)
Albania	98.46	25 963	26 369	98.80	26 067	26 383	95.31	22 456	23 562	4 979	5 214
Argentina	86.04	441 434	513 079	87.28	447 824	513 079	89.26	375 701	420 904	3 940	4 450
Australia	80.95	197 639	244 157	93.65	228 668	244 175	84.24	161 607	191 850	5 154	6 173
Austria	99.38	86 062	86 601	100.00	86 601	86 601	91.64	65 562	71 547	4 745	5 164
Belgium	69.12	81 453	117 836	85.52	100 833	117 911	93.30	88 816	95 189	6 648	7 103
Brazil	97.38	2 425 608	2 490 788	97.96	2 439 152	2 489 942	87.15	1 463 000	1 678 789	4 885	5 613
Bulgaria	99.33	87 004	87 589	99.41	87 030	87 546	90.83	79 520	87 545	4 666	5 142
Canada	87.91	335 100	381 165	93.31	355 644	381 161	84.89	276 233	325 386	29 461	33 736
Chile	97.69	220 466	225 685	100.00	225 685	225 685	96.16	209 100	217 452	4 912	5 111
Czech Republic	95.30	123 345	129 422	99.01	128 551	129 841	92.76	115 371	124 372	5 343	5 769
Denmark	83.66	42 027	50 236	94.86	47 689	50 271	91.64	37 171	40 564	4 212	4 592
Finland	96.82	63 783	65 875	100.00	65 875	65 875	92.80	58 303	62 826	4 864	5 237
France	94.66	704 971	744 754	95.23	709 454	744 982	91.19	634 276	695 523	4 657	5 115
Germany	94.71	885 792	935 222	94.71	885 792	935 222	85.65	666 794	778 516	4 983	5 788
Greece	83.91	92 824	110 622	99.77	130 555	130 851	96.83	136 919	141 404	4 672	4 819
Hong Kong-China	66.60	50 992	76 566	92.63	70 926	76 566	91.63	59 418	64 846	4 388	4 797
Hungary	98.67	209 153	211 969	98.67	209 153	211 969	95.31	100 807	105 769	4 883	5 111
Iceland	99.88	4 015	4 020	99.88	4 015	4 020	87.09	3 372	3 872	3 372	3 872
Indonesia	96.23	5 803 095	6 030 135	100.00	6 024 643	6 024 643	94.81	1 703 746	1 796 969	7 368	7 806
Ireland	85.56	53 164	62 138	87.53	54 388	62 138	85.59	42 088	49 172	3 786	4 424
Israel	79.87	79 052	98 972	91.90	90 978	98 999	86.81	59 119	68 105	4 416	5 108
Italy	97.90	550 932	562 763	100.00	562 755	562 755	93.08	475 446	510 792	4 984	5 369
Japan	82.05	1 165 576	1 420 533	90.05	1 279 121	1 420 533	96.34	1 267 367	1 315 462	5 256	5 450
Korea	100.00	589 018	589 018	100.00	589 018	589 018	98.84	572 767	579 470	4 982	5 045
Latvia	82.39	29 354	35 628	88.51	31 560	35 656	90.73	24 403	26 895	3 915	4 305
Liechtenstein	100.00	327	327	100.00	327	327	96.62	314	325	314	325
Luxembourg	93.04	3 852	4 140	93.04	3 852	4 140	89.19	3 434	3 850	3 434	3 850
FYR Macedonia	100.00	20 135	20 135	100.00	20 135	20 135	96.11	19 224	20 001	4 511	4 696
Mexico	92.69	985 745	1 063 524	100.00	1 063 524	1 063 524	93.95	903 100	961 283	4 600	4 882
New Zealand	77.65	39 328	50 645	86.37	43 744	50 645	88.23	35 616	40 369	3 667	4 163
Norway	85.95	43 207	50 271	92.25	46 376	50 271	89.28	40 908	45 821	4 147	4 665
Peru	94.49	348 960	369 310	100.00	369 516	369 516	91.58	261 537	285 595	4 499	4 892
Poland	79.11	432 603	546 842	83.21	455 870	547 847	87.70	393 675	448 904	3 639	4 169
Portugal	95.27	120 521	126 505	95.27	120 521	126 505	86.28	82 395	95 493	4 517	5 232
Russian Federation	98.84	4 445 841	4 498 235	99.29	4 466 335	4 498 235	96.21	1 903 348	1 978 266	6 701	6 981
Spain	95.41	423 900	444 288	100.00	444 288	444 288	91.78	366 301	399 100	6 214	6 764
Sweden	99.96	100 534	100 578	99.96	100 534	100 578	87.96	82 956	94 312	4 416	5 017
Switzerland	91.81	89 208	97 162	95.84	92 888	96 924	95.13	65 677	69 037	6 084	6 389
Thailand	94.82	712 097	751 009	99.97	750 988	751 225	97.19	519 549	534 590	5 340	5 461
United Kingdom	61.27	400 737	654 095	82.14	537 219	654 022	80.97	419 713	518 358	9 250	11 300
United States	56.42	2 013 101	3 567 961	70.33	2 503 666	3 559 661	84.99	1 801 229	2 119 392	3 700	4 320
Netherlands[1]	27.13	49 019	180 697	55.50	100 283	180 697	84.03	72 656	86 462	2 503	2 958

1. Response rate is too low to ensure comparability (see above).

- **Column 6** shows the *weighted number of schools sampled after school replacement* (including both responding and nonresponding schools).

- **Column 7** shows the *weighted student participation rate after replacement.* This is obtained by dividing Column 8 by Column 9.

- **Column 8** shows the *weighted number of students assessed*.

- **Column 9** shows the *weighted number of students sampled* (including both students that were assessed and students who were absent on the day of the assessment).

- **Column 10** shows the *unweighted number of students assessed*.

- **Column 11** shows the *unweighted number of students sampled* (including both students that were assessed and students who were absent on the day of the assessment).

Annex A4: Standard errors, significance tests and multiple comparisons

The statistics in this report represent *estimates* of national performance based on samples of students rather than values that could be calculated if every student in every country had answered every question. Consequently, it is important to have measures of the degree of uncertainty of the estimates. In PISA 2000, each estimate has an associated degree of uncertainty, which is expressed through a *standard error*. The use of *confidence intervals* provides a way to make inferences about the population means and proportions in a manner that reflects the uncertainty associated with the sample estimates. From an observed sample statistic it can, under the assumption of a normal distribution, be inferred that the corresponding population result would lie within the confidence interval in 95 out of 100 replications of the measurement on different samples drawn from the same population.

In many cases, readers are primarily interested in whether a given value in a particular country is different from a second value in the same or another country, *e.g.*, whether females in a country perform better than males in the same country. In the tables and charts used in this report, differences are labelled as *statistically significant* when a difference of that size, or larger, would be observed less than 5 per cent of the time, if there was actually no difference in corresponding population values. Similarly, the risk of reporting as significant if there is, in fact, no correlation between to measures is contained at 5 per cent.

Although the probability that a particular difference will falsely be declared to be statistically significant is low (5 per cent) in each single comparison, the probability of making such an error increases when several comparisons are made simultaneously.

It is possible to make an adjustment for this which reduces to 5 per cent the maximum probability that differences will be falsely declared as statistically significant at least once among all the comparisons that are made. Such an adjustment, based on the Bonferroni method, has been incorporated into the multiple comparison charts in Chapters 2 and 3 since the likely interest of readers in those contexts is to compare a country's performance with that of all other countries.

For all other tables and charts readers should note that, if there were no real differences on a given measure, then the *multiple comparison* in conjunction with a 5 per cent significance level, would erroneously identify differences on 0.05 times the number of comparisons made, occasions. For example, even though the significance tests applied in PISA for identifying gender differences ensure that, for each country, the likelihood of identifying a gender difference erroneously is less than 5 per cent, a comparison showing differences for 27 countries would, on average, identify 1.4 cases (0.05 times 27) with significant gender differences, even if there were no real gender difference in any of the countries. The same applies for other statistics for which significance tests have been undertaken in this publication, such as correlations and regression coefficients.

Annex A5: Quality assurance

Quality assurance procedures were implemented in all parts of PISA.

The consistent quality and linguistic equivalence of the PISA assessment instruments were facilitated by providing countries with equivalent source versions of the assessment instruments in English and French and requiring countries (other than those assessing students in English and French) to prepare and consolidate two independent translations using both source versions. Precise translation guidelines were also supplied, including a description of what each item was intended to measure as well as instructions for the selection and training of the translators. For each country, the translation and format of the assessment instruments were verified by experts from the PISA Consortium (whose mother tongue was the language of instruction in the country concerned and knowledgeable about education systems) before they were used in the PISA Field Trial and Main Study. Experts from participating countries were required to translate and submit the marking guidelines for verification. For further information on the PISA translation procedures see the *PISA 2000 Technical Report (OECD, 2002a)*.

The survey was implemented through standardised procedures. The PISA Consortium provided comprehensive manuals that explained the implementation of the survey, including precise instructions for the work of School Co-ordinators and scripts for Test Administrators for use during the assessment sessions. The PISA Consortium verified the national translation and adaptation of these manuals.

To establish the credibility of PISA as valid and as unbiased and to encourage uniformity in the administration of the assessment sessions, Test Administrators in participating countries were selected using the following criteria: It was *required* that the Test Administrator not be the reading, mathematics, or science instructor of any students in the sessions he or she would administer for PISA; it was *recommended* that the Test Administrator not be a member of the staff of any school where he or she would administer PISA, and it was considered *preferable* that the Test Administrator not be a member of the staff of any school in the PISA sample. Participating countries organised an in-person training session for Test Administrators.

Participating countries were not allowed to introduce modifications in the assessment session script and instructions described in the Test Administrator Manual without prior approval by the PISA Consortium. Participating countries were required to ensure that: Test Administrators worked with the School Co-ordinator to prepare the assessment session, including updating student tracking forms and identifying excluded students; no extra time was given for the cognitive items (while it was permissible to give extra time for the student questionnaire); no instrument was administered before the two 1-hour parts of the cognitive session; Test Administrators recorded the student participation status on the student tracking forms and filled in a Session Report Form; no cognitive instrument was photocopied or lent by the Test Administrator to any person before the assessment session; and that Test Administrators returned the material to the national centre immediately after the assessment sessions.

National Project Managers were encouraged to organise a follow-up session when more than 15 per cent of the PISA sample was not able to attend the original assessment session.

National Quality Monitors from the PISA Consortium visited all national centres to review data-collection procedures. Finally, School Quality Monitors from the PISA Consortium visited a sample of 25 per cent of the schools during the assessment. For further information on the field operations see the *PISA 2000 Technical Report (OECD, 2002a)*.

Software specially designed for PISA 2000 facilitated data entry, detected common errors during data entry, and facilitated the process of data cleaning. Training sessions familiarised National Project Managers with these procedures.

For a description of the quality assurance procedures applied in PISA and the results see the *PISA 2000 Technical Report (OECD, 2002a)*.

Annex A6: Development of the PISA assessment instruments

The development of the PISA 2000 assessment instruments was an interactive process between the PISA Consortium, the various expert committees, governments of participating countries and national experts. A panel of international experts led, in close consultation with participating countries, the identification of the range of skills and competencies that were, in the respective assessment domains, considered to be crucial for an individual's capacity to fully participate in and contribute to a successful modern society. A description of the assessment domains – the assessment framework – was then used by participating countries, and other test development professionals, as they contributed assessment materials. The development of this assessment framework involved the following steps:

- development of a working definition for the domain and description of the assumptions that underlay that definition;

- evaluation of how to organise the set of tasks constructed in order to report to policy-makers and researchers on performance in each assessment domain among 15-year-old students in participating countries;

- identification of a set of key characteristics to be taken into account when assessment tasks were constructed for international use;

- operationalisation of the set of key characteristics to be used in test construction, with definitions based on existing literature and the experience of other large-scale assessments;

- validation of the variables, and assessment of the contribution which each made to the understanding of task difficulty in participating countries; and

- preparation of an interpretative scheme for the results.

The frameworks were agreed at both scientific and policy levels and subsequently provided the basis for the development of the assessment instruments (OECD, 1999a). They provided a common language and a vehicle for participating countries to develop a consensus as to the measurement goals of PISA.

Assessment items were then developed to reflect the intentions of the frameworks and were piloted in a Field Trial in all participating countries before a final set of items was selected for the PISA 2000 Main Study. Tables A6.1-A6-3 show the distribution of PISA 2000 assessment items by the various dimensions of the PISA frameworks.

Due attention was paid to reflecting the national, cultural and linguistic variety among countries. As part of this effort the PISA Consortium included, in addition to the items that were developed by the PISA Consortium, assessment material contributed by participating countries that the Consortium's multi-national team of test developers deemed appropriate given the requirements laid out by the PISA assessment frameworks. As a result, the item pool included assessment items from Australia, Austria, Belgium, Czech Republic, Denmark, Finland, France, Germany, Greece, Ireland, Italy, Japan, Korea, New Zealand, Norway, the Russian Federation, Sweden Switzerland the United Kingdom and the United States. The share of items submitted by participating countries was slightly more than 50 per cent in both the Field Trial and the Main Study.

Approximately 290 units and 1169 items were contributed or developed for the Field Trial, including about 150 Reading Units comprising some 781 Reading Items. After the first consultation process, the Field Trial included 69 Reading Units with 342 Reading Items. Of these Reading Units, the stimulus material for 24 came from national contributions, 26 originated with the PISA Consortium, and 19 units came from the International Adult Literacy Survey (IALS). Material was drawn from IALS because countries wanted to have the possibility of comparing results from it with PISA results.

Each item included in the assessment pool was then rated by each country: for potential cultural, gender or other bias; for relevance to 15-year-olds in school and non-school contexts; and for familiarity and level of interest. A first consultation of countries on the item pool was undertaken as part of the process of developing the Field Trial assessment instruments. A second consultation was undertaken after the Field Trial to assist in the final selection of items for the Main Study and completed by a review of the assessment material by an international cultural fairness panel.

Following the Field Trial, in which all items were tested in all participating countries, test developers and expert groups considered a variety of aspects in selecting the items for the Main Study: *i)* the results from the Field Trial, *ii)* the outcome of the item review from countries, and *iii)* queries received during the Field Trial marking process. The test developers and expert groups selected a final set of items in October 1999 which, following a period of negotiation, was adopted by participating countries at both scientific and policy levels.

The Main Study included 37 Reading Units with 141 items (counting different parts of questions as separate items). The stimulus for 14 of these units came from national contributions, the PISA Consortium was the source of the stimulus material for 13 units, and 10 units came from the International Adult Literacy Survey. The Main Study instruments also included 16 Mathematics Units (32 Items) and 14 Science Units (35 Items).

Five item types were used in the PISA assessment instruments:

- *Multiple-choice items*: these items required students to circle a letter to indicate one choice among four or five alternatives, each of which might be a number, a word, a phrase or a sentence. They were scored dichotomously.

- *Complex multiple-choice items*: in these items, the student made a series of choices, usually binary. Students indicated their answer by circling a word or short phrase (for example *yes* or *no*) for each point. These items were scored dichotomously for each choice, yielding the possibility of full or partial credit for the whole item.

- *Closed constructed-response items*: these items required students to construct their own responses, there being a limited range of acceptable answers. Most of these items were scored dichotomously with a few items included in the marking process.

- *Short response items*: as in the closed constructed-response items, students were to provide a brief answer, but there was a wide range of possible answers. These items were hand-marked, thus allowing for dichotomous as well as partial credit.

- *Open constructed-response items*: in these items, students constructed a longer response, allowing for the possibility of a broad range of divergent, individual responses and differing viewpoints. These items usually asked students to relate information or ideas in the stimulus text to their own experience or opinions, with the acceptability depending less on the position taken by the student than on the ability to use what they had read when justifying or explaining that position. Partial credit was often permitted for partially correct or less sophisticated answers, and all of these items were marked by hand.

PISA 2000 was designed to yield group-level information in a broad range of content. The PISA assessment of reading included material allowing for a total of 270 minutes of assessment time, of which 45 per cent was devoted to items requiring open-ended responses. The mathematics and science assessments included 60 minutes of assessment time, of which 35 per cent was assessed through open-ended items. Each student, however, sat assessments lasting a total of 120 minutes.

In order to cover the intended broad range of content while meeting the limit of 120 minutes of individual assessment time, the assessment in each domain was divided into clusters, organised into nine booklets. There were nine 30-minute reading clusters, four 15-minute mathematics clusters and four 15-minute science clusters. In PISA 2000, every student answered reading items, and over half the students answered items on science and mathematics.

This assessment design had a number of particular features. First, the majority of the reading material was presented in a balanced way in order to avoid position effects and to ensure that each item had equal weight in the assessment. Second, seven of the nine booklets began with reading, and all booklets contained at least 60 minutes of reading. Five booklets also contained science items, and five contained mathematics items. Third, PISA 2000 included a link between PISA and IALS through two reading blocks containing only IALS items, which were presented in six of the nine booklets. Finally, the design ensured that a representative sample of students responded to each block of items.

For further information on the development of the PISA assessment instruments and the PISA assessment design, see the *PISA 2000 Technical Report (OECD, 2002a)*.

Table A6.1
Distribution of items by the dimensions of the PISA framework for the assessment of reading literacy

Context	Number of items[1]	Number of multiple-choice items	Number of complex multiple-choice items	Number of closed constructed-response items	Number of open constructed-response items	Number of short response items
Distribution of reading items by text structure						
Continuous	89	42	3	3	34	7
Non-continuous	52	14	4	12	9	13
Total	*141*	*56*	*7*	*15*	*43*	*20*
Distribution of reading items by type of task (process)						
Interpreting texts	70	43	3	5	14	5
Reflection and evaluation	29	3	2	-	23	1
Retrieving information	42	10	2	10	6	14
Total	*141*	*56*	*7*	*15*	*43*	*20*
Distribution of reading items by text type						
Advertisements	4	-	-	-	1	3
Argumentative and persuasive	18	7	1	2	8	-
Charts and graphs	16	8	-	2	3	3
Descriptive	13	7	1	-	4	1
Expository	31	17	1	-	9	4
Forms	8	1	1	4	1	1
Injunctive	9	3	-	1	5	-
Maps	4	1	-	-	1	2
Narrative	18	8	-	-	8	2
Schematics	5	2	2	-	-	1
Tables	15	2	1	6	3	3
Total	*141*	*56*	*7*	*15*	*43*	*20*
Distribution of reading items by context						
Educational	39	22	4	1	4	8
Occupational	22	4	1	4	9	4
Personal	26	10	-	3	10	3
Public	54	20	2	7	20	5
Total	*141*	*56*	*7*	*15*	*43*	*20*

1. Nine items were eliminated from subsequent analysis.

Table A6.2
Distribution of items by the dimensions of the PISA framework for the assessment of mathematical literacy

Context	Number of items	Number of multiple-choice items	Number of closed-constructed response items[1]	Number of open-constructed response items
Distribution of mathematics items by 'main mathematical theme'				
Change and relationship	5	1	2	2
Growth and change	8	4	2	2
Space and shape	20	4	13	3
Total	*33*	*9*	*17*	*7*
Distribution of mathematics items by competency class				
Class 1: Reproduction	15	4	11	-
Class 2: Connections	15	5	6	4
Class 3: Reflection	3	-	-	3
Total	*33*	*9*	*17*	*7*
Distribution of mathematics items by context				
Community	4	-	2	2
Educational	5	1	4	-
Occupational	2	-	2	-
Personal	9	4	2	3
Public	4	1	2	1
Scientific	9	3	5	1
Total	*33*	*9*	*17*	*7*

1. Includes short-response items.

Table A6.3
Distribution of items by the dimensions of the PISA framework for the assessment of scientific literacy

Context	Number of items	Number of multiple-choice items	Number of complex multiple-choice items	Number of open-constructed response items
Distribution of science items by science processes				
Communicating to other valid conclusions from evidence and data	2	-	-	2
Demonstrating understanding scientific knowledge	18	9	3	6
Drawing and evaluating conclusions	7	1	2	4
Identifying evidence and data	5	3	1	1
Recognising questions	3	1	2	0
Total	*35*	*14*	*8*	*13*
Distribution of science items by science area				
Earth and environment	12	2	3	7
Life and health	12	7	1	4
Technology	11	5	4	2
Total	*35*	*14*	*8*	*13*
Distribution of science items by science application				
Atmospheric change	3	-	-	3
Biodiversity	1	1	-	-
Chemical and physical change	1	-	-	1
Earth and universe	7	2	3	2
Ecosystems	4	2	-	2
Energy transfer	4	-	2	2
Forces and movement	1	1	-	-
Form and function	1	1	-	-
Genetic control	2	1	1	-
Geological change	1	-	-	1
Human biology	4	2	-	2
Structure of matter	6	4	2	-
Total	*35*	*14*	*8*	*13*

Annex A7: Reliability of the marking of open-ended items

The process of marking open-ended items was an important step in ensuring the quality and comparability of results from PISA.

Detailed guidelines contributed to a marking process that was accurate and consistent across countries. The marking guidelines consisted of: marking manuals, training materials for recruiting markers, and workshop materials used for the training of national markers. Before national training, the PISA Consortium organised training sessions to present the material and train the marking co-ordinators from the participating countries, who were later responsible for training their national markers.

For each assessment item, the relevant marking manual described the aim of the question and how to code students' responses to each item. This description included the credit labels – full credit, partial credit or no credit – attached to the possible categories of responses. PISA 2000 also included a system of double-digit coding for the mathematics and science items in which the first digit represented the score and the second digit represented different strategies or approaches that students used to solve the problem. The second digit generated national profiles of student strategies and misconceptions. By way of illustration, the marking manuals also included real examples of students' responses (drawn from the Field Trial) accompanied by a rationale for their classification.

In each country, a sub-sample of assessment booklets was marked independently by four markers and examined by the PISA Consortium. In order to examine the consistency of this marking process in more detail within each country and to estimate the magnitude of the variance components associated with the use of markers, the PISA Consortium conducted an inter-marker reliability study on a sub-sample of assessment booklets. Homogeneity analysis was applied to the national sets of multiple marking and compared with the results of the Field Trial. For details see the *PISA 2000 Technical Report (OECD, 2002a)*.

DATA TABLES

Table 1.1
Typical entry age and duration of different levels of schooling

	Entrance age			Duration		
	Primary	Lower secondary	Upper secondary	Primary	Lower secondary	Upper secondary
Albania	6	10	14	4	4	4
Argentina	6	12	15	6	3	3
Australia	5	12	16	7	4	2
Austria	6	10	14	4	4	4
Belgium	6	12	14	6	2	4
Brazil	7	11	15	4	4	3
Bulgaria	7	11	15	4	4	3
Canada	6	12	15	6	3	3
Chile	6	12	14	6	2	4
Czech Republic	6	11	15	5	4	4
Denmark	7	13	16	6	3	3
Finland	7	13	16	6	3	3
France	6	11	15	5	4	3
Germany	6	10	16	4	6	3
Greece	6	12	15	6	3	3
Hong Kong-China	6	12	15	6	3	4
Hungary	7	11	15	4	4	4
Iceland	6	12	15	6	3	2
Indonesia	7	13	16	6	3	3
Ireland	6	13	16	7	3	4
Israel	6	12	15	6	3	3
Italy	6	11	14	5	3	5
Japan	6	12	15	6	3	3
Korea	6	12	15	6	3	3
Latvia	7	11	16	4	5	3
Liechtenstein	6	11	14	5	3	3
Luxembourg	6	12	15	6	3	4
FYR Macedonia	7	11	15	4	4	4
Mexico	6	12	15	6	3	3
Netherlands	6	12	15	6	3	3
New Zealand	5	11	15	6	4	3
Norway	6	13	16	7	3	3
Peru	6	12	15	6	3	2
Poland	7	13	15	6	2	4
Portugal	6	12	15	6	3	3
Russian Federation	6	10	15	4	5	2
Spain	6	12	16	6	4	2
Sweden	7	13	16	6	3	3
Switzerland	7	13	16	6	3	4
Thailand	6	12	15	6	3	3
United Kingdom	5	11	14	6	3	4
United States	6	12	15	6	3	3
OECD average	6	12	15	6	3	4

Source: UNESCO Institute for Statistics (UIS), October 2002.

Table 1.2
Transition rate from primary to secondary education, total and by gender, 1999

	Transition rate from primary to secondary education		
	Total	**Males**	**Females**
Albania	94.0	93.2	94.9
Argentina	94.1 [a,b]	92.7 [a,b]	95.5 [a,b]
Australia	m	m	m
Austria	m	m	m
Belgium	m	m	m
Brazil	m	m	m
Bulgaria	97.3	97.2	97.4
Canada	m	m	m
Chile	97.5	96.8	98.3
Czech Republic	99.2	99.0	99.5
Denmark	99.6 [b]	99.6 [b]	99.6 [b]
Finland	100.2	100.3	100.1
France	98.7 [a,b]	99.1 [a,b]	98.3 [a,b]
Germany	98.8	98.7	100.4
Greece	m	m	m
Hong Kong-China	m	m	m
Hungary	100.0	99.6	100.4
Iceland	m	m	m
Indonesia	80.0 [b]	80.1 [b]	79.9 [b]
Ireland	m	m	m
Israel	m	m	m
Italy	101.6	101.8	101.4
Japan	m	m	m
Korea	99.6	99.6	99.7
Latvia	98.4 [a]	98.0 [a]	98.8 [a]
Liechtenstein	m	m	m
Luxembourg	m	m	m
FYR Macedonia	m	m	m
Mexico	90.2	91.5	88.9
Netherlands	101.2	100.2	102.4
New Zealand	m	m	m
Norway	m	m	m
Peru	92.5 [a]	93.6 [a]	91.3 [a]
Poland	99.6	m	m
Portugal	m	m	m
Russian Federation	m	m	m
Spain	m	m	m
Sweden	m	m	m
Switzerland	102.1	101.8	102.4
Thailand	86.5	89.8	83.0
United Kingdom	m	m	m
United States	m	m	m
OECD average	99.2	99.2	99.2

a. Data for 1998.
b. Based on UIS estimation.
Source: UNESCO Institute for Statistics (UIS)
Note: The transition rates greater than 100 per cent are due to immigration.

Table 1.3
Enrolment in secondary and tertiary education

	Net enrolment ratio (%) in secondary education[a]			Enrolment in upper secondary (including post-secondary non-tertiary) school by type of programme (%) [b]			Gross enrolment ratio (%) tertiary level education[b]	
	Total	Males	Females	General	Technical/Vocational	Total	Males	Females
Albania	71	70	73	86	14	15	11	18
Argentina	76	73	79	42	58	48	36	60
Australia	87 c	86 c	88 c	34	66	63	57	70
Austria	89 c	89 c	89 c	22	71	56	54	59
Belgium	95 c	95 c	96 c	33	67	57	54	61
Brazil	68	66	71	82	18	15	13	17
Bulgaria	86	87	85	m	m	43	36	50
Canada	98	98	98	91	m	60	52	69
Chile	72	70	73	58	42	38	39	36
Czech Republic	84	84	85	19	80	29	28	29
Denmark	89	88	91	45	55	56	47	65
Finland	95 c	94 c	96 c	45	55	84	76	92
France	93	92	94	43	57	53	47	58
Germany	88 c	87 c	88 c	37	63	46 d	47 d	45 d
Greece	86	84	88	68	32	55	53	56
Hong Kong-China	70	68	71	95	5	25	24	25
Hungary	87	87	88	36	10	37	33	40
Iceland	100 c	97 c	100 c	77	m	46	42	51
Indonesia	48 c	49 c	46 c	61	39	m	m	m
Ireland	76	75	78	37	32	46	35	58
Israel	88 c	87 c	89 c	68	32	50	42	59
Italy	88 c	89 c	86 c	36	25	47	41	53
Japan	100 c	100 c	100 c	74	25	46	50	42
Korea	94	94	94	64	36	72	90	52
Latvia	84	83	85	m	m	50 d	38 d	62 d
Liechtenstein	m	m	m	m	m	m	m	m
Luxembourg	82 c	80 c	85 c	37	64	9 c	8 c	10 c
FYR Macedonia	79 d,c	80 d,c	78 d,c	m	m	25	19	30
Mexico	57 c	57 c	58 c	87	13	20	20	19
Netherlands	92	92	92	32	68	52	51	53
New Zealand	m	m	m	m	m	66	53	80
Norway	95 c	95 c	96 c	43	57	68	56	82
Peru	61 d	62 d	61 d	75	25	29 d	43 d	15 d
Poland	88 c	86 c	90 c	36	64	50	42	59
Portugal	87 c	84 c	91 c	72	28	47	40	54
Russian Federation	m	m	m	m	m	65	57	73
Spain	91 c	90 c	92 c	67	34	58	53	62
Sweden	96	94	98	51	49	66	54	79
Switzerland	88	91	86	34	66	39 d	44 d	33 d
Thailand	55	54	57	70	30	32	29	34
United Kingdom	94	92	95	33	67	58	52	64
United States	87	86	88	m	m	72	62	81
OECD average	89	88	89	48	47	50	47	55

Note: The school year 1998/1999 and 1999/2000 corresponds in some cases to the calendar year 1998 and 1999.
a. Net enrolment data refer to 1999/2000.
b. Data for 2000.
c. Based on UIS estimation.
d. Data for 1998/1999.
Enrolment ratios of 100 have been adjusted.
Source: UNESCO Institute for Statistics (UIS), October 2002.

Table 1.4
Gini index of income distribution and percentage share of income or consumption

	Year surveyed	Gini index	Percentage share of income or consumption						
			Lowest 10%	Lowest 20%	Second 20%	Third 20%	Fourth 20%	Highest 20%	Highest 10%
Albania		m	m	m	m	m	m	m	m
Argentina		m	m	m	m	m	m	m	m
Australia	1994 [b]	35.2	2.0	5.9	12.0	17.2	23.6	41.3	25.4
Austria	1995 [b]	30.5	2.3	7.0	13.2	17.9	24.0	37.9	22.4
Belgium	1996 [b]	25.0	2.9	8.3	14.1	17.7	22.7	37.3	22.6
Brazil	1998 [b]	59.1	0.5	2.0	5.7	10.0	18.0	64.4	46.7
Bulgaria	2001 [b]	31.9	2.4	6.7	13.1	17.9	23.4	38.9	23.7
Canada	1997 [b]	31.5	2.7	7.3	12.9	17.4	23.1	39.3	23.9
Chile	1998 [b]	57.5	1.1	3.2	6.7	10.7	18.1	61.3	45.4
Czech Republic	1996 [b]	25.4	4.3	10.3	14.5	17.7	21.7	35.9	22.4
Denmark	1997 [b]	24.7	2.6	8.3	14.7	18.2	22.9	35.8	21.3
Finland	1995 [b]	25.6	4.1	10.1	14.7	17.9	22.3	35.0	20.9
France	1995 [b]	32.7	2.8	7.2	12.6	17.2	22.8	40.2	25.1
Germany	1998 [b]	38.2	2.0	5.7	10.5	15.7	23.4	44.7	28.0
Greece	1998 [b]	35.4	2.9	7.1	11.4	15.8	22.0	43.6	28.5
Hong Kong-China	1996 [b]	43.4	2.0	5.3	9.4	13.9	20.7	50.7	34.9
Hungary	1998 [a]	24.4	4.1	10.0	14.7	18.3	22.7	34.4	20.5
Indonesia	2000 [a]	30.3	3.6	8.4	11.9	15.4	21.0	43.3	28.5
Ireland	1987 [b]	35.9	2.5	6.7	11.6	16.4	22.4	42.9	27.4
Israel	1997 [b]	35.5	2.4	6.9	11.4	16.3	22.9	44.3	28.2
Italy	1998 [b]	36.0	1.9	6.0	12.0	16.8	22.6	42.6	27.4
Japan	1993 [b]	24.9	4.8	10.6	14.2	17.6	22.0	35.7	21.7
Korea	1998 [a]	31.6	2.9	7.9	13.6	18.0	23.1	37.5	22.5
Latvia	1998 [b]	32.4	2.9	7.6	12.9	17.1	22.1	40.3	25.9
Liechtenstein		m	m	m	m	m	m	m	m
Luxembourg	1998 [b]	30.8	3.2	8.0	12.8	16.9	22.5	39.7	24.7
FYR Macedonia	1998 [a]	28.2	3.3	8.4	14.0	17.7	23.1	36.7	22.1
Mexico	1998 [b]	51.9	1.2	3.4	7.4	12.1	19.5	57.6	41.6
Netherlands	1994 [b]	32.6	2.8	7.3	12.7	17.2	22.8	40.1	25.1
New Zealand	1997 [b]	36.2	2.2	6.4	11.4	15.8	22.6	43.8	27.8
Norway	1995 [b]	25.8	4.1	9.7	14.3	17.9	22.2	35.8	21.8
Peru	1996 [b]	46.2	1.6	4.4	9.1	14.1	21.3	51.2	35.4
Poland	1998 [a]	31.6	3.2	7.8	12.8	17.1	22.6	39.7	24.7
Portugal	1997 [b]	38.5	2.0	5.8	11.0	15.5	21.9	45.9	29.8
Russian Federation	2000 [a]	45.6	1.8	4.9	9.5	14.1	20.3	51.3	36.0
Spain	1990 [b]	32.5	2.8	7.5	12.6	17.0	22.6	40.3	25.2
Sweden	1995 [b]	25.0	3.4	9.1	14.5	18.4	23.4	34.5	20.1
Switzerland	1992 [b]	33.1	2.6	6.9	12.7	17.3	22.9	40.3	25.2
Thailand	2000 [a]	43.2	2.5	6.1	9.5	13.5	20.9	50.0	33.8
United Kingdom	1995 [b]	36.0	2.1	6.1	11.7	16.3	22.7	43.2	27.5
United States	1997 [b]	40.8	1.8	5.2	10.5	15.6	22.4	46.4	30.5
OECD average		33.2	2.8	7.3	12.4	16.7	22.4	41.2	26.1

a. Refers to expenditure shares by percentiles of population and ranked by per capita expenditure.
b. Refers to income shares by percentiles of population and ranked by per capita income.
Source: World Development Indicators 2003, World Bank.

Table 2.1a
Percentage of students at each level of proficiency on the combined reading literacy scale

	Proficiency levels											
	Below Level 1 (less than 335 score points)		Level 1 (from 335 to 407 score points)		Level 2 (from 408 to 480 score points)		Level 3 (from 481 to 552 score points)		Level 4 (from 553 to 625 score points)		Level 5 (above 625 score points)	
	%	S.E.	%	S.E.	%	S.E.	%	S.E.	%	S.E.	%	S.E.
Albania	43.5	(1.5)	26.8	(0.9)	20.6	(0.9)	7.7	(0.5)	1.3	(0.2)	0.1	(0.1)
Argentina	22.6	(3.2)	21.3	(2.0)	25.5	(1.6)	20.3	(2.0)	8.6	(1.3)	1.7	(0.5)
Australia	3.3	(0.5)	9.1	(0.8)	19.0	(1.1)	25.7	(1.1)	25.3	(0.9)	17.6	(1.2)
Austria	4.4	(0.4)	10.2	(0.6)	21.7	(0.9)	29.9	(1.2)	24.9	(1.0)	8.8	(0.8)
Belgium	7.7	(1.0)	11.3	(0.7)	16.8	(0.7)	25.8	(0.9)	26.3	(0.9)	12.0	(0.7)
Brazil	23.3	(1.4)	32.5	(1.2)	27.7	(1.3)	12.9	(1.1)	3.1	(0.5)	0.6	(0.2)
Bulgaria	17.9	(1.3)	22.4	(1.3)	27.0	(1.4)	21.5	(1.4)	9.0	(1.0)	2.2	(0.6)
Canada	2.4	(0.3)	7.2	(0.3)	18.0	(0.4)	28.0	(0.5)	27.7	(0.6)	16.8	(0.5)
Chile	19.9	(1.3)	28.3	(1.2)	30.0	(1.2)	16.6	(1.0)	4.8	(0.5)	0.5	(0.1)
Czech Republic	6.1	(0.6)	11.4	(0.7)	24.8	(1.2)	30.9	(1.1)	19.8	(0.8)	7.0	(0.6)
Denmark	5.9	(0.6)	12.0	(0.7)	22.5	(0.9)	29.5	(1.0)	22.0	(0.9)	8.1	(0.5)
Finland	1.7	(0.5)	5.2	(0.4)	14.3	(0.7)	28.7	(0.8)	31.6	(0.9)	18.5	(0.9)
France	4.2	(0.6)	11.0	(0.8)	22.0	(0.8)	30.6	(1.0)	23.7	(0.9)	8.5	(0.6)
Germany	9.9	(0.7)	12.7	(0.6)	22.3	(0.8)	26.8	(1.0)	19.4	(1.0)	8.8	(0.5)
Greece	8.7	(1.2)	15.7	(1.4)	25.9	(1.4)	28.1	(1.7)	16.7	(1.4)	5.0	(0.7)
Hong Kong-China	2.6	(0.5)	6.5	(0.7)	17.1	(0.9)	33.1	(1.1)	31.3	(1.1)	9.5	(0.8)
Hungary	6.9	(0.7)	15.8	(1.2)	25.0	(1.1)	28.8	(1.3)	18.5	(1.1)	5.1	(0.8)
Iceland	4.0	(0.3)	10.5	(0.6)	22.0	(0.8)	30.8	(0.9)	23.6	(1.1)	9.1	(0.7)
Indonesia	31.1	(1.9)	37.6	(1.7)	24.8	(1.7)	6.1	(1.1)	0.4	(0.2)	0.0	(0.0)
Ireland	3.1	(0.5)	7.9	(0.8)	17.9	(0.9)	29.7	(1.1)	27.1	(1.1)	14.2	(0.8)
Israel	14.9	(2.3)	18.3	(1.7)	24.1	(1.5)	24.0	(1.5)	14.6	(1.7)	4.2	(0.8)
Italy	5.4	(0.9)	13.5	(0.9)	25.6	(1.0)	30.6	(1.0)	19.5	(1.1)	5.3	(0.5)
Japan	2.7	(0.6)	7.3	(1.1)	18.0	(1.3)	33.3	(1.3)	28.8	(1.7)	9.9	(1.1)
Korea	0.9	(0.2)	4.8	(0.6)	18.6	(0.9)	38.8	(1.1)	31.1	(1.2)	5.7	(0.6)
Latvia	12.7	(1.3)	17.9	(1.3)	26.3	(1.1)	25.2	(1.3)	13.8	(1.1)	4.1	(0.6)
Liechtenstein	7.6	(1.5)	14.5	(2.1)	23.2	(2.9)	30.1	(3.4)	19.5	(2.2)	5.1	(1.6)
Luxembourg	14.2	(0.7)	20.9	(0.8)	27.5	(1.3)	24.6	(1.1)	11.2	(0.5)	1.7	(0.3)
FYR Macedonia	34.5	(1.0)	28.1	(0.9)	24.4	(0.9)	11.1	(0.5)	1.8	(0.2)	0.1	(0.1)
Mexico	16.1	(1.2)	28.1	(1.4)	30.3	(1.1)	18.8	(1.2)	6.0	(0.7)	0.9	(0.2)
New Zealand	4.8	(0.5)	8.9	(0.5)	17.2	(0.9)	24.6	(1.1)	25.8	(1.1)	18.7	(1.0)
Norway	6.3	(0.6)	11.2	(0.8)	19.5	(0.8)	28.1	(0.8)	23.7	(0.9)	11.2	(0.7)
Peru	54.1	(2.1)	25.5	(1.2)	14.5	(1.1)	4.9	(0.6)	1.0	(0.2)	0.1	(0.1)
Poland	8.7	(1.0)	14.6	(1.0)	24.1	(1.4)	28.2	(1.3)	18.6	(1.3)	5.9	(1.0)
Portugal	9.6	(1.0)	16.7	(1.2)	25.3	(1.0)	27.5	(1.2)	16.8	(1.1)	4.2	(0.5)
Russian Federation	9.0	(1.0)	18.5	(1.1)	29.2	(0.8)	26.9	(1.1)	13.3	(1.0)	3.2	(0.5)
Spain	4.1	(0.5)	12.2	(0.9)	25.7	(0.7)	32.8	(1.0)	21.1	(0.9)	4.2	(0.5)
Sweden	3.3	(0.4)	9.3	(0.6)	20.3	(0.7)	30.4	(1.0)	25.6	(1.0)	11.2	(0.7)
Switzerland	7.0	(0.7)	13.3	(0.9)	21.4	(1.0)	28.0	(1.0)	21.0	(1.0)	9.2	(1.0)
Thailand	10.4	(1.1)	26.6	(1.2)	36.8	(1.1)	20.8	(1.0)	4.8	(0.6)	0.5	(0.2)
United Kingdom	3.6	(0.4)	9.2	(0.5)	19.6	(0.7)	27.5	(0.9)	24.4	(0.9)	15.6	(1.0)
United States	6.4	(1.2)	11.5	(1.2)	21.0	(1.2)	27.4	(1.3)	21.5	(1.4)	12.2	(1.4)
OECD average	*6.0*	*(0.1)*	*11.9*	*(0.2)*	*21.7*	*(0.2)*	*28.7*	*(0.2)*	*22.3*	*(0.2)*	*9.5*	*(0.1)*
OECD total	*6.2*	*(0.4)*	*12.1*	*(0.4)*	*21.8*	*(0.4)*	*28.6*	*(0.4)*	*21.8*	*(0.4)*	*9.4*	*(0.4)*

Table 2.1b
Percentage of students at each level of proficiency on the reading/retrieving information scale

	Proficiency levels											
	Below Level 1 (less than 335 score points)		Level 1 (from 335 to 407 score points)		Level 2 (from 408 to 480 score points)		Level 3 (from 481 to 552 score points)		Level 4 (from 553 to 625 score points)		Level 5 (above 625 score points)	
	%	S.E.	%	S.E.	%	S.E.	%	S.E.	%	S.E.	%	S.E.
Albania	48.3	(1.4)	24.0	(1.0)	18.2	(0.9)	7.8	(0.5)	1.7	(0.3)	0.1	(0.1)
Argentina	27.0	(3.5)	20.7	(1.9)	22.6	(1.7)	17.8	(2.0)	9.1	(1.2)	2.8	(0.6)
Australia	3.7	(0.4)	8.8	(0.8)	17.2	(1.0)	24.7	(1.0)	24.7	(1.0)	20.9	(1.2)
Austria	5.2	(0.5)	11.1	(0.7)	22.6	(0.9)	29.1	(1.0)	23.5	(0.9)	8.6	(0.7)
Belgium	9.1	(1.0)	10.3	(0.6)	15.4	(0.7)	22.2	(0.8)	25.2	(0.9)	17.8	(0.7)
Brazil	37.1	(1.6)	30.4	(1.3)	20.5	(1.2)	9.4	(0.6)	2.2	(0.5)	0.4	(0.2)
Bulgaria	22.5	(1.5)	20.6	(1.0)	24.9	(1.1)	19.6	(1.2)	9.4	(1.0)	3.1	(0.6)
Canada	3.4	(0.3)	8.4	(0.3)	18.5	(0.5)	26.8	(0.6)	25.5	(0.6)	17.4	(0.6)
Chile	31.4	(1.6)	26.3	(0.9)	24.0	(1.1)	13.4	(0.9)	4.2	(0.4)	0.7	(0.1)
Czech Republic	9.0	(0.7)	13.8	(0.8)	24.5	(0.8)	27.1	(0.8)	17.6	(1.0)	8.0	(0.6)
Denmark	6.9	(0.7)	12.4	(0.6)	21.0	(0.8)	27.8	(0.8)	21.7	(0.8)	10.2	(0.7)
Finland	2.3	(0.5)	5.6	(0.4)	13.9	(0.9)	24.3	(1.2)	28.3	(0.8)	25.5	(0.9)
France	4.9	(0.6)	10.5	(0.9)	19.2	(0.8)	27.0	(0.9)	25.2	(1.1)	13.2	(1.0)
Germany	10.5	(0.8)	12.6	(0.7)	21.8	(0.9)	26.8	(1.1)	19.0	(1.0)	9.3	(0.5)
Greece	15.1	(1.6)	17.9	(1.1)	25.3	(1.2)	24.1	(1.2)	13.5	(1.0)	4.1	(0.6)
Hong Kong-China	3.8	(0.6)	7.8	(0.6)	18.5	(0.9)	29.9	(1.2)	27.6	(1.0)	12.4	(1.0)
Hungary	10.2	(0.9)	15.7	(1.1)	23.0	(0.9)	25.3	(1.2)	18.1	(1.2)	7.8	(0.9)
Iceland	6.5	(0.4)	12.0	(0.6)	21.6	(0.9)	28.4	(1.2)	21.0	(0.9)	10.6	(0.6)
Indonesia	42.9	(2.1)	31.5	(1.2)	19.5	(1.5)	5.5	(1.0)	0.6	(0.3)	0.0	(0.0)
Ireland	4.0	(0.5)	8.7	(0.7)	18.2	(0.9)	28.1	(1.0)	25.8	(0.9)	15.2	(0.8)
Israel	22.6	(2.7)	17.8	(1.3)	22.1	(1.2)	20.6	(1.6)	12.3	(1.3)	4.6	(0.8)
Italy	7.6	(0.8)	13.4	(0.8)	23.4	(0.9)	28.1	(0.9)	19.2	(0.9)	8.4	(0.6)
Japan	3.8	(0.8)	7.8	(1.0)	17.3	(1.1)	29.8	(1.1)	26.7	(1.3)	14.5	(1.2)
Korea	1.5	(0.3)	6.3	(0.6)	18.6	(0.9)	32.4	(1.0)	29.7	(1.0)	11.6	(0.8)
Latvia	17.1	(1.6)	17.7	(1.2)	23.6	(1.1)	21.6	(1.0)	14.1	(1.1)	5.9	(0.7)
Liechtenstein	8.6	(1.6)	12.6	(2.1)	19.9	(2.5)	28.3	(3.6)	21.8	(3.6)	8.8	(1.6)
Luxembourg	17.9	(0.7)	21.1	(0.9)	25.4	(0.8)	22.2	(0.9)	11.1	(0.8)	2.4	(0.4)
FYR Macedonia	39.6	(1.3)	24.3	(1.2)	21.3	(1.1)	11.5	(0.7)	3.0	(0.4)	0.3	(0.1)
Mexico	26.1	(1.4)	25.6	(1.3)	25.5	(1.0)	15.8	(1.1)	5.8	(0.8)	1.2	(0.3)
New Zealand	5.6	(0.5)	8.6	(0.6)	15.7	(0.7)	22.7	(1.2)	25.2	(1.1)	22.2	(1.0)
Norway	7.4	(0.6)	10.8	(0.6)	19.5	(0.9)	26.7	(1.3)	23.0	(1.2)	12.6	(0.8)
Peru	65.4	(1.9)	19.7	(1.3)	10.8	(1.0)	3.4	(0.4)	0.7	(0.2)	0.0	(0.0)
Poland	11.5	(1.1)	15.1	(1.0)	22.7	(1.2)	24.5	(1.1)	18.2	(1.3)	8.0	(1.2)
Portugal	13.9	(1.3)	18.2	(1.1)	24.3	(1.0)	24.5	(1.2)	14.8	(1.0)	4.4	(0.5)
Russian Federation	14.4	(1.3)	19.4	(0.8)	26.0	(0.8)	22.9	(1.0)	12.4	(0.9)	4.9	(0.6)
Spain	6.4	(0.6)	13.9	(1.0)	25.6	(0.8)	30.5	(1.0)	19.0	(0.9)	4.8	(0.4)
Sweden	4.9	(0.4)	10.2	(0.8)	19.9	(0.9)	26.8	(0.9)	23.5	(0.9)	14.6	(0.8)
Switzerland	8.8	(0.8)	12.5	(0.8)	19.3	(0.9)	25.9	(1.1)	21.6	(0.9)	12.1	(1.1)
Thailand	20.3	(1.3)	29.6	(1.2)	30.7	(1.1)	15.0	(1.0)	3.8	(0.6)	0.5	(0.2)
United Kingdom	4.4	(0.4)	9.4	(0.6)	18.6	(0.7)	26.9	(0.9)	24.1	(0.9)	16.5	(0.9)
United States	8.3	(1.4)	12.2	(1.1)	20.7	(1.0)	25.6	(1.2)	20.8	(1.4)	12.6	(1.4)
OECD average	8.1	(0.2)	12.3	(0.2)	20.7	(0.2)	26.1	(0.2)	21.2	(0.2)	11.6	(0.2)
OECD total	8.5	(0.4)	12.4	(0.3)	20.7	(0.3)	26.1	(0.4)	21.0	(0.4)	11.4	(0.4)

Table 2.1c
Percentage of students at each level of proficiency on the reading/interpreting texts scale

| | Proficiency levels | | | | | | | | | | |
| | Below Level 1 (less than 335 score points) | | Level 1 (from 335 to 407 score points) | | Level 2 (from 408 to 480 score points) | | Level 3 (from 481 to 552 score points) | | Level 4 (from 553 to 625 score points) | | Level 5 (above 625 score points) | |
	%	S.E.	%	S.E.	%	S.E.	%	S.E.	%	S.E.	%	S.E.
Albania	42.2	(1.5)	29.4	(1.0)	20.6	(1.2)	6.9	(0.5)	0.9	(0.2)	0.0	(0.0)
Argentina	22.1	(3.0)	23.3	(2.1)	26.7	(1.8)	19.2	(2.2)	7.3	(1.1)	1.4	(0.4)
Australia	3.7	(0.4)	9.7	(0.7)	19.3	(1.0)	25.6	(1.1)	24.0	(1.2)	17.7	(1.3)
Austria	4.0	(0.4)	10.7	(0.6)	21.8	(1.0)	30.0	(1.1)	23.8	(1.0)	9.7	(0.8)
Belgium	6.3	(0.7)	11.5	(0.8)	17.8	(0.7)	25.3	(0.9)	25.7	(0.9)	13.4	(0.7)
Brazil	21.5	(1.3)	33.2	(1.4)	28.1	(1.5)	13.4	(1.0)	3.3	(0.5)	0.6	(0.2)
Bulgaria	15.8	(1.3)	23.3	(1.5)	28.3	(1.5)	21.6	(1.4)	9.1	(1.1)	2.0	(0.5)
Canada	2.4	(0.2)	7.8	(0.4)	18.4	(0.4)	28.6	(0.6)	26.4	(0.5)	16.4	(0.5)
Chile	16.6	(1.3)	27.4	(1.2)	31.5	(1.0)	18.2	(1.1)	5.5	(0.5)	0.6	(0.2)
Czech Republic	5.4	(0.6)	10.7	(0.6)	23.2	(0.9)	30.3	(0.7)	21.7	(0.9)	8.7	(0.7)
Denmark	6.2	(0.6)	12.6	(0.8)	23.5	(0.8)	28.7	(0.9)	20.8	(1.0)	8.2	(0.7)
Finland	1.9	(0.5)	5.1	(0.4)	13.8	(0.8)	26.0	(0.9)	29.7	(0.9)	23.6	(0.9)
France	4.0	(0.5)	11.5	(0.8)	21.8	(0.9)	30.3	(1.0)	23.4	(1.1)	9.0	(0.7)
Germany	9.3	(0.8)	13.2	(0.9)	22.0	(1.0)	26.4	(1.0)	19.7	(0.7)	9.5	(0.5)
Greece	6.6	(1.1)	16.0	(1.4)	27.3	(1.2)	30.1	(1.5)	16.2	(1.2)	3.7	(0.6)
Hong Kong-China	2.3	(0.5)	6.9	(0.6)	18.2	(0.9)	34.4	(1.2)	30.2	(1.1)	8.1	(0.8)
Hungary	6.0	(0.7)	15.9	(1.3)	26.0	(1.1)	29.9	(1.3)	17.9	(1.1)	4.3	(0.6)
Iceland	3.6	(0.4)	10.1	(0.6)	21.1	(0.7)	29.2	(1.1)	24.4	(1.0)	11.7	(0.6)
Indonesia	27.6	(1.7)	40.3	(2.1)	26.1	(1.8)	5.7	(1.1)	0.3	(0.1)	0.0	(0.0)
Ireland	3.5	(0.5)	8.3	(0.7)	18.2	(0.9)	28.8	(1.1)	26.1	(1.1)	15.2	(1.0)
Israel	12.6	(2.2)	18.8	(1.9)	24.9	(1.8)	24.5	(1.6)	15.3	(1.8)	3.9	(0.7)
Italy	4.1	(0.7)	13.1	(0.8)	26.9	(1.2)	32.3	(1.3)	18.8	(0.9)	4.8	(0.4)
Japan	2.4	(0.7)	7.9	(1.1)	19.7	(1.4)	34.2	(1.5)	27.5	(1.6)	8.3	(1.0)
Korea	0.7	(0.2)	4.8	(0.6)	19.5	(1.0)	38.7	(1.4)	30.5	(1.2)	5.8	(0.6)
Latvia	11.1	(1.2)	18.6	(1.4)	27.2	(1.3)	26.6	(1.2)	13.1	(1.2)	3.4	(0.6)
Liechtenstein	6.6	(1.7)	15.2	(2.7)	23.9	(3.3)	29.7	(3.0)	19.8	(2.3)	4.9	(1.2)
Luxembourg	13.8	(0.6)	19.5	(0.9)	27.7	(1.0)	24.3	(0.9)	12.3	(0.6)	2.3	(0.4)
FYR Macedonia	30.5	(0.9)	30.4	(1.1)	25.8	(0.8)	11.5	(0.5)	1.9	(0.3)	0.1	(0.1)
Mexico	14.5	(0.9)	31.0	(1.5)	32.3	(1.3)	17.6	(1.2)	4.4	(0.6)	0.3	(0.1)
New Zealand	5.2	(0.5)	9.9	(0.7)	17.7	(0.7)	23.9	(1.1)	23.9	(0.9)	19.5	(0.9)
Norway	6.3	(0.5)	11.3	(0.8)	20.2	(0.7)	27.7	(0.8)	23.0	(0.9)	11.5	(0.7)
Peru	48.1	(2.1)	28.5	(1.1)	16.7	(1.3)	5.4	(0.6)	1.1	(0.2)	0.1	(0.1)
Poland	7.5	(0.9)	14.6	(0.9)	24.5	(1.4)	28.7	(1.3)	18.7	(1.3)	6.0	(0.9)
Portugal	7.8	(0.9)	16.9	(1.3)	26.9	(1.1)	27.9	(1.2)	16.6	(1.1)	4.0	(0.5)
Russian Federation	8.0	(0.9)	18.0	(0.8)	28.3	(0.9)	27.8	(1.1)	14.2	(1.1)	3.8	(0.6)
Spain	3.8	(0.5)	12.6	(0.9)	26.5	(0.8)	32.8	(1.1)	20.1	(0.8)	4.1	(0.4)
Sweden	3.1	(0.3)	9.5	(0.6)	19.7	(0.8)	28.6	(1.0)	25.4	(1.0)	13.7	(0.8)
Switzerland	6.7	(0.6)	12.9	(0.9)	22.3	(0.9)	27.4	(1.1)	21.4	(1.0)	9.3	(1.1)
Thailand	7.8	(0.8)	25.2	(1.5)	38.2	(1.4)	22.8	(1.1)	5.5	(0.8)	0.5	(0.2)
United Kingdom	4.4	(0.5)	11.0	(0.6)	21.1	(0.7)	26.6	(0.7)	22.9	(0.9)	14.0	(0.9)
United States	6.3	(1.2)	11.6	(1.1)	21.7	(1.2)	26.5	(1.2)	21.2	(1.5)	12.7	(1.3)
OECD average	5.5	(0.1)	12.2	(0.2)	22.3	(0.2)	28.4	(0.3)	21.7	(0.2)	9.9	(0.1)
OECD total	5.8	(0.4)	12.6	(0.4)	22.7	(0.4)	28.4	(0.4)	21.2	(0.4)	9.3	(0.4)

Table 2.1d
Percentage of students at each level of proficiency on the reading/reflection and evaluation scale

	Proficiency levels											
	Below Level 1 (less than 335 score points)		Level 1 (from 335 to 407 score points)		Level 2 (from 408 to 480 score points)		Level 3 (from 481 to 552 score points)		Level 4 (from 553 to 626 score points)		Level 5 (above 626 score points)	
	%	S.E.	%	S.E.	%	S.E.	%	S.E.	%	S.E.	%	S.E.
Albania	43.8	(1.5)	23.8	(1.2)	18.6	(1.0)	10.1	(0.7)	3.2	(0.4)	0.5	(0.1)
Argentina	21.7	(3.0)	18.8	(2.0)	23.9	(2.0)	20.7	(1.7)	11.0	(1.5)	3.9	(0.6)
Australia	3.4	(0.4)	9.1	(0.7)	19.0	(0.9)	26.9	(1.2)	25.6	(1.2)	15.9	(1.2)
Austria	5.0	(0.5)	10.1	(0.5)	20.0	(0.9)	28.2	(1.1)	25.2	(1.3)	11.6	(1.0)
Belgium	9.8	(1.2)	11.5	(0.8)	17.5	(0.7)	26.2	(1.0)	24.3	(0.8)	10.7	(0.6)
Brazil	18.7	(1.2)	27.2	(1.1)	29.3	(1.1)	17.7	(1.0)	6.0	(0.7)	1.2	(0.2)
Bulgaria	21.2	(1.5)	19.9	(1.2)	23.5	(1.3)	19.5	(1.3)	10.9	(1.0)	4.9	(0.9)
Canada	2.1	(0.2)	6.6	(0.4)	16.2	(0.4)	27.5	(0.5)	28.3	(0.5)	19.4	(0.5)
Chile	20.7	(1.3)	26.8	(1.2)	28.8	(1.1)	17.0	(1.0)	5.8	(0.6)	0.9	(0.2)
Czech Republic	7.5	(0.7)	13.2	(0.9)	24.9	(0.9)	28.3	(0.8)	19.0	(1.0)	7.2	(0.7)
Denmark	6.2	(0.6)	11.7	(0.7)	21.3	(0.8)	29.0	(1.0)	21.9	(0.8)	9.9	(0.8)
Finland	2.4	(0.5)	6.4	(0.5)	16.2	(0.7)	30.3	(0.9)	30.6	(0.9)	14.1	(0.7)
France	5.9	(0.7)	12.5	(0.8)	23.4	(0.8)	28.7	(1.1)	21.0	(1.0)	8.6	(0.6)
Germany	13.0	(0.8)	13.5	(0.7)	20.4	(1.1)	24.0	(0.9)	18.9	(0.8)	10.2	(0.6)
Greece	8.9	(1.1)	13.3	(1.1)	21.6	(1.1)	23.8	(1.1)	19.8	(1.2)	12.5	(1.1)
Hong Kong-China	2.9	(0.6)	6.1	(0.6)	14.6	(0.8)	28.6	(1.0)	32.4	(1.2)	15.5	(1.1)
Hungary	8.2	(0.8)	15.2	(1.3)	23.6	(1.3)	27.9	(1.1)	18.8	(1.2)	6.3	(0.8)
Iceland	4.8	(0.5)	11.0	(0.6)	23.1	(0.8)	30.9	(0.9)	22.1	(0.8)	8.1	(0.5)
Indonesia	32.5	(1.7)	28.7	(1.2)	24.3	(1.1)	11.2	(1.0)	2.9	(0.5)	0.4	(0.2)
Ireland	2.4	(0.4)	6.6	(0.8)	16.8	(1.0)	30.3	(1.0)	29.5	(1.0)	14.5	(0.9)
Israel	13.5	(2.2)	15.6	(1.4)	22.3	(1.4)	24.3	(1.6)	17.3	(1.9)	7.0	(1.2)
Italy	8.0	(0.9)	14.3	(1.1)	24.1	(1.3)	28.0	(1.0)	19.1	(0.8)	6.5	(0.6)
Japan	3.9	(0.8)	7.9	(0.9)	16.6	(1.1)	28.2	(1.1)	27.3	(1.2)	16.2	(1.4)
Korea	1.2	(0.3)	5.4	(0.5)	19.0	(1.0)	36.7	(1.2)	29.5	(1.2)	8.2	(0.7)
Latvia	15.6	(1.5)	16.6	(1.1)	23.4	(1.6)	24.1	(1.6)	14.2	(1.2)	6.0	(0.9)
Liechtenstein	11.9	(2.0)	16.1	(3.1)	24.4	(3.3)	24.8	(2.8)	17.0	(2.9)	5.8	(1.3)
Luxembourg	17.0	(0.7)	17.9	(0.8)	25.4	(1.1)	23.3	(0.8)	12.9	(0.5)	3.6	(0.4)
FYR Macedonia	39.8	(1.2)	24.4	(1.1)	22.0	(0.8)	11.2	(0.6)	2.4	(0.5)	0.2	(0.1)
Mexico	16.0	(0.9)	20.7	(1.0)	25.6	(0.9)	21.1	(0.8)	11.8	(0.9)	4.8	(0.6)
New Zealand	4.5	(0.5)	8.5	(0.6)	17.5	(0.9)	25.4	(1.2)	25.6	(1.0)	18.5	(1.2)
Norway	7.3	(0.7)	10.8	(0.7)	18.8	(0.8)	27.1	(0.9)	23.8	(1.0)	12.2	(0.8)
Peru	54.6	(2.0)	22.0	(1.0)	14.7	(1.0)	6.5	(0.6)	1.8	(0.3)	0.4	(0.2)
Poland	11.0	(1.1)	14.4	(1.2)	22.6	(1.8)	26.2	(1.4)	18.1	(1.3)	7.7	(1.1)
Portugal	9.1	(0.9)	15.0	(1.2)	24.4	(1.2)	26.2	(1.1)	19.0	(1.1)	6.4	(0.7)
Russian Federation	11.7	(1.1)	19.3	(1.0)	28.1	(1.1)	24.9	(0.9)	12.3	(0.8)	3.7	(0.5)
Spain	3.9	(0.4)	11.0	(0.7)	22.1	(1.1)	31.1	(1.2)	23.6	(0.9)	8.4	(0.6)
Sweden	4.3	(0.4)	10.2	(0.6)	20.7	(0.7)	30.4	(0.8)	24.3	(0.9)	10.1	(0.7)
Switzerland	9.9	(0.9)	13.6	(0.9)	21.6	(1.1)	25.2	(1.0)	19.1	(0.9)	10.5	(1.1)
Thailand	11.7	(1.1)	22.7	(1.2)	32.7	(1.3)	24.5	(1.1)	7.3	(0.8)	1.0	(0.2)
United Kingdom	2.6	(0.3)	7.2	(0.6)	17.4	(0.7)	26.7	(0.7)	26.5	(0.9)	19.6	(1.0)
United States	6.2	(1.1)	11.2	(1.2)	20.6	(1.1)	27.3	(1.1)	22.2	(1.7)	12.5	(1.3)
OECD average	*6.8*	*(0.1)*	*11.4*	*(0.2)*	*20.7*	*(0.2)*	*27.6*	*(0.2)*	*22.5*	*(0.2)*	*10.9*	*(0.2)*
OECD total	*6.9*	*(0.3)*	*11.5*	*(0.3)*	*20.6*	*(0.3)*	*27.3*	*(0.4)*	*22.3*	*(0.5)*	*11.5*	*(0.4)*

Table 2.2a
Multiple comparisons of mean performance on the reading / retrieving information subscale

Reading / retrieving information subscale

Country	Mean	S.E.
Finland	556	(2.8)
Australia	536	(3.7)
New Zealand	535	(2.8)
Canada	530	(1.7)
Korea	530	(2.5)
Japan	526	(5.5)
Ireland	524	(3.3)
United Kingdom	523	(2.5)
Hong Kong-China	522	(3.2)
Sweden	516	(2.4)
France	515	(3.0)
Belgium	515	(3.9)
Norway	505	(2.9)
Austria	502	(2.3)
Iceland	500	(1.6)
United States	499	(7.4)
Switzerland	498	(4.4)
Denmark	498	(2.8)
Liechtenstein	492	(4.9)
Italy	488	(3.1)
Spain	483	(3.0)
Germany	483	(2.4)
Czech Republic	481	(2.7)
Hungary	478	(4.4)
Poland	475	(5.0)
Portugal	455	(4.9)
Latvia	451	(5.7)
Russian Federation	451	(4.9)
Greece	450	(5.4)
Luxembourg	433	(1.6)
Israel	431	(9.2)
Bulgaria	422	(5.4)
Argentina	407	(10.8)
Thailand	406	(3.5)
Mexico	402	(3.9)
Chile	383	(4.0)
Brazil	365	(3.4)
FYR Macedonia	362	(2.8)
Indonesia	350	(4.5)
Albania	336	(3.5)
Peru	289	(5.0)

Instructions: Read across the row for a country to compare performance with the countries listed along the top of the chart. The symbols indicate whether the average performance of the country in the row is significantly lower than that of the comparison country, significantly higher than that of the comparison country, or if there is no statistically significant difference between the average achievement of the two countries.

▲ Mean performance statistically significantly higher than in comparison country.
○ No statistically significant difference from comparison country.
▽ Mean performance statistically significantly lower than in comparison country.

OECD countries
Non-OECD countries

Statistically significantly above the OECD average
Not statistically significantly different from the OECD average
Statistically significantly below the OECD average

Low- and middle-income countries

Table 2.2b
Multiple comparisons of mean performance on the reading / interpreting texts subscale

Reading/ interpreting texts scale	Mean	S.E.	Finland 555 (2.9)	Canada 532 (1.6)	Australia 527 (3.5)	Ireland 526 (3.3)	New Zealand 526 (2.7)	Korea 525 (2.3)	Hong Kong-China 522 (2.8)	Sweden 522 (2.1)	Japan 518 (5.0)	Iceland 514 (1.4)	United Kingdom 514 (2.5)	Belgium 512 (3.2)	Austria 508 (2.4)	France 506 (2.7)	Norway 505 (2.8)	United States 505 (7.1)	Czech Republic 500 (2.4)	Switzerland 496 (4.2)	Denmark 494 (2.4)	Spain 491 (2.6)	Italy 489 (2.6)	Germany 488 (2.5)	Liechtenstein 484 (4.5)	Poland 482 (4.3)	Hungary 480 (3.8)	Greece 475 (4.5)	Portugal 473 (4.3)	Russian Federation 468 (4.0)	Latvia 459 (4.9)	Israel 458 (8.0)	Luxembourg 446 (1.6)	Thailand 439 (3.1)	Bulgaria 434 (4.7)	Chile 419 (3.4)	Mexico 419 (2.9)	Argentina 415 (9.0)	Brazil 400 (3.0)	FYR Macedonia 381 (1.1)	Indonesia 375 (3.6)	Albania 352 (3.0)	Peru 342 (4.1)

Country	Mean	S.E.
Finland	555	(2.9)
Canada	532	(1.6)
Australia	527	(3.5)
Ireland	526	(3.3)
New Zealand	526	(2.7)
Korea	525	(2.3)
Hong Kong-China	522	(2.8)
Sweden	522	(2.1)
Japan	518	(5.0)
Iceland	514	(1.4)
United Kingdom	514	(2.5)
Belgium	512	(3.2)
Austria	508	(2.4)
France	506	(2.7)
Norway	505	(2.8)
United States	505	(7.1)
Czech Republic	500	(2.4)
Switzerland	496	(4.2)
Denmark	494	(2.4)
Spain	491	(2.6)
Italy	489	(2.6)
Germany	488	(2.5)
Liechtenstein	484	(4.5)
Poland	482	(4.3)
Hungary	480	(3.8)
Greece	475	(4.5)
Portugal	473	(4.3)
Russian Federation	468	(4.0)
Latvia	459	(4.9)
Israel	458	(8.0)
Luxembourg	446	(1.6)
Thailand	439	(3.1)
Bulgaria	434	(4.7)
Chile	419	(3.4)
Mexico	419	(2.9)
Argentina	415	(9.0)
Brazil	400	(3.0)
FYR Macedonia	381	(1.1)
Indonesia	375	(3.6)
Albania	352	(3.0)
Peru	342	(4.1)

Instructions: Read across the row for a country to compare performance with the countries listed along the top of the chart. The symbols indicate whether the average performance of the country in the row is significantly lower than that of the comparison country, significantly higher than that of the comparison country, or if there is no statistically significant difference between the average achievement of the two countries.

▲ Mean performance statistically significantly higher than in comparison country.

○ No statistically significant difference from comparison country.

▽ Mean performance statistically significantly lower than in comparison country.

OECD countries

Non-OECD countries

Low- and middle-income Countries

Statistically significantly above the OECD average

Not statistically significantly different from the OECD average

Statistically significantly below the OECD average

Table 2.2c

Multiple comparisons of mean performance on the reading / reflection and evaluation subscale

Reading/reflection and evaluation scale

Country	Mean	S.E.
Canada	542	(1.6)
United Kingdom	539	(2.5)
Hong Kong-China	538	(3.2)
Ireland	533	(3.1)
Finland	533	(2.7)
Japan	530	(5.5)
New Zealand	529	(2.9)
Australia	526	(3.5)
Korea	526	(2.6)
Austria	512	(2.7)
Sweden	510	(2.3)
United States	507	(7.1)
Norway	506	(3.0)
Spain	506	(2.8)
Iceland	501	(1.3)
Denmark	500	(2.6)
Belgium	497	(4.3)
France	496	(2.9)
Greece	495	(5.6)
Switzerland	488	(4.8)
Czech Republic	485	(2.6)
Italy	483	(3.1)
Hungary	481	(4.3)
Portugal	480	(4.5)
Germany	478	(2.9)
Poland	477	(4.7)
Liechtenstein	468	(5.7)
Israel	467	(9.0)
Latvia	458	(5.9)
Russian Federation	455	(4.0)
Mexico	446	(3.7)
Luxembourg	442	(1.9)
Thailand	439	(3.5)
Bulgaria	431	(5.6)
Argentina	430	(10.3)
Brazil	417	(3.3)
Chile	412	(3.7)
Indonesia	378	(4.2)
FYR Macedonia	360	(1.8)
Albania	350	(3.7)
Peru	323	(5.0)

Instructions: Read across the row for a country to compare performance with the countries listed along the top of the chart. The symbols indicate whether the average performance of the country in the row is significantly lower than that of the comparison country, significantly higher than that of the comparison country, or if there is no statistically significant difference between the average achievement of the two countries.

▲   Mean performance statistically significantly higher than in comparison country.

○   No statistically significant difference from comparison country.

▽   Mean performance statistically significantly lower than in comparison country.

OECD countries

Non-OECD countries

Low- and middle-income Countries

Statistically significantly above the OECD average

Not statistically significantly different from the OECD average

Statistically significantly below the OECD average

Table 2.3a
Variation in student performance on the combined reading literacy scale

| | Mean | | Standard deviation | | Percentiles | | | | | | | | | | | |
| | | | | | 5th | | 10th | | 25th | | 75th | | 90th | | 95th | |
	Score	S.E.	S.D.	S.E.	Score	S.E.	Score	S.E.	Score	S.E.	Score	S.E.	Score	S.E.	Score	S.E.
Albania	349	(3.3)	99	(1.9)	182	(8.8)	216	(6.4)	279	(4.9)	421	(3.2)	476	(2.9)	506	(4.2)
Argentina	418	(9.9)	109	(3.4)	232	(11.2)	270	(11.5)	344	(13.2)	495	(8.8)	554	(9.6)	589	(10.0)
Australia	528	(3.5)	102	(1.6)	354	(4.8)	394	(4.4)	458	(4.4)	602	(4.6)	656	(4.2)	685	(4.5)
Austria	507	(2.4)	93	(1.6)	341	(5.4)	383	(4.2)	447	(2.8)	573	(3.0)	621	(3.2)	648	(3.7)
Belgium	507	(3.6)	107	(2.4)	308	(10.3)	354	(8.9)	437	(6.6)	587	(2.3)	634	(2.5)	659	(2.4)
Brazil	396	(3.1)	86	(1.9)	255	(5.0)	288	(4.5)	339	(3.4)	452	(3.4)	507	(4.2)	539	(5.5)
Bulgaria	430	(4.9)	102	(3.0)	258	(7.7)	295	(6.6)	361	(5.8)	502	(6.6)	560	(7.4)	594	(9.0)
Canada	534	(1.6)	95	(1.1)	371	(3.8)	410	(2.4)	472	(2.0)	600	(1.5)	652	(1.9)	681	(2.7)
Chile	410	(3.6)	90	(1.7)	257	(6.9)	291	(5.3)	350	(4.4)	472	(3.9)	524	(3.8)	555	(4.8)
Czech Republic	492	(2.4)	96	(1.9)	320	(7.9)	368	(4.9)	433	(2.8)	557	(2.9)	610	(3.2)	638	(3.6)
Denmark	497	(2.4)	98	(1.8)	326	(6.2)	367	(5.0)	434	(3.3)	566	(2.7)	617	(2.9)	645	(3.6)
Finland	546	(2.6)	89	(2.6)	390	(5.8)	429	(5.1)	492	(2.9)	608	(2.6)	654	(2.8)	681	(3.4)
France	505	(2.7)	92	(1.7)	344	(6.2)	381	(5.2)	444	(4.5)	570	(2.4)	619	(2.9)	645	(3.7)
Germany	484	(2.5)	111	(1.9)	284	(9.4)	335	(6.3)	417	(4.6)	563	(3.1)	619	(2.8)	650	(3.2)
Greece	474	(5.0)	97	(2.7)	305	(8.2)	342	(8.4)	409	(7.4)	543	(4.5)	595	(5.1)	625	(6.0)
Hong Kong-China	525	(2.9)	84	(2.4)	369	(9.1)	413	(7.3)	477	(3.8)	584	(2.7)	624	(2.9)	646	(3.9)
Hungary	480	(4.0)	94	(2.1)	320	(5.6)	354	(5.5)	414	(5.3)	549	(4.5)	598	(4.4)	626	(5.5)
Iceland	507	(1.5)	92	(1.4)	345	(5.0)	383	(3.6)	447	(3.1)	573	(2.2)	621	(3.5)	647	(3.7)
Indonesia	371	(4.0)	72	(2.5)	250	(4.8)	277	(4.0)	321	(4.3)	422	(5.7)	464	(6.9)	489	(7.2)
Ireland	527	(3.2)	94	(1.7)	360	(6.3)	401	(6.4)	468	(4.3)	593	(3.6)	641	(4.0)	669	(3.4)
Israel	452	(8.5)	109	(4.0)	259	(15.9)	305	(13.0)	379	(11.1)	532	(8.1)	587	(7.1)	618	(7.9)
Italy	487	(2.9)	91	(2.7)	331	(8.5)	368	(5.8)	429	(4.1)	552	(3.2)	601	(2.7)	627	(3.1)
Japan	522	(5.2)	86	(3.0)	366	(11.4)	407	(9.8)	471	(7.0)	582	(4.4)	625	(4.6)	650	(4.3)
Korea	525	(2.4)	70	(1.6)	402	(5.2)	433	(4.4)	481	(2.9)	574	(2.6)	608	(2.9)	629	(3.2)
Latvia	458	(5.3)	102	(2.3)	283	(9.7)	322	(8.2)	390	(6.9)	530	(5.3)	586	(5.8)	617	(6.6)
Liechtenstein	483	(4.1)	96	(3.9)	310	(15.9)	350	(11.8)	419	(9.4)	551	(5.8)	601	(7.1)	626	(8.2)
Luxembourg	441	(1.6)	100	(1.5)	267	(5.1)	311	(4.4)	378	(2.8)	513	(2.0)	564	(2.8)	592	(3.5)
FYR Macedonia	373	(1.9)	94	(1.2)	216	(4.7)	249	(3.9)	307	(3.5)	442	(2.0)	493	(2.5)	521	(3.4)
Mexico	422	(3.3)	86	(2.1)	284	(4.4)	311	(3.4)	360	(3.6)	482	(4.8)	535	(5.5)	565	(6.3)
New Zealand	529	(2.8)	108	(2.0)	337	(7.4)	382	(5.2)	459	(4.1)	606	(3.0)	661	(4.4)	693	(6.1)
Norway	505	(2.8)	104	(1.7)	320	(5.9)	364	(5.5)	440	(4.5)	579	(2.7)	631	(3.1)	660	(4.6)
Peru	327	(4.4)	96	(2.2)	175	(6.5)	205	(4.9)	259	(5.2)	392	(5.5)	452	(5.6)	489	(6.5)
Poland	479	(4.5)	100	(3.1)	304	(8.7)	343	(6.8)	414	(5.8)	551	(6.0)	603	(6.6)	631	(6.0)
Portugal	470	(4.5)	97	(1.8)	300	(6.2)	337	(6.2)	403	(6.4)	541	(4.5)	592	(4.2)	620	(3.9)
Russian Federation	462	(4.2)	92	(1.8)	306	(6.9)	340	(5.4)	400	(5.1)	526	(4.5)	579	(4.4)	608	(5.3)
Spain	493	(2.7)	85	(1.2)	344	(5.8)	379	(5.0)	436	(4.6)	553	(2.6)	597	(2.6)	620	(2.9)
Sweden	516	(2.2)	92	(1.2)	354	(4.5)	392	(4.0)	456	(3.1)	581	(3.1)	630	(2.9)	658	(3.1)
Switzerland	494	(4.3)	102	(2.0)	316	(5.5)	355	(5.8)	426	(5.5)	567	(4.7)	621	(5.5)	651	(5.3)
Thailand	431	(3.2)	77	(1.7)	301	(4.9)	333	(4.8)	381	(4.0)	482	(3.3)	526	(4.6)	555	(5.5)
United Kingdom	523	(2.6)	100	(1.5)	352	(4.9)	391	(4.1)	458	(2.8)	595	(3.5)	651	(4.3)	682	(4.9)
United States	504	(7.1)	105	(2.7)	320	(11.7)	363	(11.4)	436	(8.8)	577	(6.8)	636	(6.5)	669	(6.8)
OECD average	500	(0.6)	100	(0.4)	324	(1.3)	366	(1.1)	435	(1.0)	571	(0.7)	623	(0.8)	652	(0.8)
OECD total	499	(2.0)	100	(0.8)	322	(3.4)	363	(3.3)	433	(2.5)	569	(1.6)	622	(2.0)	653	(2.1)

Table 2.3b
Variation in student performance on the reading/retrieving information scale

| | Mean | | Standard deviation | | Percentiles | | | | | | | | | | | | |
| | | | | | 5th | | 10th | | 25th | | 75th | | 90th | | 95th | |
	Score	S.E.	S.D.	S.E.	Score	S.E.	Score	S.E.	Score	S.E.	Score	S.E.	Score	S.E.	Score	S.E.
Albania	336	(3.5)	111	(1.9)	149	(6.0)	189	(6.4)	259	(5.7)	416	(3.6)	478	(3.4)	513	(4.0)
Argentina	407	(10.8)	125	(3.9)	189	(14.5)	235	(13.5)	326	(16.7)	497	(10.6)	562	(8.2)	601	(8.1)
Australia	536	(3.7)	108	(1.6)	351	(5.3)	393	(4.7)	462	(5.0)	612	(3.7)	671	(5.0)	704	(5.5)
Austria	502	(2.3)	96	(1.5)	332	(5.5)	374	(4.6)	440	(3.2)	571	(2.8)	619	(3.1)	648	(3.4)
Belgium	515	(3.9)	120	(2.7)	293	(9.9)	343	(8.5)	437	(7.0)	603	(2.6)	656	(2.6)	685	(3.0)
Brazil	365	(3.4)	97	(2.1)	203	(6.3)	239	(5.2)	300	(5.1)	428	(4.3)	489	(3.5)	524	(6.6)
Bulgaria	422	(5.4)	116	(3.1)	222	(9.7)	265	(7.5)	346	(6.7)	504	(6.8)	566	(7.8)	604	(9.9)
Canada	530	(1.7)	102	(1.2)	355	(4.1)	397	(2.9)	463	(2.3)	601	(1.8)	657	(2.4)	690	(2.8)
Chile	383	(4.0)	106	(1.9)	202	(7.6)	245	(6.3)	314	(5.5)	458	(4.9)	518	(4.5)	552	(4.3)
Czech Republic	481	(2.7)	107	(1.9)	294	(8.4)	343	(5.6)	415	(3.1)	555	(3.4)	614	(3.9)	647	(3.5)
Denmark	498	(2.8)	105	(1.9)	313	(7.5)	359	(5.9)	430	(3.7)	572	(2.9)	626	(3.3)	657	(4.1)
Finland	556	(2.8)	102	(2.1)	377	(6.9)	423	(4.7)	492	(3.8)	627	(3.0)	682	(3.2)	713	(3.7)
France	515	(3.0)	101	(2.1)	335	(7.8)	376	(6.4)	449	(4.8)	588	(2.8)	638	(4.0)	668	(3.8)
Germany	483	(2.4)	114	(2.0)	274	(10.5)	331	(6.2)	415	(4.1)	563	(2.9)	621	(3.1)	652	(3.2)
Greece	450	(5.4)	109	(3.0)	259	(11.6)	306	(9.2)	378	(8.0)	527	(4.4)	585	(5.0)	617	(6.2)
Hong Kong-China	522	(3.2)	95	(2.5)	350	(7.7)	396	(7.0)	465	(4.4)	588	(3.3)	635	(3.7)	663	(4.8)
Hungary	478	(4.4)	107	(2.2)	294	(7.3)	333	(6.2)	404	(5.8)	555	(4.8)	613	(4.9)	645	(5.8)
Iceland	500	(1.6)	103	(1.3)	319	(4.6)	362	(4.2)	433	(2.8)	572	(2.7)	628	(2.9)	659	(3.6)
Indonesia	350	(4.5)	85	(2.7)	212	(5.2)	241	(4.0)	291	(4.2)	409	(6.7)	460	(7.1)	488	(8.9)
Ireland	524	(3.3)	100	(1.7)	348	(7.2)	392	(6.5)	462	(4.4)	596	(3.2)	647	(3.3)	675	(3.9)
Israel	431	(9.2)	126	(4.1)	211	(15.0)	262	(14.1)	345	(12.1)	522	(7.9)	584	(9.0)	621	(8.8)
Italy	488	(3.1)	104	(3.0)	309	(10.1)	352	(5.8)	422	(4.0)	560	(2.9)	617	(4.0)	649	(3.7)
Japan	526	(5.5)	97	(3.1)	353	(12.2)	397	(10.2)	468	(7.7)	592	(4.5)	644	(4.7)	674	(5.2)
Korea	530	(2.5)	82	(1.6)	386	(5.0)	421	(4.3)	476	(3.1)	588	(3.1)	631	(3.4)	655	(3.5)
Latvia	451	(5.7)	117	(2.4)	250	(10.1)	296	(8.5)	373	(7.3)	535	(6.2)	599	(5.7)	633	(6.7)
Liechtenstein	492	(4.9)	106	(4.7)	303	(18.6)	345	(13.9)	422	(10.8)	567	(7.8)	620	(7.7)	653	(14.0)
Luxembourg	433	(1.6)	109	(1.4)	244	(5.5)	290	(4.3)	364	(3.0)	513	(2.5)	567	(2.6)	599	(3.3)
FYR Macedonia	362	(2.8)	110	(2.2)	177	(7.9)	217	(5.8)	286	(4.6)	441	(3.5)	504	(3.0)	537	(3.1)
Mexico	402	(3.9)	101	(2.2)	239	(4.7)	270	(4.5)	331	(4.3)	472	(5.3)	533	(6.0)	570	(7.2)
New Zealand	535	(2.8)	116	(2.1)	327	(6.6)	377	(6.3)	460	(4.1)	616	(3.9)	677	(3.9)	708	(6.9)
Norway	505	(2.9)	110	(1.9)	307	(6.8)	356	(6.5)	437	(4.6)	583	(2.8)	637	(3.3)	667	(4.3)
Peru	289	(5.0)	111	(2.6)	107	(8.3)	149	(6.3)	213	(5.8)	366	(5.9)	433	(5.8)	471	(6.5)
Poland	475	(5.0)	112	(3.3)	278	(9.6)	324	(8.6)	401	(6.0)	557	(6.2)	615	(7.1)	648	(8.6)
Portugal	455	(4.9)	107	(2.2)	268	(8.1)	311	(7.9)	383	(6.2)	534	(4.9)	588	(4.3)	621	(4.7)
Russian Federation	451	(4.9)	108	(2.1)	269	(7.1)	309	(7.1)	378	(6.0)	526	(5.2)	587	(5.6)	624	(6.5)
Spain	483	(3.0)	92	(1.2)	320	(5.2)	361	(4.9)	424	(4.1)	549	(3.0)	597	(2.8)	623	(3.4)
Sweden	516	(2.4)	104	(1.5)	335	(4.6)	378	(4.3)	448	(3.7)	591	(2.8)	645	(2.7)	676	(3.4)
Switzerland	498	(4.4)	113	(2.1)	295	(7.3)	344	(6.4)	423	(5.5)	578	(4.9)	636	(5.2)	668	(5.8)
Thailand	406	(3.5)	86	(1.9)	263	(6.4)	296	(4.9)	349	(4.0)	464	(3.9)	516	(5.4)	546	(6.3)
United Kingdom	523	(2.5)	105	(1.5)	342	(5.9)	384	(4.5)	455	(3.3)	597	(3.0)	656	(4.3)	687	(4.5)
United States	499	(7.4)	112	(2.7)	302	(13.0)	348	(12.0)	427	(9.3)	577	(6.4)	638	(6.0)	672	(7.3)
OECD average	498	(0.7)	111	(0.4)	303	(1.5)	349	(1.3)	426	(1.1)	576	(0.7)	634	(0.9)	667	(0.8)
OECD total	496	(2.1)	111	(0.9)	300	(3.8)	346	(3.5)	425	(2.8)	574	(1.8)	632	(1.8)	665	(2.2)

Table 2.3c
Variation in student performance on the reading/interpreting texts scale

	Mean		Standard deviation		Percentiles											
					5th		10th		25th		75th		90th		95th	
	Score	S.E.	S.D.	S.E.	Score	S.E.	Score	S.E.	Score	S.E.	Score	S.E.	Score	S.E.	Score	S.E.
Albania	352	(3.0)	92	(2.0)	198	(6.5)	232	(5.5)	288	(4.1)	418	(3.1)	470	(3.2)	499	(4.2)
Argentina	415	(9.0)	102	(3.0)	242	(13.0)	279	(9.7)	346	(12.2)	488	(8.7)	546	(7.8)	578	(7.8)
Australia	527	(3.5)	104	(1.5)	349	(5.0)	389	(4.9)	456	(3.9)	601	(4.5)	659	(4.8)	689	(4.9)
Austria	508	(2.4)	93	(1.6)	347	(5.3)	384	(3.6)	447	(3.2)	575	(3.2)	624	(3.9)	650	(3.7)
Belgium	512	(3.2)	105	(2.0)	322	(6.5)	363	(6.2)	440	(5.9)	591	(2.4)	638	(2.6)	665	(2.9)
Brazil	400	(3.0)	84	(1.8)	264	(5.3)	295	(4.4)	345	(3.7)	455	(4.1)	511	(4.9)	543	(5.1)
Bulgaria	434	(4.7)	96	(2.8)	273	(6.1)	307	(5.9)	367	(5.5)	501	(5.5)	559	(7.6)	591	(8.0)
Canada	532	(1.6)	95	(1.0)	368	(3.8)	406	(2.8)	469	(2.1)	599	(1.5)	651	(2.1)	682	(2.3)
Chile	419	(3.4)	87	(1.6)	275	(6.5)	306	(5.1)	361	(4.1)	479	(3.7)	530	(4.4)	562	(4.8)
Czech Republic	500	(2.4)	96	(1.6)	331	(7.8)	374	(4.9)	440	(3.4)	568	(3.0)	619	(3.3)	649	(4.0)
Denmark	494	(2.4)	99	(1.7)	324	(6.9)	362	(4.5)	430	(4.1)	563	(2.6)	617	(3.7)	647	(3.7)
Finland	555	(2.9)	97	(3.3)	390	(6.4)	429	(4.4)	496	(3.1)	622	(2.7)	671	(2.8)	701	(2.9)
France	506	(2.7)	92	(1.7)	345	(5.4)	381	(5.0)	444	(4.2)	571	(2.8)	621	(3.3)	649	(4.2)
Germany	488	(2.5)	109	(1.8)	294	(4.8)	340	(6.0)	417	(4.3)	564	(2.9)	623	(2.3)	654	(2.9)
Greece	475	(4.5)	89	(2.4)	322	(7.4)	356	(7.3)	415	(6.8)	538	(4.4)	588	(4.3)	615	(4.9)
Hong Kong-China	522	(2.8)	81	(2.2)	372	(7.6)	414	(6.3)	474	(3.5)	579	(2.7)	618	(3.2)	640	(4.3)
Hungary	480	(3.8)	90	(1.9)	327	(6.2)	359	(4.6)	418	(5.1)	545	(4.2)	594	(4.5)	621	(4.9)
Iceland	514	(1.4)	95	(1.4)	349	(4.5)	387	(3.8)	451	(2.2)	581	(2.2)	633	(3.1)	664	(4.2)
Indonesia	375	(3.6)	67	(2.2)	266	(3.8)	289	(3.2)	329	(3.1)	422	(5.2)	463	(6.5)	485	(6.4)
Ireland	526	(3.3)	97	(1.7)	354	(6.7)	396	(5.8)	464	(4.7)	595	(3.4)	646	(3.3)	676	(3.8)
Israel	458	(8.0)	103	(3.5)	283	(12.7)	320	(11.9)	388	(9.7)	533	(8.2)	587	(5.4)	616	(7.1)
Italy	489	(2.6)	86	(2.4)	343	(6.9)	376	(5.3)	432	(3.5)	549	(3.2)	598	(2.9)	625	(3.0)
Japan	518	(5.0)	83	(2.9)	370	(9.5)	406	(9.4)	467	(6.5)	575	(4.3)	618	(4.6)	644	(4.5)
Korea	525	(2.3)	69	(1.5)	404	(4.5)	434	(3.8)	480	(2.9)	574	(2.5)	609	(2.7)	630	(3.0)
Latvia	459	(4.9)	95	(2.0)	294	(7.2)	332	(7.6)	395	(6.0)	528	(5.0)	580	(5.3)	611	(6.2)
Liechtenstein	484	(4.5)	94	(3.6)	320	(18.2)	356	(12.1)	419	(9.5)	551	(7.5)	597	(8.8)	627	(11.1)
Luxembourg	446	(1.6)	101	(1.3)	271	(4.8)	314	(3.6)	381	(2.5)	519	(2.6)	571	(2.6)	600	(3.9)
FYR Macedonia	381	(1.1)	87	(1.0)	239	(4.4)	268	(2.4)	320	(2.6)	444	(1.6)	494	(2.7)	522	(3.4)
Mexico	419	(2.9)	78	(1.7)	294	(3.8)	319	(3.3)	363	(3.1)	472	(4.3)	521	(4.9)	550	(5.8)
New Zealand	526	(2.7)	111	(2.0)	333	(6.3)	376	(4.3)	453	(3.8)	606	(3.4)	665	(4.4)	699	(6.7)
Norway	505	(2.8)	104	(1.6)	322	(5.0)	364	(5.0)	438	(4.2)	579	(2.9)	633	(2.8)	662	(3.5)
Peru	342	(4.1)	90	(2.0)	200	(6.1)	229	(5.3)	280	(4.6)	402	(5.0)	458	(5.8)	494	(6.2)
Poland	482	(4.3)	97	(2.7)	314	(7.1)	350	(6.4)	418	(4.9)	552	(5.5)	604	(6.2)	633	(6.5)
Portugal	473	(4.3)	93	(1.6)	315	(5.9)	348	(5.9)	408	(5.8)	541	(4.6)	591	(4.4)	617	(4.5)
Russian Federation	468	(4.0)	92	(1.8)	313	(5.9)	346	(5.6)	404	(4.7)	531	(3.9)	586	(4.4)	615	(4.5)
Spain	491	(2.6)	84	(1.1)	347	(4.9)	380	(3.6)	435	(3.7)	551	(2.6)	595	(2.2)	620	(3.0)
Sweden	522	(2.1)	96	(1.3)	355	(4.2)	393	(3.8)	458	(3.1)	590	(2.8)	641	(2.7)	669	(3.4)
Switzerland	496	(4.2)	101	(2.0)	320	(4.7)	359	(5.9)	429	(5.6)	569	(4.6)	622	(5.5)	653	(5.9)
Thailand	439	(3.1)	74	(1.6)	316	(4.7)	344	(4.1)	390	(3.5)	488	(3.6)	534	(4.4)	559	(5.0)
United Kingdom	514	(2.5)	102	(1.4)	341	(5.0)	380	(4.0)	445	(3.3)	586	(3.1)	644	(4.1)	678	(4.8)
United States	505	(7.1)	106	(2.6)	322	(11.2)	363	(10.5)	435	(8.3)	579	(6.8)	640	(6.6)	672	(7.5)
OECD average	501	(0.6)	100	(0.4)	330	(1.1)	368	(1.1)	435	(1.0)	571	(0.7)	625	(0.7)	656	(1.0)
OECD total	498	(2.0)	99	(0.8)	327	(3.3)	365	(3.1)	432	(2.4)	568	(1.8)	622	(2.1)	654	(2.4)

Table 2.3d
Variation in student performance on the reading/reflection and evaluation scale

	Mean		Standard deviation		Percentiles											
					5th		10th		25th		75th		90th		95	
	Score	S.E.	S.D.	S.E.	Score	S.E.	Score	S.E.	Score	S.E.	Score	S.E.	Score	S.E.	Score	S.E.
Albania	350	(3.7)	117	(2.2)	157	(7.5)	197	(6.7)	267	(4.9)	433	(3.9)	502	(3.8)	538	(4.2)
Argentina	430	(10.3)	118	(3.6)	229	(15.5)	269	(14.3)	348	(14.3)	514	(10.3)	577	(8.1)	614	(7.4)
Australia	526	(3.5)	100	(1.5)	356	(5.6)	393	(5.3)	459	(4.0)	596	(3.9)	651	(4.7)	683	(5.5)
Austria	512	(2.7)	100	(1.8)	335	(5.1)	379	(5.0)	449	(3.5)	582	(3.2)	633	(4.6)	663	(5.3)
Belgium	497	(4.3)	114	(4.1)	283	(16.0)	336	(9.4)	426	(7.3)	579	(2.4)	629	(2.4)	656	(3.0)
Brazil	417	(3.3)	93	(2.2)	264	(6.2)	298	(5.2)	355	(4.1)	480	(4.2)	536	(5.6)	569	(6.1)
Bulgaria	431	(5.6)	121	(3.4)	228	(7.7)	274	(6.6)	350	(6.3)	515	(6.6)	584	(8.5)	625	(9.6)
Canada	542	(1.6)	96	(1.0)	377	(3.9)	416	(3.1)	481	(2.0)	609	(1.6)	661	(1.8)	691	(2.4)
Chile	412	(3.7)	95	(1.8)	251	(5.9)	287	(5.5)	348	(4.3)	476	(4.3)	534	(3.9)	566	(4.1)
Czech Republic	485	(2.6)	103	(1.8)	304	(7.9)	354	(5.0)	422	(3.4)	557	(3.1)	611	(3.9)	641	(4.7)
Denmark	500	(2.6)	102	(2.1)	321	(6.8)	365	(5.5)	436	(3.7)	571	(2.9)	625	(4.0)	657	(3.6)
Finland	533	(2.7)	91	(3.9)	374	(7.3)	415	(5.0)	480	(2.9)	595	(2.2)	640	(2.5)	665	(3.7)
France	496	(2.9)	98	(1.8)	325	(7.3)	365	(6.1)	432	(4.4)	566	(2.7)	618	(3.5)	649	(3.4)
Germany	478	(2.9)	124	(1.8)	254	(7.7)	311	(7.4)	401	(4.8)	566	(3.0)	627	(3.1)	662	(3.4)
Greece	495	(5.6)	115	(3.1)	293	(10.4)	343	(9.3)	418	(7.7)	577	(5.8)	638	(5.8)	675	(6.5)
Hong Kong-China	538	(3.2)	92	(2.7)	368	(9.2)	415	(7.2)	485	(4.4)	601	(2.8)	645	(4.0)	670	(4.3)
Hungary	481	(4.3)	100	(2.2)	307	(8.2)	347	(5.6)	413	(6.3)	553	(4.4)	606	(4.5)	636	(5.1)
Iceland	501	(1.3)	93	(1.3)	337	(5.6)	378	(3.8)	442	(2.7)	567	(2.2)	616	(2.5)	645	(4.1)
Indonesia	378	(4.2)	96	(2.5)	219	(5.8)	254	(5.4)	313	(5.3)	444	(5.4)	500	(6.0)	535	(6.8)
Ireland	533	(3.1)	90	(1.7)	373	(7.1)	414	(6.3)	478	(4.3)	595	(3.2)	642	(3.3)	671	(3.3)
Israel	467	(9.0)	115	(4.1)	266	(14.8)	313	(13.6)	391	(11.4)	551	(8.7)	609	(7.3)	642	(8.8)
Italy	483	(3.1)	101	(2.9)	307	(7.9)	348	(6.3)	418	(4.8)	555	(2.9)	607	(3.1)	636	(4.0)
Japan	530	(5.5)	100	(3.3)	352	(12.6)	397	(9.1)	469	(7.2)	599	(4.7)	651	(4.7)	680	(5.8)
Korea	526	(2.6)	76	(1.7)	395	(6.0)	428	(4.5)	479	(3.5)	577	(2.7)	619	(3.0)	642	(3.9)
Latvia	458	(5.9)	113	(2.3)	261	(8.1)	305	(7.3)	381	(7.6)	538	(6.1)	598	(7.1)	634	(7.0)
Liechtenstein	468	(5.7)	108	(4.3)	277	(18.3)	323	(12.9)	398	(8.9)	548	(8.8)	603	(9.6)	633	(13.0)
Luxembourg	442	(1.9)	115	(1.8)	243	(6.1)	293	(4.9)	371	(3.3)	523	(2.9)	581	(3.6)	613	(3.9)
FYR Macedonia	360	(1.8)	108	(1.7)	176	(4.1)	214	(4.3)	283	(4.0)	440	(2.0)	497	(2.8)	527	(4.7)
Mexico	446	(3.7)	109	(2.2)	267	(5.6)	303	(4.4)	370	(3.8)	521	(5.2)	586	(6.5)	624	(6.3)
New Zealand	529	(2.9)	107	(1.8)	340	(5.9)	387	(5.1)	460	(3.8)	605	(3.7)	662	(4.7)	692	(5.6)
Norway	506	(3.0)	108	(1.8)	313	(5.5)	357	(5.2)	439	(4.4)	582	(3.0)	636	(3.1)	667	(4.2)
Peru	323	(5.0)	114	(2.4)	139	(7.6)	179	(5.9)	244	(5.5)	401	(5.2)	471	(6.3)	511	(6.6)
Poland	477	(4.7)	110	(3.2)	279	(9.7)	328	(8.0)	406	(6.4)	556	(6.2)	613	(6.4)	642	(7.0)
Portugal	480	(4.5)	101	(1.7)	304	(5.1)	342	(6.8)	411	(6.5)	554	(4.2)	607	(3.8)	634	(4.5)
Russian Federation	455	(4.0)	98	(1.7)	289	(5.3)	326	(6.2)	389	(5.1)	523	(4.0)	580	(4.2)	612	(4.8)
Spain	506	(2.8)	91	(1.2)	346	(4.7)	383	(4.3)	446	(4.3)	570	(2.8)	618	(2.7)	646	(4.1)
Sweden	510	(2.3)	95	(1.2)	343	(4.4)	382	(4.1)	449	(3.0)	576	(2.7)	626	(4.0)	654	(3.7)
Switzerland	488	(4.8)	113	(2.2)	291	(7.2)	336	(6.5)	414	(6.1)	568	(5.4)	629	(6.0)	663	(6.7)
Thailand	439	(3.5)	86	(1.7)	293	(6.1)	326	(5.2)	382	(4.1)	498	(3.8)	545	(4.7)	573	(5.6)
United Kingdom	539	(2.5)	99	(1.6)	369	(5.7)	408	(4.5)	473	(3.4)	608	(3.1)	664	(3.5)	695	(4.8)
United States	507	(7.1)	105	(2.7)	323	(11.5)	367	(11.9)	438	(8.5)	580	(6.3)	638	(6.3)	669	(7.6)
OECD average	502	(0.7)	106	(0.4)	315	(1.5)	361	(1.4)	435	(1.0)	576	(0.7)	630	(0.9)	661	(0.9)
OECD total	503	(1.9)	107	(0.8)	314	(3.5)	361	(3.2)	435	(2.5)	577	(1.8)	633	(2.1)	665	(1.9)

Table 3.1
Variation in student performance on the mathematical literacy scale

	Mean		Standard deviation		Percentiles											
					5th		10th		25th		75th		90th		95th	
	Score	S.E.	S.D.	S.E.	Score	S.E.	Score	S.E.	Score	S.E.	Score	S.E.	Score	S.E.	Score	S.E.
Albania	381	(3.1)	107	(1.7)	202	(6.0)	240	(6.4)	308	(4.8)	457	(3.7)	515	(4.9)	551	(4.9)
Argentina	388	(9.4)	120	(4.1)	180	(12.9)	229	(12.0)	307	(11.8)	474	(8.8)	536	(8.3)	574	(10.6)
Australia	533	(3.5)	90	(1.6)	380	(6.4)	418	(6.4)	474	(4.4)	594	(4.5)	647	(5.7)	679	(5.8)
Austria	515	(2.5)	92	(1.7)	355	(5.3)	392	(4.6)	455	(3.5)	581	(3.8)	631	(3.6)	661	(5.2)
Belgium	520	(3.9)	106	(2.9)	322	(11.0)	367	(8.6)	453	(6.5)	597	(3.0)	646	(3.9)	672	(3.5)
Brazil	334	(3.7)	97	(2.3)	179	(5.5)	212	(5.2)	266	(4.2)	399	(5.5)	464	(7.5)	499	(8.9)
Bulgaria	430	(5.7)	110	(3.5)	243	(9.9)	283	(8.1)	358	(6.7)	505	(7.0)	568	(8.3)	603	(10.3)
Canada	533	(1.4)	85	(1.1)	390	(3.2)	423	(2.5)	477	(2.0)	592	(1.7)	640	(1.9)	668	(2.6)
Chile	384	(3.7)	94	(1.9)	222	(6.8)	258	(5.9)	321	(5.1)	449	(4.5)	502	(3.7)	532	(4.2)
Czech Republic	498	(2.8)	96	(1.9)	335	(5.4)	372	(4.2)	433	(4.1)	564	(3.9)	623	(4.8)	655	(5.6)
Denmark	514	(2.4)	87	(1.7)	366	(6.1)	401	(5.1)	458	(3.1)	575	(3.1)	621	(3.7)	649	(4.6)
Finland	536	(2.2)	80	(1.4)	400	(6.5)	433	(3.6)	484	(4.1)	592	(2.5)	637	(3.2)	664	(3.5)
France	517	(2.7)	89	(1.9)	364	(6.4)	399	(5.4)	457	(4.7)	581	(3.1)	629	(3.2)	656	(4.6)
Germany	490	(2.5)	103	(2.4)	311	(7.9)	349	(6.9)	423	(3.9)	563	(2.7)	619	(3.6)	649	(3.9)
Greece	447	(5.6)	108	(2.9)	260	(9.0)	303	(8.1)	375	(8.1)	524	(6.7)	586	(7.8)	617	(8.6)
Hong Kong-China	560	(3.3)	94	(2.5)	390	(10.3)	434	(7.6)	502	(4.5)	626	(3.9)	673	(5.1)	699	(5.0)
Hungary	488	(4.0)	98	(2.4)	327	(7.1)	360	(5.7)	419	(4.8)	558	(5.2)	615	(6.4)	648	(6.9)
Iceland	514	(2.3)	85	(1.4)	372	(5.7)	407	(4.7)	459	(3.5)	572	(3.0)	622	(3.1)	649	(5.5)
Indonesia	367	(4.5)	85	(2.8)	229	(5.7)	259	(4.9)	308	(4.6)	424	(5.6)	478	(8.8)	508	(10.2)
Ireland	503	(2.7)	84	(1.8)	357	(6.4)	394	(4.7)	449	(4.1)	561	(3.6)	606	(4.3)	630	(5.0)
Israel	433	(9.3)	131	(4.4)	206	(15.0)	257	(13.5)	345	(14.1)	527	(9.7)	596	(10.7)	637	(8.9)
Italy	457	(2.9)	90	(2.4)	301	(8.4)	338	(5.5)	398	(3.5)	520	(3.5)	570	(4.4)	600	(6.1)
Japan	557	(5.5)	87	(3.1)	402	(11.2)	440	(9.1)	504	(7.4)	617	(5.2)	662	(4.9)	688	(6.1)
Korea	547	(2.8)	84	(2.0)	400	(6.1)	438	(5.0)	493	(4.2)	606	(3.4)	650	(4.3)	676	(5.3)
Latvia	463	(4.5)	103	(2.6)	288	(9.0)	328	(8.9)	393	(5.7)	536	(6.2)	593	(5.6)	625	(6.6)
Liechtenstein	514	(7.0)	96	(6.0)	343	(19.7)	380	(18.9)	454	(15.5)	579	(7.5)	635	(16.9)	665	(15.0)
Luxembourg	446	(2.0)	93	(1.8)	281	(7.4)	328	(4.2)	390	(3.8)	509	(3.4)	559	(3.2)	588	(3.9)
FYR Macedonia	381	(2.7)	98	(1.7)	214	(7.6)	252	(6.0)	315	(3.5)	450	(3.5)	506	(3.9)	538	(5.4)
Mexico	387	(3.4)	83	(1.9)	254	(5.5)	281	(3.6)	329	(4.1)	445	(5.2)	496	(5.6)	527	(6.6)
New Zealand	537	(3.1)	99	(1.9)	364	(6.1)	405	(5.4)	472	(3.9)	607	(4.0)	659	(4.2)	689	(5.2)
Norway	499	(2.8)	92	(1.7)	340	(7.0)	379	(5.2)	439	(4.0)	565	(3.9)	613	(4.5)	643	(4.5)
Peru	292	(4.4)	108	(2.4)	116	(9.3)	156	(6.3)	220	(5.4)	363	(6.4)	431	(6.2)	470	(7.9)
Poland	470	(5.5)	103	(3.8)	296	(12.2)	335	(9.2)	402	(7.0)	542	(6.8)	599	(7.7)	632	(8.5)
Portugal	454	(4.1)	91	(1.8)	297	(7.3)	332	(6.1)	392	(5.7)	520	(4.3)	570	(4.3)	596	(5.0)
Russian Federation	478	(5.5)	104	(2.5)	305	(9.0)	343	(7.4)	407	(6.6)	552	(6.6)	613	(6.8)	648	(7.8)
Spain	476	(3.1)	91	(1.5)	323	(5.8)	358	(4.3)	416	(5.3)	540	(4.0)	592	(3.9)	621	(3.1)
Sweden	510	(2.5)	93	(1.6)	347	(5.8)	386	(4.0)	450	(3.3)	574	(2.6)	626	(3.3)	656	(5.5)
Switzerland	529	(4.4)	100	(2.2)	353	(9.1)	398	(6.0)	466	(4.8)	601	(5.2)	653	(5.8)	682	(4.8)
Thailand	432	(3.6)	83	(2.2)	302	(6.0)	332	(5.2)	378	(4.3)	484	(4.7)	539	(6.2)	574	(7.5)
United Kingdom	529	(2.5)	92	(1.6)	374	(5.9)	412	(3.6)	470	(3.2)	592	(3.2)	646	(4.3)	676	(5.9)
United States	493	(7.6)	98	(2.4)	327	(11.7)	361	(9.6)	427	(9.7)	562	(7.5)	620	(7.7)	652	(7.9)
OECD average	500	(0.7)	100	(0.4)	326	(1.5)	367	(1.4)	435	(1.1)	571	(0.8)	625	(0.9)	655	(1.1)
OECD total	498	(2.1)	103	(0.9)	318	(3.1)	358	(3.4)	429	(3.0)	572	(2.1)	628	(1.9)	658	(2.1)

Table 3.2
Variation in student performance on the scientific literacy scale

	Mean		Standard deviation		Percentiles											
					5th		10th		25th		75th		90th		95th	
	Score	S.E.	S.D.	S.E.	Score	S.E.	Score	S.E.	Score	S.E.	Score	S.E.	Score	S.E.	Score	S.E.
Albania	376	(2.9)	94	(2.1)	221	(6.4)	256	(7.2)	315	(6.2)	438	(3.6)	497	(4.4)	531	(5.2)
Argentina	396	(8.6)	109	(3.8)	206	(15.6)	248	(15.1)	323	(13.6)	474	(7.8)	531	(6.4)	570	(10.0)
Australia	528	(3.5)	94	(1.6)	368	(5.1)	402	(4.7)	463	(4.6)	596	(4.8)	646	(5.1)	675	(4.8)
Austria	519	(2.6)	91	(1.7)	363	(5.7)	398	(4.0)	456	(3.8)	584	(3.5)	633	(4.1)	659	(4.3)
Belgium	496	(4.3)	111	(3.8)	292	(13.5)	346	(10.2)	424	(6.6)	577	(3.5)	630	(2.6)	656	(3.0)
Brazil	375	(3.3)	90	(2.3)	230	(5.5)	262	(5.9)	315	(3.7)	432	(4.9)	492	(7.8)	531	(8.2)
Bulgaria	448	(4.6)	96	(2.6)	291	(7.1)	325	(7.0)	383	(4.9)	515	(5.6)	572	(6.7)	605	(6.6)
Canada	529	(1.6)	89	(1.1)	380	(3.7)	412	(3.4)	469	(2.2)	592	(1.8)	641	(2.2)	670	(3.0)
Chile	415	(3.4)	95	(1.7)	263	(6.5)	296	(5.2)	351	(4.4)	479	(4.2)	538	(5.1)	574	(5.2)
Czech Republic	511	(2.4)	94	(1.5)	355	(5.6)	389	(4.0)	449	(3.6)	577	(3.8)	632	(4.1)	663	(4.9)
Denmark	481	(2.8)	103	(2.0)	310	(6.0)	347	(5.3)	410	(4.8)	554	(3.5)	613	(4.4)	645	(4.7)
Finland	538	(2.5)	86	(1.2)	391	(5.2)	425	(4.2)	481	(3.5)	598	(3.0)	645	(4.3)	674	(4.3)
France	500	(3.2)	102	(2.0)	329	(6.1)	363	(5.4)	429	(5.3)	575	(4.0)	631	(4.2)	663	(4.9)
Germany	487	(2.4)	102	(2.0)	314	(9.5)	350	(6.0)	417	(4.9)	560	(3.3)	618	(3.5)	649	(4.7)
Greece	461	(4.9)	97	(2.6)	300	(9.3)	334	(8.3)	393	(7.0)	530	(5.3)	585	(5.3)	616	(5.8)
Hong Kong-China	541	(3.0)	85	(2.3)	391	(7.5)	426	(6.6)	488	(4.5)	600	(3.7)	645	(3.9)	671	(5.8)
Hungary	496	(4.2)	103	(2.3)	328	(7.5)	361	(4.9)	423	(5.5)	570	(4.8)	629	(5.1)	659	(8.5)
Iceland	496	(2.2)	88	(1.6)	351	(7.0)	381	(4.3)	436	(3.7)	558	(3.1)	607	(4.1)	635	(4.8)
Indonesia	393	(3.9)	75	(2.6)	274	(5.0)	300	(4.4)	343	(3.7)	443	(5.7)	491	(8.3)	519	(10.5)
Ireland	513	(3.2)	92	(1.7)	361	(6.5)	394	(5.7)	450	(4.4)	578	(3.4)	630	(4.6)	661	(5.4)
Israel	434	(9.0)	125	(3.2)	233	(14.1)	277	(13.2)	347	(10.9)	524	(11.8)	596	(11.1)	640	(9.8)
Italy	478	(3.1)	98	(2.6)	315	(7.1)	349	(6.2)	411	(4.4)	547	(3.5)	602	(4.0)	633	(4.4)
Japan	550	(5.5)	90	(3.0)	391	(11.3)	430	(9.9)	495	(7.2)	612	(5.0)	659	(4.7)	688	(5.7)
Korea	552	(2.7)	81	(1.8)	411	(5.3)	442	(5.3)	499	(4.0)	610	(3.4)	652	(3.9)	674	(5.7)
Latvia	460	(5.6)	98	(3.0)	299	(10.1)	334	(8.8)	393	(7.7)	528	(5.7)	585	(7.2)	620	(8.0)
Liechtenstein	476	(7.1)	94	(5.4)	314	(23.5)	357	(20.0)	409	(12.3)	543	(12.7)	595	(12.4)	629	(24.0)
Luxembourg	443	(2.3)	96	(2.0)	278	(7.2)	320	(6.8)	382	(3.4)	510	(2.8)	563	(4.4)	593	(4.0)
FYR Macedonia	401	(2.1)	83	(1.8)	267	(6.3)	293	(4.7)	343	(3.2)	458	(3.6)	509	(4.7)	538	(5.3)
Mexico	422	(3.2)	77	(2.1)	303	(4.8)	325	(4.6)	368	(3.1)	472	(4.7)	525	(5.5)	554	(7.0)
New Zealand	528	(2.4)	101	(2.3)	357	(5.6)	392	(5.2)	459	(3.8)	600	(3.4)	653	(5.0)	683	(5.1)
Norway	500	(2.8)	96	(2.0)	338	(7.3)	377	(6.6)	437	(4.0)	569	(3.5)	619	(3.9)	649	(6.2)
Peru	333	(4.0)	90	(1.8)	187	(7.6)	221	(4.3)	273	(4.6)	393	(5.0)	446	(6.3)	481	(6.8)
Poland	483	(5.1)	97	(2.7)	326	(9.2)	359	(5.8)	415	(5.5)	553	(7.3)	610	(7.6)	639	(7.5)
Portugal	459	(4.0)	89	(1.6)	317	(5.0)	343	(5.1)	397	(5.2)	521	(4.7)	575	(5.0)	604	(5.3)
Russian Federation	460	(4.7)	99	(2.0)	298	(6.5)	333	(5.4)	392	(6.2)	529	(5.8)	591	(5.9)	625	(5.7)
Spain	491	(3.0)	95	(1.8)	333	(5.1)	367	(4.3)	425	(4.4)	558	(3.5)	613	(3.9)	643	(5.5)
Sweden	512	(2.5)	93	(1.4)	357	(5.7)	390	(4.6)	446	(4.1)	578	(3.0)	630	(3.4)	660	(4.5)
Switzerland	496	(4.4)	100	(2.4)	332	(5.8)	366	(5.4)	427	(5.1)	567	(6.4)	626	(6.4)	656	(9.0)
Thailand	436	(3.1)	77	(1.9)	315	(5.2)	343	(4.9)	386	(3.4)	485	(3.7)	535	(6.3)	569	(6.8)
United Kingdom	532	(2.7)	98	(2.0)	366	(6.8)	401	(6.0)	466	(3.8)	602	(3.9)	656	(4.7)	687	(5.0)
United States	499	(7.3)	101	(2.9)	330	(11.7)	368	(10.0)	430	(9.6)	571	(8.0)	628	(7.0)	658	(8.4)
OECD average	500	(0.7)	100	(0.5)	332	(1.5)	368	(1.0)	431	(1.0)	572	(0.8)	627	(0.8)	657	(1.2)
OECD total	502	(2.0)	102	(0.9)	332	(3.3)	368	(3.1)	431	(2.8)	576	(2.1)	631	(1.9)	662	(2.3)

© OECD/UNESCO-UIS 2003

Table 3.3
Student performance on the combined reading, scientific, mathematical literacy scales and national income

	Performance on the combined reading literacy scale		Performance on the mathematical literacy scale		Performance on the scientific literacy scale		GDP per capita (US dollars[1])	Cumulative expenditure on educational institutions per student
	Mean score	S.E.	Mean score	S.E.	Mean score	S.E.	(2000)	(US dollars[1]) (1999)
Albania	349	(3.3)	381	(3.1)	376	(2.9)	3 506	m
Argentina	418	(9.9)	388	(9.4)	396	(8.6)	12 377	18 893
Australia	528	(3.5)	533	(3.5)	528	(3.5)	26 325	55 987
Austria	507	(2.4)	515	(2.5)	519	(2.6)	28 070	77 027
Belgium	507	(3.6)	520	(3.9)	496	(4.3)	26 392	49 489
Brazil	396	(3.1)	334	(3.7)	375	(3.3)	7 625	10 269 [2,3]
Bulgaria	430	(4.9)	430	(5.7)	448	(4.6)	5 710	m
Canada	534	(1.6)	533	(1.4)	529	(1.6)	28 130	59 808
Chile	410	(3.6)	384	(3.7)	415	(3.4)	9 417	17 820
Czech Republic	492	(2.4)	498	(2.8)	511	(2.4)	13 806	22 606
Denmark	497	(2.4)	514	(2.4)	481	(2.8)	28 755	65 244
Finland	546	(2.6)	536	(2.2)	538	(2.5)	25 357	47 854
France	505	(2.7)	517	(2.7)	500	(3.2)	25 090	55 086
Germany	484	(2.5)	490	(2.5)	487	(2.4)	26 139	44 800
Greece	474	(5.0)	447	(5.6)	461	(4.9)	15 885	24 671 [2]
Hong Kong-China	525	(2.9)	560	(3.3)	541	(3.0)	25 153	m
Hungary	480	(4.0)	488	(4.0)	496	(4.2)	12 204	21 997 [2]
Iceland	507	(1.5)	514	(2.3)	496	(2.2)	28 143	m
Indonesia	371	(4.0)	367	(4.5)	393	(3.9)	3 043	1 164 [4]
Ireland	527	(3.2)	503	(2.7)	513	(3.2)	28 285	34 329
Israel	452	(8.5)	433	(9.3)	434	(9.0)	20 131	m
Italy	487	(2.9)	457	(2.9)	478	(3.1)	25 095	58 868 [2]
Japan	522	(5.2)	557	(5.5)	550	(5.5)	26 011	54 737
Korea	525	(2.4)	547	(2.8)	552	(2.7)	15 186	30 246
Latvia	458	(5.3)	463	(4.5)	460	(5.6)	7 045	m
Liechtenstein	483	(4.1)	514	(7.0)	476	(7.1)	m	m
Luxembourg	441	(1.6)	446	(2.0)	443	(2.3)	48 239	m
FYR Macedonia	373	(1.9)	381	(2.7)	401	(2.1)	5 086	m
Mexico	422	(3.3)	387	(3.4)	422	(3.2)	9 117	12 189
New Zealand	529	(2.8)	537	(3.1)	528	(2.4)	20 372	m
Norway	505	(2.8)	499	(2.8)	500	(2.8)	36 242	63 599
Peru	327	(4.4)	292	(4.4)	333	(4.0)	4 799	3 479
Poland	479	(4.5)	470	(5.5)	483	(5.1)	9 547	18 586
Portugal	470	(4.5)	454	(4.1)	459	(4.0)	16 780	41 166 [2]
Russian Federation	462	(4.2)	478	(5.5)	460	(4.7)	8 377	m
Spain	493	(2.7)	476	(3.1)	491	(3.0)	20 195	41 267
Sweden	516	(2.2)	510	(2.5)	512	(2.5)	26 161	54 845
Switzerland	494	(4.3)	529	(4.4)	496	(4.4)	29 617	66 214 [2]
Thailand	431	(3.2)	432	(3.6)	436	(3.1)	6 402	m
United Kingdom	523	(2.6)	529	(2.5)	532	(2.7)	24 964	46 175
United States	504	(7.1)	493	(7.6)	499	(7.3)	34 602	72 119 [5]
OECD average	*500*	*(0.6)*	*500*	*(0.7)*	*500*	*(0.7)*		
OECD total	*499*	*(2.0)*	*498*	*(2.1)*	*502*	*(2.0)*		

1. US dollars converted using PPPs.
2. Public institutions only.
3. Year of reference 1998.
4. Year of reference 2000.
5. Public and independent private institutions only.
Source: OECD (2003c) for OECD countries and World Bank (2002) for non-OECD countries

Table 4.1
Index of sense of belonging and performance on the combined reading literacy scale, by national quarters of the index
Results based on students' self-reports

| | Index of sense of belonging[1] | | | | | | | | | | | | | |
| | All students | | Males | | Females | | Bottom quarter | | Second quarter | | Third quarter | | Top quarter | |
	Mean index	S.E.	Mean index	S.E.	Mean index	S.E.	Mean index	S.E.	Mean index	S.E.	Mean index	S.E.	Mean index	S.E.
Albania	-0.41	(0.02)	-0.41	(0.02)	-0.40	(0.02)	-1.26	(0.01)	-0.73	(0.01)	-0.32	(0.01)	0.68	(0.03)
Argentina	0.18	(0.04)	0.21	(0.04)	0.16	(0.04)	-1.07	(0.02)	-0.30	(0.01)	0.47	(0.01)	1.64	(0.02)
Australia	-0.05	(0.02)	-0.06	(0.03)	-0.04	(0.02)	-1.04	(0.01)	-0.54	(0.00)	0.09	(0.01)	1.29	(0.02)
Austria	0.26	(0.02)	0.29	(0.03)	0.23	(0.03)	-1.14	(0.02)	-0.11	(0.01)	0.65	(0.01)	1.64	(0.01)
Belgium	-0.21	(0.01)	-0.26	(0.02)	-0.16	(0.02)	-1.21	(0.01)	-0.62	(0.00)	-0.04	(0.01)	1.01	(0.02)
Brazil	0.22	(0.02)	0.17	(0.04)	0.25	(0.03)	-0.92	(0.01)	-0.30	(0.01)	0.46	(0.01)	1.63	(0.02)
Bulgaria	-0.19	(0.02)	-0.19	(0.03)	-0.18	(0.02)	-1.14	(0.01)	-0.56	(0.01)	-0.01	(0.01)	0.96	(0.02)
Canada	0.12	(0.01)	0.10	(0.02)	0.15	(0.01)	-1.08	(0.01)	-0.43	(0.00)	0.34	(0.00)	1.66	(0.01)
Chile	0.20	(0.02)	0.18	(0.03)	0.21	(0.03)	-1.10	(0.01)	-0.31	(0.01)	0.52	(0.01)	1.68	(0.02)
Czech Republic	-0.29	(0.02)	-0.29	(0.02)	-0.29	(0.02)	-1.13	(0.01)	-0.62	(0.00)	-0.17	(0.01)	0.76	(0.02)
Denmark	0.13	(0.02)	0.19	(0.03)	0.08	(0.03)	-1.07	(0.01)	-0.32	(0.01)	0.36	(0.01)	1.56	(0.02)
Finland	0.02	(0.01)	0.10	(0.02)	-0.05	(0.02)	-1.08	(0.01)	-0.42	(0.01)	0.31	(0.01)	1.28	(0.02)
France	-0.14	(0.02)	-0.12	(0.02)	-0.16	(0.02)	-1.21	(0.01)	-0.54	(0.01)	0.09	(0.01)	1.10	(0.02)
Germany	0.18	(0.02)	0.21	(0.03)	0.16	(0.02)	-1.15	(0.01)	-0.23	(0.01)	0.52	(0.01)	1.58	(0.01)
Greece	-0.02	(0.02)	-0.04	(0.03)	0.00	(0.02)	-1.06	(0.01)	-0.46	(0.01)	0.16	(0.01)	1.27	(0.02)
Hong Kong-China	-0.42	(0.01)	-0.42	(0.02)	-0.41	(0.02)	-1.17	(0.01)	-0.65	(0.00)	-0.44	(0.01)	0.59	(0.02)
Hungary	0.14	(0.02)	0.13	(0.02)	0.15	(0.02)	-0.99	(0.02)	-0.28	(0.01)	0.39	(0.01)	1.44	(0.02)
Iceland	0.14	(0.02)	0.17	(0.03)	0.11	(0.03)	-1.15	(0.02)	-0.32	(0.01)	0.42	(0.01)	1.61	(0.02)
Indonesia	-0.21	(0.02)	-0.21	(0.02)	-0.21	(0.02)	-0.99	(0.01)	-0.51	(0.00)	-0.11	(0.01)	0.78	(0.02)
Ireland	0.08	(0.02)	0.09	(0.03)	0.08	(0.02)	-1.02	(0.01)	-0.43	(0.00)	0.31	(0.01)	1.48	(0.02)
Israel	0.45	(0.03)	0.26	(0.06)	0.58	(0.03)	-1.03	(0.02)	0.07	(0.01)	0.83	(0.01)	1.94	(0.02)
Italy	0.00	(0.02)	-0.01	(0.02)	0.01	(0.02)	-1.08	(0.01)	-0.40	(0.01)	0.26	(0.01)	1.21	(0.02)
Japan	-0.35	(0.02)	-0.37	(0.02)	-0.33	(0.02)	-1.34	(0.01)	-0.71	(0.00)	-0.20	(0.01)	0.86	(0.02)
Korea	-0.39	(0.02)	-0.32	(0.02)	-0.47	(0.02)	-1.29	(0.01)	-0.75	(0.00)	-0.22	(0.01)	0.70	(0.02)
Latvia	-0.36	(0.02)	-0.36	(0.02)	-0.35	(0.03)	-1.23	(0.01)	-0.68	(0.01)	-0.25	(0.01)	0.72	(0.03)
Liechtenstein	0.21	(0.05)	0.17	(0.09)	0.27	(0.07)	-1.22	(0.06)	-0.22	(0.03)	0.64	(0.03)	1.66	(0.05)
Luxembourg	0.05	(0.02)	0.05	(0.03)	0.05	(0.03)	-1.26	(0.02)	-0.44	(0.01)	0.37	(0.01)	1.53	(0.02)
FYR Macedonia	0.03	(0.02)	0.00	(0.02)	0.06	(0.02)	-1.07	(0.01)	-0.44	(0.01)	0.23	(0.01)	1.39	(0.02)
Mexico	0.09	(0.02)	0.04	(0.03)	0.13	(0.03)	-1.03	(0.01)	-0.39	(0.01)	0.33	(0.01)	1.44	(0.02)
New Zealand	-0.02	(0.02)	-0.02	(0.02)	-0.02	(0.02)	-1.06	(0.01)	-0.49	(0.00)	0.17	(0.01)	1.30	(0.02)
Norway	0.12	(0.02)	0.16	(0.03)	0.09	(0.03)	-1.11	(0.01)	-0.31	(0.01)	0.39	(0.01)	1.51	(0.02)
Peru	-0.20	(0.02)	-0.23	(0.03)	-0.17	(0.03)	-1.28	(0.01)	-0.68	(0.00)	-0.01	(0.01)	1.18	(0.02)
Poland	-0.39	(0.02)	-0.42	(0.03)	-0.37	(0.03)	-1.30	(0.01)	-0.76	(0.01)	-0.27	(0.01)	0.76	(0.03)
Portugal	0.01	(0.02)	0.02	(0.03)	0.01	(0.02)	-0.97	(0.01)	-0.40	(0.01)	0.22	(0.01)	1.20	(0.02)
Russian Federation	-0.24	(0.02)	-0.27	(0.01)	-0.22	(0.02)	-1.15	(0.01)	-0.65	(0.00)	-0.10	(0.00)	0.94	(0.01)
Spain	-0.01	(0.02)	-0.05	(0.02)	0.03	(0.02)	-1.06	(0.01)	-0.42	(0.00)	0.26	(0.01)	1.19	(0.02)
Sweden	0.27	(0.02)	0.39	(0.02)	0.15	(0.02)	-1.00	(0.01)	-0.09	(0.01)	0.55	(0.01)	1.63	(0.02)
Switzerland	0.20	(0.02)	0.25	(0.03)	0.16	(0.03)	-1.09	(0.01)	-0.23	(0.01)	0.55	(0.01)	1.57	(0.02)
Thailand	-0.31	(0.02)	-0.34	(0.02)	-0.28	(0.02)	-1.10	(0.01)	-0.65	(0.00)	-0.25	(0.01)	0.77	(0.02)
United Kingdom	0.13	(0.01)	0.15	(0.02)	0.11	(0.02)	-0.98	(0.01)	-0.37	(0.01)	0.35	(0.00)	1.52	(0.02)
United States	-0.06	(0.03)	-0.12	(0.05)	-0.01	(0.03)	-1.24	(0.01)	-0.56	(0.00)	0.04	(0.01)	1.51	(0.03)
OECD average	*0.00*	*(0.00)*	*0.01*	*(0.01)*	*-0.01*	*(0.01)*	*-1.14*	*(0.00)*	*-0.45*	*(0.00)*	*0.24*	*(0.00)*	*1.34*	*(0.00)*
OECD total	*-0.08*	*(0.01)*	*-0.09*	*(0.01)*	*-0.06*	*(0.01)*	*-1.20*	*(0.00)*	*-0.53*	*(0.00)*	*0.11*	*(0.00)*	*1.29*	*(0.01)*
Netherlands[3]	-0.01	(0.03)	-0.04	(0.04)	0.02	(0.03)	-0.99	(0.02)	-0.38	(0.01)	0.29	(0.01)	1.03	(0.03)

1. For the definition of the index see Annex A1.
2. For explained variation see Annex A2. Unit changes marked in bold are statistically significant. Where bottom and top quarters are marked in bold this indicates that their difference is statistically significant.
3. Response rate is too low to ensure comparability (see Annex A3)

Table 4.1 (continued)
Index of sense of belonging and performance on the combined reading literacy scale, by national quarters of the index
Results based on students' self-reports

| | Performance on the combined reading literacy scale. by national quarters of the index of sense of belonging[2] | | | | | | | | Change in the combined reading literacy score per unit of the index of sense of belonging[2] | |
| | Bottom quarter | | Second quarter | | Third quarter | | Top quarter | | | |
	Mean score	S.E.	Mean score	S.E.	Mean score	S.E.	Mean score	S.E	Change	S.E.
Albania	332	(4.1)	350	(6.8)	373	(3.8)	360	(4.3)	10.5	(2.75)
Argentina	373	(9.7)	424	(11.6)	434	(7.3)	457	(8.0)	25.2	(2.51)
Australia	519	(5.0)	531	(4.5)	534	(4.7)	532	(4.5)	3.7	(1.73)
Austria	497	(3.8)	507	(3.5)	516	(3.8)	512	(3.5)	5.1	(1.73)
Belgium	487	(5.0)	515	(4.7)	515	(3.4)	523	(4.3)	9.8	(1.87)
Brazil	385	(4.3)	389	(4.3)	399	(4.0)	419	(4.1)	12.5	(1.67)
Bulgaria	401	(6.8)	429	(5.7)	449	(4.9)	460	(6.1)	24.9	(2.90)
Canada	524	(2.3)	539	(2.2)	541	(1.9)	536	(2.0)	3.3	(0.84)
Chile	383	(5.5)	403	(4.2)	422	(3.8)	435	(3.8)	16.6	(1.37)
Czech Republic	472	(4.1)	487	(3.4)	499	(3.8)	513	(3.4)	19.3	(2.18)
Denmark	486	(3.9)	500	(3.6)	503	(3.7)	505	(3.3)	5.8	(1.65)
Finland	549	(3.9)	547	(3.2)	552	(2.8)	541	(4.0)	-2.5	(1.52)
France	491	(4.2)	510	(3.8)	515	(3.4)	514	(3.6)	5.7	(1.69)
Germany	464	(5.0)	488	(4.1)	499	(3.7)	492	(3.8)	8.3	(2.05)
Greece	453	(7.1)	480	(6.2)	481	(4.5)	487	(5.3)	11.1	(2.17)
Hong Kong-China	506	(4.3)	527	(3.9)	534	(3.4)	538	(3.1)	12.9	(1.96)
Hungary	459	(5.4)	473	(4.6)	493	(4.8)	500	(4.5)	16.8	(2.13)
Iceland	502	(3.2)	513	(3.2)	510	(3.2)	511	(3.3)	2.1	(1.53)
Indonesia	344	(4.4)	373	(4.7)	379	(4.3)	388	(4.0)	21.2	(2.19)
Ireland	527	(4.7)	527	(4.2)	531	(4.0)	527	(3.8)	-0.2	(1.64)
Israel	433	(11.4)	466	(8.4)	471	(11.5)	466	(8.2)	8.7	(2.75)
Italy	480	(4.7)	492	(3.4)	499	(3.3)	484	(3.5)	-0.7	(1.57)
Japan	508	(5.9)	525	(5.6)	530	(5.8)	533	(5.3)	8.4	(1.84)
Korea	514	(3.6)	521	(3.3)	531	(3.0)	533	(3.0)	9.4	(1.72)
Latvia	435	(6.4)	463	(6.6)	466	(6.7)	476	(5.6)	16.6	(2.75)
Liechtenstein	456	(11.5)	481	(10.8)	497	(9.3)	499	(9.8)	13.4	(4.74)
Luxembourg	415	(3.7)	447	(3.4)	460	(3.0)	470	(3.0)	16.6	(1.71)
FYR Macedonia	338	(3.5)	375	(3.3)	392	(4.1)	402	(2.9)	21.1	(1.53)
Mexico	392	(3.8)	414	(3.7)	434	(4.8)	447	(4.4)	20.7	(1.96)
New Zealand	516	(4.9)	531	(3.5)	540	(4.0)	536	(3.7)	5.6	(1.90)
Norway	491	(4.4)	510	(4.0)	519	(4.1)	509	(3.8)	6.6	(1.86)
Peru	290	(5.9)	316	(4.9)	342	(4.9)	371	(4.6)	29.3	(2.34)
Poland	452	(6.3)	474	(5.5)	498	(5.2)	507	(5.2)	21.4	(2.79)
Portugal	427	(6.3)	468	(5.3)	491	(4.5)	501	(4.3)	29.4	(2.30)
Russian Federation	450	(5.9)	453	(3.9)	466	(4.3)	481	(4.6)	13.8	(1.78)
Spain	481	(3.8)	496	(3.3)	499	(3.4)	499	(3.4)	5.4	(1.58)
Sweden	516	(3.6)	520	(3.2)	521	(3.1)	511	(3.3)	-2.1	(1.42)
Switzerland	470	(5.5)	499	(4.5)	508	(4.9)	507	(5.2)	12.3	(1.57)
Thailand	400	(4.1)	430	(3.4)	442	(3.3)	452	(4.2)	22.6	(1.86)
United Kingdom	513	(4.4)	525	(3.9)	535	(2.9)	530	(3.3)	6.3	(1.57)
United States	474	(10.7)	513	(6.3)	516	(7.6)	526	(6.6)	12.8	(2.70)
OECD average	*484*	*(0.9)*	*504*	*(0.8)*	*510*	*(0.7)*	*509*	*(0.8)*	*7.8*	*(0.35)*
OECD total	*481*	*(2.9)*	*504*	*(2.1)*	*509*	*(2.0)*	*509*	*(1.9)*	*8.3*	*(0.88)*
Netherlands[3]	512	(6.3)	533	(4.3)	544	(4.4)	540	(4.1)	13.6	(3.28)

1. For the definition of the index see Annex A1.
2. For explained variation see Annex A2. Unit changes marked in bold are statistically significant. Where bottom and top quarters are marked in bold this indicates that their difference is statistically significant.
3. Response rate is too low to ensure comparability (see Annex A3).

Table 4.2
Student attendance at school
Results based on students' self-reports

| | Number of times that students report skipping class in the last two weeks | | | | | | | | | | | | | | | |
| | None[1] | | | | 1 or 2 | | | | 3 or 4 | | | | 5 or more[1] | | | |
	%	S.E.	Mean score	S.E.	%	S.E.	Mean score	S.E.	%	S.E.	Mean score	S.E.	%	S.E.	Mean score	S.E.
Korea	79.5	(0.8)	529	(2.4)	13.8	(0.5)	516	(3.9)	3.4	(0.3)	502	(6.6)	3.0	(0.3)	494	(8.3)
Hong Kong-China	89.7	(0.6)	529	(2.7)	8.8	(0.6)	506	(6.7)	0.7	c	c	c	0.4	c	c	c
Japan	86.4	(1.7)	529	(4.7)	8.8	(0.7)	491	(9.7)	1.1	(0.2)	459	(23.4)	5.8	(0.6)	412	(13.4)
Italy	43.9	(1.2)	511	(2.7)	41.5	(0.9)	482	(3.2)	8.3	(0.4)	448	(5.9)	5.8	(0.6)	466	(10.8)
United Kingdom	64.6	(0.9)	537	(2.7)	27.9	(0.8)	508	(3.3)	4.1	(0.3)	485	(9.4)	2.7	(0.3)	466	(10.8)
Albania	63.9	(1.2)	364	(3.3)	25.5	(0.7)	336	(4.8)	4.4	(0.5)	323	(8.5)	2.1	(0.3)	310	(12.4)
Liechtenstein	80.6	(2.0)	491	(4.9)	13.4	(1.7)	451	(19.4)	2.5	c	c	c	2.3	c	c	c
France	63.9	(1.0)	521	(2.6)	25.6	(0.7)	494	(3.7)	4.8	(0.4)	458	(6.7)	3.7	(0.3)	421	(8.7)
Ireland	56.8	(0.9)	537	(3.5)	33.5	(0.9)	521	(3.7)	6.1	(0.4)	499	(8.3)	2.7	(0.3)	481	(11.4)
Czech Republic	46.8	(1.1)	515	(2.6)	38.2	(0.8)	502	(2.8)	7.4	(0.4)	472	(4.3)	7.4	(0.5)	439	(5.5)
Thailand	56.1	(1.3)	449	(3.4)	35.5	(1.1)	411	(3.6)	5.8	(0.4)	399	(5.8)	1.8	(0.2)	374	(8.2)
Indonesia	68.1	(1.6)	376	(4.5)	23.2	(1.1)	359	(4.0)	2.1	(0.3)	372	(8.7)	1.4	(0.2)	347	(8.7)
Australia	56.9	(1.1)	539	(4.1)	34.3	(1.1)	517	(4.0)	5.4	(0.4)	521	(8.3)	2.9	(0.3)	493	(12.0)
Hungary	65.7	(0.9)	488	(3.9)	23.0	(0.8)	477	(4.9)	4.4	(0.3)	470	(8.9)	5.6	(0.3)	424	(10.1)
Belgium	69.2	(0.9)	528	(3.2)	20.2	(0.9)	487	(5.5)	4.5	(0.4)	430	(11.8)	3.3	(0.3)	420	(11.3)
Chile	51.6	(1.1)	424	(3.7)	32.8	(0.8)	410	(4.4)	7.3	(0.5)	386	(6.9)	7.3	(0.5)	345	(5.4)
Switzerland	66.7	(0.8)	497	(4.5)	25.0	(0.7)	505	(5.0)	4.1	(0.3)	463	(9.7)	2.7	(0.3)	443	(12.5)
Germany	72.9	(0.8)	501	(2.6)	21.3	(0.7)	483	(4.2)	3.2	(0.3)	447	(12.7)	1.9	(0.2)	434	(12.5)
FYR Macedonia	59.9	(0.8)	382	(2.1)	27.1	(0.8)	375	(3.2)	4.8	(0.4)	364	(7.1)	4.6	(0.4)	344	(7.0)
Finland	56.0	(0.9)	554	(3.1)	32.5	(0.8)	546	(2.7)	6.5	(0.4)	515	(8.4)	3.8	(0.3)	512	(6.7)
Austria	62.7	(1.0)	507	(2.8)	31.3	(0.9)	515	(3.2)	3.2	(0.3)	506	(8.7)	2.0	(0.2)	446	(16.3)
Luxembourg	71.2	(0.7)	455	(1.9)	20.7	(0.6)	429	(3.7)	3.1	(0.3)	401	(12.3)	3.1	(0.3)	392	(10.7)
Peru	55.4	(1.2)	337	(4.9)	30.5	(0.9)	320	(5.1)	7.8	(0.5)	322	(6.9)	3.8	(0.4)	310	(12.0)
Canada	52.1	(0.4)	544	(1.5)	37.0	(0.5)	533	(1.7)	6.6	(0.2)	511	(4.5)	3.6	(0.2)	484	(6.8)
Sweden	61.6	(0.8)	521	(2.6)	29.1	(0.8)	514	(3.2)	5.6	(0.3)	508	(7.1)	2.8	(0.2)	488	(9.0)
Brazil	44.2	(1.4)	411	(3.6)	36.1	(1.2)	394	(4.0)	7.6	(0.7)	395	(6.7)	9.6	(0.7)	359	(5.0)
Norway	64.1	(1.0)	514	(2.7)	26.2	(0.8)	502	(4.5)	5.7	(0.5)	484	(9.5)	3.0	(0.3)	436	(11.2)
United States	54.8	(1.9)	523	(5.9)	30.4	(1.3)	496	(8.7)	4.5	(0.4)	454	(15.7)	3.1	(0.5)	411	(9.4)
Iceland	62.4	(0.8)	516	(1.9)	22.2	(0.8)	505	(3.3)	6.2	(0.5)	507	(6.9)	8.4	(0.5)	470	(5.9)
Denmark	49.0	(0.8)	506	(2.9)	33.1	(0.7)	501	(3.0)	9.0	(0.5)	479	(5.8)	6.9	(0.3)	469	(7.9)
Mexico	65.2	(1.0)	429	(3.8)	26.8	(0.8)	411	(3.9)	3.5	(0.3)	412	(7.6)	1.2	(0.2)	359	(14.2)
Argentina	46.7	(1.8)	442	(9.3)	32.7	(0.7)	428	(9.8)	6.8	(1.2)	359	(10.7)	9.4	(1.0)	346	(9.0)
Portugal	81.6	(0.7)	476	(4.4)	13.3	(0.6)	453	(7.2)	1.6	(0.2)	425	(13.9)	1.2	(0.2)	404	(17.6)
New Zealand	54.1	(1.1)	544	(3.1)	32.8	(0.9)	529	(3.8)	7.2	(0.5)	494	(8.1)	4.3	(0.3)	452	(10.0)
Poland	53.9	(1.5)	494	(4.9)	29.9	(1.0)	478	(4.9)	6.2	(0.5)	449	(10.3)	6.4	(0.6)	444	(10.0)
Latvia	60.4	(1.5)	467	(5.3)	28.9	(1.0)	454	(6.6)	4.7	(0.4)	454	(13.1)	3.8	(0.5)	421	(13.7)
Greece	67.5	(1.0)	485	(4.2)	23.4	(0.8)	468	(7.4)	3.0	(0.3)	455	(10.7)	3.9	(0.5)	388	(11.2)
Russian Federation	62.8	(1.0)	471	(4.5)	25.4	(0.9)	455	(4.5)	4.4	(0.3)	452	(7.9)	4.6	(0.4)	437	(6.0)
Bulgaria	53.0	(1.3)	451	(5.0)	27.2	(0.8)	432	(6.0)	5.0	(0.4)	415	(8.9)	10.6	(0.7)	385	(7.7)
Spain	65.4	(0.9)	505	(2.8)	25.3	(0.7)	479	(3.9)	4.5	(0.3)	454	(5.4)	6.8	(0.6)	439	(7.7)
Israel	41.5	(1.3)	453	(8.7)	38.8	(1.0)	465	(9.8)	10.0	(0.7)	461	(11.6)	6.8	(0.6)	439	(10.8)
OECD average	64.0	(0.6)	512	(1.7)	25.6	(0.4)	489	(2.8)	4.2	(0.1)	461	(4.7)	2.9	(0.2)	431	(3.8)
OECD total	63.6	(0.2)	510	(0.7)	26.4	(0.1)	496	(0.8)	4.8	(0.1)	475	(1.7)	3.6	(0.1)	445	(2.1)
Netherlands[2]	62.3	(1.2)	543	(3.2)	28.2	(1.1)	525	(4.5)	4.9	(0.5)	501	(9.0)	3.8	(0.5)	463	(13.7)

1. Figures in bold indicate that there is a significant difference between the performance of students who reported "none" and those who reported "5 or more".
2. Response rate is too low to ensure comparability (see Annex A3).

Table 4.2 (continued)
Student attendance at school
Results based on students' self-reports

| | Number of times that students report arriving late for school in the last two weeks | | | | | | | | | | | | | | | |
| | None[1] | | | | 1 or 2 | | | | 3 or 4 | | | | 5 or more[1] | | | |
	%	S.E.	Mean score	S.E.	%	S.E.	Mean score	S.E.	%	S.E.	Mean score	S.E.	%	S.E.	Mean score	S.E.
Korea	94.4	(0.5)	**528**	(2.3)	3.6	(0.3)	488	(5.3)	0.8	(0.1)	450	(15.0)	0.4	c	c	c
Hong Kong-China	96.7	(0.4)	**527**	(2.8)	2.2	(0.3)	511	(16.9)	0.3	c	c	c	0.5	c	c	c
Japan	92.6	(1.8)	**528**	(4.7)	2.9	(0.4)	451	(13.0)	0.6	c	c	c	0.6	c	c	c
Italy	88.3	(0.6)	**494**	(2.6)	8.0	(0.5)	455	(7.4)	1.5	(0.2)	402	(18.9)	0.9	(0.1)	**405**	(20.1)
United Kingdom	88.9	(0.5)	**530**	(2.4)	7.4	(0.4)	487	(6.5)	1.3	(0.2)	484	(13.9)	1.0	(0.2)	**436**	(14.3)
Albania	78.9	(0.9)	**358**	(3.2)	13.0	(0.6)	342	(4.8)	1.6	(0.2)	322	(13.9)	1.0	(0.2)	**281**	(13.8)
Liechtenstein	90.3	(1.8)	**487**	(4.5)	5.1	c	c	c	1.3	c	c	c	1.0	c	c	c
France	88.5	(0.7)	**510**	(2.7)	7.2	(0.4)	488	(6.6)	1.1	(0.2)	473	(13.1)	1.1	(0.2)	**410**	(16.5)
Ireland	86.2	(0.7)	**530**	(3.2)	8.8	(0.6)	515	(6.4)	1.9	(0.2)	526	(14.1)	1.1	(0.2)	**471**	(18.2)
Czech Republic	90.8	(0.5)	**504**	(2.2)	6.3	(0.5)	478	(6.8)	0.8	(0.2)	425	(13.9)	1.2	(0.2)	**442**	(11.9)
Thailand	74.7	(1.1)	**441**	(3.5)	19.9	(1.0)	405	(4.4)	3.0	(0.5)	389	(9.1)	1.2	(0.2)	**372**	(12.2)
Indonesia	74.3	(1.6)	370	(3.9)	16.9	(0.8)	374	(4.8)	1.9	(0.2)	392	(12.0)	1.3	(0.2)	374	(16.9)
Australia	85.1	(0.7)	**532**	(3.5)	10.4	(0.7)	515	(7.0)	2.3	(0.4)	516	(16.7)	1.3	(0.2)	**472**	(16.8)
Hungary	82.8	(0.9)	**489**	(3.6)	13.0	(0.7)	453	(6.4)	1.5	(0.2)	411	(14.1)	1.3	(0.2)	**386**	(19.4)
Belgium	88.8	(0.8)	**518**	(3.4)	6.1	(0.4)	443	(8.1)	1.0	(0.1)	409	(13.1)	1.3	(0.1)	**408**	(13.4)
Chile	76.3	(0.9)	**415**	(3.7)	17.8	(0.8)	404	(5.4)	2.6	(0.3)	382	(11.5)	1.5	(0.2)	**354**	(11.4)
Switzerland	85.1	(0.6)	**497**	(4.1)	9.6	(0.5)	501	(9.7)	1.8	(0.3)	472	(19.7)	1.5	(0.2)	**449**	(10.9)
Germany	86.8	(0.7)	**498**	(2.5)	9.3	(0.6)	476	(10.2)	1.4	(0.2)	462	(11.5)	1.6	(0.2)	**435**	(13.8)
FYR Macedonia	76.3	(0.8)	**384**	(1.8)	14.2	(0.6)	364	(4.0)	2.6	(0.3)	319	(8.2)	1.7	(0.2)	**329**	(12.2)
Finland	79.7	(0.8)	**552**	(2.8)	14.2	(0.6)	536	(4.6)	2.9	(0.3)	507	(8.5)	1.8	(0.2)	**487**	(13.9)
Austria	84.7	(1.0)	**508**	(2.4)	10.2	(0.8)	519	(5.9)	2.4	(0.3)	505	(9.6)	1.8	(0.3)	**454**	(15.1)
Luxembourg	89.5	(0.5)	**450**	(1.5)	5.2	(0.4)	420	(8.9)	1.1	(0.2)	394	(22.9)	1.9	(0.2)	**410**	(12.9)
Peru	65.3	(1.1)	**340**	(4.7)	23.2	(0.9)	321	(5.3)	2.6	(0.3)	314	(11.3)	2.0	(0.2)	**253**	(24.1)
Canada	75.7	(0.5)	**541**	(1.5)	17.4	(0.4)	525	(2.3)	3.8	(0.2)	509	(5.3)	2.2	(0.1)	**470**	(6.3)
Sweden	77.8	(0.8)	**521**	(2.2)	15.1	(0.7)	508	(4.6)	3.8	(0.4)	507	(8.2)	2.3	(0.3)	**462**	(13.0)
Brazil	74.7	(1.4)	**403**	(3.4)	16.9	(1.0)	389	(4.8)	2.7	(0.4)	375	(8.4)	2.3	(0.3)	**356**	(8.4)
Norway	85.0	(0.7)	**515**	(2.7)	8.9	(0.7)	484	(6.9)	2.2	(0.2)	458	(11.5)	2.3	(0.2)	**398**	(11.1)
United States	74.6	(1.8)	**513**	(7.0)	13.0	(0.6)	494	(7.6)	2.5	(0.3)	487	(14.2)	2.3	(0.4)	**439**	(21.4)
Iceland	80.7	(0.7)	**517**	(1.6)	13.2	(0.6)	481	(3.9)	2.8	(0.3)	469	(10.8)	2.4	(0.3)	**426**	(10.3)
Denmark	74.1	(0.8)	**505**	(2.4)	16.1	(0.7)	493	(4.0)	4.0	(0.4)	457	(11.1)	2.5	(0.3)	**431**	(12.4)
Mexico	63.3	(1.2)	**424**	(3.7)	25.3	(1.1)	429	(4.5)	2.7	(0.3)	428	(8.9)	2.5	(0.4)	**377**	(12.2)
Argentina	77.4	(1.6)	435	(8.9)	9.9	(1.3)	383	(12.1)	2.0	(0.4)	384	(17.2)	2.6	(0.7)	379	(27.3)
Portugal	59.9	(0.8)	**474**	(4.4)	30.7	(0.8)	474	(5.2)	4.5	(0.3)	448	(10.2)	2.9	(0.3)	**431**	(12.0)
New Zealand	72.8	(0.9)	**539**	(2.9)	17.1	(0.7)	520	(5.3)	4.7	(0.4)	501	(9.0)	3.2	(0.3)	**484**	(13.1)
Poland	71.1	(1.3)	**492**	(4.6)	18.3	(0.9)	469	(5.5)	3.5	(0.4)	446	(14.9)	3.2	(0.4)	**422**	(12.4)
Latvia	63.2	(1.2)	**469**	(5.4)	26.1	(1.0)	451	(7.5)	5.4	(0.4)	437	(10.3)	3.3	(0.4)	**413**	(9.9)
Greece	56.8	(1.4)	**484**	(5.2)	29.8	(0.9)	472	(6.0)	6.8	(0.5)	459	(7.0)	4.5	(0.4)	**422**	(10.0)
Russian Federation	61.1	(1.1)	**471**	(4.0)	26.2	(0.8)	454	(4.8)	5.6	(0.3)	444	(8.7)	4.9	(0.3)	**440**	(9.2)
Bulgaria	53.1	(1.2)	**448**	(5.2)	31.7	(0.9)	429	(5.3)	6.5	(0.4)	408	(7.7)	5.5	(0.5)	**392**	(9.0)
Spain	50.7	(1.1)	**503**	(3.2)	34.2	(0.8)	489	(3.0)	7.9	(0.6)	475	(5.3)	6.1	(0.4)	**471**	(5.6)
Israel	55.8	(2.2)	450	(8.5)	27.2	(1.6)	469	(9.6)	7.6	(0.7)	468	(14.2)	6.5	(0.7)	467	(14.3)
OECD average	*79.7*	*(0.5)*	*508*	*(1.8)*	*12.3*	*(0.2)*	*477*	*(2.5)*	*2.2*	*(0.1)*	*467*	*(5.1)*	*1.9*	*(0.1)*	*430*	*(7.3)*
OECD total	*79.8*	*(0.2)*	*508*	*(0.6)*	*13.4*	*(0.1)*	*483*	*(1.3)*	*2.7*	*(0.1)*	*468*	*(2.1)*	*2.0*	*(0.1)*	*436*	*(2.7)*
Netherlands[2]	84.7	(1.1)	**534**	(3.2)	11.1	(0.9)	531	(6.5)	2.3	(0.4)	516	(15.4)	0.9	c	c	c

1. Figures in bold indicate that there is a significant difference between the performance of students who reported "none" and those who reported "5 or more".
2. Response rate is too low to ensure comparability (see Annex A3).

Table 4.3
Effort, persistence and motivation of students to learn
Results based on students' self-reports

| | Frequency with which students report that "When studying, I work as hard as possible" | | | | | | | | | | | | | | | |
| | Almost never[1] | | | | Sometimes | | | | Often | | | | Almost always[1] | | | |
	%	S.E.	Mean score	S.E.	%	S.E.	Mean score	S.E.	%	S.E.	Mean score	S.E.	%	S.E.	Mean score	S.E.
Albania	5.5	(0.4)	**330**	(7.8)	17.9	(0.9)	333	(6.0)	36.4	(1.0)	363	(3.8)	35.3	(1.1)	**356**	(5.9)
Australia	4.8	(0.4)	484	(7.9)	32.3	(0.8)	527	(4.7)	39.4	(0.8)	536	(3.7)	21.0	(0.8)	540	(5.0)
Austria	7.8	(0.5)	511	(5.6)	32.7	(0.9)	514	(3.3)	36.1	(0.7)	511	(3.0)	21.2	(0.7)	498	(3.4)
Belgium (Fl.)	7.2	(0.5)	517	(12.9)	36.3	(1.0)	541	(5.2)	34.3	(0.9)	540	(4.1)	17.6	(0.7)	525	(5.0)
Brazil	4.5	(0.4)	**344**	(6.3)	14.5	(0.8)	403	(4.5)	37.7	(1.1)	400	(3.5)	35.4	(1.1)	**412**	(3.5)
Bulgaria	5.3	(0.4)	**387**	(7.4)	23.8	(0.6)	411	(6.4)	34.2	(0.9)	448	(5.4)	33.7	(0.9)	**448**	(4.9)
Chile	4.3	(0.3)	**394**	(6.5)	20.5	(0.7)	393	(4.4)	31.5	(0.7)	412	(3.9)	40.5	(0.9)	**425**	(3.8)
Czech Republic	7.2	(0.4)	497	(6.3)	43.2	(0.9)	505	(2.7)	32.9	(0.7)	505	(2.6)	13.1	(0.5)	494	(3.9)
Denmark	4.8	(0.4)	452	(10.3)	32.7	(0.8)	490	(3.0)	38.1	(0.9)	507	(2.8)	22.3	(0.7)	516	(3.8)
Finland	6.9	(0.4)	515	(5.3)	44.4	(0.8)	545	(3.0)	37.2	(0.8)	554	(2.9)	9.8	(0.4)	562	(6.1)
Germany	7.1	(0.3)	478	(6.6)	34.6	(0.7)	497	(3.0)	35.9	(0.8)	500	(3.2)	19.5	(0.6)	494	(4.1)
Hong Kong-China	3.3	(0.3)	**468**	(10.3)	41.8	(0.8)	510	(3.8)	36.8	(0.7)	543	(2.6)	17.5	(0.6)	**541**	(3.6)
Hungary	3.0	(0.3)	447	(15.8)	24.4	(0.7)	471	(4.8)	50.5	(0.8)	494	(4.2)	18.7	(0.8)	477	(5.5)
Iceland	7.8	(0.5)	485	(6.4)	37.5	(0.8)	507	(2.7)	34.6	(0.8)	519	(2.5)	18.0	(0.7)	511	(3.9)
Ireland	8.6	(0.5)	505	(7.3)	33.5	(0.8)	530	(3.8)	33.5	(0.8)	534	(3.9)	22.5	(0.7)	528	(4.3)
Israel	8.7	(0.7)	473	(12.7)	24.7	(1.3)	479	(7.9)	28.6	(1.1)	468	(10.8)	26.3	(1.4)	455	(6.3)
Italy	5.6	(0.4)	462	(11.2)	28.4	(0.7)	486	(4.0)	41.0	(0.8)	491	(3.0)	24.4	(0.8)	490	(3.5)
Korea	8.0	(0.4)	**500**	(5.8)	40.1	(0.8)	515	(2.6)	34.6	(0.7)	537	(2.5)	17.0	(0.6)	**535**	(3.4)
Latvia	7.3	(0.5)	**426**	(9.0)	43.4	(1.0)	462	(5.9)	35.3	(0.9)	465	(5.8)	12.0	(0.6)	**464**	(7.4)
Liechtenstein	5.1	c	c	c	34.5	(2.7)	477	(7.8)	36.9	(2.4)	488	(8.3)	20.1	(2.4)	494	(12.5)
Luxembourg	9.1	(0.5)	439	(6.0)	31.7	(0.8)	454	(2.9)	32.3	(0.7)	460	(3.2)	19.1	(0.8)	448	(3.3)
FYR Macedonia	3.0	(0.3)	**327**	(13.6)	13.7	(0.6)	358	(4.8)	31.9	(0.8)	376	(2.7)	47.5	(0.8)	**388**	(2.2)
Mexico	6.8	(0.5)	419	(6.3)	37.5	(0.9)	422	(4.0)	28.9	(0.7)	432	(3.6)	22.0	(0.8)	414	(4.8)
New Zealand	5.2	(0.4)	515	(8.2)	34.7	(0.8)	533	(3.6)	38.2	(0.8)	540	(3.3)	17.5	(0.7)	534	(6.0)
Norway	10.5	(0.6)	**469**	(7.1)	37.5	(0.7)	511	(3.5)	35.2	(0.8)	521	(3.3)	12.5	(0.5)	**514**	(5.5)
Portugal	3.0	(0.3)	460	(12.6)	28.4	(0.9)	467	(5.5)	36.1	(0.7)	469	(4.9)	30.9	(0.8)	478	(4.2)
Russian Federation	5.5	(0.3)	**436**	(6.9)	34.0	(0.7)	456	(5.0)	35.7	(0.5)	470	(4.4)	22.2	(0.6)	**473**	(4.7)
Sweden	6.3	(0.4)	491	(7.3)	33.9	(0.9)	518	(2.7)	40.9	(0.7)	521	(2.6)	17.2	(0.7)	522	(4.2)
Switzerland	6.6	(0.4)	488	(7.8)	35.3	(0.8)	500	(4.9)	36.6	(0.7)	500	(4.6)	18.2	(0.6)	492	(5.2)
Thailand	10.4	(0.6)	428	(5.5)	54.4	(1.3)	431	(3.5)	28.3	(0.9)	434	(3.7)	6.1	(0.6)	429	(7.2)
United Kingdom	2.6	(0.4)	492	(17.7)	27.9	(1.0)	520	(4.0)	43.1	(1.1)	533	(5.1)	26.0	(0.8)	528	(5.6)
United States	7.5	(0.7)	488	(11.5)	32.7	(1.3)	514	(6.9)	30.2	(1.3)	520	(7.2)	16.6	(0.9)	503	(9.1)
OECD average	*6.9*	*(0.3)*	*478*	*(5.3)*	*34.1*	*(0.6)*	*497*	*(3.1)*	*33.2*	*(0.6)*	*506*	*(2.9)*	*18.7*	*(0.4)*	*491*	*(3.8)*
OECD total	*6.5*	*(0.1)*	*479*	*(1.9)*	*35.2*	*(0.2)*	*501*	*(0.8)*	*36.4*	*(0.2)*	*509*	*(0.9)*	*18.6*	*(0.1)*	*501*	*(1.2)*
Netherlands[2]	6.3	(0.6)	534	(7.8)	41.7	(0.9)	541	(3.5)	37.3	(1.1)	531	(4.3)	12.8	(0.8)	512	(7.1)

1. Figures in bold indicate that there is a significant difference between the performance of students who reported "almost never" and those who reported "almost always".
2. Response rate is too low to ensure comparability (see Annex A3)

Table 4.3 (continued)
Effort, persistence and motivation of students to learn
Results based on students' self-reports

	Frequency with which students report that "When studying, I keep working even if the material is difficult"															
	Almost never[1]				Sometimes				Often				Almost always[1]			
	%	S.E.	Mean score	S.E.	%	S.E.	Mean score	S.E.	%	S.E.	Mean score	S.E.	%	S.E.	Mean score	S.E.
Albania	8.0	(0.5)	**325**	(6.5)	26.2	(0.8)	340	(3.9)	37.6	(0.9)	359	(4.6)	23.6	(0.8)	**370**	(5.6)
Australia	7.4	(0.6)	**497**	(7.3)	37.4	(0.8)	518	(3.8)	39.1	(0.9)	542	(4.4)	13.7	(0.7)	**557**	(5.7)
Austria	6.4	(0.4)	**473**	(7.1)	29.9	(0.8)	498	(3.4)	39.3	(0.9)	511	(3.2)	22.7	(0.7)	**532**	(3.5)
Belgium (Fl.)	7.7	(0.5)	515	(11.2)	37.2	(0.9)	538	(4.9)	33.8	(0.7)	542	(4.4)	16.7	(0.7)	530	(7.2)
Brazil	8.5	(0.6)	**366**	(6.0)	21.7	(0.9)	386	(4.7)	35.7	(0.9)	407	(3.4)	26.2	(0.8)	**421**	(3.4)
Bulgaria	15.4	(0.5)	434	(7.6)	40.4	(0.8)	439	(5.3)	26.2	(0.8)	433	(5.3)	15.4	(0.6)	429	(6.1)
Chile	3.1	(0.3)	**372**	(8.1)	23.1	(0.7)	395	(4.9)	33.7	(0.7)	416	(3.9)	36.3	(0.8)	**425**	(3.8)
Czech Republic	5.5	(0.4)	**472**	(5.8)	41.4	(0.8)	491	(2.4)	37.1	(0.9)	515	(2.6)	12.0	(0.5)	**526**	(4.4)
Denmark	6.8	(0.4)	**456**	(7.1)	34.5	(0.8)	485	(3.1)	37.9	(0.7)	511	(3.0)	17.8	(0.6)	**527**	(4.0)
Finland	5.6	(0.4)	**505**	(5.3)	39.6	(0.8)	530	(2.7)	41.5	(0.9)	563	(2.5)	11.4	(0.6)	**583**	(7.2)
Germany	6.4	(0.4)	**449**	(6.7)	34.4	(0.7)	480	(3.4)	39.8	(0.7)	507	(2.9)	16.2	(0.5)	**525**	(4.0)
Hong Kong-China	5.5	(0.4)	**472**	(7.7)	53.0	(0.9)	519	(2.9)	31.5	(0.8)	543	(3.4)	9.5	(0.5)	**544**	(4.6)
Hungary	5.3	(0.4)	**428**	(11.8)	33.9	(1.0)	470	(4.1)	41.6	(0.9)	496	(4.5)	16.5	(0.8)	**495**	(5.1)
Iceland	7.8	(0.4)	**462**	(6.6)	37.4	(0.9)	495	(2.5)	35.4	(0.9)	522	(2.4)	16.7	(0.7)	**544**	(4.0)
Ireland	13.0	(0.7)	**494**	(5.2)	37.2	(0.9)	523	(4.0)	31.2	(0.9)	540	(4.0)	16.6	(0.6)	**549**	(4.5)
Israel	4.9	(0.5)	445	(16.6)	27.1	(1.4)	469	(8.8)	29.6	(1.2)	472	(8.6)	25.3	(1.0)	470	(7.3)
Italy	10.7	(0.5)	**458**	(6.0)	34.9	(0.9)	478	(3.6)	38.6	(0.8)	498	(3.5)	14.9	(0.6)	**506**	(4.3)
Korea	23.4	(0.8)	**501**	(2.9)	46.1	(0.8)	526	(2.7)	22.1	(0.7)	541	(3.4)	8.2	(0.5)	**544**	(5.0)
Latvia	8.1	(0.6)	**432**	(9.3)	42.2	(1.0)	456	(5.5)	35.3	(0.8)	471	(6.2)	11.8	(0.5)	**471**	(6.8)
Liechtenstein	5.8	c	c	c	32.9	(2.7)	450	(9.7)	42.6	(2.9)	500	(7.6)	16.9	(2.1)	527	(9.9)
Luxembourg	7.7	(0.5)	**423**	(5.9)	33.1	(0.9)	443	(2.5)	33.0	(0.9)	463	(3.0)	16.9	(0.6)	**472**	(4.0)
FYR Macedonia	6.7	(0.5)	**333**	(9.6)	28.0	(0.8)	361	(3.2)	33.7	(0.8)	386	(2.2)	27.2	(0.7)	**396**	(2.9)
Mexico	7.2	(0.5)	**397**	(6.0)	40.6	(0.8)	413	(3.1)	30.3	(0.7)	436	(3.9)	17.2	(0.7)	**435**	(5.8)
New Zealand	7.0	(0.5)	**500**	(8.3)	38.6	(0.8)	526	(3.4)	36.7	(0.9)	545	(3.4)	13.5	(0.7)	**556**	(6.8)
Norway	8.4	(0.5)	**450**	(6.6)	33.5	(1.1)	493	(4.0)	37.9	(0.9)	527	(2.9)	15.1	(0.6)	**546**	(4.5)
Portugal	5.2	(0.4)	**432**	(8.0)	40.9	(1.0)	450	(4.8)	33.3	(0.9)	484	(4.9)	19.2	(0.7)	**504**	(5.0)
Russian Federation	7.6	(0.4)	**429**	(7.3)	39.1	(0.6)	450	(4.0)	34.2	(0.6)	478	(5.1)	15.9	(0.6)	**485**	(4.5)
Sweden	5.1	(0.3)	**467**	(7.2)	30.2	(0.7)	495	(3.0)	43.2	(0.9)	525	(2.6)	19.9	(0.6)	**551**	(3.4)
Switzerland	6.1	(0.4)	**468**	(9.1)	35.5	(0.9)	486	(4.3)	41.3	(0.9)	505	(4.5)	13.9	(0.7)	**521**	(6.6)
Thailand	3.1	(0.3)	**384**	(8.8)	40.6	(1.0)	418	(3.6)	42.6	(0.8)	441	(3.2)	12.0	(0.8)	**453**	(5.0)
United Kingdom	5.9	(0.6)	**477**	(9.1)	31.4	(0.9)	509	(5.5)	42.1	(1.1)	539	(3.8)	20.0	(0.8)	**547**	(6.0)
United States	7.4	(0.5)	**465**	(10.6)	32.6	(1.0)	497	(6.8)	31.2	(1.4)	527	(5.6)	15.4	(0.9)	**534**	(10.1)
OECD average	*8.6*	*(0.3)*	*465*	*(3.9)*	*35.9*	*(0.4)*	*485*	*(2.8)*	*33.0*	*(0.6)*	*511*	*(2.5)*	*15.2*	*(0.4)*	*517*	*(4.7)*
OECD total	*7.9*	*(0.1)*	*468*	*(1.4)*	*37.4*	*(0.2)*	*491*	*(0.9)*	*36.0*	*(0.2)*	*514*	*(0.9)*	*15.3*	*(0.1)*	*524*	*(1.3)*
Netherlands[2]	11.2	(0.7)	517	(5.6)	48.2	(1.1)	533	(3.6)	30.9	(1.0)	544	(4.1)	8.3	(0.6)	508	(9.3)

1. Figures in bold indicate that there is a significant difference between the performance of students who reported "almost never" and those who reported "almost always".
2. Response rate is too low to ensure comparability (see Annex A3).

Table 4.3 (continued)
Effort, persistence and motivation of students to learn
Results based on students' self-reports

	Frequency with which students report that "I study to get a good job"															
	Almost never[1]				Sometimes				Often				Almost always[1]			
	%	S.E.	Mean score	S.E.	%	S.E.	Mean score	S.E.	%	S.E.	Mean score	S.E.	%	S.E.	Mean score	S.E.
Albania	5.0	(0.7)	340	(9.9)	14.1	(0.7)	351	(4.5)	30.2	(0.9)	355	(3.8)	44.0	(1.2)	358	(5.2)
Australia	8.6	(0.6)	543	(7.4)	27.2	(0.9)	521	(4.8)	33.6	(0.9)	528	(4.0)	27.5	(0.8)	543	(4.9)
Austria	6.2	(0.4)	538	(7.8)	15.0	(0.6)	512	(4.6)	30.2	(0.8)	509	(3.5)	45.9	(0.8)	506	(2.3)
Belgium (Fl.)	7.0	(0.5)	544	(8.1)	19.7	(0.6)	537	(6.6)	32.9	(0.7)	537	(4.4)	34.7	(0.8)	533	(5.0)
Brazil	5.4	(0.5)	340	(8.7)	7.5	(0.5)	385	(7.4)	33.3	(0.8)	393	(3.3)	44.8	(1.0)	421	(3.0)
Bulgaria	7.6	(0.5)	429	(8.0)	17.6	(0.7)	426	(6.8)	25.7	(0.7)	438	(4.9)	44.6	(1.0)	439	(5.1)
Chile	5.0	(0.4)	447	(7.8)	14.0	(0.6)	403	(5.9)	25.3	(0.8)	409	(4.3)	50.4	(1.0)	417	(3.5)
Czech Republic	5.3	(0.4)	515	(7.2)	21.5	(0.7)	487	(4.0)	36.7	(0.9)	503	(2.8)	32.0	(0.7)	515	(2.7)
Denmark	6.6	(0.4)	511	(8.1)	23.4	(0.8)	493	(4.0)	36.0	(0.8)	504	(3.3)	29.7	(0.7)	505	(3.2)
Finland	3.2	(0.3)	526	(10.5)	19.5	(0.7)	527	(3.8)	43.2	(0.8)	544	(2.8)	32.2	(0.8)	569	(3.4)
Germany	6.7	(0.4)	519	(6.9)	20.1	(0.6)	497	(5.1)	33.3	(0.8)	497	(3.0)	36.4	(0.7)	494	(3.2)
Hong Kong-China	8.5	(0.4)	523	(5.5)	35.1	(0.9)	521	(4.3)	29.9	(0.8)	527	(3.8)	25.7	(0.8)	536	(3.0)
Hungary	3.5	(0.4)	492	(11.3)	14.1	(0.6)	476	(8.1)	35.2	(0.9)	485	(4.5)	43.0	(1.0)	486	(4.5)
Iceland	7.1	(0.5)	511	(6.6)	20.4	(0.7)	487	(3.8)	32.8	(0.8)	512	(2.5)	36.6	(0.7)	523	(2.4)
Ireland	11.9	(0.6)	523	(6.4)	20.3	(0.7)	520	(4.6)	27.7	(0.8)	531	(4.4)	37.9	(0.9)	535	(3.6)
Israel	14.4	(1.2)	488	(9.1)	19.2	(1.0)	468	(8.5)	21.8	(0.7)	466	(8.5)	30.1	(1.3)	464	(8.3)
Italy	11.1	(0.6)	505	(7.3)	20.0	(0.8)	492	(4.1)	36.0	(0.7)	484	(3.8)	31.6	(0.7)	486	(2.9)
Korea	11.6	(0.5)	511	(4.7)	23.7	(0.6)	510	(3.7)	30.5	(0.8)	531	(2.7)	33.8	(0.8)	534	(2.4)
Latvia	2.5	(0.3)	420	(9.4)	18.5	(0.7)	431	(8.1)	37.6	(0.8)	460	(5.4)	37.7	(0.8)	483	(5.3)
Liechtenstein	8.3	c	c	c	22.5	(2.3)	471	(12.8)	36.7	(2.5)	489	(8.3)	28.7	(2.6)	490	(9.5)
Luxembourg	5.7	(0.4)	440	(7.9)	17.9	(0.6)	439	(4.0)	29.0	(0.9)	457	(2.7)	35.4	(0.8)	465	(2.5)
FYR Macedonia	8.0	(0.4)	385	(6.1)	17.5	(0.7)	385	(3.8)	26.7	(0.7)	383	(2.7)	42.6	(0.8)	373	(2.8)
Mexico	7.6	(0.4)	423	(7.4)	19.7	(0.6)	406	(3.8)	29.4	(0.7)	423	(3.4)	38.0	(0.8)	433	(4.1)
New Zealand	9.4	(0.5)	553	(6.7)	25.9	(0.9)	525	(4.9)	31.5	(0.8)	530	(3.2)	27.9	(1.0)	548	(4.3)
Norway	6.3	(0.5)	475	(9.2)	21.4	(0.7)	483	(4.8)	37.0	(0.9)	516	(3.5)	28.8	(0.8)	538	(3.4)
Portugal	3.1	(0.3)	475	(11.9)	18.5	(0.8)	445	(6.3)	33.6	(0.7)	466	(4.8)	42.9	(1.0)	487	(4.4)
Russian Federation	2.3	(0.2)	431	(13.0)	12.9	(0.5)	429	(5.9)	33.5	(0.8)	461	(4.1)	47.5	(0.9)	479	(4.3)
Sweden	4.2	(0.3)	513	(8.7)	15.2	(0.6)	507	(4.7)	30.6	(0.7)	513	(3.0)	47.8	(0.9)	527	(2.4)
Switzerland	7.1	(0.4)	513	(9.9)	21.5	(0.8)	494	(5.3)	37.5	(0.7)	498	(4.4)	29.1	(0.8)	501	(4.8)
Thailand	2.0	(0.2)	389	(10.3)	22.4	(0.8)	401	(3.7)	41.6	(1.1)	432	(3.5)	33.3	(1.1)	452	(3.5)
United Kingdom	4.2	(0.5)	528	(12.3)	16.8	(0.9)	506	(6.3)	32.2	(1.1)	517	(4.6)	46.1	(1.2)	541	(4.7)
United States	12.7	(0.9)	530	(7.3)	28.0	(0.9)	507	(6.7)	25.6	(1.2)	512	(7.3)	18.9	(0.9)	512	(8.6)
OECD average	*10.0*	*(0.4)*	*514*	*(4.3)*	*23.9*	*(0.4)*	*494*	*(3.5)*	*29.6*	*(0.6)*	*497*	*(2.8)*	*28.3*	*(0.5)*	*497*	*(2.6)*
OECD total	*7.1*	*(0.1)*	*510*	*(1.7)*	*21.2*	*(0.2)*	*494*	*(1.2)*	*33.2*	*(0.2)*	*503*	*(0.8)*	*34.3*	*(0.2)*	*509*	*(0.9)*
Netherlands[2]	5.4	(0.5)	564	(10.0)	19.7	(0.9)	531	(5.9)	40.1	(1.1)	537	(3.7)	33.3	(1.1)	525	(4.3)

1. Figures in bold indicate that there is a significant difference between the performance of students who reported "almost never" and those who reported "almost always".

2. Response rate is too low to ensure comparability (see Annex A3).

Table 4.4.
**Index of engagement in reading and performance on the combined reading literacy scale,
by national quarters of the index**

See next page

Table 4.4
Index of engagement in reading and performance on the combined reading literacy scale, by national quarters of the index
Results based on students' self-reports

	Index of engagement in reading[1]													
	All students		Males		Females		Bottom quarter		Second quarter		Third quarter		Top quarter	
	Mean index	S.E.	Mean index	S.E.	Mean index	S.E.	Mean index	S.E.	Mean index	S.E.	Mean index	S.E.	Mean index	S.E.
Albania	0.36	(0.01)	0.22	(0.02)	0.48	(0.01)	-0.47	(0.01)	0.14	(0.00)	0.55	(0.00)	1.22	(0.02)
Argentina	-0.13	(0.05)	-0.35	(0.04)	0.04	(0.06)	-1.41	(0.04)	-0.47	(0.01)	0.15	(0.01)	1.20	(0.03)
Australia	-0.04	(0.03)	-0.18	(0.04)	0.11	(0.03)	-1.29	(0.02)	-0.33	(0.01)	0.28	(0.01)	1.18	(0.02)
Austria	-0.08	(0.03)	-0.35	(0.03)	0.17	(0.03)	-1.39	(0.02)	-0.44	(0.01)	0.29	(0.01)	1.20	(0.02)
Belgium	-0.28	(0.02)	-0.48	(0.03)	-0.07	(0.02)	-1.61	(0.02)	-0.63	(0.01)	0.05	(0.01)	1.06	(0.02)
Brazil	0.11	(0.02)	-0.17	(0.02)	0.36	(0.02)	-1.02	(0.02)	-0.21	(0.01)	0.37	(0.01)	1.31	(0.02)
Bulgaria	0.19	(0.03)	-0.04	(0.03)	0.43	(0.04)	-0.91	(0.02)	-0.15	(0.00)	0.43	(0.01)	1.40	(0.02)
Canada	0.01	(0.01)	-0.23	(0.02)	0.24	(0.01)	-1.34	(0.01)	-0.31	(0.00)	0.35	(0.00)	1.32	(0.01)
Chile	-0.11	(0.02)	-0.35	(0.03)	0.10	(0.03)	-1.38	(0.02)	-0.45	(0.01)	0.18	(0.01)	1.21	(0.02)
Czech Republic	0.02	(0.02)	-0.29	(0.03)	0.29	(0.02)	-1.17	(0.02)	-0.25	(0.01)	0.32	(0.01)	1.16	(0.02)
Denmark	0.26	(0.02)	0.02	(0.02)	0.50	(0.03)	-1.00	(0.02)	-0.05	(0.01)	0.56	(0.01)	1.53	(0.02)
Finland	0.46	(0.02)	0.08	(0.03)	0.82	(0.02)	-0.79	(0.02)	0.14	(0.01)	0.73	(0.01)	1.75	(0.02)
France	-0.18	(0.02)	-0.33	(0.03)	-0.03	(0.02)	-1.48	(0.02)	-0.45	(0.01)	0.16	(0.01)	1.04	(0.02)
Germany	-0.26	(0.02)	-0.53	(0.03)	0.01	(0.02)	-1.67	(0.02)	-0.62	(0.01)	0.16	(0.01)	1.09	(0.02)
Greece	-0.09	(0.02)	-0.17	(0.02)	0.00	(0.02)	-0.99	(0.01)	-0.30	(0.00)	0.12	(0.00)	0.83	(0.02)
Hong Kong-China	0.39	(0.02)	0.30	(0.02)	0.49	(0.02)	-0.56	(0.01)	0.14	(0.00)	0.59	(0.00)	1.41	(0.02)
Hungary	0.03	(0.02)	-0.15	(0.03)	0.21	(0.02)	-1.09	(0.02)	-0.22	(0.00)	0.31	(0.01)	1.12	(0.02)
Iceland	0.27	(0.01)	0.08	(0.02)	0.46	(0.02)	-0.89	(0.02)	-0.03	(0.01)	0.52	(0.01)	1.49	(0.02)
Indonesia	0.29	(0.02)	0.19	(0.02)	0.39	(0.02)	-0.61	(0.02)	0.04	(0.01)	0.49	(0.01)	1.26	(0.02)
Ireland	-0.20	(0.02)	-0.43	(0.03)	0.03	(0.03)	-1.49	(0.02)	-0.48	(0.01)	0.13	(0.01)	1.06	(0.02)
Israel	0.13	(0.06)	-0.12	(0.05)	0.31	(0.07)	-1.21	(0.04)	-0.23	(0.01)	0.44	(0.01)	1.54	(0.04)
Italy	-0.08	(0.02)	-0.27	(0.03)	0.10	(0.02)	-1.28	(0.02)	-0.36	(0.01)	0.22	(0.01)	1.09	(0.02)
Japan	0.20	(0.03)	0.11	(0.03)	0.28	(0.03)	-0.99	(0.01)	-0.19	(0.01)	0.43	(0.01)	1.53	(0.02)
Korea	0.21	(0.02)	0.19	(0.03)	0.23	(0.03)	-0.94	(0.02)	-0.11	(0.00)	0.45	(0.00)	1.44	(0.02)
Latvia	-0.04	(0.02)	-0.27	(0.04)	0.17	(0.02)	-1.04	(0.02)	-0.27	(0.01)	0.21	(0.01)	0.93	(0.03)
Liechtenstein	-0.13	(0.05)	-0.36	(0.07)	0.13	(0.09)	-1.35	(0.06)	-0.50	(0.02)	0.22	(0.02)	1.15	(0.05)
Luxembourg	-0.19	(0.02)	-0.39	(0.03)	0.01	(0.02)	-1.52	(0.02)	-0.51	(0.01)	0.16	(0.01)	1.12	(0.02)
FYR Macedonia	0.42	(0.02)	0.29	(0.02)	0.56	(0.02)	-0.63	(0.02)	0.13	(0.01)	0.64	(0.00)	1.54	(0.02)
Mexico	0.07	(0.01)	-0.03	(0.02)	0.17	(0.02)	-0.85	(0.02)	-0.17	(0.00)	0.28	(0.00)	1.03	(0.02)
New Zealand	0.05	(0.02)	-0.09	(0.02)	0.20	(0.02)	-1.12	(0.02)	-0.21	(0.01)	0.33	(0.01)	1.22	(0.02)
Norway	0.09	(0.02)	-0.16	(0.03)	0.35	(0.02)	-1.07	(0.02)	-0.25	(0.01)	0.35	(0.01)	1.34	(0.02)
Peru	0.32	(0.02)	0.29	(0.02)	0.36	(0.03)	-0.66	(0.01)	0.04	(0.00)	0.52	(0.00)	1.39	(0.02)
Poland	-0.10	(0.02)	-0.28	(0.03)	0.09	(0.02)	-1.16	(0.02)	-0.35	(0.01)	0.13	(0.01)	0.99	(0.02)
Portugal	0.13	(0.02)	-0.11	(0.03)	0.36	(0.02)	-0.96	(0.02)	-0.11	(0.00)	0.40	(0.00)	1.21	(0.02)
Russian Federation	0.17	(0.02)	-0.02	(0.02)	0.37	(0.02)	-0.89	(0.01)	-0.09	(0.00)	0.43	(0.00)	1.24	(0.01)
Spain	-0.23	(0.02)	-0.38	(0.03)	-0.09	(0.03)	-1.46	(0.02)	-0.49	(0.01)	0.09	(0.01)	0.95	(0.02)
Sweden	0.14	(0.02)	-0.08	(0.03)	0.37	(0.02)	-1.09	(0.02)	-0.20	(0.01)	0.43	(0.01)	1.42	(0.02)
Switzerland	0.00	(0.03)	-0.31	(0.04)	0.31	(0.03)	-1.43	(0.02)	-0.32	(0.01)	0.37	(0.01)	1.36	(0.02)
Thailand	0.31	(0.02)	0.15	(0.02)	0.43	(0.02)	-0.51	(0.01)	0.11	(0.00)	0.50	(0.00)	1.16	(0.02)
United Kingdom	-0.10	(0.02)	-0.24	(0.02)	0.03	(0.03)	-1.33	(0.02)	-0.37	(0.00)	0.22	(0.01)	1.08	(0.02)
United States	-0.14	(0.03)	-0.32	(0.04)	0.04	(0.04)	-1.46	(0.02)	-0.45	(0.01)	0.17	(0.01)	1.19	(0.03)
OECD average	*0.00*	*(0.01)*	*-0.19*	*(0.01)*	*0.19*	*(0.01)*	*-1.25*	*(0.00)*	*-0.30*	*(0.00)*	*0.29*	*(0.00)*	*1.23*	*(0.00)*
OECD total	*-0.05*	*(0.01)*	*-0.20*	*(0.01)*	*0.11*	*(0.01)*	*-1.30*	*(0.01)*	*-0.34*	*(0.00)*	*0.25*	*(0.00)*	*1.20*	*(0.01)*
Netherlands[3]	-0.17	(0.04)	-0.38	(0.04)	0.04	(0.04)	-1.40	(0.02)	-0.48	(0.01)	0.12	(0.01)	1.09	(0.02)

1. For the definition of the index see Annex A1.
2. For explained variation see Annex A2. Unit changes marked in bold are statistically significant. Where bottom and top quarters are marked in bold this indicates that their difference is statistically significant.
3. Response rate is too low to ensure comparability (see Annex A3).

Table 4.4 (continued)

Index of engagement in reading and performance on the combined reading literacy scale, by national quarters of the index

Results based on students' self-reports

| | Performance on the combined reading literacy scale, by national quarters of the index of engagement in reading[2] | | | | | | | | Change in the combined reading literacy score per unit of the index of engagement[2] | |
| | Bottom quarter | | Second quarter | | Third quarter | | Top quarter | | | |
	Mean score	S.E.	Mean score	S.E.	Mean score	S.E.	Mean score	S.E	Change	S.E.
Albania	323	(4.5)	351	(6.6)	367	(3.9)	376	(3.8)	26.4	(3.0)
Argentina	391	(9.9)	400	(7.6)	437	(11.1)	464	(10.3)	27.5	(2.4)
Australia	472	(3.8)	507	(4.1)	548	(4.2)	589	(4.0)	42.5	(2.1)
Austria	458	(3.2)	489	(3.3)	525	(3.1)	559	(3.4)	36.8	(1.8)
Belgium	462	(4.3)	493	(4.2)	524	(4.8)	565	(4.5)	35.8	(1.7)
Brazil	370	(4.2)	386	(3.9)	405	(3.9)	431	(4.8)	23.8	(2.1)
Bulgaria	392	(5.6)	420	(6.5)	451	(5.2)	480	(7.0)	35.7	(2.7)
Canada	485	(2.0)	519	(1.9)	551	(1.7)	586	(2.1)	35.1	(0.9)
Chile	378	(3.8)	393	(4.2)	422	(4.5)	450	(4.5)	26.8	(1.5)
Czech Republic	451	(3.0)	485	(2.6)	521	(2.9)	548	(3.2)	38.1	(1.6)
Denmark	440	(4.0)	486	(3.6)	516	(3.7)	551	(3.0)	41.0	(1.8)
Finland	487	(4.2)	533	(3.7)	565	(2.4)	603	(2.7)	42.5	(1.5)
France	467	(3.6)	494	(3.6)	519	(3.5)	552	(2.9)	31.2	(1.5)
Germany	444	(4.2)	469	(2.9)	513	(3.5)	551	(3.3)	37.6	(1.8)
Greece	444	(5.4)	469	(6.3)	480	(5.2)	508	(6.0)	33.3	(3.2)
Hong Kong-China	486	(4.5)	520	(3.3)	538	(3.1)	560	(3.8)	34.9	(2.3)
Hungary	429	(4.1)	466	(5.3)	496	(5.0)	532	(4.7)	43.7	(2.1)
Iceland	451	(3.2)	496	(3.1)	528	(2.9)	561	(3.3)	42.1	(1.7)
Indonesia	351	(3.9)	368	(4.5)	380	(5.1)	387	(5.2)	17.6	(2.5)
Ireland	482	(3.7)	507	(4.2)	541	(3.7)	580	(3.8)	35.2	(1.8)
Israel	434	(10.4)	444	(11.8)	465	(9.2)	493	(8.0)	17.6	(2.7)
Italy	454	(4.4)	475	(3.5)	500	(3.8)	525	(2.9)	28.5	(1.9)
Japan	488	(5.9)	512	(5.5)	534	(4.9)	562	(4.7)	26.9	(1.7)
Korea	490	(3.3)	517	(2.9)	536	(2.7)	556	(2.7)	25.0	(1.3)
Latvia	417	(6.6)	449	(5.3)	472	(5.1)	501	(7.7)	36.2	(5.0)
Liechtenstein	427	(8.7)	452	(9.8)	516	(9.3)	536	(9.7)	43.8	(4.8)
Luxembourg	420	(3.0)	436	(3.2)	452	(3.5)	486	(3.5)	22.0	(2.2)
FYR Macedonia	353	(3.6)	379	(3.3)	385	(3.3)	391	(3.1)	12.3	(1.9)
Mexico	392	(4.1)	415	(4.2)	428	(3.8)	452	(4.6)	26.9	(2.3)
New Zealand	481	(3.7)	516	(3.9)	546	(4.0)	583	(4.2)	39.7	(2.0)
Norway	447	(5.2)	489	(3.7)	523	(3.3)	569	(3.5)	47.2	(2.3)
Peru	314	(6.8)	324	(4.9)	338	(4.5)	345	(5.6)	11.6	(3.1)
Poland	446	(5.9)	471	(5.0)	490	(4.8)	520	(6.3)	30.8	(2.9)
Portugal	428	(4.7)	461	(5.1)	480	(5.4)	516	(4.7)	35.1	(2.1)
Russian Federation	430	(5.2)	454	(4.1)	476	(4.5)	489	(4.7)	24.8	(1.7)
Spain	453	(3.6)	480	(3.0)	503	(2.7)	539	(2.6)	32.4	(1.4)
Sweden	463	(3.3)	498	(3.4)	533	(3.2)	574	(3.2)	41.5	(1.7)
Switzerland	435	(4.3)	475	(4.4)	514	(4.5)	557	(5.2)	41.2	(1.9)
Thailand	395	(3.9)	422	(3.2)	442	(3.9)	465	(4.2)	41.3	(2.5)
United Kingdom	477	(3.1)	510	(4.0)	542	(3.3)	575	(4.2)	38.0	(1.7)
United States	460	(7.5)	494	(7.7)	525	(7.3)	552	(7.0)	29.3	(2.3)
OECD average	457	(0.8)	485	(0.8)	515	(0.7)	552	(0.7)	35.7	(0.4)
OECD total	460	(2.2)	487	(2.0)	512	(2.3)	546	(2.0)	31.0	(0.9)
Netherlands[3]	487	(4.4)	519	(4.3)	545	(4.3)	578	(4.5)	34.1	(2.2)

1. For the definition of the index see Annex A1.

2. For explained variation see Annex A2. Unit changes marked in bold are statistically significant. Where bottom and top quarters are marked in bold this indicates that their difference is statistically significant.

3. Response rate is too low to ensure comparability (see Annex A3).

© OECD/UNESCO-UIS 2003

Table 4.5

Time students usually spend each day reading for enjoyment and performance on the combined reading literacy scale

Results based on students' self-reports

	Students report not reading for enjoyment[1]				Students report reading 30 minutes or less each day				Students report reading between 30 and 60 minutes each day				Students report reading between 1 and 2 hours each day				Students report reading more than 2 hours each day[1]			
	%	S.E.	Mean score	S.E.	%	S.E.	Mean score	S.E.	%	S.E.	Mean score	S.E.	%	S.E.	Mean score	S.E.	%	S.E.	Mean score	S.E.
Albania	8.6	(0.6)	**358**	(8.5)	19.1	(0.7)	372	(4.8)	30.6	(0.9)	373	(4.6)	27.6	(0.9)	373	(3.9)	14.0	(0.5)	**335**	(4.7)
Argentina	29.3	(0.9)	402	(11.6)	30.8	(1.9)	421	(7.2)	21.5	(1.7)	452	(11.3)	11.4	(0.7)	445	(10.8)	7.0	(0.7)	437	(15.8)
Australia	33.1	(1.2)	**484**	(3.9)	30.5	(0.9)	537	(3.9)	20.5	(0.9)	564	(4.7)	11.8	(0.5)	575	(5.5)	4.1	(0.3)	**558**	(9.8)
Austria	41.1	(1.1)	**477**	(2.5)	28.7	(0.8)	528	(3.0)	18.1	(0.7)	539	(4.2)	9.0	(0.5)	540	(5.6)	3.1	(0.4)	**532**	(7.9)
Belgium	42.2	(0.9)	**487**	(3.4)	24.7	(0.7)	534	(4.1)	21.4	(0.6)	541	(4.1)	9.1	(0.4)	546	(6.5)	2.6	(0.3)	511	(12.1)
Brazil	19.3	(1.0)	**385**	(3.8)	21.3	(0.8)	393	(4.5)	31.4	(1.1)	409	(4.2)	16.8	(0.7)	410	(5.8)	11.2	(0.6)	**410**	(5.3)
Bulgaria	31.3	(1.0)	**410**	(5.3)	19.0	(0.7)	449	(5.9)	20.4	(0.8)	464	(5.6)	19.6	(0.8)	454	(6.3)	9.8	(0.6)	**447**	(7.4)
Canada	32.7	(0.4)	**498**	(1.6)	33.7	(0.4)	544	(1.8)	20.4	(0.4)	564	(2.1)	9.6	(0.3)	575	(3.4)	3.6	(0.2)	550	(4.9)
Chile	26.3	(0.8)	**389**	(3.6)	27.8	(0.8)	407	(4.2)	26.9	(0.7)	430	(4.7)	12.2	(0.6)	429	(5.5)	6.8	(0.4)	**432**	(6.8)
Czech Republic	26.2	(0.8)	**458**	(3.0)	29.7	(0.8)	509	(2.9)	25.7	(0.7)	524	(2.8)	12.9	(0.6)	521	(4.3)	5.5	(0.5)	**518**	(6.2)
Denmark	26.8	(0.8)	**464**	(3.3)	36.1	(1.0)	512	(3.3)	23.3	(0.6)	519	(3.5)	9.4	(0.5)	520	(5.7)	4.4	(0.4)	487	(8.5)
Finland	22.4	(0.7)	**498**	(3.4)	29.1	(0.7)	542	(3.2)	26.3	(0.7)	568	(3.2)	18.2	(0.6)	577	(4.1)	4.1	(0.3)	**584**	(6.0)
France	30.0	(0.8)	**472**	(3.4)	27.5	(0.7)	519	(2.9)	28.6	(0.8)	533	(3.1)	10.6	(0.5)	539	(4.3)	3.4	(0.3)	514	(10.0)
Germany	41.6	(0.9)	**459**	(3.0)	27.0	(0.7)	518	(3.6)	18.0	(0.6)	532	(3.9)	8.8	(0.4)	543	(4.4)	4.6	(0.3)	**501**	(7.4)
Greece	22.0	(0.8)	**459**	(5.9)	26.6	(0.7)	486	(5.8)	22.7	(0.8)	501	(6.3)	20.0	(0.7)	478	(4.7)	8.7	(0.5)	454	(8.0)
Hong Kong-China	24.1	(0.9)	**493**	(4.7)	35.8	(0.8)	533	(2.7)	23.2	(0.7)	545	(3.5)	11.5	(0.5)	540	(5.0)	5.4	(0.4)	**536**	(6.9)
Hungary	26.0	(0.9)	**448**	(4.3)	28.3	(0.7)	494	(4.2)	24.2	(0.8)	504	(5.1)	13.4	(0.6)	501	(6.3)	8.1	(0.5)	**468**	(6.9)
Iceland	29.8	(0.7)	**466**	(2.9)	38.0	(0.8)	519	(2.2)	22.5	(0.7)	543	(3.5)	6.9	(0.4)	539	(6.1)	2.9	(0.3)	528	(10.7)
Indonesia	13.5	(1.1)	**364**	(5.3)	36.0	(1.3)	384	(4.4)	26.0	(1.3)	396	(5.2)	16.7	(1.0)	405	(6.9)	7.8	(0.6)	**404**	(9.0)
Ireland	33.4	(0.9)	**491**	(4.1)	30.9	(0.7)	536	(3.8)	20.4	(0.7)	558	(3.9)	11.6	(0.5)	556	(5.2)	3.8	(0.4)	541	(11.4)
Israel	37.0	(2.4)	**450**	(9.3)	20.2	(0.8)	475	(9.2)	19.1	(1.1)	477	(8.6)	16.3	(1.1)	464	(12.2)	7.4	(0.7)	458	(14.0)
Italy	30.7	(1.1)	**461**	(3.7)	30.2	(0.6)	498	(3.3)	22.5	(0.7)	509	(3.6)	13.0	(0.7)	502	(4.7)	3.7	(0.3)	509	(9.6)
Japan	55.0	(1.2)	**514**	(5.2)	17.8	(0.8)	539	(5.5)	15.4	(0.7)	537	(6.4)	8.2	(0.4)	541	(6.4)	3.5	(0.3)	530	(8.8)
Korea	30.6	(0.8)	**503**	(2.7)	29.6	(0.7)	529	(3.1)	21.9	(0.7)	536	(3.2)	12.0	(0.5)	544	(3.5)	6.0	(0.4)	539	(5.2)
Latvia	18.0	(1.1)	**409**	(8.6)	25.7	(1.1)	462	(6.2)	29.5	(1.2)	482	(5.9)	19.7	(0.9)	476	(5.7)	7.3	(0.5)	**470**	(7.6)
Liechtenstein	40.0	(2.8)	**447**	(6.4)	34.2	(2.7)	504	(9.5)	16.6	(2.2)	536	(11.4)	5.2	(1.2)	c	c	4.0	(1.1)	c	c
Luxembourg	38.4	(0.8)	**437**	(2.2)	25.6	(0.7)	460	(3.7)	19.6	(0.7)	463	(3.6)	11.9	(0.6)	462	(6.1)	4.5	(0.4)	465	(9.0)
FYR Macedonia	11.8	(0.6)	**383**	(3.7)	19.9	(0.7)	402	(4.2)	29.6	(0.7)	392	(3.3)	24.1	(0.8)	385	(3.1)	14.6	(0.6)	**358**	(4.5)
Mexico	13.6	(0.7)	420	(6.0)	43.7	(1.1)	423	(3.6)	27.2	(0.7)	439	(3.9)	11.5	(0.6)	426	(5.4)	4.0	(0.4)	406	(7.6)
New Zealand	29.9	(0.9)	**494**	(4.1)	36.6	(0.7)	544	(3.4)	19.4	(0.7)	563	(4.4)	10.4	(0.6)	570	(6.5)	3.7	(0.3)	**553**	(8.0)
Norway	35.3	(0.8)	**471**	(3.9)	34.7	(0.8)	528	(3.3)	20.1	(0.7)	538	(4.3)	7.7	(0.4)	536	(5.7)	2.2	(0.3)	506	(11.8)
Peru	8.7	(0.6)	**345**	(7.2)	23.6	(0.8)	330	(5.4)	32.9	(0.8)	345	(4.3)	21.3	(0.7)	330	(5.2)	13.4	(0.6)	**323**	(6.5)
Poland	24.2	(1.1)	**449**	(4.9)	22.7	(0.9)	488	(5.4)	28.7	(0.8)	502	(5.1)	16.5	(0.7)	498	(6.3)	8.0	(0.7)	497	(10.0)
Portugal	18.4	(0.8)	**432**	(5.1)	39.1	(0.8)	474	(4.3)	26.5	(0.9)	495	(5.3)	12.4	(0.6)	494	(6.0)	3.7	(0.4)	468	(10.7)
Russian Federation	19.4	(0.7)	**434**	(5.9)	24.6	(0.7)	455	(5.2)	25.8	(0.6)	474	(4.2)	17.4	(0.6)	483	(3.6)	12.7	(0.5)	**481**	(5.4)
Spain	31.8	(0.9)	**460**	(3.3)	32.9	(0.7)	505	(3.1)	24.2	(0.8)	519	(3.0)	8.8	(0.4)	514	(5.1)	2.4	(0.2)	499	(10.1)
Sweden	36.0	(1.0)	**483**	(2.8)	30.8	(0.8)	527	(3.6)	21.0	(0.6)	547	(3.1)	8.8	(0.5)	556	(4.9)	3.4	(0.3)	529	(8.8)
Switzerland	35.2	(1.2)	**450**	(4.1)	33.0	(0.8)	515	(4.8)	20.5	(0.6)	533	(4.7)	8.3	(0.5)	533	(7.8)	3.0	(0.3)	499	(12.8)
Thailand	11.9	(0.9)	**408**	(3.8)	39.8	(0.8)	431	(3.3)	25.9	(0.7)	444	(4.1)	16.1	(0.7)	445	(4.0)	6.3	(0.4)	**450**	(6.9)
United Kingdom	29.1	(0.7)	**485**	(3.0)	35.7	(0.8)	533	(3.1)	22.9	(0.7)	559	(3.5)	9.4	(0.5)	556	(5.6)	2.9	(0.3)	528	(9.8)
United States	40.7	(1.3)	**479**	(7.0)	31.2	(1.1)	530	(7.3)	16.2	(0.8)	531	(8.4)	8.1	(0.6)	539	(12.2)	3.9	(0.5)	511	(10.8)
OECD average	*31.7*	*(0.2)*	*474*	*(0.8)*	*30.9*	*(0.1)*	*513*	*(0.8)*	*22.2*	*(0.2)*	*527*	*(0.9)*	*11.1*	*(0.1)*	*526*	*(1.0)*	*4.2*	*(0.1)*	*506*	*(2.0)*
OECD total	*35.4*	*(0.5)*	*481*	*(2.2)*	*29.8*	*(0.3)*	*511*	*(2.3)*	*20.6*	*(0.3)*	*522*	*(2.0)*	*10.0*	*(0.2)*	*524*	*(2.7)*	*4.1*	*(0.1)*	*505*	*(3.9)*
Netherlands[2]	43.3	(1.5)	508	(3.7)	31.4	(1.1)	554	(4.5)	16.7	(0.9)	562	(5.3)	5.8	(0.7)	549	(9.6)	2.9	(0.4)	530	(12.6)

1. Figures in bold indicate that there is a significant difference between the performance of students who reported "not reading for enjoyment" and those who reported "reading more than 2 hours each day".
2. Response rate is too low to ensure comparability (see Annex A3).

Table 4.6.
**Index of interest in reading and performance on the combined reading literacy scale,
by national quarters of the index**

See next page

Table 4.6
Index of interest in reading and performance on the combined reading literacy scale, by national quarters of the index
Results based on students' self-reports

| | Index of interest in reading[1] | | | | | | | | | | | | | |
| | All students | | Males | | Females | | Bottom quarter | | Second quarter | | Third quarter | | Top quarter | |
	Mean index	S.E.	Mean index	S.E.	Mean index	S.E.	Mean index	S.E.	Mean index	S.E.	Mean index	S.E.	Mean index	S.E.
Albania	0.57	(0.02)	0.41	(0.02)	0.72	(0.02)	-0.34	(0.02)	0.33	(0.01)	0.82	(0.01)	1.48	(0.01)
Australia	-0.02	(0.02)	-0.16	(0.02)	0.13	(0.03)	-1.03	(0.02)	-0.25	(0.01)	0.21	(0.01)	1.00	(0.02)
Austria	-0.09	(0.03)	-0.41	(0.02)	0.20	(0.03)	-1.44	(0.01)	-0.44	(0.01)	0.20	(0.01)	1.31	(0.02)
Belgium (Fl.)	-0.32	(0.02)	-0.54	(0.03)	-0.07	(0.03)	-1.60	(0.01)	-0.55	(0.01)	0.01	(0.01)	0.86	(0.02)
Brazil	0.31	(0.02)	0.12	(0.02)	0.46	(0.02)	-0.70	(0.02)	0.06	(0.01)	0.48	(0.01)	1.39	(0.02)
Bulgaria	0.18	(0.02)	-0.03	(0.02)	0.39	(0.03)	-0.96	(0.02)	-0.14	(0.01)	0.43	(0.01)	1.38	(0.01)
Chile	-0.01	(0.02)	-0.17	(0.02)	0.13	(0.02)	-1.05	(0.02)	-0.26	(0.01)	0.21	(0.00)	1.07	(0.02)
Czech Republic	0.11	(0.02)	-0.31	(0.03)	0.48	(0.03)	-1.29	(0.02)	-0.27	(0.01)	0.43	(0.01)	1.58	(0.01)
Denmark	0.19	(0.02)	-0.07	(0.02)	0.45	(0.03)	-1.13	(0.02)	-0.19	(0.01)	0.50	(0.01)	1.58	(0.01)
Finland	0.19	(0.02)	-0.26	(0.02)	0.61	(0.02)	-1.12	(0.01)	-0.18	(0.01)	0.48	(0.01)	1.58	(0.01)
Germany	-0.06	(0.02)	-0.38	(0.03)	0.25	(0.02)	-1.44	(0.01)	-0.43	(0.01)	0.24	(0.01)	1.38	(0.02)
Hong Kong-China	0.33	(0.01)	0.20	(0.03)	0.46	(0.02)	-0.69	(0.01)	0.08	(0.01)	0.47	(0.01)	1.46	(0.01)
Hungary	-0.06	(0.02)	-0.32	(0.03)	0.20	(0.03)	-1.43	(0.02)	-0.43	(0.01)	0.22	(0.01)	1.40	(0.01)
Iceland	-0.06	(0.02)	-0.26	(0.02)	0.14	(0.02)	-1.20	(0.02)	-0.35	(0.01)	0.17	(0.01)	1.14	(0.02)
Ireland	0.04	(0.03)	-0.24	(0.03)	0.32	(0.03)	-1.40	(0.01)	-0.33	(0.01)	0.37	(0.01)	1.54	(0.01)
Israel	-0.03	(0.05)	-0.27	(0.03)	0.14	(0.06)	-1.39	(0.01)	-0.33	(0.01)	0.29	(0.01)	1.33	(0.02)
Italy	-0.11	(0.03)	-0.39	(0.03)	0.18	(0.03)	-1.43	(0.01)	-0.44	(0.01)	0.22	(0.01)	1.22	(0.01)
Korea	-0.31	(0.02)	-0.32	(0.03)	-0.29	(0.04)	-1.47	(0.01)	-0.62	(0.00)	-0.11	(0.01)	0.95	(0.02)
Latvia	0.23	(0.02)	-0.04	(0.02)	0.50	(0.03)	-0.91	(0.02)	-0.12	(0.01)	0.49	(0.01)	1.48	(0.01)
Liechtenstein	-0.07	(0.05)	-0.28	(0.07)	0.15	(0.08)	-1.33	(0.04)	-0.38	(0.02)	0.18	(0.02)	1.23	(0.06)
Luxembourg	-0.07	(0.02)	-0.28	(0.03)	0.14	(0.03)	-1.35	(0.02)	-0.39	(0.01)	0.20	(0.01)	1.25	(0.02)
FYR Macedonia	0.47	(0.01)	0.27	(0.02)	0.67	(0.02)	-0.57	(0.02)	0.21	(0.01)	0.73	(0.01)	1.51	(0.01)
Mexico	0.15	(0.01)	0.04	(0.02)	0.25	(0.02)	-0.64	(0.02)	-0.05	(0.00)	0.28	(0.00)	0.99	(0.01)
New Zealand	0.07	(0.02)	-0.10	(0.03)	0.25	(0.02)	-1.16	(0.02)	-0.25	(0.01)	0.33	(0.01)	1.38	(0.02)
Norway	0.01	(0.02)	-0.30	(0.03)	0.33	(0.03)	-1.38	(0.01)	-0.36	(0.01)	0.32	(0.01)	1.46	(0.01)
Portugal	0.23	(0.02)	-0.14	(0.02)	0.57	(0.02)	-1.00	(0.01)	-0.05	(0.01)	0.49	(0.01)	1.46	(0.01)
Russian Federation	0.15	(0.02)	-0.07	(0.02)	0.35	(0.03)	-1.15	(0.02)	-0.21	(0.01)	0.44	(0.01)	1.51	(0.01)
Sweden	0.09	(0.01)	-0.08	(0.02)	0.26	(0.02)	-0.85	(0.02)	-0.10	(0.00)	0.26	(0.00)	1.07	(0.02)
Switzerland	0.04	(0.02)	-0.29	(0.03)	0.36	(0.03)	-1.24	(0.02)	-0.28	(0.01)	0.30	(0.01)	1.39	(0.02)
Thailand	0.35	(0.01)	0.25	(0.02)	0.43	(0.02)	-0.40	(0.01)	0.15	(0.00)	0.48	(0.00)	1.19	(0.02)
United States	0.02	(0.03)	-0.16	(0.04)	0.19	(0.03)	-1.22	(0.02)	-0.29	(0.01)	0.27	(0.01)	1.34	(0.02)
OECD average	*0.00*	*(0.00)*	*-0.24*	*(0.01)*	*0.26*	*(0.01)*	*-1.23*	*(0.00)*	*-0.31*	*(0.00)*	*0.28*	*(0.00)*	*1.30*	*(0.00)*
OECD total	*-0.01*	*(0.01)*	*-0.20*	*(0.02)*	*0.19*	*(0.02)*	*-1.20*	*(0.01)*	*-0.31*	*(0.00)*	*0.24*	*(0.00)*	*1.25*	*(0.01)*
Netherlands[3]	-0.17	(0.04)	-0.52	(0.04)	0.18	(0.04)	-1.53	(0.02)	-0.54	(0.01)	0.13	(0.01)	1.27	(0.02)

1. For the definition of the index see Annex A1.
2. For explained variation see Annex A2. Unit changes marked in bold are statistically significant. Where bottom and top quarters are marked in bold this indicates that their difference is statistically significant.
3. Response rate is too low to ensure comparability (see Annex A3).

Table 4.6 (continued)
Index of interest in reading and performance on the combined reading literacy scale, by national quarters of the index
Results based on students' self-reports

| | Performance on the combined reading literacy scale, by national quarters of the index of interest in reading[2] | | | | | | | | Change in the combined reading literacy score per unit of the index of interest in reading[2] | |
| | Bottom quarter | | Second quarter | | Third quarter | | Top quarter | | | |
	Mean score	S.E.	Mean score	S.E.	Mean score	S.E.	Mean score	S.E.	Change	S.E.
Albania	329	(5.5)	356	(3.6)	364	(4.1)	367	(5.5)	21.4	(3.23)
Australia	495	(4.0)	505	(4.3)	540	(4.7)	588	(4.6)	41.1	(2.37)
Austria	481	(3.1)	485	(3.5)	514	(3.4)	557	(3.5)	28.5	(1.48)
Belgium (Fl.)	515	(4.5)	516	(6.1)	544	(5.3)	570	(6.0)	22.6	(2.05)
Brazil	397	(4.3)	395	(3.5)	399	(4.5)	419	(4.3)	10.0	(2.11)
Bulgaria	412	(5.1)	420	(6.3)	438	(5.8)	468	(6.7)	22.7	(2.40)
Chile	396	(3.6)	405	(3.9)	421	(4.6)	434	(5.8)	19.0	(2.15)
Czech Republic	471	(2.6)	484	(3.0)	512	(3.2)	548	(3.1)	26.7	(1.29)
Denmark	472	(3.3)	479	(3.4)	503	(3.6)	551	(3.5)	29.6	(1.58)
Finland	502	(2.7)	527	(4.6)	564	(2.8)	599	(3.2)	36.1	(1.18)
Germany	468	(3.7)	471	(3.7)	500	(4.2)	552	(3.8)	30.0	(1.65)
Hong Kong-China	501	(3.8)	520	(3.8)	527	(3.2)	558	(3.5)	25.3	(1.70)
Hungary	451	(3.8)	466	(5.4)	489	(5.2)	529	(4.4)	27.8	(1.55)
Iceland	475	(3.2)	493	(3.1)	514	(3.4)	560	(3.3)	35.3	(1.85)
Ireland	495	(3.8)	503	(4.0)	536	(4.1)	580	(3.7)	30.0	(1.46)
Israel	472	(9.3)	450	(9.5)	462	(10.1)	492	(7.8)	7.7	(3.21)
Italy	463	(4.2)	474	(4.2)	490	(3.5)	524	(3.3)	22.5	(1.51)
Korea	493	(2.8)	519	(3.2)	536	(3.5)	551	(2.6)	22.6	(1.27)
Latvia	429	(6.6)	440	(6.5)	464	(5.3)	512	(5.6)	32.5	(2.21)
Liechtenstein	454	(10.0)	463	(9.6)	494	(10.2)	528	(10.8)	29.5	(5.13)
Luxembourg	444	(3.0)	438	(3.5)	451	(3.0)	490	(3.4)	17.0	(1.77)
FYR Macedonia	363	(3.3)	377	(3.3)	376	(4.1)	397	(2.9)	13.2	(2.08)
Mexico	422	(4.1)	420	(3.9)	418	(3.7)	433	(5.0)	8.8	(2.61)
New Zealand	506	(3.5)	509	(4.5)	534	(4.8)	593	(4.0)	34.5	(1.70)
Norway	473	(5.0)	487	(4.0)	516	(3.7)	569	(3.2)	34.5	(1.85)
Portugal	442	(4.7)	454	(6.1)	473	(4.7)	513	(4.7)	26.7	(1.61)
Russian Federation	440	(5.1)	453	(3.5)	468	(4.8)	498	(5.3)	20.4	(1.16)
Sweden	479	(3.1)	501	(3.2)	524	(3.3)	568	(2.8)	43.8	(2.01)
Switzerland	464	(4.2)	479	(4.6)	499	(5.7)	548	(5.1)	31.5	(1.94)
Thailand	413	(4.4)	431	(3.6)	438	(3.7)	442	(3.9)	17.6	(2.38)
United States	488	(8.1)	495	(6.5)	507	(7.9)	558	(6.9)	27.0	(2.37)
OECD average	*474*	*(0.8)*	*485*	*(1.1)*	*508*	*(1.1)*	*549*	*(0.9)*	*27.9*	*(0.41)*
OECD total	*474*	*(3.2)*	*482*	*(3.0)*	*497*	*(3.4)*	*537*	*(3.3)*	*23.6*	*(1.16)*
Netherlands[3]	510	(4.8)	516	(4.9)	534	(4.7)	572	(4.6)	22.8	(1.93)

1. For the definition of the index see Annex A1.

2. For explained variation see Annex A2. Unit changes marked in bold are statistically significant. Where bottom and top quarters are marked in bold this indicates that their difference is statistically significant.

3. Response rate is too low to ensure comparability (see Annex A3).

Table 4.7
Index of interest in mathematics and performance on the mathematical literacy scale, by national quarters of the index
Results based on students' self-reports

	Index of interest in mathematics[1]												
	All students		Males		Females		Bottom quarter		Second quarter		Third quarter		Top quarter	
	Mean index	S.E.	Mean index	S.E.	Mean index	S.E.	Mean index	S.E.	Mean index	S.E.	Mean index	S.E.	Mean index	S.E.
Albania	0.51	(0.03)	0.52	(0.03)	0.49	(0.03)	-0.59	(0.02)	0.24	(0.01)	0.71	(0.01)	1.67	(0.02)
Australia	0.04	(0.02)	0.14	(0.02)	-0.08	(0.03)	-0.94	(0.03)	-0.17	(0.01)	0.28	(0.01)	0.99	(0.03)
Austria	-0.23	(0.03)	-0.03	(0.03)	-0.42	(0.03)	-1.35	(0.02)	-0.48	(0.01)	0.02	(0.01)	0.89	(0.03)
Belgium (Fl.)	-0.11	(0.03)	-0.06	(0.04)	-0.16	(0.03)	-1.21	(0.03)	-0.32	(0.01)	0.11	(0.01)	1.00	(0.03)
Brazil	0.69	(0.02)	0.75	(0.03)	0.65	(0.03)	-0.38	(0.02)	0.38	(0.01)	0.87	(0.01)	1.91	(0.02)
Bulgaria	0.22	(0.03)	0.21	(0.04)	0.23	(0.04)	-1.14	(0.03)	-0.12	(0.01)	0.51	(0.01)	1.62	(0.03)
Chile	0.41	(0.02)	0.52	(0.04)	0.31	(0.03)	-0.95	(0.03)	0.06	(0.01)	0.73	(0.01)	1.81	(0.02)
Czech Republic	-0.07	(0.02)	0.05	(0.03)	-0.17	(0.02)	-1.24	(0.02)	-0.30	(0.01)	0.18	(0.01)	1.09	(0.02)
Denmark	0.47	(0.03)	0.62	(0.04)	0.31	(0.04)	-0.98	(0.03)	0.17	(0.01)	0.76	(0.01)	1.92	(0.02)
Finland	-0.07	(0.02)	0.06	(0.03)	-0.19	(0.03)	-1.28	(0.02)	-0.35	(0.01)	0.18	(0.01)	1.17	(0.03)
Germany	-0.07	(0.03)	0.11	(0.04)	-0.23	(0.03)	-1.32	(0.03)	-0.34	(0.01)	0.19	(0.01)	1.22	(0.03)
Hong Kong-China	0.59	(0.03)	0.70	(0.04)	0.47	(0.03)	-0.68	(0.03)	0.26	(0.01)	0.81	(0.01)	1.96	(0.02)
Hungary	-0.04	(0.03)	-0.03	(0.04)	-0.06	(0.03)	-1.25	(0.02)	-0.36	(0.01)	0.15	(0.01)	1.28	(0.03)
Iceland	0.11	(0.02)	0.09	(0.03)	0.12	(0.02)	-1.00	(0.03)	-0.17	(0.01)	0.32	(0.01)	1.27	(0.03)
Ireland	-0.01	(0.02)	0.06	(0.03)	-0.08	(0.04)	-1.31	(0.02)	-0.31	(0.01)	0.29	(0.01)	1.28	(0.03)
Israel	0.08	(0.03)	0.16	(0.05)	0.03	(0.04)	-0.92	(0.04)	-0.23	(0.01)	0.30	(0.01)	1.19	(0.03)
Italy	0.00	(0.03)	0.03	(0.04)	-0.03	(0.04)	-1.29	(0.03)	-0.29	(0.01)	0.29	(0.01)	1.31	(0.03)
Korea	-0.27	(0.03)	-0.25	(0.05)	-0.29	(0.05)	-1.66	(0.01)	-0.66	(0.01)	-0.01	(0.01)	1.27	(0.03)
Latvia	0.40	(0.04)	0.42	(0.04)	0.39	(0.04)	-0.76	(0.03)	0.10	(0.01)	0.68	(0.01)	1.61	(0.03)
Liechtenstein	-0.03	(0.07)	0.22	(0.08)	-0.26	(0.09)	-0.96	(0.09)	-0.24	(0.02)	0.17	(0.01)	0.96	(0.09)
Luxembourg	-0.18	(0.03)	-0.05	(0.03)	-0.30	(0.04)	-1.43	(0.02)	-0.48	(0.01)	0.08	(0.01)	1.11	(0.03)
FYR Macedonia	0.34	(0.02)	0.31	(0.03)	0.37	(0.03)	-0.91	(0.03)	0.02	(0.01)	0.65	(0.01)	1.61	(0.02)
Mexico	0.39	(0.02)	0.38	(0.03)	0.40	(0.03)	-0.47	(0.02)	0.18	(0.01)	0.53	(0.00)	1.32	(0.02)
New Zealand	0.09	(0.03)	0.20	(0.04)	-0.01	(0.03)	-1.15	(0.03)	-0.17	(0.01)	0.37	(0.01)	1.31	(0.02)
Norway	-0.28	(0.03)	-0.04	(0.04)	-0.51	(0.04)	-1.74	(0.02)	-0.60	(0.01)	0.09	(0.01)	1.13	(0.03)
Portugal	0.26	(0.02)	0.20	(0.03)	0.31	(0.03)	-0.96	(0.02)	0.01	(0.01)	0.52	(0.01)	1.48	(0.02)
Russian Federation	0.13	(0.03)	0.11	(0.03)	0.14	(0.03)	-1.05	(0.02)	-0.20	(0.01)	0.38	(0.01)	1.37	(0.02)
Sweden	-0.21	(0.02)	-0.08	(0.03)	-0.34	(0.03)	-1.34	(0.02)	-0.37	(0.01)	0.04	(0.01)	0.85	(0.03)
Switzerland	-0.03	(0.03)	0.20	(0.03)	-0.26	(0.03)	-1.21	(0.02)	-0.30	(0.01)	0.24	(0.01)	1.17	(0.02)
Thailand	0.38	(0.02)	0.37	(0.03)	0.38	(0.03)	-0.54	(0.01)	0.11	(0.01)	0.57	(0.00)	1.38	(0.02)
United States	0.08	(0.03)	0.10	(0.05)	0.05	(0.03)	-1.18	(0.04)	-0.19	(0.01)	0.36	(0.01)	1.32	(0.03)
OECD average	*0.00*	*(0.00)*	*0.09*	*(0.01)*	*-0.09*	*(0.01)*	*-1.22*	*(0.01)*	*-0.27*	*(0.00)*	*0.25*	*(0.00)*	*1.22*	*(0.01)*
OECD total	*0.05*	*(0.01)*	*0.10*	*(0.02)*	*0.01*	*(0.02)*	*-1.15*	*(0.02)*	*-0.22*	*(0.01)*	*0.30*	*(0.01)*	*1.28*	*(0.01)*
Netherlands[3]	-0.03	(0.03)	0.26	(0.05)	-0.32	(0.04)	-1.38	(0.03)	-0.31	(0.01)	0.34	(0.01)	1.28	(0.03)

1. For the definition of the index see Annex A1.
2. For explained variation see Annex A2. Unit changes marked in bold are statistically significant. Where bottom and top quarters are marked in bold this indicates that their difference is statistically significant.
3. Response rate is too low to ensure comparability (see Annex A3).

Table 4.7 (continued)
Index of interest in mathematics and performance on the mathematical literacy scale, by national quarters of the index
Results based on students' self-reports

| | Performance on the mathematical literacy scale, by national quarters of the index of interest in mathematics[2] | | | | | | | | Change in the mathematical literacy score per unit of the index of interest in mathematics[2] | |
| | Bottom quarter | | Second quarter | | Third quarter | | Top quarter | | | |
	Mean score	S.E.	Mean score	S.E.	Mean score	S.E.	Mean score	S.E.	Change	S.E.
Albania	367	(4.8)	382	(5.0)	401	(5.6)	392	(6.8)	10.4	(3.16)
Australia	529	(6.1)	525	(4.8)	530	(4.8)	560	(5.3)	15.0	(3.10)
Austria	510	(4.3)	519	(4.4)	510	(5.0)	526	(4.8)	7.8	(2.37)
Belgium (Fl.)	533	(5.1)	546	(5.9)	545	(6.6)	564	(7.5)	12.5	(3.12)
Brazil	328	(4.9)	334	(5.4)	340	(5.8)	359	(7.0)	13.4	(2.95)
Bulgaria	421	(6.4)	421	(7.8)	432	(5.6)	464	(8.3)	15.8	(2.62)
Chile	378	(4.5)	376	(4.8)	385	(5.4)	414	(5.1)	12.2	(1.76)
Czech Republic	497	(4.4)	495	(4.5)	509	(4.3)	527	(4.7)	13.5	(2.13)
Denmark	496	(3.9)	507	(3.8)	521	(4.6)	548	(4.4)	17.1	(1.80)
Finland	508	(3.5)	527	(3.8)	541	(3.7)	575	(3.4)	25.0	(1.75)
Germany	497	(4.4)	487	(4.0)	494	(5.0)	514	(4.7)	8.9	(1.97)
Hong Kong-China	529	(5.2)	546	(4.6)	572	(4.7)	598	(4.4)	26.8	(2.37)
Hungary	477	(5.6)	483	(4.7)	492	(5.5)	513	(5.9)	14.0	(2.33)
Iceland	499	(4.1)	502	(4.1)	520	(4.1)	549	(4.3)	22.9	(2.16)
Ireland	501	(3.9)	500	(4.4)	499	(5.1)	519	(4.6)	7.8	(2.08)
Israel	455	(11.2)	453	(13.5)	445	(9.9)	442	(10.3)	-4.4	(4.59)
Italy	447	(4.1)	455	(5.4)	454	(4.5)	475	(5.1)	9.3	(2.29)
Korea	503	(4.0)	537	(3.6)	564	(4.6)	584	(4.1)	26.7	(1.74)
Latvia	442	(6.0)	463	(7.9)	465	(6.4)	492	(6.1)	18.3	(3.16)
Liechtenstein	511	(13.9)	511	(16.9)	506	(15.0)	532	(15.3)	7.6	(10.26)
Luxembourg	465	(3.9)	454	(4.5)	451	(4.5)	465	(4.5)	0.5	(2.15)
FYR Macedonia	374	(4.3)	383	(4.8)	393	(5.1)	398	(5.4)	9.7	(2.53)
Mexico	385	(5.3)	386	(4.2)	387	(4.5)	396	(5.6)	9.5	(3.05)
New Zealand	532	(5.0)	539	(5.0)	534	(5.1)	566	(6.1)	13.5	(2.78)
Norway	475	(4.1)	492	(4.5)	502	(4.7)	544	(4.3)	22.6	(1.67)
Portugal	433	(4.8)	451	(5.3)	459	(5.3)	474	(5.7)	15.5	(2.16)
Russian Federation	460	(6.8)	466	(5.8)	482	(7.2)	513	(5.3)	20.3	(2.75)
Sweden	495	(3.3)	509	(4.2)	508	(4.4)	534	(4.6)	16.0	(2.10)
Switzerland	525	(6.5)	533	(6.0)	531	(5.5)	541	(5.6)	6.9	(2.54)
Thailand	419	(4.6)	427	(5.3)	432	(4.4)	452	(5.6)	17.7	(2.77)
United States	491	(9.5)	493	(6.2)	489	(10.8)	525	(9.8)	12.0	(3.09)
OECD average	489	(1.2)	496	(1.2)	501	(1.1)	524	(1.3)	10.7	(0.63)
OECD total	476	(3.9)	481	(3.0)	484	(4.3)	509	(4.5)	6.1	(1.55)
Netherlands[3]	555	(6.1)	555	(6.5)	569	(6.4)	580	(5.8)	9.6	(3.28)

1. For the definition of the index see Annex A1.
2. For explained variation see Annex A2. Unit changes marked in bold are statistically significant. Where bottom and top quarters are marked in bold this indicates that their difference is statistically significant.
3. Response rate is too low to ensure comparability (see Annex A3).

Table 4.8
Performance on the combined reading literacy scale and percentages of students by reading profile cluster

	Cluster 1 Least diversified readers				Cluster 2 Moderately diversified readers				Cluster 3 Diversified readers in short texts				Cluster 4 Diversified readers in long texts			
	Mean Score	S.E.	%	S.E.	Mean Score	S.E.	%	S.E.	Mean Score	S.E.	%	S.E.	Mean Score	S.E.	%	S.E.
Albania	348	(5.4)	29.1	(0.9)	340	(6.0)	15.9	(0.8)	377	(4.2)	28.6	(1.2)	368	(4.4)	26.4	(0.8)
Argentina	383	(7.9)	27.2	(1.8)	438	(7.6)	23.2	(1.4)	435	(6.6)	28.2	(1.4)	465	(12.9)	21.5	(2.0)
Australia	494	(4.9)	18.5	(0.9)	514	(3.7)	35.0	(1.1)	522	(6.3)	10.8	(0.6)	569	(4.4)	35.7	(1.2)
Austria	474	(4.6)	16.6	(0.7)	503	(2.4)	41.9	(0.9)	509	(3.5)	17.0	(0.5)	545	(3.6)	24.6	(0.8)
Belgium	487	(4.4)	36.3	(0.6)	503	(5.4)	19.6	(0.6)	537	(3.4)	31.8	(0.7)	556	(5.5)	12.3	(0.5)
Brazil	370	(4.4)	29.5	(1.1)	407	(5.1)	15.1	(0.8)	413	(4.3)	27.5	(1.0)	418	(3.6)	27.9	(1.1)
Bulgaria	372	(7.5)	10.0	(0.7)	429	(4.4)	32.5	(0.8)	429	(5.6)	18.9	(0.8)	474	(5.6)	38.6	(1.2)
Canada	507	(2.3)	24.3	(0.4)	528	(1.7)	30.8	(0.5)	531	(2.5)	16.2	(0.3)	572	(1.9)	28.7	(0.5)
Chile	381	(4.0)	29.4	(1.0)	425	(4.7)	21.7	(0.7)	419	(3.7)	27.8	(0.8)	439	(5.1)	21.1	(0.7)
Czech Republic	482	(3.5)	22.0	(0.7)	492	(2.8)	35.6	(0.9)	494	(3.4)	18.7	(0.6)	543	(2.9)	23.8	(0.7)
Denmark	453	(5.0)	17.5	(0.8)	464	(6.0)	10.1	(0.6)	511	(2.3)	56.2	(1.0)	541	(5.2)	16.2	(0.6)
Finland	485	(14.6)	6.9	(0.5)	522	(4.4)	14.2	(0.6)	550	(2.2)	66.6	(0.9)	597	(3.5)	12.3	(0.5)
France	488	(4.1)	32.6	(0.9)	503	(3.4)	19.2	(0.7)	528	(2.9)	31.3	(0.9)	534	(4.1)	16.8	(0.7)
Germany	464	(4.2)	24.1	(0.8)	485	(2.8)	38.0	(0.8)	499	(5.9)	11.6	(0.6)	541	(3.1)	26.3	(0.7)
Greece	464	(5.3)	35.4	(0.9)	474	(6.6)	21.3	(0.8)	478	(5.8)	21.5	(0.7)	505	(5.2)	21.8	(0.9)
Hong Kong-China	474	(8.4)	6.6	(0.4)	512	(3.2)	23.4	(0.6)	522	(3.3)	40.8	(0.9)	557	(3.6)	29.2	(0.9)
Hungary	450	(4.8)	25.1	(1.0)	479	(4.3)	25.1	(0.8)	470		20.1	(0.7)	525	(4.7)	29.6	(1.0)
Iceland	449	(6.5)	6.6	(0.5)	492	(2.6)	28.6	(0.7)	520	(2.1)	49.7	(0.8)	537	(4.3)	15.1	(0.6)
Indonesia	353	(4.1)	24.1	(1.2)	376	(4.0)	21.6	(0.7)	383	(4.9)	37.7	(1.1)	385	(6.3)	16.6	(0.9)
Ireland	510	(5.9)	16.3	(0.7)	515	(3.3)	47.0	(0.8)	507	(5.9)	8.9	(0.6)	571	(3.6)	27.8	(1.0)
Israel	419	(10.8)	14.6	(0.9)	475	(10.1)	33.5	(2.3)	452	(10.3)	25.6	(1.4)	483	(9.1)	26.4	(1.4)
Italy	469		25.8	(0.9)	485	(3.3)	27.9	(0.7)	505	(3.3)	26.5	(0.8)	503	(4.1)	19.8	(0.7)
Japan	482	(8.2)	14.5	(0.9)	514	(7.2)	8.1	(0.5)	532	(4.6)	74.4	(0.9)	573	(7.7)	3.0	(0.3)
Korea	495	(3.9)	18.8	(0.6)	525	(3.7)	14.6	(0.6)	531	(2.4)	53.1	(1.1)	545	(3.8)	13.6	(0.7)
Latvia	412	(8.2)	13.8	(0.8)	464	(5.3)	39.9	(1.3)	433	(8.7)	15.2	(0.9)	499	(5.7)	31.1	(1.4)
Liechtenstein	442	(11.0)	21.9	(2.1)	478	(8.0)	40.7	(2.5)	524	(12.6)	14.3	(2.1)	526	(11.7)	23.2	(2.5)
Luxembourg	434	(2.5)	39.4	(0.8)	454	(4.3)	21.3	(0.6)	461	(4.0)	19.2	(0.7)	486	(3.8)	20.0	(0.6)
FYR Macedonia	345	(4.5)	14.4	(0.8)	397	(2.9)	29.2	(0.8)	389	(2.5)	35.8	(0.9)	384	(4.1)	20.7	(0.8)
Mexico	403	(3.6)	37.5	(1.3)	426	(5.9)	15.6	(0.8)	438	(4.3)	22.2	(5.9)	443	(4.9)	24.7	(0.7)
New Zealand	499	(4.8)	18.0	(0.7)	529	(3.1)	30.1	(0.9)	500	(6.4)	12.4	(0.6)	564	(3.7)	39.4	(1.0)
Norway	433	(7.1)	8.5	(0.6)	492	(4.2)	20.2	(0.7)	520	(2.7)	58.0	(0.9)	546	(4.3)	13.3	(0.5)
Peru	311	(5.6)	24.8	(1.0)	344	(7.8)	13.3	(0.6)	350	(4.7)	31.6	(1.0)	346	(6.1)	30.3	(1.0)
Poland	445	(7.0)	16.7	(0.9)	491	(4.2)	48.0	(1.1)	474	(6.6)	11.4	(0.7)	511	(6.3)	24.0	(1.1)
Portugal	449	(5.8)	29.8	(0.9)	477	(4.1)	25.9	(0.7)	487	(5.8)	24.4	(0.6)	489	(5.8)	19.8	(0.6)
Russian Federation	426	(6.3)	11.5	(0.5)	451	(5.1)	17.1	(0.6)	432	(4.8)	21.6	(1.2)	495	(3.9)	49.7	(1.1)
Spain	474	(3.4)	36.2	(1.1)	492	(3.6)	23.0	(0.7)	503	(3.4)	17.5	(0.7)	526	(2.9)	23.3	(0.7)
Sweden	469	(4.8)	11.1	(0.5)	502	(2.8)	30.3	(0.8)	518	(2.8)	37.3	(0.8)	564	(3.6)	21.3	(0.7)
Switzerland	455	(4.6)	22.1	(0.9)	487	(4.3)	30.3	(0.8)	519	(5.1)	25.4	(0.8)	534	(5.2)	22.2	(0.8)
Thailand	387	(4.6)	16.2	(1.0)	424	(5.5)	6.7	(0.5)	443	(3.3)	54.2	(1.3)	437	(4.4)	22.9	(0.9)
United Kingdom	503	(4.3)	17.1	(0.6)	512	(2.7)	39.4	(0.9)	488	(5.3)	8.4	(0.5)	566	(3.7)	35.1	(1.0)
United States	478	(7.6)	28.4	(1.3)	520	(5.8)	32.1	(1.5)	482	(10.9)	10.8	(1.1)	544	(6.0)	28.7	(1.5)
OECD average	*468*	*(1.0)*	*22.4*	*(0.2)*	*498*	*(0.7)*	*27.1*	*(0.1)*	*514*	*(0.9)*	*28.3*	*(0.2)*	*539*	*(0.9)*	*22.2*	*(0.2)*
Netherlands[1]	494	(5.4)	24.7	(1.3)	530	(4.5)	25.8	(1.0)	544	(4.0)	33.1	(1.2)	573	(4.9)	16.5	(0.9)

1. Response rate is too low to ensure comparability.

Table 4.9.
**Index of control strategies and performance on the combined reading literacy scale,
by national quarters of the index**

See next page

Table 4.9
Index of control strategies and performance on the combined reading literacy scale, by national quarters of the index
Results based on students' self-reports

	Index of control strategies[1]													
	All students		Males		Females		Bottom quarter		Second quarter		Third quarter		Top quarter	
	Mean index	S.E.	Mean index	S.E.	Mean index	S.E.	Mean index	S.E.	Mean index	S.E.	Mean index	S.E.	Mean index	S.E.
Albania	0.45	(0.02)	0.28	(0.03)	0.61	(0.02)	-0.58	(0.02)	0.20	(0.00)	0.67	(0.01)	1.51	(0.02)
Australia	0.02	(0.02)	-0.05	(0.02)	0.10	(0.03)	-1.20	(0.02)	-0.26	(0.01)	0.30	(0.01)	1.24	(0.02)
Austria	0.40	(0.02)	0.31	(0.03)	0.48	(0.02)	-0.72	(0.02)	0.12	(0.01)	0.64	(0.01)	1.54	(0.02)
Belgium (Fl.)	0.14	(0.02)	0.07	(0.02)	0.21	(0.03)	-0.96	(0.02)	-0.11	(0.01)	0.37	(0.01)	1.25	(0.02)
Brazil	0.22	(0.03)	0.12	(0.04)	0.30	(0.03)	-1.15	(0.03)	-0.02	(0.01)	0.51	(0.01)	1.53	(0.02)
Bulgaria	0.19	(0.02)	0.06	(0.03)	0.33	(0.02)	-0.99	(0.03)	-0.09	(0.01)	0.47	(0.00)	1.36	(0.02)
Chile	0.41	(0.02)	0.32	(0.03)	0.48	(0.02)	-0.80	(0.02)	0.11	(0.01)	0.69	(0.01)	1.63	(0.02)
Czech Republic	0.27	(0.02)	0.11	(0.03)	0.42	(0.02)	-0.84	(0.01)	-0.02	(0.00)	0.50	(0.01)	1.45	(0.02)
Denmark	-0.23	(0.01)	-0.24	(0.02)	-0.22	(0.02)	-1.25	(0.02)	-0.48	(0.01)	0.00	(0.01)	0.81	(0.02)
Finland	-0.47	(0.02)	-0.52	(0.02)	-0.42	(0.02)	-1.54	(0.02)	-0.71	(0.01)	-0.21	(0.01)	0.58	(0.02)
Germany	0.24	(0.02)	0.14	(0.04)	0.33	(0.02)	-0.94	(0.02)	-0.05	(0.01)	0.48	(0.00)	1.45	(0.03)
Hong Kong-China	-0.28	(0.02)	-0.28	(0.03)	-0.29	(0.02)	-1.34	(0.02)	-0.59	(0.00)	-0.03	(0.01)	0.82	(0.02)
Hungary	0.21	(0.02)	0.09	(0.03)	0.33	(0.03)	-0.91	(0.02)	-0.05	(0.01)	0.45	(0.01)	1.34	(0.02)
Iceland	-0.35	(0.02)	-0.36	(0.03)	-0.34	(0.02)	-1.53	(0.02)	-0.60	(0.01)	-0.08	(0.01)	0.79	(0.02)
Ireland	0.07	(0.02)	-0.10	(0.04)	0.23	(0.03)	-1.28	(0.03)	-0.22	(0.01)	0.37	(0.01)	1.39	(0.02)
Israel	0.30	(0.04)	0.14	(0.05)	0.42	(0.06)	-1.03	(0.03)	-0.05	(0.01)	0.59	(0.01)	1.71	(0.02)
Italy	0.23	(0.02)	0.05	(0.04)	0.41	(0.02)	-0.94	(0.03)	-0.04	(0.01)	0.48	(0.00)	1.41	(0.01)
Korea	-0.44	(0.02)	-0.47	(0.03)	-0.41	(0.03)	-1.74	(0.02)	-0.70	(0.01)	-0.12	(0.01)	0.79	(0.02)
Latvia	-0.12	(0.02)	-0.22	(0.03)	-0.03	(0.02)	-1.10	(0.02)	-0.34	(0.01)	0.12	(0.01)	0.85	(0.01)
Liechtenstein	0.15	(0.05)	0.10	(0.08)	0.21	(0.08)	-1.06	(0.07)	-0.17	(0.02)	0.41	(0.02)	1.39	(0.07)
Luxembourg	0.05	(0.02)	-0.10	(0.03)	0.19	(0.03)	-1.26	(0.03)	-0.23	(0.01)	0.33	(0.01)	1.34	(0.03)
FYR Macedonia	0.33	(0.02)	0.19	(0.02)	0.48	(0.02)	-0.84	(0.02)	0.06	(0.01)	0.62	(0.01)	1.50	(0.02)
Mexico	0.16	(0.02)	0.06	(0.03)	0.25	(0.02)	-0.98	(0.01)	-0.18	(0.01)	0.39	(0.01)	1.41	(0.02)
New Zealand	0.07	(0.03)	-0.03	(0.03)	0.17	(0.03)	-1.12	(0.02)	-0.23	(0.01)	0.30	(0.01)	1.32	(0.02)
Norway	-0.58	(0.02)	-0.50	(0.03)	-0.66	(0.02)	-1.76	(0.02)	-0.81	(0.01)	-0.28	(0.01)	0.54	(0.02)
Portugal	0.19	(0.02)	0.03	(0.02)	0.34	(0.02)	-0.90	(0.02)	-0.13	(0.01)	0.39	(0.01)	1.41	(0.02)
Russian Federation	0.08	(0.02)	0.00	(0.02)	0.17	(0.02)	-1.00	(0.02)	-0.18	(0.01)	0.32	(0.00)	1.19	(0.02)
Sweden	0.03	(0.02)	0.04	(0.03)	0.02	(0.02)	-1.09	(0.02)	-0.22	(0.01)	0.29	(0.01)	1.17	(0.02)
Switzerland	0.11	(0.02)	0.00	(0.03)	0.22	(0.03)	-1.00	(0.02)	-0.15	(0.00)	0.35	(0.01)	1.26	(0.03)
Thailand	-0.38	(0.02)	-0.44	(0.03)	-0.33	(0.02)	-1.22	(0.01)	-0.61	(0.00)	-0.18	(0.01)	0.51	(0.02)
United States	-0.08	(0.03)	-0.26	(0.04)	0.09	(0.04)	-1.44	(0.03)	-0.40	(0.01)	0.24	(0.01)	1.30	(0.03)
OECD average	*0.00*	*(0.01)*	*-0.09*	*(0.01)*	*0.09*	*(0.01)*	*-1.17*	*(0.01)*	*-0.28*	*(0.00)*	*0.26*	*(0.00)*	*1.19*	*(0.01)*
OECD total	*0.01*	*(0.02)*	*-0.12*	*(0.02)*	*0.14*	*(0.02)*	*-1.24*	*(0.02)*	*-0.29*	*(0.01)*	*0.29*	*(0.00)*	*1.28*	*(0.01)*
Netherlands[3]	-0.07	(0.02)	-0.09	(0.03)	-0.05	(0.03)	-1.09	(0.03)	-0.29	(0.01)	0.19	(0.01)	0.90	(0.03)

1. For the definition of the index see Annex A1.
2. For explained variation see Annex A2. Unit changes marked in bold are statistically significant. Where bottom and top quarters are marked in bold this indicates that their difference is statistically significant.
3. Response rate is too low to ensure comparability (see Annex A3).

Table 4.9 (continued)
Index of control strategies and performance on the combined reading literacy scale, by national quarters of the index
Results based on students' self-reports

	Performance on the combined reading literacy scale, by national quarters of the index of control strategies[2]								Change in the combined reading literacy score per unit of the index of control strategies[2]	
	Bottom quarter		Second quarter		Third quarter		Top quarter			
	Mean score	S.E.	Mean score	S.E.	Mean score	S.E.	Mean score	S.E	Change	S.E.
Albania	318	(4.1)	349	(4.2)	367	(4.4)	370	(6.1)	25.0	-(2.12)
Australia	494	(4.5)	525	(4.6)	540	(4.3)	564	(5.8)	23.8	(2.06)
Austria	485	(4.3)	502	(3.1)	517	(3.9)	531	(3.5)	18.2	(1.95)
Belgium (Fl.)	512	(7.2)	543	(4.2)	542	(5.3)	545	(5.0)	13.4	(3.15)
Brazil	368	(4.4)	395	(4.0)	414	(4.0)	425	(4.3)	20.6	(1.67)
Bulgaria	410	(6.5)	432	(5.6)	441	(5.2)	453	(5.5)	17.1	-(2.00)
Chile	383	(4.2)	412	(4.5)	425	(3.9)	430	(4.0)	16.6	-(1.68)
Czech Republic	464	(3.1)	497	(3.0)	518	(3.3)	532	(2.9)	26.6	(1.36)
Denmark	481	(3.8)	497	(3.6)	507	(3.3)	514	(3.3)	14.9	(1.73)
Finland	527	(3.8)	546	(2.9)	556	(3.6)	562	(3.6)	15.8	(1.64)
Germany	459	(4.3)	495	(4.0)	508	(3.6)	519	(3.3)	22.4	(1.80)
Hong Kong-China	490	(4.2)	525	(3.4)	537	(3.5)	554	(3.6)	24.4	-(1.75)
Hungary	456	(5.8)	483	(4.4)	495	(4.3)	496	(5.6)	17.9	(2.79)
Iceland	490	(3.2)	509	(3.2)	513	(3.1)	526	(3.6)	13.6	(2.03)
Ireland	499	(4.3)	525	(5.1)	537	(4.0)	553	(3.8)	18.6	(1.65)
Israel	460	(9.7)	462	(7.7)	475	(9.9)	471	(7.1)	5.7	-(2.95)
Italy	461	(5.1)	485	(3.8)	499	(3.4)	505	(3.2)	17.5	(1.88)
Korea	496	(3.4)	521	(2.9)	534	(3.1)	548	(3.0)	20.2	(1.54)
Latvia	430	(6.4)	465	(6.3)	463	(6.7)	482	(5.6)	23.2	(2.74)
Liechtenstein	462	(9.9)	479	(10.9)	477	(9.7)	520	(9.7)	20.6	(5.90)
Luxembourg	424	(3.3)	453	(3.0)	456	(3.3)	475	(3.3)	16.6	(1.75)
FYR Macedonia	348	(4.3)	369	(3.3)	389	(2.6)	402	(3.2)	23.7	-(2.14)
Mexico	394	(3.4)	415	(3.9)	432	(4.3)	449	(4.7)	21.4	(1.80)
New Zealand	494	(4.2)	531	(3.7)	540	(3.6)	572	(5.0)	27.7	(2.15)
Norway	494	(5.2)	505	(3.5)	521	(4.4)	518	(4.1)	13.7	(2.05)
Portugal	419	(5.6)	464	(5.0)	483	(4.4)	515	(4.4)	35.5	(2.30)
Russian Federation	431	(5.0)	462	(4.9)	476	(4.7)	485	(4.7)	23.7	(1.83)
Sweden	491	(3.2)	515	(3.2)	527	(3.9)	539	(3.0)	19.3	(1.51)
Switzerland	469	(4.9)	492	(4.9)	503	(4.8)	522	(6.1)	20.6	(2.63)
Thailand	410	(4.4)	428	(3.5)	434	(3.9)	452	(4.1)	21.1	-(2.45)
United States	477	(7.4)	505	(8.3)	528	(5.7)	534	(8.3)	18.3	(2.51)
OECD average	*474*	*(1.0)*	*500*	*(1.0)*	*512*	*(0.8)*	*526*	*(1.0)*	*15.6*	*(0.43)*
OECD total	*465*	*(3.2)*	*492*	*(3.5)*	*510*	*(2.6)*	*520*	*(3.6)*	*15.8*	*(1.31)*
Netherlands[3]	511	(5.6)	542	(4.2)	541	(3.7)	536	(4.9)	9.4	(2.61)

1. For the definition of the index see Annex A1.
2. For explained variation see Annex A2. Unit changes marked in bold are statistically significant. Where bottom and top quarters are marked in bold this indicates that their difference is statistically significant.
3. Response rate is too low to ensure comparability (see Annex A3).

Table 4.10

Index of memorisation strategies and performance on the combined reading literacy scale, by national quarters of the index

Results based on students' self-reports

| | Index of memorisation strategies[1] | | | | | | | | | | | | |
| | All students | | Males | | Females | | Bottom quarter | | Second quarter | | Third quarter | | Top quarter | |
	Mean index	S.E.	Mean index	S.E.	Mean index	S.E.	Mean index	S.E.	Mean index	S.E.	Mean index	S.E.	Mean index	S.E.
Albania	0.82	(0.02)	0.67	(0.02)	0.97	(0.02)	-0.12	(0.02)	0.56	(0.01)	1.03	(0.01)	1.83	(0.02)
Australia	0.14	(0.02)	0.11	(0.03)	0.18	(0.03)	-0.96	(0.02)	-0.10	(0.01)	0.39	(0.01)	1.25	(0.02)
Austria	-0.03	(0.02)	-0.18	(0.03)	0.11	(0.02)	-1.30	(0.02)	-0.28	(0.01)	0.26	(0.01)	1.22	(0.02)
Belgium (Fl.)	0.06	(0.02)	-0.01	(0.03)	0.14	(0.03)	-1.20	(0.02)	-0.26	(0.01)	0.32	(0.01)	1.38	(0.02)
Brazil	0.22	(0.02)	0.17	(0.03)	0.27	(0.03)	-1.02	(0.03)	0.00	(0.01)	0.52	(0.01)	1.39	(0.02)
Bulgaria	0.21	(0.01)	0.16	(0.02)	0.27	(0.03)	-0.82	(0.02)	-0.02	(0.01)	0.47	(0.00)	1.23	(0.02)
Chile	0.00	(0.02)	0.06	(0.03)	-0.06	(0.03)	-1.41	(0.02)	-0.31	(0.01)	0.33	(0.01)	1.37	(0.02)
Czech Republic	-0.06	(0.02)	-0.22	(0.03)	0.09	(0.03)	-1.21	(0.02)	-0.37	(0.01)	0.19	(0.01)	1.17	(0.02)
Denmark	0.05	(0.01)	0.08	(0.02)	0.01	(0.02)	-0.89	(0.02)	-0.14	(0.01)	0.24	(0.01)	0.98	(0.01)
Finland	-0.10	(0.01)	-0.15	(0.02)	-0.07	(0.02)	-1.07	(0.01)	-0.33	(0.00)	0.16	(0.00)	0.83	(0.02)
Germany	0.03	(0.02)	-0.11	(0.02)	0.17	(0.02)	-1.21	(0.02)	-0.26	(0.01)	0.30	(0.01)	1.28	(0.02)
Hong Kong-China	0.07	(0.02)	-0.01	(0.02)	0.16	(0.02)	-0.92	(0.02)	-0.23	(0.01)	0.25	(0.00)	1.19	(0.02)
Hungary	0.89	(0.02)	0.75	(0.03)	1.03	(0.03)	-0.12	(0.02)	0.57	(0.00)	1.08	(0.01)	2.04	(0.02)
Iceland	-0.27	(0.02)	-0.27	(0.02)	-0.27	(0.02)	-1.39	(0.02)	-0.50	(0.01)	0.01	(0.01)	0.79	(0.02)
Ireland	0.27	(0.02)	0.14	(0.03)	0.40	(0.02)	-0.96	(0.02)	0.00	(0.01)	0.54	(0.01)	1.50	(0.02)
Israel	0.13	(0.05)	0.01	(0.05)	0.22	(0.06)	-1.25	(0.02)	-0.19	(0.01)	0.42	(0.01)	1.55	(0.04)
Italy	-0.69	(0.02)	-0.69	(0.03)	-0.69	(0.02)	-1.79	(0.02)	-1.01	(0.01)	-0.42	(0.01)	0.48	(0.01)
Korea	-0.15	(0.02)	-0.18	(0.02)	-0.11	(0.02)	-1.29	(0.02)	-0.40	(0.01)	0.11	(0.01)	0.97	(0.02)
Latvia	0.17	(0.01)	0.10	(0.02)	0.23	(0.02)	-0.71	(0.02)	-0.04	(0.01)	0.39	(0.01)	1.03	(0.02)
Liechtenstein	-0.08	(0.05)	-0.16	(0.07)	-0.01	(0.06)	-1.14	(0.06)	-0.37	(0.02)	0.10	(0.02)	1.07	(0.08)
Luxembourg	-0.09	(0.02)	-0.29	(0.03)	0.11	(0.03)	-1.50	(0.03)	-0.39	(0.01)	0.23	(0.01)	1.30	(0.02)
FYR Macedonia	-0.25	(0.02)	-0.27	(0.03)	-0.22	(0.03)	-1.51	(0.02)	-0.68	(0.01)	0.03	(0.01)	1.17	(0.02)
Mexico	0.06	(0.02)	0.08	(0.03)	0.04	(0.03)	-1.07	(0.02)	-0.26	(0.01)	0.29	(0.01)	1.30	(0.02)
New Zealand	0.24	(0.02)	0.18	(0.03)	0.30	(0.03)	-0.83	(0.02)	-0.05	(0.01)	0.46	(0.01)	1.38	(0.02)
Norway	-0.60	(0.02)	-0.47	(0.03)	-0.73	(0.03)	-1.96	(0.02)	-0.77	(0.01)	-0.25	(0.01)	0.59	(0.02)
Portugal	0.03	(0.02)	0.02	(0.02)	0.05	(0.02)	-1.03	(0.02)	-0.27	(0.01)	0.25	(0.01)	1.19	(0.02)
Russian Federation	0.36	(0.02)	0.29	(0.02)	0.44	(0.02)	-0.60	(0.01)	0.13	(0.01)	0.55	(0.00)	1.38	(0.02)
Sweden	0.17	(0.02)	0.21	(0.03)	0.12	(0.03)	-0.94	(0.02)	-0.09	(0.00)	0.42	(0.01)	1.28	(0.02)
Switzerland	-0.02	(0.02)	-0.10	(0.03)	0.06	(0.02)	-1.09	(0.02)	-0.27	(0.01)	0.22	(0.00)	1.07	(0.02)
Thailand	-0.07	(0.01)	-0.11	(0.02)	-0.04	(0.01)	-0.77	(0.01)	-0.28	(0.00)	0.12	(0.00)	0.67	(0.01)
United States	0.09	(0.02)	-0.02	(0.04)	0.19	(0.03)	-1.15	(0.03)	-0.23	(0.01)	0.36	(0.01)	1.36	(0.02)
OECD average	*0.00*	*(0.00)*	*-0.05*	*(0.01)*	*0.06*	*(0.01)*	*-1.14*	*(0.01)*	*-0.27*	*(0.00)*	*0.26*	*(0.00)*	*1.16*	*(0.01)*
OECD total	*0.00*	*(0.01)*	*-0.07*	*(0.02)*	*0.08*	*(0.02)*	*-1.18*	*(0.01)*	*-0.29*	*(0.01)*	*0.26*	*(0.00)*	*1.23*	*(0.01)*
Netherlands[3]	-0.03	(0.02)	-0.04	(0.03)	-0.01	(0.02)	-1.01	(0.02)	-0.22	(0.01)	0.20	(0.01)	0.94	(0.02)

1. For the definition of the index see Annex A1.

2. For explained variation see Annex A2. Unit changes marked in bold are statistically significant. Where bottom and top quarters are marked in bold this indicates that their difference is statistically significant.

3. Response rate is too low to ensure comparability (see Annex A3).

Table 4.10 (continued)
Index of memorisation strategies and performance on the combined reading literacy scale, by national quarters of the index
Results based on students' self-reports

	Performance on the combined reading literacy scale, by national quarters of the index of memorisation strategies[2]								Change in the combined reading literacy score per unit of the index of memorisation strategies[2]	
	Bottom quarter		Second quarter		Third quarter		Top quarter			
	Mean score	S.E.	Mean score	S.E.	Mean score	S.E.	Mean score	S.E	Change	S.E.
Albania	327	(3.9)	346	(5.2)	362	(5.1)	368	(4.0)	20.7	(1.91)
Australia	515	(4.7)	528	(4.4)	535	(4.9)	545	(4.9)	10.1	(2.27)
Austria	529	(3.8)	510	(3.7)	502	(3.0)	494	(2.9)	-11.8	(1.53)
Belgium (Fl.)	547	(7.1)	538	(4.9)	536	(4.8)	519	(5.3)	-8.4	(2.49)
Brazil	380	(3.8)	400	(4.3)	408	(4.0)	414	(4.2)	12.8	(1.72)
Bulgaria	437	(7.8)	436	(5.1)	437	(5.1)	426	(6.0)	-4.8	(2.88)
Chile	443	(4.4)	408	(4.5)	397	(4.1)	400	(3.9)	-15.9	(1.51)
Czech Republic	522	(3.8)	500	(3.4)	497	(2.9)	492	(3.1)	-11.1	(1.46)
Denmark	488	(3.8)	507	(3.3)	500	(3.9)	502	(3.3)	5.7	(2.41)
Finland	539	(3.7)	544	(3.7)	553	(2.9)	554	(4.0)	7.7	(2.24)
Germany	496	(4.0)	499	(3.4)	495	(3.5)	492	(3.3)	-1.4	(1.57)
Hong Kong-China	503	(4.8)	523	(3.5)	531	(3.6)	549	(3.0)	18.7	(1.83)
Hungary	460	(6.1)	480	(5.1)	498	(4.6)	490	(4.9)	15.5	(3.48)
Iceland	516	(3.5)	506	(3.3)	513	(3.0)	502	(3.1)	-2.2	(2.40)
Ireland	524	(5.0)	526	(3.9)	529	(3.8)	535	(3.8)	6.0	(1.86)
Israel	491	(8.8)	471	(8.3)	448	(10.2)	456	(8.3)	-11.4	(3.17)
Italy	505	(4.2)	498	(3.2)	481	(3.8)	466	(4.9)	-15.4	(1.99)
Korea	512	(3.5)	528	(3.4)	529	(2.8)	530	(2.6)	6.5	(1.20)
Latvia	443	(7.5)	466	(7.2)	464	(4.9)	466	(5.7)	11.8	(3.22)
Liechtenstein	490	(10.6)	490	(10.8)	476	(10.2)	481	(10.8)	-2.5	(6.23)
Luxembourg	456	(3.1)	450	(3.2)	452	(3.5)	448	(3.3)	-2.6	(1.55)
FYR Macedonia	418	(3.6)	393	(2.9)	363	(2.9)	332	(3.1)	-28.4	(1.54)
Mexico	428	(5.0)	415	(3.9)	419	(3.5)	427	(4.7)	-1.0	(1.98)
New Zealand	516	(4.5)	532	(4.3)	540	(3.6)	549	(4.3)	12.9	(2.26)
Norway	515	(4.0)	513	(4.2)	510	(3.8)	501	(4.5)	-2.6	(2.00)
Portugal	475	(6.4)	468	(5.3)	463	(5.0)	476	(4.8)	-1.2	(2.08)
Russian Federation	442	(5.6)	464	(4.7)	475	(4.4)	472	(4.5)	14.5	(2.04)
Sweden	505	(3.4)	517	(3.2)	524	(3.4)	526	(3.2)	8.1	(1.49)
Switzerland	496	(5.9)	489	(5.4)	501	(4.6)	501	(4.9)	2.5	(2.22)
Thailand	416	(4.0)	425	(3.6)	438	(3.8)	444	(4.5)	18.1	(3.07)
United States	503	(9.2)	513	(7.4)	514	(7.0)	510	(7.2)	1.9	(2.62)
OECD average	501	(1.1)	503	(1.0)	504	(1.0)	503	(1.0)	0.5	(0.47)
OECD total	494	(3.9)	498	(3.2)	498	(3.2)	496	(3.1)	0.5	(1.21)
Netherlands[3]	535	(5.0)	536	(4.7)	540	(4.6)	518	(5.4)	-6.0	(2.49)

1. For the definition of the index see Annex A1.
2. For explained variation see Annex A2. Unit changes marked in bold are statistically significant. Where bottom and top quarters are marked in bold this indicates that their difference is statistically significant.
3. Response rate is too low to ensure comparability (see Annex A3).

Table 4.11
Index of elaboration strategies and performance on the combined reading literacy scale, by national quarters of the index
Results based on students' self-reports

	Index of elaboration strategies[1]													
	All students		Males		Females		Bottom quarter		Second quarter		Third quarter		Top quarter	
	Mean index	S.E.	Mean index	S.E.	Mean index	S.E.	Mean index	S.E.	Mean index	S.E.	Mean index	S.E.	Mean index	S.E.
Albania	0.48	(0.02)	0.39	(0.02)	0.57	(0.02)	-0.52	(0.01)	0.24	(0.01)	0.74	(0.01)	1.48	(0.02)
Australia	0.07	(0.02)	0.12	(0.02)	0.02	(0.03)	-1.12	(0.03)	-0.19	(0.01)	0.39	(0.01)	1.21	(0.02)
Austria	0.16	(0.02)	0.23	(0.03)	0.09	(0.03)	-1.16	(0.02)	-0.12	(0.01)	0.49	(0.01)	1.44	(0.02)
Belgium (Fl.)	-0.16	(0.02)	-0.07	(0.03)	-0.26	(0.03)	-1.44	(0.02)	-0.48	(0.01)	0.18	(0.01)	1.10	(0.02)
Brazil	0.47	(0.02)	0.41	(0.03)	0.52	(0.03)	-0.85	(0.02)	0.25	(0.01)	0.80	(0.01)	1.69	(0.02)
Bulgaria	0.39	(0.02)	0.34	(0.03)	0.45	(0.03)	-0.87	(0.02)	0.10	(0.01)	0.70	(0.01)	1.64	(0.02)
Chile	0.44	(0.02)	0.44	(0.03)	0.44	(0.02)	-0.87	(0.02)	0.11	(0.01)	0.78	(0.01)	1.74	(0.02)
Czech Republic	0.10	(0.02)	0.12	(0.03)	0.08	(0.02)	-1.09	(0.02)	-0.20	(0.01)	0.39	(0.01)	1.30	(0.02)
Denmark	-0.12	(0.02)	-0.06	(0.03)	-0.18	(0.02)	-1.24	(0.02)	-0.44	(0.01)	0.18	(0.01)	1.02	(0.02)
Finland	-0.15	(0.02)	-0.09	(0.02)	-0.21	(0.02)	-1.24	(0.02)	-0.47	(0.01)	0.16	(0.00)	0.94	(0.02)
Germany	0.05	(0.02)	0.09	(0.03)	0.01	(0.02)	-1.19	(0.02)	-0.22	(0.01)	0.38	(0.01)	1.24	(0.02)
Hong Kong-China	-0.21	(0.02)	-0.14	(0.03)	-0.28	(0.02)	-1.18	(0.02)	-0.57	(0.01)	-0.01	(0.01)	0.93	(0.02)
Hungary	0.15	(0.02)	0.20	(0.03)	0.10	(0.03)	-1.04	(0.02)	-0.11	(0.01)	0.49	(0.01)	1.26	(0.02)
Iceland	-0.24	(0.02)	-0.19	(0.02)	-0.29	(0.03)	-1.54	(0.02)	-0.54	(0.01)	0.10	(0.01)	1.02	(0.02)
Ireland	-0.09	(0.02)	-0.12	(0.03)	-0.07	(0.03)	-1.48	(0.02)	-0.39	(0.01)	0.28	(0.01)	1.24	(0.02)
Israel	-0.03	(0.04)	0.10	(0.05)	-0.12	(0.05)	-1.56	(0.03)	-0.39	(0.01)	0.35	(0.01)	1.49	(0.04)
Italy	-0.11	(0.02)	-0.09	(0.03)	-0.13	(0.03)	-1.49	(0.03)	-0.41	(0.01)	0.29	(0.01)	1.18	(0.02)
Korea	-0.03	(0.03)	-0.02	(0.04)	-0.04	(0.04)	-1.38	(0.02)	-0.28	(0.01)	0.30	(0.01)	1.25	(0.02)
Latvia	0.04	(0.02)	0.06	(0.02)	0.03	(0.02)	-0.97	(0.02)	-0.16	(0.01)	0.28	(0.01)	1.04	(0.02)
Liechtenstein	0.00	(0.06)	0.11	(0.07)	-0.10	(0.09)	-1.26	(0.08)	-0.28	(0.03)	0.32	(0.03)	1.20	(0.06)
Luxembourg	-0.12	(0.02)	-0.15	(0.03)	-0.09	(0.03)	-1.40	(0.03)	-0.44	(0.01)	0.21	(0.01)	1.14	(0.02)
FYR Macedonia	0.57	(0.02)	0.49	(0.03)	0.66	(0.02)	-0.67	(0.02)	0.30	(0.01)	0.85	(0.01)	1.81	(0.02)
Mexico	0.33	(0.02)	0.29	(0.03)	0.36	(0.02)	-0.85	(0.02)	0.01	(0.01)	0.58	(0.01)	1.58	(0.02)
New Zealand	0.10	(0.02)	0.11	(0.02)	0.09	(0.03)	-1.05	(0.02)	-0.16	(0.01)	0.39	(0.01)	1.22	(0.02)
Norway	-0.22	(0.02)	-0.12	(0.03)	-0.32	(0.03)	-1.44	(0.03)	-0.49	(0.01)	0.13	(0.01)	0.94	(0.02)
Portugal	0.17	(0.02)	0.15	(0.03)	0.18	(0.02)	-0.88	(0.02)	-0.14	(0.01)	0.41	(0.01)	1.27	(0.02)
Russian Federation	0.14	(0.02)	0.19	(0.02)	0.10	(0.02)	-1.08	(0.01)	-0.14	(0.01)	0.45	(0.01)	1.34	(0.01)
Sweden	0.01	(0.02)	0.15	(0.02)	-0.13	(0.03)	-1.19	(0.02)	-0.30	(0.01)	0.34	(0.01)	1.20	(0.02)
Switzerland	0.09	(0.02)	0.10	(0.03)	0.08	(0.02)	-1.07	(0.02)	-0.15	(0.01)	0.41	(0.01)	1.18	(0.02)
Thailand	0.02	(0.02)	0.00	(0.02)	0.04	(0.02)	-0.90	(0.01)	-0.19	(0.01)	0.25	(0.00)	0.94	(0.01)
United States	0.01	(0.03)	-0.04	(0.04)	0.06	(0.03)	-1.28	(0.02)	-0.32	(0.01)	0.34	(0.01)	1.32	(0.03)
OECD average	*0.00*	*(0.00)*	*0.04*	*(0.01)*	*-0.02*	*(0.01)*	*-1.22*	*(0.01)*	*-0.29*	*(0.00)*	*0.33*	*(0.00)*	*1.20*	*(0.00)*
OECD total	*0.05*	*(0.01)*	*0.04*	*(0.02)*	*0.06*	*(0.02)*	*-1.21*	*(0.01)*	*-0.25*	*(0.00)*	*0.37*	*(0.00)*	*1.31*	*(0.01)*
Netherlands[3]	-0.19	(0.02)	-0.11	(0.03)	-0.28	(0.03)	-1.32	(0.02)	-0.47	(0.01)	0.13	(0.01)	0.90	(0.02)

1. For the definition of the index see Annex A1.

2. For explained variation see Annex A2. Unit changes marked in bold are statistically significant. Where bottom and top quarters are marked in bold this indicates that their difference is statistically significant.

3. Response rate is too low to ensure comparability (see Annex A3).

Table 4.11 (continued)

Index of elaboration strategies and performance on the combined reading literacy scale, by national quarters of the index

Results based on students' self-reports

| | Performance on the combined reading literacy scale, by national quarters of the index of elaboration strategies[2] | | | | | | | | Change in the combined reading literacy score per unit of the index of elaboration strategies[2] | |
| | Bottom quarter | | Second quarter | | Third quarter | | Top quarter | | | |
	Mean score	S.E.	Mean score	S.E.	Mean score	S.E.	Mean score	S.E	Change	S.E.
Albania	330	(3.8)	352	(4.8)	356	(4.5)	370	(5.6)	18.6	(2.55)
Australia	517	(4.4)	523	(4.2)	533	(4.6)	551	(5.3)	13.0	(1.96)
Austria	501	(3.6)	500	(3.3)	509	(3.2)	526	(2.7)	9.8	(1.44)
Belgium (Fl.)	532	(6.6)	536	(4.7)	540	(4.5)	534	(6.1)	0.4	(2.23)
Brazil	382	(4.3)	394	(3.4)	410	(4.1)	418	(3.9)	15.9	(1.70)
Bulgaria	413	(6.4)	425	(4.7)	437	(5.4)	460	(6.3)	17.2	(2.12)
Chile	393	(4.1)	405	(4.5)	420	(4.4)	431	(4.3)	14.3	(1.62)
Czech Republic	485	(3.4)	491	(3.0)	506	(3.0)	529	(3.2)	18.2	(1.42)
Denmark	482	(3.9)	492	(4.1)	514	(3.1)	514	(3.3)	13.6	(1.66)
Finland	535	(3.9)	537	(3.2)	553	(3.0)	566	(4.6)	15.4	(1.81)
Germany	474	(4.4)	486	(3.4)	499	(4.4)	525	(3.1)	20.1	(1.77)
Hong Kong-China	509	(4.4)	522	(3.2)	531	(3.2)	544	(4.1)	15.7	(1.71)
Hungary	466	(5.7)	484	(5.8)	490	(5.4)	490	(5.0)	10.7	(2.96)
Iceland	498	(3.5)	501	(2.7)	507	(3.4)	533	(3.6)	12.4	(1.95)
Ireland	521	(4.5)	527	(4.4)	528	(3.8)	539	(4.1)	6.0	(1.62)
Israel	474	(8.2)	465	(8.2)	464	(10.1)	467	(8.1)	-0.8	(2.28)
Italy	483	(4.1)	480	(4.2)	487	(3.9)	501	(3.6)	6.4	(1.71)
Korea	492	(3.1)	518	(3.1)	537	(2.5)	552	(3.1)	22.4	(1.29)
Latvia	447	(6.3)	459	(6.2)	463	(6.8)	473	(6.0)	11.8	(2.81)
Liechtenstein	473	(9.6)	485	(11.0)	476	(11.0)	505	(10.3)	12.3	(4.84)
Luxembourg	441	(3.2)	449	(3.3)	456	(3.2)	467	(3.2)	8.8	(1.69)
FYR Macedonia	356	(3.9)	368	(4.1)	383	(2.8)	401	(2.8)	17.9	(1.93)
Mexico	414	(3.8)	413	(3.9)	425	(4.4)	439	(4.8)	10.9	(1.76)
New Zealand	525	(4.7)	533	(4.4)	538	(3.8)	544	(5.3)	8.7	(2.48)
Norway	490	(4.6)	504	(3.5)	517	(4.2)	529	(4.3)	16.9	(1.77)
Portugal	441	(5.5)	463	(4.8)	476	(5.0)	502	(5.1)	25.2	(2.37)
Russian Federation	450	(4.7)	459	(5.1)	468	(5.2)	478	(4.3)	10.6	(1.49)
Sweden	504	(3.0)	513	(3.3)	518	(2.9)	536	(3.1)	12.4	(1.39)
Switzerland	477	(4.7)	493	(4.4)	506	(5.4)	513	(6.1)	15.2	(2.19)
Thailand	415	(4.1)	427	(3.8)	432	(4.1)	448	(4.6)	16.9	(2.55)
United States	500	(7.6)	505	(8.5)	520	(6.8)	521	(8.1)	7.7	(2.59)
OECD average	*488*	*(1.1)*	*497*	*(0.9)*	*508*	*(0.9)*	*521*	*(1.1)*	*10.5*	*(0.46)*
OECD total	*482*	*(3.2)*	*490*	*(3.7)*	*503*	*(3.1)*	*513*	*(3.4)*	*8.1*	*(1.24)*
Netherlands[3]	531	(4.3)	528	(4.9)	539	(4.2)	533	(5.3)	1.6	(2.00)

1. For the definition of the index see Annex A1.

2. For explained variation see Annex A2. Unit changes marked in bold are statistically significant. Where bottom and top quarters are marked in bold this indicates that their difference is statistically significant.

3. Response rate is too low to ensure comparability (see Annex A3).

Table 4.12
Index of co-operative learning and performance on the combined reading literacy scale, by national quarters of the index
Results based on students' self-reports

| | Index of co-operative learning[1] | | | | | | | | | | | | | |
| | All students | | Males | | Females | | Bottom quarter | | Second quarter | | Third quarter | | Top quarter | |
	Mean index	S.E.	Mean index	S.E.	Mean index	S.E.	Mean index	S.E.	Mean index	S.E.	Mean index	S.E.	Mean index	S.E.
Albania	0.24	(0.02)	0.18	(0.03)	0.29	(0.03)	-1.09	(0.01)	-0.19	(0.01)	0.56	(0.01)	1.67	(0.02)
Australia	0.04	(0.01)	-0.03	(0.02)	0.11	(0.02)	-0.76	(0.01)	-0.16	(0.01)	0.09	(0.01)	0.97	(0.02)
Austria	-0.10	(0.02)	-0.26	(0.03)	0.04	(0.02)	-1.14	(0.01)	-0.45	(0.01)	0.11	(0.01)	1.07	(0.02)
Belgium (Fl.)	-0.15	(0.02)	-0.25	(0.02)	-0.03	(0.02)	-0.98	(0.01)	-0.37	(0.00)	-0.05	(0.00)	0.81	(0.02)
Brazil	0.47	(0.02)	0.34	(0.02)	0.58	(0.03)	-0.72	(0.02)	0.08	(0.01)	0.67	(0.01)	1.86	(0.02)
Bulgaria	0.09	(0.03)	-0.06	(0.03)	0.24	(0.03)	-1.15	(0.02)	-0.32	(0.01)	0.32	(0.01)	1.49	(0.02)
Chile	0.54	(0.02)	0.36	(0.03)	0.70	(0.03)	-0.81	(0.02)	0.13	(0.01)	0.84	(0.01)	2.02	(0.02)
Czech Republic	-0.06	(0.02)	-0.23	(0.03)	0.10	(0.02)	-1.09	(0.02)	-0.35	(0.01)	0.13	(0.01)	1.09	(0.02)
Denmark	0.50	(0.02)	0.45	(0.02)	0.56	(0.03)	-0.62	(0.01)	0.19	(0.01)	0.74	(0.01)	1.70	(0.02)
Finland	0.04	(0.02)	-0.11	(0.02)	0.18	(0.02)	-1.00	(0.01)	-0.23	(0.01)	0.22	(0.01)	1.19	(0.02)
Germany	-0.21	(0.02)	-0.33	(0.03)	-0.09	(0.02)	-1.33	(0.02)	-0.52	(0.01)	-0.03	(0.01)	1.05	(0.03)
Hong Kong-China	0.05	(0.02)	-0.01	(0.02)	0.11	(0.02)	-1.02	(0.02)	-0.22	(0.01)	0.24	(0.01)	1.19	(0.02)
Hungary	-0.34	(0.02)	-0.45	(0.03)	-0.22	(0.02)	-1.36	(0.02)	-0.70	(0.01)	-0.18	(0.01)	0.88	(0.03)
Iceland	-0.29	(0.02)	-0.38	(0.03)	-0.20	(0.02)	-1.38	(0.02)	-0.53	(0.01)	-0.10	(0.01)	0.85	(0.02)
Ireland	0.22	(0.02)	0.01	(0.03)	0.43	(0.03)	-1.09	(0.02)	-0.17	(0.01)	0.50	(0.01)	1.65	(0.02)
Israel	-0.05	(0.04)	-0.21	(0.05)	0.06	(0.05)	-1.18	(0.02)	-0.40	(0.01)	0.16	(0.01)	1.22	(0.03)
Italy	0.20	(0.03)	-0.04	(0.04)	0.45	(0.03)	-1.07	(0.03)	-0.15	(0.01)	0.51	(0.01)	1.52	(0.02)
Korea	-0.85	(0.01)	-0.81	(0.02)	-0.90	(0.02)	-1.87	(0.02)	-1.15	(0.00)	-0.69	(0.01)	0.31	(0.03)
Latvia	0.24	(0.04)	0.08	(0.04)	0.39	(0.05)	-1.00	(0.02)	-0.14	(0.01)	0.51	(0.01)	1.60	(0.03)
Liechtenstein	-0.01	(0.05)	-0.09	(0.07)	0.08	(0.07)	-0.95	(0.07)	-0.26	(0.02)	0.12	(0.02)	1.01	(0.09)
Luxembourg	-0.40	(0.02)	-0.58	(0.03)	-0.22	(0.03)	-1.66	(0.02)	-0.75	(0.01)	-0.18	(0.01)	0.97	(0.03)
FYR Macedonia	-0.04	(0.02)	-0.08	(0.03)	0.01	(0.02)	-1.28	(0.02)	-0.51	(0.01)	0.22	(0.01)	1.43	(0.02)
Mexico	0.22	(0.02)	0.12	(0.02)	0.32	(0.03)	-0.79	(0.01)	-0.11	(0.01)	0.30	(0.01)	1.47	(0.02)
New Zealand	0.29	(0.02)	0.17	(0.03)	0.40	(0.03)	-0.85	(0.02)	-0.09	(0.01)	0.53	(0.01)	1.57	(0.02)
Norway	0.17	(0.03)	0.00	(0.03)	0.34	(0.03)	-1.16	(0.02)	-0.17	(0.01)	0.47	(0.01)	1.54	(0.02)
Portugal	0.59	(0.03)	0.41	(0.03)	0.76	(0.02)	-0.61	(0.02)	0.23	(0.01)	0.86	(0.01)	1.88	(0.02)
Russian Federation	-0.23	(0.02)	-0.33	(0.02)	-0.13	(0.02)	-1.41	(0.02)	-0.55	(0.01)	0.03	(0.01)	1.02	(0.01)
Sweden	-0.21	(0.01)	-0.23	(0.02)	-0.18	(0.02)	-1.06	(0.02)	-0.42	(0.00)	-0.06	(0.00)	0.72	(0.02)
Switzerland	-0.01	(0.02)	-0.15	(0.02)	0.13	(0.02)	-1.02	(0.02)	-0.29	(0.01)	0.17	(0.01)	1.12	(0.02)
Thailand	0.32	(0.02)	0.19	(0.03)	0.41	(0.03)	-0.76	(0.01)	-0.05	(0.00)	0.55	(0.01)	1.53	(0.02)
United States	0.35	(0.03)	0.13	(0.05)	0.55	(0.03)	-1.07	(0.04)	-0.07	(0.01)	0.64	(0.01)	1.89	(0.02)
OECD average	*0.00*	*(0.00)*	*-0.13*	*(0.01)*	*0.14*	*(0.01)*	*-1.09*	*(0.01)*	*-0.31*	*(0.00)*	*0.20*	*(0.00)*	*1.22*	*(0.01)*
OECD total	*0.10*	*(0.02)*	*-0.07*	*(0.02)*	*0.26*	*(0.02)*	*-1.11*	*(0.02)*	*-0.26*	*(0.01)*	*0.32*	*(0.01)*	*1.45*	*(0.02)*
Netherlands[3]	-0.14	(0.03)	-0.02	(0.03)	0.31	(0.03)	-1.00	(0.02)	-0.18	(0.01)	0.39	(0.01)	1.36	(0.02)

1. For the definition of the index see Annex A1.
2. For explained variation see Annex A2. Unit changes marked in bold are statistically significant. Where bottom and top quarters are marked in bold this indicates that their difference is statistically significant.
3. Response rate is too low to ensure comparability (see Annex A3).

Table 4.12 (continued)
Index of co-operative learning and performance on the combined reading literacy scale, by national quarters of the index
Results based on students' self-reports

| | Performance on the combined reading literacy scale, by national quarters of the index of co-operative learning[2] | | | | | | | | Change in the combined reading literacy score per unit of the index of co-operative learning[2] | |
| | Bottom quarter | | Second quarter | | Third quarter | | Top quarter | | | |
	Mean score	S.E.	Mean score	S.E.	Mean score	S.E.	Mean score	S.E.	Change	S.E.
Albania	349	(5.1)	357	(4.1)	355	(5.3)	354	(4.9)	3.4	(2.01)
Australia	527	(5.5)	528	(4.5)	529	(4.9)	543	(4.3)	6.4	(2.75)
Austria	486	(4.5)	511	(3.3)	518	(3.0)	521	(3.5)	12.2	(2.19)
Belgium (Fl.)	524	(5.9)	545	(4.2)	536	(6.3)	538	(6.1)	3.6	(3.15)
Brazil	390	(4.6)	399	(4.1)	414	(3.6)	406	(4.3)	6.7	(1.59)
Bulgaria	403	(5.3)	438	(6.6)	450	(5.7)	447	(5.0)	15.0	(1.73)
Chile	398	(4.8)	411	(3.8)	422	(4.1)	423	(4.9)	8.3	(1.95)
Czech Republic	482	(3.7)	505	(2.9)	512	(3.0)	517	(3.3)	12.9	(1.74)
Denmark	488	(5.0)	505	(3.3)	511	(3.3)	501	(3.5)	5.4	(2.52)
Finland	531	(3.2)	546	(3.5)	555	(2.8)	561	(4.7)	11.6	(1.97)
Germany	477	(3.9)	501	(3.6)	502	(3.5)	508	(3.5)	9.0	(1.88)
Hong Kong-China	509	(4.5)	529	(3.7)	534	(3.0)	535	(3.6)	10.5	(1.79)
Hungary	475	(4.6)	488	(5.1)	490	(5.8)	481	(5.1)	1.3	(2.63)
Iceland	493	(3.3)	510	(2.7)	517	(3.3)	521	(2.6)	11.3	(1.63)
Ireland	521	(5.1)	536	(3.7)	532	(4.3)	525	(4.1)	1.1	(1.61)
Israel	470	(10.6)	466	(9.5)	472	(8.7)	466	(6.5)	-0.2	(3.64)
Italy	478	(5.9)	488	(4.1)	493	(3.0)	492	(3.3)	3.9	(2.22)
Korea	509	(3.4)	525	(3.0)	534	(3.2)	532	(2.5)	9.5	(1.34)
Latvia	432	(6.3)	462	(6.2)	469	(5.9)	483	(6.4)	17.0	(2.05)
Liechtenstein	478	(10.9)	486	(11.4)	479	(10.7)	492	(9.9)	3.1	(6.76)
Luxembourg	445	(3.3)	450	(3.1)	468	(3.2)	456	(3.6)	2.2	(1.54)
FYR Macedonia	380	(3.3)	392	(3.2)	382	(3.3)	358	(3.8)	-7.5	(1.62)
Mexico	410	(4.4)	424	(4.0)	427	(3.9)	431	(4.8)	8.3	(1.80)
New Zealand	522	(4.5)	536	(3.3)	546	(4.9)	538	(4.8)	6.1	(2.31)
Norway	479	(5.3)	513	(4.3)	525	(3.5)	527	(3.5)	17.6	(2.06)
Portugal	447	(6.9)	471	(5.5)	484	(4.5)	480	(4.7)	13.7	(2.52)
Russian Federation	447	(4.4)	458	(4.6)	473	(5.0)	479	(5.1)	12.4	(1.30)
Sweden	515	(3.1)	522	(2.9)	518	(3.5)	517	(3.4)	2.2	(1.93)
Switzerland	473	(5.7)	506	(5.2)	504	(4.8)	506	(4.4)	12.8	(1.96)
Thailand	410	(4.0)	432	(3.6)	442	(3.6)	439	(4.0)	12.8	(1.45)
United States	483	(9.6)	509	(7.8)	528	(5.5)	528	(6.1)	13.7	(1.79)
OECD average	*488*	*(1.1)*	*505*	*(1.0)*	*511*	*(1.0)*	*511*	*(1.0)*	*6.5*	*(0.52)*
OECD total	*477*	*(3.9)*	*497*	*(3.3)*	*507*	*(2.7)*	*508*	*(2.7)*	*7.8*	*(0.85)*
Netherlands[1]	516	(6.6)	538	(6.0)	536	(3.6)	541	(3.8)	8.0	(2.90)

1. For the definition of the index see Annex A1.
2. For explained variation see Annex A2. Unit changes marked in bold are statistically significant. Where bottom and top quarters are marked in bold this indicates that their difference is statistically significant.
3. Response rate is too low to ensure comparability (see Annex A3).

Table 4.13
Index of competitive learning and performance on the combined reading literacy scale, by national quarters of the index
Results based on students' self-reports

	Index of competitive learning[1]													
	All students		Males		Females		Bottom quarter		Second quarter		Third quarter		Top quarter	
	Mean index	S.E.	Mean index	S.E.	Mean index	S.E.	Mean index	S.E.	Mean index	S.E.	Mean index	S.E.	Mean index	S.E.
Albania	0.47	(0.02)	0.39	(0.03)	0.53	(0.03)	-0.75	(0.02)	0.15	(0.01)	0.74	(0.01)	1.73	(0.02)
Australia	0.10	(0.02)	0.20	(0.02)	0.00	(0.03)	-0.83	(0.01)	-0.20	(0.01)	0.27	(0.01)	1.17	(0.03)
Austria	-0.19	(0.02)	-0.13	(0.02)	-0.25	(0.03)	-1.32	(0.02)	-0.51	(0.01)	0.04	(0.01)	1.02	(0.02)
Belgium (Fl.)	-0.38	(0.02)	-0.29	(0.02)	-0.48	(0.02)	-1.34	(0.02)	-0.65	(0.01)	-0.18	(0.01)	0.66	(0.02)
Brazil	-0.03	(0.02)	0.09	(0.03)	-0.12	(0.03)	-1.23	(0.02)	-0.37	(0.01)	0.22	(0.01)	1.29	(0.03)
Bulgaria	0.31	(0.02)	0.24	(0.03)	0.38	(0.03)	-1.01	(0.02)	-0.06	(0.01)	0.62	(0.01)	1.68	(0.02)
Chile	0.49	(0.02)	0.54	(0.02)	0.45	(0.02)	-0.74	(0.02)	0.15	(0.01)	0.74	(0.01)	1.82	(0.01)
Czech Republic	0.14	(0.02)	0.14	(0.02)	0.14	(0.02)	-0.94	(0.01)	-0.17	(0.01)	0.35	(0.01)	1.33	(0.02)
Denmark	0.19	(0.02)	0.33	(0.03)	0.04	(0.03)	-1.09	(0.02)	-0.15	(0.01)	0.42	(0.01)	1.57	(0.02)
Finland	-0.25	(0.02)	-0.13	(0.02)	-0.35	(0.02)	-1.35	(0.02)	-0.55	(0.00)	-0.01	(0.01)	0.92	(0.02)
Germany	-0.07	(0.02)	-0.01	(0.03)	-0.14	(0.02)	-1.14	(0.02)	-0.38	(0.01)	0.13	(0.01)	1.11	(0.02)
Hong Kong-China	0.67	(0.02)	0.65	(0.03)	0.69	(0.03)	-0.42	(0.02)	0.31	(0.00)	0.90	(0.01)	1.88	(0.01)
Hungary	0.10	(0.02)	0.07	(0.03)	0.13	(0.02)	-1.05	(0.02)	-0.23	(0.00)	0.34	(0.01)	1.32	(0.02)
Iceland	0.01	(0.02)	0.13	(0.03)	-0.09	(0.03)	-1.20	(0.02)	-0.34	(0.01)	0.26	(0.01)	1.34	(0.02)
Ireland	0.15	(0.02)	0.35	(0.03)	-0.06	(0.03)	-1.25	(0.02)	-0.28	(0.01)	0.47	(0.01)	1.66	(0.02)
Israel	0.18	(0.03)	0.24	(0.04)	0.14	(0.03)	-0.84	(0.02)	-0.16	(0.01)	0.36	(0.01)	1.37	(0.02)
Italy	-0.01	(0.02)	0.06	(0.03)	-0.07	(0.03)	-1.33	(0.02)	-0.36	(0.01)	0.31	(0.01)	1.37	(0.02)
Korea	-0.14	(0.02)	-0.10	(0.03)	-0.19	(0.03)	-1.31	(0.02)	-0.51	(0.01)	0.07	(0.01)	1.19	(0.02)
Latvia	0.22	(0.02)	0.16	(0.03)	0.27	(0.03)	-0.89	(0.02)	-0.07	(0.01)	0.44	(0.01)	1.38	(0.02)
Liechtenstein	-0.20	(0.05)	-0.07	(0.08)	-0.34	(0.06)	-1.18	(0.06)	-0.48	(0.02)	0.02	(0.02)	0.81	(0.07)
Luxembourg	-0.18	(0.02)	-0.16	(0.03)	-0.20	(0.03)	-1.38	(0.02)	-0.49	(0.01)	0.07	(0.01)	1.07	(0.02)
FYR Macedonia	0.60	(0.02)	0.52	(0.02)	0.69	(0.03)	-0.73	(0.02)	0.26	(0.01)	0.94	(0.01)	1.93	(0.01)
Mexico	0.54	(0.02)	0.59	(0.02)	0.49	(0.02)	-0.46	(0.01)	0.23	(0.00)	0.70	(0.01)	1.70	(0.02)
New Zealand	0.29	(0.02)	0.40	(0.03)	0.17	(0.03)	-0.94	(0.02)	-0.07	(0.01)	0.53	(0.01)	1.63	(0.02)
Norway	-0.03	(0.02)	0.12	(0.03)	-0.19	(0.03)	-1.38	(0.02)	-0.40	(0.01)	0.24	(0.01)	1.41	(0.02)
Portugal	-0.22	(0.02)	-0.04	(0.03)	-0.39	(0.03)	-1.48	(0.02)	-0.58	(0.01)	0.07	(0.01)	1.10	(0.02)
Russian Federation	0.13	(0.02)	0.06	(0.02)	0.21	(0.02)	-1.05	(0.02)	-0.20	(0.01)	0.40	(0.01)	1.38	(0.02)
Sweden	-0.01	(0.02)	0.09	(0.02)	-0.12	(0.02)	-1.02	(0.02)	-0.34	(0.01)	0.20	(0.01)	1.10	(0.02)
Switzerland	-0.26	(0.02)	-0.14	(0.02)	-0.38	(0.02)	-1.34	(0.02)	-0.53	(0.01)	-0.02	(0.00)	0.86	(0.02)
Thailand	0.32	(0.02)	0.27	(0.03)	0.36	(0.02)	-0.61	(0.01)	0.04	(0.00)	0.47	(0.00)	1.40	(0.02)
United States	0.27	(0.03)	0.30	(0.04)	0.25	(0.03)	-1.02	(0.02)	-0.08	(0.01)	0.52	(0.01)	1.68	(0.02)
OECD average	*0.00*	*(0.00)*	*0.10*	*(0.01)*	*-0.08*	*(0.01)*	*-1.16*	*(0.00)*	*-0.32*	*(0.00)*	*0.25*	*(0.00)*	*1.27*	*(0.01)*
OECD total	*0.16*	*(0.01)*	*0.21*	*(0.02)*	*0.12*	*(0.01)*	*-1.02*	*(0.01)*	*-0.18*	*(0.01)*	*0.39*	*(0.00)*	*1.47*	*(0.01)*
Netherlands[3]	-0.25	(0.03)	-0.07	(0.04)	-0.43	(0.04)	-1.55	(0.03)	-0.60	(0.01)	0.05	(0.01)	1.10	(0.03)

1. For the definition of the index see Annex A1.

2. For explained variation see Annex A2. Unit changes marked in bold are statistically significant. Where bottom and top quarters are marked in bold this indicates that their difference is statistically significant.

3. Response rate is too low to ensure comparability (see Annex A3).

Table 4.13 (continued)
Index of competitive learning and performance on the combined reading literacy scale, by national quarters of the index
Results based on students' self-reports

| | Performance on the combined reading literacy scale, by national quarters of the index of competitive learning[2] | | | | | | | | Change in the combined reading literacy score per unit of the index of competitive learning[2] | |
| | Bottom quarter | | Second quarter | | Third quarter | | Top quarter | | | |
	Mean score	S.E.	Mean score	S.E.	Mean score	S.E.	Mean score	S.E.	Change	S.E.
Albania	342	(5.0)	359	(3.7)	362	(4.6)	353	(6.1)	5.5	(2.55)
Australia	515	(4.8)	522	(4.5)	530	(4.3)	559	(5.6)	21.7	(2.37)
Austria	502	(3.5)	501	(4.1)	510	(3.8)	522	(3.0)	9.5	(1.64)
Belgium (Fl.)	537	(6.0)	542	(4.1)	539	(5.0)	526	(6.7)	-2.9	(2.22)
Brazil	405	(4.5)	401	(3.7)	397	(4.2)	405	(4.6)	-1.0	(1.35)
Bulgaria	415	(5.9)	434	(5.5)	439	(5.4)	449	(6.5)	12.6	(1.45)
Chile	409	(5.6)	406	(3.9)	416	(4.0)	424	(4.2)	4.3	(1.69)
Czech Republic	483	(3.2)	498	(3.1)	513	(3.5)	521	(3.2)	16.7	(1.58)
Denmark	481	(3.5)	493	(3.6)	502	(3.4)	527	(4.1)	15.9	(1.65)
Finland	530	(4.4)	539	(3.8)	549	(3.3)	574	(3.0)	18.1	(1.85)
Germany	476	(3.9)	498	(3.5)	502	(4.1)	514	(3.3)	15.5	(1.71)
Hong Kong-China	497	(4.9)	526	(3.6)	537	(3.4)	547	(3.1)	21.2	(2.27)
Hungary	460	(5.1)	479	(5.2)	497	(5.2)	498	(4.5)	18.5	(1.86)
Iceland	489	(2.9)	500	(3.6)	514	(3.6)	538	(3.5)	19.5	(1.78)
Ireland	511	(4.7)	520	(4.4)	537	(3.9)	547	(4.3)	13.5	(1.63)
Israel	453	(8.1)	478	(9.0)	482	(9.6)	461	(8.7)	4.2	(3.70)
Italy	485	(4.5)	481	(4.0)	488	(3.7)	497	(3.7)	4.3	(1.57)
Korea	495	(3.6)	525	(2.6)	532	(2.9)	547	(2.6)	18.5	(1.16)
Latvia	429	(6.7)	454	(6.3)	467	(5.2)	495	(5.7)	27.8	(2.28)
Liechtenstein	485	(9.3)	477	(11.8)	498	(9.7)	478	(11.4)	-0.5	(6.85)
Luxembourg	448	(3.3)	456	(3.5)	456	(3.1)	461	(3.4)	3.0	(2.00)
FYR Macedonia	371	(3.2)	383	(3.2)	380	(3.2)	378	(3.3)	2.4	(1.47)
Mexico	409	(4.5)	416	(4.0)	430	(4.5)	437	(4.7)	12.7	(1.97)
New Zealand	512	(4.2)	528	(3.6)	540	(4.0)	560	(5.1)	18.9	(2.09)
Norway	477	(4.6)	496	(3.9)	520	(4.2)	551	(3.7)	24.5	(1.70)
Portugal	481	(5.0)	466	(5.3)	468	(5.5)	467	(5.3)	-5.5	(1.60)
Russian Federation	442	(4.7)	454	(4.3)	471	(5.3)	490	(4.6)	19.0	(1.50)
Sweden	507	(3.6)	511	(2.8)	518	(3.5)	535	(3.4)	12.9	(1.83)
Switzerland	503	(5.4)	496	(5.7)	495	(5.2)	496	(5.1)	-3.1	(1.98)
Thailand	412	(3.8)	430	(3.9)	437	(3.9)	444	(4.4)	15.1	(2.15)
United States	478	(9.4)	505	(6.6)	519	(6.3)	547	(6.2)	24.7	(2.42)
OECD average	*488*	*(1.0)*	*498*	*(0.9)*	*507*	*(1.0)*	*521*	*(1.0)*	*11.1*	*(0.45)*
OECD total	*474*	*(4.0)*	*492*	*(2.9)*	*503*	*(2.8)*	*521*	*(2.7)*	*13.2*	*(1.05)*
Netherlands[1]	538	(5.5)	527	(4.8)	532	(5.1)	534	(4.6)	-0.8	(2.15)

1. For the definition of the index see Annex A1.
2. For explained variation see Annex A2. Unit changes marked in bold are statistically significant. Where bottom and top quarters are marked in bold this indicates that their difference is statistically significant.
3. Response rate is too low to ensure comparability (see Annex A3).

Table 5.1
Percentage of students by socio-occupational categories, by gender

	All students				Males				Females			
	White-collar high-skilled	White-collar low-skilled	Blue-collar high-skilled	Blue-collar low-skilled	White-collar high-skilled	White-collar low-skilled	Blue-collar high-skilled	Blue-collar low-skilled	White-collar high-skilled	White-collar low-skilled	Blue-collar high-skilled	Blue-collar low-skilled
	%	%	%	%	%	%	%	%	%	%	%	%
Albania	84.1	3.7	6.5	5.7	74.1	2.7	14.1	9.1	92.2	4.6	0.3	2.9
Argentina	79.7	7.2	1.9	11.2	74.3	7.3	4.4	14.1	83.6	7.1	0.1	9.1
Australia	65.0	11.7	10.4	12.9	62.4	6.0	19.0	12.7	67.8	17.9	1.2	13.1
Austria	55.3	17.2	11.7	15.8	56.3	8.6	21.9	13.3	54.8	25.1	2.2	17.9
Belgium	65.6	14.2	15.4	4.9	58.5	7.6	27.9	6.0	73.1	21.3	1.8	3.7
Brazil	87.4	7.8	2.4	2.3	86.0	4.7	4.5	4.8	88.6	10.4	0.7	0.2
Bulgaria	55.0	8.9	4.9	31.2	48.2	6.5	7.1	38.2	62.2	11.4	2.6	23.8
Canada	70.9	10.2	7.1	11.8	64.6	9.7	13.0	12.8	77.1	10.8	1.2	10.8
Chile	68.9	10.2	7.6	13.3	64.8	5.7	14.5	15.0	72.6	14.2	1.5	11.8
Czech Republic	44.5	22.0	16.2	17.3	41.1	11.9	28.3	18.7	47.6	31.1	5.3	16.0
Denmark	58.5	17.5	19.6	4.3	50.5	10.9	34.1	4.5	67.7	25.1	2.9	4.2
Finland	60.4	15.8	12.2	11.5	55.5	9.1	21.4	14.0	65.0	22.0	3.7	9.2
France	48.9	14.7	9.9	26.5	44.1	8.5	18.7	28.7	53.4	20.5	1.7	24.4
Germany	48.8	20.9	17.2	13.2	44.7	13.3	30.1	11.9	53.1	28.0	4.6	14.3
Greece	72.3	11.7	9.4	6.6	66.0	8.6	17.9	7.6	78.5	14.6	1.3	5.6
Hong Kong-China	58.6	17.2	0.6	23.7	54.1	19.5	0.6	25.8	63.1	14.9	0.5	21.5
Hungary	52.7	19.0	16.6	11.7	50.3	9.5	28.0	12.2	55.3	28.5	5.1	11.1
Iceland	59.2	12.6	7.9	20.3	60.3	6.4	13.5	19.8	58.4	18.5	2.4	20.7
Indonesia	76.2	6.8	3.8	13.2	78.2	1.3	6.0	14.5	74.2	12.1	1.7	12.0
Ireland	64.1	12.2	11.7	12.1	57.5	7.2	22.6	12.7	70.3	16.9	1.3	11.5
Israel	63.7	5.6	1.1	29.7	64.8	3.5	2.2	29.5	62.9	7.0	0.3	29.8
Italy	69.1	15.2	5.8	9.9	66.6	11.9	10.6	10.9	71.6	18.7	0.9	8.8
Japan	45.8	12.9	4.0	37.4	43.3	7.7	7.3	41.7	48.2	17.9	0.7	33.2
Korea	71.2	13.2	1.6	13.9	71.1	13.4	2.4	13.0	71.4	13.0	0.6	15.0
Latvia	63.1	18.0	13.4	5.5	55.0	13.8	22.7	8.5	70.5	21.8	5.0	2.7
Liechtenstein	36.3	17.1	14.2	32.4	40.6	13.9	24.4	21.1	32.2	20.4	3.1	44.2
Luxembourg	59.6	14.3	8.7	17.4	55.7	11.3	15.4	17.6	63.0	16.9	2.8	17.2
FYR Macedonia	75.4	9.5	5.5	9.6	71.9	8.1	10.1	9.9	78.7	10.7	1.2	9.4
Mexico	86.0	3.6	2.1	8.2	84.0	2.5	3.4	10.1	88.0	4.7	0.8	6.4
New Zealand	67.0	15.1	8.5	9.4	61.3	11.8	16.5	10.4	72.4	18.3	0.8	8.4
Norway	57.4	12.7	12.9	17.1	55.0	6.4	23.2	15.4	60.1	18.9	2.3	18.7
Peru	84.1	7.9	6.2	1.8	82.9	2.6	11.0	3.4	85.2	13.1	1.4	0.2
Poland	68.8	15.4	14.2	1.7	63.3	9.4	24.4	2.9	74.5	21.7	3.5	0.4
Portugal	76.5	9.5	5.1	9.0	72.7	7.0	9.8	10.5	79.8	11.7	0.8	7.7
Russian Federation	58.6	6.9	11.0	23.5	47.6	4.8	15.9	31.7	69.1	9.0	6.2	15.7
Spain	66.6	12.2	8.2	13.1	61.2	7.7	16.1	15.0	71.7	16.6	0.7	11.0
Sweden	63.2	10.3	8.1	18.5	62.0	5.8	13.6	18.6	64.5	14.8	2.4	18.3
Switzerland	45.3	16.4	15.0	23.3	42.7	11.5	26.9	18.8	47.6	21.0	3.9	27.4
Thailand	43.3	17.4	10.9	28.4	33.5	12.5	22.0	32.0	49.8	20.8	3.4	26.0
United Kingdom	57.1	16.3	7.6	19.0	51.0	14.0	14.5	20.5	63.0	18.6	0.8	17.6
United States	80.5	8.2	5.1	6.2	74.4	7.5	9.8	8.4	85.8	8.8	1.0	4.3
OECD average	62.2	13.9	10.1	13.8	58.4	9.1	18.2	14.4	66.1	18.6	2.1	13.2
Netherlands[1]	57.6	18.6	8.4	15.5	58.6	9.4	15.7	16.3	56.4	28.1	0.8	14.7

1. Response rate is too low to ensure comparability (see Annex A3).

Table 5.2a
Student performance on the combined reading, mathematical and scientific literacy scales, by gender

	Reading literacy Males Mean Score	S.E.	Females Mean Score	S.E.	Difference[1] Score dif.	S.E.	Mathematical literacy Males Mean Score	S.E.	Females Mean Score	S.E.	Difference[1] Score dif.	S.E.	Scientific literacy Males Mean Score	S.E.	Females Mean Score	S.E.	Difference[1] Score dif.	S.E.	Correlation between gender and reading performance[2] Correl.	S.E.
Albania	319	(4.2)	378	(2.7)	**-58**	(3.8)	372	(4.8)	390	(3.5)	**-18**	(5.7)	366	(4.4)	387	(3.3)	**-22**	(5.3)	0.29	(0.02)
Argentina	393	(7.7)	437	(12.3)	**-44**	(10.7)	386	(8.0)	389	(12.6)	-3	(11.0)	388	(8.1)	402	(10.0)	-14	(7.9)	0.20	(0.05)
Australia	513	(4.0)	546	(4.7)	**-34**	(5.4)	539	(4.1)	527	(5.1)	12	(6.2)	526	(3.9)	529	(4.8)	-3	(5.3)	0.17	(0.03)
Austria	495	(3.2)	520	(3.6)	**-26**	(5.2)	530	(4.0)	503	(3.7)	**27**	(5.9)	526	(3.8)	514	(4.3)	12	(6.3)	0.14	(0.03)
Belgium	492	(4.2)	525	(4.9)	**-33**	(6.0)	524	(4.6)	518	(5.2)	6	(6.1)	496	(5.2)	498	(5.6)	-2	(6.7)	0.15	(0.03)
Brazil	388	(3.9)	404	(3.4)	**-17**	(4.0)	349	(4.7)	322	(4.7)	**27**	(5.6)	376	(4.8)	376	(3.8)	0	(5.6)	0.10	(0.02)
Bulgaria	407	(4.9)	455	(6.3)	**-47**	(5.6)	428	(6.5)	432	(6.9)	-4	(7.1)	446	(4.5)	451	(6.4)	-5	(6.1)	0.23	(0.03)
Canada	519	(1.8)	551	(1.7)	**-32**	(1.6)	539	(1.8)	529	(1.6)	**10**	(1.9)	529	(1.9)	531	(1.7)	-2	(1.9)	0.17	(0.01)
Chile	396	(4.3)	421	(4.6)	**-25**	(5.6)	388	(4.8)	380	(4.7)	8	(5.9)	418	(4.7)	412	(4.6)	6	(6.2)	0.14	(0.03)
Czech Republic	473	(4.1)	510	(2.5)	**-37**	(4.7)	504	(4.4)	492	(3.0)	12	(5.2)	512	(3.8)	511	(3.2)	1	(5.1)	0.20	(0.02)
Denmark	485	(3.0)	510	(2.9)	**-25**	(3.3)	522	(3.1)	507	(3.0)	**15**	(3.7)	488	(3.9)	476	(3.5)	12	(4.8)	0.13	(0.02)
Finland	520	(3.0)	571	(2.8)	**-51**	(2.6)	537	(2.8)	536	(2.6)	1	(3.3)	534	(3.5)	541	(2.7)	-6	(3.8)	0.29	(0.02)
France	490	(3.5)	519	(2.7)	**-29**	(3.4)	525	(4.1)	511	(2.8)	14	(4.2)	504	(4.2)	498	(3.8)	6	(4.8)	0.16	(0.02)
Germany	468	(3.2)	502	(3.9)	**-35**	(5.2)	498	(3.1)	483	(4.0)	**15**	(5.1)	489	(3.4)	487	(3.4)	3	(4.7)	0.16	(0.02)
Greece	456	(6.1)	493	(4.6)	**-37**	(5.0)	451	(7.7)	444	(5.4)	7	(7.4)	457	(6.1)	464	(5.2)	-7	(5.7)	0.19	(0.02)
Hong Kong-China	518	(4.8)	533	(3.6)	**-16**	(6.1)	569	(5.3)	551	(4.3)	18	(7.2)	545	(4.9)	536	(3.7)	9	(6.4)	0.09	(0.04)
Hungary	465	(5.3)	496	(4.3)	**-32**	(5.7)	492	(5.2)	485	(4.9)	7	(6.2)	496	(5.8)	497	(5.0)	-2	(6.9)	0.17	(0.03)
Iceland	488	(2.1)	528	(2.1)	**-40**	(3.1)	513	(3.1)	518	(2.9)	-5	(4.0)	495	(3.4)	499	(3.0)	-5	(4.7)	0.22	(0.02)
Indonesia	360	(3.7)	380	(4.6)	**-20**	(3.4)	369	(4.3)	364	(5.9)	5	(4.8)	396	(3.9)	391	(4.8)	5	(3.8)	a	a
Ireland	513	(4.2)	542	(3.6)	**-29**	(4.6)	510	(4.0)	497	(3.4)	13	(5.1)	511	(4.2)	517	(4.2)	-6	(5.5)	0.15	(0.02)
Israel	444	(10.9)	459	(8.1)	-16	(9.1)	442	(10.4)	430	(9.4)	12	(9.1)	446	(12.9)	426	(9.7)	20	(13.0)	0.14	(0.02)
Italy	469	(5.1)	507	(3.6)	**-38**	(7.0)	462	(5.3)	454	(3.8)	8	(7.3)	474	(5.6)	483	(3.9)	-9	(7.7)	0.21	(0.04)
Japan	507	(6.7)	537	(5.4)	**-30**	(6.4)	561	(7.3)	553	(5.9)	8	(7.4)	547	(7.2)	554	(5.9)	-7	(7.2)	0.17	(0.04)
Korea	519	(3.8)	533	(3.7)	**-14**	(6.0)	559	(4.6)	532	(5.1)	**27**	(7.8)	561	(4.3)	541	(5.1)	**19**	(7.6)	0.10	(0.04)
Latvia	432	(5.5)	485	(5.4)	**-53**	(4.2)	467	(5.3)	460	(5.6)	6	(5.8)	449	(6.4)	472	(5.8)	**-23**	(5.4)	0.07	(0.04)
Liechtenstein	468	(7.3)	500	(6.8)	**-31**	(11.5)	521	(11.5)	510	(11.1)	12	(17.7)	484	(10.9)	468	(9.3)	16	(14.7)	0.16	(0.06)
Luxembourg	429	(2.6)	456	(2.3)	**-27**	(3.8)	454	(3.0)	439	(3.2)	**15**	(4.7)	441	(3.6)	448	(3.2)	-7	(5.0)	0.13	(0.02)
FYR Macedonia	348	(2.5)	399	(2.5)	**-50**	(3.2)	381	(3.6)	384	(3.5)	-3	(4.7)	393	(3.4)	409	(2.6)	**-16**	(4.4)	0.27	(0.02)
Mexico	411	(4.2)	432	(3.8)	**-20**	(4.3)	393	(4.5)	382	(3.8)	11	(4.9)	423	(4.2)	419	(3.9)	4	(4.8)	0.12	(0.03)
New Zealand	507	(4.2)	553	(3.8)	**-46**	(6.3)	536	(5.0)	539	(4.1)	-3	(6.7)	523	(4.6)	535	(3.8)	-12	(7.0)	0.21	(0.03)
Norway	486	(3.8)	529	(2.9)	**-43**	(4.0)	506	(3.8)	495	(2.9)	**11**	(4.0)	499	(4.1)	505	(3.3)	-7	(5.0)	0.21	(0.02)
Peru	324	(6.3)	330	(5.3)	-7	(7.5)	301	(6.1)	285	(6.3)	16	(8.8)	339	(5.3)	328	(4.9)	11	(6.7)	0.03	(0.04)
Poland	461	(6.0)	498	(5.5)	**-36**	(7.0)	472	(7.5)	468	(6.3)	5	(8.5)	486	(6.1)	480	(6.5)	6	(7.4)	0.18	(0.03)
Portugal	458	(5.0)	482	(4.6)	**-25**	(3.8)	464	(4.7)	446	(4.7)	**19**	(4.9)	456	(4.8)	462	(4.2)	-6	(4.3)	0.13	(0.02)
Russian Federation	443	(4.5)	481	(4.1)	**-38**	(2.9)	478	(5.7)	479	(6.2)	-2	(4.8)	453	(5.4)	467	(5.2)	**-14**	(4.5)	0.21	(0.02)
Spain	481	(3.4)	505	(2.8)	**-24**	(3.2)	487	(4.3)	469	(3.3)	**18**	(4.5)	492	(3.5)	491	(3.6)	1	(4.0)	0.14	(0.02)
Sweden	499	(2.6)	536	(2.5)	**-37**	(2.7)	514	(3.2)	507	(3.0)	7	(4.0)	512	(3.5)	513	(2.9)	0	(3.9)	0.20	(0.02)
Switzerland	480	(4.9)	510	(4.5)	**-30**	(4.2)	537	(5.3)	523	(4.8)	14	(5.0)	500	(5.7)	493	(4.7)	7	(5.4)	0.17	(0.02)
Thailand	406	(3.9)	448	(3.1)	**-41**	(3.8)	429	(4.9)	435	(3.9)	-6	(5.1)	429	(4.2)	442	(3.4)	**-13**	(4.6)	0.26	(0.02)
United Kingdom	512	(3.0)	537	(3.4)	**-26**	(4.3)	534	(3.5)	526	(3.7)	8	(5.0)	535	(3.4)	531	(4.0)	4	(5.2)	0.13	(0.02)
United States	490	(8.4)	518	(6.2)	**-29**	(4.1)	497	(8.9)	490	(7.3)	7	(5.4)	497	(8.9)	502	(6.5)	-5	(5.3)	0.14	(0.02)
OECD average	*485*	*(0.8)*	*517*	*(0.7)*	*-32*	*(0.9)*	*506*	*(1.0)*	*495*	*(0.9)*	*11*	*(1.2)*	*501*	*(0.9)*	*501*	*(0.8)*	*0*	*(1.0)*		
OECD total	*485*	*(2.3)*	*514*	*(2.0)*	*-29*	*(1.6)*	*504*	*(2.6)*	*493*	*(2.3)*	*11*	*(2.3)*	*502*	*(2.5)*	*503*	*(2.0)*	*0*	*(2.0)*		
Netherlands[3]	517	(4.8)	547	(3.8)	**-30**	(5.7)	569	(4.9)	558	(4.6)	11	(6.2)	529	(6.3)	529	(5.1)	1	(8.1)	0.17	(0.03)

1. Positive differences indicate that males perform better than females, negative differences indicate that females perform better than males. Differences that are statistically significant are indicated in bold.

2. The OECD median correlation is 0.16 and the standard deviation is 0.04.

3. Response rate is too low to ensure comparability (see Annex A3).

Table 5.2b
Student performance on the retrieving information, interpreting texts and reflection and evaluation scales, by gender

	Retrieving information						Interpreting texts						Reflection and evaluation					
	Males		Females		Difference[1]		Males		Females		Difference[1]		Males		Females		Difference[1]	
	Mean score	S.E.	Mean score	S.E.	Score dif.	S.E.	Mean score	S.E.	Mean score	S.E.	Score dif.	S.E.	Mean score	S.E.	Mean score	S.E.	Score dif.	S.E.
Albania	308	(4.5)	363	(3.2)	**-55**	(4.5)	327	(3.7)	376	(2.6)	**-49**	(3.2)	309	(4.4)	390	(3.2)	**-80**	(4.1)
Argentina	383	(8.8)	426	(13.3)	-43	(11.4)	393	(6.9)	433	(11.4)	-40	(10.2)	400	(8.1)	454	(12.4)	-54	(10.5)
Australia	523	(4.3)	551	(5.0)	-28	(5.7)	511	(4.1)	545	(4.9)	-34	(5.7)	507	(4.0)	548	(4.7)	-42	(5.5)
Austria	495	(3.3)	510	(3.6)	-16	(5.4)	497	(3.1)	520	(3.8)	-23	(5.3)	493	(3.5)	532	(3.8)	-39	(5.5)
Belgium	504	(4.7)	529	(5.4)	-25	(6.6)	498	(3.9)	529	(4.7)	-31	(6.1)	475	(5.2)	522	(5.3)	-47	(6.4)
Brazil	360	(4.3)	370	(4.0)	**-10**	(4.5)	393	(3.8)	408	(3.5)	**-14**	(4.1)	404	(4.2)	429	(3.7)	**-25**	(4.3)
Bulgaria	397	(5.5)	448	(6.9)	**-51**	(6.2)	415	(4.6)	454	(5.9)	**-39**	(5.0)	400	(5.5)	465	(7.3)	**-66**	(6.3)
Canada	519	(1.9)	543	(1.8)	-25	(1.8)	518	(1.8)	547	(1.7)	-29	(1.6)	521	(1.8)	566	(1.7)	-45	(1.7)
Chile	373	(4.8)	393	(5.3)	-20	(6.5)	408	(4.1)	429	(4.3)	**-21**	(5.3)	392	(4.4)	429	(4.6)	-37	(5.6)
Czech Republic	467	(4.7)	495	(2.8)	-27	(5.4)	483	(4.1)	517	(2.6)	-34	(4.6)	457	(4.3)	511	(2.6)	-54	(4.7)
Denmark	491	(3.4)	506	(3.2)	-14	(3.5)	485	(3.1)	506	(2.9)	-21	(3.4)	480	(3.2)	523	(3.3)	-43	(3.6)
Finland	534	(3.4)	578	(3.1)	-44	(3.4)	529	(3.3)	579	(3.2)	**-51**	(3.1)	501	(3.0)	564	(3.1)	-63	(2.8)
France	503	(3.8)	527	(3.0)	-23	(3.6)	492	(3.5)	519	(2.7)	-27	(3.3)	477	(3.7)	515	(2.9)	-39	(3.9)
Germany	471	(3.0)	497	(4.0)	-26	(5.2)	472	(2.9)	505	(3.8)	-33	(4.8)	455	(3.5)	503	(4.2)	-48	(5.5)
Greece	435	(6.7)	466	(5.0)	-32	(5.6)	459	(5.5)	492	(4.2)	-33	(4.6)	468	(6.8)	522	(5.4)	-54	(6.1)
Hong Kong-China	518	(5.1)	526	(3.9)	-8	(6.4)	517	(4.4)	527	(3.4)	**-11**	(5.6)	522	(5.1)	553	(3.7)	**-31**	(6.4)
Hungary	465	(6.0)	491	(4.8)	-25	(6.3)	466	(5.1)	494	(4.1)	-28	(5.4)	460	(5.7)	503	(4.5)	-43	(5.8)
Iceland	485	(2.4)	517	(2.2)	-32	(3.3)	497	(2.1)	535	(2.1)	-38	(3.0)	476	(2.0)	529	(1.9)	-54	(2.8)
Indonesia	341	(4.2)	358	(5.3)	**-17**	(4.0)	366	(3.3)	384	(4.2)	**-18**	(3.2)	363	(4.3)	393	(4.6)	**-30**	(4.0)
Ireland	514	(4.2)	536	(3.6)	-22	(4.7)	513	(4.3)	541	(3.6)	-27	(4.7)	515	(4.0)	552	(3.3)	-37	(4.3)
Israel	424	(11.8)	437	(8.8)	-13	(9.7)	453	(10.0)	463	(8.0)	-9	(8.6)	451	(11.4)	480	(8.6)	-29	(9.3)
Italy	474	(5.7)	504	(4.0)	-31	(7.8)	470	(4.6)	509	(3.3)	-39	(6.4)	460	(5.5)	507	(3.8)	-47	(7.6)
Japan	512	(7.0)	539	(5.8)	-27	(6.8)	505	(6.3)	530	(5.3)	-25	(6.1)	508	(7.2)	551	(5.5)	-42	(7.0)
Korea	527	(4.1)	533	(4.3)	-6	(6.9)	521	(3.7)	530	(3.6)	-9	(5.9)	514	(3.7)	541	(3.5)	-27	(5.8)
Latvia	428	(6.1)	474	(6.0)	**-46**	(4.9)	434	(5.0)	485	(5.0)	**-51**	(3.8)	423	(5.7)	493	(6.1)	**-71**	(4.7)
Liechtenstein	484	(8.2)	504	(7.7)	-20	(12.3)	474	(7.8)	497	(6.9)	-23	(11.6)	447	(8.9)	492	(8.6)	-45	(13.3)
Luxembourg	424	(2.6)	444	(2.5)	-20	(4.0)	433	(2.6)	460	(2.3)	-27	(3.9)	423	(3.0)	464	(2.8)	-40	(4.5)
FYR Macedonia	341	(3.7)	386	(3.1)	**-45**	(3.8)	360	(1.8)	405	(1.8)	**-46**	(2.8)	325	(2.7)	397	(2.2)	**-72**	(3.5)
Mexico	396	(5.0)	408	(4.4)	-12	(5.1)	410	(3.8)	427	(3.3)	-17	(3.9)	428	(4.9)	463	(4.5)	-35	(5.6)
New Zealand	516	(4.7)	555	(4.1)	-39	(7.1)	506	(4.3)	549	(3.9)	-43	(6.6)	502	(4.2)	559	(3.9)	-57	(6.4)
Norway	490	(3.9)	523	(2.9)	-32	(4.0)	487	(3.7)	527	(2.7)	-40	(3.8)	479	(4.0)	539	(2.9)	-60	(4.1)
Peru	288	(7.1)	291	(6.1)	-3	(8.5)	340	(5.8)	344	(5.0)	-4	(7.0)	314	(7.1)	331	(6.1)	**-17**	(8.5)
Poland	461	(6.6)	489	(6.2)	-28	(7.8)	465	(5.5)	500	(5.5)	-35	(6.6)	451	(6.4)	504	(5.8)	-53	(7.4)
Portugal	447	(5.5)	464	(5.0)	-16	(4.2)	461	(4.7)	485	(4.3)	-24	(3.5)	461	(5.1)	497	(4.5)	-36	(3.8)
Russian Federation	434	(5.5)	468	(4.8)	**-34**	(3.7)	450	(4.4)	486	(3.9)	**-36**	(3.1)	431	(4.2)	480	(4.0)	**-49**	(2.8)
Spain	477	(3.7)	493	(3.1)	-16	(3.8)	481	(3.3)	502	(2.8)	-21	(3.4)	487	(3.5)	526	(2.9)	-39	(3.5)
Sweden	501	(2.7)	532	(2.9)	-30	(3.2)	505	(2.5)	540	(2.5)	-34	(2.8)	486	(2.7)	536	(2.5)	-51	(2.6)
Switzerland	487	(5.2)	510	(4.7)	-22	(4.7)	484	(4.8)	510	(4.4)	-26	(4.2)	465	(5.4)	511	(5.1)	-46	(4.5)
Thailand	384	(4.1)	422	(3.5)	-38	(4.2)	417	(3.7)	454	(3.1)	-37	(3.8)	406	(4.1)	462	(2.9)	-55	(3.9)
United Kingdom	515	(3.1)	534	(3.4)	-19	(4.4)	503	(2.9)	527	(3.5)	-24	(4.3)	522	(3.0)	557	(3.4)	-35	(4.4)
United States	486	(8.8)	512	(6.5)	-26	(4.5)	491	(8.4)	518	(6.4)	-27	(4.2)	488	(8.4)	524	(6.3)	-36	(4.5)
OECD average	*486*	*(0.9)*	*510*	*(0.8)*	*-24*	*(1.1)*	*487*	*(0.8)*	*516*	*(0.7)*	*-29*	*(0.9)*	*480*	*(0.8)*	*525*	*(0.8)*	*-45*	*(1.0)*
OECD total	*485*	*(2.4)*	*508*	*(2.1)*	*-23*	*(1.8)*	*485*	*(2.3)*	*512*	*(2.0)*	*-26*	*(1.6)*	*483*	*(2.3)*	*523*	*(2.0)*	*-40*	*(1.8)*
Netherlands[2]	537	(5.4)	559	(4.4)	-22	(6.6)	519	(5.0)	551	(4.1)	-32	(6.1)	508	(4.3)	543	(3.5)	-35	(5.4)

1. Positive differences indicate that males perform better than females, negative differences indicate that females perform better than males. Differences that are statistically significant are indicated in bold.
2. Response rate is too low to ensure comparability (see Annex A3).

Table 5.3a
Percentage of students at each level of proficiency on the combined reading literacy scale, by gender

	Males											
	Below Level 1 (less than 335 score points)		Level 1 (from 335 to 407 score points)		Level 2 (from 408 to 480 score points)		Level 3 (from 481 to 552 score points)		Level 4 (from 553 to 626 score points)		Level 5 (above 626 score points)	
	%	S.E	%	S.E	%	S.E	%	S.E	%	S.E	%	S.E
Albania	56.7	(1.9)	23.9	(1.5)	14.1	(1.1)	4.4	(0.6)	0.8	(0.2)	0.1	(0.1)
Argentina	30.3	(3.4)	23.0	(2.1)	24.7	(2.5)	15.2	(1.4)	5.9	(1.1)	0.9	(0.4)
Australia	4.7	(0.7)	11.3	(1.0)	21.3	(1.8)	26.0	(1.8)	22.5	(1.2)	14.2	(1.1)
Austria	5.9	(0.8)	11.9	(1.0)	23.3	(1.4)	30.3	(1.6)	21.9	(1.6)	6.7	(0.9)
Belgium	9.7	(1.3)	13.1	(1.0)	18.7	(1.1)	25.7	(1.2)	23.0	(1.1)	9.9	(0.9)
Brazil	27.4	(1.9)	32.1	(1.5)	25.5	(1.6)	11.9	(1.4)	2.8	(0.7)	0.4	(0.2)
Bulgaria	24.1	(1.9)	26.2	(1.8)	25.3	(1.7)	16.6	(1.4)	6.5	(0.8)	1.2	(0.4)
Canada	3.3	(0.3)	9.4	(0.4)	20.4	(0.6)	28.8	(0.7)	25.3	(0.7)	12.9	(0.6)
Chile	24.4	(1.6)	29.2	(1.4)	28.3	(1.5)	14.6	(1.4)	3.2	(0.5)	0.4	(0.2)
Czech Republic	9.0	(1.2)	14.6	(1.1)	26.9	(1.5)	28.6	(1.8)	15.6	(1.2)	5.3	(0.7)
Denmark	7.6	(0.8)	14.2	(1.1)	23.5	(1.1)	28.5	(1.3)	19.5	(1.1)	6.8	(0.7)
Finland	2.5	(0.6)	8.5	(0.7)	19.7	(1.0)	31.8	(1.1)	26.5	(1.2)	11.0	(0.9)
France	6.0	(0.9)	13.9	(1.2)	22.9	(1.3)	29.8	(1.3)	21.0	(1.3)	6.4	(0.7)
Germany	12.6	(0.9)	13.9	(0.9)	24.3	(1.3)	26.9	(1.6)	15.6	(1.4)	6.7	(0.8)
Greece	12.7	(1.7)	18.2	(1.6)	26.6	(1.5)	25.2	(2.1)	13.7	(1.4)	3.6	(0.7)
Hong Kong-China	3.7	(0.7)	8.1	(1.1)	18.2	(1.3)	31.6	(1.5)	29.4	(1.8)	9.0	(1.1)
Hungary	9.4	(1.2)	17.9	(1.6)	27.2	(1.7)	27.2	(1.6)	14.9	(1.4)	3.5	(0.8)
Iceland	5.7	(0.6)	14.4	(0.9)	24.4	(1.3)	29.9	(1.3)	19.2	(1.5)	6.4	(1.0)
Indonesia	36.0	(2.0)	38.6	(2.0)	20.7	(1.9)	4.5	(1.0)	0.2	(0.2)	a	a
Ireland	4.0	(0.6)	9.5	(1.1)	21.4	(1.5)	29.9	(1.5)	24.1	(1.5)	11.2	(1.1)
Israel	18.7	(3.2)	17.8	(2.1)	22.5	(1.6)	22.6	(2.4)	14.3	(2.5)	4.2	(1.1)
Italy	8.0	(1.4)	16.6	(1.5)	28.3	(1.7)	28.1	(1.6)	15.2	(1.4)	3.7	(0.6)
Japan	4.4	(1.1)	9.9	(1.6)	20.2	(1.5)	32.6	(1.7)	25.4	(2.1)	7.5	(1.3)
Korea	1.3	(0.4)	6.1	(0.9)	19.4	(1.4)	39.3	(1.4)	29.6	(1.9)	4.4	(0.7)
Latvia	18.4	(2.1)	22.3	(1.8)	25.8	(1.6)	21.7	(1.8)	9.3	(1.1)	2.5	(0.5)
Liechtenstein	9.9	(2.6)	17.2	(4.1)	23.4	(3.7)	27.6	(4.1)	18.0	(3.7)	3.9	(1.9)
Luxembourg	17.6	(1.1)	22.5	(1.2)	26.6	(1.5)	22.9	(1.3)	9.2	(0.8)	1.2	(0.5)
FYR Macedonia	45.1	(1.3)	27.2	(1.3)	18.8	(1.1)	7.6	(0.7)	1.1	(0.3)	0.0	(0.1)
Mexico	20.0	(1.6)	29.9	(1.9)	27.8	(1.4)	16.5	(1.4)	5.0	(0.9)	0.8	(0.3)
New Zealand	7.3	(0.9)	11.1	(0.9)	19.1	(1.5)	26.1	(1.8)	22.6	(1.3)	13.7	(1.2)
Norway	8.8	(1.0)	14.4	(1.4)	21.0	(1.4)	27.6	(1.2)	20.2	(1.2)	8.1	(0.8)
Peru	55.3	(3.0)	25.3	(1.8)	13.8	(1.6)	4.6	(0.9)	0.8	(0.3)	0.1	(0.2)
Poland	12.2	(1.5)	18.1	(1.9)	23.4	(1.7)	26.1	(1.9)	16.0	(1.7)	4.1	(0.8)
Portugal	12.3	(1.4)	19.1	(1.4)	25.9	(1.5)	24.7	(1.6)	14.3	(1.2)	3.8	(0.6)
Russian Federation	12.9	(1.6)	22.2	(1.2)	29.9	(1.0)	22.8	(1.2)	10.0	(0.8)	2.3	(0.5)
Spain	5.8	(0.7)	14.6	(1.3)	27.2	(1.2)	30.1	(1.2)	18.7	(1.5)	3.6	(0.7)
Sweden	4.6	(0.6)	12.2	(1.0)	23.3	(1.0)	29.8	(1.2)	22.7	(1.6)	7.4	(0.8)
Switzerland	8.3	(0.9)	16.4	(1.2)	23.7	(1.4)	26.3	(1.4)	18.1	(1.2)	7.3	(0.9)
Thailand	17.2	(1.8)	33.9	(1.6)	31.6	(1.6)	13.7	(1.2)	3.2	(0.7)	0.3	(0.2)
United Kingdom	5.0	(0.6)	10.4	(0.7)	21.8	(1.2)	27.4	(1.3)	22.2	(1.1)	13.2	(1.1)
United States	9.3	(1.8)	13.7	(1.6)	21.8	(1.2)	25.5	(1.6)	18.8	(1.6)	11.0	(1.6)
OECD average	8.0	(0.2)	14.2	(0.2)	23.3	(0.3)	27.9	(0.3)	19.4	(0.2)	7.2	(0.2)
OECD total	8.5	(0.5)	14.2	(0.5)	22.9	(0.5)	27.5	(0.5)	19.2	(0.5)	7.7	(0.4)
Netherlands[2]	3.0	(0.9)	10.2	(1.5)	18.8	(2.1)	29.9	(2.1)	27.5	(2.0)	10.6	(1.4)

1. Values that are statistically significant are indicated in bold.
2. Response rate is too low to ensure comparability (see Annex A3).

Table 5.3a (continued)
Percentage of students at each level of proficiency on the combined reading literacy scale, by gender

	Females												Increased likeli-hood for males to perform at level 1 or below[1]	
	Below Level 1 (less than 335 score points)		Level 1 (from 335 to 407 score points)		Level 2 (from 408 to 480 score points)		Level 3 (from 481 to 552 score points)		Level 4 (from 553 to 626 score points)		Level 5 (above 626 score points)			
	%	S.E	%	S.E	%	S.E	%	S.E	%	S.E	%	S.E	Ratio	S.E
Albania	1.3	(0.0)	30.9	(1.4)	29.6	(1.4)	26.9	(1.2)	10.9	(0.9)	1.8	(0.4)	0.10	(0.10)
Argentina	1.5	(0.2)	16.6	(3.4)	20.0	(3.1)	26.1	(1.6)	24.2	(3.1)	10.6	(1.6)	2.30	(0.80)
Australia	1.7	(0.4)	6.7	(0.9)	16.5	(1.2)	25.3	(1.5)	28.3	(1.4)	21.6	(2.0)	1.75	(0.20)
Austria	2.8	(0.5)	8.3	(0.7)	20.2	(1.3)	29.8	(1.5)	28.0	(1.4)	10.9	(1.1)	1.65	(0.18)
Belgium	5.3	(1.0)	8.9	(1.0)	14.6	(1.0)	26.3	(1.1)	30.4	(1.4)	14.5	(1.0)	1.63	(0.19)
Brazil	19.3	(1.4)	32.8	(1.7)	29.9	(1.8)	13.9	(1.5)	3.4	(0.7)	0.7	(0.3)	**1.14**	(0.04)
Bulgaria	1.7	(0.1)	11.4	(1.4)	18.4	(1.6)	28.7	(1.7)	26.7	(2.0)	11.6	(1.5)	**3.30**	(1.00)
Canada	1.3	(0.3)	4.7	(0.4)	15.3	(0.6)	27.3	(0.6)	30.5	(0.7)	21.0	(0.7)	2.06	(0.13)
Chile	1.2	(0.1)	16.0	(1.5)	27.4	(1.6)	31.4	(1.5)	18.4	(1.5)	6.2	(0.8)	0.60	(0.20)
Czech Republic	3.2	(0.4)	8.3	(0.7)	22.9	(1.3)	33.2	(1.2)	23.8	(1.0)	8.6	(0.8)	2.10	(0.21)
Denmark	3.8	(0.6)	9.6	(0.9)	21.6	(1.3)	30.6	(1.5)	24.8	(1.3)	9.6	(0.9)	1.69	(0.13)
Finland	1.0	(0.6)	2.2	(0.4)	9.1	(0.8)	25.8	(1.3)	36.4	(1.5)	25.5	(1.4)	3.19	(0.59)
France	2.3	(0.5)	8.2	(0.8)	21.1	(1.2)	31.4	(1.3)	26.5	(1.2)	10.5	(0.8)	1.78	(0.14)
Germany	6.8	(1.1)	11.3	(0.9)	20.2	(1.2)	26.9	(1.2)	23.5	(1.2)	11.1	(0.8)	1.45	(0.12)
Greece	4.7	(1.0)	13.0	(1.6)	25.0	(2.0)	31.1	(1.8)	19.8	(1.7)	6.4	(0.9)	1.82	(0.16)
Hong Kong-China	1.9	(0.3)	1.5	(0.5)	4.8	(0.7)	15.9	(1.2)	34.5	(1.3)	33.1	(1.4)	**10.10**	(1.20)
Hungary	4.5	(0.7)	13.4	(1.6)	22.7	(1.8)	30.5	(1.6)	22.2	(1.6)	6.7	(1.0)	1.64	(0.16)
Iceland	1.8	(0.5)	6.2	(0.7)	19.6	(1.0)	32.1	(1.2)	28.4	(1.4)	11.9	(0.9)	2.40	(0.23)
Indonesia	1.2	(0.0)	26.4	(2.2)	36.7	(2.1)	28.8	(1.9)	7.5	(1.5)	0.6	(0.4)	a	a
Ireland	2.0	(0.5)	6.2	(0.9)	14.3	(1.0)	29.6	(1.3)	30.4	(1.4)	17.4	(1.2)	1.62	(0.19)
Israel	1.2	(0.1)	11.8	(2.0)	18.8	(2.3)	25.2	(1.9)	25.1	(1.8)	14.9	(1.9)	**4.20**	(1.00)
Italy	2.5	(0.6)	10.1	(1.1)	22.9	(1.3)	33.5	(1.4)	24.0	(1.7)	7.0	(0.7)	1.97	(0.31)
Japan	1.1	(0.4)	4.9	(0.9)	15.8	(1.6)	34.1	(1.6)	32.1	(2.0)	12.1	(1.5)	2.51	(0.43)
Korea	0.5	(0.2)	3.3	(0.6)	17.6	(1.6)	38.1	(1.6)	33.1	(2.0)	7.4	(1.0)	1.98	(0.41)
Latvia	6.7	(1.1)	13.5	(1.2)	26.8	(1.5)	28.9	(1.4)	18.2	(1.6)	5.8	(1.0)	**2.09**	(0.15)
Liechtenstein	5.0	(2.2)	10.8	(3.2)	23.0	(4.9)	33.4	(4.8)	21.5	(3.3)	6.4	(2.6)	1.54	(0.35)
Luxembourg	10.5	(0.8)	18.5	(1.0)	28.2	(1.7)	27.0	(1.5)	13.5	(0.8)	2.2	(0.4)	1.36	(0.07)
FYR Macedonia	1.4	(0.1)	23.0	(1.3)	29.2	(1.5)	30.4	(1.4)	14.8	(0.9)	2.5	(0.4)	0.20	(0.10)
Mexico	12.5	(1.4)	26.4	(1.5)	32.4	(1.6)	20.8	(1.5)	6.9	(0.9)	0.9	(0.3)	1.28	(0.06)
New Zealand	2.0	(0.4)	6.3	(0.6)	15.3	(1.1)	23.2	(1.2)	29.2	(1.6)	24.0	(1.6)	2.34	(0.28)
Norway	3.1	(0.6)	7.3	(0.8)	18.0	(1.0)	29.1	(1.4)	27.7	(1.2)	14.7	(1.0)	2.17	(0.19)
Peru	1.0	(0.0)	52.7	(2.5)	25.7	(1.7)	15.1	(1.4)	5.2	(0.9)	1.2	(0.3)	0.10	(0.10)
Poland	5.0	(1.2)	10.9	(1.3)	24.8	(2.0)	30.4	(1.8)	21.2	(1.8)	7.7	(1.3)	1.80	(0.23)
Portugal	6.9	(1.0)	14.3	(1.6)	24.8	(1.3)	30.2	(1.4)	19.1	(1.4)	4.7	(0.7)	1.47	(0.09)
Russian Federation	5.0	(0.7)	14.7	(1.4)	28.6	(1.2)	31.1	(1.4)	16.6	(1.4)	4.1	(0.6)	**1.87**	(0.09)
Spain	2.2	(0.5)	9.3	(1.0)	24.1	(1.2)	35.8	(1.7)	23.8	(1.3)	4.9	(0.5)	1.77	(0.14)
Sweden	1.8	(0.4)	6.0	(0.6)	17.1	(1.1)	31.2	(1.4)	28.7	(1.2)	15.1	(1.1)	2.13	(0.21)
Switzerland	5.5	(0.8)	10.2	(1.0)	19.0	(1.2)	29.9	(1.3)	24.1	(1.3)	11.3	(1.4)	1.57	(0.13)
Thailand	1.9	(0.1)	5.7	(0.8)	21.6	(1.4)	40.4	(1.7)	25.8	(1.3)	5.9	(0.9)	0.60	(0.20)
United Kingdom	2.2	(0.4)	7.6	(0.8)	17.2	(1.0)	27.8	(1.3)	26.8	(1.2)	18.3	(1.3)	1.58	(0.16)
United States	3.7	(0.8)	9.5	(1.1)	20.2	(1.9)	29.2	(1.9)	24.0	(1.6)	13.4	(1.6)	1.80	(0.13)
OECD average	*3.7*	*(0.1)*	*9.3*	*(0.2)*	*20.0*	*(0.2)*	*29.6*	*(0.3)*	*25.4*	*(0.3)*	*11.9*	*(0.2)*	*1.71*	*(0.03)*
OECD total	*3.9*	*(0.3)*	*9.8*	*(0.4)*	*20.6*	*(0.6)*	*29.8*	*(0.6)*	*24.6*	*(0.6)*	*11.3*	*(0.5)*	*1.67*	*(0.05)*
Netherlands[2]	1.4	(0.6)	4.4	(1.2)	14.7	(1.3)	29.2	(2.2)	32.3	(2.2)	18.1	(1.5)	2.17	(0.50)

1. Values that are statistically significant are indicated in bold.
2. Response rate is too low to ensure comparability (see Annex A3).

Table 5.3b.
**Percentage of students scoring below 400 points and above 600 points
on the mathematical literacy scale**

See next page

Table 5.3b
Percentage of students scoring below 400 points and above 600 points on the mathematical literacy scale

| | Percentage of students scoring below 400 points on the mathematical literacy scale | | | | | | Increased likelihood for males to score below 400 on the mathematical literacy scale[1] | | Percentage of students scoring above 600 points on the mathematical literacy scale | | | | | | Increased likelihood for males to score above 600 points on the mathematical literacy scale[1] | |
| | All students | | Males | | Females | | | | All students | | Males | | Females | | | |
	%	S.E.	%	S.E.	%	S.E.	Ratio	S.E.	%	S.E.	%	S.E.	%	S.E.	Ratio	S.E.
Albania	55.3	(1.3)	58.9	(2.2)	52.0	(1.7)	**1.13**	(0.06)	1.5	(0.3)	1.7	(0.5)	1.4	(0.4)	1.18	(0.49)
Argentina	51.9	(3.7)	53.5	(3.3)	50.6	(4.8)	1.06	(0.09)	2.9	(0.7)	3.5	(1.1)	2.4	(0.7)	1.46	(0.49)
Australia	7.0	(0.8)	7.0	(1.0)	8.0	(1.3)	0.89	(0.16)	23.0	(1.6)	25.0	(1.9)	21.0	(2.3)	1.17	(0.13)
Austria	11.0	(0.7)	9.0	(1.1)	13.0	(1.1)	**0.76**	(0.11)	18.0	(1.2)	23.0	(1.8)	13.0	(1.6)	**1.73**	(0.24)
Belgium	14.0	(1.3)	15.0	(1.4)	13.0	(1.7)	1.18	(0.14)	24.0	(1.1)	27.0	(1.6)	21.0	(1.6)	**1.34**	(0.12)
Brazil	75.0	(1.6)	70.0	(2.4)	79.0	(2.1)	**0.86**	(0.02)	0.0	(0.2)	1.0	(0.3)	0.0	(0.2)	6.85	(6.61)
Bulgaria	38.0	(2.2)	40.1	(2.5)	35.8	(3.0)	1.12	(0.10)	5.3	(1.0)	6.2	(1.2)	4.3	(1.1)	1.44	(0.36)
Canada	6.0	(0.4)	6.0	(0.6)	6.0	(0.4)	0.96	(0.08)	22.0	(0.6)	25.0	(0.9)	19.0	(0.7)	**1.28**	(0.05)
Chile	55.5	(1.8)	53.2	(2.4)	57.4	(2.4)	0.93	(0.05)	0.6	(0.2)	0.8	(0.4)	0.3	(0.2)	3.16	(4.58)
Czech Republic	16.0	(0.9)	15.0	(1.5)	16.0	(1.2)	0.87	(0.11)	16.0	(0.9)	19.0	(1.2)	12.0	(1.2)	**1.65**	(0.17)
Denmark	10.0	(0.9)	9.0	(1.1)	10.0	(1.2)	0.82	(0.10)	22.0	(1.0)	22.0	(1.2)	21.0	(1.3)	1.06	(0.07)
Finland	5.0	(0.7)	5.0	(1.0)	4.0	(0.8)	1.14	(0.24)	22.0	(1.0)	22.0	(1.2)	21.0	(1.3)	**1.36**	(0.12)
France	10.0	(0.9)	10.0	(1.1)	11.0	(1.1)	0.90	(0.12)	18.0	(1.1)	21.0	(1.4)	15.0	(1.3)	**1.36**	(0.12)
Germany	19.0	(1.1)	18.0	(1.2)	21.0	(1.9)	**0.86**	(0.07)	14.0	(0.8)	16.0	(1.4)	12.0	(0.9)	**1.28**	(0.15)
Greece	32.0	(2.2)	32.0	(2.9)	32.0	(2.3)	1.04	(0.09)	7.0	(1.2)	9.0	(1.8)	6.0	(1.1)	1.48	(0.37)
Hong Kong-China	5.9	(0.9)	6.3	(1.1)	5.5	(1.1)	1.14	(0.26)	36.6	(1.5)	42.6	(2.5)	30.6	(2.0)	**1.39**	(0.13)
Hungary	19.0	(1.4)	19.0	(1.8)	20.0	(1.9)	0.88	(0.10)	13.0	(1.4)	14.0	(1.9)	12.0	(1.6)	1.33	(0.17)
Iceland	8.0	(0.7)	9.0	(0.9)	8.0	(1.1)	1.09	(0.17)	16.0	(0.9)	16.0	(1.3)	16.0	(1.3)	1.09	(0.12)
Indonesia	65.1	(2.4)	64.3	(2.5)	65.9	(3.0)	0.98	(0.04)	0.2	(0.1)	0.2	(0.2)	0.2	(0.2)	7.75	(30.27)
Ireland	11.0	(0.9)	10.0	(1.2)	12.0	(1.3)	0.84	(0.13)	12.0	(1.2)	14.0	(1.8)	9.0	(1.2)	**1.63**	(0.20)
Israel	38.3	(3.1)	37.0	(3.4)	38.8	(3.5)	0.96	(0.09)	9.6	(1.3)	12.0	(1.9)	8.0	(1.7)	1.52	(0.36)
Italy	26.0	(1.2)	25.0	(2.1)	26.0	(1.9)	1.00	(0.12)	5.0	(0.8)	6.0	(1.1)	4.0	(0.7)	**2.06**	(0.41)
Japan	5.0	(1.0)	6.0	(1.6)	4.0	(1.0)	1.46	(0.50)	32.0	(2.4)	36.0	(3.4)	28.0	(2.6)	1.24	(0.12)
Korea	5.0	(0.6)	4.0	(0.9)	6.0	(1.1)	0.69	(0.16)	27.0	(1.5)	32.0	(2.4)	21.0	(2.2)	1.46	(0.19)
Latvia	27.0	(1.9)	26.0	(2.4)	27.0	(2.2)	0.97	(0.08)	9.0	(0.9)	10.0	(1.3)	8.0	(1.3)	**1.47**	(0.19)
Liechtenstein	13.0	(3.0)	11.0	(4.2)	14.0	(3.8)	0.88	(0.31)	18.0	(3.1)	21.0	(4.6)	15.0	(4.6)	1.64	(0.56)
Luxembourg	28.0	(1.1)	26.0	(1.5)	30.0	(1.6)	**0.85**	(0.06)	4.0	(0.5)	5.0	(0.7)	2.0	(0.6)	**2.26**	(0.60)
FYR Macedonia	56.2	(1.3)	56.2	(1.7)	55.6	(1.9)	1.01	(0.05)	0.8	(0.2)	0.8	(0.3)	0.8	(0.3)	1.07	(0.73)
Mexico	56.0	(1.9)	54.0	(2.5)	59.0	(2.4)	0.94	(0.04)	0.0	(0.2)	0.0	(0.2)	0.0	(0.2)	1.82	(1.27)
New Zealand	9.0	(0.8)	10.0	(1.3)	8.0	(1.0)	1.41	(0.28)	28.0	(1.6)	28.0	(1.9)	27.0	(2.3)	0.97	(0.08)
Norway	14.0	(1.1)	14.0	(1.4)	13.0	(1.2)	1.05	(0.11)	14.0	(1.1)	16.0	(1.7)	11.0	(1.1)	**1.54**	(0.17)
Peru	84.6	(1.4)	83.0	(2.0)	85.9	(1.8)	0.97	(0.03)	0.2	(0.1)	0.4	(0.2)	0.0	(0.1)	a	a
Poland	24.0	(1.8)	26.0	(2.6)	23.0	(2.5)	1.15	(0.16)	10.0	(1.6)	12.0	(2.2)	8.0	(1.4)	**1.66**	(0.30)
Portugal	28.0	(1.8)	25.0	(2.0)	30.0	(2.3)	**0.85**	(0.07)	4.0	(0.6)	6.0	(1.1)	3.0	(0.7)	**2.07**	(0.48)
Russian Federation	23.0	(1.8)	24.0	(2.1)	22.0	(1.9)	1.03	(0.06)	13.0	(1.4)	13.0	(1.4)	12.0	(1.7)	1.18	(0.12)
Spain	20.0	(1.3)	18.0	(1.6)	21.0	(1.9)	0.95	(0.09)	9.0	(0.8)	12.0	(1.5)	5.0	(0.8)	**2.62**	(0.39)
Sweden	12.0	(0.9)	12.0	(1.2)	13.0	(1.1)	0.87	(0.09)	16.0	(0.9)	18.0	(1.2)	15.0	(1.2)	1.09	(0.10)
Switzerland	10.0	(0.9)	9.0	(1.0)	11.0	(1.2)	0.91	(0.11)	25.0	(1.8)	28.0	(2.1)	22.0	(2.1)	**1.21**	(0.10)
Thailand	35.4	(1.6)	37.4	(2.3)	34.0	(1.8)	1.10	(0.08)	2.9	(0.6)	3.1	(0.9)	2.7	(0.6)	1.15	(0.37)
United Kingdom	8.0	(0.7)	8.0	(0.8)	8.0	(1.0)	1.07	(0.16)	23.0	(1.2)	25.0	(1.8)	20.0	(1.7)	1.20	(0.12)
United States	18.0	(2.4)	18.0	(2.9)	17.0	(2.4)	1.07	(0.12)	14.0	(1.7)	16.0	(2.1)	12.0	(1.7)	1.27	(0.15)
OECD average	*16.0*	*(0.3)*	*15.0*	*(0.3)*	*16.0*	*(0.4)*	*0.95*	*(0.02)*	*16.0*	*(0.2)*	*18.0*	*(0.3)*	*14.0*	*(0.3)*	*1.34*	*(0.03)*
OECD total	*18.0*	*(0.7)*	*18.0*	*(0.9)*	*18.0*	*(0.8)*	*0.99*	*(0.04)*	*17.0*	*(0.5)*	*19.0*	*(0.7)*	*14.0*	*(0.6)*	*1.33*	*(0.06)*
Netherlands[2]	4.0	(1.0)	4.0	(1.3)	4.0	(1.2)	1.03	(0.28)	37.0	(2.1)	40.0	(2.6)	34.0	(2.7)	1.09	(0.08)

1. Values that are statistically significant are indicated in bold.
2. Response rate is too low to ensure comparability (see Annex A3).

© OECD/ UNESCO-UIS 2003

Table 5.4
Correlation between gender and performance on the combined reading literacy scale and engagement in reading

	Gender			
	Performance	S.E.	Engagement in reading[1]	S.E.
Albania	0.29	(0.02)	0.19	(0.02)
Argentina	0.20	(0.05)	0.18	(0.03)
Australia	0.17	(0.03)	0.14	(0.02)
Austria	0.14	(0.03)	0.25	(0.02)
Belgium	0.15	(0.03)	0.19	(0.02)
Brazil	0.10	(0.02)	0.28	(0.01)
Bulgaria	0.23	(0.03)	0.25	(0.02)
Canada	0.17	(0.01)	0.22	(0.01)
Chile	0.14	(0.03)	0.21	(0.02)
Czech Republic	0.20	(0.02)	0.30	(0.02)
Denmark	0.13	(0.02)	0.23	(0.02)
Finland	0.29	(0.02)	0.36	(0.01)
France	0.16	(0.02)	0.15	(0.02)
Germany	0.16	(0.02)	0.25	(0.01)
Greece	0.19	(0.02)	0.11	(0.02)
Hong Kong-China	0.09	(0.04)	0.11	(0.02)
Hungary	0.17	(0.03)	0.20	(0.02)
Iceland	0.22	(0.02)	0.20	(0.01)
Indonesia	m	m	m	m
Ireland	0.15	(0.02)	0.22	(0.02)
Israel	0.14	(0.02)	0.13	(0.02)
Italy	0.21	(0.04)	0.19	(0.02)
Japan	0.17	(0.04)	0.08	(0.02)
Korea	0.10	(0.04)	0.02	(0.02)
Latvia	0.07	(0.04)	0.19	(0.03)
Liechtenstein	0.16	(0.06)	0.25	(0.06)
Luxembourg	0.13	(0.02)	0.19	(0.02)
FYR Macedonia	0.27	(0.02)	0.15	(0.02)
Mexico	0.12	(0.03)	0.13	(0.02)
New Zealand	0.21	(0.03)	0.15	(0.02)
Norway	0.21	(0.02)	0.27	(0.02)
Peru	0.03	(0.04)	0.04	(0.02)
Poland	0.18	(0.03)	0.21	(0.02)
Portugal	0.13	(0.02)	0.27	(0.02)
Russian Federation	0.21	(0.02)	0.23	(0.01)
Spain	0.14	(0.02)	0.15	(0.02)
Sweden	0.20	(0.02)	0.23	(0.02)
Switzerland	0.15	(0.02)	0.28	(0.02)
Thailand	0.26	(0.02)	0.21	(0.02)
United Kingdom	0.13	(0.02)	0.14	(0.01)
United States	0.14	(0.02)	0.17	(0.02)
OECD median	0.16		0.20	
SD of correlation	0.04		0.07	
Netherlands[2]	0.17	(0.03)	0.21	(0.02)

1. Index of engagement in reading as used in OECD (2002b) which includes the following three components: frequency of reading, diversity of reading and the interest in reading.
2. Response rate is too low to ensure comparability (see Annex A3).

Table 5.5
Time students usually spend each day reading for enjoyment

	Students report not reading for enjoyment				Students report reading 30 minutes or less each day				Students report reading between 30 and 60 minutes each day			
	Females		Males		Females		Males		Females		Males	
	%	S.E.	%	S.E.	%	S.E.	%	S.E.	%	S.E.	%	S.E.
Albania	6.6	(0.6)	11.1	(1.1)	16.9	(0.9)	21.8	(1.2)	29.0	(1.2)	32.5	(1.3)
Argentina	22.9	(1.2)	37.8	(1.3)	29.2	(3.0)	32.9	(1.3)	24.9	(2.8)	17.0	(1.5)
Australia	25.4	(1.5)	40.1	(1.7)	31.4	(1.3)	29.7	(1.3)	24.3	(1.1)	17.1	(1.3)
Austria	30.3	(1.0)	52.9	(1.4)	30.5	(1.0)	26.8	(1.2)	22.3	(1.0)	13.5	(0.8)
Belgium	30.6	(0.7)	53.1	(1.4)	28.0	(0.9)	21.7	(1.0)	25.7	(0.9)	17.4	(0.8)
Brazil	12.8	(0.9)	27.1	(1.4)	17.9	(1.2)	25.4	(0.9)	32.4	(1.2)	30.1	(1.4)
Bulgaria	23.1	(1.3)	39.8	(1.2)	16.2	(0.9)	21.8	(0.9)	23.3	(1.1)	17.4	(1.0)
Canada	23.0	(0.5)	42.6	(0.7)	36.7	(0.6)	30.7	(0.5)	24.6	(0.6)	16.1	(0.5)
Chile	20.7	(1.0)	32.7	(1.1)	24.9	(1.0)	31.2	(1.1)	29.7	(0.9)	23.5	(1.2)
Czech Republic	15.1	(0.7)	38.7	(1.4)	29.1	(1.0)	30.4	(1.2)	31.3	(1.0)	19.5	(0.9)
Denmark	17.4	(1.0)	35.8	(1.3)	37.5	(1.2)	34.7	(1.3)	27.9	(1.0)	18.8	(0.7)
Finland	10.3	(0.6)	35.3	(1.1)	27.3	(1.0)	31.0	(0.9)	32.0	(1.2)	20.1	(0.8)
France	21.2	(0.9)	39.5	(1.1)	28.0	(1.0)	27.0	(0.9)	33.4	(1.3)	23.3	(1.0)
Germany	29.1	(0.9)	54.5	(1.2)	30.3	(1.1)	23.7	(0.9)	23.0	(0.9)	12.7	(0.7)
Greece	19.4	(0.9)	24.6	(1.4)	26.7	(1.0)	26.6	(1.2)	23.7	(1.0)	21.7	(1.1)
Hong Kong-China	20.0	(0.9)	28.2	(1.3)	37.4	(1.1)	34.2	(1.2)	24.0	(0.9)	22.4	(1.0)
Hungary	18.8	(1.0)	33.3	(1.2)	29.0	(1.2)	27.6	(0.9)	27.3	(1.1)	21.1	(1.1)
Iceland	22.7	(1.0)	37.0	(1.0)	38.4	(1.1)	37.5	(1.1)	27.3	(1.1)	17.6	(1.0)
Indonesia	11.9	(1.5)	15.3	(1.1)	33.2	(1.7)	39.4	(1.6)	27.9	(1.8)	23.8	(1.4)
Ireland	24.5	(1.0)	42.4	(1.4)	32.0	(1.0)	29.7	(0.9)	23.8	(1.1)	17.0	(0.9)
Israel	29.9	(2.9)	48.1	(2.0)	20.1	(1.0)	20.4	(1.1)	20.0	(1.5)	17.8	(1.5)
Italy	23.3	(1.1)	38.0	(1.3)	28.4	(0.8)	31.8	(1.0)	25.5	(1.0)	19.5	(0.9)
Japan	54.9	(1.5)	55.2	(1.6)	17.8	(0.9)	17.9	(1.1)	15.4	(1.0)	15.5	(0.9)
Korea	29.7	(1.4)	31.2	(1.2)	32.7	(1.2)	27.1	(0.7)	22.5	(0.9)	21.5	(0.9)
Latvia	9.5	(0.9)	26.8	(1.6)	23.4	(1.3)	28.0	(1.3)	34.7	(1.3)	24.1	(1.8)
Liechtenstein	31.5	(3.9)	48.5	(3.9)	33.4	(3.6)	35.0	(3.9)	22.7	(3.5)	10.6	(2.5)
Luxembourg	28.5	(1.1)	48.7	(1.2)	26.5	(1.0)	24.6	(1.0)	24.4	(1.2)	14.6	(0.9)
FYR Macedonia	7.2	(0.6)	16.7	(1.0)	18.2	(0.9)	21.7	(1.1)	30.3	(1.0)	28.9	(1.1)
Mexico	8.9	(0.8)	18.4	(1.1)	41.8	(1.3)	45.7	(1.4)	29.2	(1.0)	25.1	(1.0)
New Zealand	23.1	(1.0)	36.8	(1.3)	36.8	(1.1)	36.5	(0.9)	23.3	(1.1)	15.3	(0.8)
Norway	24.7	(1.1)	45.6	(1.3)	38.9	(1.1)	30.5	(1.1)	23.6	(1.1)	16.8	(1.0)
Peru	7.8	(0.7)	9.6	(0.9)	19.5	(1.1)	27.8	(1.1)	33.6	(1.1)	32.2	(1.1)
Poland	16.1	(1.0)	32.2	(1.8)	21.6	(1.3)	23.8	(1.2)	31.0	(1.2)	26.4	(1.2)
Portugal	8.3	(0.6)	29.4	(1.3)	36.1	(1.0)	42.4	(1.2)	32.2	(1.2)	20.1	(1.0)
Russian Federation	13.9	(0.7)	25.0	(0.9)	21.7	(1.0)	27.6	(0.8)	27.7	(0.9)	23.9	(1.0)
Spain	22.4	(1.1)	41.5	(1.2)	33.0	(0.9)	32.8	(1.1)	30.5	(1.0)	17.6	(0.8)
Sweden	27.0	(1.3)	44.9	(1.2)	33.9	(1.1)	27.7	(1.1)	25.1	(0.9)	17.1	(0.7)
Switzerland	21.5	(1.1)	48.9	(1.6)	35.4	(0.9)	30.6	(1.2)	27.7	(1.0)	13.2	(0.8)
Thailand	8.6	(0.8)	17.0	(1.7)	39.2	(1.0)	40.7	(1.4)	27.3	(0.9)	23.7	(1.1)
United Kingdom	22.6	(0.9)	35.8	(1.0)	36.4	(1.1)	34.8	(1.0)	26.2	(1.0)	19.5	(0.8)
United States	32.0	(1.5)	50.1	(1.8)	35.2	(1.6)	26.8	(1.2)	18.7	(0.9)	13.6	(1.1)
OECD average	23.3	(0.2)	40.2	(0.3)	31.8	(0.2)	30.0	(0.2)	26.1	(0.2)	18.2	(0.2)
OECD total	28.5	(0.5)	42.6	(0.6)	31.2	(0.5)	28.3	(0.4)	23.4	(0.4)	17.8	(0.3)
Netherlands[1]	29.3	(1.8)	57.1	(2.2)	36.9	(1.7)	25.9	(1.6)	22.3	(1.4)	11.1	(1.0)

1. Response rate is too low to ensure comparability (see Annex A3).

Table 5.5 (continued)
Time students usually spend each day reading for enjoyment

	Students report reading between 1 and 2 hours each day				Students report reading more than 2 hours each day			
	Females		Males		Females		Males	
	%	S.E.	%	S.E.	%	S.E.	%	S.E.
Albania	31.6	(1.1)	22.9	(1.2)	15.9	(0.8)	11.8	(0.9)
Argentina	14.5	(1.1)	7.2	(0.7)	8.4	(0.8)	5.2	(0.8)
Australia	13.9	(0.9)	9.9	(0.6)	5.1	(0.5)	3.2	(0.4)
Austria	12.4	(0.8)	5.3	(0.6)	4.5	(0.6)	1.5	(0.3)
Belgium	12.4	(0.6)	5.9	(0.4)	3.4	(0.4)	1.9	(0.3)
Brazil	21.1	(0.9)	11.6	(1.0)	15.8	(0.9)	5.7	(0.6)
Bulgaria	24.1	(1.2)	14.9	(0.9)	13.3	(1.0)	6.2	(0.6)
Canada	11.4	(0.3)	7.8	(0.4)	4.3	(0.3)	2.8	(0.2)
Chile	15.5	(0.9)	8.4	(0.7)	9.1	(0.6)	4.2	(0.4)
Czech Republic	16.9	(1.0)	8.4	(0.6)	7.6	(0.7)	3.1	(0.4)
Denmark	11.8	(0.8)	7.2	(0.8)	5.4	(0.6)	3.4	(0.4)
Finland	24.9	(0.9)	11.0	(0.7)	5.5	(0.5)	2.6	(0.3)
France	13.3	(0.7)	7.6	(0.7)	4.2	(0.5)	2.5	(0.3)
Germany	11.6	(0.7)	5.8	(0.6)	5.9	(0.4)	3.3	(0.4)
Greece	20.7	(1.1)	19.2	(1.0)	9.5	(0.7)	7.9	(0.6)
Hong Kong-China	12.7	(0.7)	10.3	(0.7)	5.9	(0.5)	4.9	(0.4)
Hungary	16.5	(0.9)	10.2	(0.7)	8.4	(0.7)	7.8	(0.7)
Iceland	8.0	(0.6)	5.8	(0.5)	3.6	(0.5)	2.0	(0.4)
Indonesia	18.5	(1.3)	14.7	(1.1)	8.6	(0.9)	6.8	(0.9)
Ireland	14.6	(0.8)	8.5	(0.7)	5.1	(0.6)	2.4	(0.4)
Israel	21.1	(1.3)	8.6	(0.9)	8.9	(1.0)	5.1	(0.9)
Italy	18.1	(0.9)	7.9	(0.6)	4.6	(0.4)	2.8	(0.4)
Japan	8.5	(0.6)	7.8	(0.7)	3.4	(0.4)	3.7	(0.4)
Korea	10.7	(0.8)	13.0	(0.7)	4.5	(0.5)	7.1	(0.6)
Latvia	23.9	(1.1)	15.2	(1.2)	8.5	(0.8)	6.0	(0.8)
Liechtenstein	8.4	(2.0)	1.9	(1.1)	4.0	(1.6)	4.0	(1.6)
Luxembourg	15.1	(1.0)	8.7	(0.8)	5.6	(0.6)	3.4	(0.5)
FYR Macedonia	27.2	(0.9)	20.8	(1.2)	17.2	(0.9)	11.9	(0.8)
Mexico	15.0	(0.9)	7.9	(0.7)	5.1	(0.7)	2.8	(0.4)
New Zealand	12.4	(0.9)	8.4	(0.7)	4.3	(0.4)	3.0	(0.4)
Norway	10.1	(0.8)	5.4	(0.5)	2.7	(0.4)	1.6	(0.3)
Peru	24.5	(1.1)	18.1	(1.1)	14.6	(0.9)	12.3	(0.9)
Poland	21.2	(0.9)	11.6	(0.8)	9.9	(0.9)	6.0	(0.7)
Portugal	17.9	(1.0)	6.3	(0.7)	5.5	(0.6)	1.8	(0.3)
Russian Federation	21.3	(1.0)	13.4	(0.5)	15.4	(0.6)	10.0	(0.7)
Spain	11.5	(0.6)	5.9	(0.4)	2.6	(0.3)	2.2	(0.3)
Sweden	10.2	(0.7)	7.4	(0.6)	3.8	(0.5)	3.0	(0.4)
Switzerland	11.6	(0.7)	5.1	(0.5)	3.7	(0.4)	2.2	(0.3)
Thailand	17.5	(0.9)	13.9	(0.9)	7.3	(0.7)	4.8	(0.5)
United Kingdom	11.2	(0.7)	7.6	(0.6)	3.5	(0.4)	2.3	(0.4)
United States	9.6	(0.8)	6.4	(0.7)	4.5	(0.6)	3.2	(0.5)
OECD average	13.8	(0.2)	8.3	(0.1)	5.1	(0.1)	3.4	(0.1)
OECD total	12.2	(0.3)	7.9	(0.2)	4.8	(0.2)	3.5	(0.2)
Netherlands[1]	7.7	(0.9)	3.9	(0.8)	3.8	(0.7)	2.0	(0.4)

1. Response rate is too low to ensure comparability (see Annex A3).

Table 5.6
Diversity of reading materials, by gender / How often do you read these materials because you want to?
Agree or strongly agree

	Magazines				Comics				Fiction books			
	Female		Male		Female		Male		Female		Male	
	%	SE	%	SE	%	SE	%	SE	%	SE	%	SE
Albania	59.7	1.2	48.0	1.9	33.0	1.5	30.6	1.6	61.1	1.4	41.5	1.7
Argentina	67.9	2.0	55.6	2.1	29.7	2.2	30.1	1.8	34.6	1.6	20.8	1.6
Australia	62.2	1.2	64.0	1.2	5.3	0.6	15.1	0.9	40.2	1.6	23.2	1.2
Austria	69.2	1.2	73.8	1.0	9.8	0.6	22.7	1.0	38.1	1.1	12.8	0.9
Belgium	72.3	1.2	64.1	1.1	33.0	1.0	43.3	1.0	28.8	1.0	13.5	1.1
Brazil	71.5	1.1	46.3	1.3	28.9	1.5	31.1	1.5	45.7	1.4	16.5	0.9
Bulgaria	76.8	1.2	64.4	1.4	17.3	0.9	19.2	1.0	43.5	1.2	22.5	1.0
Canada	71.8	0.6	62.2	0.6	12.7	0.5	19.9	0.5	38.8	0.7	23.0	0.6
Chile	61.5	1.0	48.7	1.2	28.2	0.9	31.5	1.3	35.8	1.1	20.9	1.1
Czech Republic	82.8	0.8	75.4	0.9	13.3	0.7	21.2	1.1	44.6	1.3	11.5	0.7
Denmark	79.1	1.1	69.1	1.1	57.8	1.2	65.9	1.1	43.0	1.3	20.9	1.0
Finland	83.0	0.8	66.8	1.0	57.2	1.0	75.2	1.1	41.2	1.1	12.2	0.7
France	61.5	1.1	63.0	1.2	23.1	0.9	42.8	1.3	28.7	0.9	17.7	0.9
Germany	68.3	1.2	63.2	1.4	6.7	0.6	17.2	1.0	39.7	1.1	13.8	0.8
Greece	60.8	1.4	60.8	1.2	18.8	1.0	27.4	1.1	31.6	1.1	15.6	1.0
Hong Kong-China	71.2	0.9	66.3	0.9	29.6	1.0	54.8	1.3	42.4	1.3	27.8	1.3
Hungary	75.9	1.1	67.8	1.3	16.9	1.0	19.0	1.0	35.4	1.5	15.0	1.2
Iceland	81.5	1.0	76.5	1.0	43.9	1.0	55.1	1.3	29.9	1.0	13.9	0.8
Indonesia	54.4	1.6	43.9	1.3	41.8	1.5	38.1	1.5	41.8	1.5	31.1	1.1
Ireland	64.9	1.1	58.0	1.3	6.6	0.7	10.8	0.8	34.0	1.1	18.2	1.3
Israel	54.4	1.7	41.2	1.4	29.7	1.8	25.7	1.7	39.3	2.4	26.0	1.9
Italy	72.5	0.9	59.5	1.3	22.6	0.9	32.8	1.2	40.1	1.2	23.4	0.8
Japan	81.0	0.9	82.7	0.9	79.7	1.0	88.2	0.8	30.1	1.2	24.9	1.0
Korea	37.4	1.0	40.8	1.1	52.1	1.4	71.0	1.3	33.8	1.5	35.8	1.0
Latvia	84.5	1.0	67.9	1.4	12.3	1.4	15.8	1.0	41.0	1.5	21.1	1.3
Liechtenstein	71.9	3.1	70.4	3.6	8.5	2.4	21.0	3.1	36.1	3.6	16.1	3.4
Luxembourg	65.5	1.2	63.3	1.1	15.2	0.7	32.6	1.1	39.1	1.2	16.5	1.0
FYR Macedonia	84.8	0.9	66.7	1.2	30.0	1.3	37.7	1.1	45.1	1.3	30.8	1.1
Mexico	48.9	1.5	43.8	1.5	19.1	0.9	30.5	1.1	39.9	1.0	32.9	1.1
New Zealand	70.1	1.1	70.5	1.2	6.7	0.7	16.5	1.0	42.7	1.1	26.8	1.0
Norway	77.6	1.1	61.4	1.3	47.6	1.3	67.7	1.3	36.3	1.2	12.6	0.8
Peru	36.1	1.7	40.3	1.5	34.9	1.3	38.7	1.3	44.3	1.3	38.7	1.1
Poland	74.7	1.3	67.0	1.5	8.0	0.9	13.5	0.9	26.8	1.5	10.6	0.9
Portugal	78.1	0.8	64.4	1.5	22.0	1.0	26.9	1.1	43.4	0.9	19.5	1.1
Russian Federation	82.1	0.8	67.3	1.2	25.1	1.4	24.5	1.5	64.3	1.0	42.2	1.3
Spain	66.5	1.1	56.1	1.3	11.2	0.7	26.4	1.1	31.7	1.1	18.2	0.8
Sweden	75.4	1.0	61.5	1.1	25.2	1.0	46.5	1.1	45.1	1.1	22.5	1.2
Switzerland	68.7	1.0	64.2	1.2	19.3	0.8	33.3	1.2	45.6	1.2	15.0	1.0
Thailand	43.6	1.3	29.7	1.3	62.6	1.2	57.8	1.9	55.3	1.1	43.6	1.4
United Kingdom	67.6	1.2	69.3	1.1	4.1	0.4	10.7	0.7	36.6	1.3	20.9	0.9
United States	73.3	1.5	62.5	2.0	7.4	1.1	15.7	1.5	33.9	1.5	22.0	1.4
OECD average	*70.7*	*0.3*	*64.1*	*0.3*	*23.5*	*0.2*	*34.7*	*0.3*	*37.2*	*0.2*	*19.2*	*0.2*
OECD total	*68.7*	*0.5*	*62.9*	*0.6*	*23.2*	*0.6*	*34.0*	*0.6*	*34.8*	*0.5*	*22.1*	*0.4*
Netherlands[1]	85.4	1.3	72.4	1.4	25.8	1.8	46.0	1.6	34.0	1.9	12.6	1.3

1. Response rate is too low to ensure comparability (see Annex A3).

Table 5.6 (continued)
Diversity of reading materials, by gender / How often do you read these materials because you want to?
Agree or strongly agree

	Non-fiction books				E-mail & Web				Newspapers			
	Female		Male		Female		Male		Female		Male	
	%	SE	%	SE	%	SE	%	SE	%	SE	%	SE
Albania	18.2	0.8	18.7	1.3	14.8	0.8	20.2	1.1	47.5	1.4	58.7	1.4
Argentina	31.5	2.5	21.9	1.6	28.0	2.9	30.0	2.9	59.4	2.2	58.2	2.1
Australia	19.7	1.1	19.4	1.1	55.4	1.5	62.4	1.6	63.2	1.3	68.3	1.5
Austria	13.1	0.7	24.5	1.0	51.1	1.4	57.4	1.5	73.0	1.2	73.4	1.2
Belgium	17.8	0.8	14.6	0.8	32.2	1.2	43.8	1.2	41.4	1.0	50.5	0.8
Brazil	38.3	1.2	33.9	1.4	16.8	1.5	23.3	1.7	50.9	1.7	50.7	1.6
Bulgaria	39.4	1.2	29.5	1.2	51.2	2.0	61.6	1.5	86.5	0.9	79.2	1.1
Canada	18.5	0.5	14.9	0.4	62.6	0.6	65.8	0.6	54.8	0.6	60.4	0.7
Chile	27.7	0.9	21.6	1.1	24.4	1.4	28.3	1.6	60.7	1.3	55.0	1.5
Czech Republic	11.8	0.7	14.7	0.8	22.1	1.4	34.4	1.3	55.3	1.1	69.9	1.0
Denmark	26.2	1.2	29.3	1.3	57.7	1.5	71.2	1.2	59.7	1.4	68.7	1.2
Finland	11.2	0.7	17.9	0.9	62.9	1.3	63.5	1.3	85.3	0.8	84.8	0.9
France	19.5	0.8	21.8	0.9	15.1	0.9	27.4	1.3	46.1	1.3	48.6	1.3
Germany	15.3	0.7	18.6	1.0	28.5	0.9	45.0	1.1	60.3	1.1	65.6	1.4
Greece	26.7	1.2	26.1	1.2	13.5	0.8	31.9	1.3	30.2	1.3	62.2	1.3
Hong Kong-China	37.5	1.2	35.1	1.2	79.6	1.0	81.2	0.9	89.3	0.9	86.8	0.8
Hungary	27.7	1.0	35.4	1.3	26.6	1.6	36.6	1.6	60.4	1.4	61.5	1.7
Iceland	21.9	0.9	13.8	0.7	61.5	1.3	76.7	1.1	88.6	0.8	89.9	0.8
Indonesia	23.2	1.1	20.5	1.2	8.7	1.1	10.7	1.0	65.6	1.3	68.6	1.3
Ireland	17.9	1.0	11.6	0.9	27.9	1.4	36.5	1.6	72.5	1.1	78.1	1.0
Israel	29.0	2.1	22.8	1.7	34.7	2.6	54.1	2.1	79.8	1.5	79.2	1.6
Italy	13.1	0.8	15.1	0.8	21.5	1.0	37.0	1.1	56.2	1.4	66.0	1.2
Japan	9.9	0.6	9.7	0.6	43.7	1.4	43.3	1.4	65.9	1.4	74.0	1.2
Korea	23.9	1.0	22.4	0.8	64.5	1.5	67.2	1.2	65.0	1.5	73.4	1.2
Latvia	18.2	1.5	18.0	2.0	11.0	0.9	20.2	1.5	79.7	1.1	73.1	1.5
Liechtenstein	17.3	2.8	13.4	3.0	55.9	3.6	62.2	3.5	58.8	4.4	77.0	3.6
Luxembourg	13.7	0.8	18.8	0.9	40.2	1.1	54.6	1.2	37.2	1.2	47.7	1.2
FYR Macedonia	12.4	0.9	19.7	1.0	41.7	1.4	48.8	1.3	78.0	1.2	75.1	1.1
Mexico	21.2	1.0	23.2	1.1	16.6	1.5	20.4	2.1	44.5	1.9	47.7	1.8
New Zealand	24.6	1.2	25.7	1.1	50.4	1.6	53.0	1.3	65.0	1.3	68.0	1.2
Norway	17.9	0.9	24.4	1.0	58.4	1.5	67.7	1.3	83.1	1.0	85.8	0.9
Peru	39.3	1.2	39.1	1.5	27.2	1.8	27.2	1.7	62.1	1.5	65.8	1.3
Poland	17.3	1.0	17.0	1.0	16.9	1.3	29.7	1.9	78.8	1.1	69.7	1.3
Portugal	18.3	1.1	7.4	0.6	23.4	1.3	43.1	1.5	38.9	1.2	67.9	1.5
Russian Federation	53.9	0.8	43.2	1.2	7.9	0.5	14.1	0.8	78.4	1.1	73.8	1.1
Spain	25.2	0.9	20.7	1.2	17.2	1.1	28.2	1.3	37.1	1.4	56.1	1.2
Sweden	11.5	0.9	13.9	0.8	72.1	1.0	78.7	0.9	82.0	0.9	83.2	0.9
Switzerland	14.8	0.7	18.8	0.8	44.2	1.6	53.9	1.5	61.4	1.3	71.0	1.1
Thailand	50.1	1.2	40.7	1.9	22.4	2.2	22.5	1.8	78.5	1.3	66.3	2.1
United Kingdom	21.7	1.0	20.2	1.0	41.1	1.1	55.4	1.1	65.1	1.3	77.4	0.8
United States	20.7	1.3	16.0	1.3	64.8	1.7	65.4	1.3	55.6	1.8	56.4	1.9
OECD average	*18.5*	*0.2*	*19.1*	*0.2*	*39.3*	*0.3*	*49.2*	*0.3*	*61.0*	*0.2*	*68.0*	*0.2*
OECD total	*18.4*	*0.4*	*17.6*	*0.4*	*41.8*	*0.6*	*48.3*	*0.5*	*57.6*	*0.6*	*63.1*	*0.5*
Netherlands[1]	16.3	1.2	9.4	1.2	49.1	2.3	64.0	1.6	55.4	1.5	66.0	2.0

1. Response rate is too low to ensure comparability (see Annex A3).

Table 5.7
Percentage of students in each reading profile cluster by gender

	Cluster 1 Least diversified readers		Cluster 2 Moderately diversified readers		Cluster 3 Diversified readers in short texts		Cluster 4 Diversified readers in long texts	
	Males (%)	Females (%)	Males (%)	Females (%)	Males (%)	Females (%)	Males (%)	Females (%)
Albania	27.3	30.7	20.1	12.3	29.5	27.8	23.1	29.2
Argentina	31.0	24.2	25.8	21.1	29.5	27.1	13.7	27.5
Australia	17.4	19.7	39.0	30.7	15.5	5.7	28.2	43.9
Austria	16.9	16.0	42.1	42.0	23.6	10.9	17.4	31.2
Belgium	34.2	38.5	22.1	16.9	36.3	26.9	7.4	17.6
Brazil	33.4	26.2	19.5	11.4	29.4	25.9	17.7	36.5
Bulgaria	13.5	6.4	37.3	27.5	20.6	17.2	28.6	48.9
Canada	24.7	23.9	34.3	27.2	19.4	13.1	21.6	35.8
Chile	33.7	25.7	23.1	20.4	28.7	27.0	14.5	26.8
Czech Republic	19.4	24.3	44.8	27.3	22.9	14.9	12.9	33.5
Denmark	18.2	16.8	11.7	8.4	60.3	52.1	9.7	22.8
Finland	8.1	5.8	12.2	15.9	74.1	59.7	5.6	18.6
France	31.7	33.5	16.7	21.6	41.2	22.2	10.4	22.8
Germany	23.3	24.8	42.6	33.3	16.7	6.7	17.4	35.2
Greece	24.7	46.0	29.6	12.9	27.4	15.7	18.3	25.3
Hong Kong-China	8.0	5.1	19.7	27.2	52.0	29.7	20.3	38.0
Hungary	25.8	24.3	28.3	22.0	21.6	18.7	24.3	35.0
Iceland	6.5	6.8	29.0	28.2	55.2	44.3	9.4	20.7
Indonesia	24.4	23.9	25.1	18.3	35.1	40.2	15.4	17.7
Ireland	15.7	16.9	53.7	40.6	11.2	6.7	19.5	35.8
Israel	15.4	14.0	37.6	30.5	24.2	26.6	22.8	28.9
Italy	23.4	28.0	30.0	25.9	31.0	21.9	15.5	24.3
Japan	12.2	16.7	6.4	9.7	79.5	69.5	1.9	4.0
Korea	16.6	21.5	13.1	16.4	60.3	44.1	10.0	18.1
Latvia	17.0	10.8	42.3	37.5	16.7	13.8	23.9	37.8
Liechtenstein	17.3	24.8	51.1	31.1	17.9	10.9	13.7	33.2
Luxembourg	36.2	42.5	23.6	19.1	27.4	11.3	12.8	27.1
FYR Macedonia	17.2	11.5	27.1	31.3	38.3	33.3	17.4	24.0
Mexico	36.9	38.0	15.4	15.8	26.8	17.7	20.9	28.5
New Zealand	18.2	17.9	33.9	26.5	17.6	7.2	30.4	48.4
Norway	8.6	8.3	19.6	20.7	66.0	49.9	5.8	21.0
Peru	24.1	25.5	14.6	11.9	33.8	29.5	27.6	33.2
Poland	21.0	12.3	48.1	48.0	14.6	8.2	16.3	31.6
Portugal	22.9	36.0	37.2	15.7	27.8	21.4	12.1	26.9
Russian Federation	15.4	7.7	21.4	13.0	22.1	21.3	41.0	58.1
Spain	30.7	41.5	27.9	18.4	25.1	10.4	16.4	29.8
Sweden	11.9	10.2	29.5	31.1	45.0	29.5	13.6	29.2
Switzerland	20.2	23.9	34.2	26.5	32.7	18.2	13.0	31.3
Thailand	22.5	11.8	6.6	6.8	51	56.5	19.8	24.9
United Kingdom	13.9	20.2	46.0	33.1	12.5	4.4	27.6	42.3
United States	30.4	26.5	33.2	31.1	15.0	7.0	21.4	35.4
OECD average	*20.9*	*23.6*	*29.8*	*24.7*	*33.8*	*22.9*	*15.5*	*28.8*
Netherlands[1]	24.5	25.0	27.2	24.3	41.4	24.3	6.9	26.3

1. Response rate is too low to ensure comparability (see Annex A3).

Table 5.8a.
**Index of self-concept in reading, by gender and performance on the combined reading literacy scale,
by national quarters of the index**

See next page

Table 5.8a
**Index of self-concept in reading, by gender and performance on the combined reading literacy scale,
by national quarters of the index**
Results based on students' self-reports

	Index of self-concept in reading[1]														
	Males		Females		Difference[2]		Bottom quarter		Second quarter		Third quarter		Top quarter	
	Mean index	S.E.	Mean index	S.E.	Differ-ence	S.E.	Mean index	S.E.	Mean index	S.E.	Mean index	S.E.	Mean index	S.E.
Albania	-0.11	(0.03)	0.37	(0.03)	-0.48	(0.03)	-0.92	(0.01)	-0.27	(0.01)	0.29	(0.01)	1.45	(0.01)
Australia	-0.11	(0.02)	0.06	(0.03)	-0.17	(0.03)	-0.94	(0.02)	-0.24	(0.01)	0.00	(0.01)	1.06	(0.02)
Austria	-0.15	(0.03)	0.21	(0.03)	-0.35	(0.05)	-1.23	(0.02)	-0.37	(0.01)	0.25	(0.01)	1.50	(0.01)
Belgium	-0.24	(0.02)	-0.11	(0.02)	-0.13	(0.03)	-1.12	(0.02)	-0.38	(0.01)	-0.06	(0.00)	0.83	(0.02)
Brazil	0.11	(0.03)	-0.17	(0.03)	0.28	(0.03)	-1.12	(0.02)	-0.35	(0.01)	0.17	(0.01)	1.22	(0.02)
Bulgaria	-0.21	(0.03)	0.24	(0.03)	-0.45	(0.04)	-1.25	(0.02)	-0.44	(0.01)	0.24	(0.01)	1.48	(0.01)
Chile	-0.10	(0.03)	0.21	(0.03)	-0.31	(0.04)	-1.11	(0.01)	-0.37	(0.01)	0.24	(0.01)	1.49	(0.01)
Czech Republic	-0.45	(0.03)	-0.09	(0.02)	-0.36	(0.04)	-1.43	(0.02)	-0.61	(0.01)	-0.04	(0.01)	1.04	(0.02)
Denmark	0.20	(0.03)	0.52	(0.03)	-0.32	(0.04)	-0.91	(0.02)	-0.01	(0.01)	0.66	(0.01)	1.70	(0.01)
Finland	-0.28	(0.02)	0.14	(0.03)	-0.42	(0.03)	-1.19	(0.01)	-0.40	(0.01)	0.15	(0.01)	1.19	(0.02)
Germany	-0.34	(0.02)	0.11	(0.03)	-0.45	(0.03)	-1.35	(0.02)	-0.50	(0.01)	0.13	(0.01)	1.28	(0.02)
Hong Kong-China	-0.39	(0.02)	-0.21	(0.02)	-0.18	(0.03)	-1.30	(0.01)	-0.60	(0.01)	-0.12	(0.01)	0.83	(0.02)
Hungary	-0.30	(0.03)	0.02	(0.03)	-0.32	(0.04)	-1.24	(0.02)	-0.56	(0.01)	0.10	(0.01)	1.14	(0.02)
Iceland	-0.15	(0.02)	0.05	(0.02)	-0.20	(0.03)	-1.26	(0.02)	-0.39	(0.01)	0.16	(0.01)	1.29	(0.02)
Ireland	0.20	(0.04)	0.35	(0.04)	-0.15	(0.05)	-1.12	(0.02)	-0.16	(0.01)	0.66	(0.01)	1.71	(0.01)
Israel	-0.17	(0.05)	-0.01	(0.04)	-0.17	(0.06)	-1.23	(0.03)	-0.53	(0.01)	0.09	(0.01)	1.36	(0.02)
Italy	0.08	(0.03)	0.52	(0.03)	-0.44	(0.04)	-1.12	(0.02)	-0.10	(0.01)	0.67	(0.01)	1.73	(0.01)
Korea	-0.34	(0.02)	-0.36	(0.03)	0.02	(0.05)	-1.33	(0.01)	-0.63	(0.01)	-0.22	(0.01)	0.81	(0.02)
Latvia	0.36	(0.04)	-0.15	(0.02)	0.51	(0.04)	-1.07	(0.02)	-0.31	(0.01)	0.34	(0.01)	1.49	(0.02)
Liechtenstein	0.08	(0.07)	-0.29	(0.06)	0.37	(0.10)	-1.15	(0.04)	-0.40	(0.02)	0.05	(0.02)	1.07	(0.08)
Luxembourg	0.06	(0.03)	0.26	(0.03)	-0.21	(0.04)	-1.16	(0.02)	-0.27	(0.01)	0.43	(0.01)	1.65	(0.01)
FYR Macedonia	0.17	(0.02)	0.54	(0.02)	-0.37	(0.04)	-0.83	(0.02)	-0.10	(0.01)	0.68	(0.01)	1.67	(0.01)
Mexico	-0.10	(0.02)	0.11	(0.02)	-0.21	(0.03)	-0.88	(0.02)	-0.27	(0.01)	0.11	(0.01)	1.06	(0.02)
New Zealand	-0.26	(0.02)	0.03	(0.03)	-0.29	(0.04)	-1.39	(0.02)	-0.49	(0.01)	0.08	(0.01)	1.35	(0.02)
Norway	-0.23	(0.03)	0.15	(0.03)	-0.38	(0.04)	-1.27	(0.02)	-0.44	(0.01)	0.19	(0.01)	1.35	(0.02)
Portugal	-0.23	(0.03)	0.08	(0.03)	-0.31	(0.03)	-1.21	(0.02)	-0.42	(0.01)	0.17	(0.01)	1.20	(0.02)
Russian Federation	0.37	(0.03)	-0.15	(0.02)	0.52	(0.03)	-1.14	(0.01)	-0.32	(0.01)	0.39	(0.01)	1.52	(0.01)
Sweden	-0.11	(0.02)	0.19	(0.02)	-0.30	(0.03)	-0.94	(0.02)	-0.22	(0.01)	0.21	(0.01)	1.10	(0.02)
Switzerland	-0.20	(0.02)	0.11	(0.03)	-0.31	(0.03)	-1.12	(0.01)	-0.37	(0.01)	0.13	(0.01)	1.18	(0.02)
Thailand	-0.20	(0.02)	0.00	(0.03)	-0.20	(0.02)	-0.95	(0.01)	-0.38	(0.00)	0.08	(0.01)	0.92	(0.01)
United States	0.05	(0.04)	0.44	(0.04)	-0.39	(0.04)	-1.11	(0.02)	-0.23	(0.01)	0.64	(0.01)	1.73	(0.01)
OECD average	*-0.14*	*(0.01)*	*0.15*	*(0.01)*	*-0.29*	*(0.01)*	*-1.17*	*(0.00)*	*-0.35*	*(0.00)*	*0.23*	*(0.00)*	*1.30*	*(0.01)*
OECD total	*-0.09*	*(0.02)*	*0.24*	*(0.02)*	*-0.33*	*(0.02)*	*-1.13*	*(0.01)*	*-0.31*	*(0.00)*	*0.35*	*(0.01)*	*1.41*	*(0.01)*
Netherlands[3]	0.13	(0.04)	-0.11	(0.04)	0.25	(0.05)	-1.11	(0.02)	-0.33	(0.01)	0.19	(0.01)	1.30	(0.02)

1. For the definition of the index, see Annex A1.
2. Positive differences indicate that males have a better self-concept in reading than females, negative differences indicate that females have a better self concept in reading than males. Differences that are statistically significant are indicated in bold.
3. Response rate is too low to ensure comparability (see Annex A3).

Table 5.8a (continued)
Index of self-concept in reading, by gender and performance on the combined reading literacy scale, by national quarters of the index
Results based on students' self-reports

	Performance on the combined reading literacy scale by national quarters of the index of self-concept in reading							
	Bottom quarter		Second quarter		Third quarter		Top quarter	
	Mean score	S.E.	Mean score	S.E.	Mean score	S.E.	Mean score	S.E.
Albania	326	(4.7)	341	(4.3)	350	(5.0)	399	(4.8)
Australia	499	(4.6)	519	(4.9)	538	(4.4)	572	(4.5)
Austria	484	(3.8)	492	(4.1)	513	(3.6)	547	(3.3)
Belgium	514	(6.6)	529	(5.2)	553	(4.4)	548	(5.1)
Brazil	391	(4.3)	392	(3.8)	401	(3.4)	424	(5.1)
Bulgaria	411	(5.7)	414	(6.4)	438	(5.3)	475	(5.9)
Chile	390	(4.9)	396	(4.2)	419	(4.1)	450	(3.9)
Czech Republic	478	(3.8)	490	(3.2)	511	(3.1)	536	(3.1)
Denmark	456	(3.9)	491	(3.5)	510	(3.2)	548	(3.4)
Finland	509	(3.1)	531	(3.9)	560	(3.2)	593	(3.6)
Germany	477	(3.8)	476	(4.0)	503	(3.6)	534	(3.8)
Hong Kong-China	516	(3.5)	519	(3.9)	529	(3.7)	543	(3.8)
Hungary	458	(4.1)	464	(5.4)	491	(4.8)	521	(5.0)
Iceland	474	(3.2)	495	(3.4)	522	(3.2)	551	(3.3)
Ireland	513	(4.4)	527	(3.8)	533	(4.3)	542	(4.8)
Israel	461	(9.5)	438	(10.7)	467	(8.3)	508	(7.2)
Italy	452	(5.4)	484	(3.6)	501	(3.1)	514	(3.7)
Korea	498	(3.1)	518	(2.9)	531	(3.3)	552	(2.4)
Latvia	425	(6.8)	441	(6.8)	467	(5.6)	513	(5.4)
Liechtenstein	458	(10.6)	472	(9.8)	494	(11.1)	515	(8.6)
Luxembourg	417	(3.3)	442	(3.6)	471	(2.9)	492	(3.2)
FYR Macedonia	349	(3.2)	349	(3.3)	390	(2.7)	426	(2.7)
Mexico	410	(4.9)	415	(4.7)	425	(4.0)	441	(4.2)
New Zealand	514	(3.9)	510	(4.1)	544	(4.8)	573	(4.4)
Norway	470	(4.8)	490	(4.5)	523	(3.4)	561	(3.9)
Portugal	433	(5.9)	454	(5.2)	483	(4.5)	512	(5.0)
Russian Federation	435	(5.3)	447	(4.0)	471	(4.3)	505	(5.1)
Sweden	481	(3.0)	503	(2.8)	528	(3.2)	559	(3.5)
Switzerland	473	(4.9)	482	(5.6)	511	(4.6)	524	(5.2)
Thailand	412	(4.0)	421	(3.6)	435	(4.6)	456	(3.9)
United States	469	(9.0)	496	(6.3)	526	(7.0)	558	(6.2)
OECD average	*474*	*(1.0)*	*490*	*(1.1)*	*513*	*(1.0)*	*539*	*(1.0)*
OECD total	*465*	*(3.6)*	*484*	*(2.9)*	*507*	*(3.1)*	*533*	*(3.0)*
Netherlands[1]	515	(6.8)	529	(5.0)	538	(4.6)	549	(4.2)

1. For the definition of the index, see Annex A1.

2. Positive differences indicate that males have a better self-concept in reading than females, negative differences indicate that females have a better self concept in reading than males. Differences that are statistically significant are indicated in bold.

3. Response rate is too low to ensure comparability (see Annex A3).

Table 5.8b
**Index of self-concept in mathematics, by gender and performance on the mathematical literacy scale,
by national quarters of the index**
Results based on students' self-reports

	Males		Females		Difference[2]		Bottom quarter		Second quarter		Third quarter		Top quarter	
	Mean index	S.E.	Mean index	S.E.	Differ-ence	S.E.	Mean index	S.E.	Mean index	S.E.	Mean index	S.E.	Mean index	S.E.
Albania	0.35	(0.03)	0.27	(0.03)	0.08	(0.04)	-0.86	(0.02)	0.07	(0.01)	0.64	(0.01)	1.38	(0.02)
Australia	0.27	(0.02)	0.04	(0.03)	0.23	(0.04)	-0.84	(0.02)	-0.07	(0.01)	0.39	(0.01)	1.19	(0.02)
Austria	0.09	(0.03)	-0.20	(0.03)	0.29	(0.04)	-1.29	(0.02)	-0.38	(0.01)	0.22	(0.01)	1.21	(0.02)
Belgium	0.09	(0.03)	-0.09	(0.03)	0.18	(0.04)	-1.04	(0.02)	-0.26	(0.01)	0.32	(0.01)	1.02	(0.02)
Brazil	0.29	(0.04)	0.04	(0.04)	**0.25**	(0.05)	-1.06	(0.03)	-0.15	(0.01)	0.45	(0.01)	1.37	(0.02)
Bulgaria	-0.03	(0.04)	-0.09	(0.05)	0.06	(0.06)	-1.40	(0.02)	-0.43	(0.01)	0.30	(0.01)	1.30	(0.02)
Chile	0.18	(0.03)	-0.07	(0.03)	0.25	(0.05)	-1.23	(0.01)	-0.28	(0.01)	0.40	(0.01)	1.32	(0.02)
Czech Republic	0.02	(0.03)	-0.24	(0.03)	0.26	(0.04)	-1.29	(0.01)	-0.41	(0.01)	0.16	(0.01)	1.08	(0.02)
Denmark	0.68	(0.03)	0.29	(0.03)	0.39	(0.04)	-0.88	(0.02)	0.26	(0.01)	0.91	(0.01)	1.67	(0.01)
Finland	0.15	(0.03)	-0.20	(0.03)	0.35	(0.04)	-1.41	(0.01)	-0.41	(0.01)	0.31	(0.01)	1.39	(0.02)
Germany	0.24	(0.03)	-0.18	(0.03)	0.42	(0.04)	-1.29	(0.02)	-0.32	(0.01)	0.34	(0.01)	1.35	(0.02)
Hong Kong-China	0.14	(0.04)	-0.24	(0.03)	0.38	(0.05)	-1.38	(0.01)	-0.39	(0.01)	0.31	(0.01)	1.26	(0.02)
Hungary	-0.25	(0.04)	-0.37	(0.03)	**0.12**	(0.05)	-1.49	(0.01)	-0.68	(0.01)	-0.09	(0.01)	1.03	(0.02)
Iceland	0.11	(0.04)	-0.09	(0.03)	0.20	(0.05)	-1.36	(0.01)	-0.39	(0.01)	0.38	(0.01)	1.41	(0.02)
Ireland	-0.02	(0.02)	-0.11	(0.04)	0.09	(0.04)	-1.40	(0.01)	-0.40	(0.01)	0.26	(0.01)	1.27	(0.02)
Israel	0.36	(0.04)	0.29	(0.04)	0.07	(0.05)	-0.81	(0.02)	-0.02	(0.01)	0.61	(0.01)	1.51	(0.02)
Italy	0.14	(0.04)	-0.04	(0.03)	**0.17**	(0.05)	-1.36	(0.01)	-0.30	(0.01)	0.43	(0.01)	1.45	(0.02)
Korea	-0.42	(0.04)	-0.57	(0.04)	0.15	(0.06)	-1.62	(0.00)	-1.06	(0.01)	-0.24	(0.01)	0.97	(0.03)
Latvia	0.14	(0.03)	-0.04	(0.04)	**0.18**	(0.05)	-1.2	(0.02)	-0.18	(0.02)	0.42	(0.01)	1.17	(0.02)
Liechtenstein	0.28	(0.09)	-0.11	(0.09)	**0.39**	(0.12)	-0.92	(0.07)	-0.22	(0.03)	0.35	(0.03)	1.16	(0.08)
Luxembourg	0.11	(0.03)	-0.17	(0.04)	0.28	(0.05)	-1.33	(0.02)	-0.34	(0.01)	0.30	(0.01)	1.25	(0.02)
FYR Macedonia	0.18	(0.03)	0.09	(0.04)	0.09	(0.06)	-1.27	(0.02)	-0.20	(0.01)	0.55	(0.01)	1.47	(0.01)
Mexico	0.17	(0.03)	0.12	(0.03)	**0.05**	(0.03)	-0.81	(0.02)	-0.15	(0.01)	0.38	(0.01)	1.15	(0.02)
New Zealand	0.30	(0.04)	0.04	(0.04)	0.26	(0.04)	-1.21	(0.02)	-0.18	(0.01)	0.53	(0.01)	1.53	(0.01)
Norway	0.17	(0.04)	-0.33	(0.04)	0.50	(0.06)	-1.49	(0.01)	-0.49	(0.01)	0.27	(0.01)	1.36	(0.02)
Portugal	-0.14	(0.03)	-0.28	(0.03)	0.13	(0.04)	-1.50	(0.01)	-0.64	(0.01)	0.17	(0.01)	1.11	(0.02)
Russian Federation	0.04	(0.03)	0.02	(0.04)	**0.01**	(0.04)	-1.32	(0.02)	-0.32	(0.01)	0.43	(0.01)	1.34	(0.01)
Sweden	0.13	(0.02)	-0.23	(0.03)	0.36	(0.04)	-1.16	(0.02)	-0.33	(0.01)	0.20	(0.01)	1.11	(0.02)
Switzerland	0.32	(0.03)	-0.18	(0.03)	0.50	(0.04)	-1.13	(0.02)	-0.23	(0.01)	0.39	(0.01)	1.26	(0.02)
Thailand	0.06	(0.04)	-0.14	(0.03)	0.21	(0.05)	-1.06	(0.02)	-0.35	(0.01)	0.22	(0.01)	0.97	(0.02)
United States	0.38	(0.05)	0.29	(0.04)	0.09	(0.06)	-0.98	(0.04)	0.08	(0.01)	0.67	(0.01)	1.58	(0.01)
OECD average	*0.12*	*(0.01)*	*-0.13*	*(0.01)*	*0.25*	*(0.01)*	*-1.25*	*(0.01)*	*-0.34*	*(0.00)*	*0.31*	*(0.00)*	*1.27*	*(0.01)*
OECD total	*0.19*	*(0.02)*	*0.04*	*(0.02)*	*0.15*	*(0.03)*	*-1.12*	*(0.02)*	*-0.2*	*(0.01)*	*0.43*	*(0.01)*	*1.36*	*(0.01)*
Netherlands[3]	0.29	(0.05)	-0.36	(0.05)	**0.65**	(0.07)	-1.40	(0.02)	-0.42	(0.01)	0.34	(0.01)	1.39	(0.03)

1. For a definition of the index see Annex A1.

2. Positive differences indicate that males have a better self-concept in mathematics than females, negative differences indicate that females have a better self concept in mathematics than males. Differences that are statistically significant are indicated in bold.

3. Response rate is too low to ensure comparability (see Annex A3).

Table 5.8b (continued)
Index of self-concept in mathematics, by gender and performance on the mathematical literacy scale, by national quarters of the index
Results based on students' self-reports

| | Performance on the mathematical literacy scale, by national quarters of the index of self-concept in mathematics | | | | | | | |
| | Bottom quarter | | Second quarter | | Third quarter | | Top quarter | |
	Mean score	S.E.	Mean score	S.E.	Mean score	S.E.	Mean score	S.E.
Albania	385	(4.9)	373	(5.3)	392	(6.5)	403	(6.1)
Australia	507	(4.8)	521	(5.0)	544	(5.2)	572	(4.9)
Austria	496	(3.9)	507	(4.4)	513	(4.5)	550	(4.5)
Belgium	530	(6.6)	545	(5.0)	555	(5.8)	560	(7.6)
Brazil	326	(5.9)	335	(6.5)	342	(6.5)	361	(6.4)
Bulgaria	414	(6.7)	424	(6.9)	436	(6.9)	471	(8.3)
Chile	379	(4.7)	377	(5.3)	383	(4.6)	415	(5.8)
Czech Republic	477	(4.1)	495	(5.2)	514	(4.4)	542	(4.5)
Denmark	476	(3.6)	512	(4.3)	529	(3.7)	557	(5.0)
Finland	497	(3.4)	515	(3.7)	547	(2.9)	593	(3.0)
Germany	482	(4.7)	486	(5.1)	498	(5.7)	529	(3.9)
Hong Kong-China	542	(4.5)	548	(4.9)	562	(4.8)	595	(5.1)
Hungary	465	(4.4)	482	(5.5)	497	(5.0)	524	(6.9)
Iceland	478	(4.3)	498	(3.6)	521	(3.8)	573	(4.0)
Ireland	484	(3.4)	495	(4.0)	509	(4.6)	533	(5.0)
Israel	438	(10.1)	432	(11.9)	446	(11.9)	484	(11.6)
Italy	434	(3.8)	445	(5.4)	464	(4.3)	488	(4.8)
Korea	512	(3.9)	535	(4.4)	556	(4.3)	584	(4.0)
Latvia	439	(6.2)	455	(6.6)	466	(6.1)	504	(6.8)
Liechtenstein	488	(15.8)	519	(12.9)	503	(16.1)	554	(14.8)
Luxembourg	455	(4.0)	457	(4.5)	455	(3.9)	474	(5.1)
FYR Macedonia	382	(4.4)	384	(4.4)	379	(4.8)	408	(5.9)
Mexico	382	(4.8)	384	(3.9)	389	(5.1)	401	(5.3)
New Zealand	506	(4.3)	525	(4.5)	543	(5.0)	598	(4.9)
Norway	456	(4.7)	488	(4.1)	507	(5.0)	563	(4.2)
Portugal	424	(4.1)	453	(5.6)	460	(6.2)	480	(5.6)
Russian Federation	453	(7.6)	459	(6.4)	488	(6.0)	523	(5.9)
Sweden	475	(3.6)	489	(4.0)	521	(4.4)	562	(4.6)
Switzerland	514	(6.0)	527	(7.0)	532	(5.1)	559	(5.4)
Thailand	427	(4.5)	434	(5.2)	423	(4.8)	445	(5.9)
United States	473	(7.0)	488	(9.1)	496	(10.1)	545	(8.0)
OECD average	*475*	*(1.2)*	*492*	*(1.1)*	*507*	*(1.2)*	*539*	*(1.5)*
OECD total	*464*	*(3.0)*	*477*	*(3.9)*	*489*	*(4.2)*	*523*	*(3.7)*
Netherlands[3]	556	(7.1)	552	(6.0)	564	(6.3)	588	(5.2)

1. For a definition of the index see Annex A1.
2. Positive differences indicate that males have a better self-concept in mathematics than females, negative differences indicate that females have a better self concept in mathematics than males. Differences that are statistically significant are indicated in bold.
3. Response rate is too low to ensure comparability (see Annex A3).

Table 6.1a
International socio-economic index of occupational status (ISEI) and performance on the combined reading literacy scale, by national quarters of the index
Results based on students' self-reports

| | International socio-economic index of occupational status[1] | | | | | | | | | |
| | All students | | Bottom quarter | | Second quarter | | Third quarter | | Top quarter | |
	Mean index	S.E.	Mean index	S.E.	Mean index	S.E.	Mean index	S.E.	Mean index	S.E.
Albania	45.5	(0.5)	24.5	(0.2)	34.6	(0.1)	49.0	(0.3)	74.0	(0.2)
Argentina	43.3	(1.0)	24.2	(0.3)	33.3	(0.2)	47.5	(0.3)	68.4	(0.7)
Australia	52.3	(0.5)	31.1	(0.2)	46.3	(0.1)	58.4	(0.2)	73.2	(0.3)
Austria	49.7	(0.3)	32.9	(0.2)	44.7	(0.1)	52.2	(0.1)	69.1	(0.3)
Belgium	49.0	(0.4)	28.4	(0.1)	42.1	(0.1)	53.5	(0.1)	71.8	(0.2)
Brazil	43.9	(0.6)	24.6	(0.2)	34.5	(0.2)	49.6	(0.2)	67.1	(0.4)
Bulgaria	50.0	(0.6)	31.8	(0.2)	44.2	(0.1)	52.2	(0.1)	71.8	(0.2)
Canada	52.8	(0.2)	31.3	(0.1)	48.1	(0.1)	58.9	(0.1)	72.9	(0.1)
Chile	39.9	(0.4)	23.3	(0.2)	30.9	(0.1)	43.2	(0.2)	62.1	(0.3)
Czech Republic	48.3	(0.3)	31.2	(0.2)	44.4	(0.1)	51.5	(0.0)	66.1	(0.3)
Denmark	49.7	(0.4)	29.0	(0.2)	44.0	(0.1)	54.9	(0.2)	71.1	(0.3)
Finland	50.0	(0.4)	29.7	(0.2)	43.4	(0.1)	55.1	(0.1)	71.8	(0.2)
France	48.3	(0.4)	27.7	(0.2)	41.1	(0.2)	53.1	(0.1)	71.2	(0.3)
Germany	48.9	(0.3)	30.0	(0.2)	42.6	(0.1)	52.5	(0.1)	70.2	(0.2)
Greece	47.8	(0.6)	25.6	(0.3)	40.2	(0.2)	53.0	(0.1)	72.3	(0.4)
Hong Kong-China	42.3	(0.4)	28.1	(0.2)	37.0	(0.1)	45.8	(0.1)	58.2	(0.4)
Hungary	49.5	(0.5)	30.4	(0.2)	42.6	(0.1)	53.7	(0.1)	71.5	(0.2)
Iceland	52.7	(0.3)	31.4	(0.2)	47.3	(0.1)	58.6	(0.2)	73.8	(0.2)
Indonesia	36.4	(0.8)	16.0	(0.0)	26.5	(0.1)	42.6	(0.5)	60.4	(0.4)
Ireland	48.4	(0.5)	28.5	(0.2)	42.7	(0.2)	53.2	(0.1)	69.4	(0.2)
Israel	55.3	(0.8)	33.3	(0.3)	51.4	(0.1)	62.3	(0.4)	74.2	(0.5)
Italy	47.1	(0.3)	28.5	(0.1)	40.6	(0.1)	50.3	(0.1)	68.9	(0.4)
Japan[4]	m	m	m	m	m	m	m	m	m	m
Korea	42.8	(0.4)	26.5	(0.1)	35.9	(0.1)	46.0	(0.1)	62.9	(0.5)
Latvia	50.2	(0.5)	27.7	(0.1)	40.4	(0.2)	58.5	(0.3)	74.1	(0.3)
Liechtenstein	47.5	(0.9)	28.0	(0.6)	41.8	(0.4)	52.1	(0.2)	68.2	(0.9)
Luxembourg	44.8	(0.3)	25.1	(0.1)	37.5	(0.1)	50.6	(0.1)	66.1	(0.4)
FYR Macedonia	46.8	(0.3)	27.5	(0.2)	38.6	(0.1)	50.0	(0.1)	71.1	(0.3)
Mexico	42.5	(0.7)	24.4	(0.1)	32.3	(0.1)	46.8	(0.2)	66.5	(0.5)
New Zealand	52.2	(0.4)	30.5	(0.3)	47.1	(0.1)	57.7	(0.2)	73.6	(0.2)
Norway	53.9	(0.4)	35.6	(0.2)	47.1	(0.1)	59.0	(0.2)	73.9	(0.2)
Peru	40.4	(0.5)	23.9	(0.1)	31.2	(0.1)	42.1	(0.1)	64.5	(0.4)
Poland	46.0	(0.5)	27.3	(0.2)	40.0	(0.1)	49.8	(0.1)	67.0	(0.4)
Portugal	43.9	(0.6)	26.8	(0.2)	34.5	(0.1)	48.4	(0.1)	65.7	(0.5)
Russian Federation	49.4	(0.5)	30.0	(0.2)	40.3	(0.1)	53.4	(0.2)	73.9	(0.2)
Spain	45.0	(0.6)	26.8	(0.1)	36.2	(0.1)	49.6	(0.1)	67.3	(0.5)
Sweden	50.6	(0.4)	30.4	(0.2)	44.1	(0.1)	55.7	(0.1)	72.1	(0.2)
Switzerland	49.2	(0.5)	29.3	(0.2)	42.5	(0.1)	53.2	(0.1)	71.9	(0.3)
Thailand	33.0	(0.6)	21.2	(0.1)	23.3	(0.0)	31.5	(0.1)	56.0	(0.6)
United Kingdom	51.3	(0.3)	30.7	(0.2)	45.7	(0.1)	56.9	(0.2)	71.8	(0.2)
United States	52.4	(0.8)	30.3	(0.2)	47.4	(0.2)	59.5	(0.2)	72.5	(0.3)
OECD average	*48.9*	*(0.1)*	*29.3*	*(0.0)*	*42.4*	*(0.0)*	*53.6*	*(0.0)*	*70.2*	*(0.1)*
OECD total	*49.0*	*(0.2)*	*29.1*	*(0.1)*	*42.5*	*(0.1)*	*54.0*	*(0.1)*	*70.3*	*(0.1)*
Netherlands[5]	50.9	(0.5)	29.5	(0.2)	45.3	(0.2)	57.3	(0.3)	71.3	(0.2)

1. For the definition of the index see Annex A1.
2. For explained variation see Annex A2. Unit changes marked in bold are statistically significant. Where bottom and top quarters are marked in bold this indicates that their difference is statistically significant. 16.3 units on the index corresponds to one international standard deviation.
3. Ratios statistically significantly greater than 1 are marked in bold.
4. Japan was excluded from this comparison because of a high proportion of missing data.
5. Response rate is too low to ensure comparability (see Annex A3)

Table 6.1a (continued)
International socio-economic index of occupational status (ISEI) and performance on the combined reading literacy scale, by national quarters of the index
Results based on students' self-reports

	Performance on the combined reading literacy scale, by national quarters of the international socio-economic index of occupational status[2]								Change in the combined reading literacy score per 16.3 units of the international socio-economic index of occupational status[2]		Increased likelihood of students in the bottom quarter of the ISEI distribution scoring in the bottom quarter of the national reading literacy performance distribution[3]	
	Bottom quarter		Second quarter		Third quarter		Top quarter					
	Mean score	S.E.	Mean score	S.E.	Mean score	S.E.	Mean score	S.E.	Change	S.E.	Ratio	S.E.
Albania	311	(4.5)	340	(4.7)	365	(3.8)	400	(3.9)	27.7	(1.79)	2.0	(0.15)
Argentina	379	(7.1)	393	(9.9)	440	(9.6)	483	(6.3)	37.5	(2.61)	1.9	(0.28)
Australia	490	(3.8)	523	(4.5)	538	(4.2)	576	(5.4)	31.7	(2.10)	1.9	(0.14)
Austria	467	(3.9)	500	(3.3)	522	(3.4)	547	(3.5)	35.2	(2.07)	2.1	(0.10)
Belgium	457	(6.2)	497	(4.5)	537	(3.2)	560	(3.4)	38.2	(2.23)	2.4	(0.14)
Brazil	368	(3.9)	387	(3.8)	413	(4.0)	435	(4.5)	26.1	(1.94)	1.9	(0.13)
Bulgaria	394	(5.4)	409	(4.9)	454	(5.0)	488	(7.8)	39.1	(3.91)	1.9	(0.17)
Canada	503	(2.2)	529	(1.9)	545	(1.9)	570	(2.0)	25.7	(0.98)	1.9	(0.06)
Chile	373	(3.8)	388	(4.3)	420	(4.6)	466	(3.5)	39.1	(1.79)	1.9	(0.13)
Czech Republic	445	(3.1)	487	(2.8)	499	(3.5)	543	(2.9)	43.2	(1.68)	2.3	(0.13)
Denmark	465	(3.3)	490	(3.3)	511	(3.2)	543	(3.6)	29.1	(1.89)	1.8	(0.11)
Finland	524	(4.5)	535	(3.3)	555	(3.1)	576	(3.3)	20.8	(1.76)	1.5	(0.08)
France	469	(4.3)	496	(3.2)	520	(3.1)	552	(3.6)	30.8	(1.91)	2.2	(0.13)
Germany	427	(5.4)	471	(4.0)	513	(3.4)	541	(3.5)	45.3	(2.10)	2.6	(0.19)
Greece	440	(5.6)	460	(7.2)	486	(5.5)	519	(5.5)	28.1	(2.51)	1.8	(0.16)
Hong Kong-China	508	(4.0)	527	(3.4)	533	(3.7)	548	(4.7)	19.6	(3.10)	1.5	(0.10)
Hungary	435	(4.9)	461	(4.5)	504	(3.8)	531	(5.9)	39.2	(2.38)	2.2	(0.16)
Iceland	487	(3.1)	496	(3.2)	513	(3.2)	540	(2.6)	19.3	(1.45)	1.5	(0.09)
Indonesia	341	(4.9)	361	(3.8)	385	(5.0)	403	(6.8)	21.2	(2.77)	1.9	(0.22)
Ireland	491	(4.3)	520	(4.3)	535	(3.7)	570	(3.7)	30.3	(1.79)	1.9	(0.10)
Israel	418	(8.2)	470	(8.8)	475	(7.7)	509	(8.6)	34.2	(2.28)	2.2	(0.29)
Italy	457	(4.3)	481	(3.3)	494	(3.6)	525	(3.9)	26.4	(1.84)	1.8	(0.13)
Japan[4]	m	m	m	m	m	m	m	m	m	m	m	m
Korea	509	(4.5)	524	(2.9)	531	(2.8)	542	(3.4)	14.6	(2.12)	1.5	(0.11)
Latvia	428	(6.4)	449	(5.0)	479	(6.7)	492	(6.6)	21.3	(2.22)	1.8	(0.12)
Liechtenstein	437	(11.0)	491	(11.9)	495	(9.1)	523	(9.3)	32.6	(5.15)	2.1	(0.40)
Luxembourg	394	(4.1)	428	(3.4)	473	(3.3)	497	(2.8)	39.2	(2.02)	2.5	(0.15)
FYR Macedonia	339	(3.5)	354	(3.1)	396	(3.0)	420	(3.4)	32.6	(1.47)	2.0	(0.12)
Mexico	385	(4.1)	408	(3.7)	435	(4.0)	471	(5.9)	31.8	(2.28)	1.9	(0.18)
New Zealand	489	(4.3)	523	(3.8)	549	(3.4)	574	(4.5)	31.9	(2.14)	2.0	(0.12)
Norway	477	(4.1)	494	(3.8)	514	(3.8)	547	(4.2)	29.7	(2.02)	1.6	(0.09)
Peru	283	(5.9)	317	(4.3)	338	(4.7)	383	(5.8)	35.9	(2.28)	2.2	(0.17)
Poland	445	(5.6)	472	(4.8)	493	(5.3)	534	(6.4)	35.4	(2.72)	2.0	(0.16)
Portugal	431	(4.9)	452	(4.9)	485	(4.3)	527	(5.0)	38.4	(2.14)	2.0	(0.13)
Russian Federation	429	(5.5)	450	(3.8)	472	(4.7)	502	(3.9)	26.5	(1.86)	1.8	(0.09)
Spain	461	(3.5)	482	(3.6)	507	(2.7)	529	(3.0)	26.5	(1.61)	1.9	(0.11)
Sweden	485	(2.9)	509	(3.2)	522	(3.1)	558	(3.3)	27.1	(1.50)	1.8	(0.10)
Switzerland	434	(4.3)	492	(4.6)	513	(4.3)	549	(5.3)	40.2	(2.17)	2.7	(0.17)
Thailand	419	(4.2)	422	(3.7)	427	(4.3)	465	(5.8)	21.2	(2.61)	1.3	(0.10)
United Kingdom	481	(3.1)	513	(3.1)	543	(3.5)	579	(3.6)	38.4	(1.60)	2.1	(0.11)
United States	466	(7.5)	507	(5.9)	528	(6.1)	556	(5.9)	33.5	(2.71)	2.1	(0.20)
OECD average	463	(0.9)	491	(0.8)	515	(0.7)	545	(0.9)	33.6	(0.44)	2.0	(0.02)
OECD total	462	(2.3)	492	(1.7)	515	(1.9)	543	(2.1)	34.0	(0.90)	2.0	(0.06)
Netherlands[5]	495	(5.6)	525	(5.2)	555	(3.6)	566	(4.4)	29.9	(2.45)	2.2	(0.20)

1. For the definition of the index see Annex A1.
2. For explained variation see Annex A2. Unit changes marked in bold are statistically significant. Where bottom and top quarters are marked in bold this indicates that their difference is statistically significant. 16.3 units on the index corresponds to one international standard deviation.
3. Ratios statistically significantly greater than 1 are marked in bold.
4. Japan was excluded from this comparison because of a high proportion of missing data.
5. Response rate is too low to ensure comparability (see Annex A3).

Table 6.1b
International socio-economic index of occupational status (ISEI) and performance on the mathematical literacy scale, by national quarters of the index
Results based on students' self-reports

| | International socio-economic index of occupational status[1] | | | | | | | | | |
| | All students | | Bottom quarter | | Second quarter | | Third quarter | | Top quarter | |
	Mean index	S.E.	Mean index	S.E.	Mean index	S.E.	Mean index	S.E.	Mean index	S.E.
Albania	45.70	(0.50)	24.60	(0.20)	34.70	(0.10)	49.60	(0.40)	73.90	(0.30)
Argentina	43.20	(1.10)	24.50	(0.30)	32.90	(0.20)	46.90	(0.50)	68.40	(0.70)
Australia	52.32	(0.64)	30.65	(0.31)	46.19	(0.15)	58.66	(0.22)	73.83	(0.33)
Austria	49.83	(0.35)	33.17	(0.24)	44.86	(0.10)	52.26	(0.08)	69.11	(0.38)
Belgium	49.07	(0.44)	28.26	(0.18)	42.50	(0.16)	53.59	(0.12)	71.95	(0.25)
Brazil	44.00	(0.70)	24.64	(0.24)	34.33	(0.25)	49.72	(0.30)	67.37	(0.53)
Bulgaria	49.60	(0.70)	31.50	(0.20)	43.80	(0.10)	51.90	(0.10)	71.30	(0.30)
Canada	52.94	(0.25)	31.44	(0.12)	48.21	(0.09)	59.07	(0.10)	73.03	(0.16)
Chile	40.00	(0.50)	23.50	(0.20)	31.00	(0.10)	43.30	(0.20)	62.20	(0.30)
Czech Republic	48.24	(0.31)	31.29	(0.22)	44.45	(0.17)	51.52	(0.04)	65.74	(0.38)
Denmark	49.80	(0.48)	29.24	(0.21)	44.01	(0.17)	54.96	(0.18)	70.99	(0.36)
Finland	49.99	(0.47)	29.48	(0.22)	43.14	(0.17)	55.40	(0.18)	71.97	(0.26)
France	48.39	(0.50)	27.72	(0.20)	41.37	(0.24)	53.18	(0.07)	71.32	(0.31)
Germany	49.11	(0.34)	29.99	(0.20)	42.67	(0.15)	52.80	(0.08)	70.99	(0.27)
Greece	48.29	(0.63)	25.58	(0.30)	40.94	(0.20)	53.78	(0.15)	72.91	(0.39)
Hong Kong-China	42.50	(0.50)	28.10	(0.30)	37.30	(0.10)	45.90	(0.10)	58.70	(0.50)
Hungary	49.80	(0.49)	30.50	(0.25)	42.97	(0.13)	53.99	(0.17)	71.78	(0.36)
Iceland	52.44	(0.38)	31.43	(0.35)	47.06	(0.18)	57.92	(0.27)	73.39	(0.35)
Indonesia	36.20	(0.80)	16.00	(0.00)	26.40	(0.20)	42.00	(0.50)	60.50	(0.40)
Ireland	48.00	(0.51)	28.53	(0.20)	42.48	(0.20)	52.74	(0.09)	68.29	(0.34)
Israel	55.00	(0.80)	32.60	(0.40)	51.30	(0.10)	62.40	(0.50)	73.90	(0.50)
Italy	46.94	(0.39)	28.22	(0.17)	40.41	(0.19)	50.34	(0.07)	68.81	(0.44)
Japan[4]	m	m	m	m	m	m	m	m	m	m
Korea	42.98	(0.51)	26.65	(0.15)	36.21	(0.12)	46.14	(0.19)	62.96	(0.45)
Latvia	49.89	(0.61)	27.76	(0.19)	39.93	(0.20)	57.67	(0.38)	74.26	(0.35)
Liechtenstein	46.69	(1.30)	28.41	(0.70)	40.21	(0.54)	51.29	(0.52)	67.39	(1.33)
Luxembourg	44.37	(0.35)	24.99	(0.19)	36.92	(0.20)	50.11	(0.17)	65.50	(0.46)
FYR Macedonia	47.00	(0.40)	27.40	(0.20)	38.60	(0.20)	50.30	(0.10)	71.50	(0.40)
Mexico	42.72	(0.71)	24.71	(0.17)	32.74	(0.15)	47.13	(0.21)	66.32	(0.54)
New Zealand	52.40	(0.45)	30.62	(0.36)	46.90	(0.15)	58.02	(0.28)	74.12	(0.28)
Norway	53.71	(0.42)	35.65	(0.26)	47.01	(0.16)	58.51	(0.27)	73.71	(0.31)
Peru	40.50	(0.60)	23.70	(0.10)	31.20	(0.10)	42.00	(0.20)	64.90	(0.50)
Poland	45.88	(0.46)	27.15	(0.20)	40.07	(0.17)	49.88	(0.13)	66.52	(0.54)
Portugal	44.20	(0.68)	27.00	(0.18)	34.81	(0.16)	48.65	(0.13)	66.38	(0.57)
Russian Federation	49.80	(0.54)	30.02	(0.29)	40.71	(0.12)	54.25	(0.22)	74.26	(0.22)
Spain	44.87	(0.66)	26.78	(0.17)	35.96	(0.15)	49.48	(0.15)	67.32	(0.63)
Sweden	50.30	(0.48)	29.93	(0.18)	43.76	(0.16)	55.64	(0.20)	71.89	(0.28)
Switzerland	48.96	(0.63)	29.04	(0.23)	41.92	(0.10)	52.85	(0.10)	72.05	(0.51)
Thailand	32.80	(0.60)	21.00	(0.10)	23.30	(0.00)	31.20	(0.20)	55.50	(0.50)
United Kingdom	51.22	(0.35)	30.57	(0.21)	45.66	(0.18)	56.89	(0.22)	71.75	(0.25)
United States	52.33	(0.81)	30.47	(0.32)	47.26	(0.26)	59.22	(0.27)	72.47	(0.39)
OECD average	*48.86*	*(0.10)*	*29.28*	*(0.06)*	*42.38*	*(0.05)*	*53.56*	*(0.05)*	*70.26*	*(0.07)*
OECD total	*48.97*	*(0.24)*	*29.15*	*(0.10)*	*42.56*	*(0.13)*	*53.94*	*(0.15)*	*70.30*	*(0.15)*
Netherlands[5]	50.91	(0.54)	29.45	(0.27)	45.46	(0.26)	57.14	(0.35)	71.68	(0.31)

1. For the definition of the index see Annex A1.
2. For explained variation see Annex A2. Unit changes marked in bold are statistically significant. Where bottom and top quarters are marked in bold this indicates that their difference is statistically significant. 16.3 units on the index corresponds to one international standard deviation.
3. Ratios statistically significantly greater than 1 are marked in bold.
4. Japan was excluded from this comparison because of a high proportion of missing data.
5. Response rate is too low to ensure comparability (see Annex A3).

Table 6.1b (continued)
International socio-economic index of occupational status (ISEI) and performance on the mathematical literacy scale, by national quarters of the index
Results based on students' self-reports

| | Performance on the mathematical literacy scale, by national quarters of the international socio-economic index of occupational status[2] | | | | | | | | Change in the mathematical literacy score per 16.3 units of the international socio-economic index of occupational status[2] | | Increased likelihood of students in the bottom quarter of the ISEI distribution scoring in the bottom quarter of the national mathematical literacy performance distribution[3] | |
| | Bottom quarter | | Second quarter | | Third quarter | | Top quarter | | | | | |
	Mean score	S.E.	Mean score	S.E.	Mean score	S.E.	Mean score	S.E.	Change	S.E.	Ratio	S.E.
Albania	346	(5.0)	372	(5.5)	398	(4.4)	429	(5.4)	27.7	(2.28)	1.8	(0.20)
Argentina	330	(8.5)	369	(11.6)	413	(11.0)	462	(8.0)	45.6	(3.75)	2.5	(0.41)
Australia	495	(4.3)	527	(4.7)	545	(4.6)	578	(6.1)	29.2	(2.25)	2.1	(0.22)
Austria	479	(5.0)	509	(4.1)	528	(4.8)	549	(4.3)	31.1	(2.66)	1.8	(0.15)
Belgium	473	(6.7)	507	(4.8)	547	(4.0)	574	(4.4)	38.1	(2.71)	2.3	(0.17)
Brazil	299	(5.1)	315	(4.7)	353	(6.0)	385	(7.6)	33.1	(3.19)	2.0	(0.17)
Bulgaria	391	(7.7)	412	(7.0)	456	(5.9)	490	(9.2)	40.8	(4.73)	2.0	(0.20)
Canada	509	(2.1)	527	(2.2)	541	(2.3)	563	(2.3)	21.2	(1.03)	1.8	(0.06)
Chile	347	(5.5)	363	(5.0)	395	(4.4)	440	(3.9)	37.5	(2.28)	1.9	(0.18)
Czech Republic	454	(4.3)	491	(3.6)	507	(4.0)	545	(4.3)	41.8	(2.36)	2.1	(0.15)
Denmark	489	(3.8)	505	(3.9)	531	(4.2)	553	(4.5)	24.8	(2.04)	2.0	(0.17)
Finland	513	(3.6)	528	(3.3)	543	(3.1)	565	(3.7)	19.3	(1.61)	1.6	(0.10)
France	486	(4.8)	512	(3.9)	530	(3.6)	560	(3.8)	26.9	(2.18)	2.0	(0.16)
Germany	438	(5.3)	481	(5.5)	513	(4.0)	541	(4.3)	39.9	(2.46)	2.6	(0.22)
Greece	411	(6.5)	430	(7.9)	456	(6.6)	499	(7.7)	30.5	(3.24)	1.7	(0.19)
Hong Kong-China	547	(4.9)	562	(4.1)	569	(5.4)	580	(6.1)	16.3	(4.08)	1.4	(0.14)
Hungary	439	(4.7)	468	(5.2)	513	(4.5)	543	(6.9)	41.6	(2.95)	2.2	(0.16)
Iceland	496	(4.7)	511	(4.3)	518	(4.3)	540	(3.8)	16.5	(2.10)	1.5	(0.12)
Indonesia	341	(5.4)	358	(4.5)	377	(6.4)	398	(8.7)	19.6	(3.59)	1.6	(0.19)
Ireland	472	(4.1)	498	(4.4)	513	(4.1)	536	(4.4)	25.9	(2.22)	1.8	(0.12)
Israel	380	(9.8)	448	(7.0)	465	(10.5)	501	(11.1)	45.6	(3.42)	2.4	(0.36)
Italy	433	(5.1)	449	(4.4)	467	(4.5)	486	(5.0)	21.3	(2.49)	1.6	(0.13)
Japan[4]	m	m	m	m	m	m	m	m	m	m	m	m
Korea	523	(4.2)	549	(3.6)	553	(4.1)	573	(4.2)	21.9	(2.30)	1.8	(0.14)
Latvia	438	(6.9)	459	(5.2)	486	(8.1)	481	(6.5)	14.2	(2.38)	1.5	(0.14)
Liechtenstein	486	(14.2)	514	(17.0)	532	(13.5)	546	(15.0)	23.3	(8.17)	c	c
Luxembourg	408	(5.2)	434	(4.4)	470	(4.1)	494	(3.7)	33.2	(2.04)	2.1	(0.17)
FYR Macedonia	348	(5.2)	367	(4.3)	403	(4.3)	425	(4.8)	29.3	(2.12)	1.8	(0.15)
Mexico	354	(4.8)	375	(4.7)	398	(5.0)	433	(5.9)	30.0	(2.58)	1.8	(0.19)
New Zealand	500	(5.9)	529	(4.5)	555	(4.2)	584	(4.7)	31.0	(2.56)	1.9	(0.13)
Norway	476	(5.0)	485	(4.5)	506	(4.4)	537	(4.4)	25.9	(2.41)	1.5	(0.13)
Peru	254	(6.4)	283	(5.5)	297	(5.6)	345	(7.6)	34.2	(3.10)	1.8	(0.19)
Poland	438	(7.0)	459	(6.5)	488	(6.9)	525	(6.4)	35.3	(2.97)	1.8	(0.17)
Portugal	420	(5.3)	441	(4.9)	464	(4.8)	507	(4.9)	33.9	(2.40)	1.9	(0.17)
Russian Federation	451	(7.4)	466	(6.4)	488	(6.6)	515	(5.0)	23.7	(2.33)	1.7	(0.14)
Spain	443	(4.8)	465	(4.3)	493	(3.5)	513	(4.8)	27.6	(2.35)	1.9	(0.13)
Sweden	474	(4.2)	499	(4.5)	518	(3.5)	555	(3.9)	30.6	(2.00)	2.0	(0.15)
Switzerland	478	(4.7)	531	(5.3)	541	(5.9)	578	(5.3)	34.0	(2.00)	2.3	(0.18)
Thailand	415	(5.1)	424	(5.0)	427	(4.5)	472	(7.2)	24.5	(3.26)	1.3	(0.17)
United Kingdom	488	(3.3)	524	(3.5)	547	(4.1)	578	(4.0)	34.5	(1.94)	2.3	(0.14)
United States	452	(7.6)	495	(8.0)	513	(6.8)	551	(6.9)	35.9	(3.19)	2.3	(0.21)
OECD average	465	(1.2)	491	(0.9)	513	(1.0)	542	(1.2)	32.6	(0.55)	1.7	(0.18)
OECD total	458	(2.7)	489	(2.3)	509	(2.1)	539	(2.5)	34.2	(1.17)	2.0	(0.06)
Netherlands[5]	531	(5.7)	558	(6.4)	582	(4.6)	597	(4.4)	27.2	(2.62)	1.8	(0.23)

1. For the definition of the index see Annex A1.
2. For explained variation see Annex A2. Unit changes marked in bold are statistically significant. Where bottom and top quarters are marked in bold this indicates that their difference is statistically significant. 16.3 units on the index corresponds to one international standard deviation.
3. Ratios statistically significantly greater than 1 are marked in bold.
4. Japan was excluded from this comparison because of a high proportion of missing data.
5. Response rate is too low to ensure comparability (see Annex A3).

Table 6.1c
**International socio-economic index of occupational status (ISEI) and performance on the scientific literacy scale,
by national quarters of the index**
Results based on students' self-reports

| | International socio-economic index of occupational status[1] | | | | | | | | | |
| | All students | | Bottom quarter | | Second quarter | | Third quarter | | Top quarter | |
	Mean index	S.E.	Mean index	S.E.	Mean index	S.E.	Mean index	S.E.	Mean index	S.E.
Albania	45.90	(0.60)	24.60	(0.20)	34.80	(0.10)	49.90	(0.40)	74.30	(0.30)
Argentina	43.70	(1.10)	23.70	(0.40)	34.00	(0.20)	48.40	(0.30)	68.70	(0.60)
Australia	51.97	(0.56)	31.07	(0.20)	46.33	(0.13)	58.38	(0.17)	73.23	(0.27)
Austria	49.52	(0.37)	32.94	(0.22)	44.69	(0.08)	52.24	(0.06)	69.06	(0.28)
Belgium	48.94	(0.41)	28.38	(0.13)	42.08	(0.13)	53.52	(0.08)	71.83	(0.20)
Brazil	44.04	(0.66)	24.56	(0.23)	34.50	(0.19)	49.60	(0.18)	67.12	(0.37)
Bulgaria	49.70	(0.70)	31.20	(0.20)	43.90	(0.10)	52.10	(0.10)	71.50	(0.40)
Canada	52.74	(0.25)	31.32	(0.08)	48.14	(0.07)	58.94	(0.08)	72.94	(0.13)
Chile	40.00	(0.50)	23.20	(0.30)	30.90	(0.10)	43.30	(0.20)	62.40	(0.30)
Czech Republic	48.46	(0.28)	31.19	(0.20)	44.40	(0.12)	51.53	(0.02)	66.14	(0.28)
Denmark	49.56	(0.49)	29.01	(0.19)	44.03	(0.13)	54.85	(0.15)	71.08	(0.28)
Finland	50.05	(0.43)	29.65	(0.18)	43.40	(0.12)	55.14	(0.13)	71.84	(0.20)
France	48.50	(0.46)	27.69	(0.17)	41.09	(0.16)	53.07	(0.06)	71.21	(0.28)
Germany	48.86	(0.36)	30.04	(0.20)	42.64	(0.13)	52.52	(0.06)	70.21	(0.23)
Greece	46.72	(0.70)	25.55	(0.26)	40.22	(0.21)	52.99	(0.10)	72.33	(0.37)
Hong Kong-China	42.10	(0.40)	28.00	(0.20)	36.60	(0.10)	45.70	(0.10)	58.00	(0.40)
Hungary	49.39	(0.56)	30.39	(0.19)	42.62	(0.10)	53.67	(0.12)	71.45	(0.24)
Iceland	52.88	(0.41)	31.36	(0.24)	47.26	(0.12)	58.57	(0.21)	73.76	(0.25)
Indonesia	36.70	(0.80)	16.00	(0.00)	26.60	(0.20)	43.50	(0.50)	60.60	(0.50)
Ireland	48.47	(0.50)	28.45	(0.18)	42.72	(0.15)	53.22	(0.08)	69.36	(0.25)
Israel	55.80	(0.80)	34.90	(0.40)	51.60	(0.10)	62.10	(0.40)	74.50	(0.60)
Italy	47.24	(0.40)	28.47	(0.15)	40.64	(0.13)	50.30	(0.06)	68.91	(0.37)
Japan[4]	m	m	m	m	m	m	m	m	m	m
Korea	43.00	(0.45)	26.50	(0.14)	35.89	(0.10)	45.97	(0.14)	62.87	(0.45)
Latvia	50.01	(0.70)	27.68	(0.15)	40.41	(0.19)	58.46	(0.31)	74.07	(0.27)
Liechtenstein	48.77	(1.18)	28.01	(0.63)	41.82	(0.38)	52.11	(0.24)	68.22	(0.92)
Luxembourg	45.07	(0.39)	25.09	(0.14)	37.46	(0.14)	50.55	(0.12)	66.06	(0.37)
FYR Macedonia	46.80	(0.50)	27.60	(0.20)	38.60	(0.20)	50.00	(0.10)	71.10	(0.50)
Mexico	42.40	(0.75)	24.36	(0.13)	32.33	(0.11)	46.79	(0.16)	66.46	(0.48)
New Zealand	52.10	(0.46)	30.53	(0.27)	47.05	(0.12)	57.66	(0.20)	73.56	(0.20)
Norway	53.90	(0.46)	35.59	(0.25)	47.14	(0.13)	58.97	(0.18)	73.94	(0.22)
Peru	40.60	(0.60)	24.00	(0.10)	31.30	(0.10)	42.30	(0.10)	65.00	(0.40)
Poland	46.18	(0.59)	27.32	(0.17)	39.97	(0.12)	49.82	(0.09)	67.02	(0.43)
Portugal	43.38	(0.60)	26.80	(0.16)	34.47	(0.10)	48.40	(0.11)	65.74	(0.55)
Russian Federation	49.22	(0.45)	30.03	(0.18)	40.27	(0.08)	53.39	(0.17)	73.85	(0.18)
Spain	45.10	(0.67)	26.82	(0.11)	36.23	(0.14)	49.63	(0.12)	67.30	(0.49)
Sweden	50.38	(0.46)	30.40	(0.16)	44.08	(0.12)	55.71	(0.13)	72.10	(0.20)
Switzerland	49.15	(0.54)	29.26	(0.19)	42.49	(0.09)	53.21	(0.06)	71.94	(0.30)
Thailand	32.70	(0.50)	21.20	(0.10)	23.30	(0.00)	31.10	(0.10)	55.20	(0.80)
United Kingdom	51.13	(0.37)	30.66	(0.17)	45.68	(0.14)	56.92	(0.19)	71.82	(0.19)
United States	52.56	(0.91)	30.29	(0.22)	47.36	(0.19)	59.50	(0.22)	72.48	(0.30)
OECD average	48.81	(0.10)	29.24	(0.06)	42.32	(0.06)	53.51	(0.05)	70.21	(0.08)
OECD total	49.02	(0.27)	29.09	(0.10)	42.55	(0.12)	54.15	(0.13)	70.36	(0.16)
Netherlands[5]	50.26	(0.56)	29.52	(0.21)	45.34	(0.16)	57.29	(0.28)	71.27	(0.22)

1. For the definition of the index see Annex A1.

2. For explained variation see Annex A2. Unit changes marked in bold are statistically significant. Where bottom and top quarters are marked in bold this indicates that their difference is statistically significant. 16.3 units on the index corresponds to one international standard deviation.

3. Ratios statistically significant greater than 1 are marked in bold.

4. Japan was excluded from this comparison because of a high proportion of missing data.

5. Response rate is too low to ensure comparability (see Annex A3).

Table 6.1c (continued)
International socio-economic index of occupational status (ISEI) and performance on the scientific literacy scale, by national quarters of the index
Results based on students' self-reports

| | Performance on the scientific literacy scale, by national quarters of the international socio-economic index of occupational status[2] | | | | | | | | Change in the scientific literacy score per 16.3 units of the international socio-economic index of occupational status[2] | | Increased likelihood of students in the bottom quarter of the ISEI distribution scoring in the bottom quarter of the national scientific literacy performance distribution[3] | |
| | Bottom quarter | | Second quarter | | Third quarter | | Top quarter | | | | | |
	Mean score	S.E.	Mean score	S.E.	Mean score	S.E.	Mean score	S.E.	Change	S.E.	Ratio	S.E.
Albania	347	(5.2)	366	(4.7)	386	(4.1)	424	(5.0)	24.5	(2.12)	1.8	(0.16)
Argentina	361	(7.9)	373	(11.5)	416	(10.7)	456	(6.9)	34.2	(3.59)	1.8	(0.32)
Australia	498	(4.9)	522	(4.7)	531	(4.6)	571	(6.2)	26.2	(2.41)	2.0	(0.16)
Austria	479	(4.7)	511	(3.5)	534	(3.7)	556	(4.1)	34.1	(2.59)	2.3	(0.14)
Belgium	444	(9.0)	486	(4.6)	524	(3.6)	552	(4.1)	40.2	(2.87)	2.4	(0.18)
Brazil	346	(5.6)	363	(5.1)	391	(5.1)	414	(6.7)	25.7	(3.21)	1.8	(0.14)
Bulgaria	419	(6.7)	431	(4.8)	466	(5.0)	496	(7.9)	32.6	(3.75)	1.7	(0.21)
Canada	501	(2.7)	524	(2.2)	538	(2.1)	563	(2.4)	23.3	(1.27)	1.8	(0.07)
Chile	383	(5.1)	394	(4.7)	421	(5.1)	471	(4.2)	37.5	(2.28)	1.7	(0.18)
Czech Republic	468	(4.1)	504	(3.8)	519	(4.0)	561	(3.9)	41.7	(2.41)	2.2	(0.14)
Denmark	445	(4.5)	473	(5.1)	493	(4.1)	532	(5.3)	32.1	(2.56)	1.8	(0.14)
Finland	517	(4.2)	526	(3.8)	546	(4.4)	565	(4.3)	18.4	(2.17)	1.3	(0.11)
France	460	(4.5)	488	(5.0)	518	(4.5)	556	(4.5)	33.9	(2.20)	2.0	(0.15)
Germany	437	(5.4)	473	(5.9)	512	(3.8)	539	(3.9)	40.7	(2.51)	2.3	(0.19)
Greece	429	(6.0)	443	(7.7)	477	(5.6)	498	(7.0)	25.9	(3.02)	1.7	(0.18)
Hong Kong-China	518	(4.2)	541	(3.9)	549	(4.2)	568	(5.9)	24.5	(3.26)	1.6	(0.15)
Hungary	444	(6.6)	478	(5.2)	519	(4.5)	554	(5.9)	43.3	(3.24)	2.2	(0.16)
Iceland	487	(4.4)	484	(4.3)	497	(3.9)	519	(4.2)	13.5	(2.27)	1.2	(0.10)
Indonesia	371	(4.2)	387	(4.0)	403	(5.8)	421	(7.9)	17.9	(3.10)	1.6	(0.18)
Ireland	482	(4.8)	504	(4.9)	523	(4.5)	553	(4.5)	28.9	(2.15)	1.7	(0.13)
Israel	404	(10.3)	441	(12.8)	460	(8.5)	491	(10.5)	34.2	(3.75)	1.8	(0.31)
Italy	451	(5.0)	471	(4.5)	480	(5.1)	514	(4.2)	24.4	(2.18)	1.5	(0.13)
Japan[4]	m	m	m	m	m	m	m	m	m	m	m	m
Korea	534	(5.1)	549	(4.5)	559	(3.8)	575	(4.7)	18.8	(2.74)	1.5	(0.14)
Latvia	433	(7.1)	451	(5.9)	483	(7.7)	490	(8.2)	19.3	(2.90)	1.6	(0.17)
Liechtenstein	437	(14.7)	472	(12.8)	495	(12.3)	523	(15.4)	35.7	(7.69)	2.4	(0.64)
Luxembourg	403	(5.3)	434	(4.8)	466	(4.2)	490	(5.4)	33.3	(3.00)	2.2	(0.19)
FYR Macedonia	374	(3.3)	388	(4.3)	417	(3.6)	439	(4.5)	26.1	(1.79)	1.8	(0.17)
Mexico	392	(4.1)	410	(3.8)	430	(4.5)	461	(6.4)	25.8	(2.49)	1.7	(0.14)
New Zealand	490	(5.5)	518	(3.6)	546	(3.9)	575	(4.1)	31.7	(2.45)	2.2	(0.18)
Norway	473	(4.5)	498	(4.7)	507	(4.3)	536	(4.4)	25.7	(2.46)	1.6	(0.11)
Peru	310	(5.8)	329	(4.8)	333	(5.5)	372	(6.3)	22.8	(2.77)	1.5	(0.17)
Poland	452	(6.0)	475	(6.7)	493	(6.3)	535	(7.9)	32.8	(2.90)	1.7	(0.18)
Portugal	426	(4.5)	445	(5.2)	475	(3.9)	504	(5.3)	32.4	(2.30)	1.9	(0.17)
Russian Federation	431	(5.6)	448	(5.6)	469	(5.4)	499	(5.4)	24.0	(2.20)	1.6	(0.12)
Spain	455	(4.4)	477	(4.9)	506	(3.8)	533	(4.7)	30.3	(2.25)	1.9	(0.14)
Sweden	485	(3.7)	498	(4.3)	519	(4.1)	552	(3.8)	25.2	(1.83)	1.5	(0.12)
Switzerland	442	(4.8)	485	(5.8)	510	(5.0)	554	(5.9)	40.2	(2.45)	2.5	(0.16)
Thailand	430	(4.4)	427	(4.2)	431	(4.6)	470	(5.9)	21.2	(2.28)	1.1	(0.12)
United Kingdom	492	(4.1)	522	(3.2)	548	(4.5)	588	(3.9)	37.5	(2.28)	2.2	(0.14)
United States	464	(8.4)	497	(6.5)	521	(6.9)	555	(7.8)	33.4	(3.33)	2.2	(0.19)
OECD average	465	(0.9)	490	(0.9)	512	(0.9)	543	(1.1)	31.9	(0.49)	1.9	(0.03)
OECD total	465	(2.6)	492	(1.9)	514	(2.2)	545	(2.5)	32.6	(1.06)	1.9	(0.03)
Netherlands[5]	496	(8.3)	519	(5.9)	554	(5.2)	564	(5.8)	29.2	(3.57)	2.1	(0.20)

1. For the definition of the index see Annex A1.
2. For explained variation see Annex A2. Unit changes marked in bold are statistically significant. Where bottom and top quarters are marked in bold this indicates that their difference is statistically significant. 16.3 units on the index corresponds to one international standard deviation.
3. Ratios statistically significant greater than 1 are marked in bold.
4. Japan was excluded from this comparison because of a high proportion of missing data.
5. Response rate is too low to ensure comparability (see Annex A3).

Table 6.2
Index of family wealth and performance on the combined reading literacy scale, by national quarters of the index
Results based on students' self-reports

	Index of family wealth[1]									
	All students		Bottom quarter		Second quarter		Third quarter		Top quarter	
	Mean index	S.E.	Mean index	S.E.	Mean index	S.E.	Mean index	S.E.	Mean index	S.E.
Albania	-1.56	(0.02)	-2.59	(0.01)	-1.89	(0.01)	-1.32	(0.01)	-0.45	(0.02)
Argentina	-1.06	(0.07)	-2.37	(0.02)	-1.45	(0.01)	-0.72	(0.01)	0.31	(0.04)
Australia	0.42	(0.02)	-0.64	(0.02)	0.15	(0.01)	0.66	(0.01)	1.53	(0.02)
Austria	0.25	(0.02)	-0.70	(0.02)	0.00	(0.00)	0.45	(0.01)	1.24	(0.02)
Belgium	-0.09	(0.02)	-1.03	(0.01)	-0.35	(0.00)	0.11	(0.00)	0.90	(0.02)
Brazil	-1.39	(0.04)	-2.69	(0.01)	-1.79	(0.01)	-1.13	(0.01)	0.05	(0.03)
Bulgaria	-0.99	(0.03)	-2.11	(0.03)	-1.30	(0.01)	-0.72	(0.01)	0.17	(0.02)
Canada	0.41	(0.01)	-0.67	(0.01)	0.15	(0.00)	0.66	(0.00)	1.51	(0.01)
Chile	-0.97	(0.03)	-2.20	(0.02)	-1.31	(0.01)	-0.67	(0.01)	0.32	(0.03)
Czech Republic	-0.86	(0.02)	-1.92	(0.01)	-1.12	(0.01)	-0.61	(0.01)	0.20	(0.02)
Denmark	0.49	(0.02)	-0.46	(0.02)	0.26	(0.01)	0.72	(0.00)	1.46	(0.01)
Finland	0.22	(0.02)	-0.71	(0.02)	0.03	(0.00)	0.47	(0.00)	1.10	(0.01)
France	-0.15	(0.02)	-1.08	(0.01)	-0.38	(0.01)	0.08	(0.00)	0.77	(0.01)
Germany	0.20	(0.02)	-0.85	(0.02)	-0.07	(0.01)	0.43	(0.01)	1.30	(0.02)
Greece	-0.45	(0.03)	-1.49	(0.02)	-0.73	(0.01)	-0.22	(0.01)	0.63	(0.04)
Hong Kong-China	-0.38	(0.02)	-1.19	(0.02)	-0.50	(0.00)	-0.22	(0.00)	0.39	(0.02)
Hungary	-0.87	(0.03)	-1.96	(0.02)	-1.16	(0.01)	-0.59	(0.01)	0.25	(0.01)
Iceland	0.53	(0.01)	-0.45	(0.02)	0.30	(0.01)	0.78	(0.01)	1.52	(0.01)
Indonesia	-2.07	(0.03)	-3.16	(0.03)	-2.30	(0.00)	-1.83	(0.00)	-0.99	(0.03)
Ireland	0.05	(0.03)	-1.03	(0.01)	-0.21	(0.01)	0.31	(0.01)	1.11	(0.02)
Israel	-0.05	(0.08)	-1.56	(0.07)	-0.28	(0.01)	0.36	(0.01)	1.28	(0.02)
Italy	0.12	(0.02)	-0.85	(0.02)	-0.13	(0.01)	0.34	(0.01)	1.13	(0.02)
Japan	-0.14	(0.02)	-0.99	(0.01)	-0.31	(0.00)	0.08	(0.00)	0.67	(0.01)
Korea	-0.27	(0.02)	-1.14	(0.02)	-0.42	(0.01)	-0.02	(0.00)	0.49	(0.01)
Latvia	-1.46	(0.03)	-2.63	(0.03)	-1.71	(0.01)	-1.18	(0.01)	-0.31	(0.02)
Liechtenstein	0.26	(0.05)	-0.73	(0.05)	0.02	(0.01)	0.52	(0.02)	1.27	(0.05)
Luxembourg	0.32	(0.02)	-0.80	(0.02)	0.05	(0.01)	0.58	(0.01)	1.45	(0.02)
FYR Macedonia	-0.96	(0.02)	-2.14	(0.03)	-1.24	(0.00)	-0.70	(0.01)	0.23	(0.02)
Mexico	-1.44	(0.06)	-2.81	(0.02)	-1.90	(0.01)	-1.14	(0.01)	0.10	(0.06)
New Zealand	0.22	(0.02)	-0.88	(0.02)	-0.06	(0.01)	0.50	(0.01)	1.34	(0.02)
Norway	0.56	(0.02)	-0.37	(0.02)	0.34	(0.01)	0.77	(0.01)	1.50	(0.01)
Peru	-1.82	(0.04)	-3.15	(0.02)	-2.21	(0.01)	-1.51	(0.01)	-0.39	(0.03)
Poland	-1.00	(0.03)	-2.23	(0.02)	-1.30	(0.01)	-0.72	(0.01)	0.24	(0.03)
Portugal	-0.13	(0.03)	-1.37	(0.02)	-0.45	(0.01)	0.19	(0.01)	1.12	(0.02)
Russian Federation	-1.79	(0.03)	-2.87	(0.02)	-2.04	(0.01)	-1.54	(0.01)	-0.70	(0.02)
Spain	-0.14	(0.03)	-1.16	(0.01)	-0.43	(0.01)	0.09	(0.01)	0.93	(0.02)
Sweden	0.65	(0.02)	-0.37	(0.02)	0.43	(0.00)	0.93	(0.01)	1.63	(0.02)
Switzerland	0.05	(0.03)	-0.98	(0.01)	-0.23	(0.01)	0.28	(0.01)	1.14	(0.04)
Thailand	-1.70	(0.05)	-2.98	(0.02)	-2.15	(0.01)	-1.49	(0.01)	-0.18	(0.04)
United Kingdom	0.42	(0.02)	-0.61	(0.02)	0.15	(0.01)	0.66	(0.00)	1.51	(0.02)
United States	0.61	(0.06)	-0.60	(0.02)	0.35	(0.01)	0.91	(0.01)	1.80	(0.02)
OECD average	*0.00*	*(0.00)*	*-1.04*	*(0.01)*	*-0.26*	*(0.01)*	*0.25*	*(0.01)*	*1.06*	*(0.01)*
OECD total	*0.00*	*(0.02)*	*-1.08*	*(0.02)*	*-0.26*	*(0.01)*	*0.26*	*(0.02)*	*1.09*	*(0.02)*
Netherlands[4]	0.18	(0.03)	-0.69	(0.02)	-0.01	(0.01)	0.40	(0.01)	1.03	(0.02)

1. For the definition of the index see Annex A1.
2. For explained variation see Annex A2. Unit changes marked in bold are statistically significant. Where bottom and top quarters are marked in bold this indicates that their difference is statistically significant.
3. Ratios statistically significantly greater than 1 are marked in bold.
4. Response rate is too low to ensure comparability (see Annex A3)

Table 6.2 (continued)
Index of family wealth and performance on the combined reading literacy scale, by national quarters of the index
Results based on students' self-reports

| | Performance on the combined reading literacy scale, by national quarters of the index of family wealth[2] | | | | | | | | Change in the combined reading literacy score per unit of the index of family wealth[2] | | Increased likelihood of students in the bottom quarter of the wealth distribution scoring in the bottom quarter of the national reading literacy performance distribution[3] | |
| | Bottom quarter | | Second quarter | | Third quarter | | Top quarter | | | | | |
	Mean score	S.E.	Mean score	S.E.	Mean score	S.E.	Mean score	S.E.	Change	S.E.	Ratio	S.E.
Albania	353	(4.6)	342	(4.2)	357	(4.8)	347	(5.9)	1.0	(2.65)	1.0	(0.09)
Argentina	380	(7.8)	397	(6.9)	430	(13.9)	471	(10.9)	33.3	(4.75)	1.7	(0.31)
Australia	510	(4.3)	523	(4.6)	538	(4.7)	544	(5.0)	16.6	(2.64)	1.4	(0.11)
Austria	495	(3.9)	508	(3.4)	514	(3.7)	514	(3.8)	10.8	(2.37)	1.3	(0.07)
Belgium	494	(5.9)	509	(4.6)	516	(3.1)	515	(3.7)	9.6	(2.98)	1.3	(0.08)
Brazil	370	(3.6)	385	(3.7)	396	(4.5)	437	(5.7)	25.2	(2.15)	1.6	(0.12)
Bulgaria	416	(5.5)	427	(5.0)	431	(5.7)	457	(8.4)	16.6	(4.41)	1.2	(0.11)
Canada	514	(2.4)	538	(2.0)	543	(1.9)	546	(2.2)	13.8	(1.19)	1.4	(0.05)
Chile	378	(4.3)	390	(4.0)	411	(4.3)	460	(3.8)	31.5	(1.77)	1.7	(0.14)
Czech Republic	475	(2.9)	491	(3.8)	499	(3.0)	502	(4.0)	11.6	(2.03)	1.3	(0.07)
Denmark	485	(3.8)	492	(3.8)	511	(3.6)	506	(3.8)	12.1	(2.42)	1.3	(0.08)
Finland	535	(5.6)	544	(2.9)	551	(3.2)	556	(3.8)	12.2	(4.20)	1.2	(0.08)
France	478	(4.5)	501	(3.8)	514	(3.3)	528	(3.3)	26.2	(2.56)	1.6	(0.10)
Germany	451	(5.3)	484	(3.5)	497	(4.0)	506	(4.1)	25.2	(3.96)	1.7	(0.14)
Greece	459	(7.0)	469	(5.6)	474	(5.8)	495	(6.6)	15.1	(3.45)	1.3	(0.11)
Hong Kong-China	512	(3.5)	526	(3.8)	531	(3.5)	533	(5.5)	15.7	(3.93)	1.4	(0.10)
Hungary	456	(5.9)	469	(4.7)	494	(5.0)	502	(5.1)	22.2	(3.05)	1.6	(0.13)
Iceland	515	(3.1)	508	(3.3)	508	(3.1)	501	(3.1)	-5.6	(2.33)	0.9	(0.06)
Indonesia	349	(3.7)	366	(4.1)	373	(4.5)	394	(6.8)	19.1	(3.08)	1.5	(0.13)
Ireland	513	(4.1)	523	(4.2)	531	(4.2)	543	(4.8)	11.9	(2.47)	1.3	(0.08)
Israel	414	(12.0)	450	(8.7)	472	(8.1)	491	(12.6)	23.5	(5.15)	1.9	(0.31)
Italy	476	(4.0)	487	(3.6)	488	(4.8)	500	(3.5)	9.9	(2.02)	1.2	(0.08)
Japan	521	(6.7)	526	(5.5)	526	(5.1)	527	(5.6)	3.9	(3.14)	1.1	(0.07)
Korea	509	(4.0)	525	(3.0)	531	(2.9)	534	(3.2)	15.3	(2.90)	1.6	(0.10)
Latvia	449	(5.7)	455	(5.4)	468	(7.2)	465	(7.8)	7.5	(3.27)	1.2	(0.11)
Liechtenstein	468	(11.9)	478	(11.0)	495	(11.6)	490	(11.1)	14.9	(7.17)	c	c
Luxembourg	405	(3.7)	447	(3.8)	455	(3.2)	464	(3.5)	25.0	(1.76)	1.9	(0.13)
FYR Macedonia	361	(4.2)	380	(3.2)	379	(3.2)	377	(3.4)	8.1	(2.49)	1.2	(0.10)
Mexico	392	(4.1)	408	(4.2)	424	(3.5)	464	(6.9)	24.4	(2.37)	1.6	(0.15)
New Zealand	497	(4.6)	529	(4.3)	540	(4.1)	552	(4.2)	21.8	(2.39)	1.8	(0.09)
Norway	496	(4.1)	515	(4.2)	511	(5.5)	504	(4.0)	4.2	(2.96)	1.2	(0.08)
Peru	301	(5.3)	311	(4.7)	329	(5.2)	371	(6.1)	26.8	(2.40)	1.4	(0.12)
Poland	464	(4.7)	483	(5.8)	490	(5.8)	488	(6.3)	8.8	(2.62)	1.3	(0.09)
Portugal	432	(4.9)	457	(5.1)	486	(4.9)	507	(5.2)	29.8	(2.39)	1.8	(0.12)
Russian Federation	449	(6.1)	460	(4.4)	464	(4.9)	477	(3.7)	12.1	(2.64)	1.4	(0.08)
Spain	472	(3.8)	491	(4.2)	499	(2.9)	512	(3.1)	17.2	(1.98)	1.5	(0.10)
Sweden	508	(3.7)	518	(3.3)	520	(3.2)	522	(3.4)	8.2	(2.10)	1.3	(0.07)
Switzerland	476	(5.5)	497	(4.2)	502	(4.6)	504	(6.7)	13.5	(2.52)	1.5	(0.10)
Thailand	419	(3.5)	422	(3.4)	427	(3.3)	454	(7.4)	13.2	(2.62)	1.2	(0.10)
United Kingdom	508	(3.8)	520	(3.7)	531	(3.4)	541	(3.7)	14.9	(1.93)	1.3	(0.08)
United States	455	(8.4)	503	(6.3)	525	(6.6)	540	(6.9)	32.0	(3.06)	2.3	(0.14)
OECD average	*481*	*(0.9)*	*499*	*(0.9)*	*508*	*(0.8)*	*515*	*(0.8)*	*19.8*	*(0.54)*	*1.4*	*(0.02)*
OECD total	*472*	*(2.7)*	*497*	*(1.8)*	*509*	*(1.9)*	*520*	*(2.2)*	*25.1*	*(0.89)*	*1.6*	*(0.03)*
Netherlands[4]	532	(5.6)	539	(4.6)	532	(5.1)	525	(4.6)	-3.9	(4.27)	1.0	(0.11)

1. For the definition of the index see Annex A1.
2. For explained variation see Annex A2. Unit changes marked in bold are statistically significant. Where bottom and top quarters are marked in bold this indicates that their difference is statistically significant.
3. Ratios statistically significantly greater than 1 are marked in bold.
4. Response rate is too low to ensure comparability (see Annex A3).

Table 6.3
Index of possessions in the family home related to "classical" culture and performance on the combined reading literacy scale, by national quarters of the index
Results based on students' self-reports

	All students		Bottom quarter		Second quarter		Third quarter		Top quarter	
	Mean index	S.E.	Mean index	S.E.	Mean index	S.E.	Mean index	S.E.	Mean index	S.E.
Albania	0.03	(0.02)	-0.87	(0.02)	-0.29	(0.01)	0.14	(0.00)	1.15	(0.00)
Argentina	0.06	(0.04)	-1.18	(0.02)	-0.19	(0.02)	0.45	(0.03)	1.16	(0.00)
Australia	-0.09	(0.03)	-1.38	(0.02)	-0.50	(0.01)	0.38	(0.02)	Max	
Austria	0.01	(0.02)	-1.24	(0.02)	-0.30	(0.01)	0.41	(0.02)	Max	
Belgium	-0.41	(0.02)	-1.65	(0.00)	-0.76	(0.01)	-0.15	(0.01)	0.93	(0.01)
Brazil	-0.41	(0.02)	-1.65	(0.00)	-0.68	(0.01)	-0.06	(0.01)	0.77	(0.02)
Bulgaria	0.55	(0.02)	-0.59	(0.03)	0.48	(0.02)	1.16	(0.00)	1.16	(0.00)
Canada	-0.12	(0.01)	-1.39	(0.01)	-0.56	(0.00)	0.33	(0.01)	Max	
Chile	-0.20	(0.02)	-1.44	(0.01)	-0.55	(0.01)	0.11	(0.00)	1.07	(0.01)
Czech Republic	0.18	(0.02)	-1.06	(0.02)	-0.08	(0.01)	0.72	(0.02)	Max	
Denmark	-0.11	(0.02)	-1.31	(0.02)	-0.55	(0.01)	0.28	(0.01)	Max	
Finland	0.12	(0.02)	-1.18	(0.02)	-0.25	(0.01)	0.75	(0.02)	Max	
France	-0.30	(0.02)	-1.65	(0.00)	-0.65	(0.01)	0.12	(0.00)	1.00	(0.01)
Germany	-0.02	(0.02)	-1.30	(0.02)	-0.33	(0.01)	0.39	(0.01)	Max	
Greece	0.20	(0.03)	-0.96	(0.02)	-0.02	(0.01)	0.63	(0.02)	Max	
Hong Kong-China	-0.59	(0.03)	-1.65	(0.00)	-1.04	(0.02)	-0.32	(0.01)	0.66	(0.02)
Hungary	0.33	(0.02)	-0.84	(0.03)	0.12	(0.00)	0.90	(0.01)	Max	
Iceland	0.67	(0.01)	-0.44	(0.02)	0.83	(0.02)	1.15	(0.00)	Max	
Indonesia	-0.60	(0.02)	-1.65	(0.00)	-0.87	(0.02)	-0.33	(0.01)	0.46	(0.02)
Ireland	-0.08	(0.03)	-1.39	(0.02)	-0.43	(0.01)	0.36	(0.01)	Max	
Israel	-0.04	(0.03)	-1.14	(0.02)	-0.41	(0.01)	0.23	(0.01)	1.16	(0.00)
Italy	0.34	(0.02)	-0.98	(0.02)	0.12	(0.00)	1.07	(0.01)	Max	
Japan	-0.27	(0.03)	-1.63	(0.00)	-0.62	(0.00)	0.09	(0.00)	1.09	(0.01)
Korea	0.24	(0.02)	-1.02	(0.02)	0.06	(0.01)	0.75	(0.02)	Max	
Latvia	0.55	(0.02)	-0.53	(0.03)	0.44	(0.02)	1.15	(0.00)	Max	
Liechtenstein	-0.03	(0.05)	-1.24	(0.05)	-0.28	(0.04)	0.27	(0.04)	Max	
Luxembourg	-0.11	(0.02)	-1.50	(0.01)	-0.48	(0.01)	0.38	(0.01)	Max	
FYR Macedonia	0.19	(0.02)	-1.01	(0.02)	-0.06	(0.01)	0.66	(0.02)	1.16	(0.00)
Mexico	-0.58	(0.03)	-1.65	(0.00)	-1.15	(0.01)	-0.29	(0.01)	0.77	(0.02)
New Zealand	-0.22	(0.02)	-1.51	(0.01)	-0.62	(0.00)	0.10	(0.01)	Max	
Norway	0.14	(0.02)	-1.21	(0.02)	-0.25	(0.01)	0.86	(0.02)	Max	
Peru	0.04	(0.02)	-1.11	(0.02)	-0.14	(0.01)	0.25	(0.01)	1.16	(0.00)
Poland	0.18	(0.02)	-1.03	(0.02)	0.00	(0.01)	0.60	(0.02)	Max	
Portugal	-0.10	(0.03)	-1.44	(0.01)	-0.38	(0.01)	0.25	(0.01)	Max	
Russian Federation	0.44	(0.03)	-0.44	(0.03)	0.12	(0.00)	0.95	(0.01)	Max	
Spain	0.17	(0.03)	-1.16	(0.02)	-0.04	(0.01)	0.73	(0.02)	Max	
Sweden	0.05	(0.02)	-1.18	(0.02)	-0.34	(0.01)	0.57	(0.02)	Max	
Switzerland	-0.08	(0.03)	-1.37	(0.01)	-0.42	(0.01)	0.31	(0.01)	Max	
Thailand	-0.10	(0.03)	-1.40	(0.01)	-0.49	(0.01)	0.33	(0.01)	1.16	(0.00)
United Kingdom	-0.07	(0.02)	-1.50	(0.01)	-0.43	(0.01)	0.48	(0.02)	Max	
United States	-0.12	(0.04)	-1.49	(0.02)	-0.51	(0.01)	0.35	(0.02)	Max	
OECD average	0.00	(0.00)	-1.27	(0.00)	-0.31	(0.00)	0.47	(0.00)	1.12	(0.00)
OECD total	-0.10	(0.01)	-1.40	(0.01)	-0.45	(0.01)	0.35	(0.01)	1.10	(0.00)
Netherlands[3]	-0.45	(0.02)	-1.65	(0.00)	-0.68	(0.01)	-0.21	(0.02)	0.77	(0.03)

Index of cultural possessions in the family home[1]

1. For the definition of the index see Annex A1. "Max" is used for countries with more than 25 per cent of students at the highest value of this index, which is 1.15.
2. For explained variation see Annex A2. Unit changes marked in bold are statistically significant. Where bottom and top quarters are marked in bold this indicates that their difference is statistically significant.
3. Response rate is too low to ensure comparability (see Annex A3)

Table 6.3 (continued)
Index of possessions in the family home related to "classical" culture and performance on the combined reading literacy scale, by national quarters of the index
Results based on students' self-reports

| | Performance on the combined reading literacy scale, by national quarters of the index of cultural possessions in the family home[2] | | | | | | | | Change in the combined reading literacy score per unit of the index of cultural possessions[2] | |
| | Bottom quarter | | Second quarter | | Third quarter | | Top quarter | | | |
	Mean score	S.E.	Mean score	S.E.	Mean score	S.E.	Mean score	S.E.	Change	S.E.
Albania	317	(5.4)	331	(4.9)	354	(4.6)	403	(4.1)	39.70	(2.68)
Argentina	383	(8.9)	413	(9.4)	422	(13.6)	463	(9.1)	31.50	(4.73)
Australia	492	(3.8)	511	(4.9)	541	(4.2)	572	(4.5)	32.30	(2.09)
Austria	485	(4.0)	492	(3.4)	512	(3.8)	542	(3.7)	22.92	(2.08)
Belgium	466	(5.2)	504	(4.3)	517	(3.8)	549	(3.3)	31.61	(1.81)
Brazil	380	(3.7)	386	(4.1)	405	(4.1)	423	(5.1)	19.94	(2.33)
Bulgaria	384	(4.7)	436	(5.7)	456	(5.4)	459	(5.1)	42.60	(2.71)
Canada	508	(2.2)	524	(2.0)	543	(2.2)	567	(1.8)	22.84	(0.94)
Chile	384	(4.4)	391	(4.3)	417	(4.2)	449	(4.3)	26.40	(1.95)
Czech Republic	453	(3.8)	489	(3.6)	509	(3.3)	522	(3.5)	30.89	(2.68)
Denmark	466	(4.1)	490	(2.9)	506	(3.7)	534	(3.3)	25.98	(1.78)
Finland	516	(4.4)	543	(3.1)	563	(3.3)	565	(3.3)	21.57	(1.62)
France	456	(4.2)	498	(3.5)	530	(3.0)	538	(3.2)	31.94	(1.76)
Germany	448	(6.8)	467	(6.1)	491	(4.6)	532	(4.1)	33.94	(3.32)
Greece	435	(6.7)	470	(4.6)	489	(5.6)	505	(5.5)	32.08	(2.99)
Hong Kong-China	508	(4.5)	519	(3.3)	533	(3.6)	543	(5.2)	14.20	(2.66)
Hungary	426	(4.7)	477	(5.7)	506	(4.5)	513	(4.2)	42.08	(2.58)
Iceland	484	(3.7)	511	(3.3)	520	(3.4)	518	(3.2)	22.23	(2.42)
Indonesia	368	(4.0)	373	(3.9)	367	(4.2)	378	(5.4)	3.50	(1.91)
Ireland	502	(4.4)	517	(4.6)	536	(3.9)	556	(4.0)	22.02	(2.17)
Israel	421	(10.7)	458	(8.5)	453	(9.0)	496	(9.9)	28.50	(3.43)
Italy	456	(4.0)	486	(4.0)	506	(3.7)	503	(3.2)	23.26	(2.02)
Japan	493	(6.8)	525	(4.9)	538	(5.0)	544	(5.2)	18.86	(2.00)
Korea	502	(3.5)	524	(2.9)	534	(3.1)	541	(2.9)	16.73	(1.68)
Latvia	421	(6.6)	462	(6.0)	483	(7.0)	474	(5.9)	34.31	(3.40)
Liechtenstein	450	(10.8)	472	(10.2)	493	(9.8)	520	(10.7)	27.34	(6.10)
Luxembourg	395	(3.8)	429	(3.6)	456	(3.5)	495	(2.9)	36.71	(1.75)
FYR Macedonia	358	(3.2)	371	(3.9)	377	(3.7)	400	(3.1)	17.80	(1.84)
Mexico	400	(3.3)	405	(3.2)	422	(4.0)	464	(5.6)	27.28	(2.31)
New Zealand	505	(3.8)	519	(4.1)	525	(3.9)	572	(4.9)	24.26	(2.27)
Norway	464	(4.2)	501	(4.0)	524	(4.4)	539	(3.9)	29.70	(2.01)
Peru	314	(5.2)	335	(6.2)	331	(4.8)	348	(5.6)	12.60	(2.57)
Poland	437	(5.5)	490	(5.5)	494	(5.4)	506	(6.7)	30.28	(3.02)
Portugal	426	(5.2)	454	(5.0)	495	(4.4)	508	(5.0)	33.68	(2.02)
Russian Federation	440	(4.8)	466	(5.4)	473	(4.7)	476	(3.6)	24.06	(2.35)
Spain	455	(3.7)	493	(3.3)	510	(2.6)	516	(3.2)	25.60	(1.58)
Sweden	484	(3.0)	509	(2.9)	530	(3.7)	545	(3.2)	26.21	(1.47)
Switzerland	465	(4.2)	485	(4.2)	496	(5.7)	536	(5.7)	26.65	(2.22)
Thailand	427	(4.4)	428	(4.2)	429	(3.9)	439	(3.8)	4.00	(1.41)
United Kingdom	489	(2.9)	505	(3.1)	540	(4.3)	566	(4.8)	29.07	(1.95)
United States	465	(6.3)	488	(10.2)	519	(7.7)	552	(6.8)	32.79	(2.59)
OECD average	466	(0.9)	493	(0.9)	513	(0.8)	534	(0.8)	27.02	(0.44)
OECD total	464	(1.9)	490	(2.8)	512	(2.3)	535	(2.0)	28.94	(0.87)
Netherlands[3]	509	(5.2)	526	(4.6)	535	(4.3)	560	(4.2)	20.61	(1.91)

1. For the definition of the index see Annex A1. "Max" is used for countries with more than 25 per cent of students at the highest value of this index, which is 1.15.
2. For explained variation see Annex A2. Unit changes marked in bold are statistically significant. Where bottom and top quarters are marked in bold this indicates that their difference is statistically significant.
3. Response rate is too low to ensure comparability (see Annex A3).

Table 6.4
Percentage of students and performance on the combined reading, mathematical and scientific literacy scales by levels of mothers' education
Results based on students' self-reports

	Mothers with completed primary or lower secondary education (ISCED levels 1 or 2)								Mothers with completed upper secondary education (ISCED level 3)							
	Performance[2]									Performance[2]						
	Percentage of students[1]		Combined reading literacy scale		Mathematical literacy scale		Scientific literacy scale		Percentage of students[1]		Combined reading literacy scale		Mathematical literacy scale		Scientific literacy scale	
		S.E.	Mean score	S.E.	Mean score	S.E.	Mean score	S.E.		S.E.	Mean score	S.E.	Mean score	S.E.	Mean score	S.E.
Albania	32.3	(1.2)	315	(3.9)	353	(4.2)	356	(4.0)	45.5	(1.2)	375	(3.1)	402	(4.0)	390	(3.4)
Argentina	56.3	(2.8)	391	(8.1)	356	(8.2)	367	(5.9)	23.1	(2.9)	454	(10.0)	428	(8.9)	428	(9.9)
Australia	29.0	(1.2)	502	(4.0)	508	(4.5)	505	(4.2)	40.0	(0.9)	530	(3.7)	531	(4.5)	529	(3.5)
Austria	28.1	(0.8)	482	(3.8)	491	(4.6)	497	(4.8)	53.7	(0.9)	517	(2.9)	520	(3.3)	526	(3.3)
Belgium	24.3	(1.0)	463	(5.3)	474	(5.6)	452	(5.9)	43.0	(0.8)	536	(3.2)	547	(3.7)	523	(3.4)
Brazil	65.8	(1.5)	379	(3.0)	316	(3.4)	358	(3.6)	21.9	(0.9)	431	(4.2)	372	(6.9)	403	(5.9)
Bulgaria	6.6	(0.7)	349	(12.6)	347	(15.3)	386	(14.1)	59.8	(1.6)	418	(4.0)	421	(5.0)	437	(3.9)
Canada	14.9	(0.4)	496	(2.4)	502	(2.6)	493	(2.9)	35.6	(0.4)	531	(1.9)	529	(1.8)	527	(2.0)
Chile	41.0	(1.4)	372	(3.7)	348	(4.3)	381	(3.7)	43.9	(1.2)	428	(3.7)	399	(3.9)	430	(4.2)
Czech Republic	6.6	(0.5)	421	(12.2)	444	(10.8)	461	(10.9)	79.4	(0.8)	492	(2.3)	494	(2.8)	509	(2.4)
Denmark	22.9	(0.9)	447	(4.5)	476	(5.2)	430	(6.4)	32.6	(0.9)	498	(2.7)	517	(3.5)	480	(4.0)
Finland	31.0	(0.9)	529	(2.8)	520	(3.2)	523	(3.4)	42.2	(0.9)	553	(3.3)	540	(2.9)	539	(3.4)
France	32.0	(0.9)	480	(4.0)	495	(4.2)	470	(5.0)	35.8	(0.7)	518	(2.9)	532	(3.4)	512	(3.9)
Germany	20.0	(0.8)	408	(5.5)	420	(5.9)	432	(6.0)	60.1	(0.9)	507	(2.5)	509	(2.7)	504	(3.0)
Greece	42.1	(1.2)	446	(5.5)	414	(6.0)	436	(5.6)	32.5	(1.1)	490	(4.9)	464	(6.3)	470	(5.5)
Hong Kong-China	72.7	(1.3)	518	(2.7)	554	(3.2)	533	(2.8)	23.1	(1.0)	546	(4.3)	578	(5.5)	559	(5.4)
Hungary	16.8	(1.1)	424	(5.7)	426	(5.7)	435	(7.9)	62.1	(1.1)	481	(3.6)	486	(3.6)	496	(4.0)
Iceland	46.7	(0.8)	495	(2.2)	502	(3.1)	485	(3.1)	30.7	(0.9)	516	(2.8)	525	(3.7)	499	(4.2)
Indonesia	75.8	(1.8)	365	(3.2)	361	(3.8)	388	(2.9)	19.6	(1.5)	400	(7.9)	396	(8.9)	415	(8.8)
Ireland	40.7	(1.3)	511	(3.5)	486	(3.1)	493	(3.8)	31.8	(1.0)	536	(3.7)	516	(3.7)	522	(4.3)
Israel	21.2	(2.0)	402	(10.1)	364	(13.0)	381	(11.1)	36.3	(2.0)	453	(7.5)	435	(8.6)	423	(9.5)
Italy	45.5	(1.0)	468	(3.8)	442	(4.1)	457	(4.6)	40.6	(0.9)	504	(3.2)	471	(3.7)	493	(4.3)
Japan[4]	m	m	m	m	m	m	m	m	m	m	m	m	m	m	m	m
Korea	41.9	(1.3)	509	(3.1)	527	(3.2)	536	(3.2)	45.1	(1.0)	535	(2.5)	557	(3.3)	559	(3.4)
Latvia	8.2	(0.6)	401	(8.5)	413	(13.4)	395	(9.8)	55.9	(1.4)	457	(5.1)	462	(4.3)	458	(5.2)
Liechtenstein	56.6	(2.7)	468	(6.2)	503	(8.6)	462	(7.8)	35.9	(2.4)	520	(7.9)	545	(11.8)	514	(10.8)
Luxembourg	52.3	(1.0)	424	(2.5)	434	(3.2)	429	(3.3)	31.4	(0.9)	467	(3.2)	470	(4.3)	463	(3.7)
FYR Macedonia	30.7	(1.2)	320	(3.0)	330	(4.4)	359	(4.0)	48.9	(1.2)	398	(1.8)	406	(3.1)	418	(2.5)
Mexico	73.6	(1.8)	404	(2.9)	371	(3.0)	407	(2.7)	14.0	(0.8)	479	(5.0)	436	(6.6)	463	(5.8)
New Zealand	17.3	(0.7)	499	(5.0)	508	(6.5)	491	(6.0)	37.5	(1.0)	539	(3.3)	542	(4.3)	535	(3.8)
Norway	19.1	(0.8)	485	(4.5)	482	(6.7)	478	(5.5)	39.0	(0.9)	509	(3.0)	504	(3.0)	504	(4.3)
Peru	59.2	(1.6)	302	(4.0)	269	(3.9)	316	(4.0)	23.2	(1.0)	355	(5.4)	321	(6.6)	344	(5.4)
Poland	8.1	(0.5)	447	(5.8)	454	(9.5)	452	(9.4)	73.6	(0.9)	478	(4.1)	467	(5.3)	481	(5.1)
Portugal	72.3	(1.5)	460	(4.2)	445	(3.7)	450	(3.7)	13.5	(0.7)	488	(7.1)	460	(8.7)	484	(7.4)
Russian Federation	6.3	(0.4)	413	(6.3)	445	(10.1)	417	(9.3)	57.6	(1.1)	461	(4.1)	477	(6.0)	456	(4.7)
Spain	62.1	(1.5)	478	(3.0)	461	(3.3)	472	(3.4)	21.3	(0.8)	516	(2.8)	501	(5.3)	516	(4.4)
Sweden	15.9	(0.7)	490	(3.8)	486	(5.7)	490	(5.4)	36.8	(0.8)	523	(2.6)	518	(3.8)	514	(3.6)
Switzerland	43.1	(1.3)	458	(4.2)	497	(4.9)	456	(4.5)	39.5	(1.0)	532	(4.0)	563	(4.7)	532	(5.0)
Thailand	85.0	(1.2)	425	(2.8)	425	(3.3)	430	(2.7)	8.8	(0.8)	459	(6.7)	470	(7.6)	464	(8.5)
United Kingdom	17.4	(0.7)	490	(5.0)	497	(5.7)	494	(6.3)	44.1	(1.1)	527	(2.8)	534	(3.1)	538	(3.3)
United States	12.1	(1.9)	449	(6.4)	432	(7.2)	446	(9.6)	54.3	(1.4)	508	(5.1)	496	(6.0)	500	(6.1)
OECD average	*32.3*	*(0.3)*	*467*	*(0.9)*	*464*	*(0.9)*	*465*	*(0.9)*	*41.1*	*(0.2)*	*511*	*(0.8)*	*510*	*(0.9)*	*510*	*(0.9)*
OECD total	*28.7*	*(0.7)*	*453*	*(1.4)*	*443*	*(1.5)*	*455*	*(1.7)*	*44.8*	*(0.5)*	*509*	*(1.9)*	*503*	*(2.2)*	*507*	*(2.3)*
Netherlands[5]	54.5	(1.5)	522	(3.6)	555	(4.7)	515	(4.5)	26.1	(1.2)	553	(6.0)	586	(5.9)	552	(6.8)

1. Percentage of students participating in the assessment of reading literacy with the respective level of mothers' education.
2. Mean scores marked in bold indicate that the difference in performance between students whose mothers have completed upper secondary education and those whose mothers have not is statistically significant.
3. Ratios statistically significantly greater than 1 are marked in bold.
4. Japan was excluded from this comparison because of a high proportion of missing data.
5. Response rate is too low to ensure comparability (see Annex A3).

Table 6.4 (continued)
Percentage of students and performance on the combined reading, mathematical and scientific literacy scales by levels of mothers' education
Results based on students' self-reports

	Mothers with tertiary education (ISCED levels 5 or 6)								Increased likelihood of students whose mothers have not completed upper secondary education scoring in the bottom quarter of the national reading literacy performance distribution[3]	
			Performance							
			Combined reading literacy scale		Mathematical literacy scale		Scientific literacy scale			
	Percentage of students[1]	S.E.	Mean score	S.E.	Mean score	S.E.	Mean score	S.E.	Ratio	S.E.
Albania	22.2	(0.9)	376	(6.7)	407	(7.3)	399	(7.0)	**2.1**	(0.20)
Argentina	20.6	(1.9)	464	(10.0)	439	(17.2)	445	(10.1)	**2.3**	(0.44)
Australia	31.0	(1.1)	560	(5.0)	565	(4.6)	554	(5.6)	**1.6**	(0.11)
Austria	18.2	(0.8)	539	(3.9)	551	(5.1)	547	(4.8)	**1.7**	(0.09)
Belgium	32.8	(0.9)	525	(4.5)	540	(4.6)	515	(5.4)	**2.3**	(0.15)
Brazil	12.3	(0.9)	440	(6.3)	378	(10.2)	428	(8.1)	**2.4**	(0.22)
Bulgaria	33.7	(1.7)	478	(6.9)	476	(8.0)	490	(6.4)	**2.6**	(0.30)
Canada	49.5	(0.5)	553	(1.8)	549	(1.9)	547	(1.8)	**1.7**	(0.06)
Chile	15.1	(0.7)	465	(4.0)	442	(4.7)	466	(5.6)	**2.5**	(0.21)
Czech Republic	14.0	(0.7)	540	(6.2)	553	(6.7)	563	(6.7)	**2.1**	(0.18)
Denmark	44.5	(1.1)	531	(2.8)	540	(3.2)	516	(3.7)	**2.4**	(0.14)
Finland	26.8	(1.0)	563	(3.7)	553	(3.4)	557	(4.4)	**1.4**	(0.07)
France	32.3	(1.0)	528	(3.4)	535	(4.1)	530	(4.3)	**1.9**	(0.13)
Germany	20.0	(0.7)	534	(3.8)	535	(5.0)	537	(5.2)	**3.0**	(0.22)
Greece	25.3	(1.2)	503	(6.9)	483	(9.1)	492	(7.8)	**1.9**	(0.14)
Hong-Kong, China	4.2	(0.5)	563	(11.3)	597	(15.2)	594	(11.4)	**1.7**	(0.17)
Hungary	21.1	(1.1)	533	(5.8)	550	(6.7)	557	(6.5)	**2.4**	(0.19)
Iceland	22.6	(0.8)	539	(3.3)	544	(4.6)	528	(5.0)	**1.5**	(0.08)
Indonesia	4.7	(0.4)	402	(9.0)	393	(13.3)	417	(13.4)	**1.6**	(0.21)
Ireland	27.5	(1.0)	545	(5.0)	517	(4.6)	539	(5.4)	**1.4**	(0.10)
Israel	42.5	(2.3)	496	(9.4)	481	(12.1)	487	(9.5)	**2.4**	(0.29)
Italy	13.9	(0.8)	514	(5.2)	482	(5.6)	511	(5.9)	**1.6**	(0.12)
Japan[4]	m	m	m	m	m	m	m	m	m	m
Korea	13.0	(1.0)	540	(5.0)	576	(6.9)	579	(7.5)	**1.6**	(0.11)
Latvia	35.9	(1.4)	479	(7.0)	482	(6.5)	486	(8.1)	**2.1**	(0.19)
Liechtenstein	7.6	(1.6)	c	c	580	(30.5)	c	c	c	c
Luxembourg	16.3	(0.7)	485	(4.9)	477	(6.9)	490	(6.8)	**2.1**	(0.14)
FYR Macedonia	20.4	(0.7)	411	(3.3)	421	(5.2)	439	(3.7)	**3.2**	(0.22)
Mexico	12.4	(1.2)	474	(7.5)	436	(6.8)	469	(8.0)	**3.7**	(0.57)
New Zealand	45.2	(1.0)	553	(4.0)	564	(3.7)	552	(3.8)	**1.6**	(0.10)
Norway	41.9	(1.0)	522	(4.1)	511	(4.0)	516	(3.9)	**1.5**	(0.09)
Peru	17.6	(1.1)	389	(6.2)	351	(7.3)	382	(7.2)	**2.3**	(0.23)
Poland	18.3	(0.9)	535	(8.1)	530	(9.2)	530	(8.7)	**1.4**	(0.14)
Portugal	14.2	(1.1)	520	(7.9)	501	(7.7)	495	(8.6)	**1.6**	(0.16)
Russian Federation	36.2	(1.1)	477	(4.8)	494	(6.0)	478	(6.3)	**2.0**	(0.11)
Spain	16.5	(1.2)	535	(3.3)	517	(4.8)	540	(5.0)	**2.2**	(0.16)
Sweden	47.4	(1.1)	527	(2.8)	518	(3.5)	522	(3.4)	**1.5**	(0.08)
Switzerland	17.3	(0.9)	518	(7.5)	553	(7.3)	524	(7.6)	**2.5**	(0.17)
Thailand	6.1	(0.7)	486	(7.6)	499	(10.2)	500	(8.7)	**1.9**	(0.23)
United Kingdom	38.5	(1.0)	551	(3.8)	555	(4.0)	557	(3.8)	**1.7**	(0.12)
United States	33.5	(2.2)	537	(7.4)	528	(8.3)	536	(8.5)	**2.1**	(0.20)
OECD average	*26.6*	*(0.2)*	*534*	*(0.9)*	*533*	*(1.0)*	*532*	*(1.1)*	*1.7*	*(0.03)*
OECD total	*26.5*	*(0.7)*	*534*	*(2.9)*	*530*	*(3.3)*	*535*	*(3.2)*	*1.7*	*(0.07)*
Netherlands[5]	19.4	(1.0)	554	(5.5)	582	(7.6)	561	(7.3)	**1.7**	(0.17)

1. Percentage of students participating in the assessment of reading literacy with the respective level of mothers' education.
2. Mean scores marked in bold indicate that the difference in performance between students whose mothers have completed upper secondary education and those whose mothers have not is statistically significant.
3. Ratios statistically significantly greater than 1 are marked in bold.
4. Japan was excluded from this comparison because of a high proportion of missing data.
5. Response rate is too low to ensure comparability (see Annex A3).

Table 6.5
**Index of social communication with parents and performance
on the combined reading literacy scale, by national quarters of the index**
Results based on students' self-reports

	Index of social communication[1]									
	All students		Bottom quarter		Second quarter		Third quarter		Top quarter	
	Mean index	S.E.	Mean index	S.E.	Mean index	S.E.	Mean index	S.E.	Mean index	S.E.
Albania	0.10	(0.02)	-1.16	(0.02)	-0.18	(0.01)	0.56	(0.02)	Max	
Argentina	0.17	(0.05)	-1.28	(0.02)	-0.23	(0.01)	0.98	(0.02)	Max	
Australia	-0.31	(0.02)	-1.49	(0.02)	-0.68	(0.01)	-0.12	(0.01)	1.05	(0.01)
Austria	-0.27	(0.01)	-1.37	(0.02)	-0.64	(0.01)	-0.09	(0.01)	1.03	(0.01)
Belgium	-0.12	(0.02)	-1.28	(0.02)	-0.54	(0.00)	0.16	(0.01)	Max	
Brazil	0.10	(0.03)	-1.51	(0.03)	-0.34	(0.01)	1.06	(0.01)	Max	
Bulgaria	0.44	(0.02)	-0.97	(0.03)	0.35	(0.02)	Max	(0.00)	Max	
Canada	-0.20	(0.01)	-1.34	(0.01)	-0.58	(0.00)	-0.05	(0.00)	1.16	(0.00)
Chile	0.36	(0.02)	-1.07	(0.02)	0.13	(0.01)	Max	(0.00)	Max	
Czech Republic	0.28	(0.02)	-0.99	(0.02)	-0.09	(0.01)	0.99	(0.02)	Max	
Denmark	0.20	(0.02)	-0.92	(0.02)	-0.11	(0.01)	0.63	(0.02)	Max	
Finland	-0.20	(0.01)	-1.10	(0.01)	-0.51	(0.00)	-0.05	(0.01)	0.86	(0.02)
France	0.16	(0.02)	-1.03	(0.02)	-0.20	(0.01)	0.67	(0.02)	Max	
Germany	-0.24	(0.02)	-1.27	(0.01)	-0.58	(0.01)	-0.09	(0.01)	0.99	(0.01)
Greece	0.10	(0.02)	-1.12	(0.02)	-0.22	(0.01)	0.53	(0.02)	Max	
Hong Kong-China	-0.24	(0.02)	-1.41	(0.01)	-0.66	(0.01)	-0.07	(0.01)	Max	
Hungary	0.54	(0.02)	-0.69	(0.02)	0.46	(0.02)	1.20	(0.00)	Max	
Iceland	-0.09	(0.02)	-1.20	(0.02)	-0.51	(0.01)	0.15	(0.01)	Max	
Indonesia	-0.60	(0.03)	-2.03	(0.02)	-1.05	(0.01)	-0.32	(0.01)	1.01	(0.01)
Ireland	-0.05	(0.02)	-1.25	(0.02)	-0.44	(0.01)	0.30	(0.02)	Max	
Israel	-0.32	(0.03)	-1.50	(0.02)	-0.73	(0.01)	-0.12	(0.01)	1.06	(0.01)
Italy	0.77	(0.02)	-0.42	(0.02)	1.09	(0.01)	1.20	(0.00)	Max	
Japan	-0.19	(0.03)	-1.47	(0.02)	-0.65	(0.01)	0.14	(0.01)	Max	
Korea	-0.18	(0.03)	-1.61	(0.02)	-0.65	(0.01)	0.34	(0.02)	Max	
Latvia	0.10	(0.03)	-1.10	(0.02)	-0.25	(0.01)	0.57	(0.03)	Max	
Liechtenstein	-0.34	(0.05)	-1.28	(0.02)	-0.70	(0.02)	-0.16	(0.02)	0.79	(0.07)
Luxembourg	-0.19	(0.02)	-1.37	(0.02)	-0.58	(0.01)	-0.02	(0.01)	1.19	(0.00)
FYR Macedonia	0.08	(0.02)	-1.26	(0.03)	-0.20	(0.01)	0.61	(0.02)	Max	
Mexico	-0.05	(0.02)	-1.45	(0.02)	-0.47	(0.01)	0.54	(0.02)	Max	
New Zealand	-0.28	(0.02)	-1.48	(0.02)	-0.69	(0.01)	-0.09	(0.01)	1.13	(0.01)
Norway	-0.01	(0.02)	-1.18	(0.02)	-0.36	(0.01)	0.30	(0.02)	Max	
Peru	-0.26	(0.02)	-1.66	(0.02)	-0.72	(0.01)	0.14	(0.01)	Max	
Poland	0.04	(0.02)	-1.26	(0.02)	-0.32	(0.01)	0.54	(0.02)	Max	
Portugal	0.38	(0.02)	-0.92	(0.02)	0.04	(0.01)	1.20	(0.00)	Max	
Russian Federation	0.47	(0.02)	-0.90	(0.02)	0.39	(0.02)	1.20	(0.00)	Max	
Spain	0.19	(0.02)	-1.12	(0.01)	-0.18	(0.01)	0.86	(0.01)	Max	
Sweden	-0.04	(0.02)	-1.14	(0.01)	-0.47	(0.01)	0.27	(0.02)	Max	
Switzerland	-0.25	(0.02)	-1.25	(0.01)	-0.60	(0.01)	-0.11	(0.01)	0.95	(0.01)
Thailand	-0.27	(0.02)	-1.62	(0.03)	-0.67	(0.01)	0.02	(0.01)	Max	
United Kingdom	0.01	(0.02)	-1.27	(0.02)	-0.36	(0.01)	0.46	(0.02)	Max	
United States	0.06	(0.03)	-1.44	(0.02)	-0.36	(0.01)	0.85	(0.02)	Max	
OECD average	*0.00*	*(0.00)*	*-1.20*	*(0.00)*	*-0.34*	*(0.00)*	*0.40*	*(0.00)*	*1.15*	*(0.00)*
OECD total	*0.01*	*(0.01)*	*-1.30*	*(0.01)*	*-0.36*	*(0.01)*	*0.53*	*(0.01)*	*1.18*	*(0.00)*
Netherlands[3]	0.29	(0.03)	-1.07	(0.04)	-0.10	(0.01)	1.14	(0.01)	Max	

1. For the definition of the index see Annex A1. "Max" is used to represent countries which have more than 25 per cent of students at the highest value of this index, which is 1.20.

2. For explained variation see Annex A2. Unit changes marked in bold are statistically significant. Where bottom and top quarters are marked in bold this indicates that their difference is statistically significant.

3. Response rate is too low to ensure comparability (see Annex A3).

Table 6.5 (continued)
Index of social communication with parents and performance on the combined reading literacy scale, by national quarters of the index
Results based on students' self-reports

| | Performance on the combined reading literacy scale, by national quarters of the index of social communication[2] | | | | | | | | Change in the combined reading literacy score per unit of the index of social communication[2] | |
| | Bottom quarter | | Second quarter | | Third quarter | | Top quarter | | | |
	Mean score	S.E	Mean score	S.E.	Mean score	S.E.	Mean score	S.E.	Change	S.E.
Albania	308	(4.9)	365	(4.3)	362	(4.6)	376	(3.6)	25.90	(2.12)
Argentina	383	(12.9)	431	(8.7)	431	(10.2)	440	(7.9)	19.90	(3.71)
Australia	502	(4.6)	526	(5.0)	545	(3.9)	545	(4.8)	17.41	(1.97)
Austria	493	(4.4)	504	(3.2)	520	(3.4)	514	(2.9)	10.98	(1.65)
Belgium	492	(5.4)	516	(3.9)	520	(3.7)	513	(3.9)	10.49	(1.99)
Brazil	372	(4.1)	402	(3.9)	405	(4.7)	413	(3.7)	12.33	(1.51)
Bulgaria	398	(6.7)	447	(5.1)	443	(5.1)	449	(6.0)	24.20	(2.55)
Canada	515	(2.4)	536	(2.1)	543	(2.2)	548	(1.7)	13.80	(0.94)
Chile	384	(4.8)	416	(4.0)	422	(4.5)	420	(4.2)	15.60	(1.63)
Czech Republic	487	(3.3)	503	(3.3)	505	(2.8)	509	(3.1)	9.87	(1.46)
Denmark	469	(4.4)	505	(3.6)	508	(3.0)	516	(3.3)	21.28	(2.23)
Finland	535	(5.1)	551	(3.2)	554	(3.4)	549	(3.4)	7.42	(2.72)
France	486	(4.6)	511	(3.0)	516	(3.4)	511	(3.1)	12.43	(1.93)
Germany	479	(3.8)	497	(3.7)	504	(3.3)	498	(3.5)	7.95	(1.71)
Greece	457	(6.8)	484	(5.4)	477	(4.3)	480	(5.8)	9.60	(2.12)
Hong Kong-China	493	(4.3)	524	(3.6)	538	(3.6)	548	(3.3)	22.30	(1.68)
Hungary	465	(5.2)	479	(4.8)	491	(5.5)	488	(4.5)	13.96	(2.22)
Iceland	491	(3.4)	509	(3.3)	516	(3.2)	518	(3.3)	11.96	(1.85)
Indonesia	349	(3.7)	360	(4.0)	386	(4.7)	391	(4.9)	13.80	(1.51)
Ireland	515	(4.8)	526	(4.2)	535	(4.0)	536	(4.1)	9.99	(1.78)
Israel	450	(9.4)	458	(9.9)	468	(9.8)	458	(9.5)	3.60	(2.23)
Italy	480	(4.6)	488	(4.7)	493	(3.4)	491	(3.4)	8.66	(2.65)
Japan	491	(7.4)	525	(5.4)	534	(5.1)	546	(5.0)	20.05	(2.24)
Korea	492	(3.4)	524	(2.8)	540	(2.3)	545	(3.4)	18.26	(1.55)
Latvia	444	(9.0)	464	(6.5)	463	(5.3)	467	(6.5)	9.62	(2.49)
Liechtenstein	462	(11.1)	488	(10.5)	491	(10.0)	494	(10.4)	14.42	(7.13)
Luxembourg	424	(4.0)	451	(3.6)	459	(3.4)	446	(3.1)	11.64	(2.02)
FYR Macedonia	338	(4.7)	391	(2.9)	385	(3.0)	394	(3.0)	22.40	(1.95)
Mexico	397	(3.7)	422	(3.9)	429	(4.7)	440	(4.6)	14.54	(1.78)
New Zealand	511	(4.3)	525	(3.5)	545	(4.4)	541	(4.3)	13.79	(1.89)
Norway	480	(4.4)	509	(4.1)	526	(4.0)	513	(4.2)	16.47	(2.22)
Peru	304	(5.8)	321	(5.5)	346	(4.8)	353	(4.7)	17.00	(1.78)
Poland	457	(6.0)	489	(4.5)	494	(5.8)	489	(5.2)	14.75	(2.10)
Portugal	442	(5.7)	468	(5.4)	488	(4.7)	485	(5.1)	22.00	(1.69)
Russian Federation	444	(5.4)	466	(4.7)	471	(4.5)	472	(3.6)	13.04	(1.58)
Spain	475	(3.8)	500	(3.5)	499	(3.4)	500	(3.1)	11.05	(1.38)
Sweden	506	(3.1)	520	(3.5)	521	(3.3)	521	(3.6)	5.43	(1.83)
Switzerland	473	(6.0)	498	(5.1)	508	(4.7)	504	(5.0)	14.69	(2.30)
Thailand	417	(4.2)	429	(3.6)	435	(3.7)	442	(4.2)	8.40	(1.31)
United Kingdom	503	(3.6)	529	(3.4)	532	(3.5)	538	(3.9)	13.70	(1.55)
United States	480	(8.1)	515	(7.6)	516	(6.8)	515	(8.4)	12.43	(2.16)
OECD average	*481*	*(0.9)*	*504*	*(0.8)*	*512*	*(0.7)*	*511*	*(0.9)*	*10.01*	*(0.38)*
OECD total	*477*	*(2.4)*	*505*	*(2.1)*	*510*	*(1.9)*	*512*	*(2.4)*	*11.93*	*(0.79)*
Netherlands[3]	493	(6.2)	547	(4.2)	545	(4.1)	546	(5.0)	23.25	(2.68)

1. For the definition of the index see Annex A1. "Max" is used to represent countries which have more than 25 per cent of students at the highest value of this index, which is 1.20.
2. For explained variation see Annex A2. Unit changes marked in bold are statistically significant. Where bottom and top quarters are marked in bold this indicates that their difference is statistically significant.
3. Response rate is too low to ensure comparability (see Annex A3).

Table 6.6
**Index of communication with parents related to aspects of culture and performance
on the combined reading literacy scale, by national quarters of the index**
Results based on students' self-reports

	Index of cultural communication[1]									
	All students		Bottom quarter		Second quarter		Third quarter		Top quarter	
	Mean index	S.E.	Mean index	S.E.	Mean index	S.E.	Mean index	S.E.	Mean index	S.E.
Albania	0.19	(0.02)	-1.00	(0.03)	-0.06	(0.01)	0.54	(0.01)	1.29	(0.01)
Argentina	0.54	(0.04)	-0.71	(0.03)	0.35	(0.01)	0.98	(0.01)	1.54	(0.02)
Australia	-0.13	(0.03)	-1.47	(0.03)	-0.39	(0.01)	0.27	(0.01)	1.09	(0.02)
Austria	-0.15	(0.02)	-1.42	(0.02)	-0.39	(0.01)	0.21	(0.01)	1.01	(0.01)
Belgium	-0.24	(0.02)	-1.67	(0.01)	-0.49	(0.01)	0.15	(0.01)	1.03	(0.01)
Brazil	0.17	(0.03)	-1.31	(0.02)	-0.09	(0.01)	0.63	(0.01)	1.48	(0.02)
Bulgaria	0.29	(0.02)	-0.96	(0.03)	0.08	(0.01)	0.66	(0.01)	1.40	(0.02)
Canada	0.08	(0.01)	-1.17	(0.01)	-0.14	(0.00)	0.42	(0.00)	1.21	(0.01)
Chile	0.31	(0.02)	-1.07	(0.02)	0.07	(0.01)	0.78	(0.00)	1.47	(0.01)
Czech Republic	-0.15	(0.02)	-1.35	(0.02)	-0.37	(0.01)	0.19	(0.01)	0.95	(0.01)
Denmark	0.11	(0.02)	-1.22	(0.02)	-0.10	(0.01)	0.55	(0.01)	1.21	(0.01)
Finland	-0.01	(0.02)	-1.11	(0.02)	-0.17	(0.00)	0.27	(0.01)	0.96	(0.01)
France	0.27	(0.02)	-0.94	(0.02)	0.08	(0.01)	0.65	(0.01)	1.30	(0.01)
Germany	-0.14	(0.02)	-1.42	(0.02)	-0.35	(0.01)	0.23	(0.01)	0.98	(0.01)
Greece	0.19	(0.02)	-0.92	(0.02)	0.00	(0.01)	0.52	(0.01)	1.18	(0.01)
Hong Kong-China	0.21	(0.02)	-1.18	(0.02)	0.02	(0.01)	0.68	(0.01)	1.32	(0.01)
Hungary	0.33	(0.02)	-0.82	(0.02)	0.15	(0.01)	0.65	(0.01)	1.35	(0.01)
Iceland	0.08	(0.02)	-1.26	(0.02)	-0.14	(0.01)	0.44	(0.01)	1.28	(0.02)
Indonesia	-0.30	(0.04)	-2.02	(0.01)	-0.71	(0.01)	0.18	(0.01)	1.33	(0.02)
Ireland	-0.09	(0.02)	-1.35	(0.02)	-0.30	(0.01)	0.24	(0.01)	1.05	(0.01)
Israel	0.34	(0.03)	-1.07	(0.05)	0.13	(0.01)	0.79	(0.01)	1.52	(0.02)
Italy	0.41	(0.02)	-0.84	(0.02)	0.23	(0.01)	0.84	(0.00)	1.41	(0.01)
Japan	0.09	(0.03)	-1.48	(0.03)	-0.08	(0.01)	0.56	(0.01)	1.34	(0.02)
Korea	-0.59	(0.03)	-2.20	(0.00)	-1.08	(0.02)	-0.05	(0.01)	0.99	(0.02)
Latvia	0.25	(0.02)	-1.01	(0.02)	0.02	(0.01)	0.64	(0.01)	1.36	(0.02)
Liechtenstein	-0.20	(0.05)	-1.43	(0.07)	-0.46	(0.02)	0.14	(0.02)	0.96	(0.05)
Luxembourg	-0.20	(0.02)	-1.55	(0.02)	-0.44	(0.01)	0.17	(0.01)	1.03	(0.02)
FYR Macedonia	0.17	(0.02)	-1.02	(0.02)	-0.08	(0.01)	0.50	(0.01)	1.29	(0.02)
Mexico	0.00	(0.02)	-1.29	(0.02)	-0.28	(0.01)	0.33	(0.01)	1.23	(0.01)
New Zealand	0.07	(0.02)	-1.23	(0.02)	-0.15	(0.01)	0.44	(0.01)	1.22	(0.02)
Norway	-0.22	(0.02)	-1.51	(0.02)	-0.47	(0.01)	0.13	(0.01)	0.99	(0.02)
Peru	0.42	(0.02)	-0.97	(0.02)	0.14	(0.01)	0.86	(0.01)	1.65	(0.02)
Poland	-0.03	(0.02)	-1.35	(0.03)	-0.24	(0.01)	0.33	(0.01)	1.15	(0.02)
Portugal	-0.02	(0.03)	-1.32	(0.02)	-0.23	(0.01)	0.36	(0.01)	1.13	(0.01)
Russian Federation	0.19	(0.02)	-1.22	(0.02)	-0.06	(0.01)	0.62	(0.01)	1.43	(0.01)
Spain	0.17	(0.02)	-0.97	(0.02)	-0.02	(0.01)	0.49	(0.01)	1.18	(0.01)
Sweden	-0.14	(0.02)	-1.38	(0.02)	-0.36	(0.01)	0.18	(0.01)	0.99	(0.01)
Switzerland	-0.01	(0.02)	-1.29	(0.02)	-0.24	(0.01)	0.35	(0.01)	1.14	(0.02)
Thailand	0.28	(0.03)	-1.25	(0.02)	0.02	(0.01)	0.77	(0.01)	1.58	(0.02)
United Kingdom	0.06	(0.02)	-1.10	(0.02)	-0.12	(0.00)	0.35	(0.01)	1.11	(0.02)
United States	0.22	(0.04)	-1.23	(0.03)	-0.01	(0.01)	0.65	(0.01)	1.48	(0.02)
OECD average	*0.00*	*(0.00)*	*-1.29*	*(0.01)*	*-0.23*	*(0.00)*	*0.37*	*(0.00)*	*1.15*	*(0.00)*
OECD total	*0.07*	*(0.01)*	*-1.29*	*(0.01)*	*-0.15*	*(0.00)*	*0.47*	*(0.00)*	*1.26*	*(0.01)*
Netherlands[3]	-0.35	(0.03)	-1.85	(0.02)	-0.61	(0.01)	0.11	(0.01)	0.95	(0.02)

1. For the definition of the index see Annex A1.
2. For explained variation see Annex A2. Unit changes marked in bold are statistically significant. Where bottom and top quarters are marked in bold this
   indicates that their difference is statistically significant.
3. Response rate is too low to ensure comparability (see Annex A3)

Table 6.6 (continued)
Index of communication with parents related to aspects of culture and performance on the combined reading literacy scale, by national quarters of the index
Results based on students' self-reports

| | Performance on the combined reading literacy scale, by national quarters of the index of cultural communication[2] | | | | | | | | Change in the combined reading literacy score per unit of the index of cultural communication[2] | |
| | Bottom quarter | | Second quarter | | Third quarter | | Top quarter | | | |
	Mean score	S.E.	Mean score	S.E.	Mean score	S.E.	Mean score	S.E.	Change	S.E.
Albania	329	(4.5)	354	(5.0)	361	(4.4)	369	(4.2)	17.30	(1.85)
Argentina	375	(9.5)	411	(10.2)	456	(8.3)	447	(10.5)	29.20	(4.39)
Australia	488	(4.1)	515	(4.7)	543	(4.1)	573	(4.8)	30.84	(1.77)
Austria	474	(3.3)	503	(3.6)	520	(3.7)	535	(3.2)	24.44	(1.82)
Belgium	490	(4.1)	508	(3.5)	514	(4.5)	531	(4.2)	13.63	(1.41)
Brazil	371	(3.7)	384	(4.1)	411	(4.1)	435	(4.7)	19.87	(1.64)
Bulgaria	398	(5.9)	436	(5.9)	449	(5.7)	458	(6.1)	24.50	(2.73)
Canada	507	(1.9)	528	(2.0)	542	(2.0)	564	(2.1)	22.06	(0.88)
Chile	378	(4.5)	393	(4.1)	431	(4.4)	443	(4.1)	25.40	(1.76)
Czech Republic	474	(3.2)	494	(3.3)	507	(2.9)	530	(2.9)	21.76	(1.56)
Denmark	459	(3.8)	488	(3.2)	511	(3.6)	540	(3.3)	33.11	(1.77)
Finland	514	(4.7)	544	(2.8)	558	(3.0)	573	(3.1)	26.20	(2.49)
France	474	(4.4)	500	(3.3)	519	(3.3)	532	(3.2)	22.93	(1.99)
Germany	460	(3.3)	492	(4.2)	504	(2.7)	522	(5.3)	23.70	(1.82)
Greece	448	(5.6)	468	(5.7)	487	(5.1)	498	(6.3)	22.81	(2.47)
Hong Kong-China	499	(3.6)	522	(3.9)	538	(3.9)	545	(3.2)	18.20	(1.65)
Hungary	457	(4.5)	480	(4.6)	489	(4.2)	497	(6.1)	18.21	(2.66)
Iceland	480	(3.2)	505	(3.2)	516	(3.2)	533	(3.5)	19.14	(1.78)
Indonesia	357	(3.5)	369	(4.1)	371	(5.0)	391	(5.4)	9.40	(1.49)
Ireland	502	(4.2)	522	(3.7)	535	(4.3)	554	(4.1)	18.68	(1.98)
Israel	434	(9.2)	460	(8.7)	471	(9.8)	468	(11.9)	13.90	(2.77)
Italy	459	(3.9)	486	(3.7)	505	(4.1)	503	(4.3)	18.85	(1.68)
Japan	493	(7.5)	519	(5.3)	539	(4.8)	545	(4.9)	18.40	(2.08)
Korea	509	(3.2)	521	(3.2)	529	(2.7)	544	(3.5)	10.52	(1.14)
Latvia	437	(7.4)	448	(5.7)	475	(5.8)	479	(7.0)	16.78	(2.37)
Liechtenstein	465	(10.6)	471	(10.3)	475	(10.9)	528	(11.7)	21.63	(6.13)
Luxembourg	414	(3.7)	450	(3.6)	451	(3.3)	466	(3.6)	16.90	(1.89)
FYR Macedonia	351	(4.3)	388	(3.0)	392	(3.3)	384	(3.3)	14.60	(2.18)
Mexico	395	(3.4)	416	(4.1)	433	(4.2)	450	(5.1)	22.02	(1.95)
New Zealand	508	(3.8)	522	(4.3)	540	(3.8)	552	(5.3)	16.97	(2.31)
Norway	467	(4.4)	499	(4.2)	516	(3.9)	545	(4.1)	29.68	(1.69)
Peru	311	(5.0)	322	(6.7)	348	(5.0)	349	(5.0)	13.60	(1.75)
Poland	455	(5.1)	479	(5.2)	495	(4.9)	501	(6.4)	16.17	(2.24)
Portugal	423	(4.9)	463	(4.7)	486	(4.3)	513	(5.1)	34.97	(1.97)
Russian Federation	440	(5.6)	461	(4.4)	475	(4.4)	483	(3.9)	14.30	(1.30)
Spain	454	(3.8)	487	(3.6)	507	(3.0)	528	(2.8)	31.79	(1.48)
Sweden	483	(2.8)	512	(3.4)	528	(2.8)	546	(3.6)	23.93	(1.50)
Switzerland	457	(4.9)	489	(4.4)	507	(5.0)	531	(5.5)	27.53	(2.04)
Thailand	414	(3.5)	427	(4.0)	438	(4.1)	445	(4.5)	9.90	(1.45)
United Kingdom	493	(2.8)	520	(3.3)	531	(3.4)	561	(4.6)	28.24	(2.03)
United States	471	(7.4)	499	(7.6)	526	(6.7)	529	(8.7)	20.66	(1.96)
OECD average	471	(0.9)	497	(0.8)	513	(0.8)	530	(0.9)	20.50	(0.38)
OECD total	470	(2.2)	495	(2.0)	515	(2.0)	526	(2.5)	19.56	(0.79)
Netherlands[3]	500	(4.4)	525	(4.2)	541	(4.4)	568	(4.3)	22.00	(1.88)

1. For the definition of the index see Annex A1.
2. For explained variation see Annex A2. Unit changes marked in bold are statistically significant. Where bottom and top quarters are marked in bold this indicates that their difference is statistically significant.
3. Response rate is too low to ensure comparability (see Annex A3).

Table 6.7
Family structure and performance on the combined reading literacy scale,
by type of family structure
Results based on students' self-reports

	Students from single-parent families[1]				Students from other types of families[1]				Increased likelihood of students from single-parent families scoring in the bottom quarter of the national reading literacy performance distribution[2]	
	Percentage of students	S.E.	Mean reading score	S.E.	Percentage of students	S.E.	Mean reading score	S.E.	Ratio	S.E.
Albania	7.9	(0.5)	347	(6.5)	92.1	(0.5)	350	(3.4)	1.0	(0.16)
Argentina	18.9	(0.7)	419	(10.5)	81.1	(0.7)	421	(9.4)	1.0	(0.16)
Australia	16.2	(0.7)	521	(4.7)	83.8	(0.7)	530	(3.8)	1.1	(0.09)
Austria	12.6	(0.5)	508	(5.2)	87.4	(0.5)	507	(2.5)	0.9	(0.07)
Belgium	12.8	(0.5)	487	(5.5)	87.2	(0.5)	512	(3.6)	1.3	(0.08)
Brazil	18.1	(0.7)	396	(5.4)	81.9	(0.7)	398	(3.0)	0.9	(0.09)
Bulgaria	13.0	(0.8)	437	(7.4)	87.0	(0.8)	432	(4.7)	1.0	(0.08)
Canada	15.6	(0.3)	527	(2.5)	84.4	(0.3)	537	(1.6)	1.1	(0.05)
Chile	20.0	(0.7)	407	(4.8)	80.0	(0.7)	411	(3.7)	1.0	(0.10)
Czech Republic	11.0	(0.5)	494	(6.4)	89.0	(0.5)	492	(2.3)	1.0	(0.09)
Denmark	16.9	(0.7)	484	(5.8)	83.1	(0.7)	501	(2.4)	1.3	(0.11)
Finland	18.7	(0.7)	529	(6.8)	81.4	(0.7)	551	(2.2)	1.4	(0.09)
France	15.0	(0.6)	488	(4.7)	85.0	(0.6)	508	(2.7)	1.3	(0.08)
Germany	15.3	(0.7)	478	(5.4)	84.8	(0.7)	485	(2.6)	1.1	(0.09)
Greece	8.7	(0.5)	473	(8.3)	91.3	(0.5)	475	(4.9)	1.1	(0.12)
Hong Kong-China	10.4	(0.4)	519	(5.4)	89.6	(0.4)	527	(2.9)	1.1	(0.13)
Hungary	17.2	(0.6)	474	(4.6)	82.8	(0.6)	482	(4.2)	1.1	(0.09)
Iceland	13.2	(0.6)	507	(4.5)	86.8	(0.6)	508	(1.7)	1.0	(0.09)
Indonesia	5.6	(0.5)	378	(5.9)	94.4	(0.5)	370	(3.8)	0.8	(0.10)
Ireland	12.3	(0.6)	508	(6.2)	87.7	(0.6)	530	(3.2)	1.3	(0.12)
Israel	8.5	(0.8)	434	(13.8)	91.5	(0.8)	458	(8.7)	1.3	(0.23)
Italy	19.7	(0.6)	481	(4.5)	80.3	(0.6)	490	(2.7)	1.2	(0.08)
Japan	10.8	(0.7)	510	(8.6)	89.2	(0.7)	527	(5.0)	1.2	(0.15)
Korea	7.8	(0.4)	510	(5.6)	92.2	(0.4)	526	(2.4)	1.4	(0.11)
Latvia	20.6	(0.9)	451	(8.7)	79.4	(0.9)	461	(4.9)	1.2	(0.09)
Liechtenstein	12.6	(1.5)	468	(16.5)	87.4	(1.5)	485	(4.4)	1.4	(0.40)
Luxembourg	10.8	(0.6)	432	(5.5)	89.2	(0.6)	444	(1.7)	1.2	(0.12)
FYR Macedonia	8.2	(0.5)	373	(5.6)	91.8	(0.5)	374	(2.0)	0.9	(0.14)
Mexico	17.4	(0.7)	420	(4.4)	82.6	(0.7)	423	(3.6)	1.1	(0.09)
New Zealand	20.5	(0.7)	513	(4.9)	79.5	(0.7)	535	(2.8)	1.3	(0.08)
Norway	16.0	(0.6)	489	(5.5)	84.0	(0.6)	510	(2.9)	1.3	(0.10)
Peru	19.3	(0.8)	328	(4.9)	80.7	(0.8)	327	(4.7)	0.9	(0.08)
Poland	9.6	(0.6)	479	(6.2)	90.4	(0.6)	482	(4.7)	1.1	(0.11)
Portugal	11.2	(0.4)	468	(5.7)	88.8	(0.4)	472	(4.5)	1.1	(0.08)
Russian Federation	19.5	(0.6)	462	(4.8)	80.5	(0.6)	462	(4.1)	1.0	(0.06)
Spain	16.9	(0.6)	486	(3.6)	83.1	(0.6)	495	(2.8)	1.1	(0.09)
Sweden	16.8	(0.6)	501	(4.0)	83.2	(0.6)	521	(2.1)	1.3	(0.09)
Switzerland	13.0	(0.5)	496	(6.0)	87.0	(0.5)	495	(4.4)	1.0	(0.08)
Thailand	9.3	(0.5)	444	(5.1)	90.7	(0.5)	429	(3.3)	0.7	(0.12)
United Kingdom	20.5	(0.6)	502	(3.2)	79.6	(0.6)	531	(2.9)	1.4	(0.08)
United States	21.0	(0.9)	484	(8.6)	79.0	(0.9)	512	(7.4)	1.4	(0.11)
OECD average	*14.7*	*(0.1)*	*491*	*(1.0)*	*85.3*	*(0.1)*	*503*	*(0.6)*	*1.2*	*(0.02)*
OECD total	*16.2*	*(0.3)*	*485*	*(3.0)*	*83.8*	*(0.3)*	*503*	*(1.9)*	*1.3*	*(0.04)*
Netherlands[3]	10.3	(0.8)	503	(8.4)	89.7	(0.8)	535	(3.3)	1.5	(0.17)

1. For the definition of the index see Annex A1.
2. For explained variation see Annex A2. Unit changes marked in bold are statistically significant. Where bottom and top quarters are marked in bold this indicates that their difference is statistically significant.
3. Response rate is too low to ensure comparability (see Annex A3).

Table 6.8
Percentage of students and performance on the combined reading, mathematical and scientific literacy scales, by students' nationality and the nationality of their parents
Results based on students' self-reports

	Native students (students who were born in the country of assessment with at least one of their parents born in the same country)							First-generation students (students who were born in the country of assessment but whose parents were foreign-born)						
			Performance[2]								Performance[2]				
			Combined reading literacy scale		Mathematical literacy scale		Scientific literacy scale				Combined reading literacy scale		Mathematical literacy scale		Scientific literacy scale	
	Percent-age of students	S.E.	Mean score	S.E.	Mean score	S.E.	Mean score	S.E.	Percent-age of students	S.E.	Mean score	S.E.	Mean score	S.E.	Mean score	S.E.
Albania	99.2	(0.2)	351	(3.3)	383	(3.1)	**379**	(2.9)	0.4	(0.1)	311	(26.7)	364	(41.6)	**303**	(30.0)
Argentina	97.7	(0.5)	**422**	(9.2)	**391**	(9.2)	**401**	(7.6)	1.9	(0.4)	**360**	(26.2)	**342**	(22.2)	**320**	(24.9)
Australia	77.4	(1.8)	532	(3.6)	536	(3.6)	531	(3.5)	10.7	(1.1)	528	(7.1)	535	(7.3)	523	(9.0)
Austria	90.4	(0.9)	515	(2.4)	523	(2.6)	528	(2.5)	3.7	(0.4)	453	(9.4)	462	(12.9)	447	(13.6)
Belgium	88.0	(1.1)	522	(3.8)	536	(4.0)	511	(4.6)	8.6	(0.9)	411	(8.7)	418	(10.3)	401	(9.0)
Brazil	99.6	(0.1)	398	(3.0)	337	(3.7)	377	(3.2)	0.3	(0.1)	c	c	c	c	c	c
Bulgaria	99.6	(0.1)	434	(4.9)	**434**	(5.6)	**451**	(4.6)	0.1	(0.1)	492	(51.7)	315	(45.9)	**529**	(35.6)
Canada	79.5	(1.0)	538	(1.5)	536	(1.4)	535	(1.6)	10.8	(0.5)	539	(3.1)	530	(3.6)	521	(4.1)
Chile	99.7	(0.1)	411	(3.6)	384	(3.6)	416	(3.4)	0.0	(0.0)	369	(23.7)	399	(65.2)	470	(51.5)
Czech Republic	98.9	(0.2)	501	(2.1)	504	(2.7)	518	(2.4)	0.6	(0.1)	c	c	c	c	c	c
Denmark	93.8	(0.6)	**504**	(2.2)	520	(2.3)	488	(2.7)	2.4	(0.4)	409	(13.9)	448	(15.9)	395	(17.4)
Finland	98.7	(0.2)	548	(2.6)	537	(2.1)	539	(2.5)	0.2	(0.1)	c	c	c	c	c	c
France	88.0	(0.9)	512	(2.8)	523	(2.8)	510	(3.3)	9.8	(0.7)	471	(6.2)	487	(7.0)	451	(7.4)
Germany	84.8	(0.8)	507	(2.3)	**510**	(2.5)	507	(2.5)	5.1	(0.5)	432	(9.0)	437	(7.7)	423	(12.0)
Greece	95.2	(0.9)	478	(4.7)	452	(5.6)	464	(4.8)	0.5	(0.1)	c	c	c	c	c	c
Hong Kong-China	56.2	(1.0)	531	(3.3)	570	(3.9)	545	(3.7)	26.4	(0.8)	532	(3.2)	567	(4.2)	549	(4.2)
Hungary	98.3	(0.2)	482	(4.0)	489	(4.0)	498	(4.2)	0.1	(0.0)	c	c	c	c	a	a
Iceland	99.2	(0.2)	509	(1.5)	516	(2.2)	497	(2.2)	0.2	(0.1)	c	c	c	c	c	c
Indonesia	99.6	(0.1)	**372**	(3.7)	**367**	(4.3)	394	(3.6)	0.2	(0.1)	303	(14.4)	255	(36.1)	272	(28.8)
Ireland	97.7	(0.3)	528	(3.2)	503	(2.7)	514	(3.2)	0.9	(0.2)	519	(20.2)	c	c	c	c
Israel	75.0	(1.7)	456	(9.6)	436	(11.3)	435	(10.1)	16.1	(1.2)	461	(9.1)	441	(11.7)	432	(10.9)
Italy	99.1	(0.2)	489	(2.9)	459	(2.9)	479	(2.9)	0.2	(0.1)	c	c	c	c	c	c
Japan	99.9	(0.1)	525	(5.1)	559	(5.5)	553	(5.5)	0.0	(0.0)	c	c	c	c	c	c
Korea[1]	a	a	a	a	a	a	a	a	a	a	a	a	a	a	a	a
Latvia	77.9	(2.4)	**462**	(6.0)	466	(5.4)	466	(6.0)	1.5	(0.3)	423	(15.1)	c	c	433	(20.9)
Liechtenstein	79.4	(2.1)	**500**	(5.0)	528	(7.9)	492	(7.4)	10.2	(1.8)	**446**	(14.8)	c	c	c	c
Luxembourg	65.8	(0.7)	474	(1.7)	472	(2.3)	473	(2.5)	17.8	(0.7)	399	(4.6)	422	(5.4)	407	(5.3)
FYR Macedonia	95.6	(0.5)	380	(1.7)	389	(2.6)	408	(1.8)	0.9	(0.2)	355	(17.3)	365	(24.2)	388	(19.3)
Mexico	96.4	(0.4)	427	(3.3)	391	(3.4)	425	(3.2)	1.1	(0.2)	378	(15.3)	c	c	380	(14.5)
New Zealand	80.4	(1.1)	538	(2.7)	543	(3.2)	536	(2.4)	6.4	(0.5)	507	(10.3)	503	(12.0)	506	(11.2)
Norway	95.4	(0.4)	510	(2.7)	503	(2.7)	506	(2.7)	1.5	(0.2)	464	(10.6)	481	(15.9)	437	(13.0)
Peru	99.7	(0.1)	331	(4.3)	296	(4.3)	**335**	(4.0)	0.2	(0.1)	328	(62.2)	332	(83.5)	113	(49.2)
Poland	99.7	(0.1)	482	(4.4)	474	(5.1)	485	(5.1)	0.0	(0.0)	c	c	c	c	c	c
Portugal	96.9	(0.3)	472	(4.5)	456	(4.0)	461	(4.1)	1.8	(0.2)	463	(14.3)	434	(20.3)	438	(14.1)
Russian Federation	95.4	(0.6)	463	(4.3)	480	(5.6)	461	(4.9)	1.8	(0.3)	452	(9.9)	473	(11.7)	452	(12.7)
Spain	98.0	(0.4)	494	(2.6)	478	(3.0)	493	(2.9)	0.6	(0.1)	450	(15.9)	c	c	c	c
Sweden	89.5	(0.9)	523	(2.1)	517	(2.3)	518	(2.6)	4.7	(0.6)	485	(7.3)	466	(9.0)	486	(10.7)
Switzerland	79.3	(0.9)	514	(4.0)	548	(4.2)	514	(4.4)	9.3	(0.6)	460	(6.8)	489	(8.8)	454	(8.5)
Thailand	99.3	(0.5)	432	(3.2)	**433**	(3.6)	437	(3.1)	0.7	(0.5)	401	(23.4)	**397**	(16.2)	394	(25.1)
United Kingdom	90.4	(1.2)	528	(2.6)	534	(2.5)	537	(2.7)	7.0	(0.9)	510	(9.4)	**505**	(11.1)	519	(10.2)
United States	86.4	(2.1)	511	(6.5)	500	(7.2)	506	(6.7)	7.4	(1.4)	478	(19.4)	467	(20.2)	462	(22.6)
OECD average	*91.3*	*(0.6)*	*503*	*(1.9)*	*500*	*(2.0)*	*505*	*(1.9)*	*4.6*	*(0.4)*	*479*	*(9.1)*	*476*	*(10.0)*	*467*	*(11.1)*
OECD total	*91.0*	*(0.2)*	*506*	*(0.6)*	*504*	*(0.7)*	*504*	*(0.7)*	*4.3*	*(0.1)*	*467*	*(2.8)*	*474*	*(2.9)*	*462*	*(3.4)*
Netherlands[4]	88.1	(1.8)	542	(3.0)	575	(3.2)	541	(3.7)	7.4	(1.2)	470	(14.2)	494	(16.0)	441	(17.4)

1. Percentage of students participating in the assessment of reading literacy in the respective category.
2. Mean scores marked in bold indicate that the difference in performance between native and first-generation students is statistically significant.
3. This question was not asked in Korea.
4. Response rate is too low to ensure comparability (see Annex A3).

Table 6.8 (continued)
Percentage of students and performance on the combined reading, mathematical and scientific literacy scales, by students' nationality and the nationality of their parents
Results based on students' self-reports

	Non-native students (students who were foreign-born and whose parents were also foreign-born)								
			Performance						
			Combined reading literacy scale		Mathematical literacy scale		Scientific literacy scale		
	Percentage of students[1]	S.E.	Mean score	S.E.	Mean score	S.E.	Mean score	S.E.	
Albania	0.4	(0.1)	282	(21.9)	300	(32.8)	337	(22.7)
Argentina	0.4	(0.1)	382	(26.0)	315	(36.3)	339	(37.9)
Australia	11.9	(1.2)	513	(9.3)	526	(9.5)	514	(10.5)
Austria	5.9	(0.6)	422	(8.2)	429	(9.9)	434	(9.8)
Belgium	3.4	(0.4)	431	(9.5)	432	(11.1)	419	(10.7)
Brazil	0.1	(0.1)	c	c	c	c	c	c
Bulgaria	0.3	(0.1)	356	(59.2)	312	(77.3)	390	(52.2)
Canada	9.8	(0.6)	511	(4.9)	522	(5.1)	503	(5.4)
Chile	0.2	(0.1)	444	(31.4)	430	(42.3)	465	(45.4)
Czech Republic	0.5	(0.1)	c	c	c	c	c	c
Denmark	3.8	(0.4)	433	(7.6)	447	(9.1)	413	(11.6)
Finland	1.0	(0.2)	468	(12.9)	c	c	459	(17.0)
France	2.2	(0.3)	434	(11.5)	441	(13.9)	408	(16.8)
Germany	10.1	(0.6)	419	(7.5)	423	(9.7)	410	(7.9)
Greece	4.3	(0.9)	403	(17.5)	351	(17.5)	386	(18.5)
Hong Kong-China	17.4	(0.8)	504	(4.8)	528	(6.1)	522	(5.8)
Hungary	1.6	(0.2)	486	(11.6)	491	(18.2)	472	(14.8)
Iceland	0.6	(0.1)	c	c	c	c	c	c
Indonesia	0.2	(0.1)	286	(30.5)	243	(38.6)	229	(47.0)
Ireland	1.4	(0.3)	573	(9.2)	c	c	572	(14.9)
Israel	8.9	(1.1)	456	(15.2)	450	(14.3)	454	(15.9)
Italy	0.8	(0.2)	445	(15.1)	c	c	c	c
Japan	0.1	(0.1)	c	c	c	c	c	c
Korea[3]	a	a	a	a	a	a	a	a
Latvia	20.6	(2.4)	454	(7.3)	464	(8.2)	451	(8.4)
Liechtenstein	10.4	(1.6)	392	(21.4)	c	c	c	c
Luxembourg	16.4	(0.6)	370	(4.7)	385	(5.7)	374	(6.5)
FYR Macedonia	3.5	(0.5)	282	(12.3)	296	(14.1)	303	(9.3)
Mexico	2.5	(0.3)	329	(8.2)	309	(13.9)	355	(11.0)
New Zealand	13.2	(0.8)	507	(7.6)	538	(8.4)	510	(7.9)
Norway	3.1	(0.3)	449	(8.5)	436	(12.4)	443	(9.6)
Peru	0.1	(0.0)	338	(59.4)	290	(84.2)	342	(78.0)
Poland	0.2	(0.1)	c	c	c	c	c	c
Portugal	1.4	(0.2)	450	(15.8)	c	c	420	(16.1)
Russian Federation	2.8	(0.4)	458	(9.6)	461	(15.3)	467	(12.7)
Spain	1.4	(0.3)	460	(17.8)	459	(25.0)	434	(23.6)
Sweden	5.9	(0.6)	450	(7.2)	446	(12.1)	439	(9.1)
Switzerland	11.4	(0.7)	402	(6.1)	443	(7.1)	407	(6.6)
Thailand	0.0	(0.0)	a	a	a	a	a	a
United Kingdom	2.6	(0.4)	456	(15.1)	483	(18.0)	457	(16.5)
United States	6.1	(0.9)	466	(10.0)	451	(10.7)	473	(14.2)
OECD average	*4.1*	*(0.3)*	*452*	*(4.9)*	*450*	*(5.6)*	*453*	*(6.5)*
OECD total	*4.7*	*(0.1)*	*446*	*(2.5)*	*456*	*(3.0)*	*444*	*(3.0)*
Netherlands[4]	4.5	(0.8)	453	(15.6)	470	(19.9)	437	(15.4)

1. Percentage of students participating in the assessment of reading literacy in the respective category.
2. Mean scores marked in bold indicate that the difference in performance between native and first-generation students is statistically significant.
3. This question was not asked in Korea.
4. Response rate is too low to ensure comparability (see Annex A3).

Table 6.9
Student performance on the combined reading, mathematical and scientific literacy scales by language spoken at home
Results based on students' self-reports

	Language spoken at home most of the time IS DIFFERENT from the language of assessment, from other official languages or from other national dialects							
			Performance[2]					
	Percentage of students[1]	S.E.	Combined reading literacy scale		Mathematical literacy scale		Scientific literacy scale	
			Mean score	S.E.	Mean score	S.E.	Mean score	S.E.
Albania	0.5	(0.1)	355	(22.3)	397	(32.2)	380	(26.3)
Argentina	0.3	(0.1)	409	(37.7)	402	(49.9)	439	(41.9)
Australia	17.0	(1.6)	504	(7.6)	522	(6.8)	496	(9.4)
Austria	6.7	(0.7)	434	(7.2)	443	(9.2)	439	(9.7)
Belgium	4.9	(0.6)	403	(8.6)	420	(10.6)	381	(9.4)
Brazil	0.8	(0.2)	c	c	c	c	c	c
Bulgaria	3.8	(0.7)	**317**	(16.1)	**350**	(20.2)	**358**	(16.7)
Canada	9.4	(0.6)	506	(3.8)	522	(4.3)	498	(4.5)
Chile	0.4	(0.1)	402	(22.3)	385	(29.6)	420	(33.2)
Czech Republic	0.8	(0.2)	c	c	c	c	c	c
Denmark	6.7	(0.4)	425	(8.1)	446	(8.7)	405	(11.5)
Finland	1.3	(0.2)	470	(12.5)	469	(19.2)	472	(19.1)
France	4.0	(0.5)	442	(7.7)	463	(8.8)	431	(9.8)
Germany	7.9	(0.8)	386	(13.9)	395	(11.4)	390	(10.3)
Greece	2.8	(0.6)	407	(18.3)	371	(17.4)	379	(20.8)
Hong Kong-China	5.3	(0.4)	**466**	(6.5)	**497**	(10.9)	**484**	(8.5)
Hungary	m	m	m	m	m	m	m	m
Iceland	1.9	(0.3)	463	(13.4)	c	c	471	(21.5)
Indonesia	2.7	(0.4)	354	(11.3)	362	(17.6)	377	(13.6)
Ireland	0.9	(0.2)	c	c	c	c	c	c
Israel	9.8	(1.0)	448	(13.9)	445	(16.4)	430	(15.0)
Italy	0.7	(0.2)	c	c	c	c	c	c
Japan	0.3	(0.1)	c	c	c	c	c	c
Korea[4]	a	a	a	a	a	a	a	a
Latvia	0.0	(0.0)	a	a	a	a	a	a
Liechtenstein	20.7	(2.2)	**441**	(14.3)	490	(18.6)	432	(18.6)
Luxembourg	18.3	(0.7)	367	(4.1)	389	(5.6)	377	(5.3)
FYR Macedonia	1.7	(0.3)	**346**	(13.9)	365	(17.7)	368	(18.1)
Mexico	0.2	(0.1)	c	c	c	c	c	c
New Zealand	9.6	(0.6)	469	(9.6)	511	(10.2)	474	(9.6)
Norway	5.3	(0.4)	459	(8.4)	456	(11.1)	449	(9.4)
Peru	0.0	(0.0)	a	a	a	a	a	a
Poland	0.5	(0.2)	c	c	c	c	c	c
Portugal	1.5	(0.2)	416	(13.8)	424	(21.1)	385	(15.4)
Russian Federation	7.3	(2.1)	**432**	(9.3)	465	(14.9)	**437**	(10.2)
Spain	1.2	(0.2)	456	(16.0)	437	(25.5)	442	(23.2)
Sweden	6.7	(0.6)	456	(7.1)	448	(10.9)	450	(9.3)
Switzerland	13.6	(0.6)	414	(6.1)	455	(7.3)	419	(6.4)
Thailand	1.9	(0.9)	428	(19.2)	439	(21.0)	**389**	(22.6)
United Kingdom	4.1	(0.7)	470	(12.8)	476	(14.1)	481	(16.4)
United States	10.8	(2.4)	438	(13.1)	430	(11.3)	440	(16.0)
OECD average	*5.5*	*(0.2)*	*440*	*(2.6)*	*454*	*(3.0)*	*438*	*(2.8)*
OECD total	*5.5*	*(0.7)*	*443*	*(8.2)*	*443*	*(8.5)*	*443*	*(9.6)*
Netherlands[5]	6.3	(1.1)	466	(13.1)	496	(14.9)	457	(13.9)

1. Percentage of students participating in the assessment of reading literacy in the respective category.
2. Mean scores marked in bold indicate that the difference in performance between students who do not speak the language of assessment at home and those who do is statistically significant.
3. Ratios statistically significant greater than 1 are marked in bold.
4. This question was not asked in Korea.
5. Response rate is too low to ensure comparability (see Annex A3)

Table 6.9 (continued)
Student performance on the combined reading, mathematical and scientific literacy scales by language spoken at home
Results based on students' self-reports

	Language spoken at home most of the time IS THE SAME as the language of assessment, other official languages or another national dialects								Increased likelihood of students who do not speak the language of assessment at home scoring in the bottom quarter of the national reading literacy performance distribution[3]	
	Percentage of students[1]	S.E.	Performance[2]							
			Combined reading literacy scale		Mathematical literacy scale		Scientific literacy scale			
			Mean score	S.E.	Mean score	S.E.	Mean score	S.E.	Ratio	S.E.
Albania	99.5	(0.1)	351	(3.2)	383	(3.1)	378	(2.8)	0.8	(0.32)
Argentina	99.7	(0.1)	420	(9.6)	388	(9.6)	399	(8.3)	1.4	(0.66)
Australia	83.0	(1.6)	534	(3.6)	537	(3.6)	534	(3.2)	1.6	(0.12)
Austria	93.3	(0.7)	515	(2.4)	523	(2.5)	527	(2.4)	2.3	(0.18)
Belgium	95.2	(0.6)	518	(3.7)	531	(3.9)	507	(4.5)	2.8	(0.23)
Brazil	99.2	(0.2)	397	(3.0)	335	(3.7)	376	(3.3)	c	c
Bulgaria	96.2	(0.7)	**438**	(4.8)	**437**	(5.4)	**455**	(4.5)	**3.2**	(0.35)
Canada	90.6	(0.6)	540	(1.5)	536	(1.4)	534	(1.6)	1.6	(0.07)
Chile	99.6	(0.1)	410	(3.6)	384	(3.7)	415	(3.5)	1.2	(0.46)
Czech Republic	99.2	(0.2)	494	(2.2)	499	(2.7)	513	(2.4)	c	c
Denmark	93.3	(0.4)	503	(2.2)	520	(2.4)	488	(2.7)	2.5	(0.17)
Finland	98.7	(0.2)	548	(2.6)	537	(2.1)	539	(2.4)	c	c
France	96.0	(0.5)	510	(2.6)	521	(2.7)	506	(3.1)	2.3	(0.21)
Germany	92.1	(0.8)	500	(2.9)	505	(2.6)	504	(2.6)	2.9	(0.29)
Greece	97.2	(0.6)	477	(4.8)	451	(5.6)	464	(4.6)	2.3	(0.41)
Hong Kong-China	94.7	(0.4)	**530**	(2.9)	**566**	(3.2)	**545**	(3.0)	**2.2**	(0.20)
Hungary	m	m	m	m	m	m	m	m	m	m
Iceland	98.1	(0.3)	509	(1.5)	516	(2.2)	497	(2.2)	c	c
Indonesia	97.3	(0.4)	373	(3.8)	368	(4.4)	394	(3.7)	**1.5**	(0.24)
Ireland	99.1	(0.2)	527	(3.2)	503	(2.7)	514	(3.1)	c	c
Israel	90.2	(1.0)	458	(8.8)	437	(10.2)	437	(9.5)	1.3	(0.21)
Italy	99.3	(0.2)	491	(3.0)	460	(3.1)	481	(3.1)	c	c
Japan	99.7	(0.1)	525	(5.2)	559	(5.5)	553	(5.5)	c	c
Korea[4]	a	a	a	a	a	a	a	a	a	a
Latvia	100.0	(0.0)	460	(5.2)	464	(4.4)	462	(5.5)	a	a
Liechtenstein	79.3	(2.2)	**494**	(5.1)	520	(8.3)	**488**	(7.4)	c	c
Luxembourg	81.7	(0.7)	460	(1.6)	462	(2.2)	459	(2.4)	2.8	(0.13)
FYR Macedonia	98.3	(0.3)	**375**	(1.9)	384	(2.6)	403	(2.1)	1.6	(0.38)
Mexico	99.8	(0.1)	422	(3.4)	388	(3.4)	422	(3.3)	c	c
New Zealand	90.4	(0.6)	541	(2.6)	545	(3.2)	540	(2.4)	2.1	(0.15)
Norway	94.7	(0.4)	510	(2.8)	504	(2.9)	506	(2.9)	1.8	(0.15)
Peru	100.0	(0.0)	329	(4.2)	295	(4.4)	334	(3.8)	a	a
Poland	99.5	(0.2)	482	(4.4)	474	(5.1)	486	(5.2)	c	c
Portugal	98.5	(0.2)	471	(4.6)	455	(4.0)	461	(4.0)	c	c
Russian Federation	92.7	(2.1)	**465**	(4.3)	480	(5.8)	**462**	(5.1)	**1.5**	(0.22)
Spain	98.8	(0.2)	495	(2.6)	478	(3.0)	493	(2.8)	c	c
Sweden	93.3	(0.6)	523	(2.0)	517	(2.3)	519	(2.5)	2.1	(0.19)
Switzerland	86.4	(0.6)	509	(4.1)	543	(4.3)	508	(4.5)	2.8	(0.15)
Thailand	98.1	(0.9)	433	(3.2)	435	(3.6)	**439**	(3.0)	0.9	(0.43)
United Kingdom	95.9	(0.7)	528	(2.5)	534	(2.5)	536	(2.6)	1.9	(0.24)
United States	89.2	(2.4)	514	(5.8)	503	(6.7)	509	(6.2)	2.1	(0.22)
OECD average	*94.5*	*(0.2)*	*506*	*(0.6)*	*503*	*(0.7)*	*504*	*(0.7)*	*2.1*	*(0.05)*
OECD total	*94.5*	*(0.7)*	*503*	*(1.8)*	*500*	*(1.9)*	*505*	*(1.8)*	*2.0*	*(0.12)*
Netherlands[5]	93.7	(1.1)	539	(2.7)	571	(3.0)	538	(3.3)	2.2	(0.29)

1. Percentage of students participating in the assessment of reading literacy in the respective category.
2. Mean scores marked in bold indicate that the difference in performance between students who do not speak the language of assessment at home and those who do is statistically significant.
3. Ratios statistically significant greater than 1 are marked in bold.
4. This question was not asked in Korea.
5. Response rate is too low to ensure comparability (see Annex A3).

Table 6.10
**Relationship between student performance on the combined reading literacy scale
and family economic, social and cultural backgrounds**

	Unadjust mean score	Mean score if index of students' socio-economic status is equal to the OECD average		Slope of socio-economic gradients		Length of the projection of gradient line
	Mean score	Mean score	S.E.	Coefficient	S.E.	
Albania	349	382	(2.95)	39	(2.01)	3.3
Argentina	418	454	(7.24)	41	(2.93)	4.1
Australia	528	513	(3.10)	46	(2.36)	2.9
Austria	507	507	(2.62)	41	(2.26)	2.7
Belgium	507	520	(2.84)	48	(2.35)	3.1
Brazil	396	434	(3.28)	38	(2.60)	4.0
Bulgaria	430	448	(3.81)	52	(3.57)	2.9
Canada	534	527	(1.52)	37	(1.31)	2.8
Chile	410	441	(3.25)	41	(2.24)	3.8
Czech Republic	492	500	(2.42)	50	(2.22)	2.7
Denmark	497	498	(2.32)	42	(2.07)	2.8
Finland	546	546	(2.22)	30	(2.40)	2.9
France	505	512	(2.48)	47	(2.17)	2.9
Germany	484	476	(3.80)	60	(3.44)	2.8
Greece	474	484	(4.12)	38	(3.05)	3.3
Hong Kong, China	525	546	(3.14)	28	(2.60)	3.0
Hungary	480	488	(3.46)	53	(2.89)	2.9
Iceland	507	492	(2.13)	24	(2.05)	2.8
Indonesia	371	419	(7.40)	33	(5.41)	3.5
Ireland	527	526	(2.89)	38	(2.22)	2.9
Israel	452	454	(6.63)	46	(4.00)	3.4
Italy	487	487	(3.11)	32	(2.35)	3.1
Japan	522	533	(4.62)	21	(2.87)	2.6
Korea	525	534	(2.22)	21	(2.37)	2.9
Latvia	458	471	(2.72)	29	(1.75)	3.0
Liechtenstein	483	478	(5.31)	49	(6.30)	2.5
Luxembourg	441	447	(2.10)	46	(1.69)	3.4
FYR Macedonia	373	392	(1.49)	34	(2.14)	3.6
Mexico	422	459	(3.04)	35	(2.47)	4.4
New Zealand	529	524	(2.52)	45	(2.27)	3.1
Norway	505	487	(3.03)	41	(1.83)	2.9
Peru	327	383	(4.26)	50	(3.52)	3.6
Poland	479	496	(4.36)	36	(3.40)	3.2
Portugal	470	488	(3.76)	40	(2.09)	3.6
Russian Federation	462	480	(3.20)	31	(2.79)	3.0
Spain	493	504	(2.23)	32	(1.52)	3.3
Sweden	516	504	(1.97)	36	(1.86)	2.7
Switzerland	494	499	(3.55)	49	(2.24)	3.0
Thailand	431	468	(4.72)	31	(3.68)	3.9
United Kingdom	523	519	(2.31)	49	(1.87)	2.9
United States	504	497	(4.79)	48	(2.75)	3.3
OECD average	*500*	*505*	*(1.31)*	*41*	*(0.97)*	*3.0*
Netherlands		534	(1.77)	38	(2.61)	2.8

Table 6.11
Effects of student individual and family characteristics and reading engagement on the combined reading literacy score

Parameter	Mean	Model 1: Effects of individual and socio-economic background		Model 2: Added effects of engagement		Model 3: Differential effects of engagement in reading by socio-economic back-ground and country's level of wealth	
		Effects	S.E.	Effects	S.E.	Effects	S.E.
Intercept		491.9	(32.87)	493.4	(32.73)	488.9	(29.21)
Individual and family characteristics							
Female student	0.507	32.1	(8.44)	23.6	(4.93)	22.3	(9.05)
Native or first-generation student	0.952	13.1	(25.28)	17.0	(24.34)	27.5	(28.97)
Student from single-parent family	0.147	-0.7	(5.76)	0.3	(5.82)	2.9	(4.65)
Number of siblings	1.986	-8.0	(0.88)	-8.2	(1.18)	-8.9	(3.93)
Index of family economic, social and cultural status	-0.235	36.2	(2.12)	31.8	(0.55)	32.1	(6.42)
Student from low- or middle-income country	0.357	-53.3	(8.88)	-59.2	(4.64)	-64.5	(19.54)
Reading engagement							
Index of reading engagement	0.051			21.9	(6.07)	26.4	(1.56)
Index of social background X index of reading engagement						2.4	(0.58)
Low- and middle-income country X index of engagement in reading						-10.1	(3.98)

Note: Countries were given equal weight in the model.

Table 7.1a
Between-school and within-school variation in student performance on the combined reading literacy scale

	Total variation in SP[1]	Variation expressed as a percentage of the average variation in student performance (SP) across the OECD countries							Total variation between schools expressed as a percentage of the total variation within the country[2]
		Total variation in SP expressed as a percentage of the average variation in student performance across OECD countries	Total variation in SP between schools	Total variation in SP within schools	Variation explained by the international socio-economic index of occupational status of students		Variation explained by the international socio-economic index of occupational status of students and schools		
					Between-school variation	Within-school variation	Between-school variation	Within-school variation	
Albania	9 801	105.6	43.8	63.3	7.5	2.8	26.3	2.8	40.9
Argentina	11 881	128.1	66.4	63.3	12.2	6.9	42.0	6.9	51.2
Australia	10 357	111.6	20.9	90.6	8.3	6.7	14.2	6.9	18.8
Austria	8 649	93.2	68.6	45.7	10.4	0.4	42.6	0.3	60.0
Belgium	11 455	123.5	76.0	50.9	11.0	1.8	44.2	1.9	59.9
Brazil	7 427	80.1	35.8	47.1	6.5	1.9	19.7	2.1	43.1
Bulgaria	10 404	112.1	66.1	53.1	9.4	3.5	47.7	3.5	55.4
Canada	8 955	96.5	17.1	80.1	4.6	5.0	7.8	5.1	17.6
Chile	8 100	87.3	55.5	42.3	10.0	0.8	31.5	0.8	56.7
Czech Republic	9 278	100.0	51.9	45.3	8.8	1.8	34.4	1.8	53.4
Denmark	9 614	103.6	19.6	85.9	10.2	8.0	11.6	8.1	18.6
Finland	7 994	86.2	10.7	76.5	1.5	4.6	1.7	4.6	12.3
France	m	m	m	m	m	m	m	m	m
Germany	12 368	133.3	74.8	50.2	11.7	2.3	51.5	2.3	59.8
Greece	9 436	101.7	53.8	52.9	7.0	1.1	25.0	1.1	50.4
Hong Kong-China	7 056	76.1	36.6	39.3	3.6	1.3	11.5	1.3	48.3
Hungary	8 810	95.0	71.2	34.8	8.3	0.3	49.4	0.2	67.2
Iceland	8 529	91.9	7.0	85.0	1.6	5.0	1.7	5.0	7.6
Indonesia	5 184	55.9	22.1	29.7	2.5	0.3	9.5	0.3	42.7
Ireland	8 755	94.4	17.1	79.2	5.5	5.7	10.1	5.7	17.8
Israel	11 881	128.1	55.8	74.3	9.8	14.5	31.2	14.6	42.9
Italy	8 356	90.1	50.9	43.4	3.4	0.5	23.8	0.5	54.0
Japan[3]	7 358	79.3	36.5	43.9	m	m	m	m	45.4
Korea	4 833	52.1	19.7	33.0	1.0	0.2	7.1	0.2	37.4
Latvia	10 435	112.5	35.1	77.5	4.9	4.4	16.7	4.5	31.2
Liechtenstein	m	m	m	m	m	m	m	m	43.9
Luxembourg	10 088	108.7	33.4	74.9	11.1	8.3	26.7	8.2	30.8
FYR Macedonia	8 836	95.2	42.8	52.6	8.7	2.8	27.2	2.8	44.9
Mexico	7 370	79.4	42.9	37.4	5.2	0.1	25.7	0.1	53.4
New Zealand	11 701	126.1	20.1	103.9	7.3	10.9	11.6	11.0	16.2
Norway	10 743	115.8	12.6	102.4	3.7	8.7	4.9	8.7	10.9
Peru	9 216	99.3	64.5	46.6	8.9	1.3	41.1	1.3	58.0
Poland	9 958	107.3	67.0	38.9	6.3	1.1	42.4	1.1	63.2
Portugal	9 436	101.7	37.5	64.3	10.6	4.6	23.8	4.6	36.8
Russian Federation	8 466	91.3	33.6	57.1	4.8	2.4	15.4	2.3	37.1
Spain	7 181	77.4	15.9	60.9	5.4	3.0	9.1	3.1	20.7
Sweden	8 495	91.6	8.9	83.0	4.5	6.9	5.8	6.9	9.7
Switzerland	10 408	112.2	48.7	63.7	12.7	4.0	24.3	3.9	43.4
Thailand	5 929	63.9	19.8	44.2	1.5	1.8	8.6	1.9	30.9
United Kingdom	10 098	108.9	22.4	82.3	9.6	8.4	16.0	8.7	21.4
United States	10 979	118.3	35.1	83.6	12.0	5.6	25.5	5.8	29.6
OECD average	9 277	100.0	36.2	65.1	7.3	4.2	21.6	4.2	35.2

1. The total variation in student performance is obtained as the square of the standard deviation shown in Table 2.3a. The statistical variance and not the standard deviation is used for this comparison to allow for the decomposition of the components of variation in student performance. For reasons explained in the *PISA 2000 Technical Report* (OECD 2002a), the sum of the between and within-school variance components may, for some countries, differ slightly from the square of the standard deviation shown in Table 2.3a.
2. This index is often referred to as the intra-class correlation (rho).
3. Due to the sampling methods, the between-school variance in Japan includes variation between classes within schools.

Table 7.1b
Between-school and within-school variation in student performance on the mathematical literacy and scientific literacy scales

		Mathematical literacy							
		Variation expressed as a percentage of the average variation in student performance (SP) across the OECD countries							Total variation between schools expressed as a percentage of the total variation within the country[2]
	Total variation in SP[1]	Total variation in SP expressed as a percentage of the average variation in SP across OECD countries	Total variation in SP between schools	Total variation in SP within schools	Variation explained by the international socio-economic index of occupational status of students		Variation explained by the international socio-economic index of occupational status of students and schools		
					Between-school variation	Within-school variation	Between-school variation	Within-school variation	
Albania	11 449	132.6	40.1	93.4	9.3	4.3	23.7	4.3	30.0
Argentina	14 400	166.8	72.5	88.9	14.7	8.4	46.0	8.6	44.9
Australia	8 107	93.9	16.2	76.3	7.4	6.0	10.4	6.4	17.5
Austria	8 545	99.0	58.6	53.4	8.4	0.2	29.4	0.3	52.3
Belgium	11 268	130.5	71.6	59.4	13.7	2.7	38.5	2.7	54.7
Brazil	9 493	110.0	40.0	71.5	26.8	71.8	15.5	71.0	35.9
Bulgaria	12 100	140.2	67.2	79.4	14.4	5.6	45.3	5.7	45.9
Canada	7 152	82.9	14.3	68.2	2.9	3.7	4.5	3.8	17.3
Chile	8 836	102.4	49.2	59.1	12.5	1.7	32.8	1.6	45.4
Czech Republic	9 276	107.5	45.9	59.2	9.3	2.1	25.8	2.1	43.7
Denmark	7 500	86.9	15.4	70.8	7.9	5.5	8.9	5.7	17.8
Finland	6 451	74.7	6.1	68.5	1.0	5.7	1.0	5.7	8.1
France	m	m	m	m	m	m	m	m	m
Germany	10 512	121.8	65.5	53.1	10.9	1.7	40.1	1.8	55.2
Greece	11 731	135.9	65.4	74.0	9.9	0.9	29.5	0.9	46.9
Hong Kong-China	8 836	102.4	45.4	55.2	4.3	1.0	10.8	1.0	45.1
Hungary	9 592	111.1	60.1	53.6	14.2	0.5	45.2	0.5	52.9
Iceland	7 159	82.9	4.5	78.0	1.1	4.2	1.1	4.1	5.4
Indonesia	7 225	83.7	26.3	50.7	2.3	-0.4	8.5	-0.3	34.1
Ireland	6 982	80.9	9.4	73.1	3.9	4.3	6.1	4.5	11.4
Israel	17 161	198.8	65.2	127.9	15.0	20.0	41.0	20.3	33.7
Italy	8 174	94.7	40.5	55.1	3.3	0.2	15.0	0.2	42.4
Japan[3]	7 559	87.6	43.7	44.3	m	m	m	m	49.7
Korea	7 110	82.4	32.1	50.9	2.7	0.7	13.6	0.7	38.7
Latvia	10 654	123.4	33.1	90.8	30.9	88.1	24.4	88.0	26.7
Liechtenstein	9 162	106.2	m	m	m	m	m	m	m
Luxembourg	8 566	99.2	24.9	73.4	9.5	6.9	21.0	6.8	25.3
FYR Macedonia	9 604	111.3	34.8	76.4	9.8	4.7	21.9	4.7	31.3
Mexico	6 834	79.2	41.1	39.3	6.1	0.4	23.4	0.4	51.1
New Zealand	9 748	112.9	19.8	93.7	7.8	10.1	11.7	10.2	17.5
Norway	8 383	97.1	7.8	89.1	1.5	6.2	1.6	6.2	8.1
Peru	11 664	135.1	57.4	84.2	8.3	2.6	34.1	2.6	40.5
Poland	10 510	121.8	63.3	53.5	7.5	0.3	38.8	0.2	54.2
Portugal	8 341	96.6	30.1	64.0	10.5	4.8	18.2	5.0	32.0
Russian Federation	10 837	125.6	45.5	79.9	39.6	77.2	31.8	77.2	36.3
Spain	8 192	94.9	17.1	76.1	5.9	2.5	9.0	2.6	18.3
Sweden	8 724	101.1	8.3	92.7	5.3	8.7	6.0	8.7	8.3
Switzerland	9 922	115.0	47.5	68.2	9.6	3.2	21.1	3.0	41.1
Thailand	6 889	79.8	27.6	54.0	4.4	1.8	12.8	1.9	33.8
United Kingdom	8 402	97.3	21.2	72.0	8.5	6.0	14.8	6.5	22.7
United States	9 671	112.0	35.0	74.5	12.4	6.3	24.2	6.5	32.0
OECD average	8 631								

1. The total variation in student performance is obtained as the square of the standard deviation shown in Table 3.1 for mathematical literacy and Table 3.2 for scientific literacy. The statistical variance and not the standard deviation is used for this comparison to allow for the decomposition of the components of variation in student performance. For the reasons explained in the *PISA 2000 Technical Report* (OECD 2002a), the sum of the between-school and within-school variance components may, for some countries, differ slightly from the square of the standard deviation shown in Tables 3.1 and 3.2.
2. This index is often referred to as the intra-class correlation (rho).
3. Due to the sampling methods, the between-school variance in Japan includes variation between classes within schools.

Table 7.1b (continued)
Between-school and within-school variation in student performance on the mathematical literacy and scientific literacy scales

		Scientific literacy							
		Variation expressed as a percentage of the average variation in SP across the OECD countries							Total variation between schools expressed as a percentage of the total variation within the country[2]
		Total variation in SP expressed as a percentage of the average variation in SP across OECD countries	Total variation in SP between schools	Total variation in SP within schools	Variation explained by the international socio-economic index of occupational status of students		Variation explained by the international socio-economic index of occupational status of students and schools		
	Total variation in SP[1]				Between-school variation	Within-school variation	Between-school variation	Within-school variation	
Albania	8 836	98.0	29.5	70.3	7.9	3.2	16.3	3.2	29.5
Argentina	11 881	131.7	54.8	78.3	9.7	6.2	32.9	6.5	41.1
Australia	8 879	98.4	17.2	81.0	5.7	4.5	9.6	4.8	17.5
Austria	8 327	92.3	58.7	46.5	10.5	0.6	33.4	0.5	55.8
Belgium	12 314	136.5	77.4	62.3	14.4	2.2	46.0	2.3	55.4
Brazil	8 181	90.7	25.5	65.2	7.7	0.2	14.6	0.8	28.1
Bulgaria	9 216	102.2	42.3	63.0	9.2	2.4	29.8	2.5	40.2
Canada	7 893	87.5	13.9	71.9	3.4	4.5	4.9	4.6	16.2
Chile	9 025	100.1	40.5	62.9	12.8	1.0	25.0	0.9	39.2
Czech Republic	8 821	97.8	39.2	58.0	9.9	2.0	26.1	2.1	40.3
Denmark	10 652	118.1	19.4	101.6	8.7	10.2	9.7	10.5	16.0
Finland	7 446	82.6	5.5	78.1	0.9	3.8	1.0	3.8	6.6
France	m	m	m	m	m	m	m	m	m
Germany	10 394	115.2	58.5	59.8	11.7	2.3	40.4	2.4	49.5
Greece	9 390	104.1	42.0	62.9	5.5	0.4	18.6	0.3	40.0
Hong Kong-China	7 225	80.1	36.0	44.2	4.0	1.8	11.6	1.8	44.9
Hungary	10 510	116.5	65.9	58.9	11.8	0.7	49.0	0.4	52.8
Iceland	7 705	85.4	6.4	78.3	1.0	1.4	0.8	1.5	7.6
Indonesia	5 625	62.4	19.2	38.2	1.8	0.0	6.3	0.0	33.5
Ireland	8 416	93.3	13.3	81.2	4.7	5.4	7.5	5.4	14.1
Israel	15 625	173.2	55.5	119.4	3.8	21.4	18.1	21.5	31.7
Italy	9 612	106.6	46.9	64.2	3.1	0.5	14.1	0.4	42.2
Japan[3]	8 185	90.7	40.6	50.9	m	m	m	m	44.4
Korea	6 508	72.2	27.6	44.5	1.6	0.3	10.0	0.2	38.3
Latvia	9 543	105.8	29.8	74.5	4.0	3.0	12.2	3.0	28.6
Liechtenstein	8 896	98.6	m	m	m	m	m	m	m
Luxembourg	9 281	102.9	28.0	73.4	6.9	4.6	21.6	4.5	27.6
FYR Macedonia	6 889	76.4	26.3	51.1	6.8	2.5	16.8	2.6	34.0
Mexico	5 940	65.9	26.8	38.8	5.0	-0.6	15.5	0.0	40.9
New Zealand	10 149	112.5	18.9	92.6	7.7	10.0	11.4	10.0	16.9
Norway	9 128	101.2	10.2	92.5	2.9	6.7	3.3	6.7	10.0
Peru	8 100	89.8	27.3	63.6	4.5	0.6	15.5	0.7	30.0
Poland	9 378	104.0	53.3	50.5	7.0	0.4	33.1	0.4	51.4
Portugal	7 923	87.8	27.4	60.3	8.0	3.9	16.3	3.9	31.3
Russian Federation	9 825	108.9	33.2	75.3	4.0	2.0	10.9	1.9	30.6
Spain	9 097	100.9	18.2	82.5	8.1	3.5	11.1	3.6	18.0
Sweden	8 688	96.3	8.0	90.0	3.5	6.0	4.0	6.0	8.2
Switzerland	10 012	111.0	45.4	63.9	8.7	3.7	19.5	3.6	41.6
Thailand	5 929	65.7	20.3	45.4	2.2	0.4	9.5	0.5	30.9
United Kingdom	9 639	106.9	24.6	76.7	9.0	7.1	16.0	7.6	24.3
United States	10 217	113.3	40.3	73.0	14.1	6.7	26.1	7.1	35.6
OECD average	9 019								

1. The total variation in student performance is obtained as the square of the standard deviation shown in Table 3.1 for mathematical literacy and Table 3.2 for scientific literacy. The statistical variance and not the standard deviation is used for this comparison to allow for the decomposition of the components of variation in student performance. For the reasons explained in the *PISA 2000 Technical Report* (OECD 2002a), the sum of the between-school and within-school variance components may, for some countries, differ slightly from the square of the standard deviation shown in Tables 3.1 and 3.2.
2. This index is often referred to as the intra-class correlation (rho).
3. Due to the sampling methods, the between-school variance in Japan includes variation between classes within schools.

Table 7.2
Index of the quality of the schools' physical infrastructure and performance on the combined reading literacy scale, by national quarters of the index
Results based on reports from school principals and reported proportionate to the number of 15-year-olds enrolled in the school

	Index of the quality of the schools' physical infrastructure[1]								Performance on the combined reading literacy scale by quarters of the index of the quality of the schools' physical infrastructure[2]						Change in the combined reading literacy score per unit of the index of quality of the schools' physical infrastructure[2]	
	All students		Bottom quarter		Middle half		Top quarter		Bottom quarter		Middle half		Top quarter			
	Mean index	S.E.	Mean index	S.E.	Mean index	S.E.	Mean index	S.E.	Mean score	S.E.	Mean score	S.E.	Mean score	S.E.	Change	S.E.
Albania	-0.37	(0.06)	-1.58	(0.09)	-0.37	(0.03)	0.84	(0.06)	356	(6.5)	344	(5.5)	347	(7.4)	-5.22	(4.01)
Argentina	-0.08	(0.16)	-1.49	(0.22)	0.21	(0.17)	Max		384	(9.4)	450	(11.6)	486	(14.7)	33.32	(5.98)
Australia	0.05	(0.08)	-1.11	(0.06)	0.08	(0.06)	Max		527	(9.1)	530	(4.6)	527	(7.6)	1.39	(4.82)
Austria	-0.07	(0.09)	-1.52	(0.14)	0.05	(0.05)	Max		510	(9.5)	507	(5.4)	505	(8.9)	-3.07	(4.41)
Belgium	0.33	(0.06)	-0.79	(0.06)	0.48	(0.05)	Max		490	(11.4)	516	(5.8)	510	(10.4)	15.25	(7.39)
Brazil	0.30	(0.07)	-1.14	(0.12)	0.59	(0.05)	Max		386	(7.4)	398	(4.2)	403	(9.1)	9.32	(4.38)
Bulgaria	0.20	(0.09)	-1.12	(0.11)	0.42	(0.06)	Max		441	(12.4)	434	(8.7)	415	(13.3)	-12.77	(6.51)
Canada	0.35	(0.03)	-0.80	(0.05)	0.54	(0.03)	Max		536	(3.3)	534	(2.3)	535	(3.0)	-1.30	(2.13)
Chile	0.29	(0.07)	-1.01	(0.12)	0.54	(0.06)	Max		394	(7.9)	410	(7.1)	425	(8.1)	13.55	(5.36)
Czech Republic	0.66	(0.05)	-0.32	(0.05)	0.89	(0.03)	Max		508	(8.0)	478	(3.9)	502	(8.1)	-6.09	(6.55)
Denmark	-0.07	(0.08)	-1.29	(0.08)	-0.05	(0.03)	1.07	(0.04)	498	(5.7)	492	(4.2)	500	(6.0)	-2.66	(3.27)
Finland	-0.22	(0.08)	-1.41	(0.08)	-0.24	(0.04)	0.97	(0.05)	550	(4.6)	549	(3.1)	538	(6.6)	-2.88	(3.49)
France	m	m	m	m	m	m	m	m	m	m	m	m	m	m	m	m
Germany	0.14	(0.06)	-1.00	(0.10)	0.22	(0.05)	Max		468	(13.9)	489	(7.8)	497	(9.7)	14.06	(9.22)
Greece	-1.17	(0.12)	-2.78	(0.10)	-1.35	(0.06)	0.68	(0.09)	468	(10.4)	465	(9.1)	492	(10.5)	8.01	(4.69)
Hong Kong-China	0.27	(0.06)	-0.66	(0.09)	0.32	(0.04)	Max		537	(10.0)	524	(5.7)	517	(9.7)	-12.55	(9.04)
Hungary	0.42	(0.07)	-0.61	(0.15)	0.57	(0.05)	Max		462	(11.1)	492	(8.4)	471	(11.1)	11.68	(9.02)
Iceland	0.31	(0.00)	-0.85	(0.00)	0.46	(0.00)	Max		512	(3.4)	505	(2.1)	506	(2.7)	-2.18	(1.76)
Indonesia	-0.19	(0.13)	-2.25	(0.11)	0.22	(0.10)	Max		384	(8.5)	359	(5.3)	379	(10.0)	-2.46	(3.48)
Ireland	0.19	(0.09)	-1.10	(0.11)	0.35	(0.07)	Max		517	(7.4)	533	(4.8)	524	(7.3)	4.34	(4.17)
Israel	-0.40	(0.13)	-1.83	(0.17)	-0.29	(0.08)	1.04	(0.04)	447	(11.9)	450	(13.4)	465	(26.8)	0.35	(8.43)
Italy	-0.20	(0.09)	-1.67	(0.11)	-0.14	(0.06)	Max		470	(11.2)	493	(6.5)	493	(7.2)	5.92	(4.37)
Japan	-0.21	(0.08)	-1.26	(0.06)	-0.26	(0.04)	0.88	(0.06)	519	(11.4)	520	(7.6)	529	(7.9)	4.81	(5.61)
Korea	-0.36	(0.08)	-1.65	(0.12)	-0.34	(0.05)	0.83	(0.06)	518	(7.3)	525	(5.1)	526	(8.2)	2.93	(4.54)
Latvia	-0.07	(0.10)	-1.25	(0.13)	-0.09	(0.07)	Max		462	(14.8)	460	(8.3)	457	(9.0)	1.89	(6.60)
Liechtenstein	m	m	m	m	m	m	m	m	m	m	m	m	m	m	m	m
Luxembourg	-0.28	(0.00)	-1.32	(0.00)	-0.35	(0.00)	0.50	(0.00)	435	(3.6)	416	(2.3)	499	(2.3)	34.98	(1.99)
FYR Macedonia	-0.06	(0.02)	-1.56	(0.03)	0.18	(0.01)	Max		346	(3.4)	379	(3.0)	386	(2.1)	14.70	(1.32)
Mexico	-0.39	(0.09)	-1.95	(0.09)	-0.35	(0.06)	0.99	(0.05)	399	(8.5)	417	(6.2)	454	(9.4)	16.88	(3.91)
New Zealand	0.10	(0.06)	-0.96	(0.08)	0.11	(0.04)	Max		525	(8.5)	536	(4.4)	525	(6.8)	2.99	(4.86)
Norway	-0.59	(0.07)	-1.77	(0.11)	-0.58	(0.03)	0.53	(0.06)	504	(6.1)	504	(4.3)	505	(6.9)	0.49	(3.42)
Peru	-0.28	(0.08)	-1.64	(0.09)	-0.25	(0.06)	1.07	(0.03)	286	(8.8)	327	(8.0)	363	(9.5)	30.41	(4.55)
Poland	-0.15	(0.10)	-1.50	(0.19)	-0.03	(0.05)	0.91	(0.06)	502	(13.7)	480	(9.0)	454	(14.1)	-16.87	(6.72)
Portugal	0.14	(0.07)	-1.14	(0.11)	0.29	(0.06)	Max		498	(8.2)	464	(7.9)	455	(7.6)	-16.16	(4.50)
Russian Federation	-0.52	(0.09)	-2.07	(0.08)	-0.51	(0.05)	0.98	(0.03)	445	(7.9)	461	(5.9)	482	(9.4)	12.22	(3.94)
Spain	0.13	(0.07)	-1.27	(0.11)	0.33	(0.06)	Max		484	(6.1)	494	(4.2)	496	(6.3)	9.18	(3.14)
Sweden	0.01	(0.08)	-1.20	(0.08)	0.02	(0.05)	Max		506	(6.4)	519	(3.5)	521	(4.5)	6.01	(3.08)
Switzerland	0.49	(0.06)	-0.62	(0.08)	0.73	(0.05)	Max		487	(11.6)	491	(7.0)	507	(10.9)	11.11	(6.33)
Thailand	0.11	(0.08)	-1.28	(0.11)	0.31	(0.08)	Max		432	(6.1)	427	(5.1)	437	(6.9)	0.58	(2.89)
United Kingdom	-0.41	(0.08)	-1.65	(0.07)	-0.49	(0.04)	0.95	(0.05)	514	(8.4)	521	(3.6)	540	(9.6)	8.92	(4.83)
United States	0.20	(0.08)	-0.77	(0.06)	0.20	(0.05)	Max		507	(11.1)	508	(6.9)	499	(13.9)	-2.16	(6.10)
OECD average	0.00	(0.01)	-1.22	(0.02)	0.08	(0.01)	1.01	(0.01)	498	(1.8)	499	(1.1)	504	(1.6)	5.08	(0.98)
OECD total	-0.01	(0.02)	-1.19	(0.03)	0.04	(0.02)	1.03	(0.01)	495	(3.8)	499	(2.6)	502	(3.8)	6.09	(1.64)
Netherlands[3]	0.09	(0.13)	-1.28	(0.20)	0.21	(0.08)	Max		519	(15.9)	531	(7.8)	542	(12.2)	3.10	(6.40)

1. For the definition of the index see Annex A1. *The scale was inverted so that positive and high values indicate that the school's physical infrastructure is perceived less of a problem than on OECD average.* "Max" is used in cases where more than 25 per cent of the students are enrolled in schools in which the responses from school principals correspond to the highest value on the index, which is 1.12.

2. For explained variation see Annex A2. Unit changes marked in bold are statistically significant. Where bottom and top quarters are marked in bold this indicates that their difference is statistically significant.

3. Response rate is too low to ensure comparability (see Annex A3).

Table 7.3
**Index of the quality of the schools' educational resources and performance on the combined reading literacy scale,
by national quarters of the index**

Results based on reports from school principals and reported proportionate to the number of 15-year-olds enrolled in the school

| | Index of the quality of the schools' educational resources[1] | | | | | | | | Performance on the combined reading literacy scale by quarters of the index of the quality of the schools' educational resources[2] | | | | | | Change in the combined reading literacy score per unit of the index of the quality of the schools' educational resources[2] | |
| | All students | | Bottom quarter | | Middle half | | Top quarter | | Bottom quarter | | Middle half | | Top quarter | | | |
	Mean index	S.E.	Mean index	S.E.	Mean index	S.E.	Mean index	S.E.	Mean score	S.E.	Mean score	S.E.	Mean score	S.E.	Change	S.E.
Albania	-1.61	(0.04)	-2.42	(0.04)	-1.69	(0.02)	-0.65	(0.06)	330	(8.6)	351	(5.5)	364	(6.3)	17.33	(4.69)
Argentina	-0.52	(0.12)	-1.82	(0.12)	-0.52	(0.15)	1.13	(0.09)	386	(9.0)	444	(11.4)	487	(11.0)	37.68	(4.50)
Australia	0.28	(0.08)	-0.82	(0.06)	0.10	(0.05)	1.63	(0.09)	515	(6.3)	528	(5.5)	542	(6.7)	9.76	(3.33)
Austria	0.02	(0.08)	-1.09	(0.10)	0.05	(0.04)	1.02	(0.10)	503	(9.0)	512	(5.7)	503	(8.0)	2.96	(5.74)
Belgium	0.45	(0.06)	-0.77	(0.08)	0.44	(0.04)	1.69	(0.04)	491	(11.8)	514	(5.6)	516	(11.4)	9.21	(5.84)
Brazil	-0.36	(0.10)	-1.82	(0.10)	-0.44	(0.05)	1.21	(0.10)	380	(7.0)	392	(4.9)	421	(9.5)	12.70	(3.44)
Bulgaria	-0.49	(0.11)	-1.72	(0.07)	-0.61	(0.04)	1.02	(0.12)	435	(12.3)	424	(7.5)	445	(13.3)	6.87	(5.83)
Canada	0.24	(0.04)	-0.98	(0.05)	0.15	(0.02)	1.61	(0.03)	530	(3.2)	535	(2.0)	539	(3.7)	4.50	(1.49)
Chile	-0.29	(0.08)	-1.58	(0.09)	-0.31	(0.03)	1.08	(0.08)	380	(7.0)	413	(5.7)	434	(9.9)	20.44	(4.65)
Czech Republic	0.22	(0.09)	-0.92	(0.05)	0.05	(0.04)	1.68	(0.06)	489	(7.3)	495	(6.7)	487	(12.2)	0.23	(5.44)
Denmark	0.25	(0.06)	-0.77	(0.07)	0.28	(0.03)	1.18	(0.07)	485	(6.4)	498	(3.7)	503	(6.0)	6.21	(3.42)
Finland	-0.22	(0.06)	-1.17	(0.07)	-0.28	(0.03)	0.79	(0.08)	551	(5.2)	547	(3.0)	541	(6.7)	-4.39	(4.02)
France	m	m	m	m	m	m	m	m	m	m	m	m	m	m	m	m
Germany	-0.20	(0.07)	-1.31	(0.09)	-0.24	(0.04)	0.99	(0.07)	447	(16.2)	497	(9.0)	502	(10.0)	24.99	(9.01)
Greece	-0.93	(0.09)	-2.09	(0.09)	-0.99	(0.04)	0.33	(0.12)	486	(13.7)	459	(8.3)	488	(10.8)	7.92	(7.62)
Hong Kong-China	0.66	(0.10)	-0.70	(0.11)	0.75	(0.07)	1.90	(0.00)	526	(10.5)	520	(7.1)	533	(9.7)	0.59	(5.14)
Hungary	0.50	(0.08)	-0.63	(0.07)	0.44	(0.05)	1.71	(0.06)	462	(13.4)	485	(8.0)	486	(10.6)	10.06	(7.00)
Iceland	-0.19	(0.00)	-1.11	(0.00)	-0.29	(0.00)	0.91	(0.00)	509	(2.9)	500	(2.1)	519	(3.1)	6.48	(1.75)
Indonesia	-0.96	(0.08)	-2.42	(0.09)	-0.92	(0.05)	0.47	(0.11)	356	(6.9)	377	(7.2)	375	(8.2)	8.29	(3.47)
Ireland	-0.19	(0.10)	-1.45	(0.09)	-0.25	(0.05)	1.15	(0.11)	519	(7.1)	533	(5.4)	522	(6.7)	1.78	(3.73)
Israel	0.16	(0.16)	-1.32	(0.11)	0.15	(0.06)	1.72	(0.06)	431	(12.4)	460	(12.5)	462	(26.3)	8.83	(10.50)
Italy	0.07	(0.08)	-1.17	(0.07)	0.01	(0.05)	1.40	(0.09)	469	(11.9)	489	(6.0)	502	(10.2)	11.43	(5.81)
Japan	0.00	(0.07)	-0.96	(0.07)	-0.11	(0.04)	1.18	(0.09)	511	(10.5)	517	(7.7)	544	(7.1)	13.65	(4.99)
Korea	0.00	(0.08)	-1.00	(0.05)	-0.09	(0.04)	1.13	(0.11)	526	(6.0)	518	(5.0)	534	(6.9)	1.63	(4.41)
Latvia	-0.67	(0.09)	-1.85	(0.13)	-0.65	(0.05)	0.41	(0.09)	453	(14.0)	467	(8.7)	452	(11.2)	9.45	(5.09)
Liechtenstein	m	m	m	m	m	m	m	m	m	m	m	m	m	m	m	m
Luxembourg	0.11	(0.00)	-0.65	(0.00)	0.01	(0.00)	0.95	(0.00)	407	(4.2)	445	(2.1)	470	(2.5)	22.98	(2.28)
FYR Macedonia	-0.43	(0.03)	-1.86	(0.04)	-0.59	(0.01)	1.37	(0.01)	331	(2.9)	388	(2.5)	386	(3.5)	15.16	(1.75)
Mexico	-0.95	(0.10)	-2.28	(0.08)	-1.13	(0.05)	0.70	(0.13)	391	(8.7)	413	(5.1)	472	(9.7)	26.01	(3.86)
New Zealand	0.11	(0.06)	-0.83	(0.06)	-0.06	(0.03)	1.35	(0.07)	516	(7.4)	530	(3.9)	545	(7.8)	12.78	(4.03)
Norway	-0.55	(0.06)	-1.34	(0.08)	-0.63	(0.03)	0.37	(0.09)	490	(5.7)	508	(4.0)	514	(5.9)	9.09	(4.22)
Peru	-1.29	(0.08)	-2.62	(0.08)	-1.34	(0.06)	0.20	(0.11)	293	(9.9)	316	(6.1)	381	(10.7)	32.16	(4.78)
Poland	-0.17	(0.09)	-1.35	(0.08)	-0.18	(0.06)	0.98	(0.08)	464	(16.4)	476	(9.0)	498	(12.6)	8.59	(9.19)
Portugal	0.14	(0.08)	-1.06	(0.08)	0.09	(0.04)	1.42	(0.09)	458	(10.5)	474	(7.1)	474	(12.1)	5.31	(5.12)
Russian Federation	-1.27	(0.08)	-2.53	(0.06)	-1.31	(0.03)	0.04	(0.09)	455	(7.1)	459	(6.0)	473	(8.0)	9.09	(3.36)
Spain	0.15	(0.09)	-1.12	(0.09)	0.05	(0.05)	1.58	(0.07)	480	(5.8)	490	(3.6)	509	(7.0)	10.12	(2.97)
Sweden	0.00	(0.07)	-0.99	(0.06)	-0.13	(0.04)	1.22	(0.10)	509	(5.8)	513	(3.4)	530	(4.6)	6.89	(2.78)
Switzerland	0.51	(0.07)	-0.56	(0.05)	0.38	(0.05)	1.78	(0.03)	484	(13.0)	494	(6.0)	504	(7.6)	8.35	(5.04)
Thailand	-0.82	(0.11)	-2.08	(0.07)	-0.89	(0.06)	0.70	(0.18)	419	(6.3)	428	(4.0)	450	(10.4)	11.20	(4.61)
United Kingdom	-0.44	(0.07)	-1.62	(0.08)	-0.52	(0.04)	0.85	(0.11)	507	(6.0)	522	(4.7)	546	(7.0)	16.86	(3.19)
United States	0.40	(0.08)	-0.60	(0.07)	0.30	(0.05)	1.55	(0.10)	481	(7.0)	521	(9.6)	498	(12.8)	0.66	(6.56)
OECD average	*0.00*	*(0.02)*	*-1.09*	*(0.02)*	*-0.08*	*(0.01)*	*1.22*	*(0.02)*	*488*	*(2.1)*	*501*	*(1.2)*	*511*	*(1.6)*	*10.85*	*(1.00)*
OECD total	*0.01*	*(0.03)*	*-1.09*	*(0.04)*	*-0.08*	*(0.02)*	*1.27*	*(0.03)*	*480*	*(3.2)*	*502*	*(2.9)*	*511*	*(3.2)*	*16.88*	*(1.68)*
Netherlands[3]	0.10	(0.12)	-1.18	(0.18)	0.03	(0.05)	1.45	(0.13)	513	(12.7)	541	(8.9)	527	(13.7)	11.39	(7.30)

1. For the definition of the index see Annex A1. *The scale was inverted so that positive and high values indicate that the school's educational resources are not perceived as an important problem.*
2. For explained variation see Annex A2. Unit changes marked in bold are statistically significant. Where bottom and top quarters are marked in bold this indicates that their difference is statistically significant.
3. Response rate is too low to ensure comparability (see Annex A3).

Table 7.4
Index of teacher shortage and performance on the combined reading literacy scale, by national quarters of the index
Results based on reports from school principals and reported proportionate to the number of 15-year-olds enrolled in the school

	Index of teacher shortage[1]								Performance on the combined reading literacy scale, by national quarters of the index of teacher shortage[2]						Change in the combined reading literacy score per unit of the index of teacher shortage[2]	
	All students		Bottom quarter		Middle half		Top quarter		Bottom quarter		Middle half		Top quarter			
	Mean index	S.E.	Mean index	S.E.	Mean index	S.E.	Mean index	S.E.	Mean score	S.E.	Mean score	S.E.	Mean score	S.E.	Change	S.E.
Albania	-0.08	(0.06)	-1.47	(0.12)	0.10	(0.06)	Max		334	(4.0)	356	(5.4)	353	(8.4)	8.62	(3.24)
Argentina	-0.22	(0.18)	-1.51	(0.23)	-0.10	(0.21)	Max		435	(15.3)	438	(12.4)	445	(15.9)	8.13	(10.33)
Australia	-0.18	(0.08)	-1.39	(0.04)	-0.16	(0.08)	Max		510	(5.8)	534	(5.3)	534	(6.9)	13.95	(3.23)
Austria	0.53	(0.05)	-0.43	(0.08)	0.79	(0.04)	Max		478	(10.2)	514	(4.4)	523	(7.4)	27.15	(7.81)
Belgium	0.25	(0.07)	-0.89	(0.08)	0.47	(0.07)	Max		501	(11.6)	543	(7.2)	542	(14.6)	23.01	(8.05)
Brazil	-0.07	(0.07)	-1.32	(0.06)	0.03	(0.07)	Max		384	(6.9)	397	(5.9)	404	(9.0)	6.16	(3.99)
Bulgaria	0.72	(0.04)	0.03	(0.09)	0.95	(0.00)	Max		430	(13.1)	441	(8.6)	410	(9.0)	6.86	(14.17)
Canada	-0.01	(0.04)	-1.41	(0.03)	0.20	(0.04)	Max		531	(2.6)	536	(2.3)	535	(3.3)	2.11	(1.42)
Chile	0.06	(0.08)	-1.28	(0.06)	0.30	(0.06)	Max		400	(8.7)	411	(6.5)	418	(11.1)	8.34	(5.73)
Czech Republic	0.51	(0.04)	-0.36	(0.06)	0.71	(0.04)	Max		459	(11.2)	502	(4.4)	502	(10.5)	42.06	(11.26)
Denmark	0.31	(0.05)	-0.71	(0.04)	0.50	(0.05)	Max		485	(5.5)	497	(3.8)	505	(6.0)	9.29	(4.28)
Finland	0.09	(0.06)	-0.88	(0.03)	0.13	(0.04)	Max		544	(4.0)	548	(2.8)	546	(7.4)	1.23	(4.09)
France	m	m	m	m	m	m	m	m	m	m	m	m	m	m	m	m
Germany	-0.23	(0.06)	-1.47	(0.04)	-0.23	(0.04)	Max		424	(11.5)	498	(6.1)	522	(8.3)	42.31	(5.68)
Greece	-0.73	(0.14)	-2.97	(0.15)	-0.52	(0.10)	Max		476	(13.7)	458	(7.7)	504	(10.1)	2.61	(3.84)
Hong Kong-China	-0.22	(0.09)	-1.43	(0.06)	-0.20	(0.08)	Max		521	(10.0)	519	(6.9)	540	(9.7)	9.45	(5.56)
Hungary	0.29	(0.08)	-1.04	(0.12)	0.61	(0.05)	Max		460	(10.5)	490	(6.2)	477	(11.7)	12.25	(5.77)
Iceland	-0.39	(0.00)	-1.59	(0.00)	-0.47	(0.00)	Max		504	(3.3)	503	(2.2)	517	(3.2)	5.25	(1.49)
Indonesia	-0.85	(0.12)	-2.67	(0.13)	-0.80	(0.07)	0.90	(0.02)	372	(12.4)	376	(5.6)	358	(8.1)	-2.90	(4.38)
Ireland	-0.06	(0.08)	-1.35	(0.11)	0.07	(0.07)	Max		519	(7.9)	528	(4.6)	532	(7.2)	2.83	(3.65)
Israel	-0.46	(0.15)	-1.97	(0.17)	-0.39	(0.09)	Max		429	(16.4)	466	(14.1)	449	(25.1)	4.18	(9.30)
Italy	-0.28	(0.09)	-1.53	(0.07)	-0.30	(0.08)	Max		477	(9.3)	494	(6.4)	487	(8.8)	2.62	(5.05)
Japan	-0.23	(0.07)	-1.51	(0.07)	-0.19	(0.09)	Max		501	(10.7)	525	(8.0)	538	(8.9)	12.04	(4.47)
Korea	0.32	(0.06)	-0.90	(0.09)	0.62	(0.06)	Max		515	(7.8)	531	(4.6)	522	(6.0)	8.09	(4.33)
Latvia	-0.05	(0.10)	-1.18	(0.12)	0.00	(0.04)	Max		465	(12.4)	454	(7.4)	463	(12.2)	-6.96	(8.63)
Liechtenstein	m	m	m	m	m	m	m	m	m	m	m	m	m	m	m	m
Luxembourg	-0.10	(0.01)	-1.66	(0.00)	-0.14	(0.01)	c	c	467	(3.7)	422	(2.5)	473	(3.0)	-4.22	(1.45)
FYR Macedonia	0.67	(0.01)	-0.16	(0.02)	0.95	(0.00)	Max		366	(4.6)	373	(2.5)	378	(3.4)	27.48	(1.74)
Mexico	-0.53	(0.09)	-1.88	(0.08)	-0.60	(0.05)	0.94	(0.01)	411	(8.1)	430	(6.9)	419	(10.6)	3.90	(4.43)
New Zealand	-0.18	(0.07)	-1.42	(0.06)	-0.15	(0.07)	Max		512	(6.8)	529	(4.3)	550	(7.1)	12.66	(3.82)
Norway	-0.32	(0.07)	-1.42	(0.07)	-0.41	(0.05)	0.92	(0.03)	501	(6.6)	506	(3.8)	506	(6.9)	4.47	(3.66)
Peru	-0.36	(0.07)	-1.56	(0.06)	-0.37	(0.05)	0.89	(0.03)	298	(9.7)	325	(8.0)	361	(10.4)	23.78	(5.28)
Poland	0.30	(0.10)	-1.05	(0.20)	0.64	(0.05)	Max		447	(14.2)	487	(9.7)	496	(13.5)	7.75	(8.93)
Portugal	0.03	(0.08)	-0.97	(0.03)	0.05	(0.10)	Max		470	(9.0)	472	(6.7)	470	(11.7)	0.68	(6.11)
Russian Federation	-0.75	(0.10)	-2.52	(0.10)	-0.70	(0.06)	0.90	(0.03)	459	(9.2)	462	(8.3)	460	(7.1)	0.41	(3.52)
Spain	0.52	(0.06)	-0.59	(0.11)	0.85	(0.03)	Max		485	(5.3)	496	(4.4)	492	(6.1)	2.90	(3.41)
Sweden	-0.25	(0.07)	-1.54	(0.06)	-0.21	(0.06)	Max		511	(6.8)	513	(3.2)	527	(3.9)	7.88	(2.53)
Switzerland	0.35	(0.06)	-0.78	(0.07)	0.61	(0.05)	Max		479	(10.4)	497	(8.1)	503	(11.2)	18.74	(6.30)
Thailand	-1.20	(0.08)	-2.79	(0.08)	-1.18	(0.06)	0.47	(0.12)	420	(5.7)	429	(4.1)	446	(8.2)	8.40	(2.50)
United Kingdom	-0.40	(0.07)	-1.71	(0.06)	-0.42	(0.06)	Max		507	(7.3)	519	(5.4)	556	(7.5)	18.47	(3.49)
United States	0.20	(0.08)	-1.18	(0.09)	0.48	(0.07)	Max		488	(10.3)	510	(7.7)	513	(11.5)	13.54	(4.21)
OECD average	*0.00*	*(0.01)*	*-1.24*	*(0.03)*	*0.12*	*(0.01)*	*Max*		*488*	*(1.9)*	*502*	*(1.1)*	*510*	*(1.7)*	*9.36*	*(0.96)*
OECD total	*-0.01*	*(0.03)*	*-1.32*	*(0.03)*	*0.14*	*(0.02)*	*Max*		*481*	*(3.2)*	*503*	*(2.3)*	*509*	*(3.6)*	*13.65*	*(1.39)*
Netherlands[1]	-0.37	(0.09)	-1.37	(0.06)	-0.41	(0.06)	0.67	(0.08)	508	(13.8)	543	(7.0)	529	(11.6)	18.48	(7.84)

1. For the definition of the index see Annex A1. *The scale was inverted so that positive and high values indicate that teacher shortage is perceived as less of a problem than on OECD average.* "Max" is used in cases where more than 25 per cent of the students are enrolled in schools in which the responses from school principals correspond to the highest value on the index, which is 0.95.

2. For explained variation see Annex A2. Unit changes marked in bold are statistically significant. Where bottom and top quarters are marked in bold this indicates that their difference is statistically significant.

3. Response rate is too low to ensure comparability (see Annex A3).

Table 7.5
Class size in the language of assessment and performance on the combined reading literacy scale, by national quarters of of lowest to highest class size

| | Class size | | | | Mean class size | | | | | | Performance on the combined reading literacy scale, by national quartiles of class size | | | | | |
| | All students | | Share of students with ratio >50 | | Bottom quarter | | Middle half | | Top quarter | | Bottom quarter | | Middle half | | Top quarter | |
	Mean	S.E.	Mean	S.E.	Mean	S.E.	Mean	S.E.	Mean	S.E.	Mean	S.E.	Mean	S.E.	Mean	S.E.
Albania	30.5	(0.4)	1.6	(0.3)	14.6	(0.4)	31.5	(0.2)	44.1	(0.2)	308	(5.3)	364	(4.5)	394	(4.9)
Argentina	30.0	(0.6)	0.2	(0.1)	20.5	(0.5)	30.3	(0.3)	39.1	(0.5)	390	(12.7)	428	(11.9)	463	(8.9)
Australia	24.3	(0.2)	a	a	17.3	(0.3)	24.9	(0.1)	30.1	(0.1)	516	(4.6)	532	(4.7)	541	(4.7)
Austria	22.6	(0.3)	a	a	11.8	(0.4)	23.3	(0.2)	31.9	(0.2)	454	(5.0)	528	(3.5)	532	(4.4)
Belgium	18.6	(0.2)	0.0	(0.0)	11.0	(0.2)	19.1	(0.1)	25.4	(0.1)	446	(7.6)	527	(3.5)	556	(3.7)
Brazil	38.8	(0.6)	7.9	(1.5)	26.1	(0.3)	39.6	(0.2)	50.1	(0.4)	393	(5.7)	399	(4.0)	402	(5.3)
Bulgaria	22.5	(0.2)	a	a	16.8	(0.1)	23.2	(0.1)	26.9	(0.1)	406	(6.5)	441	(4.4)	462	(8.5)
Canada	25.7	(0.1)	0.3	(0.0)	17.4	(0.1)	26.7	(0.0)	31.8	(0.1)	512	(2.9)	544	(1.5)	551	(1.9)
Chile	36.1	(0.3)	a	a	25.9	(0.4)	37.4	(0.1)	43.9	(0.1)	415	(6.8)	410	(5.1)	422	(6.1)
Czech Republic	24.8	(0.2)	a	a	17.9	(0.2)	25.4	(0.1)	30.4	(0.1)	470	(4.6)	500	(3.1)	538	(4.4)
Denmark	17.4	(0.2)	a	a	12.7	(0.2)	17.6	(0.1)	21.9	(0.1)	486	(5.6)	510	(2.6)	515	(4.4)
Finland	19.5	(0.2)	a	a	14.6	(0.1)	19.4	(0.1)	24.5	(0.2)	535	(6.9)	548	(1.9)	564	(3.5)
France	27.2	(0.2)	a	a	19.4	(0.3)	27.9	(0.1)	33.8	(0.1)	451	(5.8)	508	(3.7)	567	(2.2)
Germany	24.1	(0.2)	a	a	17.5	(0.2)	24.5	(0.1)	29.8	(0.1)	455	(5.9)	501	(3.7)	527	(4.5)
Greece	24.8	(0.3)	a	a	18.3	(0.3)	25.1	(0.1)	30.8	(0.2)	448	(7.5)	484	(6.1)	493	(8.5)
Hong Kong-China	38.0	(0.2)	a	a	29.8	(0.4)	39.6	(0.0)	42.9	(0.1)	486	(7.6)	536	(2.9)	552	(4.1)
Hungary	28.1	(0.3)	a	a	19.2	(0.3)	28.9	(0.1)	35.5	(0.2)	448	(6.6)	485	(5.7)	507	(7.6)
Iceland	19.3	(0.1)	a	a	10.9	(0.1)	19.7	(0.0)	26.8	(0.1)	485	(3.5)	508	(1.9)	543	(2.8)
Indonesia	a	a	a	a	a	a	a	a	a	a	a	a	a	a	a	a
Ireland	24.1	(0.2)	a	a	16.2	(0.2)	24.9	(0.1)	30.5	(0.1)	485	(6.5)	536	(3.5)	554	(3.5)
Israel	29.8	(0.7)	0.5	(0.3)	16.5	(0.5)	31.2	(0.3)	40.3	(0.4)	421	(11.0)	485	(7.7)	472	(12.8)
Italy	22.0	(0.2)	0.0	(0.0)	16.4	(0.2)	22.3	(0.1)	27.2	(0.1)	483	(5.8)	491	(3.4)	491	(5.5)
Japan	38.8	(0.4)	0.4	(0.4)	32.0	(0.7)	39.9	(0.0)	43.1	(0.4)	504	(12.0)	537	(5.6)	534	(9.3)
Korea	37.6	(0.4)	0.6	(0.4)	24.1	(0.9)	39.9	(0.1)	46.4	(0.3)	498	(5.5)	543	(2.8)	548	(4.0)
Latvia	21.4	(0.4)	0.0	(0.0)	12.1	(0.3)	21.8	(0.2)	29.9	(0.1)	436	(8.7)	467	(6.5)	486	(7.8)
Liechtenstein	14.8	(0.1)	a	a	10.3	(0.3)	15.0	(0.1)	18.8	(0.2)	450	(10.0)	478	(6.1)	535	(8.2)
Luxembourg	20.7	(0.1)	0.1	(0.0)	13.9	(0.1)	21.2	(0.1)	26.4	(0.1)	395	(3.3)	456	(2.1)	495	(3.2)
FYR Macedonia	31.5	(0.1)	0.0	(0.0)	23.5	(0.2)	32.5	(0.0)	37.6	(0.1)	345	(3.2)	394	(2.1)	396	(3.0)
Mexico	35.0	(0.6)	7.7	(1.8)	20.1	(0.4)	35.1	(0.3)	49.6	(1.0)	393	(5.8)	422	(4.7)	462	(7.9)
New Zealand	25.0	(0.2)	a	a	17.5	(0.2)	25.9	(0.1)	30.7	(0.1)	492	(5.7)	548	(3.5)	546	(4.0)
Norway	22.7	(0.3)	0.3	(0.2)	15.8	(0.4)	23.3	(0.1)	28.6	(0.4)	496	(7.0)	510	(3.5)	515	(4.7)
Peru	33.1	(0.6)	2.1	(0.9)	19.8	(0.6)	34.1	(0.2)	44.4	(0.5)	314	(11.7)	333	(4.9)	345	(8.7)
Poland	29.4	(0.4)	a	a	22.2	(0.6)	30.3	(0.1)	34.9	(0.1)	451	(6.2)	495	(5.3)	503	(11.2)
Portugal	22.2	(0.2)	a	a	15.1	(0.2)	22.5	(0.1)	28.4	(0.1)	453	(6.8)	475	(5.6)	486	(5.7)
Russian Federation	23.5	(0.3)	a	a	15.3	(0.3)	24.2	(0.1)	30.5	(0.2)	445	(8.5)	472	(4.9)	469	(5.3)
Spain	24.4	(0.3)	a	a	16.2	(0.3)	24.9	(0.1)	31.7	(0.4)	479	(5.1)	496	(3.6)	511	(5.2)
Sweden	21.2	(0.3)	a	a	14.3	(0.2)	21.5	(0.1)	27.7	(0.2)	504	(3.9)	526	(2.7)	528	(4.2)
Switzerland	18.2	(0.2)	a	a	11.9	(0.2)	18.7	(0.1)	23.6	(0.1)	448	(5.0)	508	(5.1)	535	(5.3)
Thailand	35.2	(0.5)	4.7	(1.0)	21.6	(0.4)	35.8	(0.3)	47.7	(0.3)	422	(5.7)	430	(3.3)	459	(7.2)
United Kingdom	24.9	(0.2)	0.1	(0.1)	17.2	(0.2)	25.9	(0.1)	30.6	(0.1)	500	(6.2)	534	(3.8)	539	(3.1)
United States	23.5	(0.4)	0.3	(0.1)	14.3	(0.3)	24.0	(0.1)	31.8	(0.3)	490	(10.4)	514	(5.8)	522	(7.9)
OECD average	24.6	(0.1)	0.4	(0.1)	15.1	(0.1)	24.2	(0.0)	34.8	(0.1)	480	(1.3)	510	(0.8)	520	(1.2)
OECD total	27.7	(0.2)	0.8	(0.2)	16.5	(0.1)	27.0	(0.1)	39.9	(0.2)	483	(3.8)	509	(2.0)	516	(2.6)
Netherlands[1]	23.8	(0.3)	a	a	16.7	(0.3)	24.5	(0.1)	29.5	(0.1)	482	(7.6)	548	(3.9)	566	(4.1)

1. Response rate is too low to ensure comparability (see Annex A3).

Table 7.6
Percentage[1] of students enrolled in schools which have at least some responsibility for the following aspects of school policy and management
Results based on reports from school principals and reported proportionate to the number of 15-year-olds enrolled in the school

	Appointing teachers		Dismissing teachers		Establishing teachers' starting salaries		Determining teachers' salary increases		Formulating the school budget		Deciding on budget allocations within the school	
	%	S.E.	%	S.E.	%	S.E.	%	S.E.	%	S.E.	%	S.E.
Albania	13.3	(2.4)	14.3	(2.5)	5.4	(1.6)	5.3	(1.6)	25.7	(2.4)	42.2	(3.4)
Argentina	39.3	(8.1)	33.4	(8.5)	3.1	(1.7)	3.4	(1.8)	32.0	(6.2)	47.1	(5.9)
Australia	59.7	(2.2)	47.3	(3.1)	18.1	(2.2)	18.7	(2.6)	95.7	(1.5)	99.6	(0.2)
Austria	14.6	(2.9)	5.3	(1.7)	0.7	(0.5)	0.7	(0.5)	13.7	(2.7)	92.5	(2.0)
Belgium	95.9	(1.3)	95.0	(1.4)	6.6	(1.7)	6.9	(1.8)	97.8	(1.0)	99.2	(0.6)
Brazil	39.2	(2.7)	32.7	(2.9)	9.8	(1.7)	9.5	(1.7)	55.3	(3.4)	74.8	(2.8)
Bulgaria	99.2	(0.8)	98.6	(1.0)	15.2	(4.4)	13.2	(4.5)	27.4	(4.6)	69.3	(3.9)
Canada	81.7	(1.2)	60.6	(1.7)	33.7	(1.8)	34.0	(1.7)	77.3	(1.4)	98.7	(0.3)
Chile	48.3	(2.2)	47.0	(2.1)	30.4	(2.6)	27.3	(2.6)	61.5	(3.3)	65.1	(3.3)
Czech Republic	96.5	(1.2)	94.8	(1.3)	70.4	(3.1)	73.3	(3.1)	83.1	(2.6)	99.1	(0.6)
Denmark	97.0	(1.3)	56.8	(3.2)	13.2	(2.5)	15.3	(2.7)	89.3	(2.2)	97.9	(1.0)
Finland	35.1	(3.8)	21.3	(3.3)	1.1	(0.8)	1.7	(1.0)	56.1	(3.9)	98.7	(0.9)
France	m	m	m	m	m	m	m	m	m	m	m	m
Germany	10.1	(2.3)	3.5	(1.3)	2.0	(0.9)	11.0	(2.2)	12.8	(2.0)	95.6	(1.3)
Greece	65.2	(4.7)	69.6	(4.4)	72.6	(4.3)	76.7	(3.9)	86.7	(3.4)	94.7	(2.1)
Hong Kong-China	91.2	(1.5)	86.9	(2.3)	26.1	(3.6)	8.1	(1.8)	93.7	(2.1)	97.9	(1.2)
Hungary	100.0	(0.0)	98.5	(1.0)	41.0	(4.3)	50.4	(4.3)	60.6	(4.1)	92.2	(2.3)
Iceland	99.5	(0.0)	98.8	(0.1)	4.0	(0.1)	7.4	(0.1)	75.9	(0.2)	87.1	(0.1)
Indonesia	73.4	(4.2)	65.0	(5.2)	64.5	(4.0)	64.3	(5.3)	96.9	(1.7)	97.4	(0.9)
Ireland	87.9	(2.5)	73.3	(3.0)	4.3	(1.7)	5.4	(2.2)	79.1	(3.1)	100.0	(0.0)
Israel	96.8	(1.3)	88.8	(3.3)	51.2	(6.4)	21.1	(4.2)	79.7	(5.9)	95.0	(2.0)
Italy	10.3	(2.1)	10.9	(2.6)	1.1	(0.8)	1.0	(0.8)	93.7	(2.4)	57.1	(5.0)
Japan	33.1	(1.9)	32.5	(2.0)	32.5	(2.0)	32.5	(2.0)	50.4	(3.3)	91.2	(2.9)
Korea	32.3	(4.1)	22.1	(4.0)	14.6	(3.1)	7.0	(2.4)	88.0	(2.5)	94.7	(1.7)
Latvia	100.0	(0.0)	99.0	(0.9)	24.9	(4.2)	34.8	(5.2)	32.8	(4.5)	89.0	(3.8)
Liechtenstein	m	m	m	m	m	m	m	m	m	m	m	m
Luxembourg	m	m	m	m	m	m	m	m	100.0	(0.0)	100.0	(0.0)
FYR Macedonia	97.0	(1.5)	96.7	(0.1)	20.4	(0.4)	20.3	(0.4)	53.3	(1.0)	77.9	(0.6)
Mexico	57.1	(3.4)	47.9	(3.8)	25.8	(3.1)	27.7	(3.1)	67.6	(4.2)	77.3	(3.7)
New Zealand	100.0	(0.0)	99.2	(0.8)	17.2	(2.4)	40.8	(3.3)	97.7	(1.1)	100.0	(0.0)
Norway	m	m	m	m	m	m	m	m	m	m	m	m
Peru	75.0	(3.3)	30.6	(3.8)	14.3	(2.4)	12.0	(2.2)	79.2	(4.0)	68.3	(4.2)
Poland	m	m	m	m	m	m	m	m	m	m	m	m
Portugal	12.7	(2.1)	8.7	(1.2)	0.9	(0.7)	0.9	(0.7)	88.9	(2.9)	94.9	(2.0)
Russian Federation	99.6	(0.4)	98.5	(0.7)	41.2	(3.2)	46.9	(3.3)	47.4	(4.0)	70.1	(3.8)
Spain	37.7	(2.5)	38.7	(2.6)	9.2	(2.2)	9.0	(2.2)	89.7	(2.5)	98.2	(1.3)
Sweden	99.0	(0.8)	82.8	(3.2)	61.8	(3.6)	73.6	(3.6)	85.1	(3.1)	99.4	(0.6)
Switzerland	92.6	(1.7)	82.0	(2.3)	12.7	(2.7)	14.8	(3.0)	54.3	(3.3)	86.9	(2.9)
Thailand	30.4	(3.0)	43.8	(3.7)	26.5	(2.7)	95.4	(1.9)	75.9	(3.2)	89.6	(1.9)
United Kingdom	99.2	(0.3)	88.6	(1.3)	71.7	(3.0)	70.3	(3.1)	92.1	(0.8)	99.9	(0.1)
United States	97.1	(0.9)	97.7	(1.2)	76.2	(4.9)	74.3	(5.1)	95.9	(1.9)	98.7	(1.0)
OECD average	*61.5*	*(0.4)*	*53.6*	*(0.5)*	*23.4*	*(0.5)*	*25.9*	*(0.5)*	*76.1*	*(0.6)*	*94.5*	*(0.3)*
Cross-country correlation with country's average achievement on the combined reading literacy scale[2] — OECD countries	0.16		0.10		-0.05		-0.06		0.00		0.37	
Cross-country correlation — All PISA countries	0.14		0.13		0.00		-0.02		0.26		**0.66**	
Netherlands[3]	100.0	(0.0)	100.0	(0.0)	71.5	(5.0)	45.3	(5.6)	100.0	(0.0)	100.0	(0.0)

1. Percentages are calculated from non-missing (valid) cases only.
2. Correlation values indicated in bold are statistically significant.
3. Response rate is too low to ensure comparability (see Annex A3).

Table 7.6 (continued)
Percentage[1] of students enrolled in schools which have at least some responsibility for the following aspects of school policy and management

Results based on reports from school principals and reported proportionate to the number of 15-year-olds enrolled in the school

	Establishing student disciplinary policies		Establishing student assessment policies		Approving students for admittance to school		Choosing which textbooks are used		Determining course content		Deciding which courses are offered	
	%	S.E.	%	S.E.	%	S.E.	%	S.E.	%	S.E.	%	S.E.
Albania	75.4	(2.8)	72.2	(3.0)	78.5	(2.6)	13.9	(2.3)	12.1	(2.0)	14.0	(2.6)
Argentina	89.6	(2.7)	81.0	(4.0)	85.0	(2.7)	100.0	(0.0)	73.6	(7.7)	73.4	(4.8)
Australia	99.6	(0.2)	98.8	(0.6)	93.5	(1.6)	99.7	(0.2)	84.4	(3.2)	95.9	(1.8)
Austria	96.4	(1.6)	69.3	(3.5)	74.6	(2.9)	99.3	(0.7)	54.0	(3.6)	56.8	(3.7)
Belgium	98.7	(0.9)	99.6	(0.4)	94.7	(1.7)	98.5	(0.6)	58.6	(3.7)	60.7	(3.6)
Brazil	97.9	(0.7)	90.7	(1.8)	79.1	(3.3)	99.7	(0.3)	90.3	(2.2)	57.1	(3.4)
Bulgaria	95.7	(1.2)	85.5	(3.1)	83.9	(2.9)	95.4	(1.7)	35.8	(4.6)	85.0	(2.8)
Canada	98.5	(0.5)	94.1	(1.0)	89.2	(1.0)	89.1	(0.9)	48.9	(1.8)	89.8	(1.1)
Chile	99.3	(0.7)	98.0	(1.2)	93.5	(2.2)	90.8	(2.2)	85.8	(3.1)	93.5	(1.9)
Czech Republic	99.5	(0.5)	99.6	(0.3)	89.2	(1.7)	100.0	(0.0)	81.9	(2.9)	81.5	(2.8)
Denmark	98.9	(0.8)	86.9	(2.4)	87.1	(2.6)	100.0	(0.0)	89.8	(1.9)	76.8	(2.6)
Finland	95.6	(1.9)	89.0	(2.6)	53.8	(4.0)	100.0	(0.0)	91.4	(2.3)	94.7	(2.0)
France	m	m	m	m	m	m	m	m	m	m	m	m
Germany	95.3	(1.4)	79.3	(2.8)	79.3	(3.0)	95.5	(1.7)	34.9	(3.3)	35.1	(3.4)
Greece	96.5	(1.5)	94.2	(2.2)	89.7	(2.5)	89.8	(2.9)	91.6	(2.6)	89.3	(2.9)
Hong Kong-China	100.0	(0.0)	100.0	(0.0)	97.3	(1.3)	100.0	(0.0)	97.5	(1.3)	99.7	(0.3)
Hungary	100.0	(0.0)	98.1	(1.0)	98.7	(0.7)	99.6	(0.4)	97.0	(1.3)	98.4	(1.0)
Iceland	99.5	(0.0)	98.5	(0.1)	74.2	(0.1)	98.7	(0.0)	78.8	(0.2)	61.6	(0.2)
Indonesia	100.0	(0.0)	100.0	(0.0)	99.7	(0.3)	98.3	(0.7)	80.1	(3.4)	96.2	(1.5)
Ireland	99.4	(0.6)	98.7	(0.9)	95.2	(2.0)	100.0	(0.0)	36.9	(4.1)	97.4	(1.3)
Israel	100.0	(0.0)	99.2	(0.8)	90.3	(2.8)	99.4	(0.6)	80.9	(6.0)	92.8	(2.1)
Italy	100.0	(0.0)	100.0	(0.0)	62.7	(5.1)	100.0	(0.0)	93.2	(2.9)	21.6	(4.0)
Japan	99.6	(0.4)	100.0	(0.0)	100.0	(0.0)	99.3	(0.7)	99.3	(0.7)	97.8	(1.3)
Korea	100.0	(0.0)	98.8	(0.1)	96.5	(1.4)	99.4	(0.6)	99.4	(0.6)	93.2	(2.3)
Latvia	99.9	(0.1)	77.4	(4.6)	98.1	(1.3)	99.4	(0.6)	75.9	(4.9)	90.2	(3.5)
Liechtenstein	m	m	m	m	m	m	m	m	m	m	m	m
Luxembourg	m	m	m	m	100.0	(0.0)	m	m	m	m	m	m
FYR Macedonia	98.4	(0.0)	97.0	(0.1)	98.8	(0.0)	56.2	(0.9)	30.9	(0.6)	33.9	(0.7)
Mexico	99.3	(0.7)	92.2	(2.5)	85.9	(2.3)	81.3	(3.0)	58.8	(4.1)	58.2	(3.4)
New Zealand	100.0	(0.0)	100.0	(0.0)	94.4	(1.2)	100.0	(0.0)	87.2	(2.7)	99.9	(0.1)
Norway	m	m	m	m	m	m	m	m	m	m	m	m
Peru	99.5	(0.5)	97.4	(1.2)	97.2	(1.3)	89.1	(2.6)	84.5	(3.1)	56.4	(4.4)
Poland	m	m	m	m	m	m	m	m	m	m	m	m
Portugal	91.7	(2.2)	88.4	(2.6)	85.0	(3.1)	100.0	(0.0)	20.3	(3.4)	54.2	(4.5)
Russian Federation	100.0	(0.0)	99.6	(0.4)	99.2	(0.6)	97.4	(1.0)	94.5	(1.4)	95.5	(1.3)
Spain	99.1	(0.8)	96.6	(1.5)	89.3	(2.4)	99.6	(0.4)	86.0	(2.9)	54.4	(3.8)
Sweden	100.0	(0.0)	96.7	(1.5)	54.1	(4.0)	100.0	(0.0)	87.6	(2.8)	76.2	(3.7)
Switzerland	97.7	(1.2)	74.6	(3.6)	81.7	(3.0)	50.7	(4.1)	29.5	(3.5)	34.2	(3.4)
Thailand	98.4	(1.0)	94.9	(1.5)	98.4	(1.0)	97.7	(0.9)	92.6	(2.1)	98.2	(1.0)
United Kingdom	99.5	(0.5)	99.6	(0.2)	66.4	(3.6)	100.0	(0.0)	93.5	(1.5)	99.8	(0.1)
United States	98.5	(0.9)	93.2	(2.2)	88.9	(2.6)	92.2	(3.0)	84.0	(4.3)	97.3	(1.3)
OECD average	*94.5*	*(0.2)*	*89.4*	*(0.4)*	*83.7*	*(0.5)*	*91.7*	*(0.2)*	*69.2*	*(0.6)*	*70.9*	*(0.6)*
Cross-country correlation with country's average achievement on the combined reading literacy scale[2] — OECD countries	0.21		0.20		-0.21		0.30		0.25		**0.51**	
Cross-country correlation with country's average achievement on the combined reading literacy scale[2] — All PISA countries	**0.42**		0.21		-0.27		**0.47**		0.24		**0.36**	
Netherlands[3]	100.0	(0.0)	100.0	(0.0)	100.0	(0.0)	100.0	(0.0)	91.7	(3.2)	94.9	(2.4)

1. Percentages are calculated from non-missing (valid) cases only.
2. Correlation values indicated in bold are statistically significant.
3. Response rate is too low to ensure comparability (see Annex A3).

Table 7.7
Percentage[1] of students enrolled in schools in which teachers have the main responsibility for the following aspects of school policy and management
Results based on reports from school principals and reported proportionate to the number of 15-year-olds enrolled in the school

	Appointing teachers		Dismissing teachers		Establishing teachers' starting salaries		Determining teachers' salary increases		Formulating the school budget		Deciding on budget allocations within the school	
	%	S.E.	%	S.E.	%	S.E.	%	S.E.	%	S.E.	%	S.E.
Albania	2.4	(1.0)	1.5	(1.1)	2.5	(1.1)	3.3	(1.2)	2.8	(1.2)	3.3	(1.2)
Argentina	0.5	(0.5)	0.5	(0.5)	m	m	0.5	(0.5)	0.4	(0.5)	1.9	(1.0)
Australia	1.4	(1.0)	m	m	0.3	(0.2)	1.2	(0.7)	11.3	(2.5)	12.6	(2.6)
Austria	1.7	(0.9)	1.7	(1.0)	m	m	m	m	3.7	(1.3)	22.6	(3.0)
Belgium	0.6	(0.6)	0.4	(0.4)	m	m	m	m	3.0	(1.3)	8.1	(2.0)
Brazil	1.4	(1.3)	m	m	m	m	m	m	7.2	(2.2)	15.7	(2.8)
Bulgaria	2.7	(1.6)	0.7	(0.7)	m	m	m	m	6.1	(4.2)	5.6	(3.6)
Canada	2.2	(0.4)	m	m	1.0	(0.4)	1.1	(0.4)	7.8	(0.8)	20.4	(1.4)
Chile	1.2	(0.8)	m	m	m	m	m	m	4.9	(1.6)	6.9	(1.8)
Czech Republic	m	m	0.6	(0.6)	m	m	m	m	1.3	(0.6)	6.1	(1.8)
Denmark	19.5	(2.6)	1.6	(0.9)	m	m	0.9	(0.6)	12.7	(2.3)	21.7	(3.0)
Finland	1.0	(0.7)	1.7	(0.9)	0.4	(0.4)	m	m	15.8	(2.8)	39.0	(4.2)
France	m	m	m	m	m	m	m	m	m	m	m	m
Germany	0.9	(0.5)	0.5	(0.3)	0.5	(0.3)	0.5	(0.3)	6.8	(1.5)	38.1	(3.6)
Greece	0.4	(0.4)	0.8	(0.6)	m	m	m	m	m	m	0.1	(0.1)
Hong Kong-China	4.5	(1.8)	m	m	m	m	m	m	12.1	(2.9)	6.7	(2.1)
Hungary	m	m	0.5	(0.5)	m	m	0.8	(0.8)	2.9	(1.2)	7.4	(2.2)
Iceland	m	m	m	m	m	m	m	m	3.9	(0.1)	11.6	(0.2)
Indonesia	4.3	(1.8)	4.1	(2.1)	0.8	(0.5)	4.1	(1.6)	12.3	(3.0)	10.0	(3.3)
Ireland	0.9	(1.0)	m	m	m	m	m	m	4.2	(1.8)	7.4	(1.8)
Israel	0.0	(0.0)	m	m	m	m	m	m	0.4	(0.5)	4.3	(1.9)
Italy	m	m	m	m	m	m	m	m	m	m	m	m
Japan	0.7	(0.7)	m	m	m	m	m	m	m	m	4.7	(1.8)
Korea	0.8	(0.8)	m	m	0.8	(0.8)	0.8	(0.8)	4.1	(1.9)	2.6	(1.5)
Latvia	m	m	m	m	m	m	2.2	(1.2)	m	m	1.8	(1.0)
Liechtenstein	m	m	m	m	m	m	m	m	m	m	m	m
Luxembourg	m	m	m	m	m	m	m	m	m	m	m	m
FYR Macedonia	m	m	1.3	(0.0)	0.2	(0.0)	0.2	(0.0)	m	m	6.2	(0.1)
Mexico	2.2	(1.1)	1.2	(0.9)	m	m	m	m	2.2	(1.0)	3.1	(1.3)
New Zealand	m	m	m	m	m	m	m	m	4.9	(1.8)	6.2	(1.7)
Norway	m	m	m	m	m	m	m	m	m	m	m	m
Peru	8.5	(2.2)	0.8	(0.6)	m	m	m	m	15.1	(2.9)	14.3	(2.8)
Poland	m	m	m	m	m	m	m	m	m	m	m	m
Portugal	m	m	m	m	m	m	m	m	1.3	(0.9)	3.6	(1.6)
Russian Federation	m	m	0.4	(0.2)	m	m	1.9	(1.1)	m	m	m	m
Spain	0.6	(0.6)	0.6	(0.6)	0.6	(0.6)	0.6	(0.6)	4.5	(1.4)	5.5	(1.7)
Sweden	5.5	(1.6)	m	m	0.6	(0.5)	0.6	(0.5)	2.8	(1.4)	13.9	(2.7)
Switzerland	4.7	(1.8)	1.8	(1.2)	m	m	m	m	11.8	(2.7)	31.5	(3.3)
Thailand	m	m	m	m	m	m	1.1	(0.7)	2.0	(1.1)	3.5	(1.6)
United Kingdom	3.0	(1.3)	m	m	m	m	m	m	0.9	(0.6)	4.3	(1.6)
United States	9.5	(3.2)	m	m	8.6	(3.1)	12.4	(3.9)	13.5	(4.4)	24.2	(4.9)
OECD average	*2.2*	*(0.2)*	*0.5*	*(0.1)*	*0.4*	*(0.1)*	*0.7*	*(0.1)*	*4.8*	*(0.3)*	*12.0*	*(0.5)*
Cross-country correlation with country's average achievement on the combined reading literacy scale[2] — OECD countries	-0.09		0.25		-0.21		0.00		0.35		0.24	
All PISA countries	-0.05		-0.26		0.02		-0.01		0.04		0.28	
Netherlands[3]	3.9	(2.3)	2.4	(1.8)	m	m	0.8	(0.7)	m	m	1.8	(1.9)

1. Percentages are calculated from non-missing (valid) cases only.
2. Correlation values indicated in bold are statistically significant.
3. Response rate is too low to ensure comparability (see Annex A3).

© OECD/UNESCO-UIS 2003

Table 7.7 (continued)
Percentage[1] of students enrolled in schools in which teachers have the main responsibility for the following aspects of school policy and management
Results based on reports from school principals and reported proportionate to the number of 15-year-olds enrolled in the school

	Establishing student disciplinary policies		Establishing student assessment policies		Approving students for admittance to school		Choosing which textbooks are used		Determining course content		Deciding which courses are offered	
	%	S.E.	%	S.E.	%	S.E.	%	S.E.	%	S.E.	%	S.E.
Albania	21.6	(2.8)	63.0	(3.5)	3.7	(1.5)	10.2	(2.3)	10.0	(1.9)	7.4	(2.0)
Argentina	52.6	(6.0)	62.4	(5.8)	6.3	(2.0)	89.1	(4.9)	61.4	(5.9)	29.9	(5.7)
Australia	60.8	(3.7)	57.4	(3.9)	1.2	(0.8)	63.2	(4.4)	63.0	(3.9)	38.6	(4.1)
Austria	67.0	(3.3)	68.1	(2.9)	12.9	(2.5)	90.1	(2.1)	55.1	(3.8)	42.0	(4.0)
Belgium	45.7	(4.6)	52.4	(3.5)	17.6	(2.9)	89.0	(2.2)	59.8	(3.7)	24.5	(3.1)
Brazil	52.7	(3.8)	62.8	(3.6)	14.3	(3.0)	93.1	(1.5)	83.6	(2.4)	33.3	(4.2)
Bulgaria	56.2	(4.3)	80.7	(3.4)	26.2	(4.0)	90.5	(2.5)	35.0	(4.4)	43.8	(5.3)
Canada	58.8	(2.0)	64.1	(1.9)	1.7	(0.5)	65.8	(1.9)	47.1	(1.8)	39.0	(1.9)
Chile	52.6	(4.1)	57.9	(4.0)	26.0	(3.5)	80.5	(3.0)	74.7	(3.5)	31.2	(3.5)
Czech Republic	51.0	(3.5)	59.1	(3.5)	5.7	(1.3)	66.6	(3.3)	45.2	(3.7)	11.7	(2.5)
Denmark	59.0	(3.9)	53.4	(4.0)	13.1	(2.0)	85.7	(2.7)	88.9	(2.2)	52.4	(3.5)
Finland	86.7	(2.8)	92.4	(2.2)	5.9	(2.0)	94.2	(1.9)	97.9	(1.2)	82.1	(3.3)
France	m	m	m	m	m	m	m	m	m	m	m	m
Germany	64.7	(3.1)	79.0	(3.0)	3.1	(1.2)	52.3	(3.3)	37.3	(3.7)	22.4	(3.3)
Greece	41.5	(4.6)	25.0	(4.1)	3.3	(1.7)	9.0	(2.4)	2.7	(1.7)	3.4	(2.0)
Hong Kong-China	40.3	(4.2)	53.7	(4.2)	27.6	(3.9)	55.9	(4.1)	55.8	(4.4)	28.2	(3.7)
Hungary	59.2	(4.5)	67.6	(4.2)	16.2	(3.1)	82.7	(3.0)	81.4	(3.2)	32.7	(4.1)
Iceland	76.3	(0.2)	85.3	(0.1)	4.9	(0.1)	96.8	(0.0)	77.9	(0.2)	47.6	(0.2)
Indonesia	52.7	(4.7)	76.7	(3.9)	20.9	(3.5)	81.3	(3.0)	22.2	(3.7)	39.5	(5.7)
Ireland	72.3	(4.0)	74.3	(4.2)	15.9	(3.0)	97.6	(1.8)	47.0	(3.8)	52.1	(4.1)
Israel	35.5	(5.1)	39.8	(5.3)	4.8	(1.7)	39.8	(6.8)	32.1	(5.7)	18.0	(5.1)
Italy	16.5	(4.4)	93.3	(2.9)	2.8	(1.7)	89.3	(3.4)	55.2	(6.0)	20.7	(4.0)
Japan	25.3	(3.5)	22.0	(3.6)	6.1	(2.2)	34.5	(4.2)	24.6	(3.6)	26.2	(4.0)
Korea	9.4	(2.5)	19.8	(4.0)	0.6	(0.6)	68.8	(3.9)	87.1	(2.8)	16.5	(3.3)
Latvia	30.5	(5.0)	38.6	(4.3)	2.2	(1.3)	87.5	(3.2)	56.2	(5.7)	21.1	(3.3)
Liechtenstein	m	m	m	m	m	m	m	m	m	m	m	m
Luxembourg	m	m	m	m	m	m	m	m	m	m	m	m
FYR Macedonia	68.0	(1.2)	84.1	(0.3)	45.4	(0.8)	50.3	(0.9)	23.5	(0.5)	23.6	(0.4)
Mexico	32.8	(3.5)	49.1	(3.7)	9.7	(2.4)	62.4	(4.0)	32.8	(3.8)	18.7	(3.4)
New Zealand	37.8	(3.8)	39.2	(3.7)	1.7	(0.7)	57.4	(3.8)	49.8	(3.8)	24.1	(3.4)
Norway	m	m	m	m	m	m	m	m	m	m	m	m
Peru	45.7	(3.9)	60.2	(3.9)	20.7	(3.3)	84.7	(2.9)	78.7	(3.5)	31.3	(3.8)
Poland	m	m	m	m	m	m	m	m	m	m	m	m
Portugal	61.2	(4.5)	77.9	(3.4)	1.2	(0.9)	87.6	(2.7)	19.5	(3.3)	19.4	(3.4)
Russian Federation	3.0	(1.2)	10.0	(1.8)	1.6	(1.0)	78.6	(2.2)	18.1	(2.2)	33.7	(3.1)
Spain	36.7	(3.8)	75.1	(4.3)	0.6	(0.6)	74.2	(3.1)	73.5	(3.3)	12.4	(2.6)
Sweden	40.1	(3.9)	64.2	(3.6)	5.2	(1.8)	83.0	(3.3)	77.8	(3.1)	49.3	(4.3)
Switzerland	82.2	(2.8)	69.7	(3.4)	13.0	(2.7)	56.2	(3.7)	35.8	(4.0)	42.1	(3.5)
Thailand	11.3	(2.5)	10.6	(2.4)	2.8	(1.2)	35.8	(4.4)	51.8	(4.3)	18.4	(2.9)
United Kingdom	42.3	(4.0)	47.8	(3.9)	3.4	(1.5)	93.2	(1.3)	87.6	(2.0)	50.2	(3.9)
United States	38.2	(6.0)	35.1	(5.0)	3.1	(2.1)	71.6	(5.4)	61.3	(4.8)	47.2	(6.1)
OECD average	48.8	(0.7)	56.7	(0.8)	6.2	(0.4)	70.2	(0.6)	54.7	(0.7)	32.0	(0.8)
Cross-country correlation with country's average achievement on the combined reading literacy scale[2] — OECD countries	0.16		-0.03		-0.15		0.22		**0.46**		**0.55**	
Cross-country correlation with country's average achievement on the combined reading literacy scale[2] — All PISA countries	0.16		-0.04		**-0.42**		0.18		0.31		**0.36**	
Netherlands[3]	19.2	(5.0)	27.2	(5.6)	8.7	(3.5)	75.6	(4.1)	75.0	(4.7)	15.3	(4.3)

1. Percentages are calculated from non-missing (valid) cases only.
2. Correlation values indicated in bold are statistically significant.
3. Response rate is too low to ensure comparability (see Annex A3).

Table 7.8
Index of principals' perception of teachers' morale and commitment and performance on the combined reading literacy scale, by national quarters of the index

Results based on reports from school principals and reported proportionate to the number of 15-year-olds enrolled in the school

| | Index of school principals' perception of teachers' morale and commitment[1] | | | | | | | | Performance on the combined reading literacy scale by national quarters of the index of school principals' perception of teachers' morale and commitment[2] | | | | | | Change in the combined reading literacy score per unit of the index of school principals' perception of teachers' morale and commitment[2] | |
| | All students | | Bottom quarter | | Middle half | | Top quarter | | Bottom quarter | | Middle half | | Top quarter | | | |
	Mean index	S.E.	Mean index	S.E.	Mean index	S.E.	Mean index	S.E.	Mean score	S.E.	Mean score	S.E.	Mean score	S.E.	Change	S.E.
Albania	-0.23	(0.06)	-1.99	(0.05)	0.06	(0.04)	1.03	(0.07)	356	(6.1)	351	(5.6)	340	(6.9)	-4.21	(3.02)
Argentina	-0.17	(0.08)	-0.99	(0.10)	-0.32	(0.08)	0.97	(0.09)	412	(16.3)	419	(16.8)	438	(11.6)	**17.74**	(8.00)
Australia	0.04	(0.08)	-0.96	(0.07)	-0.08	(0.05)	1.29	(0.07)	512	(6.9)	526	(5.4)	550	(6.0)	18.24	(3.53)
Austria	0.63	(0.07)	-0.46	(0.06)	0.63	(0.04)	1.73	(0.03)	518	(8.8)	508	(5.8)	496	(8.2)	-7.83	(6.05)
Belgium	-0.20	(0.06)	-1.12	(0.06)	-0.29	(0.03)	0.95	(0.06)	457	(8.8)	513	(8.0)	553	(8.3)	35.77	(6.28)
Brazil	-0.42	(0.07)	-1.58	(0.04)	-0.50	(0.04)	0.95	(0.09)	397	(9.2)	391	(4.7)	405	(8.0)	6.91	(4.48)
Bulgaria	0.26	(0.10)	-0.97	(0.06)	0.30	(0.08)	1.44	(0.06)	421	(11.7)	428	(8.8)	447	(11.9)	**13.84**	(6.89)
Canada	0.08	(0.04)	-1.04	(0.04)	0.02	(0.03)	1.34	(0.04)	525	(4.1)	536	(2.0)	539	(2.8)	5.57	(1.96)
Chile	-0.40	(0.07)	-1.51	(0.05)	-0.49	(0.03)	0.94	(0.09)	379	(8.9)	414	(5.7)	432	(9.3)	18.75	(4.86)
Czech Republic	-0.29	(0.05)	-1.14	(0.07)	-0.31	(0.04)	0.62	(0.06)	493	(10.1)	481	(7.2)	511	(8.0)	5.31	(5.66)
Denmark	0.02	(0.06)	-0.85	(0.08)	-0.10	(0.05)	1.15	(0.07)	490	(6.8)	498	(3.6)	503	(5.7)	8.96	(4.12)
Finland	0.02	(0.06)	-0.90	(0.07)	-0.04	(0.05)	1.08	(0.09)	543	(3.6)	546	(4.4)	551	(4.7)	5.96	(2.75)
France	m	m	m	m	m	m	m	m	m	m	m	m	m	m	m	m
Germany	-0.01	(0.06)	-1.04	(0.07)	-0.01	(0.04)	1.02	(0.07)	474	(11.7)	491	(6.8)	488	(13.7)	14.25	(7.60)
Greece	0.37	(0.11)	-0.98	(0.10)	0.35	(0.08)	1.78	(0.00)	464	(12.7)	476	(8.4)	480	(9.4)	8.19	(5.13)
Hong Kong-China	-0.31	(0.08)	-1.27	(0.08)	-0.38	(0.04)	0.80	(0.10)	497	(9.7)	520	(5.8)	566	(6.9)	**30.61**	(4.87)
Hungary	0.27	(0.07)	-1.09	(0.09)	0.41	(0.04)	1.38	(0.07)	463	(8.8)	476	(8.3)	508	(10.6)	16.09	(5.80)
Iceland	0.28	(0.00)	-0.98	(0.01)	0.27	(0.00)	1.67	(0.00)	506	(3.4)	506	(2.3)	511	(3.2)	2.47	(1.68)
Indonesia	1.06	(0.14)	-0.39	(0.20)	1.44	(0.06)	1.78	(0.00)	371	(8.8)	367	(7.7)	378	(9.9)	-2.22	(5.70)
Ireland	0.19	(0.08)	-0.89	(0.10)	0.07	(0.06)	1.57	(0.05)	525	(6.2)	523	(4.9)	538	(7.0)	7.48	(3.46)
Israel	0.00	(0.08)	-0.91	(0.09)	0.04	(0.07)	1.02	(0.09)	437	(15.2)	443	(17.7)	499	(7.4)	30.78	(8.71)
Italy	-0.69	(0.07)	-1.68	(0.04)	-0.77	(0.05)	0.46	(0.08)	484	(8.9)	490	(5.6)	488	(9.3)	3.89	(5.44)
Japan	0.14	(0.11)	-1.35	(0.11)	0.14	(0.07)	1.64	(0.05)	482	(11.7)	529	(6.7)	550	(9.1)	19.99	(4.93)
Korea	-0.72	(0.08)	-1.79	(0.05)	-0.77	(0.04)	0.47	(0.10)	497	(6.2)	537	(3.7)	530	(8.2)	12.00	(4.57)
Latvia	-0.47	(0.08)	-1.49	(0.07)	-0.50	(0.04)	0.69	(0.12)	462	(12.7)	462	(8.1)	452	(11.4)	-6.14	(7.89)
Liechtenstein	m	m	m	m	m	m	m	m	m	m	m	m	m	m	m	m
Luxembourg	-0.02	(0.01)	-0.98	(0.00)	-0.09	(0.00)	1.22	(0.01)	414	(3.0)	446	(2.1)	470	(2.8)	22.66	(1.71)
FYR Macedonia	-0.27	(0.02)	-1.22	(0.00)	-0.42	(0.00)	1.05	(0.03)	359	(2.4)	369	(1.9)	393	(7.9)	**14.01**	(2.84)
Mexico	0.39	(0.09)	-1.02	(0.09)	0.42	(0.06)	1.77	(0.01)	409	(8.6)	426	(6.2)	428	(10.6)	5.45	(4.83)
New Zealand	0.22	(0.07)	-0.92	(0.09)	0.12	(0.06)	1.59	(0.04)	502	(6.5)	538	(4.6)	544	(5.5)	11.17	(4.11)
Norway	-0.09	(0.07)	-0.95	(0.08)	-0.15	(0.04)	0.91	(0.08)	505	(5.3)	506	(4.0)	505	(7.5)	1.94	(5.06)
Peru	-0.32	(0.08)	-1.50	(0.09)	-0.37	(0.04)	0.97	(0.07)	320	(9.8)	322	(7.5)	347	(10.4)	**13.20**	(5.52)
Poland	-0.53	(0.09)	-1.47	(0.07)	-0.55	(0.07)	0.53	(0.10)	456	(15.4)	468	(9.4)	527	(10.6)	30.43	(8.74)
Portugal	-0.57	(0.07)	-1.66	(0.05)	-0.59	(0.04)	0.60	(0.07)	460	(10.4)	470	(6.3)	484	(10.6)	9.89	(5.70)
Russian Federation	-0.15	(0.07)	-1.21	(0.06)	-0.22	(0.04)	1.08	(0.07)	433	(9.9)	465	(4.7)	486	(10.1)	**18.55**	(6.61)
Spain	-0.31	(0.06)	-1.46	(0.03)	-0.33	(0.05)	0.91	(0.09)	466	(5.4)	499	(3.9)	506	(5.8)	15.69	(3.02)
Sweden	0.34	(0.08)	-0.83	(0.10)	0.36	(0.03)	1.51	(0.06)	509	(7.0)	518	(3.5)	522	(4.3)	6.27	(3.84)
Switzerland	0.43	(0.07)	-0.85	(0.05)	0.43	(0.06)	1.73	(0.03)	488	(10.0)	489	(6.3)	510	(10.0)	4.04	(5.30)
Thailand	-0.38	(0.06)	-1.35	(0.09)	-0.40	(0.04)	0.63	(0.06)	419	(5.6)	433	(4.5)	439	(6.7)	8.44	(3.80)
United Kingdom	0.02	(0.07)	-1.06	(0.08)	-0.03	(0.05)	1.27	(0.08)	507	(5.9)	526	(4.3)	542	(9.9)	17.50	(4.31)
United States	-0.04	(0.11)	-1.07	(0.22)	-0.17	(0.08)	1.30	(0.13)	494	(8.5)	494	(8.9)	540	(9.7)	11.85	(6.23)
OECD average	*0.00*	*(0.01)*	*-1.10*	*(0.02)*	*-0.04*	*(0.01)*	*1.21*	*(0.02)*	*486*	*(1.8)*	*501*	*(1.1)*	*515*	*(1.7)*	*10.20*	*(0.83)*
OECD total	*-0.05*	*(0.03)*	*-1.20*	*(0.06)*	*-0.09*	*(0.02)*	*1.22*	*(0.04)*	*481*	*(3.6)*	*498*	*(2.7)*	*519*	*(3.6)*	*10.37*	*(1.92)*
Netherlands[3]	-0.19	(0.09)	-0.93	(0.10)	-0.28	(0.06)	0.75	(0.11)	522	(12.6)	534	(9.9)	533	(12.8)	11.44	(11.18)

1. For the definition of the index see Annex A1.

2. For explained variation see Annex A2. Unit changes marked in bold are statistically significant. Where bottom and top quarters are marked in bold this indicates that their difference is statistically significant.

3. Response rate is too low to ensure comparability (see Annex A3).

Table 7.9
Index of principals' perception of teacher-related factors affecting school climate and performance on the combined reading literacy scale, by national quarters of the index

Results based on reports from school principals and reported proportionate to the number of 15-year-olds enrolled in the school

| | Index of teacher-related factors affecting school climate[1] | | | | | | | | Performance on the combined reading literacy scale, by national quarters of the index of teacher-related factors affecting school climate[2] | | | | | | Change in the combined reading literacy score per unit of the index of teacher-related factors affecting school climate[2] | |
| | All students | | Bottom quarter | | Middle half | | Top quarter | | Bottom quarter | | Middle half | | Top quarter | | | |
	Mean index	S.E.	Mean index	S.E.	Mean index	S.E.	Mean index	S.E.	Mean score	S.E.	Mean score	S.E.	Mean score	S.E.	Change	S.E.
Albania	-0.05	(0.07)	-1.30	(0.06)	-0.10	(0.03)	1.30	(0.07)	351	(7.5)	345	(5.5)	354	(8.0)	-1.43	(4.27)
Argentina	-0.06	(0.09)	-1.06	(0.10)	-0.05	(0.10)	1.22	(0.10)	404	(9.6)	447	(13.0)	463	(14.7)	20.36	(8.73)
Australia	-0.11	(0.07)	-1.13	(0.04)	-0.30	(0.05)	1.26	(0.13)	503	(7.2)	532	(5.1)	546	(7.3)	15.16	(3.17)
Austria	0.11	(0.05)	-0.79	(0.05)	0.03	(0.03)	1.17	(0.10)	525	(6.5)	511	(5.2)	484	(7.8)	-14.26	(5.54)
Belgium	0.07	(0.06)	-1.17	(0.07)	0.05	(0.04)	1.34	(0.08)	467	(8.9)	511	(7.5)	543	(9.4)	24.33	(5.79)
Brazil	0.23	(0.08)	-1.31	(0.08)	0.15	(0.05)	1.88	(0.08)	385	(7.1)	394	(4.7)	410	(7.4)	6.31	(2.99)
Bulgaria	1.10	(0.09)	-0.19	(0.06)	1.14	(0.06)	2.32	(0.04)	437	(13.4)	426	(8.5)	436	(13.5)	-0.82	(8.08)
Canada	0.12	(0.03)	-0.91	(0.03)	0.02	(0.02)	1.34	(0.05)	529	(3.9)	534	(2.2)	542	(2.6)	4.62	(1.85)
Chile	-0.29	(0.07)	-1.33	(0.06)	-0.36	(0.04)	0.94	(0.08)	386	(8.0)	413	(5.9)	427	(10.1)	15.02	(5.11)
Czech Republic	0.53	(0.05)	-0.55	(0.04)	0.47	(0.04)	1.71	(0.08)	490	(12.1)	494	(6.6)	490	(7.6)	1.64	(4.65)
Denmark	0.81	(0.07)	-0.23	(0.05)	0.70	(0.03)	2.05	(0.06)	484	(6.9)	498	(3.5)	503	(5.7)	6.46	(3.53)
Finland	-0.08	(0.06)	-0.89	(0.05)	-0.10	(0.04)	0.77	(0.05)	549	(4.3)	548	(2.5)	541	(7.3)	-4.96	(4.46)
France	m	m	m	m	m	m	m	m	m	m	m	m	m	m	m	m
Germany	-0.16	(0.05)	-1.10	(0.04)	-0.14	(0.03)	0.72	(0.05)	456	(12.0)	505	(6.9)	478	(13.2)	17.09	(9.49)
Greece	-1.18	(0.13)	-2.99	(0.13)	-1.38	(0.08)	0.93	(0.17)	492	(11.7)	465	(8.4)	475	(11.4)	-2.13	(4.05)
Hong Kong-China	0.13	(0.08)	-1.14	(0.07)	0.06	(0.05)	1.57	(0.10)	512	(7.8)	519	(6.3)	549	(9.0)	15.76	(4.35)
Hungary	0.42	(0.08)	-1.01	(0.09)	0.46	(0.05)	1.69	(0.07)	464	(9.1)	483	(7.0)	487	(9.9)	10.25	(4.39)
Iceland	0.33	(0.00)	-0.73	(0.00)	0.27	(0.00)	1.47	(0.00)	499	(3.2)	509	(2.1)	512	(2.9)	6.69	(1.69)
Indonesia	-0.05	(0.13)	-1.97	(0.12)	0.04	(0.05)	1.71	(0.09)	375	(8.8)	370	(5.6)	368	(11.8)	-3.95	(4.22)
Ireland	-0.02	(0.08)	-1.15	(0.09)	-0.17	(0.04)	1.35	(0.10)	525	(6.5)	529	(4.8)	523	(7.7)	1.82	(3.58)
Israel	-0.50	(0.15)	-2.05	(0.10)	-0.38	(0.09)	1.10	(0.14)	446	(15.8)	441	(14.6)	488	(11.3)	6.04	(5.69)
Italy	0.05	(0.10)	-1.36	(0.07)	0.01	(0.05)	1.50	(0.10)	472	(10.0)	488	(6.0)	503	(10.0)	7.19	(4.57)
Japan	0.12	(0.09)	-0.99	(0.07)	-0.03	(0.03)	1.50	(0.11)	485	(10.9)	531	(7.2)	541	(9.0)	17.38	(5.92)
Korea	0.38	(0.08)	-0.69	(0.07)	0.37	(0.05)	1.45	(0.09)	519	(6.6)	523	(5.2)	534	(6.1)	9.25	(3.41)
Latvia	0.55	(0.08)	-0.51	(0.06)	0.53	(0.05)	1.63	(0.11)	472	(8.8)	455	(8.3)	454	(14.9)	-7.92	(9.12)
Liechtenstein	m	m	m	m	m	m	m	m	m	m	m	m	m	m	m	m
Luxembourg	-0.47	(0.00)	-1.40	(0.00)	-0.53	(0.00)	0.20	(0.00)	449	(3.4)	456	(2.6)	422	(2.8)	-10.68	(2.18)
FYR Macedonia	0.32	(0.02)	-0.78	(0.00)	0.35	(0.00)	1.46	(0.02)	362	(2.5)	384	(1.6)	364	(6.0)	7.09	(2.95)
Mexico	-0.65	(0.08)	-1.94	(0.09)	-0.62	(0.04)	0.56	(0.10)	416	(8.7)	426	(6.3)	420	(8.1)	-0.89	(4.57)
New Zealand	-0.05	(0.06)	-1.07	(0.09)	-0.14	(0.03)	1.13	(0.08)	512	(7.5)	532	(4.3)	547	(5.2)	16.40	(4.00)
Norway	-0.29	(0.06)	-1.06	(0.05)	-0.38	(0.03)	0.62	(0.07)	499	(6.5)	505	(3.5)	512	(6.6)	6.20	(4.52)
Peru	-0.32	(0.07)	-1.33	(0.08)	-0.31	(0.04)	0.68	(0.08)	311	(9.0)	332	(6.9)	332	(12.9)	12.23	(7.65)
Poland	0.10	(0.10)	-0.94	(0.14)	0.02	(0.05)	1.23	(0.11)	459	(15.2)	474	(8.5)	509	(12.0)	12.54	(9.82)
Portugal	-0.29	(0.08)	-1.31	(0.07)	-0.33	(0.04)	0.82	(0.11)	462	(9.2)	473	(8.0)	472	(10.1)	7.12	(6.26)
Russian Federation	-0.75	(0.09)	-2.19	(0.06)	-0.83	(0.04)	0.81	(0.12)	445	(12.2)	469	(4.7)	465	(5.9)	5.46	(3.42)
Spain	0.20	(0.07)	-1.05	(0.07)	0.13	(0.06)	1.55	(0.11)	484	(5.3)	492	(4.0)	503	(7.6)	9.41	(3.15)
Sweden	0.00	(0.07)	-1.00	(0.05)	-0.14	(0.03)	1.25	(0.10)	508	(6.0)	519	(3.9)	520	(4.2)	3.50	(2.87)
Switzerland	0.13	(0.05)	-0.74	(0.04)	0.08	(0.03)	1.09	(0.08)	483	(10.1)	504	(6.6)	483	(8.3)	-4.55	(5.76)
Thailand	-0.08	(0.07)	-1.19	(0.06)	-0.16	(0.04)	1.22	(0.12)	420	(6.1)	435	(5.3)	433	(5.5)	2.92	(2.92)
United Kingdom	-0.08	(0.07)	-1.18	(0.06)	-0.22	(0.03)	1.28	(0.09)	506	(6.5)	515	(4.1)	560	(7.8)	22.81	(3.68)
United States	-0.07	(0.10)	-1.00	(0.05)	-0.17	(0.04)	1.01	(0.13)	479	(8.5)	514	(9.3)	514	(11.0)	13.08	(5.99)
OECD average	*0.00*	*(0.01)*	*-1.09*	*(0.02)*	*-0.08*	*(0.01)*	*1.18*	*(0.02)*	*489*	*(1.9)*	*503*	*(1.1)*	*505*	*(1.9)*	*9.95*	*(1.05)*
OECD total	*-0.04*	*(0.03)*	*-1.12*	*(0.02)*	*-0.12*	*(0.02)*	*1.15*	*(0.04)*	*479*	*(3.0)*	*504*	*(2.6)*	*509*	*(3.8)*	*15.67*	*(1.53)*
Netherlands[3]	-0.63	(0.07)	-1.47	(0.05)	-0.71	(0.04)	0.33	(0.06)	486	(14.6)	540	(6.6)	554	(8.2)	33.53	(8.93)

1. For the definition of the index see Annex A1. *The scale was inverted so that positive and high values represent a positive school climate with regard to teacher-related factors.*
2. For explained variation see Annex A2. Unit changes marked in bold are statistically significant. Where bottom and top quarters are marked in bold this indicates that their difference is statistically significant.
3. Response rate is too low to ensure comparability (see Annex A3).

Table 7.10
Index of teacher support and performance on the combined reading literacy scale, by national quarters of the index
Results based on students' self-reports

	Index of teacher support[1]								Performance on the combined reading literacy scale, by national quarters of the index of teacher support[2]							Change in the combined reading literacy score per unit of the index of teacher support[2]	
	All students		Bottom quarter		Middle half		Top quarter		Bottom quarter		Middle half		Top quarter			
	Mean index	S.E.	Mean index	S.E.	Mean index	S.E.	Mean index	S.E.	Mean score	S.E.	Mean score	S.E.	Mean score	S.E.	Change	S.E.
Albania	0.33	(0.02)	0.00	(0.02)	0.33	(0.01)	0.68	(0.04)	**376**	(6.0)	344	(5.7)	**341**	(6.2)	-2.37	(2.20)
Argentina	0.21	(0.04)	-0.30	(0.05)	0.20	(0.03)	0.76	(0.02)	440	(21.4)	419	(10.4)	405	(16.7)	-3.39	(3.47)
Australia	0.41	(0.02)	0.07	(0.03)	0.41	(0.01)	0.78	(0.02)	524	(8.1)	533	(5.0)	529	(7.9)	**7.37**	(2.24)
Austria	-0.25	(0.03)	-0.75	(0.04)	-0.24	(0.02)	0.22	(0.03)	528	(9.1)	498	(5.3)	510	(9.1)	-0.62	(2.34)
Belgium	-0.28	(0.02)	-0.67	(0.02)	-0.29	(0.01)	0.11	(0.02)	526	(8.8)	514	(5.9)	485	(14.0)	**-4.83**	(2.38)
Brazil	0.38	(0.03)	-0.07	(0.04)	0.38	(0.02)	0.81	(0.02)	390	(8.1)	394	(4.7)	410	(6.6)	**4.60**	(1.79)
Bulgaria	0.24	(0.02)	-0.10	(0.03)	0.25	(0.01)	0.58	(0.04)	416	(11.7)	441	(7.8)	438	(9.8)	**7.07**	(2.16)
Canada	0.31	(0.01)	-0.08	(0.02)	0.31	(0.01)	0.69	(0.01)	536	(2.3)	536	(2.5)	534	(3.4)	**4.42**	(0.97)
Chile	0.30	(0.02)	-0.15	(0.03)	0.33	(0.02)	0.72	(0.02)	421	(8.5)	411	(5.4)	396	(10.3)	-1.77	(1.87)
Czech Republic	-0.50	(0.02)	-0.88	(0.03)	-0.49	(0.01)	-0.13	(0.03)	514	(8.1)	498	(4.9)	494	(6.5)	0.77	(2.32)
Denmark	0.17	(0.02)	-0.20	(0.03)	0.18	(0.01)	0.54	(0.02)	490	(6.4)	500	(3.0)	507	(4.1)	**11.65**	(2.34)
Finland	0.02	(0.02)	-0.33	(0.03)	0.04	(0.01)	0.36	(0.02)	543	(5.0)	551	(2.7)	543	(7.0)	**5.48**	(2.03)
France	-0.20	(0.03)	-0.62	(0.03)	-0.18	(0.01)	0.17	(0.02)	524	(8.2)	501	(5.7)	499	(9.4)	-2.53	(1.77)
Germany	-0.34	(0.02)	-0.78	(0.02)	-0.34	(0.01)	0.11	(0.02)	532	(7.2)	500	(5.1)	443	(9.6)	**-12.55**	(2.12)
Greece	0.14	(0.02)	-0.24	(0.02)	0.16	(0.01)	0.48	(0.03)	466	(12.5)	489	(9.2)	459	(9.0)	2.20	(2.42)
Hong Kong-China	-0.22	(0.02)	-0.44	(0.02)	-0.23	(0.01)	0.01	(0.02)	525	(9.4)	522	(6.8)	533	(8.7)	1.82	(2.49)
Hungary	0.05	(0.02)	-0.32	(0.03)	0.06	(0.01)	0.43	(0.04)	490	(11.3)	491	(7.6)	453	(12.9)	-2.43	(2.76)
Iceland	0.13	(0.01)	-0.27	(0.03)	0.13	(0.02)	0.55	(0.03)	507	(3.0)	506	(2.0)	514	(2.8)	**8.87**	(1.92)
Indonesia	-0.07	(0.01)	-0.35	(0.01)	-0.06	(0.01)	0.20	(0.02)	360	(10.9)	365	(6.4)	394	(7.5)	**12.17**	(2.57)
Ireland	0.13	(0.03)	-0.27	(0.02)	0.13	(0.02)	0.52	(0.02)	530	(6.1)	530	(5.1)	521	(6.9)	-0.13	(1.90)
Israel	0.08	(0.05)	-0.46	(0.04)	0.13	(0.03)	0.55	(0.03)	475	(16.0)	462	(10.1)	431	(21.8)	-7.03	(4.39)
Italy	-0.28	(0.02)	-0.65	(0.02)	-0.29	(0.01)	0.13	(0.02)	523	(7.1)	492	(6.0)	444	(8.6)	**-11.46**	(2.21)
Japan	-0.17	(0.04)	-0.72	(0.05)	-0.15	(0.02)	0.34	(0.04)	517	(12.2)	522	(8.3)	537	(7.5)	**6.23**	(2.28)
Korea	-0.67	(0.03)	-1.03	(0.02)	-0.68	(0.01)	-0.31	(0.03)	516	(6.3)	526	(4.9)	532	(7.6)	**5.56**	(1.61)
Latvia	-0.20	(0.03)	-0.52	(0.03)	-0.22	(0.01)	0.16	(0.03)	456	(11.9)	451	(6.0)	481	(9.7)	**15.56**	(2.42)
Liechtenstein	0.09	(0.05)	-0.33	(0.09)	0.07	(0.06)	0.47	(0.10)	**584**	(7.3)	480	(4.8)	**408**	(10.3)	**-14.19**	(5.19)
Luxembourg	-0.34	(0.02)	-0.64	(0.03)	-0.33	(0.03)	-0.03	(0.04)	**493**	(2.4)	426	(2.3)	**430**	(2.9)	**-5.13**	(1.48)
FYR Macedonia	0.26	(0.02)	0.01	(0.03)	0.27	(0.03)	0.50	(0.03)	371	(2.5)	379	(3.0)	373	(3.6)	2.00	(1.91)
Mexico	0.07	(0.03)	-0.30	(0.03)	0.08	(0.01)	0.45	(0.02)	435	(10.1)	422	(6.3)	410	(8.5)	-2.60	(2.29)
New Zealand	0.34	(0.02)	0.00	(0.03)	0.34	(0.02)	0.67	(0.03)	524	(6.5)	534	(4.1)	530	(8.3)	**5.26**	(2.45)
Norway	-0.03	(0.03)	-0.42	(0.04)	-0.01	(0.01)	0.34	(0.02)	502	(5.1)	511	(4.3)	504	(6.0)	**14.95**	(2.26)
Peru	0.30	(0.02)	-0.08	(0.03)	0.31	(0.01)	0.66	(0.03)	**305**	(12.6)	323	(5.6)	**367**	(10.3)	**11.82**	(2.96)
Poland	-0.39	(0.03)	-0.73	(0.03)	-0.39	(0.01)	-0.04	(0.04)	444	(12.5)	493	(8.7)	499	(12.1)	**9.20**	(2.96)
Portugal	0.47	(0.02)	0.12	(0.03)	0.48	(0.01)	0.79	(0.02)	483	(12.5)	469	(6.3)	462	(9.9)	-1.33	(2.78)
Russian Federation	0.16	(0.02)	-0.20	(0.02)	0.16	(0.01)	0.51	(0.02)	465	(5.8)	462	(7.3)	463	(8.0)	**6.40**	(1.41)
Spain	0.09	(0.03)	-0.38	(0.03)	0.09	(0.02)	0.58	(0.03)	487	(6.0)	497	(4.0)	494	(6.4)	2.53	(1.89)
Sweden	0.21	(0.02)	-0.13	(0.03)	0.23	(0.01)	0.53	(0.02)	516	(5.0)	514	(3.5)	524	(3.9)	**6.20**	(1.82)
Switzerland	0.01	(0.03)	-0.47	(0.03)	0.03	(0.01)	0.46	(0.03)	546	(9.2)	489	(5.7)	458	(7.6)	**-13.40**	(2.24)
Thailand	-0.06	(0.02)	-0.32	(0.02)	-0.06	(0.01)	0.20	(0.01)	425	(6.2)	431	(5.1)	436	(7.1)	**7.15**	(2.26)
United Kingdom	0.50	(0.02)	0.14	(0.02)	0.52	(0.01)	0.83	(0.01)	522	(6.6)	525	(6.4)	529	(7.6)	**6.66**	(1.45)
United States	0.34	(0.04)	-0.13	(0.05)	0.36	(0.02)	0.81	(0.04)	502	(12.8)	508	(8.3)	507	(12.3)	**6.87**	(2.61)
OECD average	*0.00*	*(0.01)*	*-0.40*	*(0.01)*	*0.01*	*(0.01)*	*0.39*	*(0.01)*	*508*	*(1.8)*	*503*	*(1.3)*	*495*	*(2.0)*	*2.82*	*(0.45)*
OECD total	*0.02*	*(0.01)*	*-0.41*	*(0.02)*	*0.04*	*(0.01)*	*0.44*	*(0.02)*	*503*	*(3.7)*	*502*	*(2.8)*	*496*	*(4.4)*	*2.96*	*(0.90)*
Netherlands[3]	-0.21	(0.03)	-0.52	(0.04)	-0.19	(0.01)	0.07	(0.02)	**563**	(11.5)	528	(7.3)	**510**	(13.3)	-5.54	(3.55)

1. For the definition of the index see Annex A1.
2. For explained variation see Annex A2. Unit changes marked in bold are statistically significant. Where bottom and top quarters are marked in bold this indicates that their difference is statistically significant.
3. Response rate is too low to ensure comparability (see Annex A3).

Table 7.11
Index of principals' perception of student-related factors affecting school climate and performance on the combined reading literacy scale, by national quarters of the index

Results based on reports from school principals and reported proportionate to the number of 15-year-olds enrolled in the school

| | Index of student-related factors affecting school climate[1] | | | | | | | Performance on the combined reading literacy scale, by national quarters of the index of student-related factors affecting school climate[2] | | | | | | Change in the combined reading literacy score per unit of the index of student-related factors affecting school climate[2] | |
| | All students | | Bottom quarter | | Middle half | | Top quarter | | Bottom quarter | | Middle half | | Top quarter | | | |
	Mean index	S.E.	Mean index	S.E.	Mean index	S.E.	Mean index	S.E.	Mean score	S.E.	Mean score	S.E.	Mean score	S.E.	Change	S.E.
Albania	0.56	(0.08)	-0.95	(0.13)	0.64	(0.04)	1.95	(0.07)	346	(6.9)	348	(5.9)	352	(7.7)	2.44	(4.16)
Argentina	1.03	(0.11)	-0.15	(0.14)	1.05	(0.07)	2.21	(0.12)	424	(13.1)	433	(14.3)	469	(10.9)	21.24	(6.75)
Australia	0.06	(0.06)	-1.12	(0.05)	0.01	(0.04)	1.32	(0.09)	503	(7.1)	524	(3.7)	562	(8.4)	23.35	(3.08)
Austria	-0.16	(0.06)	-1.16	(0.05)	-0.14	(0.03)	0.80	(0.06)	488	(9.1)	513	(5.9)	517	(7.5)	16.37	(5.67)
Belgium	0.26	(0.07)	-1.32	(0.10)	0.30	(0.04)	1.75	(0.07)	443	(11.5)	517	(5.6)	554	(9.5)	37.91	(4.02)
Brazil	-0.35	(0.08)	-1.83	(0.11)	-0.37	(0.04)	1.14	(0.08)	383	(6.2)	389	(5.4)	422	(6.2)	12.21	(2.70)
Bulgaria	0.63	(0.08)	-0.49	(0.06)	0.58	(0.05)	1.88	(0.09)	400	(12.3)	438	(8.1)	450	(10.6)	22.03	(6.89)
Canada	-0.27	(0.03)	-1.24	(0.04)	-0.30	(0.02)	0.77	(0.04)	519	(3.7)	539	(2.0)	543	(2.3)	12.41	(1.97)
Chile	0.20	(0.08)	-1.11	(0.10)	0.15	(0.05)	1.63	(0.10)	382	(5.4)	397	(5.9)	463	(6.8)	27.36	(3.35)
Czech Republic	0.56	(0.06)	-0.57	(0.06)	0.51	(0.04)	1.76	(0.06)	458	(10.4)	495	(4.9)	519	(7.7)	31.03	(4.84)
Denmark	0.73	(0.06)	-0.34	(0.08)	0.70	(0.04)	1.85	(0.07)	480	(6.9)	499	(4.0)	505	(5.3)	14.48	(4.70)
Finland	-0.42	(0.05)	-1.10	(0.04)	-0.46	(0.02)	0.35	(0.07)	545	(4.1)	544	(4.3)	554	(5.1)	4.30	(3.67)
France	m	m	m	m	m	m	m	m	m	m	m	m	m	m	m	m
Germany	-0.10	(0.05)	-1.04	(0.08)	-0.11	(0.02)	0.85	(0.08)	412	(11.1)	506	(8.0)	519	(8.5)	50.74	(7.09)
Greece	-1.05	(0.10)	-2.45	(0.07)	-1.22	(0.07)	0.65	(0.11)	474	(14.1)	472	(8.1)	478	(12.2)	1.49	(4.98)
Hong Kong-China	0.66	(0.09)	-0.74	(0.09)	0.62	(0.05)	2.21	(0.07)	502	(9.5)	517	(6.4)	565	(5.6)	22.26	(4.24)
Hungary	0.15	(0.09)	-1.45	(0.08)	0.23	(0.06)	1.52	(0.07)	429	(8.7)	480	(7.2)	527	(8.6)	29.41	(3.80)
Iceland	-0.22	(0.00)	-1.06	(0.00)	-0.31	(0.00)	0.77	(0.01)	502	(3.1)	505	(2.1)	517	(3.2)	8.29	(1.93)
Indonesia	0.02	(0.14)	-1.91	(0.09)	0.19	(0.05)	1.60	(0.12)	380	(8.8)	369	(6.1)	364	(10.8)	-3.06	(4.29)
Ireland	-0.22	(0.06)	-1.23	(0.06)	-0.22	(0.04)	0.73	(0.07)	502	(8.2)	528	(3.8)	548	(6.3)	21.87	(3.92)
Israel	-0.32	(0.09)	-1.46	(0.12)	-0.35	(0.07)	0.91	(0.10)	448	(19.1)	444	(14.1)	475	(11.4)	13.09	(7.45)
Italy	0.18	(0.07)	-1.06	(0.07)	0.13	(0.04)	1.47	(0.08)	445	(12.0)	489	(5.5)	526	(7.3)	33.98	(4.93)
Japan	0.69	(0.09)	-0.61	(0.08)	0.73	(0.06)	1.88	(0.08)	471	(11.1)	532	(6.5)	553	(7.9)	34.74	(4.85)
Korea	0.92	(0.08)	-0.61	(0.13)	0.98	(0.05)	2.27	(0.07)	489	(7.1)	531	(3.9)	547	(3.7)	19.55	(2.59)
Latvia	0.00	(0.07)	-1.01	(0.06)	-0.04	(0.04)	1.05	(0.14)	452	(10.5)	450	(6.3)	484	(14.6)	9.52	(7.99)
Liechtenstein	m	m	m	m	m	m	m	m	m	m	m	m	m	m	m	m
Luxembourg	-0.41	(0.00)	-1.27	(0.00)	-0.43	(0.00)	0.35	(0.00)	453	(2.5)	419	(2.6)	481	(2.9)	11.44	(2.09)
FYR Macedonia	0.39	(0.02)	-0.77	(0.00)	0.25	(0.02)	1.88	(0.01)	351	(2.5)	379	(2.6)	382	(5.2)	17.26	(2.43)
Mexico	-0.05	(0.09)	-1.62	(0.14)	0.06	(0.04)	1.27	(0.05)	407	(9.1)	430	(6.7)	423	(9.5)	4.31	(4.00)
New Zealand	-0.19	(0.05)	-1.16	(0.08)	-0.16	(0.02)	0.72	(0.06)	504	(6.5)	536	(4.6)	546	(5.9)	26.17	(4.03)
Norway	-0.21	(0.05)	-1.12	(0.07)	-0.23	(0.03)	0.71	(0.06)	503	(5.6)	505	(4.4)	509	(5.3)	5.25	(3.45)
Peru	0.11	(0.07)	-0.88	(0.10)	0.14	(0.03)	1.07	(0.06)	305	(10.0)	325	(6.3)	353	(14.3)	20.67	(9.53)
Poland	0.03	(0.11)	-1.27	(0.08)	-0.02	(0.06)	1.36	(0.11)	421	(12.2)	481	(9.4)	530	(8.5)	38.90	(6.53)
Portugal	-0.33	(0.07)	-1.35	(0.07)	-0.39	(0.04)	0.79	(0.09)	451	(9.5)	473	(6.2)	484	(11.0)	13.28	(5.50)
Russian Federation	-0.96	(0.08)	-2.46	(0.09)	-1.01	(0.06)	0.60	(0.11)	450	(6.7)	463	(6.5)	471	(8.4)	7.83	(3.20)
Spain	0.00	(0.07)	-1.33	(0.09)	-0.01	(0.04)	1.30	(0.07)	471	(5.8)	490	(4.1)	519	(5.9)	18.15	(2.53)
Sweden	-0.05	(0.06)	-0.89	(0.05)	-0.08	(0.03)	0.82	(0.07)	498	(5.7)	520	(3.2)	526	(4.9)	15.70	(3.74)
Switzerland	-0.01	(0.06)	-1.01	(0.06)	-0.06	(0.03)	1.07	(0.06)	463	(8.3)	502	(7.0)	508	(8.1)	19.05	(5.15)
Thailand	0.08	(0.07)	-0.89	(0.06)	0.03	(0.05)	1.21	(0.10)	424	(5.9)	429	(4.6)	440	(9.2)	6.51	(3.85)
United Kingdom	0.04	(0.05)	-1.01	(0.05)	-0.07	(0.03)	1.30	(0.09)	487	(5.9)	521	(3.8)	567	(7.6)	36.69	(3.12)
United States	-0.23	(0.07)	-1.19	(0.08)	-0.21	(0.05)	0.65	(0.05)	489	(13.1)	505	(7.7)	520	(10.0)	15.92	(9.23)
OECD average	*0.00*	*(0.01)*	*-1.13*	*(0.02)*	*-0.02*	*(0.01)*	*1.13*	*(0.02)*	*473*	*(1.8)*	*502*	*(1.0)*	*522*	*(1.5)*	*20.11*	*(0.85)*
OECD total	*0.09*	*(0.02)*	*-1.09*	*(0.03)*	*0.09*	*(0.02)*	*1.22*	*(0.04)*	*466*	*(3.9)*	*503*	*(2.2)*	*522*	*(3.2)*	*23.59*	*(1.78)*
Netherlands[3]	-0.11	(0.08)	-1.19	(0.09)	-0.07	(0.04)	0.87	(0.06)	458	(13.2)	545	(8.1)	572	(7.6)	52.09	(6.24)

1. For the definition of the index see Annex A1. *The scale was inverted so that positive and high values represent a positive school climate with regard to student-related factors.*
2. For explained variation see Annex A2. Unit changes marked in bold are statistically significant. Where bottom and top quarters are marked in bold this indicates that their difference is statistically significant.
3. Response rate is too low to ensure comparability (see Annex A3).

Table 7.12
Index of disciplinary climate and performance on the combined reading literacy scale, by national quarters of the index
Results based on students' self-reports

| | Index of disciplinary climate[1] | | | | | | | Performance on the combined reading literacy scale, by national quarters of the index of disciplinary climate[2] | | | | | | Change in the combined reading literacy score per unit of the index of disciplinary climate[2] | |
| | All students | | Bottom quarter | | Middle half | | Top quarter | | Bottom quarter | | Middle half | | Top quarter | | | |
	Mean index	S.E.	Mean index	S.E.	Mean index	S.E.	Mean index	S.E.	Mean score	S.E.	Mean score	S.E.	Mean score	S.E.	Change	S.E.
Albania	0.64	(0.03)	0.29	(0.03)	0.60	(0.01)	1.11	(0.05)	363	(6.4)	356	(5.6)	330	(8.7)	-4.23	(2.43)
Argentina	-0.37	(0.06)	-0.87	(0.09)	-0.36	(0.02)	0.12	(0.05)	432	(18.8)	423	(16.6)	406	(14.3)	**-12.56**	(4.84)
Australia	-0.09	(0.03)	-0.51	(0.03)	-0.10	(0.02)	0.33	(0.02)	506	(5.3)	528	(5.5)	553	(7.9)	16.69	(2.26)
Austria	0.19	(0.04)	-0.37	(0.03)	0.18	(0.02)	0.76	(0.04)	483	(8.3)	513	(5.3)	524	(8.2)	4.98	(1.99)
Belgium	-0.12	(0.03)	-0.57	(0.02)	-0.12	(0.01)	0.33	(0.02)	511	(9.2)	504	(7.1)	521	(14.9)	3.15	(2.48)
Brazil	-0.34	(0.02)	-0.72	(0.02)	-0.35	(0.01)	0.06	(0.04)	416	(7.9)	387	(4.9)	398	(6.2)	**-5.95**	(2.34)
Bulgaria	0.12	(0.04)	-0.36	(0.03)	0.09	(0.02)	0.68	(0.05)	420	(10.9)	428	(7.0)	460	(12.6)	10.02	(2.58)
Canada	-0.14	(0.01)	-0.52	(0.01)	-0.15	(0.01)	0.27	(0.01)	522	(3.9)	536	(2.0)	547	(2.7)	13.28	(0.95)
Chile	-0.32	(0.02)	-0.60	(0.02)	-0.33	(0.01)	-0.04	(0.03)	400	(8.7)	402	(5.0)	435	(10.1)	10.39	(3.58)
Czech Republic	0.14	(0.03)	-0.43	(0.04)	0.11	(0.02)	0.77	(0.03)	468	(6.0)	506	(4.6)	523	(6.7)	12.37	(1.78)
Denmark	-0.20	(0.02)	-0.57	(0.02)	-0.20	(0.01)	0.18	(0.02)	483	(5.4)	501	(4.0)	510	(5.1)	9.71	(2.41)
Finland	-0.16	(0.03)	-0.55	(0.03)	-0.18	(0.01)	0.27	(0.04)	545	(4.9)	545	(3.8)	554	(4.5)	9.56	(1.76)
France	-0.05	(0.03)	-0.49	(0.02)	-0.07	(0.01)	0.42	(0.03)	507	(8.4)	497	(5.5)	523	(10.2)	1.53	(1.72)
Germany	0.10	(0.02)	-0.39	(0.04)	0.10	(0.02)	0.55	(0.02)	467	(7.6)	496	(5.9)	515	(8.0)	10.13	(1.64)
Greece	-0.42	(0.02)	-0.78	(0.02)	-0.42	(0.02)	-0.06	(0.03)	461	(11.4)	470	(7.4)	500	(11.1)	2.96	(2.74)
Hong Kong-China	0.00	(0.03)	-0.42	(0.03)	0.01	(0.02)	0.43	(0.04)	493	(10.3)	524	(4.8)	563	(7.1)	12.38	(2.17)
Hungary	0.23	(0.04)	-0.38	(0.05)	0.23	(0.02)	0.80	(0.05)	432	(8.9)	483	(7.5)	525	(8.0)	16.05	(3.62)
Iceland	-0.08	(0.01)	-0.62	(0.03)	-0.07	(0.02)	0.44	(0.03)	493	(3.2)	513	(2.2)	515	(2.8)	8.90	(1.80)
Indonesia	0.39	(0.03)	0.01	(0.03)	0.40	(0.02)	0.78	(0.02)	373	(11.1)	366	(6.1)	379	(6.9)	-0.12	(1.71)
Ireland	0.09	(0.03)	-0.37	(0.03)	0.08	(0.02)	0.54	(0.04)	509	(7.2)	532	(4.7)	537	(6.6)	15.41	(1.67)
Israel	-0.18	(0.06)	-0.72	(0.04)	-0.19	(0.03)	0.45	(0.07)	497	(10.0)	444	(10.1)	442	(24.2)	-7.86	(4.27)
Italy	-0.24	(0.02)	-0.74	(0.03)	-0.25	(0.02)	0.28	(0.03)	442	(9.9)	493	(5.2)	521	(7.7)	14.11	(2.13)
Japan	0.49	(0.05)	-0.22	(0.05)	0.51	(0.03)	1.14	(0.05)	475	(10.5)	527	(6.1)	567	(5.9)	17.15	(2.98)
Korea	0.20	(0.03)	-0.26	(0.03)	0.20	(0.02)	0.63	(0.04)	501	(8.2)	525	(4.1)	548	(5.6)	6.88	(1.41)
Latvia	0.38	(0.03)	-0.07	(0.04)	0.40	(0.01)	0.79	(0.02)	445	(7.3)	462	(7.9)	470	(14.0)	9.04	(2.47)
Liechtenstein	0.35	(0.05)	0.05	(0.10)	0.36	(0.08)	0.52	(0.06)	512	(7.1)	527	(5.8)	414	(7.2)	-2.59	(6.04)
Luxembourg	0.12	(0.02)	-0.10	(0.04)	0.09	(0.02)	0.37	(0.04)	458	(4.0)	436	(2.0)	449	(2.4)	2.41	(1.82)
FYR Macedonia	0.33	(0.01)	0.00	(0.03)	0.32	(0.02)	0.73	(0.04)	367	(2.4)	369	(2.4)	399	(5.0)	6.85	(1.96)
Mexico	0.17	(0.03)	-0.24	(0.03)	0.15	(0.01)	0.61	(0.03)	425	(9.1)	417	(6.6)	429	(9.0)	2.03	(2.89)
New Zealand	-0.15	(0.02)	-0.48	(0.03)	-0.16	(0.02)	0.21	(0.03)	517	(7.1)	532	(3.6)	541	(7.9)	12.47	(2.58)
Norway	-0.36	(0.03)	-0.72	(0.03)	-0.38	(0.01)	0.02	(0.03)	492	(6.0)	513	(3.4)	510	(6.8)	7.79	(2.66)
Peru	-0.06	(0.02)	-0.38	(0.03)	-0.09	(0.01)	0.33	(0.03)	330	(10.4)	328	(6.7)	331	(12.0)	-2.77	(3.41)
Poland	0.37	(0.04)	-0.24	(0.04)	0.39	(0.02)	0.91	(0.04)	418	(10.1)	486	(8.2)	532	(9.3)	20.88	(2.41)
Portugal	-0.05	(0.02)	-0.32	(0.02)	-0.05	(0.01)	0.20	(0.02)	452	(12.5)	470	(6.3)	491	(8.0)	10.57	(2.15)
Russian Federation	0.45	(0.03)	0.01	(0.02)	0.42	(0.02)	0.92	(0.03)	442	(6.8)	463	(6.8)	482	(7.6)	10.06	(1.84)
Spain	-0.17	(0.03)	-0.65	(0.04)	-0.16	(0.01)	0.27	(0.03)	480	(6.4)	492	(4.5)	510	(5.3)	12.18	(1.83)
Sweden	-0.19	(0.02)	-0.57	(0.03)	-0.19	(0.01)	0.17	(0.02)	502	(4.0)	514	(3.1)	537	(4.0)	12.44	(1.81)
Switzerland	0.30	(0.03)	-0.23	(0.03)	0.30	(0.02)	0.83	(0.03)	483	(10.5)	493	(6.9)	511	(10.2)	9.81	(2.42)
Thailand	0.18	(0.02)	-0.10	(0.02)	0.18	(0.01)	0.45	(0.02)	423	(7.8)	432	(4.7)	438	(5.1)	10.14	(2.27)
United Kingdom	0.02	(0.03)	-0.44	(0.02)	0.01	(0.02)	0.49	(0.04)	503	(6.1)	524	(3.7)	548	(9.3)	20.10	(2.01)
United States	0.03	(0.03)	-0.40	(0.02)	0.01	(0.01)	0.47	(0.04)	505	(9.8)	491	(9.9)	536	(9.6)	13.17	(2.33)
OECD average	*0.00*	*(0.01)*	*-0.45*	*(0.01)*	*-0.01*	*(0.01)*	*0.45*	*(0.01)*	*483*	*(1.6)*	*501*	*(1.1)*	*522*	*(1.7)*	*9.45*	*(0.45)*
OECD total	*0.09*	*(0.01)*	*-0.40*	*(0.01)*	*0.08*	*(0.01)*	*0.57*	*(0.02)*	*482*	*(3.2)*	*497*	*(2.7)*	*527*	*(3.3)*	*11.99*	*(0.79)*
Netherlands[3]	-0.33	(0.03)	-0.73	(0.05)	-0.31	(0.02)	0.02	(0.03)	532	(12.2)	520	(6.8)	555	(12.7)	2.63	(3.86)

1. For the definition of the index see Annex A1. *The scale was inverted so that positive and high values represent a positive student perception of disciplinary climate.*
2. For explained variation see Annex A2. Unit changes marked in bold are statistically significant. Where bottom and top quarters are marked in bold this indicates that their difference is statistically significant.
3. Response rate is too low to ensure comparability (see Annex A3).

Table 7.13
Percentage of students and performance on the combined reading literacy scale, by type of school
Results based on reports from school principals and reported proportionate to the number of 15-year-olds enrolled in the school

	Government or public schools[1]						Government-dependent private schools[2]					
			Performance on the combined reading literacy scale		International socio-economic index of occupational status (ISEI)				Performance on the combined reading literacy scale		International socio-economic index of occupational status (ISEI)	
	Percent-age of students	S.E.	Mean score	S.E.	Mean index	S.E.	Percent-age of students	S.E.	Mean score	S.E.	Mean index	S.E.
Albania	96.1	(0.8)	345	(3.5)	45	(0.5)	a	a	a	a	a	a
Argentina	61.8	(7.8)	381	(8.3)	39.7	(1.1)	31.7	(8.3)	473	(13.9)	46.1	(2.7)
Australia	m	m	m	m	m	m	m	m	m	m	m	m
Austria	88.8	(2.8)	504	(3.5)	48.9	(0.4)	6.2	(2.0)	531	(15.6)	54.1	(3.2)
Belgium	m	m	m	m	m	m	m	m	m	m	m	m
Brazil	89.5	(2.2)	386	(4.0)	41.5	(0.7)	a	a	a	a	a	a
Bulgaria	99.4	(0.6)	430	(4.9)	50	(0.6)	a	a	a	a	a	a
Canada	93.8	(0.5)	532	(1.6)	52.2	(0.2)	3.8	(0.5)	573	(7.5)	59.2	(1.1)
Chile	54.3	(1.9)	387	(5.3)	35.5	(0.7)	32.8	(2.3)	415	(7.0)	39.4	(0.8)
Czech Republic	94.1	(1.6)	491	(2.7)	48.4	(0.3)	5.7	(1.6)	502	(12.5)	47.3	(1.8)
Denmark	75.5	(2.3)	497	(2.9)	49.6	(0.5)	24.5	(2.3)	496	(5.9)	50.8	(0.9)
Finland	97.2	(1.3)	547	(2.5)	49.9	(0.4)	2.8	(1.3)	555	(13.9)	55.1	(3.0)
France	m	m	m	m	m	m	m	m	m	m	m	m
Germany	95.9	(1.3)	480	(3.6)	48.7	(0.4)	4.1	(1.3)	563	(12.6)	56.9	(1.8)
Greece	95.9	(2.1)	468	(5.2)	46.3	(0.6)	a	a	a	a	a	a
Hong Kong-China	95.1	(1.0)	529	(2.8)	42.2	(0.4)	4.4	(0.7)	458	(17.0)	40.4	(1.0)
Hungary	95.2	(1.7)	480	(4.3)	49.4	(0.5)	4.4	(1.6)	494	(35.6)	52.6	(3.3)
Iceland	99.2	(0.0)	507	(1.5)	52.6	(0.3)	a	a	a	a	a	a
Indonesia	53.2	(5.4)	380	(6.4)	36.5	(1.3)	0.2	(0.2)	300	(12.1)	21.1	(0.5)
Ireland	39.5	(2.0)	501	(5.0)	44.5	(0.7)	57.7	(2.4)	541	(4.0)	50.1	(0.5)
Israel	75.4	(5.2)	452	(10.8)	54.5	(0.9)	20.3	(5.0)	463	(17.3)	55.4	(2.7)
Italy	94.1	(1.6)	486	(3.3)	46.8	(0.3)	0.8	(0.8)	c	c	c	c
Japan	69.6	(1.0)	524	(5.9)	49.2	(0.7)	0.8	(0.8)	c	c	c	c
Korea	50.7	(4.5)	519	(5.6)	42.8	(0.8)	15.7	(3.6)	522	(7.8)	40.1	(1.7)
Latvia	99.2	(0.8)	463	(6.5)	50.7	(0.7)	0.8	(0.8)	c	c	c	c
Liechtenstein	m	m	m	m	m	m	m	m	m	m	m	m
Luxembourg	87.9	(0.0)	443	(1.8)	45.5	(0.3)	12.1	(0.0)	439	(3.6)	41.4	(0.8)
FYR Macedonia	99.5	(0.0)	375	(2.0)	47	(0.3)	a	a	a	a	a	a
Mexico	85.1	(3.1)	413	(3.7)	39.7	(0.5)	a	a	a	a	a	a
New Zealand	95.1	(0.6)	528	(2.8)	51.7	(0.4)	0.1	(0.1)	c	c	c	c
Norway	98.6	(0.9)	505	(2.9)	53.8	(0.4)	1.4	(0.9)	517	(11.2)	54	(5.6)
Peru	92.5	(1.6)	314	(5.2)	37.6	(0.6)	0.8	(0.7)	392	(10.9)	42.6	(0.3)
Poland	97.1	(1.3)	478	(5.0)	45.6	(0.5)	a	a	a	a	a	a
Portugal	92.6	(0.8)	469	(4.9)	43.8	(0.6)	5.9	(0.9)	483	(16.7)	41.7	(2.1)
Russian Federation	100.0	(0.0)	461	(4.1)	49.3	(0.4)	a	a	a	a	a	a
Spain	62	(2.0)	478	(3.6)	41.3	(0.6)	28.9	(3.3)	503	(7.1)	46.5	(1.3)
Sweden	96.6	(0.7)	516	(2.3)	50.4	(0.4)	3.4	(0.7)	520	(15.9)	54.8	(2.2)
Switzerland	94.1	(1.6)	492	(4.6)	48.2	(0.4)	1.2	(0.6)	530	(20.6)	51.7	(2.7)
Thailand	80.7	(2.2)	433	(3.2)	32.3	(0.5)	1.8	(1.0)	397	(32.9)	32.8	(6.6)
United Kingdom	90.8	(1.2)	515	(2.5)	50.1	(0.4)	a	a	a	a	a	a
United States	94.6	(2.3)	501	(5.5)	51.7	(0.6)	1.1	(1.2)	523	(2.8)	47.9	(0.0)
Netherlands[6]	26.2	(5.2)	514	(13.2)	49.3	(1.3)	73.9	(5.2)	538	(7.0)	51.6	(0.8)

1. Government or public: Schools which are directly controlled or managed by: i) a public education authority or agency, or ii) by a government agency directly or by a governing body, most of whose members are either appointed by a public authority or elected by public franchise.
2. Private, government-dependent: Schools which receive more than 50 per cent of their core funding (funding that support the basic educational services of the institution) from government agencies.
3. Private, government-independent: Schools which receive less than 50 per cent of their core funding (funding that support the basic educational services of the institution) from government agencies.
4. Positive differences favour government-dependent private schools while negative differences favour public schools. Bold values are statistically significant.
5. Positive differences favour government-independent private schools while negative differences favour public schools. Bold values are statistically significant.
6. Response rate is too low to ensure comparability (see Annex A3).

Table 7.13 (continued)
Percentage of students and performance on the combined reading literacy scale, by type of school
Results based on reports from school principals and reported proportionate to the number of 15-year-olds enrolled in the school

| | Government-independent private schools[3] | | | | | | Difference in performance on the combined reading literacy scale | | | | Difference on the socio-economic index of occupational status (ISEI) | | | |
| | Percentage of students | | Performance on the combined reading literacy scale | | International socio-economic index of occupational status (ISEI) | | Government-dependent private schools and public schools[4] | | Government-independent private schools and public schools[5] | | Government-dependent private schools and public schools[4] | | Government-independent private schools and public schools[5] | |
	Percentage of students	S.E.	Mean score	S.E.	Mean index	S.E.	Difference	S.E	Difference	S.E	Difference	S.E	Difference	S.E
Albania	3.9	(0.8)	430	(9.5)	54.7	(2.3)	a	a	85	(10.6)	a	a	9.7	(2.3)
Argentina	6.5	(2.4)	498	(11.9)	64.9	(2.3)	91	(17.3)	116	(15.2)	6.4	(3.0)	25.2	(2.5)
Australia	m	m	m	m	m	m	m	m	m	m	m	m	m	m
Austria	5	(1.8)	532	(11.2)	59	(1.4)	27	(16.5)	28	(11.8)	5.2	(3.3)	10.1	(1.5)
Belgium	m	m	m	m	m	m	m	m	m	m	m	m	m	m
Brazil	10.5	(2.2)	460	(15.8)	57	(1.9)	a	a	74	(16.4)	a	a	15.4	(2.1)
Bulgaria	0.6	(0.6)	597	(5.8)	68.7	(0.0)	a	a	167	(7.1)	a	a	18.7	(0.6)
Canada	2.6	(0.4)	568	(7.2)	64.3	(0.8)	41	(7.6)	36	(7.3)	7	(1.1)	12.1	(0.8)
Chile	12.9	(1.4)	484	(7.3)	57.4	(1.8)	28	(9.1)	98	(9.4)	3.9	(1.1)	21.9	(1.9)
Czech Republic	0.2	(0.2)	c	c	c	c	11	(13.5)	c	c	-1.1	(1.9)	c	c
Denmark	a	a	a	a	a	a	-2	(6.7)	a	a	1.2	(1.1)	a	a
Finland	a	a	a	a	a	a	9	(15.0)	a	a	5.3	(3.1)	a	a
France	m	m	m	m	m	m	m	m	m	m	m	m	m	m
Germany	a	a	a	a	a	a	83	(13.8)	a	a	8.2	(1.9)	a	a
Greece	4.1	(2.1)	550	(26.2)	66.9	(2.9)	a	a	81	(26.7)	a	a	20.6	(3.0)
Hong Kong-China	0.5	(0.4)	464	(1.9)	61.5	(0.0)	-70	(17.4)	-64	(4.8)	-1.8	(1.1)	19.2	(0.4)
Hungary	0.3	(0.3)	394	(4.8)	38	(0.0)	14	(36.2)	-85	(6.3)	3.2	(3.4)	-11.4	(0.5)
Iceland	0.8	(0.0)	c	c	c	c	a	a	c	c	a	a	c	c
Indonesia	46.6	(5.4)	357	(6.2)	35.9	(1.2)	-77	(13.5)	-22	(9.5)	-15.5	(1.3)	-0.6	(1.9)
Ireland	2.9	(1.4)	587	(7.8)	62.5	(0.8)	41	(6.3)	86	(9.0)	5.5	(0.9)	18	(1.1)
Israel	4.2	(1.9)	529	(25.6)	66.2	(2.8)	12	(19.4)	77	(25.8)	0.9	(2.7)	11.7	(2.8)
Italy	5	(1.4)	513	(12.1)	53.6	(2.0)	c	c	27	(13.3)	c	c	6.8	(2.1)
Japan	29.6	(1.1)	518	(11.0)	53	(1.2)	c	c	-6	(12.5)	c	c	3.8	(1.4)
Korea	33.6	(3.8)	533	(3.6)	44.1	(0.7)	3	(11.4)	13	(7.1)	-2.6	(2.1)	1.3	(1.1)
Latvia	a	a	a	a	a	a	c	c	a	a	c	c	a	a
Liechtenstein	m	m	m	m	m	m	m	m	m	m	m	m	m	m
Luxembourg	a	a	a	a	a	a	-4	(3.8)	a	a	-4	(0.9)	a	a
FYR Macedonia	0	(0.0)	408	(8.0)	60	(1.6)	a	a	34	(8.0)	a	a	13	(1.6)
Mexico	14.9	(3.1)	491	(7.4)	58.3	(1.5)	a	a	79	(8.9)	a	a	18.5	(1.7)
New Zealand	4.8	(0.6)	598	(24.7)	64	(1.3)	c	c	71	(24.4)	c	c	12.3	(1.4)
Norway	a	a	a	a	a	a	14	(13.3)	a	a	0.2	(5.7)	a	a
Peru	6.7	(1.4)	428	(16.0)	52.4	(3.2)	79	(12.2)	113	(16.7)	5.1	(0.6)	14.8	(3.3)
Poland	2.9	(1.3)	500	(25.2)	57.9	(3.9)	a	a	22	(26.2)	a	a	12.3	(4.0)
Portugal	1.5	(0.7)	509	(47.5)	56.1	(7.0)	13	(17.5)	39	(47.3)	-2.1	(2.2)	12.3	(7.1)
Russian Federation	a	a	a	a	a	a	a	a	a	a	a	a	a	a
Spain	9.2	(2.5)	543	(6.1)	62.8	(1.4)	25	(7.9)	65	(7.1)	5.2	(1.4)	21.5	(1.5)
Sweden	a	a	a	a	a	a	3	(16.3)	a	a	4.3	(2.3)	a	a
Switzerland	4.7	(1.5)	523	(28.8)	63.3	(2.2)	38	(22.6)	31	(29.4)	3.5	(2.8)	15.1	(2.3)
Thailand	17.5	(2.8)	422	(9.8)	36.3	(1.5)	-37	(33.6)	-11	(10.4)	0.4	(6.6)	4	(1.5)
United Kingdom	9.2	(1.2)	613	(9.5)	64.8	(0.9)	a	a	98	(9.8)	a	a	14.7	(1.0)
United States	4.3	(2.1)	546	(24.2)	55.3	(3.8)	22	(6.1)	43	(26.2)	-3.9	(0.6)	3.5	(4.0)
Netherlands[6]	a	a	a	a	a	a	24	(18.5)	a	a	2.3	(1.7)	a	a

1. Government or public: Schools which are directly controlled or managed by: i) a public education authority or agency, or ii) by a government agency directly or by a governing body, most of whose members are either appointed by a public authority or elected by public franchise.

2. Private, government-dependent: Schools which receive more than 50 per cent of their core funding (funding that support the basic educational services of the institution) from government agencies.

3. Private, government-independent: Schools which receive less than 50 per cent of their core funding (funding that support the basic educational services of the institution) from government agencies.

4. Positive differences favour government-dependent private schools while negative differences favour public schools. Bold values are statistically significant.

5. Positive differences favour government-independent private schools while negative differences favour public schools. Bold values are statistically significant.

6. Response rate is too low to ensure comparability (see Annex A3).

Table 7.14

Percentage of students and performance on the combined reading literacy scale, by the community in which the school is located

Results based on reports from school principals and reported proportionate to the number of 15-year-olds enrolled in the school

| | Schools in cities with up to 15 000 people | | | | | | Schools in cities between 15 000 and 100 000 people | | | | | |
| | Percentage of students | S.E. | Performance on the combined reading literacy scale | | International socio-economic index of occupational status (ISEI) | | Percentage of students | S.E. | Performance on the combined reading literacy scale | | International socio-economic index of occupational status (ISEI) | |
			Mean score	S.E.	Mean index	S.E.			Mean score	S.E.	Mean index	S.E.
Albania	40.8	(2.8)	309	(5.0)	39.6	(0.8)	30.8	(2.8)	383	(5.3)	47.8	(0.8)
Argentina	24.3	(4.9)	379	(12.1)	36.5	(1.7)	35.1	(6.9)	434	(16.4)	42.9	(1.6)
Australia	14.3	(2.2)	510	(5.4)	45.4	(1.0)	24.8	(3.3)	526	(5.7)	50.2	(0.6)
Austria	42.1	(3.9)	500	(6.7)	47.8	(0.6)	27.1	(4.0)	522	(6.7)	50.5	(1.0)
Belgium	29.8	(3.1)	516	(11.3)	49.1	(1.0)	49.3	(2.8)	515	(5.1)	47.7	(0.6)
Brazil	15.8	(2.4)	374	(5.7)	37.6	(1.0)	26.7	(3.3)	390	(6.2)	42.4	(1.2)
Bulgaria	15.4	(2.7)	373	(14.4)	44.2	(0.9)	34.7	(4.3)	419	(6.8)	47.5	(0.6)
Canada	a	a	a	a	a	a	a	a	a	a	a	a
Chile	16.3	(2.6)	377	(9.1)	33.2	(1.1)	27.3	(3.3)	400	(7.8)	37.2	(1.1)
Czech Republic	32.3	(2.7)	474	(6.7)	45.7	(0.7)	37.6	(3.4)	500	(8.7)	48.2	(0.6)
Denmark	54.4	(3.6)	497	(2.8)	47.1	(0.4)	26.7	(3.5)	506	(5.0)	52.5	(1.0)
Finland	38.9	(2.8)	543	(2.9)	46.2	(0.6)	33.2	(3.7)	546	(5.7)	49.5	(0.7)
France	28.6	(3.2)	477	(9.5)	43.3	(1.0)	52.1	(3.8)	516	(5.3)	48.4	(0.8)
Germany	35.4	(3.2)	474	(8.1)	46.5	(0.7)	41.1	(3.7)	507	(9.4)	50.7	(0.7)
Greece	20.3	(2.9)	469	(8.5)	42.4	(1.0)	46.5	(4.4)	473	(9.6)	47.0	(1.0)
Hong Kong-China	2.1	(1.2)	442	(30.8)	36.5	(2.4)	13.5	(2.6)	502	(9.0)	40.0	(0.6)
Hungary	17.8	(2.9)	445	(12.5)	45.0	(1.4)	40.3	(3.8)	473	(8.7)	47.2	(0.8)
Iceland	a	a	a	a	a	a	a	a	a	a	a	a
Indonesia	49.9	(5.0)	358	(6.8)	31.5	(1.1)	30.0	(4.4)	397	(9.5)	41.6	(1.7)
Ireland	60.1	(4.0)	531	(3.8)	47.4	(0.6)	14.0	(2.7)	546	(9.0)	52.3	(1.6)
Israel	31.8	(5.6)	449	(16.2)	54.3	(1.6)	47.0	(6.3)	478	(9.5)	54.9	(1.2)
Italy	18.0	(3.1)	474	(11.7)	43.6	(0.9)	52.2	(3.7)	492	(4.5)	46.8	(0.5)
Japan	14.5	(4.2)	532	(20.5)	48.6	(2.6)	29.0	(6.2)	526	(9.4)	48.7	(0.8)
Korea	8.4	(2.2)	497	(10.9)	35.8	(1.6)	9.9	(2.2)	501	(14.8)	36.7	(2.1)
Latvia	43.5	(2.6)	442	(9.6)	48.8	(1.0)	26.6	(3.8)	474	(10.2)	51.6	(1.1)
Liechtenstein	100.0	(0.0)	486	(4.3)	47.5	(0.9)	a	a	a	a	a	a
Luxembourg	31.6	(0.3)	447	(2.9)	42.4	(0.5)	18.5	(0.2)	452	(3.5)	44.6	(0.5)
FYR Macedonia	13.9	(0.4)	387	(6.5)	46.0	(0.8)	57.0	(0.8)	366	(1.8)	45.0	(0.4)
Mexico	35.2	(3.1)	383	(5.4)	35.3	(0.6)	24.4	(3.1)	427	(8.3)	42.4	(1.4)
New Zealand	24.1	(2.4)	519	(4.7)	46.1	(0.6)	30.5	(3.3)	530	(3.9)	51.8	(0.6)
Norway	66.8	(3.2)	500	(3.5)	51.6	(0.4)	22.0	(3.0)	525	(5.7)	57.4	(0.9)
Peru	a	a	a	a	a	a	a	a	a	a	a	a
Poland	18.8	(3.4)	464	(11.2)	41.2	(1.1)	41.0	(4.3)	472	(10.4)	44.5	(0.9)
Portugal	39.9	(3.8)	456	(7.6)	39.9	(0.9)	38.1	(3.5)	478	(7.4)	45.3	(0.9)
Russian Federation	43.3	(3.3)	436	(7.4)	46.7	(0.8)	19.8	(2.5)	471	(7.8)	48.2	(0.7)
Spain	20.9	(3.0)	480	(5.7)	39.8	(0.9)	32.8	(3.8)	488	(5.1)	44.0	(1.1)
Sweden	48.6	(3.1)	511	(2.7)	47.1	(0.4)	34.3	(3.4)	524	(4.0)	52.5	(0.7)
Switzerland	58.1	(3.3)	487	(4.9)	46.7	(0.5)	25.3	(3.4)	507	(11.5)	50.3	(1.1)
Thailand	47.4	(2.8)	416	(4.4)	27.9	(0.5)	23.5	(3.8)	441	(7.3)	34.4	(1.3)
United Kingdom	29.7	(3.2)	532	(4.7)	52.6	(0.9)	35.4	(3.5)	529	(5.3)	50.6	(0.9)
United States	35.4	(4.6)	499	(9.9)	49.3	(1.1)	35.8	(5.2)	538	(7.0)	54.2	(0.9)
OECD average	*33.4*	*(0.6)*	*491*	*(1.5)*	*45.8*	*(0.2)*	*32.9*	*(0.7)*	*503*	*(1.6)*	*48.6*	*(0.2)*
OECD total	*28.6*	*(1.3)*	*480*	*4.4*	*45.5*	*(0.5)*	*35.0*	*(1.6)*	*507*	*(3.0)*	*49.1*	*(0.4)*
Netherlands[1]	12.1	(4.0)	530	(16.3)	45.9	(1.8)	60.5	(5.1)	540	(6.9)	51.7	(0.7)

1. Response rate is too low to ensure comparability (see Annex A3)

Table 7.14 (continued)
Percentage of students and performance on the combined reading literacy scale, by the community in which the school is located
Results based on reports from school principals and reported proportionate to the number of 15-year-olds enrolled in the school

	Schools in cities between 100 000 and 1 000 000 people						Schools in cities larger than 1 000 000 people					
	Percent-age of students	S.E.	Performance on the combined reading literacy scale		International socio-economic index of occupational status (ISEI)		Percent-age of students	S.E.	Performance on the combined reading literacy scale		International socio-economic index of occupational status (ISEI)	
			Mean score	S.E.	Mean index	S.E.			Mean score	S.E.	Mean index	S.E.
Albania	27.1	(1.2)	390	(5.2)	51.6	(0.9)	1.3	(0.5)	357	(27.9)	53.6	(2.5)
Argentina	25.9	(4.4)	425	(15.2)	45.8	(1.9)	14.8	(3.5)	471	(21.2)	51.8	(3.9)
Australia	15.8	(2.5)	540	(6.3)	53.5	(0.8)	45.1	(2.7)	540	(6.3)	55.1	(1.0)
Austria	14.8	(2.7)	520	(10.4)	51.9	(1.4)	16.0	(2.4)	501	(9.4)	51.5	(1.1)
Belgium	20.4	(2.4)	512	(8.1)	52.6	(1.0)	0.5	(0.5)	429	(5.1)	36.3	(0.0)
Brazil	34.7	(3.7)	411	(6.8)	45.1	(1.3)	22.8	(3.1)	420	(8.1)	48.7	(1.5)
Bulgaria	38.7	(5.0)	453	(9.9)	51.5	(1.1)	11.2	(2.7)	510	(15.7)	59.7	(1.7)
Canada	a	a	a	a	a	a	a	a	a	a	a	a
Chile	27.7	(3.3)	419	(8.9)	41.1	(1.3)	28.7	(3.1)	436	(8.1)	45.1	(1.1)
Czech Republic	17.4	(3.0)	499	(14.9)	49.3	(1.2)	12.7	(2.5)	517	(10.7)	53.9	(1.3)
Denmark	7	(1.7)	502	(9.3)	53.1	(1.7)	12	(1.4)	518	(7.6)	54.8	(1.3)
Finland	7	(2.1)	557	(5.5)	56.6	(1.9)	21	(2.8)	556	(4.5)	55.7	(0.8)
France	15.1	(3.1)	520	(12.9)	52.5	(2.0)	4.3	(1.4)	563	(12.4)	59.4	(1.4)
Germany	17.4	(2.7)	488	(18.8)	50.8	(1.5)	6.1	(1.5)	470	(28.4)	50.4	(2.3)
Greece	17.3	(2.6)	487	(11.2)	50.2	(1.6)	15.9	(2.7)	488	(15.2)	54.2	(2.5)
Hong Kong-China	39.9	(3.8)	536	(6.1)	42.1	(0.7)	44.5	(3.7)	535	(5.9)	43.3	(0.6)
Hungary	22.0	(3.0)	511	(9.5)	52.6	(1.4)	19.9	(2.1)	508	(9.5)	55.2	(1.3)
Iceland	a	a	a	a	a	a	a	a	a	a	a	a
Indonesia	8.1	(2.1)	373	(8.4)	41.4	(1.8)	12.0	(2.4)	382	(11.5)	41.9	(1.3)
Ireland	7.6	(2.2)	534	(12.5)	50.6	(1.9)	18.3	(3.1)	508	(8.3)	47.7	(1.4)
Israel	20.4	(4.0)	471	(23.3)	56.1	(1.8)	0.8	(0.6)	460	(16.2)	59.2	(2.5)
Italy	18.1	(3.2)	510	(10.8)	51.0	(1.4)	11.8	(2.2)	468	(12.2)	47.7	(1.1)
Japan	45.2	(6.4)	551	(9.4)	52.0	(0.9)	11.3	(4.4)	546	(26.1)	52.0	(1.8)
Korea	36.1	(2.6)	533	(4.2)	42.9	(1.0)	45.6	(2.0)	532	(3.0)	45.3	(0.4)
Latvia	24.9	(4.0)	485	(11.8)	51.3	(1.3)	5.0	(1.9)	496	(22.1)	52.8	(2.8)
Liechtenstein	a	a	a	a	a	a	a	a	a	a	a	a
Luxembourg	49.9	(0.3)	452	(2.5)	46.8	(0.4)	a	a	a	a	a	a
FYR Macedonia	27.1	(0.9)	396	(4.7)	51.0	(0.7)	2.0	(0.1)	362	(9.8)	45.8	(1.7)
Mexico	27.7	(3.9)	453	(9.5)	48.2	(1.7)	12.7	(2.5)	471	(12.3)	49.2	(2.5)
New Zealand	17.1	(2.4)	564	(7.6)	55.9	(1.0)	28.3	(2.0)	533	(6.6)	55.6	(0.8)
Norway	11.2	(2.3)	519	(5.5)	58.9	(1.0)	a	a	a	a	a	a
Peru	a	a	a	a	a	a	a	a	a	a	a	a
Poland	31.6	(3.5)	510	(8.7)	49.4	(1.0)	8.6	(2.1)	512	(17.0)	51.6	(2.1)
Portugal	14.0	(2.6)	490	(11.4)	47.4	(2.0)	8.1	(2.5)	514	(23.1)	49.7	(3.5)
Russian Federation	23.6	(2.8)	490	(6.7)	52.6	(0.8)	13.4	(1.8)	494	(8.3)	54.1	(1.5)
Spain	36.2	(3.9)	503	(4.8)	47.1	(1.2)	10.1	(1.5)	518	(10.1)	51.5	(1.9)
Sweden	10.3	(1.9)	525	(7.9)	56.4	(1.9)	6.8	(1.9)	529	(14.4)	54.8	(2.5)
Switzerland	16.6	(2.9)	516	(16.1)	54.7	(2.1)	a	a	a	a	a	a
Thailand	16.9	(3.4)	466	(8.2)	40.8	(1.6)	12.2	(3.9)	439	(14.0)	39.5	(2.2)
United Kingdom	19.3	(2.8)	525	(8.7)	50.7	(1.3)	15.5	(2.8)	535	(14.3)	52.1	(1.9)
United States	19.7	(5.1)	517	(11.1)	54.5	(1.7)	9.2	(3.2)	482	(15.3)	49.6	(1.6)
OECD average	*19.8*	*(0.6)*	*508*	*(2.1)*	*50.4*	*(0.3)*	*13.9*	*(0.5)*	*520*	*(2.3)*	*52.0*	*(0.3)*
OECD total	*23.2*	*(1.5)*	*512*	*(3.6)*	*50.5*	*(0.6)*	*13.2*	*(1.0)*	*511*	*(4.3)*	*50.2*	*(0.4)*
Netherlands[1]	27.5	(4.5)	523	(13.0)	51.4	(1.2)	a	a	a	a	a	a

1. Response rate is too low to ensure comparability (see Annex A3).

Table 7.15
Multilevel regression coefficients (model 1, without class size)[1]

	Student-level variables																
	Socio-economic background (HISEI)		Engagement in reading		Achievement pressure		Sense of belonging		Cultural communication		Disciplinary climate		Gender		Grade		Home educational resources	
	Coef.	S.E.	Coef.	S.E.	Coef.	S.E.	Coef.	S.E.	Coef.	S.E.	Coef.	S.E.	Coef.	S.E.	Coef.	S.E.	Coef.	S.E.
Albania	8.0	(1.4)	3.9	(1.5)	-1.5	(1.2)	4.8	(1.7)	-0.9	(1.5)	-0.6	(1.2)	24.3	(3.0)	26.2	(2.7)	9.1	(1.6)
Argentina	4.9	(1.9)	19.1	(1.8)	-4.6	(2.1)	6.4	(1.8)	-1.6	(3.4)	-5.0	(2.1)	19.7	(4.1)	36.8	(3.5)	2.1	(2.3)
Australia	12.2	(1.9)	24.7	(2.0)	-7.7	(1.4)	-2.7	(1.5)	9.2	(1.8)	2.7	(1.6)	17.9	(2.8)	39.9	(3.0)	3.0	(1.7)
Austria	2.3	(1.3)	18.1	(1.3)	-1.8	(1.3)	1.8	(1.4)	1.7	(1.5)	-2.0	(1.3)	6.3	(3.2)	31.0	(1.8)	2.2	(1.6)
Belgium	6.5	(1.3)	18.0	(1.0)	-1.5	(1.1)	2.0	(0.9)	1.0	(1.0)	1.5	(1.1)	4.5	(2.2)	51.7	(2.9)	2.0	(1.0)
Brazil	3.3	(1.6)	14.1	(1.4)	2.9	(1.6)	2.2	(1.2)	2.1	(1.5)	-3.6	(1.4)	0.5	(2.7)	33.8	(1.7)	3.3	(1.8)
Bulgaria	6.2	(1.3)	10.6	(1.7)	0.3	(1.3)	6.0	(1.3)	3.1	(1.4)	3.4	(1.4)	13.7	(3.3)	12.3	(3.1)	5.3	(1.5)
Canada	11.8	(0.9)	24.5	(0.8)	-6.7	(0.8)	-2.0	(0.7)	3.8	(0.8)	2.2	(0.8)	14.8	(1.6)	46.1	(1.7)	0.5	(0.8)
Chile	7.0	(1.2)	14.5	(1.2)	-10.0	(1.1)	4.6	(1.0)	4.6	(1.2)	1.0	(1.2)	0.6	(2.4)	36.1	(1.9)	-0.6	(1.0)
Czech Republic	8.0	(1.1)	17.9	(1.2)	-4.0	(1.4)	5.1	(1.0)	3.1	(1.1)	1.0	(1.1)	7.7	(2.4)	31.4	(2.6)	3.3	(1.3)
Denmark	12.4	(1.9)	29.1	(1.6)	-1.2	(1.5)	2.0	(1.3)	10.9	(1.6)	2.5	(1.4)	6.6	(2.7)	32.8	(5.2)	0.7	(1.4)
Finland	11.8	(1.2)	30.5	(1.3)	-3.3	(1.4)	-4.3	(1.3)	5.2	(1.3)	1.0	(1.3)	26.0	(2.2)	40.4	(4.2)	0.3	(1.3)
France	7.4	(1.4)	12.3	(1.1)	-2.8	(1.1)	0.4	(1.1)	1.3	(1.2)	-1.4	(1.2)	10.3	(2.0)	46.6	(3.1)	4.6	(1.0)
Germany	3.7	(1.5)	17.9	(1.6)	-1.5	(1.2)	-0.5	(1.2)	-0.1	(1.3)	-0.5	(1.4)	4.3	(2.3)	35.0	(1.8)	5.0	(2.2)
Greece	7.5	(1.6)	8.9	(1.5)	-1.3	(1.4)	3.3	(1.3)	1.7	(1.3)	-0.5	(1.4)	18.1	(2.5)	18.3	(3.9)	6.1	(1.2)
Hong Kong-China	0.6	(1.2)	12.7	(1.1)	-3.2	(1.1)	-0.2	(0.9)	1.8	(1.1)	1.1	(1.3)	5.7	(2.4)	25.1	(1.3)	3.7	(1.2)
Hungary	0.7	(1.1)	14.7	(1.0)	-0.8	(0.9)	4.4	(0.9)	-3.1	(0.9)	0.2	(1.1)	7.4	(2.3)	22.5	(1.9)	-0.3	(1.0)
Iceland	10.5	(1.5)	31.4	(1.8)	-7.9	(1.5)	-1.0	(1.4)	5.8	(1.6)	2.1	(1.4)	22.3	(2.9)	a	a	-1.8	(1.5)
Indonesia	6.5	(1.1)	4.7	(1.1)	2.2	(1.3)	5.1	(1.1)	-0.7	(1.2)	-2.5	(1.7)	6.9	(2.3)	17.2	(1.9)	-2.2	(1.6)
Ireland	13.3	(1.5)	24.5	(1.5)	-4.0	(1.3)	-2.0	(1.4)	1.7	(1.4)	7.8	(1.7)	6.6	(3.6)	24.0	(1.6)	4.8	(1.5)
Israel	9.3	(2.0)	14.6	(2.1)	-4.7	(2.1)	1.9	(2.1)	5.5	(2.2)	-2.7	(2.5)	9.6	(5.3)	20.0	(7.9)	2.5	(2.2)
Italy	3.0	(1.2)	12.4	(1.0)	-3.5	(1.1)	-0.5	(1.1)	2.8	(1.2)	-0.6	(1.2)	11.2	(2.6)	32.2	(3.0)	0.6	(1.1)
Japan[2]	m	m	m	m	m	m	m	m	m	m	m	m	m	m	m	m	m	m
Korea	-1.1	(1.2)	12.6	(1.1)	2.5	(1.0)	-0.6	(1.1)	0.0	(1.1)	1.1	(1.1)	18.3	(2.6)	13.4	(11.8)	-0.5	(1.1)
Latvia	8.4	(1.5)	14.7	(2.1)	-1.1	(1.4)	0.8	(1.7)	4.3	(1.8)	2.1	(1.8)	25.3	(3.2)	30.8	(3.1)	2.5	(1.8)
Liechtenstein[3]	c	c	c	c	c	c	c	c	c	c	c	c	c	c	c	c	c	c
Luxembourg	10.7	(1.7)	11.8	(1.9)	-1.5	(1.6)	5.3	(1.4)	1.3	(1.8)	0.1	(1.5)	13.6	(2.7)	30.7	(2.0)	8.5	(1.3)
FYR Macedonia	13.6	(1.5)	5.4	(1.6)	0.9	(1.1)	7.3	(1.3)	1.1	(1.5)	4.6	(1.5)	19.1	(3.5)	14.0	(3.4)	7.8	(1.4)
Mexico	3.4	(1.3)	9.4	(1.2)	-3.0	(1.3)	5.4	(1.3)	1.4	(1.5)	2.0	(1.2)	7.6	(2.3)	29.0	(3.0)	1.4	(1.2)
New Zealand	15.6	(1.7)	24.6	(1.8)	-8.1	(1.8)	-2.0	(1.8)	-1.4	(1.6)	-0.4	(2.0)	28.6	(3.4)	54.0	(4.7)	9.6	(1.8)
Norway	12.9	(1.6)	28.9	(2.0)	-7.6	(1.6)	-2.9	(1.7)	7.2	(1.7)	-2.0	(1.7)	19.1	(3.7)	42.6	(22.0)	10.3	(1.7)
Peru	4.1	(1.4)	5.5	(1.4)	1.1	(1.3)	11.1	(1.3)	-2.1	(1.2)	-1.1	(1.2)	-1.2	(2.5)	28.4	(1.4)	4.1	(1.3)
Poland	1.5	(1.7)	11.2	(1.8)	-3.2	(1.2)	3.0	(1.3)	-1.9	(1.3)	5.3	(1.6)	-0.5	(2.9)	a	a	2.1	(1.3)
Portugal	7.3	(1.4)	13.3	(1.5)	-3.7	(1.0)	6.3	(0.9)	5.4	(1.1)	0.9	(1.2)	2.0	(2.7)	53.3	(1.7)	2.2	(1.2)
Russian Federation	9.2	(1.3)	10.3	(1.2)	-3.2	(1.2)	1.0	(1.2)	0.3	(1.0)	-0.9	(1.1)	16.7	(2.3)	34.6	(2.8)	3.7	(1.1)
Spain	3.7	(1.1)	14.2	(1.3)	-1.4	(1.2)	-0.3	(1.0)	4.6	(1.2)	0.0	(1.4)	7.7	(1.9)	70.7	(2.2)	1.7	(1.2)
Sweden	14.1	(1.5)	30.3	(1.8)	-7.6	(1.2)	-2.8	(1.3)	6.9	(1.4)	2.8	(1.3)	19.7	(2.5)	70.3	(9.8)	1.3	(1.2)
Switzerland	9.0	(1.4)	23.4	(1.5)	1.5	(1.3)	5.2	(1.3)	1.5	(1.2)	4.8	(1.3)	6.7	(2.1)	44.0	(2.9)	4.8	(1.1)
Thailand	3.8	(1.6)	12.8	(1.5)	-1.1	(1.2)	7.0	(1.1)	-3.7	(1.2)	1.4	(1.7)	24.7	(2.4)	20.2	(2.3)	5.4	(1.6)
United Kingdom	16.7	(1.3)	19.8	(1.2)	-4.3	(1.2)	-1.8	(1.2)	3.3	(1.3)	7.4	(1.5)	13.8	(2.3)	10.5	(2.1)	3.6	(1.3)
United States	9.9	(2.0)	16.8	(2.7)	-2.0	(1.9)	2.4	(1.8)	1.1	(2.0)	6.2	(1.5)	10.7	(3.2)	37.6	(2.9)	0.2	(1.7)
Netherlands[4]	6.5	(1.6)	15.5	(1.7)	-5.8	(1.4)	1.9	(1.3)	5.2	(1.6)	-0.9	(1.5)	2.9	(2.2)	35.9	(3.7)	3.3	(2.0)

1. For reasons of comparability, the regression specification used here corresponds exactly to the one presented in OECD (2002b, Chapter 7). Variables such as quality of the schools' physical infrastructure and educational resources, teacher- and student-related factors affecting school climate, teacher shortage, teachers' morale and commitment, and the type of schools or the tracks available in the school were initially included in the model but due to their sma impact or to the percentage of missing data, these variables were removed (OECD 2002b, p.158). Coefficients for the intercept are not included in this table.

2. Japan is excluded from the analysis due to a high proportion of missing data on occupation status of parents.

3. Liechtenstein is excluded from the analysis because the number of schools in the country was considered too small to be considered as appropriate for the analyses of variance decomposition.

4. Response rate is too low to ensure comparability (see Annex A3).

Table 7.15 (continued)
Multilevel regression coefficients (model 1, without class size)[1]

| | Student-level variables | | | | | | | | | | School-level variables | | | |
| | Homework time | | Immigration status | | Family structure | | Books at home | | Teacher-student relations | | Socio-economic background at school level | | Engagement in reading at the school level | |
	Coef.	S.E.	Coef.	S.E.	Coef.	S.E.	Coef.	S.E.	Coef.	S.E.	Coef.	S.E.	Coef.	S.E.
Albania	13.3	(1.4)	-54.3	(19.7)	11.8	(4.5)	4.5	(1.4)	-10.6	(1.5)	63.6	(4.0)	0.6	(5.0)
Argentina	-2.3	(2.2)	-13.1	(18.9)	-0.9	(3.6)	5.1	(1.6)	-3.2	(1.7)	53.6	(3.2)	6.3	(4.5)
Australia	5.2	(1.9)	-29.5	(4.8)	5.0	(3.9)	4.4	(1.2)	2.0	(1.7)	42.7	(3.2)	4.4	(3.9)
Austria	-7.3	(1.3)	-30.9	(5.5)	-2.8	(3.1)	4.6	(1.0)	2.9	(1.3)	46.0	(3.5)	44.4	(3.6)
Belgium	0.8	(1.2)	-4.7	(6.0)	-4.5	(2.1)	3.5	(0.7)	-3.0	(1.1)	61.1	(2.6)	22.0	(2.3)
Brazil	0.8	(1.4)	-59.0	(40.4)	-4.7	(3.3)	0.6	(1.4)	-2.9	(1.4)	40.7	(2.7)	-1.0	(3.1)
Bulgaria	1.5	(1.7)	-12.4	(22.7)	-1.3	(3.0)	4.9	(0.9)	-2.7	(1.6)	77.1	(2.8)	35.5	(4.2)
Canada	3.2	(0.8)	-25.1	(3.6)	7.0	(1.6)	4.9	(0.6)	5.7	(0.8)	28.1	(1.9)	2.1	(2.1)
Chile	0.9	(1.1)	3.6	(21.5)	-0.5	(2.4)	2.7	(0.9)	0.1	(1.1)	42.2	(1.9)	22.6	(4.8)
Czech Republic	-6.3	(1.1)	-1.4	(18.1)	-4.0	(2.6)	6.9	(0.9)	-1.7	(1.1)	50.4	(2.5)	37.2	(3.2)
Denmark	-7.9	(1.6)	-44.7	(7.6)	5.1	(2.9)	6.5	(1.2)	4.7	(1.4)	21.3	(4.0)	15.2	(5.2)
Finland	-4.9	(1.4)	-61.8	(10.3)	10.2	(2.9)	4.1	(0.9)	5.7	(1.2)	11.1	(2.5)	17.5	(5.4)
France	3.3	(1.1)	-15.7	(7.9)	-0.6	(2.3)	5.2	(0.8)	-4.9	(1.3)	19.2	(3.6)	33.4	(6.0)
Germany	-2.3	(1.2)	-23.5	(6.3)	-4.6	(2.6)	3.9	(1.1)	0.6	(1.2)	63.7	(2.7)	44.8	(3.1)
Greece	8.5	(1.6)	2.1	(8.8)	0.8	(3.5)	3.0	(1.1)	-2.2	(1.2)	46.8	(2.6)	65.3	(3.9)
Hong Kong-China	4.2	(1.2)	21.2	(3.2)	-5.7	(3.0)	-0.2	(1.0)	2.7	(1.1)	16.5	(1.8)	89.8	(2.7)
Hungary	-0.3	(1.0)	3.0	(7.0)	-4.0	(2.3)	6.8	(0.8)	-5.8	(1.1)	61.8	(3.8)	35.8	(4.4)
Iceland	-8.6	(1.6)	-36.5	(22.5)	4.3	(3.4)	7.0	(1.1)	7.9	(1.6)	7.5	(3.9)	8.3	(6.5)
Indonesia	3.1	(1.3)	-60.9	(42.1)	1.1	(3.5)	2.3	(1.2)	-0.2	(1.3)	27.1	(2.6)	19.9	(3.0)
Ireland	2.1	(1.5)	8.7	(10.2)	8.8	(3.3)	6.7	(1.1)	0.7	(1.6)	40.5	(2.8)	12.6	(4.6)
Israel	-4.5	(2.3)	-0.2	(7.4)	-1.7	(5.0)	3.5	(1.8)	2.4	(2.8)	71.3	(5.7)	-18.7	(4.6)
Italy	1.7	(1.2)	-6.2	(17.7)	4.9	(2.1)	1.1	(0.7)	-1.4	(1.4)	54.2	(3.5)	30.9	(6.2)
Japan[2]	m	m	m	m	m	m	m	m	m	m	m	m	m	m
Korea	0.7	(1.1)	a	a	-0.5	(2.9)	5.7	(0.7)	2.4	(0.9)	17.1	(2.6)	64.3	(3.0)
Latvia	2.7	(1.9)	-5.8	(5.6)	-3.9	(3.7)	7.2	(1.4)	-0.1	(2.3)	45.0	(4.2)	23.9	(5.3)
Liechtenstein[3]	c	c	c	c	c	c	c	c	c	c	c	c	c	c
Luxembourg	-2.8	(1.3)	-21.5	(4.0)	2.4	(3.1)	6.3	(1.0)	-1.0	(1.5)	53.2	(4.8)	9.4	(8.6)
FYR Macedonia	4.3	(1.4)	-1.0	(17.7)	-0.2	(4.2)	-1.4	(1.0)	-9.1	(1.5)	64.9	(3.1)	-14.0	(6.3)
Mexico	2.2	(1.0)	-32.3	(8.6)	-5.0	(2.2)	4.6	(1.2)	0.1	(1.1)	45.8	(3.2)	9.8	(6.9)
New Zealand	3.6	(1.6)	-35.8	(4.8)	6.8	(3.1)	7.9	(1.2)	5.3	(1.7)	42.6	(3.8)	-6.1	(4.8)
Norway	-1.2	(1.7)	-41.2	(10.2)	11.9	(3.7)	5.1	(1.3)	8.7	(1.9)	10.0	(4.1)	24.2	(7.9)
Peru	-	-	14.8	(31.2)	0.0	(2.4)	4.0	(1.1)	-3.9	(1.7)	65.9	(2.9)	10.2	(6.2)
Poland	0.3	(1.6)	-29.8	(29.0)	-0.2	(3.9)	1.8	(1.0)	-3.2	(1.6)	82.6	(2.7)	58.9	(3.9)
Portugal	-3.7	(1.2)	-15.8	(10.7)	-4.6	(2.5)	3.5	(1.1)	-1.4	(1.2)	20.9	(2.4)	19.3	(4.5)
Russian Federation	9.5	(1.2)	2.5	(5.2)	-3.0	(2.1)	5.0	(0.9)	-0.5	(1.2)	48.3	(3.6)	13.7	(2.7)
Spain	5.6	(1.3)	-9.3	(9.2)	-2.3	(2.5)	6.6	(1.1)	1.0	(1.0)	18.8	(1.7)	25.0	(2.8)
Sweden	-11.3	(1.4)	-27.1	(6.5)	11.9	(2.6)	5.5	(1.1)	5.5	(1.6)	20.6	(3.2)	-2.5	(3.9)
Switzerland	-1.4	(1.2)	-43.1	(4.1)	-1.6	(2.6)	4.4	(0.9)	0.1	(1.1)	19.1	(4.4)	41.2	(4.5)
Thailand	4.8	(1.2)	22.2	(28.7)	4.4	(2.6)	2.2	(1.0)	-1.6	(1.3)	13.0	(2.7)	36.3	(2.7)
United Kingdom	8.1	(1.5)	-31.1	(8.9)	13.6	(2.6)	5.6	(1.0)	3.2	(1.3)	44.5	(3.0)	11.0	(5.6)
United States	7.4	(1.5)	-6.4	(8.1)	21.5	(3.9)	9.3	(1.2)	2.3	(1.8)	52.8	(4.3)	-7.6	(6.1)
Netherlands[4]	-1.7	(1.2)	-32.0	(8.2)	-0.6	(4.2)	3.3	(1.2)	-0.4	(1.6)	76.4	(3.1)	20.5	(3.2)

1. For reasons of comparability, the regression specification used here corresponds exactly to the one presented in OECD (2002b, Chapter 7). Variables such as quality of the schools' physical infrastructure and educational resources, teacher- and student-related factors affecting school climate, teacher shortage, teachers' morale and commitment, and the type of schools or the tracks available in the school were initially included in the model but due to their sma impact or to the percentage of missing data, these variables were removed (OECD 2002b, p.158). Coefficients for the intercept are not included in this table.
2. Japan is excluded from the analysis due to a high proportion of missing data on occupation status of parents.
3. Liechtenstein is excluded from the analysis because the number of schools in the country was considered too small to be considered as appropriate for the analyses of variance decomposition.
4. Response rate is too low to ensure comparability (see Annex A3).

Description of variables for model 1 (Table 7.15)

Individual characteristics of the student

- *Gender*: Females were recoded as 1 and males as 0.
- *Engagement in reading*: See Annex A1 for a description of the variable.

Home and family background variables

- *Family structure*: Students living with two parents/guardians were coded to 1. Other students have a 0 on this variable. It indicates whether the student lives in a nuclear family.
- *Socio-economic background*: The PISA International Socio-economic Index of Occupational Status was derived from students' responses on parental occupation. See Annex A1 for a description of the variable.
- *Books at home*: Number of books in the home. This is an indicator of literacy resources at home and reflects also the educational and socio-economic background of the family. This variable has been used as an indicator for students' socio-economic and educational background in most international studies on educational achievement (TIMSS, IEA Civic Education Study, IEA Reading Literacy Study).
- *Cultural communication with parents*: See Annex A1 for a description of the variable.
- *Home educational resources*: See Annex A1 for a description of the variable.
- *Immigration status*: Students' reports on where they and their parents were born were recoded so that 1 indicates that a student and both of his or her parents were born in another country (0 for all other students). This variable indicates whether a student comes from a 'first-generation' immigrant family. Preliminary analyses showed that the language spoken at home has a strong effect in many countries, typically those with a higher proportion of immigrants. That is, students who, most of the time, speak a language at home different from the test language on average have lower reading scores. But as this question was not included in two countries' questionnaires and as in a considerable number of countries this variable had a high percentage of non-responses it was decided not to include this variable in the final model.

Instruction and learning

- *Achievement pressure*: See Annex A1 for a description of the variable.
- *Time spent on homework*: See Annex A1 for a description of the variable.
- *Grade*: This variable contains the grade the student attends. It was recoded to reflect the difference between the student's level and the modal level for 15-year-old students in the country. It was included mainly for the purpose of controlling for different levels of instruction. Without controlling for grade level some (school-related) predictors may appear to be have an effect which is only due to grade differences.

Perceptions of school and learning climate

- *Sense of belonging to school*: This is an index measuring students' feelings about being at school. Positive values indicating a favourable perception of the school. See Annex A1 for a description of the variable.
- *Disciplinary climate*: See Annex A1 for a description of the variable.
- *Teacher-student relations*: See Annex A1 for a description of the variable.

School characteristics

- *Mean of parents' occupational status for school*: This variable indicates the average of the occupational status of parents within a school. It is an indicator for the 'intake' of a school: that is, whether its students on average come from families with a higher or a lower socio-economic status.
- *Mean of engagement in reading for school*: This variable reflects the average of the students' engagement in reading for each school.

Note: To make effect sizes comparable across countries, all continuous variables were standardised to have a national (within-country) mean of 0 and a standard deviation of 1. Aggregates of student variables at the school level were not standardised. (For further details on variables and the methodology used, see OECD 2002*a*, Annex A3.)

Table 7.16
Multilevel regression coefficients (model 2, including class size)[1]

	Socio-economic background (HISEI)		Engagement in reading		Achievement pressure		Sense of belonging		Cultural communication		Disciplinary climate	
	Coef.	S.E.	Coef.	S.E.	Coef.	S.E.	Coef.	S.E.	Coef.	S.E.	Coef.	S.E.
Albania	8.0	(1.5)	2.7	(1.5)	-1.6	(1.2)	4.4	(1.7)	-1.0	(1.5)	0.7	(1.2)
Argentina	4.7	(1.9)	19.5	(1.8)	-5.3	(2.1)	6.0	(2.0)	-1.2	(3.6)	4.4	(2.1)
Australia	12.2	(1.9)	24.5	(2.0)	-7.7	(1.4)	-3.0	(1.4)	9.1	(1.8)	-2.6	(1.6)
Austria	2.2	(1.3)	18.1	(1.3)	-1.8	(1.3)	1.6	(1.4)	1.8	(1.4)	1.6	(1.2)
Belgium	6.3	(1.3)	18.1	(1.0)	-1.6	(1.1)	1.8	(1.0)	0.9	(1.0)	-2.5	(1.1)
Brazil	3.1	(1.6)	14.1	(1.5)	2.7	(1.6)	2.3	(1.2)	2.1	(1.6)	3.5	(1.4)
Bulgaria	6.2	(1.5)	10.9	(1.8)	0.5	(1.3)	6.2	(1.3)	3.1	(1.4)	-3.6	(1.4)
Canada	11.2	(0.9)	24.2	(0.9)	-6.4	(0.8)	-2.2	(0.7)	3.9	(0.8)	-2.4	(0.8)
Chile	6.5	(1.3)	14.4	(1.2)	-9.6	(1.2)	4.1	(1.1)	4.2	(1.1)	-0.7	(1.1)
Czech Republic	8.0	(1.2)	18.1	(1.1)	-4.2	(1.4)	5.0	(1.0)	3.0	(1.1)	-0.9	(1.1)
Denmark	11.4	(1.8)	28.9	(1.5)	-1.7	(1.4)	1.5	(1.4)	10.3	(1.6)	-2.7	(1.4)
Finland	11.8	(1.2)	30.0	(1.3)	-3.4	(1.3)	-4.4	(1.3)	5.1	(1.3)	-1.3	(1.2)
France	7.0	(1.4)	12.3	(1.1)	-3.2	(1.1)	0.0	(1.0)	1.0	(1.1)	1.1	(1.2)
Germany	3.4	(1.4)	18.1	(1.5)	-2.0	(1.1)	-0.7	(1.1)	0.4	(1.2)	0.1	(1.3)
Greece	7.4	(1.6)	8.8	(1.5)	-1.8	(1.4)	3.6	(1.4)	1.9	(1.3)	-0.2	(1.5)
Hong Kong-China	0.9	(1.2)	12.7	(1.0)	-3.1	(1.0)	-0.5	(0.9)	1.9	(1.1)	-0.2	(1.3)
Hungary	0.9	(1.1)	14.8	(1.0)	-0.8	(1.0)	4.3	(0.9)	-3.2	(0.9)	-0.1	(1.1)
Iceland	8.7	(1.5)	29.7	(1.8)	-7.3	(1.5)	-1.9	(1.3)	5.7	(1.5)	-1.7	(1.4)
Indonesia	m	m	m	m	m	m	m	m	m	m	m	m
Ireland	11.9	(1.5)	24.8	(1.5)	-4.4	(1.2)	-2.6	(1.4)	1.2	(1.4)	-7.2	(1.7)
Israel	7.4	(2.2)	14.1	(2.3)	-4.4	(2.0)	0.6	(2.0)	5.7	(2.2)	3.6	(2.3)
Italy	3.0	(1.2)	12.4	(1.0)	-3.5	(1.1)	-0.6	(1.1)	3.0	(1.2)	1.0	(1.2)
Japan[2]	-2.0	(1.7)	15.7	(2.0)	-0.7	(2.0)	-2.5	(1.7)	1.1	(1.6)	-3.5	(1.8)
Korea	-1.6	(1.1)	10.9	(1.2)	2.7	(1.1)	-0.4	(1.3)	0.8	(1.2)	-2.0	(1.1)
Latvia	7.9	(1.5)	14.6	(2.2)	-1.3	(1.4)	0.3	(1.6)	4.1	(2.0)	-2.3	(1.9)
Liechtenstein[3]	c	c	c	c	c	c	c	c	c	c	c	c
Luxembourg	10.4	(1.7)	11.6	(1.9)	-1.7	(1.5)	4.6	(1.4)	1.6	(1.7)	-0.4	(1.4)
FYR Macedonia	12.8	(1.5)	6.2	(1.6)	0.1	(1.1)	6.9	(1.3)	0.7	(1.5)	-4.2	(1.5)
Mexico	3.2	(1.4)	9.7	(1.3)	-3.2	(1.3)	4.9	(1.4)	1.6	(1.5)	-2.3	(1.3)
New Zealand	14.6	(1.6)	23.8	(1.8)	-8.7	(1.7)	-2.6	(1.7)	-1.1	(1.5)	-0.4	(1.9)
Norway	13.1	(1.6)	28.6	(2.0)	-7.6	(1.6)	-3.3	(1.6)	7.2	(1.7)	1.9	(1.8)
Peru	m	m	m	m	m	m	m	m	m	m	m	m
Poland	1.8	(1.7)	11.5	(1.8)	-3.7	(1.2)	3.0	(1.4)	-2.4	(1.4)	-5.4	(1.6)
Portugal	7.4	(1.4)	13.2	(1.5)	-3.8	(1.0)	6.4	(1.0)	5.2	(1.1)	-1.0	(1.2)
Russian Federation	9.3	(1.3)	10.4	(1.3)	-3.3	(1.2)	1.1	(1.2)	0.5	(1.1)	0.9	(1.1)
Spain	3.6	(1.1)	14.1	(1.3)	-1.6	(1.2)	-0.5	(1.0)	4.6	(1.1)	0.0	(1.5)
Sweden	12.7	(1.5)	28.9	(1.9)	-6.9	(1.3)	-2.9	(1.4)	7.0	(1.5)	-2.9	(1.4)
Switzerland	7.6	(1.4)	23.0	(1.5)	1.4	(1.2)	4.5	(1.2)	1.8	(1.2)	-5.0	(1.3)
Thailand	4.3	(1.7)	12.6	(1.6)	-0.3	(1.2)	6.4	(1.2)	-3.9	(1.3)	-2.0	(1.7)
United Kingdom	15.2	(1.3)	19.2	(1.2)	-4.5	(1.3)	-2.7	(1.1)	3.8	(1.3)	-7.0	(1.4)
United States	10.0	(2.0)	17.3	(2.3)	-2.7	(1.8)	1.9	(1.9)	1.5	(1.9)	-6.4	(1.6)
Netherlands[4]	5.9	(1.4)	15.6	(1.6)	-5.9	(1.5)	1.5	(1.2)	5.3	(1.6)	-0.4	(1.3)

1. The regression specification used here corresponds exactly to the one presented in Table 7.15 and in OECD (2002b, Chapter 7) with the exception that this model also includes class size and class size squared. Coefficients for the intercept are not included in this table. Coefficients for the intercept are no included in this table.

2. Although Japan has been excluded from the previous multi-level analysis presented in table 7.15 due to high proportion of missing data, its data has been included in this analysis because the information on class size is valid.

3. Liechtenstein is excluded from the analysis because the number of schools in the country was considered too small to be considered as appropriate for the analyses of variance decomposition.

4. Response rate is too low to ensure comparability (see Annex A3).

Table 7.16 (continued)
Multilevel regression coefficients (model 2, including class size)[1]

	Student-level variables													
	Gender		Grade		Home educational resources		Homework time		Immigration status		Family structure		Books at home	
	Coef.	S.E.	Coef.	S.E.	Coef.	S.E.	Coef.	S.E.	Coef.	S.E.	Coef.	S.E.	Coef.	S.E.
Albania	25.0	(3.1)	26.6	(3.2)	8.4	(1.6)	12.0	(1.5)	-50.2	(20.5)	9.9	(4.8)	4.3	(1.4)
Argentina	16.4	(3.7)	39.1	(3.5)	1.8	(2.2)	-1.2	(2.1)	-23.3	(20.2)	-2.1	(3.3)	4.9	(1.6)
Australia	16.0	(2.7)	43.3	(3.2)	2.4	(1.7)	4.9	(1.8)	-27.5	(4.7)	4.8	(3.8)	4.4	(1.2)
Austria	5.8	(3.2)	32.5	(2.0)	2.0	(1.6)	-7.6	(1.2)	-29.1	(5.5)	-2.8	(3.1)	4.6	(1.1)
Belgium	4.2	(2.2)	51.1	(2.9)	1.1	(1.1)	0.5	(1.2)	-3.7	(6.0)	-4.5	(2.1)	3.3	(0.7)
Brazil	0.0	(2.8)	33.7	(1.6)	3.6	(1.8)	0.9	(1.4)	-60.0	(40.8)	-4.6	(3.3)	0.6	(1.4)
Bulgaria	12.9	(3.4)	14.5	(3.1)	5.4	(1.5)	0.7	(1.7)	-8.7	(24.5)	-2.7	(3.0)	4.2	(1.0)
Canada	13.7	(1.5)	44.6	(1.7)	0.1	(0.7)	1.9	(0.9)	-23.9	(3.6)	6.6	(1.6)	4.7	(0.6)
Chile	0.8	(2.8)	35.8	(2.0)	-0.6	(1.1)	1.1	(1.1)	3.3	(24.1)	0.4	(2.5)	2.5	(0.9)
Czech Republic	6.8	(2.4)	29.6	(2.5)	2.9	(1.3)	-6.3	(1.1)	-4.1	(18.6)	-4.0	(2.5)	6.7	(0.9)
Denmark	8.3	(2.8)	31.1	(5.2)	0.3	(1.4)	-8.2	(1.7)	-45.8	(7.7)	4.8	(2.9)	6.1	(1.3)
Finland	26.0	(2.2)	37.6	(4.0)	0.1	(1.2)	-6.0	(1.4)	-53.6	(11.3)	9.2	(2.9)	3.8	(0.9)
France	9.4	(2.0)	44.5	(3.1)	3.6	(1.0)	2.4	(1.0)	-17.5	(8.1)	-0.5	(2.3)	4.9	(0.8)
Germany	3.1	(2.1)	35.3	(1.9)	3.3	(1.3)	-2.9	(1.2)	-21.2	(5.2)	-4.4	(2.8)	3.4	(1.0)
Greece	18.1	(2.4)	17.9	(4.0)	6.2	(1.1)	8.1	(1.6)	0.7	(8.8)	1.0	(3.6)	2.8	(1.1)
Hong Kong-China	4.6	(2.3)	22.5	(1.3)	3.5	(1.1)	3.7	(1.1)	19.7	(3.2)	-6.1	(2.8)	-0.2	(1.0)
Hungary	7.2	(2.4)	22.7	(2.0)	-0.5	(1.1)	-0.5	(1.0)	4.3	(6.9)	-4.3	(2.4)	6.7	(0.8)
Iceland	18.7	(2.9)	a	a	-2.1	(1.6)	-8.0	(1.5)	-34.1	(23.3)	2.9	(3.4)	6.4	(1.1)
Indonesia	m	m	m	m	m	m	m	m	m	m	m	m	m	m
Ireland	3.8	(3.4)	25.5	(1.6)	3.3	(1.5)	-0.2	(1.5)	7.2	(9.9)	7.5	(3.2)	6.0	(1.1)
Israel	4.9	(5.3)	15.9	(7.2)	0.7	(2.5)	-6.5	(2.5)	-1.3	(7.9)	-1.9	(5.4)	2.6	(1.6)
Italy	10.9	(2.5)	31.5	(3.0)	0.7	(1.1)	1.8	(1.1)	-3.1	(17.8)	4.5	(2.1)	1.2	(0.7)
Japan[2]	16.4	(4.4)	a	a	1.6	(1.8)	-1.3	(1.7)	15.9	(29.6)	-2.3	(6.4)	1.5	(1.2)
Korea	16.3	(2.4)	12.7	(13.0)	-1.1	(1.1)	0.6	(1.2)	a	a	-0.7	(3.1)	5.4	(0.8)
Latvia	25.4	(3.2)	29.0	(2.9)	2.3	(1.8)	2.3	(1.8)	-7.9	(5.5)	-2.1	(3.8)	7.2	(1.4)
Liechtenstein[3]	c	c	c	c	c	c	c	c	c	c	c	c	c	c
Luxembourg	13.0	(2.5)	31.9	(2.0)	7.0	(1.3)	-4.0	(1.4)	-16.9	(3.9)	3.0	(3.3)	6.1	(1.0)
FYR Macedonia	17.8	(3.5)	12.3	(3.1)	6.3	(1.5)	3.3	(1.5)	-6.6	(17.9)	0.5	(4.4)	-0.4	(1.0)
Mexico	8.3	(2.3)	29.5	(3.0)	1.7	(1.2)	2.1	(1.0)	-33.7	(8.5)	-5.4	(2.2)	4.5	(1.2)
New Zealand	24.8	(3.4)	56.0	(4.7)	7.9	(1.8)	2.7	(1.5)	-34.4	(4.9)	6.6	(3.0)	7.3	(1.1)
Norway	19.3	(3.8)	37.1	(22.4)	9.7	(1.7)	-0.9	(1.7)	-41.1	(10.4)	11.8	(3.8)	5.3	(1.3)
Peru	m	m	m	m	m	m	m	m	m	m	m	m	m	m
Poland	-0.7	(2.9)	a	a	2.1	(1.2)	0.3	(1.7)	-15.4	(29.2)	-0.1	(4.0)	1.9	(1.1)
Portugal	1.7	(2.8)	52.9	(1.8)	2.1	(1.2)	-3.8	(1.2)	-15.0	(10.8)	-4.2	(2.5)	3.4	(1.1)
Russian Federation	15.8	(2.4)	35.1	(2.8)	3.2	(1.1)	9.4	(1.1)	4.4	(5.6)	-2.3	(2.1)	5.0	(1.0)
Spain	7.2	(2.0)	68.8	(2.3)	1.8	(1.3)	5.2	(1.3)	-9.2	(9.3)	-2.8	(2.5)	6.6	(1.0)
Sweden	18.9	(2.6)	67.7	(9.5)	0.8	(1.2)	-10.7	(1.4)	-23.2	(6.5)	11.2	(2.6)	5.7	(1.1)
Switzerland	5.3	(2.0)	43.6	(3.0)	3.8	(1.1)	-1.7	(1.2)	-40.0	(4.2)	-3.0	(2.7)	4.2	(0.9)
Thailand	23.4	(2.6)	19.5	(2.7)	5.0	(1.6)	4.7	(1.3)	23.3	(29.1)	3.8	(2.6)	2.8	(1.2)
United Kingdom	8.6	(2.2)	15.7	(2.1)	2.0	(1.1)	6.1	(1.4)	-28.1	(8.6)	13.2	(2.5)	5.1	(1.0)
United States	9.6	(3.3)	37.6	(3.0)	-0.9	(1.6)	7.0	(1.6)	-6.9	(8.3)	21.6	(3.9)	9.2	(1.1)
Netherlands[4]	2.1	(2.1)	34.8	(3.7)	2.3	(1.9)	-2.7	(1.3)	-28.1	(8.4)	-1.3	(4.2)	3.0	(1.1)

1. The regression specification used here corresponds exactly to the one presented in Table 7.15 and in OECD (2002b, Chapter 7) with the exception that this model also includes class size and class size squared. Coefficients for the intercept are not included in this table. Coefficients for the intercept are no included in this table.
2. Although Japan has been excluded from the previous multi-level analysis presented in table 7.15 due to high proportion of missing data, its data has been included in this analysis because the information on class size is valid.
3. Liechtenstein is excluded from the analysis because the number of schools in the country was considered too small to be considered as appropriate for the analyses of variance decomposition.
4. Response rate is too low to ensure comparability (see Annex A3).

Table 7.16 (continued)
Multilevel regression coefficients (model 2, including class size)

	Student-level variables						School level variables				Regression statistics			
	Student-teacher relationship		Class size		Class size squared		Socio-economic background at school level		Reading engagement at the school level		Number of students in data-base	Number of students used in the multilevel regres-sion	Ex-plained variance at the school level (%)	Ex-plained variance at the student level within school (%)
	Coef.	S.E.	Coef.	S.E.	Coef.	S.E.	Coef.	S.E.	Coef.	S.E.				
Albania	-9.9	(1.4)	36.1	(6.0)	-25.1	(6.2)	57.1	(5.1)	5.5	(5.7)	4980	3697	0.79	0.19
Argentina	-3.5	(1.7)	12.2	(9.8)	-10.0	(9.4)	50.9	(3.3)	6.0	(4.7)	3983	3107	0.82	0.17
Australia	2.4	(1.7)	22.4	(8.6)	-15.0	(8.6)	38.9	(3.0)	7.2	(3.9)	5176	4755	0.77	0.28
Austria	3.3	(1.3)	19.9	(5.5)	-12.6	(5.4)	39.9	(3.1)	39.7	(3.6)	4745	4073	0.87	0.18
Belgium	-3.1	(1.1)	15.7	(3.2)	-8.8	(2.7)	55.9	(2.7)	18.9	(2.4)	6670	5791	0.76	0.25
Brazil	-3.1	(1.4)	21.8	(5.6)	-24.4	(5.7)	40.6	(2.8)	0.6	(3.2)	4893	3975	0.77	0.18
Bulgaria	-3.2	(1.7)	18.7	(10.4)	-13.0	(10.4)	73.4	(3.0)	35.8	(4.0)	4657	3664	0.81	0.11
Canada	5.9	(0.8)	27.6	(2.5)	-20.9	(2.4)	23.5	(1.8)	4.3	(2.0)	29687	25750	0.60	0.29
Chile	-0.3	(1.1)	7.8	(6.6)	-5.9	(6.7)	43.2	(2.0)	22.0	(4.7)	4889	4052	0.90	0.18
Czech Republic	-1.9	(1.2)	17.8	(9.4)	-13.7	(8.8)	48.5	(2.5)	36.6	(3.2)	5365	4912	0.79	0.20
Denmark	4.8	(1.4)	37.9	(10.7)	-33.7	(10.5)	17.0	(3.5)	7.4	(5.0)	4235	3339	0.67	0.29
Finland	5.6	(1.1)	43.0	(8.8)	-35.1	(8.6)	7.6	(2.3)	20.6	(5.6)	4864	4500	0.35	0.35
France	-3.8	(1.3)	21.1	(8.5)	-9.6	(8.5)	12.6	(3.3)	28.0	(5.0)	4673	4022	0.91	0.20
Germany	0.3	(1.2)	43.6	(12.4)	-31.9	(11.2)	58.0	(2.9)	43.6	(3.1)	5073	4549	0.84	0.24
Greece	-2.4	(1.2)	17.2	(8.5)	-19.2	(8.7)	48.6	(3.2)	64.2	(4.0)	4672	4074	0.71	0.10
Hong Kong-China	2.9	(1.1)	6.4	(7.3)	4.7	(7.2)	23.8	(2.3)	75.0	(3.3)	4405	4112	0.65	0.20
Hungary	-5.8	(1.1)	13.0	(8.7)	-10.8	(8.6)	61.0	(3.9)	36.9	(4.4)	4887	4433	0.84	0.15
Iceland	7.1	(1.6)	-5.0	(6.4)	24.8	(6.5)	-12.0	(4.6)	9.7	(6.7)	3372	3088	0.15	0.31
Indonesia	m	m	m	m	m	m	m	m	m	m	7368	m	m	m
Ireland	1.6	(1.6)	49.4	(9.4)	-28.5	(9.4)	31.3	(2.9)	15.4	(4.4)	3854	3642	0.73	0.33
Israel	3.5	(2.9)	49.5	(7.6)	-34.3	(6.7)	67.0	(5.5)	-20.5	(4.7)	4498	2955	0.54	0.14
Italy	-1.4	(1.4)	11.2	(8.7)	-14.5	(8.7)	56.4	(3.5)	24.5	(5.8)	4984	4560	0.60	0.13
Japan[1]	6.3	(1.8)	23.3	(11.4)	-21.6	(13.4)	65.9	(5.4)	27.6	(9.1)	5256	1957	0.49	0.11
Korea	1.3	(1.0)	22.1	(4.4)	-13.8	(5.0)	18.5	(2.7)	54.6	(4.3)	4982	3869	0.77	0.11
Latvia	-0.1	(2.3)	9.2	(10.1)	-2.1	(9.5)	41.9	(4.3)	18.0	(5.1)	3893	3398	0.58	0.19
Liechtenstein[2]	3.0	(3.9)	-1.8	(21.1)	2.3	(21.5)	21.0	(17.4)	69.5	(17.7)	314	272	0.62	0.23
Luxembourg	-0.3	(1.5)	26.3	(8.0)	-17.8	(8.7)	47.0	(5.6)	7.0	(8.5)	3528	2788	0.94	0.28
FYR Macedonia	-9.5	(1.6)	20.0	(6.5)	-12.4	(7.3)	63.8	(3.4)	-17.9	(6.2)	4510	3523	0.70	0.12
Mexico	-0.3	(1.1)	9.5	(4.3)	-6.2	(4.4)	43.1	(3.1)	8.1	(7.0)	4600	3647	0.84	0.10
New Zealand	5.9	(1.6)	60.3	(8.3)	-43.5	(8.4)	32.9	(4.1)	0.6	(5.0)	3667	3297	0.74	0.31
Norway	8.9	(1.8)	12.9	(7.7)	-14.0	(7.7)	10.1	(4.5)	24.6	(7.2)	4147	3727	0.59	0.29
Peru	m	m	m	m	m	m	m	m	m	m	4429	m	m	m
Poland	-3.4	(1.5)	9.3	(12.9)	-7.3	(12.9)	82.8	(2.9)	52.5	(4.0)	3654	3001	0.76	0.05
Portugal	-1.3	(1.2)	17.0	(6.4)	-12.8	(6.4)	20.9	(2.3)	18.8	(4.5)	4585	4064	0.93	0.39
Russian Federation	-0.7	(1.3)	7.7	(7.3)	-3.5	(7.4)	43.5	(3.6)	15.7	(2.7)	6701	5892	0.46	0.18
Spain	1.1	(0.9)	12.2	(6.5)	-8.3	(6.7)	18.7	(1.9)	21.4	(3.1)	6214	5325	0.75	0.39
Sweden	5.5	(1.6)	36.5	(6.8)	-32.4	(6.5)	18.9	(3.5)	1.8	(3.7)	4416	3999	0.77	0.32
Switzerland	0.1	(1.0)	26.7	(8.9)	-11.0	(8.5)	19.0	(4.4)	33.0	(4.9)	6100	5359	0.72	0.33
Thailand	-2.2	(1.3)	-4.2	(9.9)	9.5	(10.1)	10.5	(3.0)	31.1	(3.6)	5340	4246	0.63	0.16
United Kingdom	4.0	(1.2)	42.0	(4.6)	-21.9	(4.7)	47.4	(3.0)	15.4	(6.9)	9340	8462	0.71	0.30
United States	3.3	(1.7)	17.3	(8.5)	-14.6	(9.2)	51.8	(4.7)	-7.0	(5.6)	3846	2924	0.83	0.24
Netherlands[3]	-0.5	(1.6)	43.7	(12.1)	-34.6	(11.5)	65.7	(4.3)	19.3	(3.3)	2503	2277	0.81	0.28

1. Japan is excluded from the analysis due to a high proportion of missing data on occupation status of parents.
2. Liechtenstein is excluded from the analysis because the number of schools in the country was considered too small to be considered as appropriate for the analyses of variance decomposition.
3. Response rate is too low to ensure comparability (see Annex A3).

Description of variables for model 2 (Table 7.16)

All details given for model 1 (Table 7.15) apply equally to model 2 (Table 7.16). However, two additional variables were introduced into the model. These are class size and its square. Class size is reported by individual students with respect to the class relevant for the PISA reading assessment (class of the language of assessment).

As opposed to the other continuous variables introduced at the student level, this variable was not standardised, so that the coefficients reflect the change in performance when adding one additional student. Since the relationship with perfromance is non-linear, the overall effect also depends on initial class size.

ANNEX C

Annex C1: The development and implementation of PISA – A collaborative effort

Introduction

PISA is a collaborative effort, bringing together scientific expertise from the participating countries, steered jointly by their governments on the basis of shared, policy-driven interests.

A Board of Participating Countries on which each country is represented determines, in the context of OECD objectives, the policy priorities for PISA and oversees adherence to these priorities during the implementation of the programme. This includes the setting of priorities for the development of indicators, for the establishment of the assessment instruments and for the reporting of the results.

Experts from participating countries also serve on working groups that are charged with linking policy objectives with the best internationally available technical expertise. By participating in these expert groups, countries ensure that: the instruments are internationally valid and take into account the cultural and educational contexts in participating countries; the assessment materials have strong measurement properties; and the instruments place an emphasis on authenticity and educational validity.

Through National Project Managers, participating countries implement PISA at the national level subject to the agreed administration procedures. National Project Managers play a vital role in ensuring that the implementation of the survey is of high quality, and verify and evaluate the survey results, analyses, reports and publications.

The design and implementation of the surveys, within the framework established by the Board of Participating Countries, is the responsibility of the PISA consortium, referred to as the PISA Consortium, led by the Australian Council for Educational Research (ACER). Other partners in this consortium include the Netherlands National Institute for Educational Measurement (Citogroep), The National Institute for Educational Policy Research in Japan (NIER), the Educational Testing Service in the United States (ETS), and WESTAT in the United States.

The OECD Secretariat has overall managerial responsibility for the programme, monitors its implementation on a day-to-day basis, acts as the secretariat for the Board of Participating Countries, builds consensus among countries and serves as the interlocutor between the Board of Participating Countries and the international consortium charged with the implementation of the activities. The OECD Secretariat also produces the indicators and analyses and prepares the international reports and publications in co-operation with the PISA consortium and in close consultation with Member countries both at the policy level (Board of Participating Countries) and at the level of implementation (National Project Managers).

The following lists the members of the various PISA bodies and the individual experts and consultants who have contributed to PISA during the first cycle.

Members of the PISA Board of Participating Countries (PISA 2000 and PISA Plus)

Chair: Eugene Owen

Argentina: Lilia Toranzos
Albania: Nikoleta Mika and Perparim Shera
Australia: Wendy Whitham
Austria: Friedrich Plank
Belgium: Dominique Barthélémy, Christiane Blondin, Dominique Lafontaine, Liselotte van de Perre
Brazil: Maria Helena Guimarães de Castro
Bulgaria: Alexander Petkov Lakiurski
Canada: Satya Brink, Patrick Bussière, Dianne Pennock,
Chile: Leonor Cariola
Czech Republic: Jan Koucky, Jana Strakova
Denmark: Birgitte Bovin
Finland: Ritva Jakku-Sihvonen
France: Gérard Bonnet
Germany: Jochen Schweitzer, Helga Hinke, Gudrun Stoltenberg
Greece: Vassilis Koulaidis
Hong Kong-China: Esther Sui Chu Ho
Hungary: Péter Vári
Iceland: Einar Gudmundsson
Indonesia: Ramon Mohandas, Bahrul Hayat
Ireland: Gerry Shiel
Israel: Bracha Kramarski, Zemira Mevarech
Italy: Chiara Croce, Elisabetta Midena, Benedetto Vertecchi
Japan: Ryo Watanabe
Korea: Kooghyang Ro
Latvia: Andris Kangro
Luxembourg: Jean-Paul Reeff
FYR Macedonia: Vladimir Mostrov
Mexico: Fernando Córdova Calderón
Netherlands: Arnold Spee
New Zealand: Lynne Whitney
Norway: Alette Schreiner
Peru: José Rodríguez, Giuliana Espinosa
Poland: Kazimierz Korab
Portugal: Glória Ramalho
Romania: Adrian Stoica, Roxana Mihail
Russian Federation: Galina Kovalyova
Spain: Guillermo Gil
Sweden: Anders Auer, Birgitta Fredander, Anita Wester
Switzerland: Heinz Gilomen
Thailand: Sunee Klainin

United Kingdom: Lorna Bertrand, Brian Semple
United States: Mariann Lemke

PISA National Project Managers (PISA 2000 and PISA Plus)

Argentina: Lilia Toranzos
Albania: Nikoleta Mika and Perparim Shera
Australia: Jan Lokan
Austria: Günter Haider
Belgium: Dominique Lafontaine, Luc van de Poele
Brazil: Tereza Cristina Cotta, Maria Lucia Guardia, Maria Inês Pestana
Bulgaria: Alexander Petkov Lakiurski
Canada: Marc Lachance, Dianne Pennock
Chile: Leonor Cariola
Czech Republic: Jana Straková
Denmark: Vita Bering Pruzan
Finland: Jouni Välijärvi
France: Jean-Pierre Jeantheau
Germany: Juergen Baumert, Petra Stanat
Greece: Katerina Kassotakis
Hong Kong-China: Esther Sui Chu Ho
Hungary: Péter Vári
Iceland: Julius Bjornsson, Ragna Benedikta Garðarsdóttir
Indonesia: Ramon Mohandas, Bahrul Hayat
Ireland: Judith Cosgrove
Israel: Bracha Kramarski, Zemira Mevarech
Italy: Emma Nardi
Japan: Ryo Watanabe
Korea: Kooghyang Ro
Latvia: Andris Kangro
Luxembourg: Iris Blanke, Jean-Paul Reeff
FYR Macedonia: Vladimir Mostrov
Mexico: Fernando Córdova Calderón
Netherlands: Johan Wijnstra
New Zealand: Steve May
Norway: Svein Lie
Peru: José Rodríguez, Giuliana Espinosa
Poland: Michal Federowicz
Portugal: Glória Ramalho
Romania: Adrian Stoica, Roxana Mihail
Russian Federation: Galina Kovalyova
Spain: Guillermo Gil

Sweden: Bengt-Olov Molander, Astrid Pettersson, Karin Taube
Switzerland: Huguette McCluskey
Thailand: Sunee Klainin
United Kingdom: Baljit Gill, Graham Thorpe
United States: Ghedam Bairu, Marilyn Binkley

OECD Secretariat

Andreas Schleicher (overall co-ordination of PISA and Member country relations)
Claudia Tamassia (project management)
Kooghyang Ro (project management)
Hannah Cocks (statistical support)
Sophie Vayssettes (statistical support)
Juliet Evans (administrative support)

UNESCO Institute for Statistics

Douglas Lynd
Albert Motivans
Yanhong Zhang
Marie-Hélène Lussier

PISA Expert Groups

Mathematics Functional Expert Group

Jan de Lange (Chair) (Utrecht University, The Netherlands)
Raimondo Bolletta (Istituto Nazionale di Valutazione, Italy)
Sean Close (St Patrick's College, Ireland)
Maria Luisa Moreno (IES "Lope de Vega", Spain)
Mogens Niss (IMFUFA, Roskilde University, Denmark)
Kyungmee Park (Hongik University, Korea)
Thomas A. Romberg (United States)
Peter Schüller (Federal Ministry of Education and Cultural Affairs, Austria)

Reading Functional Expert Group

Irwin Kirsch (Chair) (Educational Testing Service, United States)
Marilyn Binkley (National Center for Educational Statistics, United States)
Alan Davies (University of Edinburgh, United Kingdom)
Stan Jones (Statistics Canada, Canada)
John de Jong (Language Testing Services, The Netherlands)
Dominique Lafontaine (Université de Liège Sart Tilman, Belgium)
Pirjo Linnakylä (University of Jyväskylä, Finland)

Martine Rémond (Institut National de Recherche Pédagogique, France)
Wolfgang Schneider (University of Würzburg, Germany)
Ryo Watanabe (National Institute for Educational Research, Japan)

Science Functional Expert Group

Wynne Harlen (Chair) (University of Bristol, United Kingdom)
Peter Fensham (Monash University, Australia)
Raul Gagliardi (University of Geneva, Switzerland)
Svein Lie (University of Oslo, Norway)
Manfred Prenzel (Universität Kiel, Germany)
Senta A. Raizen (National Center for Improving Science Education (NCISE), United States)
Donghee Shin (DankooK University, Korea)
Elizabeth Stage (University of California, United States)

PISA Technical Advisory Group (PISA)

Ray Adams (ACER, Australia)
Pierre Foy (Statistics Canada, Canada)
Aletta Grisay (Belgium)
Larry Hedges (The University of Chicago, United States)
Eugene Johnson (American Institutes for Research, United States)
John de Jong (Language Testing Services, The Netherlands)
Geoff Masters (ACER, Australia)
Keith Rust (WESTAT, United States)
Norman Verhelst (Citogroep, The Netherlands)
J. Douglas Willms (University of New Brunswick, Canada)

PISA Consortium (PISA 2000 and PISA Plus)

Australian Council for Educational Research

Ray Adams (Project Director of the PISA Consortium)
Christian Monseur (Project Director of the PISA Consortium for PISA Plus, Director of the PISA Consortium for data processing, data analysis and quality monitoring for PISA 2000)
Alla Berezner (data processing, data analysis)
Claus Carstensen (data analysis)
Lynne Darkin (reading test development)
Brian Doig (mathematics test development)
Adrian Harvey-Beavis (quality monitoring, questionnaire development)
Kathryn Hill (reading test development)
John Lindsey (mathematics test development)
Jan Lokan (quality monitoring, field procedures development)
Le Tu Luc (data processing)
Greg Macaskill (data processing)
Joy McQueen (reading test development and reporting)
Gary Marks (questionnaire development)
Juliette Mendelovits (reading test development and reporting)
Gayl O'Connor (science test development)
Alla Routitsky (data processing)
Wolfram Schulz (data analysis)
Ross Turner (test analysis and reporting co-ordination)
Nikolai Volodin (data processing)
Craig Williams (data processing, data analysis)
Margaret Wu (Deputy Project Director of the PISA Consortium)

Westat

Nancy Caldwell (Director of the PISA Consortium for field operations and quality monitoring)
Ming Chen (sampling and weighting)
Fran Cohen (sampling and weighting)
Susan Fuss (sampling and weighting)
Brice Hart (sampling and weighting)
Sharon Hirabayashi (sampling and weighting)
Sheila Krawchuk (sampling and weighting)
Dward Moore (field operations and quality monitoring)
Phu Nguyen (sampling and weighting)
Monika Peters (field operations and quality monitoring)
Merl Robinson (field operations and quality monitoring)
Keith Rust (Director of the PISA Consortium for sampling and weighting)
Leslie Wallace (sampling and weighting)
Dianne Walsh (field operations and quality monitoring)
Trevor Williams (questionnaire development)

Citogroep

Steven Bakker (science test development)
Bart Bossers (reading test development)
Truus Decker (mathematics test development)
Erna van Hest (reading test development and quality monitoring)
Kees Lagerwaard (mathematics test development)
Gerben van Lent (mathematics test development)
Ico de Roo (science test development)
Maria van Toor (office support and quality monitoring)
Norman Verhelst (technical advice, data analysis)

Educational Testing Service

Irwin Kirsch (reading test development)

Other experts (PISA 2000 and PISA Plus)

Cordula Artelt (questionnaire development)
Marc Demeuse (quality monitoring)
Edward Fiske (editorial review)
Harry Ganzeboom (questionnaire development)
Aletta Grisay (technical advice, data analysis, translation, questionnaire development)
Donald Hirsch (editorial review)
Katharina Michaelowa (reporting, chapter 7)
Jules Peschar (questionnaire development)
Erich Ramseier (questionnaire development)
Gundula Schumel (questionnaire development)
Marie-Andrée Somers (data analysis and reporting)
Peter Sutton (editorial review)
Rich Tobin (questionnaire development and reporting)
J. Douglas Willms (questionnaire development, data analysis and reporting)

■ UNESCO PUBLISHING

7, place de Fontenoy, 75352 Paris 07 SP, France
UIS Ref.: UIS/AP/03-02
ISBN: 92-9189-002-2
PRINTED IN CANADA

■ OECD PUBLICATIONS

2, rue André-Pascal, 75775 Paris Cedex 16, France
OECD Code: (96 2003 07 1 P1)
ISBN: 92-64-10286-8 - n°53081 2003